Reading and Study Skills

Annotated Instructor's Edition

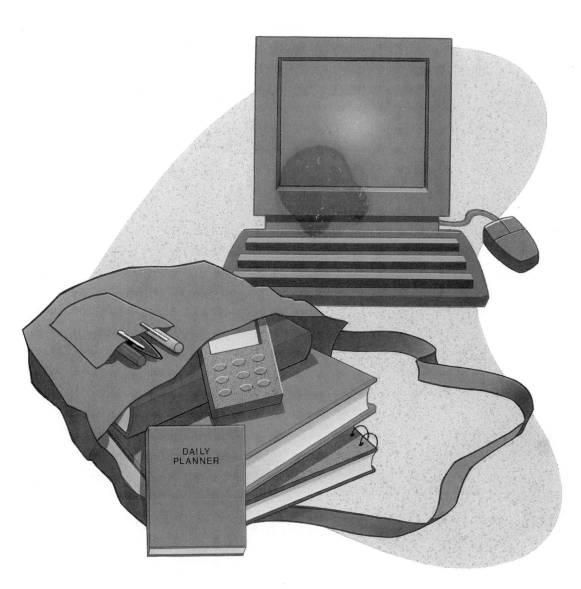

DAILY PLANNER

Praise for *Reading and Study Skills, 7th edition*

"Over the years I've tried using other texts, for variety's sake, but have found them to be less useful overall than *Reading and Study Skills.* I choose this text because of its comprehensive coverage of reading and study skills, and because its layout and format are appealing to readers. The chapters are of reasonable length, and the quantity and variety of practice exercises, and of review and mastery tests, offer students frequent opportunities to apply newly learned skills and to test their own competency."

Jamie T. Barrett, Holyoke Community College

"My students like this text. They find it easy to read and easy to resource. Teaching from it is a pleasure."

Dianne Belitsky Shames, Delaware County Community College

"I believe that this book can be very useful throughout my students' college careers. I once had a student tell me she was going to graduate school and was still using PRWR—wow!"

Denis J. Davis, Widener University

"The way Langan personalizes the approach, and his insistence from the beginning on the importance of attitude in any endeavor certainly focus the concerns of the text clearly for both student and instructor. I think students would enjoy learning from this text for these reasons, just as instructors would enjoy teaching from it for the same reasons."

Larry D. Griffin, Dyersburg State Community College

"Langan introduces each new concept with clear examples and the practice exercises provide immediate feedback about student understanding. Concepts are related to students' experiences and linked to academic success. Additional readings that emphasize various college disciplines link the content to other courses of study."

Patricia R. Grega, University of Alaska, Anchorage

"I like the book because it is comprehensive. An instructor could follow the format and feel confident that the students are being exposed to valuable information."

Beth Healander, Lexington Community College

"The text is user-friendly. The tone is relaxed and the writing style nonthreatening. Students would enjoy learning from this text and I would enjoy teaching from it."

Delores J. Cabezut-Ortiz, Merced College

Reading and Study Skills

Seventh Edition

Annotated Instructor's Edition

John Langan
Atlantic Cape Community College

McGraw Hill

Boston   Burr Ridge, IL   Dubuque, IA   Madison, WI   New York   San Francisco   St. Louis
Bangkok   Bogotá   Caracas   Kuala Lumpur   Lisbon   London   Madrid   Mexico City
Milan   Montreal   New Delhi   Santiago   Seoul   Singapore   Sydney   Taipei   Toronto

McGraw-Hill Higher Education 🐦

*A Division of The **McGraw-Hill** Companies*

READING AND STUDY SKILLS
Published by McGraw-Hill, an imprint of The McGraw-Hill Companies, Inc., 1221 Avenue of the Americas, New York, NY, 10020. Copyright © 2002, 1998, 1992, 1989, 1986, 1982, 1978, by The McGraw-Hill Companies, Inc. All rights reserved. No part of this publication may be reproduced or distributed in any form or by any means, or stored in a database or retrieval system, without the prior written consent of The McGraw-Hill Companies, Inc., including, but not limited to, in any network or other electronic storage or transmission, or broadcast for distance learning. Some ancillaries, including electronic and print components, may not be available to customers outside the United States.

This book is printed on acid-free paper.

Domestic   2 3 4 5 6 7 8 9 0 DOC/DOC 0 9 8 7 6 5 4 3 2
International   1 2 3 4 5 6 7 8 9 0 DOC/DOC 0 9 8 7 6 5 4 3 2 1

ISBN 0-07-244599-8 (student's edition)
ISBN 0-07-250324-6 (annotated instructor's edition)

Editorial director: *Phillip A. Butcher*
Executive editor: *Sarah Touborg*
Developmental editor: *Chris Narozny*
Senior marketing manager: *David S. Patterson*
Senior project manager: *Pat Frederickson*
Senior production supervisor: *Lori Koetters*
Media producer: *Gregg Di Lorenzo*
Senior designer: *Jennifer McQueen*
Supplement producer: *Susan Lombardi*
Photo research corrdinator: *Jeremy Cheshareck*
Cover illustrator: *Paul Turnbaugh*
Typeface: *11/13 Times Roman*
Compositor: *Electronic Publishing Services, Inc., TN*
Printer: *R. R. Donnelley & Sons Company*

The Library of Congress Cataloging-in-Publication Data

Langan, John 1942-
    Reading and study skills / John Langan. — 7th ed.
      p.   cm. (The Langan series)
    Includes index.
      ISBN 0-07-244599-8 (alk. paper : student ed) — ISBN 0-07-248005-X (alk. paper :
    annotated instructor's ed)
      1. Study skills. 2. Reading (Higher education) — United States. I. Title.
    LB2395.L346 2002
    428.4'071'1—dc21   2001034293

INTERNATIONAL EDITION ISBN 0-07-112138-2
Copyright © 2002. Exclusive rights by The McGraw-Hill Companies, Inc. for manufacture and export.
This book cannot be re-exported from the country to which it is sold by McGraw-Hill.
The International Edition is not available in North America.

www.mhhe.com

About the Author

John Langan has taught reading and writing at Atlantic Cape Community College near Atlantic City, New Jersey, for over twenty-five years. The author of a popular series of college textbooks on both subjects, he enjoys the challenge of developing materials that teach skills in an especially clear and lively way. Before teaching, he earned advanced degrees in writing at Rutgers University and in reading at Glassboro State College. He also spent a year writing fiction that, he says, "is now at the back of a drawer waiting to be discovered and acclaimed posthumously." While in school, he supported himself by working as a truck driver, machinist, battery assembler, hospital attendant, and apple packer. He presently lives with his wife, Judith Nadell, near Philadelphia. Among his everyday pleasures are running, working on his Macintosh computer, and watching Philadelphia sports teams on TV. He also loves to read: newspapers at breakfast, magazines at lunch, and a chapter or two of a recent book ("preferably an autobiography") at night.

The Langan Series

Essay-Level

College Writing Skills, Fifth Edition
ISBN: 0-07-228322-X (Copyright © 2000)

College Writing Skills with Readings, Fifth Edition
ISBN: 0-07-238121-3 (Copyright © 2001)

Paragraph-Level

English Skills, Seventh Edition
ISBN: 0-07-238127-2 (Copyright © 2001)

English Skills with Readings, Fifth Edition
ISBN: 0-07-248003-3 (Copyright © 2002)

Sentence-Level

Sentence Skills: A Workbook for Writers, Form A, Sixth Edition
ISBN: 0-07-036672-1 (Copyright © 1998)

Sentence Skills: A Workbook for Writers, Form B, Sixth Edition
ISBN: 0-07-037127-X (Copyright © 1999)

Sentence Skills with Readings, Second Edition
ISBN: 0-07-238132-9 (Copyright © 2001)

Grammar Review

English Brushup, Second Edition
ISBN: 0-07-037108-3 (Copyright © 1998)

Reading

Reading and Study Skills, Seventh Edition
ISBN: 0-07-244599-8 (Copyright © 2002)

Contents

To the Instructor

Key Features of the Book

Reading and Study Skills will help students learn and apply the essential reading and study skills needed for success in college work. The book also provides a brief review of important word skills that students must have. And it will help students examine their attitudes about college and about studying, set goals for themselves, and take responsibility for their own learning.

The book covers a good number of skills because, quite simply, students often need to learn or review that many. In the best of academic worlds, students would have an unlimited amount of time to spend on study skills, word skills, motivation for achievement, and so on. In such an ideal scheme of things, they could use a series of books over several semesters to strengthen their learning ability. But in reality, students usually have only one or two semesters for improving their reading and study skills, and all too often they are asked to handle regular academic subjects at the same time as their developmental course. They should, then, have a book that presents all the central skills they need to become more effective learners. The book should also be organized in self-contained units, so that students can turn quickly and easily to the skills needed in a given situation.

With *Reading and Study Skills,* an instructor can cover a wide range of skills and activities that might otherwise require several books or one limited book and a bundle of handouts and supplementary exercises. In addition to its comprehensiveness, *Reading and Study Skills* has a number of other important features:

- The book is highly *versatile.* Its eight parts, and many sections within these parts, are self-contained units that deal with distinct skills areas. An instructor can present in class those areas most suited to the general needs of students and then assign other sections for independent study. Also, because the book is so flexible, an instructor can more easily sustain students' attention by covering several skills in one session. For example, in a three-hour class period, work could be done on a study skill such as time control, a motivational skill such as setting goals, and a reading skill such as locating main ideas in short selections.

- The book is *practical.* It contains a large number and wide range of activities so that students can practice skills enough to make them habits. There are, for instance, over sixty separate exercises in the section on study skills, over fifty activities in the section on reading comprehension skills, and twenty-seven mastery tests that cover most of the skills in the book. No instructor is likely to cover all the exercises in the book, but the chances are good that an instructor will be able to select the combination of skills best suited to the needs of a reading class or individual students.

- The book is *easily used.* It has a simple conversational style and explanations that are friendly and nonpatronizing. It presents skills as processes that can be mastered in a step-by-step sequence. Besides its many activities, the book uses a question-answer format to help students learn the material. After a set of ideas is presented, one or more questions may follow so that students can check their understanding of those ideas. Such questions are signaled in the text with a bullet (•). Finally, the book features high-interest materials. For instance, selections on how people cope with conflict, on the influence of television, on fatigue in everyday life, and on the importance of education are used to practice reading skills.

- The book is *realistic.* It uses material taken from a variety of college textbooks (in one instance, an entire textbook chapter) and gives practice in common study situations. Wherever possible, students are asked to transfer skills to actual study and classroom activities. A particular value of *Reading and Study Skills* for instructors should be its emphasis on activities that help students practice and apply study skills; the lack of such activities is a drawback in many currently available texts. In the past, too much attention has been given to increasing students' skill in reading selections rapidly and answering questions about the selections. Such drill has some value, but it does not prepare students to cope with an essay, control their study time, memorize material effectively (on those still-too-frequent occasions when memory work is emphasized), take useful classroom notes, or carry out the study assignments in a textbook chapter. *Reading and Study Skills* treats all the study skills that students need to survive in their courses at the same time they are working in other parts of the book to improve their reading skills.

Changes in the Seventh Edition

The helpful comments of reading and study skills instructors who have used previous versions of *Reading and Study Skills* have prompted a number of changes in the new edition.

- A major addition is the student profiles and photographs that begin most of the study skills chapters in Part Two. Each of these profiles features a real-life student who explains just how he or she is practicing the study skill in question. The profiles help to put a human face on the practical ideas and strategies presented in the chapter. And some of the profiles do more than model a particular study skill; they serve as inspiring stories of how challenges to learning can be overcome with courage, determination, and hard work.

- Critical reading and discussion questions have been added to the ten reading selections in Part Six. In addition, five of the readings in this section are new to the book: "The Scholarship Jacket," "Dare to Think Big," "Flour Children," "From Nonreading to Reading," and "What You Need to Know to Succeed at Math." Emphasis has been placed on providing selections that will inspire and motivate students as well as give them practice in literal and critical reading comprehension.

- A chapter on the library has been revised and expanded to provide a highly practical guide to the library and the Internet. The chapter illustrates how the author of a model research paper was able to draw upon the resources of the traditional library and of the Internet. In addition, the book includes a model research paper that examines a contemporary topic and that follows the latest MLA guidelines, including the citation of sources found on the Internet.

- An earlier chapter in the book, "Learning Survival Strategies," has been expanded to include a description of different learning styles. Students are encouraged to develop an awareness of just how they learn and to take advantage of that style in their studies.

- New to the book is a chapter from the latest edition of Gelles and Levine's *Sociology*, a popular introductory text. Students are given extensive practice in reading and taking study notes on this chapter.

- The chapter on time control now includes additional suggestions for time management: close attention to the syllabus or course outline and the use of a daily planner.

- The material on studying mathematics and science in Part Eight has been reinforced by the inclusion of a new reading titled "What You Need to Know to Succeed at Math."

- Throughout the book, activities have been freshened with new practice materials. A list of recommended readings in the last part of the book has also been revised.

Helpful Learning Aids Accompany the Book

Supplements for Instructors

- An *Instructor's Edition* (ISBN 0-07-249952-4) consists of the student text complete with answers to all activities and tests, followed by an Instructor's Guide featuring teaching suggestions and a model syllabus.
- The *Instructor's Manual and Test Bank* (ISBN 0-07-251839-1) includes the Instructor's Guide along with thirty supplementary activities and tests.
- An *Online Learning Center* (**www.mhhe.com/langan**) offers a host of instructional aids and additional resources for instructors, including a comprehensive computerized test bank, the Instructor's Manual and Test Bank, online resources for writing instructors, and more.
- The online content of *Reading and Study Skills* is supported by WebCT, eCollege.com, and Blackboard. To find out more, contact your local McGraw-Hill representative or visit **http://www.mhhe.com/solutions.**
- Additionally, adopters of *Reading and Study Skills* can use McGraw's free PageOut service to get a course up and running online in a matter of hours. To find out more, contact your local McGraw-Hill representative or visit **http://www.pageout.net.**
- *WebWrite!* is an interactive peer-editing program that allows students to post papers, read comments from their peers and instructor, discuss, and edit online. To learn more, visit the online demo at **www.metatext.com/webwrite.**

Supplements for Students

- An *Online Learning Center* (**www.mhhe.com/langan**) offers a host of instructional aids and additional resources for students, including self-correcting exercises, writing activities for additional practice, a PowerPoint grammar tutorial, guides to doing research on the Internet and avoiding plagiarism, useful web links, and more.
- A *Student CD-ROM* (0-07-249951-6) offers all of the resources of the Student's Online Learning Center (described above) in a convenient offline format. This CD is available in both Windows and Macintosh formats and is free when packaged with the book.

You can contact your local McGraw-Hill representative or consult McGraw-Hill's web site at **www.mhhe.com/english** for more information on the supplements that accompany *Reading and Study Skills*, Seventh Edition.

Acknowledgments

Reviewers who have contributed to this edition through their helpful comments include

Rane Arroyo	University of Toledo
Jamie T. Barrett	Holyoke Community College
Delores J. Cabezut-Ortiz	Merced College
Denis J. Davis	Widener University
Deborah Edson	Tidewater Community College, Virginia Beach
Ann Engle	Iowa Western Community College
Jennifer Fleischer	State University of New York, Albany
Daniel Ford	Arkansas Community College at Hope
Dennis Gill	Treasure Valley Community College
Patricia Grega	University of Alaska, Anchorage
Larry D. Griffin	Dyersburg State Community College
Jeff Gundy	Bluffton College
Beth Healander	Lexington Community College
Maurice Hunt	Baylor College
Eleanor James	Montgomery County Community College
Muata Kamdibe	Rio Hondo College
Sandra Kelley	Leeward Community College
Elizabeth McConnell	Massachusetts Communications College
Pratul Pathak	California University of Pennsylvania
Sol Rabushka	St. Louis Community College at Forest Park
Ron Reed	Hazard Community College
Thomas Sadowski	Allan Hancock College
Charis Sawyer	Johnson County Community College
Dianne Belitsky Shames	Delaware County Community College
Jan Strever	Spokane Community College
Joyce Washburn	Colby Community College
Gail Watson	County College of Morris
Patricia Wells	Morgan State University

I am grateful also for help provided by Beth Johnson, Janet M. Goldstein, Susan Gamer, and Pat Frederickson as well as for the support of my McGraw-Hill editors: Sarah Touborg and Chris Narozny.

John Langan

Introduction

While working my way through school, I had all kinds of summer and part-time jobs. One of my first summer jobs was as a drill-press operator in a machine shop. When I reported to begin work, the supervisor said to me, "Langan, I want you to spend the first couple of nights going around and observing the operators and picking up everything you can. Then I'll put you on a machine." So for three nights, I walked around and watched people, was bored stiff, and learned very little. I didn't learn the skill of operating a drill press until I was actually put on a machine with a person who could teach me how to run it and I began practicing the skill. I have found that my experience in the machine shop holds true for skill mastery in general. One picks up a skill and becomes good at it when a clear explanation of the skill is followed by plenty of practice. This book, then, tries to present clearly the reading and study skills that you will need to succeed in your school or career work. And it provides abundant activities so that you can practice the skills enough to make them habits.

The skills in this book should help make you an independent learner—a person able to take on and master almost any learning challenge. However, the book cannot help you at all unless you have a personal determination to learn the skills. Back in the machine shop, I quickly learned how to run the drill press because I had plenty of motivation to learn. The job was piecework, and the more skilled I became, the more money I could make. In your case, the more reading and study skills you master, the more likely you are not only to survive but also to do well in your college courses.

1

Overview of the Book

Here are the eight parts into which this book is divided.

- *Part One: Motivational Skills*   This part describes important steps you must take to get off to a strong start with your college career.
- *Part Two: Study Skills*   Part Two explains and gives practice in all the key study skills you need to do well in your courses.
- *Part Three: A Brief Guide to Important Word Skills*   The information here will help you quickly brush up on important word skills.
- *Part Four: Reading Comprehension Skills*   Part Four explains and offers practice in comprehension skills that will help you read and take notes on your textbooks and other college materials.
- *Part Five: Skim Reading and Comprehension*   Here you will learn how to do skimming, or selective reading.
- *Part Six: Rapid Reading and Comprehension*   This part of the book will suggest a method for increasing your reading speed.
- *Part Seven: Mastery Tests*   Part Seven consists of a series of mastery tests for many of the skills in the book.
- *Part Eight: Additional Learning Skills*   This last part of the book presents other learning skills that can help you with your college work.

What Skills Do You Need to Master?

Which learning skills do you need most? To help yourself answer this question, respond to the groups of statements that follow. The statements will tell you important things about yourself as a student.

The statements will make you aware, first, of your attitude toward study. By recognizing negative feelings you may have about yourself or about student life, you can begin to deal with those feelings. The statements will also make you aware of important reading and study skills you have—or do not have—right now. You can then use the book to master the skills you need.

Read and consider each statement carefully. Check the space for *True* if a statement applies to you most of the time. Check the space for *False* if a statement does not apply to you most of the time. Remember that your answers will be of value only if they are honest and accurate.

True   False   *Attitude about Studying*

____ ____ 1. I feel there are personal problems that I have to straighten out before I can be a good student.

____ ____ 2. I seem to be so busy all the time that I don't have a chance to do my school-work regularly.

____ ____ 3. If a subject is boring to me, I don't make the full effort needed to pass the course.

____ ____ 4. I often get discouraged about how much I have to learn and how long it's going to take me.

____ ____ 5. I will let myself be distracted by almost anything rather than study.

____ ____ 6. I want to be a successful student, but I hate studying so much that I often don't bother.

____ ____ 7. I often get moody or depressed, and then I am not able to study.

____ ____ 8. I keep trying to do well in school, but I don't seem to be making any progress.

____ ____ 9. I am still trying to develop the willpower needed to study consistently.

____ ____ 10. I am not completely sure that I want to be in school at this time.

Evaluating Your Responses:

If you answered *true* more than twice in questions 1 to 10, you should read and work through all of Part One in this book. Part One will encourage you to think about the commitment you must make to become an independent learner. It will also help you set goals for yourself and will show you five important survival strategies.

It may also be important for you to discuss your situation with a counselor, a friend, a teacher, or some other person whose opinion you respect. All too often, people try to keep problems closed up inside themselves. As a result, they may limit their potential unnecessarily and waste valuable time in their lives. Talking with another person can help you get a perspective on your own situation and so help you deal better with that situation. If you care about making yourself a strong and successful person, you should take the risk of sharing your feelings and concerns with someone else.

True   False   *Taking and Studying Classroom Notes*

When I must take classroom notes,

____ ____ 11. I have trouble deciding what to write down.

____ ____ 12. While I am writing down an earlier point, I sometimes miss a new point the instructor is making.

____ ____ 13. I often get sleepy or begin to daydream when the instructor talks for long periods.

True   False

____ ____   14. I don't know how to organize my notes, and so they are often hard for me to understand later.

____ ____   15. I write down what the instructor puts on the board, but I usually don't take notes on anything else.

____ ____   16. I seldom go over my notes after a class to make them easy to understand or to fill in missing points.

____ ____   17. I don't have an effective way of studying my notes for a test.

Evaluating Your Responses: If you answered *true* more than twice in questions 11 to 17, you should read and work through the first chapter on study skills, "Taking Classroom Notes" (pages 39–69). The chapter will show you how to take effective notes in class and how to study those notes. If you are taking any content course such as business, psychology, sociology, or a science at the same time as your course in reading and study skills, you should *read this chapter first*.

True   False   *Time Control and Concentration*

____ ____   18. I never seem to have enough time to study.

____ ____   19. I don't have a schedule of regular study hours.

____ ____   20. I never make up a list of what I need to study in a given day or week.

____ ____   21. I don't write down test dates and paper deadlines in a place where I will see them every day.

____ ____   22. When I sit down to study, I have trouble concentrating.

____ ____   23. I often end up having to cram for a test.

Evaluating Your Responses: If you answered *true* more than twice in questions 18 to 23, you should read and work through "Time Control and Concentration" (pages 71–92) early in the semester. You'll learn how to use your time effectively— a key to success in college as well as in a career—and to develop consistent study habits.

True   False   *Textbook Study*

____ ____   24. I'm not sure how to preview a textbook chapter.

____ ____   25. It takes me a very long time to read and understand a textbook chapter.

____ ____   26. I'm never sure what is important when I read a textbook.

____ ____   27. I don't have a method for marking important passages while reading a textbook chapter.

True   False

____ ____   28. I don't have a really good way of taking notes on a textbook chapter.

____ ____   29. I don't have a really good way of studying my notes on a textbook chapter.

____ ____   30. I have trouble understanding tables and graphs.

Evaluating Your Responses:

If you answered *true* more than twice in questions 24 to 30, you should read and work through the entire chapter "Textbook Study I" on pages 93–112. This chapter will provide immediate help to you as you begin getting textbook assignments in other courses. Then go on to "Textbook Study II" and "Textbook Study III."

As time permits, you will then want to work through Part Four of the book, which explains and offers practice in eight key reading comprehension skills. Students often ask, "What can I do to understand and remember more of what I read?" The first five skills (pages 361–408) will help you locate and understand important points in articles and textbook chapters. The sixth and seventh skills (pages 409–438) will enable you to take down and remember those key points in the form of clear, concise study notes. The eighth skill will enable you to decipher the material displayed in tables and graphs.

True   False   *Memory Training*

____ ____   31. I have trouble concentrating and often "read words" when I try to study.

____ ____   32. I don't know any techniques to help me remember material.

____ ____   33. I often forget something almost as soon as I have studied it.

____ ____   34. I usually don't organize material in any special way before I try to study it.

____ ____   35. I don't know how to study and remember a large amount of material for a test.

Evaluating Your Responses:

If you answered *true* more than twice in questions 31 to 35, you should read and work through "Building a Powerful Memory" on pages 207–223. That chapter presents techniques to help you remember both classroom and textbook notes.

True   False   *Taking Tests*

____ ____   36. When I take a test, I often panic and forget what I have learned.

____ ____   37. Before a test, I never make a careful, organized review.

____ ____   38. When I prepare for a test, I am never sure what is important enough to study.

____ ____   39. I don't know how to go about preparing for an essay test.

True   False

____ ____   40. When I write an essay answer, I have trouble organizing my thoughts.

____ ____   41. I sometimes misread test questions and give an answer other than the one called for.

____ ____   42. I don't know any hints to keep in mind when taking a true–false or multiple-choice test.

____ ____   43. I sometimes spend too much time with some questions on a test and don't have enough time for others.

Evaluating Your Responses: If you answered *true* more than twice in questions 36 to 43, you should read and work through "Taking Objective Exams" (225–241) and "Taking Essay Exams" (243–254). These chapters show you how to prepare for both kinds of exams and explain test-taking techniques. Use them whenever exams are approaching.

True   False   *Using the Library and the Internet*

____ ____   44. I'm not sure how to look up or find a book in my library.

____ ____   45. I don't know how to use the *Readers' Guide* or other files for looking up magazine, newspaper, and journal articles.

____ ____   46. I don't know how to look up information about books or articles by using the computer terminals in my library.

____ ____   47. I don't know how to use an Internet search engine or directory.

____ ____   48. I don't know how to look for books on a topic through an online bookseller.

Evaluating Your Responses: If you answered *true* more than once in questions 44 to 48, you should read and work through "Using the Library and the Internet" on pages 255–276. You'll learn all the basics you need to know in order to use the library and the Internet for researching a topic and preparing a research paper.

True   False   *Word Skills*

____ ____   49. I'm not sure how to use prefixes, suffixes, and roots to improve my pronunciation and spelling of words.

____ ____   50. I have trouble pronouncing unfamiliar words.

____ ____   51. I'm not sure how to use the dictionary for pronouncing words.

____ ____   52. I feel that I should be a better speller.

True   False

___ ___ 53. If I see an unfamiliar word, I'm not able to guess its meaning by looking at the rest of the sentence.

___ ___ 54. I feel that my vocabulary is limited and that this keeps me from understanding my textbooks.

___ ___ 55. Very seldom, if ever, do I read a book for pleasure.

Evaluating Your Responses: If you answered *true* more than twice in questions 49 to 55, you should read and work through all of Part Three of the book. Part Three will help you improve your spelling and show you how to pronounce unfamiliar words, including specialized terms in your various subjects. You'll also learn ways to develop your vocabulary—a vital matter, because a small word base will limit your understanding of what you read. The concise information about word skills in Part Three can be supplemented with practice materials that are probably available in your college learning center.

True   False   *Other Reading Skills*

___ ___ 56. I have trouble locating definitions when I read.

___ ___ 57. I have trouble locating examples of ideas when I read.

___ ___ 58. I have trouble locating enumerations (lists of items) when I read.

___ ___ 59. I don't know how to use headings or subheadings when I read.

___ ___ 60. I don't know what kinds of words are used to signal important facts or ideas.

___ ___ 61. I have trouble locating main ideas in what I read.

___ ___ 62. I would benefit from practice in outlining and summarizing.

___ ___ 63. I don't know how to skim-read a textbook chapter effectively.

___ ___ 64. I think learning how to speed-read would help me.

___ ___ 65. I feel my lips moving as I read silently.

___ ___ 66. My eyes go back a lot to reread earlier lines on a page.

Evaluating Your Responses: If you answered *true* more than twice in questions 56 to 66, you should read and work through Parts Four, Five, and Six of the book. The chapters on textbook study in Part Two offer a quick course in becoming a better reader and note-taker; the chapters in Part Four provide a more detailed step-by-step process to strengthen your textbook reading and note-taking skills.

Part Five gives you practice in skim reading—going through a selection quickly and selectively to find important ideas. Skimming is a valuable technique when it is not necessary to read every word of a passage.

Part Six introduces you to rapid reading—processing words at a faster rate than is your normal habit. You will learn that rapid reading is not a cure-all for reading problems but simply one technique used by effective readers.

The overall purpose of Parts Four, Five, and Six is to make *you* an effective, flexible reader—able to apply "study reading," skim reading, or speed reading (or all three), depending on your purpose for reading and on the nature of the material. You will improve your comprehension, slowly but surely, if you isolate and work on important reading skills in a systematic way.

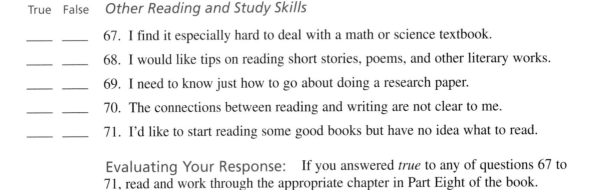

True False   *Other Reading and Study Skills*

____ ____   67. I find it especially hard to deal with a math or science textbook.

____ ____   68. I would like tips on reading short stories, poems, and other literary works.

____ ____   69. I need to know just how to go about doing a research paper.

____ ____   70. The connections between reading and writing are not clear to me.

____ ____   71. I'd like to start reading some good books but have no idea what to read.

Evaluating Your Response: If you answered *true* to any of questions 67 to 71, read and work through the appropriate chapter in Part Eight of the book.

Achieving Your Goal

You should now have a good sense of just what skills you most need to work on. Many students, I find, say that they want to improve in almost *all* the areas listed above. Whatever your specific needs, the material in this book should help.

Your goal as you begin your work is to become an independent learner—a person who can take on the challenge of any college course. Achieving the goal depends on your personal determination to do the work it takes to become a successful student. If you decide—something that only you can decide—that you want to make your college time productive and worthwhile, this book will help you reach that goal. I wish you a successful journey.

Part One

Motivational Skills

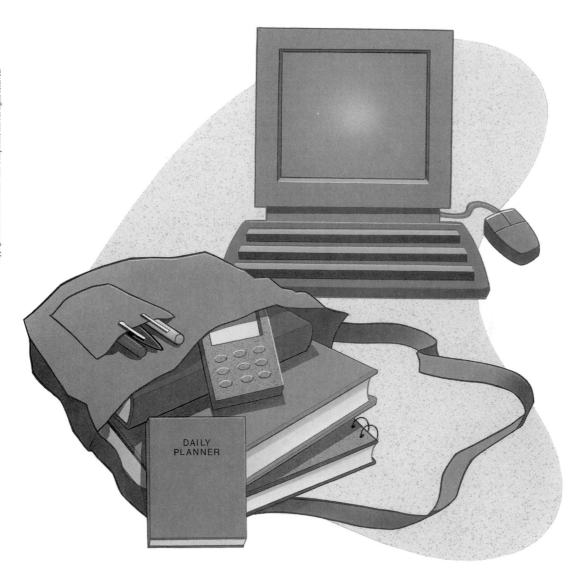

Preview

Part One is about important steps you must take to get off to a strong start in your college career. The point stressed throughout the first chapter, "Your Attitude: The Heart of the Matter," is that you must make a personal decision and commitment to do the diligent work that learning requires. The chapter describes several students who made or failed to make this a commitment, and also asks a series of questions that will help you measure your own willingness to make it. The second chapter, "Setting Goals for Yourself," will encourage you to think actively about your eventual career goal and the practical steps you should take to start working toward that goal. In the third chapter, "Learning Survival Strategies," a successful student talks about the importance of planning for a realistic career, of getting organized, of learning how to persist, of being positive, and of remaining open to growth.

Your Attitude: The Heart of the Matter

This book is chiefly about the reading and study skills you need in order to do well in your college work. But your *attitude* toward college work is even more crucial than any reading or study skill. Without the proper frame of mind, you might as well throw this book in the trash. And without the proper frame of mind, you may be wasting your time in school.

Doing the Work

Your attitude must say, "I will do the work." I have found that among the two hundred or so students I meet each year, there is almost no way of telling at first which students have this attitude and which ones do not. Some time must pass for people to reveal their attitude by what they do or do not do. What happens is that, as the semester unfolds and classes must be attended and work must be done, some people take on the work and persist even if they hit all kinds of snags and problems; others don't take on the work or don't persist when things get rough. It becomes clear which students have determined inside themselves, "I will do the work" and which have not.

The crucial matter is seldom the speed at which a person learns; the crucial matter is his or her determination—"I *will* learn." I have seen people who had this quality of determination or persistence do poorly in a course, come back and repeat it, and eventually succeed. And two years or so later, in June, I have heard their names being called out and have seen them walking up to the commencement stage to get their degrees.

For example, I have seen the woman who wrote the following piece as her first assignment in a reading and writing class go up to receive her associate of arts degree:

> Well its 10:48 and the kids are all in bed. I don't know yet what Im going to write about but I hope I think of something befor this ten minutes are up. boy I don't even like to write that much. I never send my letters or cards because I dislike writing, may be because I never took the time to sit down and really write, I've always wishes I could, put thing on paper that were in my mind. but my spelling isn't at all good, so when I had to take the time to look up a word or ask one of my children how to spell it, I said to heck with it, but, I can't do that with this any way I don't believ I can write for ten mintes straght, but Im trying I refus to stop until Ive made It. Ive always given my self credit for not being a quiter, so I guess I have to keep fighting at this and every thing else in the future, If I wish to reach my gols wich is to pass my GED and go in to nursing. I know it will take me a little longer then some one who hasn't been out of school as long as I have but no matter how long it takes I'm shure I will be well worth It and I'll be glad that I keep fighting. And Im shur my children will be very prowd of ther mother some day.

Through knowing such determined people as this woman, I have come to feel that the single most important factor for survival and success in college is not a high IQ, or plenty of money, or an easy balance between school, work, and family life. Instead, it's *an inner commitment to doing the work*. When the crunch comes—and the crunch is the plain hard work that college requires—the person with commitment meets it head-on; the person without commitment avoids it in a hundred different ways.

Doing the Work Despite Difficulties

The person who is committed to doing the work needed to succeed in college is not necessarily someone without confusion and difficulties in his or her life. A joke that is sometimes made about freshman orientation—the day or so preceding the start of the first semester, when the student is introduced to college life—is that for some people freshman orientation takes a year or more. The joke is all too often true. I can remember my own confusing first year at LaSalle College in Philadelphia. I entered as a chemistry major but soon discovered that I could not deal with the mathematics course required. As hard as I tried, I couldn't pass any of the weekly quizzes given in the class. I felt that the instructor was poor and the text unclear, but since other people were passing the tests, I felt that the problem was in me, too. It was a terribly confusing time. Because I doubted my ability to do the work, I began questioning my own self-worth.

At the same time that I doubted whether I *could* do the work in mathematics, I began to know that I did not *want* to do the work. Even if I eventually passed the course and the other mathematics courses I would have to take, I realized I did not want to spend my life working with numbers. Very quickly my career plans disintegrated. I was not going to be a chemist, and I was left in a vacuum, confused and anxious, wondering what I *was* going to be.

My career identity was not my only problem. My social identity was precarious as well. The one male friend that I had from high school had gone into the Army and was in Germany. And because I was shy, I found no one immediately at the college to share experiences with. My one female friend—or supposed friend—from high school had gone off to a school in Chicago, and we did not bother to write to each other. I realized dismally that we didn't write because we didn't really know each other anyway. We had gone together in high school for the sake of form and convenience—so we would each have a partner for social events. There had never been real communication and sharing between the two of us. I had no one to help me shape my fragile social and sexual identities, and I felt very alone. To make matters worse, in the midst of all this, my blood was burning. I yearned desperately for someone to burst into flame with—and felt lost that I had no one. In sum, my first college year was a very worried, confused, and anxious time.

I responded to my general unhappiness partly by trying to escape. One way I did this was by resorting to games. In some respects my real major that first year at LaSalle was the game room located in the student center. Before and after classes I went there to play endless games of chess and Ping-Pong. I played, I now realize, not only to find relief from my worries but also as an indirect way of trying to meet other people. For a while I had a roommate who was in college only because his parents wanted him to be; he too was desperately unhappy. We seldom talked because we had very little in common, but we would spend entire evenings playing chess together. One day, soon after midsemester grades were sent out, I came back to the dorm to find that my roommate, his clothes, his chessboard—everything—had disappeared.

The games were not enough escape for me, and so I decided to get a job. I did not absolutely need a job, but I told myself I did. Not only did I need an excuse to get away from my dismal days at the college; I also wanted to shore up my unsure self-image. If I could not be a successful student or friend or lover, I could at least be a successful wage earner. Fortunately, I did not get a full-time job but instead began working as a graphotype operator two nights a week in downtown Philadelphia. The job made me feel a little older and closer to being independent, so it helped lift my spirits.

Had I gotten a full-time job, it might have provided enough excuse for me to drop out of school, and I might have done so. As it was, I stayed, and—despite general unhappiness and partial escape through games and my part-time job—I did the work. Mathematics was hopeless, especially because there was no tutoring program or mathematics lab at the college, so I dropped the course. But I knew I would need the chemistry course that I was taking as a basic science requirement for graduation. The course meant a massive amount of work for me, and I studied and studied and went into each test hoping to get a grade that would reflect all the studying I had done. Instead, I always came out with D's. The grades were all the more discouraging because I felt so generally displeased with myself anyway. They seemed to be saying to me, "You are a 'D' person." However, I kept studying. I read and underlined the text, took lots of notes, and studied the material as best I could. I was determined to get the course behind me and, with a final grade of low C, I did.

I have known students who experienced a far rougher personal time at college than I did in my first year. And those people *who were determined to do the work,* despite all their difficulties, were the ones who succeeded. To overcome the worries, fears, and demands that may seem overwhelming during a semester, you must make a firm decision to do the work. Running from the work, you may lose precious time and opportunities in your life.

It is true that in a given situation you may decide it is better to drop a course or drop out for a semester rather than to try to do the work. You may be right, *but* it is important that you first talk to someone about your decision. One of the things that helped me stay in school during the hard first year was talking to an instructor I liked and felt I could trust. At your school you will find there are people—counselors, instructors, and others—who will care about your special situation. Talking with someone about your concerns will enable you to do something you cannot possibly do alone—get a perspective on yourself. From time to time we all need the insights into ourselves that can come from such a perspective. So if you are having trouble making yourself do the work that college requires, it is in your best interest to talk to someone about it.

Discovering the Commitment to Do the Work

I have often seen people come to college almost accidentally. Perhaps they are in doubt about what to do after high school, or are discontented with their limited job opportunities, or are looking for other interests to fill the time they once spent with their children. So they come to college uncommitted, vaguely looking for a change of pace in their lives. Without a commitment, they often drift along for a couple of weeks or months or semesters and then fade away—silent, shadowy figures in both their coming and their going.

But in some instances a spark ignites. These people discover possibilities within themselves or realize the potential meaning that college can have in their lives. As a result, they make the commitment to do the work that is absolutely essential to success in college. Here is one student's account of such a discovery:

My present feeling about college is that it will improve my life. My first attitude about college was that I didn't need it. I had been bored by high school, where it seemed we spent grades 9 to 12 just reviewing everything we had learned up through grade 8. I had a job as a bottle inspector at Wheaton's and was taking home over $225 a week. Then I was laid off and spent whole days hanging around with nothing to do. My roommate was going to Atlantic Community College and talked me into going, and now I hope I'll be thanking her one day for saving my life.

When I entered college in January I thought it was fun but that's all. I met a lot of people and walked around with college textbooks in my hand playing the game of being a college student. Some weeks I went to class and other weeks I didn't go at all and went off on trips instead. I didn't do much studying. I really wasn't into it but was just going along with the ball game.

Then two things happened. My sociology class was taught by a really cool person who asked us questions constantly, and they began getting to me. I started asking *myself* questions and looking at myself and thinking, "What am I about anyway? What do I want and what am I doing?" Also I discovered I could write. I wrote my own version of the Red Riding Hood story and it was read in class and everyone, including the instructor, roared. Now I'm really putting time into my writing and my other courses as well.

After reading my first version of this paper, the instructor asked me, "What is the point at which you changed? When was the switch thrown to 'On' in your head?" I don't know the exact moment, but it was just there, and now it seems so real I can almost touch it. I know this is my life and I want to be somebody and college is going to help me do it. I'm here to improve myself, and I'm going to give it my best shot.

Earlier in the semester things seemed so bad to me. I was busted for drugs, I got an eviction notice, and I was having man trouble too. I was going to quit school and get a job and try to get a new start. But then I realized this is my start and this is where I will begin. I can tell you with a strong mind that nothing will discourage me, and that I will make it.

Running from the Commitment to Do the Work

I said earlier that as a semester unfolds and the crunch of work comes, people are put up against the wall. Like it or not, they must define their role in college. There are only two roads to take. One road is to do the work: to leave the game table, click off the stereo or television, turn down the invitation to go out, get off the telephone, stop anything and everything else, and go off by oneself to do the essentially lonely work that study is. The other road is to avoid the work, and there are countless ways of doing this.

Here is one student's moving account of the avoidance pattern in his life and his discovery of it:

Somewhere, a little piece of me is lost and crying. Someplace, deep in the shadows of my subconscious, a piece of my soul has sat down and anchored itself in defeat and is trying to pull me down into the darkness with it. This might sound strange to someone who is not familiar with the inner conflicts of a person that can tear and pull at his soul until he begins to stop and sink in his own deep-hollow depths. But sinking doesn't take much. It takes only one little flaw which left unattended will grow and grow . . . until like cancer it consumes the soul.

My flaw, the part of me that has given up, is best seen when it is winning. Then I am lost like a rudderless ship after the storm has abated, motor gone, drifting . . . pushed about by the eddying currents in little circles of lassitude and self-doubt, just waiting . . . just waiting . . . peering at the ominous dark clouds in the sky, waiting for help to arrive.

I know now, and I have always known, that help comes first from within. I know that if one doesn't somehow come to one's own rescue, then all is lost. I know it is time for me to look at myself. I would rather avoid that. But in order to break free of my own chains, I must look at myself.

I could relate the incidents of my youth. I could tell of the many past failures and what I think caused them. But I won't, for one example will show where I'm at. At the beginning of this summer I set my goals. These goals consisted of the college courses I wanted to complete and where I wanted to be physically and mentally when the summer was over. Listed among the goals to be accomplished were courses I needed in writing and accounting. To help me become at ease with my writing, I took English Composition 101, and to clear up my deficiency in accounting, I took that course a second time. But now, at the end of July, I am so far behind in both courses it looks as if I will fail them both. I ask myself, "Why?" I know that if I work enough I can handle the courses. So, why have I been so lazy? Why is it that the things I seem to want most, I either give up or in some way do not strive for? These are the questions I must try to answer.

I remember when I was about five or six—a little, dreamy boy living in the country—a much older neighbor boy told me one rainy afternoon, just when the rain had stopped and the sun peered with glistening rays of gold through gray and white fluffy clouds, that "there is a pot of gold at the end of the rainbow." And right then a pulsating, glowing rainbow of violets, blues, and golds raced from the clouds and down past the hill. It sent me scampering across the wet, weedy field and up the hill and down the other side, where fields with rows of wet corn stood. There my rainbow had moved a little farther on. I should have known then, but I kept walking through the puddles in the muddy fields watching my rainbow fade farther and farther away with each step. I started home when the rainbow faded, but in the puddles of water I saw little rainbows and dreamed that the next time I would get the pot of gold under the big rainbow.

I think it's time for me to stop chasing rainbows in the sky. It's time to stop looking into the sky waiting for help to arrive. It's time for me to start bailing the rot out of my mind, to stop dreaming and not acting, before I have nothing left to hope for. I can see now that I've never given it the total effort, that I've always been afraid I would fail or not measure up. So I've quit early. Instead of acting on my dreams, I've lain back and just floated along. I've lived too much time in this world unfulfilled. I've got to make my dreams work. I've suffered enough in this world. I must do this now, and all it takes is the doing. Somehow I must learn to succeed at success rather than at failure, and the time to start is now.

Avoidance Tactics

Described below are some of the tactics that people may use to avoid doing the hard work that college requires. If you see yourself in any of these situations, you should do some serious thinking about whether now is the right time for you to be in college. If you are unsure of your commitment, don't coast along, trying to ignore the situation. Instead, make an appointment with a counselor, your academic adviser, or some other interested person. That way you will confront your problem and begin to deal with it.

"I Can't Do It"

The only way people will really know that they cannot do something is by first trying—giving it their best shot. The temptation is to use a defeatist attitude as an excuse for not making a real effort. Remember that many colleges can give you help if you decide to try. There may be a tutoring program and writing, reading, and mathematics labs. And you can often go to your instructor as well. If you think you "can't do it," the reason may be that you are not trying.

"I'm Too Busy"

Some people *make* themselves too busy, taking on a job that is not absolutely necessary or working more hours on a job than they need to. Others get overly involved in social activities on and off campus. Others allow personal or family problems to become so tangled and pressing that they cannot concentrate on their work. There are real cases where people are so busy or troubled that they cannot do their work. But there are many cases where people unconsciously create conflicts in order to have an excuse for not doing what they know they should do.

"I'm Too Tired"

People who use this excuse usually become tired as soon as it's time to write a paper or study a book or go to class. Their weariness clears up when the work period ends. The "sleepiness syndrome" also expresses itself in an imagined need for naps during the day and then ten hours or more of sleep at night. Such students are, often literally, closing their eyes to the hard work that college demands.

"I'll Do It Later"

Everyone tends at times to procrastinate—to put things off. Some students, however, constantly postpone doing assignments and setting aside regular study hours. Time and time again they put off what needs to be done so they can watch TV, talk to a friend, go to the movies, play cards, or do any one of a hundred other things. These students typically wind up cramming for tests and writing last-minute papers, yet they often seem surprised and angry at their low grades.

"I'm Bored with the Subject"

Students sometimes explain that they are doing poorly in a course because the instructor or the subject matter is boring. These students want education to be entertainment—an unrealistic expectation. On the whole, college courses and instructors balance out: Some are boring, some are exciting, many are in between. If a course is not interesting, students should be all the more motivated to do the work so that they can leave the course behind once and for all.

"I'm Here, and That's What Counts"

Some people spend their first weeks in school lost in a dangerous kind of fantasy. They feel, "All will be well, for I am now here in college. I have a student identification card in my pocket, a parking sticker on the bumper of my car, and textbooks under my arm. All this proves I am a college student. I have it made." Such students have succumbed to a fantasy we all at times succumb to: the belief that we will get something for nothing. But everyone knows from experience that such a hope is a false one. Life seldom gives us something for nothing—and college won't either. College, like life, is demanding. And because this is so, to get somewhere and to become someone we must be prepared and able to make a solid effort. We must accept the fact that little can be won or achieved or cherished in life without hard work. The decision that each of us must make is the commitment to do the hard work required for success in college—and ultimately in life. By making such a decision, and acting on it, we assume control of our lives.

■ Questions to Consider

Your instructor may put you into small groups of three or four and ask you to take turns reading aloud to each other the discussion about attitude on pages 11–18. The instructor may then ask you to discuss with one another the questions that follow. Every person in the group should try to contribute to the sharing of experiences. The more honest and real you can be in exchanging individual experiences, the more meaningful and valuable the discussion can be.

1. Tell the group about some skill you have learned and how you went about learning it. Do you think the basic principles involved in learning that skill could hold true with reading and study skills as well?

2. "A person who does not go to class faithfully is showing that he or she is not committed to doing the work that college requires." Give your reasons for agreeing or disagreeing with this statement.

3. Have you or has anyone you've known had a "time of decision" like the one described by the person who wrote the paper on page 15?

4. Have you or has anyone you've known ever run from the commitment to do the work, like the person who wrote the paper on pages 16–17?

5. Have you or has anyone you've known experienced the "sleepiness syndrome" described on page 18?

6. Have you or has anyone you've known ever experienced the "dangerous kind of fantasy" described on page 18?

7. Everyone uses avoidance tactics from time to time. Share with the group the ones that you may sometimes use. (You've already discussed two; four more are described on pages 17–18—and there may be other kinds of escape you can think of.) Also discuss whether you think avoidance tactics have ever prevented you from meeting your goals.

8. What is your purpose, or what are your purposes, in taking college courses? Take a few minutes to write down on a separate sheet of paper your specific goals for four months from now, one year from now, and two years from now. Then share these goals with the other members of the group.

9. Do you think your chance of reaching your goals is 100 percent? 70 percent? 30 percent? Specifically, what odds would you give on yourself—and why? Share these odds with the group, and then give your reasons for setting the odds as you do. (Describe what you see as your strengths and weaknesses.)

Your instructor may ask you to write a paper that responds *in detail* to one of the preceding questions. He or she may stress that in this paper, honesty—the expression of your real thoughts and feelings and experiences—is more important than sentence skills.

Setting Goals for Yourself

If you asked a cross section of students why they are in college, you would probably get a wide range of responses. Following are some reasons people give for going to college. Check the reasons that you feel apply to you. Be honest; think a bit about each reason before you go on to the next one.

Reasons Students Go to College	*Apply in My Case*
• To have some fun before getting a job.	————
• To prepare for a specific career.	————
• To please their families.	————
• To educate and enrich themselves.	————
• To be with friends who are going to college.	————
• To fill in time until they figure out what they want to do.	————
• To take advantage of an opportunity they didn't have before in their lives.	————
• To find a husband or wife.	————
• To see if college has anything to offer them.	————
• To do more with their lives than they've done so far.	————
• To take advantage of VA benefits or other special funding.	————
• To earn the status that they feel comes with a college degree.	————
• To get a new start in life.	————
• To set an example for their children.	————
• To be qualified for a promotion at work.	————

Get together with one or more other students to compare and discuss your responses to this list. Talk about what you feel are the "bottom-line" reasons you are in college. Make a genuine effort to be as honest about yourself as possible.

Now write in the spaces that follow the basic reason or reasons you have for being in college.

_____

_____

_____

_____

If you do not have one or more solid reasons for being in college, you may have trouble motivating yourself to do the hard work that will be required. When difficult moments occur, your concentration and effort will lag unless you can remember that you have good reasons for persisting.

Long-Term Goals

For many students, a main reason for being in college is to prepare themselves for a career—the specific kind of work they intend to do in life. If you have not been thinking actively about this long-range goal, you should begin doing so during your first year at college. Here are four specific steps you can take to start formulating a career goal.

1 If you are not sure of a major, visit the college's counseling center. The center probably administers an *interest inventory* and a *vocational preference test.* The first identifies what you like and can do well; the second points to careers that match your interests and abilities. With this information, the counseling staff at the center can help you decide on a possible major. You should begin taking courses in this prospective major as soon as you can in order to learn for sure that it is right for you.

2 Some time early in college, make an appointment to talk with a faculty member in the department of your intended major. Most department advisers set aside a certain period of time to meet with students and discuss their course of study. Ask such advisers the following questions:

   What courses are required in the major?

   What courses are recommended?

   What courses, if any, offer practical work experiences?

3 Also, plan to go to the placement office some time during your first year to get specific information on careers. Many students have the notion that placement offices provide this information only to students who are about to graduate, but

this is not the case. In fact, waiting until you are about to graduate to start investigating the job field is a poor idea. *It is important for beginning students to speak to the placement staff to obtain updated information about the future of specific fields.* For example, it would make little sense for you to plan to become a history teacher if that particular job market is expected to have few openings at the time you graduate.

4   See if your counseling center has the latest copy of the *Occupational Outlook Handbook,* which is an invaluable source of information about the many kinds of jobs currently available and the best job prospects in the future. In fact, it makes sense to order the book for your personal reference early in your school career. Write to the Bureau of Labor Statistics, Publications Sales Center, P.O. Box 2145, Chicago, IL 60690, and ask for the latest paperback edition of the *Occupational Outlook Handbook.* The book will probably cost you about $50. If you have access to the Internet, you can browse through the *Handbook* online; its address is **http://stats.bls.gov/ocohome.htm.**

Activity   Answers to items 2–5 will vary.

Answer the following questions.

1. What is a vocational preference test? _A test that points to careers that_ _match your interests and abilities._

2. Does your counseling center or library have a current copy of the *Occupational Outlook Handbook?* _____ What are three promising career fields identified in the *Handbook?*

    a. _____

    b. _____

    c. _____

3. Have you asked a counselor for his or her professional opinion on the best job opportunities in your area of the country? _____

4. Describe your long-range career goal (or what you think will be your goal):

    _____

5. Mark with a check the expected job prospects in your major at the time you graduate. (You can answer this only after you have visited the placement center or spoken to a knowledgeable person in the field.)

    _____ Excellent   _____ Good   _____ Fair   _____ Poor

Short-Term Goals

There is a familiar saying that the longest journey begins with a single step. To achieve your long-term career goal, you must set and work toward a continuing series of short-term goals. These can be as simple as a list of specific objectives that you have for your present semester in college. In Activity 1 is an example— the short-term goals that one student, Allen, set for himself.

Personal and Study Goals

Activity 1

Specific goals can consist of both *personal* and *study* goals. In the spaces beside the items on Allen's list, indicate whether the goal listed is a personal or a study goal.

Allen's Short-Term Goals

1. To get the name and phone number of at least two people in each of my classes (<u>study and/or personal</u>)

2. To earn a B in my basic math class (<u>study</u>)

3. To earn a B or better in my writing class (<u>study</u>)

4. To earn a B in my basic accounting class (<u>study</u>)

5. To get my motorcycle running again (<u>personal</u>)

6. To see my writing tutor at least once a week (<u>study</u>)

7. To go out no more than one night during the school week (<u>study and/or personal</u>)

8. To use either Saturday or Sunday as a study day each weekend (<u>study and/or personal</u>)

You can help yourself succeed in your present semester of college by setting a series of personal and study goals. The goals must be honest ones that you choose yourself—goals that you truly intend to work on and that you have the time to achieve. If necessary, you can change or add to your goals as needed. What matters is that you have a series of definite targets that will give you direction and motivation during the semester. A list of specific goals will help you do the *consistent* work that is needed for success.

Activity 2   *Answers will vary.*

Use the following space to set a series of short-term goals for yourself. Indicate in parentheses whether each goal is a personal or a study goal. Set real targets for yourself. At the same time, be realistic about how much you can achieve in one semester.

Goals for the _____ *Semester, 20____*

1. _____

2. _____

3. _____

4. _____

5. _____

6. _____

7. _____

8. _____

9. _____

10. _____

_____

_____

_____

_____

_____

_____

_____

Use the extra space provided if you decide to change or add to your goals. Refer frequently to your goals as the semester progresses. When a goal is completed, cross it out and write the date beside it.

Steps for Achieving Short-Term Goals

At the same time that you set short-term goals, you should decide on specific steps you must take to achieve those goals. By looking closely at what you must do to reach your goals, you can determine whether they are realistic and practical. You can also get a good sense of just how you will reach them.

Look at some of the specific steps Allen decided he must take to reach his goals:

Goal: <u>To take and earn B's in three courses this semester</u>.

Specific steps for achieving this goal:
I will quit my evening job at the Uni-Mart.
I will tell my boss at my day job that I can't work more than twenty hours a week.
I will make weekly grocery lists so I'm not running to the store every day.
I will get up early on weekends so I have time to study as well as do my laundry and cleaning.
I will get the phone numbers of at least two people in each class, so if I ever do have to miss a class, I can find out right away what happened.
I will be in bed by 11 P.M. on weeknights.

Activity 3   Answers will vary.

Now choose three of your most important goals and list specific steps you must take to achieve each of them.

Goal 1: _____

Specific steps for achieving goal 1:

_____

_____

_____

_____

_____

_____

Goal 2: _____

Specific steps for achieving goal 2:

_____

_____

_____

_____

_____

Goal 3: _____

Specific steps for achieving goal 3:

_____

_____

_____

_____

_____

Activity 4

Your instructor may now put you in a group with one or two other students so that you can compare your goals and discuss the steps you plan to take to achieve them. You should try to give each other feedback on what seems realistic about your goals—and what does not. *Or,* your instructor may sit down with you individually to review your goals.

Activity 5   *Answers will vary.*

Answer the following questions as honestly as you can.

- How important do you think it is that you set specific goals for yourself and consciously work toward those goals?

    Very important _____

    Fairly important _____

    Somewhat important _____

    Unimportant _____

- How important do you think it is to work out the specific steps that you must take to achieve your goals?

    Very important _____

    Fairly important _____

    Somewhat important _____

    Unimportant _____

- Are you already a disciplined person? Or will you have to make a special effort to work consistently toward your goals during the semester?

    _____

- On the basis of your present situation in life and what you know about yourself, what do you think will be your greatest obstacles in reaching your short-term goals?

    _____

    _____

    _____

- How would you rate your chance of success in achieving your short-term goals?

    Excellent _____

    Good _____

    Fair _____

    Uncertain _____

Learning
Survival
Strategies

Note: *Over the years I have spoken with a number of successful students who started college with a course in reading and study skills and then went on to earn their college degrees. Essentially, what I asked them was, "What would you want to say to students who are just starting out in college? What advice would you give? What experiences would it help to share?" The comments of one student, Jean Coleman, were especially helpful. In several conversations I had with Jean, she identified strategies for surviving in college that other students often spoke of as well. Jean's comments are presented mostly in her own words on the pages that follow.*

The Advice and Experience of a Successful Student

"Be Realistic"

The first advice that I'd give to beginning students is: "Be realistic about how college will help you get a job." Some students believe that once they have a college degree, the world will be waiting on their doorstep, ready to give them a wonderful job. But the chances are that, unless they've planned, there will be *nobody* on their doorstep.

I remember the way you dramatized this point in our first class, John. You pretended to be a student who had just been handed a college degree. You opened up an imaginary door, stepped through, and peered around in both directions outside. There was nobody to be seen. I understood the point you were making immediately. A college degree in itself isn't enough. We've got to prepare while we're in college to make sure our degree is a marketable one.

At that time I began to think seriously about (1) what I wanted to do in life and (2) whether there were jobs out there for what I wanted to do. I went to the counseling center and said, "I want to learn where the best job opportunities will be in the next ten years." The counselor referred me to a copy of the *Occupational Outlook Handbook* published by the United States government. The *Handbook* has good information on what kinds of jobs are available now and which career fields will need workers in the future. In the front of the book is a helpful section on job hunting. The counselor also gave me a vocational interest test to see where my skills and interests lay.

The result of my personal career planning was that I graduated from Atlantic Community College with a degree in accounting. I then got a job almost immediately, for I had chosen an excellent employment area. The firm that I worked for paid my tuition as I went on to get my bachelor's degree. Now, the company is paying for my work toward certification as a CPA, and my salary increases regularly.

By way of contrast, I know a woman named Sheila who majored in French. She earned a bachelor's degree with honors in French. After graduation, she spent several unsuccessful months trying to find a job in which she could use her French degree. Sheila eventually wound up going to a specialized school where she trained for six months as a paralegal assistant. She then got a job on the strength of that training—but her years of studying French were of no practical value in her career at all.

I'm not saying that college should serve only as a training ground for a job. People should take some courses just for the sake of learning and for expanding their minds in different directions. At the same time, unless they have a huge amount of money (and few of us are so lucky), they must be ready at some point to take career-oriented courses so that they can survive in the harsh world outside college.

In my own case, I started college at the age of twenty-seven. I was divorced, had a six-year-old son to care for, and was working full time as a hotel night clerk. If I had had my preference, I would have taken a straight liberal arts curriculum. As it was, I did take some general-interest courses—in art, for example. But mainly I was getting ready for the solid job I desperately needed. What I am saying, then, is that students must be realistic. If they will need a job soon after graduation, they should be sure to study in an area where jobs are available.

"Get Organized"

One of the problems that can start a student off in the wrong direction is failing to get organized right at the beginning of the semester. It's funny, but even a disorganized first day—just one day—can set a negative tone for the semester that just seems to snowball. For instance, I have seen students come to the first day of class as if the first class were some kind of unimportant rehearsal. They don't bother to bring pens or notebooks, and they let the important information they're receiving just float by. You get the feeling that they believe they'll catch up later, but they usually don't.

I think students who are disorganized like this have never learned to take responsibility for their own behavior. They have had parents, teachers, and bosses telling them what to do, so they can't cope when they're placed in an atmosphere that says, "Nobody here is going to protect you from the consequences if you don't take care of things yourself." Students like this miss classes, fail to get the notes they missed, or don't know the most basic information, such as where their instructors' offices are. Then they act surprised when their grades take a nose-dive—they feel as if they've been cheated because no one "rescued" them with warnings, reminders, or prodding.

I would tell all students to get organized right at the start of school. To help them do this, I would pass out the following checklist of important items:

_____ • Remember that the first meeting of any class is crucial. Bring two pens and a notebook with you, for many instructors not only distribute basic information about assigned textbooks and requirements—they also start lecturing the first day.

_____ • Don't put off getting your books, even if you have to wait in a long, boring line at the bookstore. You will need your books right away if you don't want to fall behind, so make the sacrifice.

_____ • Find out, early in the semester, the names and phone numbers of some students in the class. Students who feel "funny" about this or are too shy to do it are really hurting themselves. If you miss class, it's your responsibility to go *prepared* to the next class. At the college level, you can't get away with saying to a professor, "I don't have the assignment because I was absent" or "Could you tell me what I missed?" If you have some of your classmates' phone numbers, you can find out what happened in class and get the notes or assignments you missed. But of course, if you start missing too many classes or showing up late for your classes, just getting the notes won't help you keep up.

_____ • Have a specific place at home for all your school materials. In other words, have some kind of headquarters. You just can't study when you sit down to work and discover that your biology book is in the trunk of your brother's car, your lab notes are in a locker at school, and you can't find the handout the instructor gave you. All school-related materials should be kept somewhere convenient for you—a desk, a worktable, a closet, or a corner. This kind of very basic organization makes a big difference.

_____ • Decide, right from the start, how much work you can handle. If you are taking five courses, working at a full-time job, and caring for two children, for example, you're asking for a nervous breakdown—no matter how organized you are. I heard a good rule of thumb for this, and it seems accurate: For every ten hours per week you work, deduct one course from a full-time college course load. For example, if you don't work, you can do well in five courses; if you work ten hours, you should attempt only four courses; if you work twenty hours, take three courses maximum; and so on. You might have to bend this rule, however, depending on your family responsibilities and the level of difficulty of the courses you are taking.

I think what all this comes down to is that there seem to be two kinds of students—the ones who have a mature, professional attitude toward being a student and the ones who act like children who have to be taken care of. It's important to realize that college instructors aren't baby-sitters or disciplinarians. They want to teach, but they want to teach adults who meet them halfway and take responsibility for themselves. When I have seen students who have the attitude "I'm sitting in class, so I've done my job—now you make me learn something," I have wanted to ask them, "What are you doing here?" They just never accept, or choose to ignore, the fact that *they*—not the instructors—are the ones who determine whether they will succeed or fail.

"Know How You Learn"

I remember very well writing my first English paper for college. I was determined to do it right. I sat down at my desk with my nice new pen and a blank sheet of paper in front of me—and twenty minutes later I was still sitting there, and the paper was still blank. I began to panic. How was I ever going to get a five-paragraph essay done when I couldn't write a single sentence?

To calm myself down, I walked to the kitchen to make myself a cup of tea. As I waited for the water to boil, I paced around the kitchen, thinking about the paper I had to write. I've always had the habit of talking to myself when I am alone, and in my anxiety about the paper, I began lecturing to myself out loud. "Now, this paper is about *The Great Gatsby,*" I told myself. "I read the book. I liked it. What do I want to say about it?" For the next ten minutes or so I walked around my kitchen, sipping my tea and talking to myself about *The Great Gatsby.* Anyone watching me might have thought I was crazy, but I didn't care. I realized that I was doing what I couldn't do when I was sitting at my desk. I was "writing" my paper. By the time I sat down again, I had my essay almost completely composed in my head. All I had to do was write it down.

I had discovered something important about myself. I learn most easily when I'm talking or listening. That's why I have always liked classes that feature plenty of lectures and discussions more than classes that rely heavily on independent reading. As I got to know other students better, I realized that many people favor one learning style over another. For instance, my friend Darlene could never compose a paper by "talking it" as I do. But she is a wizard at the computer keyboard. She tells me, "My thoughts come together as I'm typing. Until I sit down and do the physical act of writing, I honestly don't know what I'm going to say."

I guess a learning specialist would say that I've got an auditory learning style—one that emphasizes hearing. Darlene's learning style is more tactile—she has to touch things, like a pen or the computer keyboard, in order to learn. People who absorb ideas easily through reading have a more visual style—they learn easily through what they see. The point is that not all of us learn in the same ways. If you recognize your own learning style, you can take advantage of it—whether that style emphasizes hearing, touch, sight, or another sense or combination of senses. Don't think that your style is wrong if it happens to be different from your roommate's! The important thing is whether it works for you.

"Persist"

The older I get, the more I see that life visits some hard experiences on us. There are times for each of us when simple survival becomes a deadly serious matter. We must then learn to persist—to struggle through each day and wait for better times to come, as they invariably do.

I think of one of my closest friends, Neil. After graduating from high school with me, Neil spent two years working as a stock boy at a local department store in order to save money for college tuition. He then went to the guidance office at the small college in our town. Incredibly, the counselor there told him, "Your IQ is not high enough to do college work." Neil decided to go anyway, and he earned his degree in five years—with a year out to care for his father, who had had a stroke one day at work.

Neil then got a job as a manager of a regional beauty supply firm. He met a woman who owned a salon, got married, and soon had two children. Three years later he found out that his wife was having an affair. I'll never forget the day Neil came over and sat at my kitchen table and told me what he had learned. He always seemed so much in control, but that morning he lowered his head into his hands and cried. "What's the point?" he kept saying in a low voice over and over to himself.

But Neil has endured. He divorced his wife, won custody of his children, and learned how to be a single parent. Recently, Neil and I got letters informing us of the tenth reunion of our high school graduating class. Included was a short questionnaire for us to fill out that ended with this item, "What has been your outstanding accomplishment since graduation?" Neil wrote, "My outstanding accomplishment is that I have survived." I have a feeling that most of our high school classmates, ten years out in the world, would have no trouble understanding the sad truth of his statement.

I can think of people who started college with me who had not yet learned, like Neil, the basic skill of endurance. Life hit some of them with unexpected low punches and knocked them to the floor. Stunned and dismayed, they didn't fight back and eventually dropped out of school. I remember Yvonne, still a teenager, whose parents involved her in their ugly divorce battle. Yvonne started missing classes and gave up at midsemester. There was Jeff, whose girlfriend broke off their relationship. Jeff stopped coming to class, and by the end of the semester he was failing most of his courses. I also recall Nelson, whose old car kept breaking down. After Nelson put his last $200 into it, the brakes failed and needed to be replaced. Overwhelmed by his continuing troubles with his car, Nelson dropped out of school. And there was Rita, discouraged by her luck of the draw with instructors and courses. In sociology, she had an instructor who wasn't able to express ideas clearly. She also had a mathematics instructor who talked too fast and seemed not to care at all about whether his students learned. To top it off, Rita's adviser had enrolled her in an economics course that put her to sleep. Rita told me she had expected college to be an exciting place, but instead she was getting busywork assignments and trying to cope with hostile or boring instructors. Rita decided to drop her mathematics course, and that must have set something in motion in her head, for she soon dropped her other courses as well.

In my experience, younger students seem more prone to dropping out than do older students. I think some younger students are still in the process of learning that life slams people around without warning. I'm sure they feel that being knocked about is especially unfair because the work of college is hard enough without having to cope with some of life's special hardships.

In some situations, withdrawing from college may be the best response. But there are going to be times in college when students—young or old—must simply determine, "I am going to persist." They should remember that no matter how hard their lives may be, there are many other people out there who are quietly having great difficulties also. I think of Dennis, a boy in my introductory psychology class who lived mostly on peanut butter and discount-store white bread for almost a semester in his freshman year. And I remember Estelle, who came to school because she needed a job to support her sons when her husband, who was dying of leukemia, would no longer be present. These are especially dramatic examples of the faith and hope that are sometimes necessary for us to persist.

"Be Positive"

A lot of people are their own worst enemies. They regard themselves as unlikely to succeed in college and often feel that there have been no accomplishments in their lives. In my first year of college, especially, I saw people get down on themselves all too quickly. There were two students in my developmental mathematics class who failed the first quiz and seemed to give up immediately. From that day on, they walked into the classroom carrying defeat on their shoulders the way other students carried textbooks under their arms. I'd look at them slouching in their seats, not even taking notes, and think, "What terrible things have gone on in their lives that they have quit already? They have so little faith in their ability to learn that they're not even trying." Both students hung on until about midsemester. When they disappeared for good, no one took much notice, for they had already disappeared in spirit after that first test.

They are not the only people in whom I have seen the poison of self-doubt do its ugly work. I have seen others with resignation in their eyes and have wanted to shake them by the shoulders and say, "You are not dead. Be proud and pleased that you have brought yourself here to college. Many people would not have gotten so far. Be someone. Breathe. Hope. Act." Such people should refuse to use self-doubt as an excuse for not trying. They should roll up their sleeves and get to work. They should start taking notes in class and trying to learn. They should get a tutor, go to the learning center, see a counselor. If they honestly and fully try and still can't handle a course, only then should they drop it. Above all, they should not lapse into being "zombie students"—ones who have given up in their heads but persist in hanging on for months, just going through the motions of trying.

Nothing but a little time is lost through being positive and giving school your best shot. On the other hand, people who let self-doubt limit their efforts may lose the opportunity to test their abilities to the fullest.

"Grow"

I don't think that people really have much choice about whether to grow in their lives. Not to be open to growth is to die a little each day. Grow or die—it's as simple as that.

I have a friend, Jackie, who, when she's not working, can almost always be found at home or at her mother's house. Jackie eats too much and watches TV too much. I sometimes think that when she swings open her apartment door in response to my knock, I'll be greeted by her familiar chubby body with an eight-inch-screen television set occupying the place where her head used to be.

Jackie seems quietly desperate. There is no growth or plan for growth in her life. I've said to her, "Go to school and study for a job you'll be excited about." She says, "It'll take me forever." Once Jackie said to me, "The favorite time of my life was when I was a teenager. I would lie on my bed listening to music and I would dream. I felt I had enormous power, and there seemed no way that life would stop me from realizing my biggest dreams. Now that power doesn't seem possible to me anymore."

I feel that Jackie must open some new windows in her life. If she does not, her spirit is going to die. There are many ways to open new windows, and college is one of them. For this reason, I think people who are already in school should stay long enough to give it a chance. No one should turn down lightly such an opportunity for growth.

In Conclusion

Maybe I can put all I've said into perspective by describing briefly what my life is like now. I have inner resources that I did not have when I was newly divorced. I have a secure future with the accounting firm where I work. My son is doing OK in school. I have friends. I am successful and proud and happy. I have my fears and my loneliness and my problems and my pains, to say the least, but essentially I know that I have made it. I have survived and done more than survive. I am tough, not fragile, and I can rebound if hard blows land. I feel passionately that all of us can control our own destinies. I urge every beginning student to use well the chances that college affords. Students should plan for a realistic career, get themselves organized, learn to persist, be positive, and open themselves to growth. In such ways, they can help themselves find happiness and success in this perilous but wonderful world of ours.

■ Questions to Consider

In groups of three or four, discuss the questions that follow. Every person in the group should try to contribute. The more honest you can be in sharing experiences, the more meaningful and valuable the discussion will be.

1. Do you know yet what kind of work you want to do after college?
   a. If your answer is *no,* have you visited the counseling center to take a vocational interest test?
   b. Are you thinking actively about possible careers and getting information on those careers?
   c. If your answer is *yes,* have you checked with the counseling center or instructors in the field or through your own reading about whether there will be good job opportunities available at the time you graduate?
2. Do you know any people with a recent two- or four-year college degree? How successful have they been in getting jobs? On the basis of their experiences, what areas seem to offer good job opportunities?
3. People often limit themselves by taking only career-oriented courses in college. Are there any courses you plan to take just for the sake of learning?
4. Were you aware of all the tips Jean Coleman discusses in her section on getting organized? Which of her suggestions do you practice, and which ones have you ignored? Describe how well or poorly your actions compare with the habits that Coleman recommends.
5. What is your favorite learning style? Is it like one that Jean Coleman describes, or do you have a learning style that is completely your own? Explain.

6. Are any people you know like the four Jean Coleman describes on pages 32–33 who dropped out of school when their lives became very hard? What do you think might have helped them decide to stay in school?

7. Are there any students you know who continued in school despite tough luck? What kinds of struggles did they have?

8. Do you know any students whose feelings of inferiority are keeping them from making an honest effort to learn in college? What do you think students with self-doubts could do to become more positive?

9. Do you know any "zombie students" like the ones the writer describes on page 34—students who are going through the motions of being college students but are not really committed to study? What are some of the ways they are deluding themselves?

10. Describe one person you know well who is open to growth in life and one person who is not open to such growth. How do they show their willingness or reluctance to grow in their everyday lives?

Your instructor may ask you to write a paper that responds *in detail* to one of the preceding questions.

Part Two
Study Skills

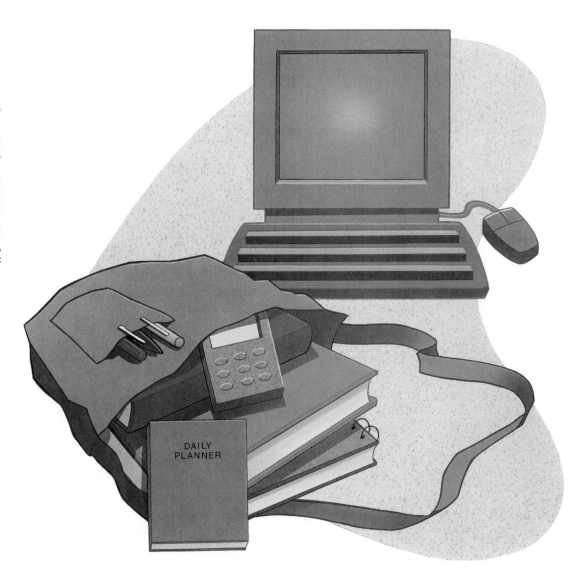

Preview

Part Two presents study skills that you need if you are to do well in your courses. Each skill is explained and illustrated, and a number of activities are given to help you practice and master it. "Taking Classroom Notes" lists a number of hints for note-taking, explains how to study your class notes, and discusses handwriting and listening efficiency. In "Time Control and Concentration," you will learn several ways to make better use of your time and to develop the persistence in your work that is vital to success in school. "Textbook Study I" describes a four-step method you can use to read and study chapters in your textbooks. "Textbook Study II" gives you practice in that method with short and medium-length textbook passages. "Textbook Study III" shows you how to apply the method to an entire textbook chapter. In "Building a Powerful Memory," you will learn seven steps you can take to improve your memory. "Taking Objective Exams" and "Taking Essay Exams" show you how to prepare for both kinds of exams and explain test-taking techniques. Finally, the chapters on "Using the Library and the Internet" and "Writing a Research Paper" will prepare you for writing projects that require research. They explain just how you can use the library and the Internet to look up information about a subject as well as an appropriate way to present this information.

Taking Classroom Notes

This chapter will show you how to:

- Take effective classroom notes
- Study and remember your notes
- Improve your handwriting and listening efficiency

Taking Classroom Notes: In Real Life

Read the profile that follows. Then ask yourself these questions:

- Why does Cheryl believe it's important to write down notes rather than just listen carefully?
- What is one of Cheryl's note-taking tips that I plan to try?

Student Profile: Cheryl Parker

"If you get a good union job at a factory and work your way up, you'll do OK. You'll be able to support yourself and a family." This was the advice that Cheryl Parker was given in high school. According to the standardized tests she took, she was "slow." She wasn't college material.

Cheryl believed what she was told. As soon as she graduated from high school, she found full-time work with a company that manufactured clothing. Always a hard worker, she eventually moved up into the company's printing department. The years passed. Occasionally Cheryl would see a newspaper article or hear a television news report about learning disabilities—disorders that can keep even highly intelligent people from doing well in school. "I wonder if that's what happened to me," Cheryl would sometimes think.

Continued

Seventeen years after Cheryl started her job, the clothing company declared bankruptcy. "I realized I was at a fork in the road," she says today. "Would I take another full-time job and just keep going the way I'd been going? Or would I challenge myself by going back to school?"

Cheryl made her decision. She approached a counselor at Rio Hondo Community College in Whittier, California, and asked two questions: Could she be tested for a learning disorder? And could she enroll in a remedial English course? The counselor, Judy Marks, encouraged

Cheryl on both counts. Cheryl took the test and enrolled in a developmental course taught by Ms. Marks herself. "By the time my test results came back, I was already hooked on school," Cheryl remembers.

Cheryl's test results showed that she was severely dyslexic—a condition that "scrambles" the perception of written words. Suddenly, Cheryl's problems in high school made sense. "It wasn't that I didn't study—I did! It wasn't that I didn't know the material—I did!" she recalls. "But it took me so much longer than the average student to read material and, especially, to write out answers in exams. It was such a relief to know there was a reason, that it wasn't that I was mentally 'slow.'"

Once Cheryl's dyslexia was identified, she and her instructors were able to make accommodations she needed. She was given extra time to take examinations. She was also allowed to tape-record lectures. Most importantly of all, Cheryl now believed in her own ability. She knew she could find ways around the obstacles that faced her.

Of all the skills Cheryl has developed in her college career, she points to note-taking as perhaps the most important of all. "I've always been an excellent listener. With my disability, I've *had* to become one," she explains. "But I've realized that *no one* can listen well enough to rely on memory alone. There's something about the act of actually writing notes down that helps them stick in your mind. Good notes are absolutely essential to college success."

Continued

Cheryl has a number of tips to share regarding note-taking:

- "First, I sit in the front row of every class. And not only in the front row, but in the *middle* of the front row," she explains. "I need not only to *hear* what the instructor's saying but to *see* everything—her gestures, her posture, her facial expressions. Her body language is as important as her words in telling me what is most important about what she's saying."

- "Next, I tape-record lectures. Even though I've taken notes throughout class, I replay the lecture that same night while it's still fresh in my mind and fill in anything that I've missed. Because I can stop and restart the tape, I can write very clearly, without hurrying."

- "When the instructor uses the blackboard, I write down everything she writes, whether it seems important at the moment or not. When an instructor bothers to write something on the board, it's often in the form of a list—and chances are good that this list is going to show up on the next exam."

- "This may not apply to people who aren't dyslexic, but occasionally I just won't be able to recognize a word on the board, even if I'm familiar with it. When that happens, I ask a classmate what it says. But rather than say 'I'm dyslexic and I can't read that,' I'll fake it a little by saying, 'I can't make that out—is that *a* or *e* or *o?*'"

- "If the instructor uses an overhead projector, I can rarely take complete notes on a transparency before she removes it. Rather than panic because I can't get it all, I ask to borrow it once she's finished. I stay a few minutes after class and copy it down."

- "My notes are full of symbols to myself. I'll write a big star to emphasize an important word. Or I'll underline or circle major points. I'll write a question mark in the margin to remind myself to ask the instructor to clarify something later."

- "Occasionally I'll ask a classmate who I know takes good notes to share his or her notes with me. I'll just compare our notes to make sure we're picking up the same major points. If so, I feel reassured; and if I'm missing something the other student has, I know I need to check into that."

- "After an exam, even if I've done well on it, I go back to my notes to compare how closely they mirror what was on the test. If they don't overlap a lot with what was on the exam, then I know I have to change

Continued

my strategy for taking notes in that class. I hear a lot of students say, 'Well, that test is over and there's nothing I can learn from it anymore.' There's always something you can learn, especially from your mistakes."

Cheryl graduated from Rio Hondo College in the spring of 1999 with a 4.0 grade point average during her career there. Now a student at California State Long Beach University, she is working toward her bachelor's degree in criminal justice.

Cheryl Parker slow? Yeah—slow like a race horse.

The Importance of Attending Class

If you really want to do well in a course, you must promise yourself that you will go to class faithfully and take good notes. This chapter will offer a series of tips on how to take effective classroom notes. However, the hints will be of no value if you do not attend class. The importance of *regular class attendance* cannot be emphasized enough. Students who cut class rarely do well in college.

The alternatives to class attendance—reading the text or using someone else's notes—can seldom substitute for the experience of being in class and hearing the instructor talk about key ideas in the course. These ideas are often the ones you will be expected to know on exams.

If you do not attend classes regularly, you may be making an unconscious decision that you do not want to attend college at this time. If you think this may be how you feel, talk to a counselor, an instructor, or a friend. Another person can often help you clarify your own thoughts and feelings so that you can achieve a perspective on your situation.

- Have you made a personal decision (be honest!) to attend all your classes

  regularly? _____

- If not, are you willing to think about why you are reluctant to make the

  commitment to college work? _____

Thirteen Hints for Taking Effective Classroom Notes

Hint 1: Keep a Written Record

Keep a written record of each class. It's important that you write down the material covered because forgetting begins almost immediately. Studies have shown that within two weeks you probably will forget 80 percent or more of what you have heard. And in four weeks you are lucky if 5 percent remains! The significance of these facts is so crucial that the point bears repeating: To guard against the relentlessness of forgetting, you must write down much of the information presented in class. Later, you will study your notes so that you understand and remember the ideas presented in class. And the more complete your notes are when you review them, the more likely you are to master the material.

How many notes should you take? If you pay attention in class, you will soon develop an instinct for what is meaningful and what is not. If you are unsure whether certain terms, facts, and ideas are significant, here is a good rule to follow: *When in doubt, write it down.* This doesn't mean you should (or could) get down every word, but you should be prepared to do a good deal of writing in class. Also, do not worry if you don't understand everything you record in your notes. Sometimes an instructor will phrase an idea several different ways, and it may turn out that it is the third version of the idea that you clearly understand. Later, it is easy to cross out the material that you don't need, but it is impossible to recover material you never recorded in the first place. Keep in mind that writing too much, rather than too little, may mean the difference between passing and failing a course or between a higher grade and a lower one.

- Explain briefly why you should keep a written record of each class.

  Because forgetting begins almost immediately _____

  _____

  _____

  _____

Hint 2: Sit Where You'll Be Seen

Sit where the instructor will always see you, and where you can see the blackboard clearly and easily. Your position near or at the front will help you stay tuned in to what the instructor does in class. If you sit behind someone, are hidden in a corner, or are otherwise out of the instructor's line of vision, it may be a reflection of your attitude—either you are worried that you may be noticed and called on (a common anxiety) or you don't really want to be in the classroom at all (something worth thinking about).

Analyze your attitude. If you're hiding, be aware that you're hiding and try to understand why. It is all right not to want to be in a class; instructors can be boring and subjects uninteresting. However, the danger in such cases is that you may slide into a passive state where you won't listen or take notes. Don't fool yourself. If a class is deadly, there is all the more reason to make yourself take good notes—that way you will pass the course and get out of the class once and for all.

- Explain briefly two reasons why you should sit near the front.

  Sitting near the front helps you stay tuned in to what the instructor does
  and encourages you to take notes.

Hint 3: Do Some Advance Reading

Ideally, read in advance about the topic to be discussed in class. All too often, students don't read assigned textbook material on a topic until after class is over. Lacking the necessary background, they have trouble understanding the new ideas discussed in class. However, if they have made an initial breakthrough on a topic by doing some advance reading, they will be able to listen and take notes more easily and with greater understanding. And they should be able to write more organized and effective notes because they will have a general sense of the topic.

If you don't know what the next topic is going to be, check with your instructor at the end of the preceding class. Simply ask, "Is there a chapter in the textbook that I can read in advance of your next class? I'd like to get a head start on what you're going to cover." At the least, you are going to make a good impression on the instructor, who will appreciate your seriousness and interest.

In particular, try to read the textbook in advance when the subject is very difficult. Reading in advance is also a good idea if you have spelling problems that hinder note-taking. As you read through the text, write down key terms and recurring words that may come up in the lecture and that you might have trouble spelling.

- Explain briefly why you should read your textbook in advance of a lecture.

  Reading in advance helps you to understand challenging material and to take

  more organized and efficient notes.

  _____

  _____

Hint 4: Record Notes Systematically

1   Use full-size 8½- by 11-inch paper. Do *not* use a small note tablet. As explained below, you will need the margin space provided by full-size paper. Also, on a single page of full-size paper you can often see groups of related ideas that might not be apparent spread over several small pages.

2   Use a ballpoint pen. You will often need to write quickly—something that you cannot do as well with a pencil or a felt-tip pen. (Don't worry about making mistakes with a pen that makes marks you can't erase. Just cross out the mistakes!)

3   Keep all the notes from each course together in a separate section of a notebook. Use a loose-leaf binder with sections indicated by dividers and index tabs, or use a large spiral notebook that has several sections. A spiral notebook is simpler. But a loose-leaf binder has the advantage of letting you insert hand-out sheets and supplementary notes at appropriate points. If you use a binder, you may want to leave previous notes safe at home and just bring to each class the last day or so of notes and some blank paper.

4   Date each day's notes.

5   Take notes on one side of the page only and leave space at the top of the page and at the left-hand margin. (You might use notebook paper that has a light red line down the left side.) Using only one side of the paper eliminates the bother, when you are studying, of having to flip pages over and then flip them back to follow the development of an idea.

    Leaving wide margins gives you space to add to your notes if desired. You may, for example, write in ideas taken from your textbook or other sources. Also, the margins can be used to prepare study notes (see pages 53–54) that will help you learn the material.

6   Write legibly. When you prepare for a test, you want to spend your time studying—not deciphering your handwriting.

7   To save time, abbreviate recurring terms. Put a key to abbreviated words in the top margin of your notes. For example, in a biology class *ch* could stand for *chromosome;* in a psychology class *o c* could stand for *operant conditioning.* (When a lecture is over, you may want to go back and fill in the words you have abbreviated.)

Also abbreviate the following common words, using the symbols shown:

+ = and	*def* = definition
w/ = with	∴ = therefore
eg = for example	*info* = information
ex = example	*1, 2, 3* = one, two, three, etc.

Note, too, that you can often omit words like *a, and,* and *the.*

8   Note prominently exams or quizzes that are announced, as well as assignments that the instructor gives. It's a good idea to circle exam dates and put a large *A* for *assignment* in the margin. (Be sure you have a definite system for keeping track of assignments. Some students record them on a separate small notepad; others record them at the back of the notebook devoted to a given course.)

- What do you consider the three most helpful suggestions for recording notes?

Answers will vary.

_____

_____

_____

Hint 5: Use an Outline for Notes

Try to write your notes in the form of an outline, as described below. By following the outline form, you'll be able to tell at a glance which are the most important points in your notes and which are less essential supportive details.

Start writing main points at the margin of the page. Indent (skip a few spaces from the margin) secondary ideas and supporting details. Further indent material subordinate to secondary points.

Main points start at the margin.
Secondary points and supporting details are indented, like this line.
Material subordinate to secondary points is indented further.

Definitions, for example, are essential to your understanding of the material, so they should always start at the margin. When a list of terms is presented, the heading should also start at the margin, but each item in the series should be set in slightly from the margin. Examples, too, should be indented under the point they illustrate.

Here is another organizational aid: When the instructor changes topics or moves from one aspect of an idea to another, show this shift by skipping a line or two, leaving a clearly visible white space.

In the fast-paced lecture, you won't always be able to tell what is a main point and what is secondary material. Be ready, though, to use the outline technique of indentation and extra space whenever you can. They are the first steps toward organizing class material.

- Explain briefly what is meant by *indentation.*

  Setting in from the margin secondary points and supporting details

  _____

  _____

  _____

Hint 6: Be Alert for Signals

Watch for signals of importance:

1 Write down whatever your instructor puts on the board. Ideally, *print* such material in capital letters. If you don't have time to print, write as you usually do and put the letters *OB* in the margin to indicate that the material was written on the board. Later, when you review your notes, you will know which ideas the instructor emphasized. The chances are good that they will come up on exams.

2 Always write down definitions and enumerations. Most people instinctively write down definitions—explanations of key terms in the subject they are learning. But they often ignore enumerations, which are often equally important. An *enumeration* is simply a list of items (marked 1, 2, 3, etc., or with other symbols) that fit under a particular heading. (See also page 368.)

Instructors use enumerations, or lists, to show the relationships among ideas. Being aware of enumerations will help you organize material as you take notes. Enumerations are signaled in such ways as: "The four steps in the process are . . . "; "There were three reasons for . . . "; "Five characteristics of . . . "; "The two effects were . . . "; and so on. When you write a list, always mark the items 1, 2, 3, or use other appropriate symbols. Also, always be sure to include a clear heading that explains what a list is about. For example, if you list and number six kinds of defense mechanisms, make sure you write at the top of the list the heading "Kinds of Defense Mechanisms."

3 Your instructor may say, "This is an important reason . . . "; or "A point that will keep coming up later . . . "; or "The chief cause was . . . "; or "The basic idea here is . . . "; or "Don't forget that . . . "; or "Pay special attention to . . . "; and so on. Be sure to write down the important statements announced by these and other emphasis words, and write in the margin *imp* or some other mark (such as * or ζ or →) to show their importance.

4 If your instructor repeats a point, you can usually assume it is important. You might write *R* for *repeated* in the margin so that you will know later that your instructor stressed this idea.

5 An instructor's voice may slow down, become louder, or otherwise signal that you are expected to write down exactly what is being said, word for word. Needless to say, do so!

- Which two signals of importance do you think will be most helpful for you to remember?

Answers will vary.

_____

_____

_____

_____

Hint 7: Write Down Examples

Write down any examples the instructor provides, and mark them with *ex.* The examples help you understand complex and abstract points. If you don't mark them with *ex,* you are likely to forget their purpose when you later review them for study. You may not have to write down every example that illustrates an idea, but you should record at least one example that makes a point clear.

Hint 8: Write Down Details That Connect or Explain

Be sure to write down the details that connect or explain main points. Too many students copy only the major points the instructor puts on the board. They do not realize that as time passes, they may forget the specifics that serve as bridges connecting key ideas. Be sure, then, to record the connecting details the instructor provides. That way you are more apt to remember the relationships among the major points in your notes.

In science and mathematics classes especially, students often fail to record the explanations that make formulas or numerical problems meaningful. Their notes may consist only of the letters and numbers the instructor chalked on the board. But to understand how the letters and numbers are related, they should also write down accompanying explanations and details.

Always take advantage of the connections instructors often make at the beginning or end of a class. They may review material already covered and preview what is to come. Write down such overviews when they are presented and label them *review* or *preview,* as the case may be. An instructor's summaries or projections will help the course come together for you.

- How often do you write down connections between ideas?

_____ Frequently   _____ Sometimes   _____ Almost never

Hint 9: Leave Some Blank Spaces

Leave blank spaces for items or ideas you miss. Right after class, ask another student to help you fill in the gaps. Ideally, you should find a person in each course who will agree to be your note-taking partner—someone with whom you can compare and fill in notes after a class. If another person is not available, you might want to tape each class and play back the tape right away to get any missing material. (Don't ever, though, fall into the trap of relying on a tape recorder to take most of your notes. In no time at all, you'll have hours and hours of tape to go through—time you probably cannot afford to take. Use a tape only to help you fill in occasional gaps.)

When you do fall behind in note-taking during class, don't give up and just stop writing. Try to get down what seem to be the main ideas rather than supporting facts and details. You may be able to fill in the supporting material later.

Hint 10: Ask Questions

Don't hesitate to ask the instructor questions if certain points are confusing to you. Probably, other students have the same questions but are reluctant to ask to have the material clarified. Remember that instructors look favorably on students who show interest and curiosity.

- How often do you ask questions in class?

_____ Frequently

_____ Sometimes

_____ Almost never

Hint 11: Take Notes during Discussions

Do not stop taking notes during discussion periods. Many valuable ideas may come up during informal discussions, ideas that your instructor may not present formally later on. If your instructor puts notes on the board during a class discussion, it's a good sign that the material is important. If he or she pursues or draws out a discussion in a given direction, it's a clue that you should be taking notes. And don't forget the advice in hint 1 on page 43: When in doubt, write it down.

Hint 12: Take Notes Right Up to the End of Class

Do not stop taking notes toward the end of a class. Because of time spent on discussions, instructors may have to cram important points they want to cover into the last minutes of a class. Be ready to write as rapidly as you can to get down this final rush of ideas.

Be prepared, also, to resist the fatigue that may settle in during class. As a lecture proceeds, the possibility of losing attention increases. You do not want to snap out of a daydream only to realize that an instructor is halfway into an important idea and you haven't even begun writing.

- Are you one of the many students whose note-taking slows down at the end of a class? _____

Hint 13: Review Your Notes Soon

Go over your notes soon after class. While the material is still clear in your mind, make your notes as clear as possible. A day later may be too late, because forgetting sets in almost at once.

As far as possible, make sure that your punctuation is clear, that unfinished ideas are completed, and that all words are readable and correctly spelled. You may also want to write out completely words that you abbreviated during the lecture. Wherever appropriate, add connecting statements and other comments to clarify the material. Make sure important items—material on the board, definitions, enumerations, and so on—are clearly marked. Improve the organization, if necessary, so that you can see at a glance the differences between main points and supporting material as well as any relationships among the main points.

This review does more than make your notes clear: It is also a vital step in the process of mastering the material. During class, you have almost certainly been too busy taking notes to absorb all the ideas. Now, as you review the notes, you can roll up your sleeves and wrestle with the ideas presented and think about the relationships among them. You can, in short, do the work needed to reach the point where you can smile and say, "Yes, I understand—and everything I understand is down clearly in my notes."

- Explain briefly why you should go over your notes soon after class.

  They are still fresh in your mind. You can make them more complete and

  better organized.

  _____

How to Study Class Notes

The best time to start studying your notes is within a day after taking them. Because of the mind's tendency to forget material rapidly, a few minutes of study soon after a class will give you more learning for less time and effort than almost any other technique you can practice.

One Effective Method for Studying Class Notes

Here is one effective way to study your notes:

1 Use the margin space at the side (or top) of each page. Jot down in the margin a series of key words or phrases from your notes. These key words or phrases, known as *recall words,* will help you pull together and remember the important ideas on the page.

On page 53 are notes from a business course. Take the time now to look them over carefully. You will notice in the side margin the recall words that the student, Janet, used for studying this page of notes.

2 To test yourself on the material, turn the recall words in the margin into questions. For instance, Janet asked herself, "What is the origin of economics?" After she could recite the answer without looking at it, she asked herself, "What is the definition of economics?" Janet then went back and retested herself on the first question. When she could recite the answers to both the first and second questions, she went on to the third one.

Shown below are most of the questions that Janet asked herself. Fill in the missing questions.

What is the origin of economics?
What is the definition of economics?
What is an important assumption of economics?

What is the definition of economic resources?
What are two types of economic resources?

What are the two kinds of property resources and their definitions?
What are the three kinds of human resources and their definitions?

Janet tested herself on each of the seven questions and retested herself on those from earlier lectures, until she could recite all of them from memory. (For more information on repeated self-testing, see page 212.)

This approach, if it is pursued regularly, will help you remember the material covered in your classes. With such a study method, you will not be left with a great deal of material to organize and learn right before an exam. Instead, you will be able to devote preexam time to a final intensive review of the subject.

Another Good Method for Studying Class Notes

Some students prefer to write out on separate sheets of paper the material they want to learn. They prepare study sheets that often use a question-and-answer format. The very act of writing out study notes is itself a step toward remembering the material. Shown on page 54 is a study sheet that Janet could have prepared.

Two Special Skills that Help Note-Taking

Two special skills that will help you take effective classroom notes are handwriting efficiency and listening efficiency. The following pages explain and offer practice in these skills.

Increasing Handwriting Efficiency

Activity 1

To check your handwriting efficiency, write as fast as you can for ten minutes. Don't stop for anything. Don't worry about spelling, punctuation, erasing mistakes, or finding exact words. If you get stuck for words, write "I am looking for something to say" or repeat words until something comes. You have two objectives in this rapid-writing activity: to write as many words as you can in the ten minutes (you will be asked to count the words later) and to write words legibly enough so that you can still understand them several weeks from now.

Count the number of words you have written in the ten minutes and record the number here: _____.

At the left are the recall words Janet placed in the margin.

Janet's Classroom Notes

	Business 101 11-29-01 ec = economic(s) res = resource
	Economics—from Greek words meaning "HOUSE" and "TO
Origin of ec	MANAGE." Meaning gradually extended to cover management
	not only of household but of business and governments.
Def of ec	Ec (definition)—STUDY OF HOW SCARCE RESOURCES ARE
	ALLOCATED IN A SOCIETY OF UNLIMITED WANTS.
	Every society provides goods + services; these are
	available in limited quantities + so have value.
Imp	One of the most imp. assumptions of ec: Though res of
assumption	world are limited, wants of people are not. This means ec system
	can never produce enough to satisfy everyone completely.
Def of ec res	Ec res—all factors that go into production of goods + services.
2 types of	Two types:
ec res	1. PROPERTY RES—2 kinds:
2 kinds of	a. LAND—all natural res (land, timber, water, oil, minerals)
property	b. CAPITAL—all machinery, tools, equipment, + building
res + defs	needed to produce goods + distribute them to consumers.
3 kinds of	2. HUMAN RES—3 kinds
human	a. LABOR—all physical and mental talents needed to produce
res + defs	goods + services
	b. MANAGEMENT ABILITY—talent needed to bring
	together land, capital, + labor to produce goods + services.
	c. TECHNOLOGY—accumulated fund of knowledge
	which helps in production of goods + services.

Sample Study Sheet

What is the origin of economics?

From Greek words "house" and "manage." Word gradually extended to include business and government.

What is economics?

Study of how scarce resources are allocated in a society of unlimited wants.

What is an important assumption of economics?

Resources are limited but people's wants are not.

What are economic resources?

All the factors that go into production of goods + services.

What are the two types of economic resources?

Property + human resources.

What are the two kinds of property resources?

a. Land—all natural resources (land, timber, water, oil, minerals).

b. Capital—all the machinery, tools, equipment, and building needed to produce goods + distribute them to consumers.

What are the three kinds of human resources?

a. Labor—all physical and mental talents needed to produce goods + services.

b. Management ability—talent needed to bring together land, capital, + labor to produce goods a services.

c. Technology—accumulated fund of knowledge which helps in production of goods + services.

Handwriting Speed and Legibility: In Activity 1, you should have been able to write at least 250 legible words in ten minutes—and ideally 100 or so more than that. Handwriting speed is important because it is basic to effective note-taking in fast-moving lectures. If you cannot write quickly enough, you are likely to miss valuable ideas presented in such classes. Also, you may have trouble writing out full answers on essay exams. And in either situation, if your handwriting is not legible, there is hardly any point in writing at all.

Improving Speed: There are several steps you can take to improve your hand-writing speed.

One step is to practice *rapid writing*—writing nonstop for ten or fifteen minutes at a time about whatever comes into your head. Try to increase the number of pages you fill with words in the limited time period. With several practice sessions, you should be able to increase your handwriting speed significantly.

Another way to increase speed is to use abbreviations. Abbreviate words that occur repeatedly in a lecture class, and put a key for such words in the top margin of your notes. For example, if the name *Linnaeus* keeps recurring in a botany class, at the top of the page write *L = Linnaeus,* and from then on in your notes that day simply use *L.*

• What keys could you make for a psychology class on Skinner and behaviorism?

S = Skinner   *beh = behaviorism*

Following is a list of other symbols that can be made part of a general "short-hand" for your writing. (Note that you can often omit *a, and, the,* and other connecting words.)

$$+ = \text{and}$$
$$\text{w/} = \text{with}$$
$$\text{eg} = \text{for example}$$
$$\text{ex} = \text{example}$$
$$\text{def} = \text{definition}$$
$$\text{imp} = \text{important}$$
$$\text{ind} = \text{individual}$$
$$\text{info} = \text{information}$$
$$\text{sc} = \text{science}$$
$$\text{soc} = \text{sociology}$$
$$\text{psy} = \text{psychology}$$
$$1, 2, 3, = \text{one, two, three, (etc.)}$$

Finally, you can write faster if you streamline your handwriting by eliminating unnecessary high and low loops in letters. For example,

Instead of	Write		Instead of	Write
b	*b*		*k*	*k*
d	*d*		*l*	*l*
f	*f*		*p*	*p*
g	*g*		*t*	*t*
h	*h*		*y*	*y*

You will find that this streamlined, print-style writing is learned easily and will help you write faster.

- Go back and put the numbers 1, 2, and 3 in front of the three methods described for increasing handwriting speed.

Improving Legibility: To improve and maintain legibility, check a sample of your writing for the four common types of faulty handwriting illustrated here. Or give your writing sample to someone else to analyze for handwriting faults.

1 Overlapping letters from one line to the next. For example:

> *One of the main types of faulty handwriting is the overlapping of letters from one line to the next.*

Note the improvement in legibility when this fault is eliminated:

> *One of the main types of faulty handwriting is the overlapping of letters from one line to the next.*

2 Slanting letters in more than one direction. For example:

> *Another kind of faulty handwriting is to slant letters in all directions instead of just one.*

Note how legibility improves when slants are consistent:

> *Another kind of faulty handwriting is to slant letters in all directions instead of just one.*

3 Making decorative capitals or loops. For example:

[handwritten:] The use of decorative capitals and loops may result in a script that

You can greatly improve legibility by *printing* capital letters and restraining your loop letters.

4 Miswriting the letters *a, e, r, n,* and *t.* Common errors include writing the letter *e* like *i* (closing the loop) and putting a loop in nonloop letters like *i* and *t.* Check your handwriting to be sure you form these letters clearly. Also, look for other letters that you may miswrite consistently.

To improve legibility, follow two other tips as well. First, always use a ballpoint pen rather than a pencil. A dull-edged pencil will slow down your writing speed and hinder legibility. You can buy a Bic pen for 45 cents. Second, be sure to hold your pen between the thumb and index finger, resting it against the middle finger. Don't grip the pen tightly, but hold it just firmly enough to keep it from slipping. And don't hold it, as some people do, too close to the tip—you won't be able to see what you're writing. Hold it about ¾ inch from the point.

If you follow these suggestions, your handwriting should become more efficient. Clear and rapid handwriting is a mechanical technique; once you decide to learn it and begin to practice, mastery is almost bound to follow. People should not allow a failure to write skillfully to limit their note-taking performance, whether in school or on the job.

Activity 2

Write again for ten minutes without stopping. Try to write more words than you did in Activity 1. At the same time, be sure to keep your words legible.

Number of words in Activity 1: _____   In Activity 2: _____

Increasing Listening Efficiency

Activity 1

To take effective classroom notes, you must be able to listen attentively. This activity will test your ability to listen carefully and to follow spoken directions. The instructor will give you a series of thirteen directions. Listen closely to each one and then do exactly what it calls for. Each direction will be spoken only once.

If you are working on this book independently, get a friend to read the directions to you, or read each direction aloud once to yourself and then try to follow it. Do the same for other activities in this section as well.

Direction 1: Do not say a word at any point during this exercise. Do not raise your hand or look at your neighbor. There will be thirteen directions in the exercise. Follow every one of them except for the last direction, which you should disregard.

Direction 2: Get out a sheet of paper and write your full name in the upper left-hand corner of the paper.

Direction 3: Write the numbers 1 to 8 down the left-hand side of the page.

Direction 4: Write beside space 2 the word *quiet,* which is spelled *q-u-i-e-t.*

Direction 5: Write down the name of the street where you live beside space 3. Do not write down the street number.

Direction 6: Think of the name of the high school that you went to. Do not write it down beside space 1.

Direction 7: Think of the name of the toothpaste that you use. Write it down on the back of your sheet of paper.

Direction 8: Listen to the following set of numbers and then put them down beside space 4. The numbers are 8, 12, 20, 31, 45.

Direction 9: Think of the name of a television show that you like, turn your paper upside down, and write the name of the show beside space 5.

Direction 10: Turn your paper back to the original position. Then count the number of people in the room, including yourself. Write out the number beside space 6.

Direction 11: Print in capital letters your first name or nickname beside space 7.

Direction 12: Write the word *banana*—spelled *b-a-n-a-n-a*—beside space 8. Then draw a picture of a pear on one side of the word *banana* and a picture of an apple under the word *banana.*

Direction 13: This is the last direction. Crumple your paper into a ball and throw it to the front of the room.

If you followed all directions correctly, you have done an effective job of attending closely. It is a skill that will help you be a good listener and note-taker.

Skills in Good Listening:
Effective listening and note-taking require not only the ability to attend but other skills as well. At the same time you are writing down what an instructor has said, you must be able to listen to what he or she is now saying and to decide whether it is important enough to write down as well. Also, in a rapid lecture you must be able at times to store one or more ideas in your memory

so that you will be able to write them down next. If you can "listen ahead" and process and remember what you hear at the same time that you are writing rapidly, you will be listening efficiently. Your brain will be able to work along with and ahead of your pen.

Activity 2

This activity will give you practice in developing your listening efficiency.

Group A: Your instructor will read each sentence in group A once, at a normal speaking speed. Listen carefully and, after the instructor has read the sentence, see if you can write down what has been said. Before starting the second sentence, the instructor will give you time to finish writing. Do not worry about getting down every little word; do try to get down the basic idea. (If there are words you cannot spell, try to spell them the way they sound. In actual note-taking situations, you can later look up correct spellings in your textbook or dictionary.) There are three practice sentences in group A.

1. Almost one in every seven Americans is affected by hypertension—that is, by high blood pressure.
2. A half hour of TV nightly news, if printed, would not fill one page of *The New York Times.*
3. In 1900 about one in thirteen marriages ended in divorce; today one in two ends in divorce.

Group B: The three examples in group B are almost twice as long as those in group A. They require, then, increased listening efficiency. Your instructor will read the two sentences in each example at a normal speaking rate. You can begin writing as soon as the instructor starts the first sentence. You will have to listen to and remember the second sentence in each example at the same time you are writing the first sentence.

1. The popular idea that you can tell the age of a rattlesnake by the number of rattles on its tail is false. A healthy snake can grow several new rattles in a single year.
2. The usual age of retirement in America is sixty-five. Many experts are now questioning the fairness of a system that removes people from their jobs no matter how qualified they are.
3. People have a great advantage over computers, for we can understand visual images drawn from our environment. Computers can process only facts that are put into numerical form.

Group C: The three examples in group C are about three times as long as those in group A. They create, then, an even more realistic note-taking situation, and they require a further increase in listening efficiency. Again your instructor will read the sentences in each example at a normal rate of speed. You will have to "listen ahead" and remember what you hear at the same time that you are writing rapidly.

1. When trapped in quicksand, do not struggle, or you will be sucked in deeper. The body floats on quicksand, so you should fall on your back, stretching out your arms at right angles, as if floating on water. Then, after working your legs free from the sand, begin rolling your entire body toward safe ground.

2. Ralph Nader has suggested that voting be required in this country, as it is in several other countries. In Australia, students learn that if they don't vote at age eighteen, they may have to pay a fine equal to about $15 in American money. The result is that about 90 percent of qualified voters go to the polls.

3. Babies seldom cry for no reason at all. They cry because of some discomfort that they feel. In the first year of life in particular, it is important that parents respond to a baby's cries rather than ignore them. A prompt response helps give the baby a sense of security and trust.

You will receive additional practice in listening when you take notes on the short lectures that appear on pages 63–69.

Practice in Taking Classroom Notes

Activity 1

Taking Notes: Evaluate your present note-taking skills by putting a check mark beside each of the thirteen note-taking hints that you already practice. Then put a check mark beside those steps that you plan to practice. Leave a space blank if you do not plan to follow a particular strategy.

Now Do	Plan to Do	
____	____	1. Take notes on classroom work.
____	____	2. Sit near the front of the class.
____	____	3. Read in advance textbook material about the topic to be presented in class.
		4. Record notes as follows:
____	____	a. Use full-size 8½- by 11-inch paper.

____ ____   b.   Use a ballpoint pen.

____ ____   c.   Use a notebook divided into parts.

____ ____   d.   Date each day's notes.

____ ____   e.   Take notes on one side of the page only.

____ ____   f.   Write legibly.

____ ____   g.   Abbreviate common words and recurring terms.

____ ____   h.   Indicate assignments and exams.

     5. Write notes in outline form as follows:

____ ____   a.   Start main points at the margin; indent secondary points.

____ ____   b.   Use white space to show shift in thought.

     6. Watch for signals of importance:

____ ____   a.   Write whatever the instructor puts on the board.

____ ____   b.   Write definitions and enumerations.

____ ____   c.   Write down points marked by emphasis words.

____ ____   d.   Record repeated points.

____ ____   e.   Note the hints given by the instructor's tone of voice.

____ ____   7. Write down examples.

____ ____   8. Write down connecting details and explanations.

     9. Do as follows when material is missed:

____ ____   a.   Leave space for notes missed.

____ ____   b.   Try to get the broad sweep of ideas when you fall behind.

____ ____   10. Question the instructor when an idea isn't clear.

____ ____   11. Do not stop taking notes during discussion periods.

____ ____   12. Do not stop taking notes toward the end of a class.

____ ____   13. Go over your notes soon after class.

Studying Notes: Now, evaluate your skills in studying class notes.

____ ____   • Jot in the margin key words to recall ideas.

____ ____   • Turn recall words into questions.

____ ____   • Use repeated self-testing to learn the material.

____ ____   • Apply this study method regularly.

Activity 2

Below is an excerpt from notes taken during an introductory lecture in a sociology class. In the margin of the notes, jot down key words or phrases that could be used to pull together and so recall the main ideas on the page.

	Sociology 101 11-21-01
5 sources of truth	In the million years or so of life on earth, human beings have sought truth in many places. FIVE SOURCES OF TRUTH in particular are important to note: (1) intuition, (2) authority, (3) tradition, (4) common sense, and (5) science.
Def. and ex. intuition	1. INTUITION—any flash of insight (true or mistaken) whose source the receiver cannot fully identify or explain. Ex.—Galen in second century made chart of human body showing exactly where it might be pierced without fatal injury. Knew which zones were fatal through intuition.
Def. of authority	2. AUTHORITY—persons who are experts in a specific field.
2 kinds of authority and defs.	Two kinds of authority: a. SACRED—rests upon faith that a certain tradition or document—eg, the Bible—is of supernatural origin. b. SECULAR—arises from human perception + is of two kinds:
2 kinds of sacred authority and defs.	(1) secular scientific—rests upon empirical observation. (2) secular humanistic—rests upon belief that certain "great people" have had special insight.

Activity 3

Turn in to your instructor a copy of one day's notes that you have taken in one of your classes. These notes should fill at least one side of a sheet of paper. If you have never taken a full page of notes in class, add a second or third day's notes until you complete at least one sheet. In the top or left-hand margin of your notes, write down key words or phrases you could use to master the material in the notes.

Activity 4

The activity that follows will give you practice in taking lecture notes. The activity is based on a short lecture on listening given in a speech class. Take notes on the lecture as your instructor or a friend reads it aloud. Items that the original lecturer put on the board are shown at the top of the lecture. As you take your notes, apply the hints you have learned in this chapter. Then answer the questions that follow the selection by referring to your notes but not to the selection itself. Write your answers on separate sheets of paper.

Lecture about Listening

On Board

Problem of losing attention	Spare time
125 wpm = talking speed	Three techniques for concentration
500 wpm = listening speed	Intend to listen

I'm going to describe to you a listening problem that many people have. I'll also explain why many people have the problem, and I'll tell you what can be done about the problem. The listening problem that many people have is that they lose attention while listening to a speaker. They get bored, their minds wander, their thoughts go elsewhere.

Everyone has had this experience of losing attention, but probably few people understand one of the main reasons why we have this trouble keeping our attention on the speaker. The reason is this: There is a great deal of difference between talking speed and listening speed. The average speaker talks at the rate of 125 words a minute. On the other hand, we can listen and think at the rate of about 500 words a minute. Picture it: The speaker is going along at 125 wpm, and we are sitting there ready to move at four times that speed. The speaker is like a tortoise plodding along slowly; we, the listeners, are like the rabbit ready to dash along at a much faster speed. The result of this gap is that we have a lot of spare time to use while listening to a speech.

Unfortunately, many of us use this time to go off on side excursions of our own. We may begin thinking about a date, a sports event, a new shirt we want to buy, balancing our budget, how to start saving money, what we must do later in the day, and a thousand other things. The result of the side excursions may be that when our attention returns to the speaker, we find that we have been left far behind. The speaker has gotten into some new idea, and we, having missed some connection, have little sense of what is being talked about. We may have to listen very closely for five minutes to get back on track. The temptation at this point is to go back to our own special world of thoughts and forget about the speaker. Then we're wasting both our time and the speaker's time. What we must do instead is work hard to keep our attention on the speaker and to concentrate on what is being said.

Here are three mental techniques you can use to keep your concentration on the speaker. First of all, summarize what the speaker has said. Do this after each new point is developed. This constant summarizing will help you pay attention. Second, try to guess where the speaker is going next. Try to anticipate what direction the speaker is going to take, based on what has already been said. This game you play with yourself arouses your curiosity and helps maintain your attention. Third, question the truth, the validity, of the speaker's words. Compare the points made with your own knowledge and experience. Keep trying to decide whether you agree or disagree with the speaker on the basis of what you know. Don't simply take as gospel whatever the speaker tells you; question it—ask yourself whether you think it is true. Remember, then, to summarize what the speaker has said, try to guess where the speaker is going next, and question the truth of what is stated.

All three techniques can make you a better listener. But even better than these techniques, I think, is making a conscious effort to listen more closely. You must intend to concentrate, intend to listen carefully. For example, you should go into your classes every day determined to pay close attention. It should be easier for you to make this important mental decision if you remember how easily attention can wander when someone else is speaking.

Questions on the Lecture

1. What is a listening problem that many people have?

   People lose attention.

   _____

2. What are common talking and listening speeds?

   Talking—125 wpm; listening—500 wpm.

   _____

3. What are three techniques to help you pay attention when someone is talking?

   Summarize. Try to guess what's next. Question the truth of what's been said.

4. What is the most important step you can take to become a better listener?

   Make a conscious effort to listen closely.

   _____

Activity 5

Follow the directions given for Activity 4.

Lecture about Propaganda Techniques

On Board

Propaganda   Testimonial   Bandwagon   Plain folks   Transfer

We all know that advertising sells products. How many times have you bought a particular item because you saw it advertised on TV? We all have, of course, and that is the power of advertising. One thing that makes ads work is propaganda. Propaganda may be defined as *messages intended to persuade audiences to adopt a certain opinion.* We know that totalitarian governments use propaganda to win people to their side. But propaganda is also used by our own politicians, editorial writers, and advertisers. Today, we will discuss four propaganda techniques often used by advertisers.

The first of these techniques is called the *testimonial.* This means that celebrities are used to pitch an idea or sell a product. For example, you may have seen ads that used celebrities like Jerry Seinfeld for American Express, or Michael Jordan and Tiger Woods for Nike. Two well-known personalities, Rosie O'Donnell and Penny Marshall, have advertised K-Mart. The testimonial is a propaganda method because the audience associates the star qualities of the celebrity with the product—whether or not the celebrity knows anything at all about the product. Our good feelings about the person, in other words, spill over to the product. You can all think of famous people who have appeared in TV or magazine or billboard ads to sell products.

Another propaganda technique used by advertisers is the *bandwagon.* This method encourages people to do or buy something because "everyone else is doing it." Advertisers, for example, tell us that "Nobody doesn't like Sara Lee" or that we should "make the switch to Burger King" because everyone else (in the ads, at least) is doing just that. Countless ads have begun with the statement "All over America, people are switching to . . . using . . . buying." You are expected to do the same if you don't want to feel "out of it." The bandwagon, then, tells us that by buying a certain product we can get "on board."

Plain folks is a third propaganda method, one in which the product being sold is associated with "ordinary" people—people we can identify with. They're not glamorous types; they're just folks like you and me. When you see "regular" people, the kind who don't seem to be actors, explaining how Anacin helped their headaches, or how Bounce made their wash softer, or how much better Pepsi tasted than Coke, you are seeing the plain folks method. Advertisers know that consumers will believe people who seem down-to-earth, honest, and just like the folks next door.

A final propaganda technique is called *transfer.* In this method, the product is associated with something else that is attractive, respectable, or admirable. For example, countless advertisements for cars show a gorgeous model leaning over the hood or sliding into a plush interior. The audience will transfer its feeling about the model ("I want her" or "She is beautiful") to the car ("I want it" or "It is beautiful"). Advertisers use transfer, too, when they associate their products with patriotic symbols, such as the bald eagle or the Liberty Bell. When we see an eagle flying over the land while a narrator tells us about the Westinghouse Corporation's philosophy of quality, we transfer our patriotic feelings to the company.

This, then, has been an introduction to some of the propaganda methods that advertisers use to sell their products.

Questions on the Lecture

1. What is propaganda?

   Messages intended to persuade audiences to adopt a certain opinion
   _____

2. What are four propaganda techniques used by advertisers?

   Testimonial, bandwagon, plain folks, transfer
   _____

3. Explain the bandwagon technique.

   People are encouraged to do or buy something because "everybody

   is doing it."

4. Explain the technique of transfer.

   Products are associated with something attractive, respected,

   or admired.

Activity 6

Follow the directions given for Activity 4.

Lecture on Effective Writing

On Board

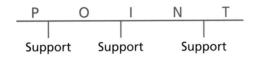

1. Make a point.
2. Support the point (BS).
3. Organize the support.
4. Write clear sentences.

Many people think that writing a good paragraph or paper is a kind of magical skill—one that some people have and others don't. When such people find that they have to do a great deal of writing themselves, either in college or on their jobs, they become angry and frustrated. Why should they have to write? After all, people aren't asked to play the piano or draw a picture if they have no training or talent. Isn't it just as unfair to be asked to write?

Probably the best-kept secret about writing is that it is a skill that can be mastered. That's right—you can learn to write a decent paper, learn to do well in writing assignments in school or on the job, no matter how much trouble you may have had with writing before. Writing consists of a series of steps that you can follow. When you finish, you should have an organized, effective paper.

The first step in writing an effective paper is to *make a point of some kind.* A point is an assertion, a statement that goes beyond a mere fact—a point has your opinion injected into it. We all make points all day long. If we could gather several points from the conversations around us, we might hear things like: "That movie was a waste of money"; "Our sociology professor is the best teacher I have ever had"; "I don't vote, because politicians are crooks"; "Going out for an evening is getting to be really expensive." Starting to write means deciding to focus on a point similar to any of these. For example, let's take a subject we all know something about: high school proms. When we were in high school, we all went to proms, or talked about people who went to proms, or stayed home from proms. We could make many points about proms; each of you would have some opinion about them. Let's take one point in particular, though. My point is that proms should be banned. If I said this to you as we were talking, I might go on to give you my reasons, or I might refuse to talk about it any more, or I might change the subject. In writing, however, once I made this point, I would have to support it.

That's the second step in writing—*supporting your point.* You saw that the first step wasn't too hard; this one isn't either. When I say support your point, I mean back it up. In other words, give reasons, details, examples, anything you can think of to make your point a convincing one. In addition, you should BS a lot. Yes, I said BS. You must remember to BS in your writing if you want to be effective. Of course, you all know what BS stands for—"Be specific." The details that support your point should be exact, precise, particular—not vague and general. In other words, they should be specific.

Let's try to come up with some specific details to support my point about proms. Perhaps I feel proms should be banned, first of all, because they cost too much money. Now I have to develop this reason with specific details. If I write "All the things a person has to buy to go to the prom are too expensive," I have failed my readers. "Too expensive" is not specific. Instead, I might write, "Attending the prom means buying a gown for $150, a bouquet of flowers for $35, a pair of tickets at $50 apiece, and a set of photographs that can cost $100 and up." Now I'm communicating better, for I have given my readers a clear idea of exactly how much money I'm talking about. Now there's a much better chance that they will eventually agree with my opening point—or at least respect my opinion. You can see, too, that specific details are a lot more interesting and lively than general ones. If you don't want your reader to fall asleep, then remember to BS.

The third step in writing a good paper is *organizing your supporting details.* Without some method of organization, your paper will sound confused and illogical, no matter how good your details are. How do you organize the details? Basically, there are two methods: *time order* and *emphatic order.* Time order means that the details are arranged as they occur in time. For example, if you were writing about a day in your life, you might start with getting up in the morning and end with watching Jay Leno through bleary eyes. My prom paper could be organized this way; I might begin with the preparations for the prom and end with prom night itself. Of course, I would weave in my reasons for banning proms along the way. I might begin with before-prom expenses and end with after-prom drinking.

The other method of organization is, again, emphatic order. Emphatic order means saving the best, most dramatic, or most important detail for last. In other words, you build up to the best. I could decide to use emphatic order for my prom paper. I would make a scratch outline of my reasons for wanting proms banned. Then I would save for last my most important reason for wanting proms banned. For me, that reason would be the drunken driving that often seems to go along with prom night. Drunken driving is more important than prom expenses or anything else.

Finally, after you have made a point, supported it, and organized your supporting details, you have one last step. You must be sure you have written *clear, correct sentences.* This means checking for mistakes in spelling, grammar, and punctuation. The importance of this step should be obvious; it won't matter how good your ideas are if no one can understand them. I can't go into detail about individual grammar skills in the time I have left. Let me just say, then, that a dictionary and an English handbook are essential for this step.

Let's end with a summary. To write an effective paper, you must take the four steps you see on the board:

1. Make a point.
2. Support the point (BS).
3. Organize the support.
4. Write clear sentences.

You can definitely learn how to follow these four steps. It's a matter of practice and a matter of thinking, planning, checking, and rewriting. If you work hard, you will produce clear and effective pieces of writing. And writing is a skill that will help you immeasurably both in school and later in your career.

Questions on the Lecture

1. What are the four steps in effective writing?

   Make a point; support your point; organize your supporting details; write

   clear, correct sentences

2. What does BS in writing refer to?

   "Be specific"

3. What are two methods of organizing details in writing?

   Time order and emphatic order

4. What is meant by emphatic order?

   Saving the best or most important detail for last

Time Control and Concentration

This chapter will show you how to manage your time by using:

- A course outline
- A large monthly calendar
- A weekly study schedule
- A "to do" list
- Hints on concentration

Time Control and Concentration: In Real Life

Read the profile that follows. Then ask yourself these questions:

- What challenges does Maria Cardenas face in managing her time?
- What solutions has she found to those challenges?
- Are any of the time-control challenges Maria has faced problems for me, too?

Student Profile: Maria Cardenas

As she talks about the challenge of making time for her students as well as her husband, three school-age children, housekeeping job, and beloved garden, Maria Cardenas—an honor student at Florida Gulf Coast University—sounds more matter-of-fact than flustered. "I just do what I have to do," she says.

Maybe the experience of growing up as a migrant worker with an abusive father puts future difficulties in perspective. The second oldest of eight children, Maria left Rio Verde, Mexico, for the United States at age seven. With the rest of her family, Maria traveled with the harvest, using

Continued

a series of false names to evade immigration authorities. Laboring like an adult in the fields, Maria often attended three or four schools each year. Her school attendance suffered as her father grew more brutal. Eventually at age sixteen, Maria, barely able to read or write, left school to marry a man as abusive as her father.

But by age twenty-nine, Maria had turned her life around. In a solid second marriage, having struggled to acquire the skills she needed to earn her GED, Maria enrolled at Edison Community College in Fort Myers, Florida. There she was a straight-A student and a member of Phi Theta

Kappa, the international honor society for two-year colleges. Now a junior at Florida Gulf Coast, Maria has a high grade point average and expects to graduate with a B.A. in elementary education. Her goal is to teach other migrant children "to stand on their own two feet, to achieve their dreams."

For Maria, the key to time management is "do a little at a time, all the time." With her weeks consisting of working at least twenty-four hours; attending to her children, now ages eight, thirteen, and eighteen; and taking three college courses, Maria rarely has the luxury of long uninterrupted study sessions. She has become a master of using what time she does have efficiently.

"I study steadily, all through the term," Maria says. "Every day after class, while the material is fresh in my mind, I review my notes and make sure I understand whatever is there. If not, I question the instructor." By never allowing herself to fall behind in class, Maria avoids the need for last-minute cramming for an exam. "I'm prepared by then. All I have to do is spend a little extra time the night before going over my notes."

When a big project or term paper is assigned, Maria approaches it in the same "do it now" fashion. "First, I make sure I know *exactly* what the instructor wants," she says. "I pay very close attention to any handouts, and I ask, ask, ask. Then I do the project a little at a time, staying in close touch with the instructor every step of the way. Whenever possible, I'll get a draft of the project done early and ask the instructor to go over

Continued

it with me before I hand in a final version." By checking in with her instructor frequently, Maria emphasizes, she saves herself the time and discouragement of having to redo her work.

As she grabs chunks of study time when and where she can, Maria has two criteria in mind: silence and solitude. "I concentrate best when the house is quiet, so I do most of my studying after the children are in bed," she says. "I sit in the living room or at the kitchen table—with the TV off!" she adds with a laugh. "Best of all is the school library, where I don't have any of the household distractions. At home, it's too easy to think, 'I really should be getting groceries.'"

In order to maintain her concentration and give herself an incentive, Maria knows she must schedule times for breaks. "If I had my way, I'd be in my garden all day with my daughter Jasmine, my gardening buddy," she admits. "So I work it into my schedule. If I've been studying well for a while, I'll tell myself, 'OK, you can have twenty minutes in the garden.' Or if I reach the point where I cannot read another word, I go for a really fast walk with one of the children. That way, I can clear my head and have some one-to-one conversation at the same time. When I come back in, my mind is rested and I can concentrate again."

Maria has one final trick for making wise use of her study time. Without a conventional high school background, she admits that she is often overwhelmed at first by the material in her textbooks, especially in the humanities. "Renoir, Beethoven, Christopher Columbus—what do I know about any of them?" she asks. "I start to read the textbook chapters, and they mean nothing to me. I could spend hours staring at those words and not understanding them. So, instead, I go to the library" (and here Maria lowers her voice to a confidential whisper) *to the juvenile section. I get out children's books about the subject and read them. They're very short, simple, and to the point. Then I return to my fat college textbooks with some idea of what's going on!"*

With Maria's record of success, nobody is going to argue with her methods.

All of us need free time, hours without demands and obligations, so we can just relax and do what we please. But it is easy to lose track of time and discover suddenly that there aren't enough hours to do what needs to be done. No skill is more basic to survival in college than time control. If you do not use your time well, your college career—and the life goals that depend on how well you do in college—will slip like sand through your fingers. This chapter describes four methods to help you gain control of your time: You will learn how to use a course outline, a large monthly calendar, a weekly study schedule, and a daily or weekly "to do" list. There is also a series of hints on concentration—how to use your study time more effectively.

Your Course Outline

At the beginning of a school semester, each of your instructors will probably pass out a course outline, or syllabus. If you do not want to take a giant step to control your time, throw this syllabus away or put it in the back of a notebook and never look at it.

The syllabus is your instructor's plan for the course. Chances are it will explain the instructor's grading system and the factors on which your grade will be based. Chances are it will give you the dates of exams and will tell you when papers or reports are due. Chances are it will outline what topics will be covered in each week of class, and it may list the chapters in the textbook that you may be expected to read.

In other words, the syllabus will put you inside your instructor's head and help you learn exactly what you must do to succeed in the course. The syllabus is often the key to doing well in a course.

Believe it or not, many students ignore the syllabus. Don't make this mistake! Instead, use the syllabus to help organize your work for the course: move the dates of exams and the due dates of papers to a large monthly calendar. Refer to the syllabus on a regular basis to make sure you are doing just what your instructor expects you to do.

A Large Monthly Calendar

You should buy or make a large monthly calendar. Such a calendar is your first method of time control because it allows you, in one quick glance, to get a clear picture of what you need to do in the weeks to come. Be sure your monthly calendar has a good-sized block of white space for each date. Then, as soon as you learn about exam dates and paper deadlines, enter them clearly in the appropriate spots on the calendar. Hang the calendar in a place where you will see it every day, perhaps on your kitchen or bedroom wall. The monthly calendar made up by one student is shown on the next page.

October

Sun.	Mon.	Tues.	Wed.	Thurs.	Fri.	Sat.
				1 computer quiz	2	3
4	5 Soc test	6	7	8	9 English essay due	10
11	12	13 Bio field trip	14	15 Psych quiz	16	17
18	19 Speech	20	21	22	23 English essay due	24
25	26 Bio test	27	28	29 Business report due	30	31

Activity

In the following spaces, write the names of the courses you are taking. Also, record the dates on which papers or other assignments are due and the dates on which exams are scheduled. Due dates are often listed in a course syllabus as well as announced by a course instructor.

Courses	Paper Due Dates	Exam Dates
_____	_____	_____
_____	_____	_____
_____	_____	_____
_____	_____	_____
_____	_____	_____
_____	_____	_____

Transfer all this information to a monthly calendar.

- Write here what you think would be the best place for you to post a monthly calendar:

  Answers will vary.

- *Complete the following statement:*

  A monthly calendar will keep you constantly aware of exam days and paper

  target days, so that you can _*prepare (or plan) for them*_

  well in advance.

A Weekly Study Schedule

Evaluating Your Use of Time

A weekly study schedule will make you aware of how much time you actually have each week and will help you use that time effectively. Before you prepare a weekly study schedule, however, you need to get a sense of how you spend your time *each day*. The activity that follows will help you do that.

Activity   *Answers will vary, but Emily could use parts of the following time slots for additional study time: 9-10, 11-1, 7:30-11*

The daily schedule of one student, Emily, follows. Emily has three classes. Assuming that every hour of class time should receive at least one hour of study time, how could Emily revise her schedule so that she would have at least three full study hours in addition to time for "rest and relaxation"? Make your suggested changes by crossing out items and adding study time to her schedule. Your instructor may have you compare answers with those of others in the class.

Emily's Daily Schedule

Time	Activity	Time	Activity
6:30–7:30	Get up, shower, breakfast	2–2:30	Read newspaper in library
7:30–8	Travel to school	2:30–3	Drive to work
8–9	Class (English)	3–6	Work at Wal-Mart
9–10	Coffee in student center	6–7:30	Travel home, eat supper, watch news
10–11	Class (Business)	7:30–9	Telephone, go on Internet, English homework
11–1	Lunch in cafeteria	9–11:30	TV
1–2	Class (sociology)	11:30	Bed

Next, use the chart that follows to record a *typical* school day in your life. Be honest: You want to see clearly what you are doing so that you will be able to plan ways to use your time more effectively.

Time	Activity

Now, honestly evaluate your use of time. Write in the number of hours you *actually* used for study in your typical day: _____ hours. Next, go back to your chart and block off time in the day that you *could* have used for study. (Remember to still allow time for "rest and relaxation," which is also needed.) Write in the number of hours you could have used for study in the day: _____ hours.

Note: People sometimes learn from their schedules that they are victims of a time overload, for they have taken too much work on themselves with too little time to do it. If you think this is your case, you should talk with your instructor or a counselor about possibly dropping one or more courses.

Emily's Weekly Schedule

	Mon.	Tues.	Wed.	Thurs.	Fri.	Sat.	Sun.	
6:00 A.M.								6:00 A.M.
7:00	B		B		B			7:00
8:00	Eng	B	Eng		Eng	B		8:00
9:00				B			B	9:00
10:00	Biz	Phys Ed	Biz		Biz	Job		10:00
11:00		↓						11:00
12:00	L	L	L	L	L			12:00
1:00 P.M.	Chem	Lab	Chem		Chem		L	1:00 P.M.
2:00								2:00
3:00		↓	Job		Job			3:00
4:00								4:00
5:00	S	S	↓	S		↓	S	5:00
6:00			S			S		6:00
7:00	Comp Prog			Psych				7:00
8:00					S			8:00
9:00	↓			↓				9:00
10:00								10:00
11:00								11:00
12:00	Bed	Bed	Bed	Bed			Bed	12:00
1:00 A.M.								1:00 A.M.
2:00	④	④	③	⑤	②	⓪	⑤	2:00

B = Breakfast   ■ = Study blocks   Psych = Psychology   Eng = English

L = Lunch   ○ = Study hours per day   Comp Prog = Computer Programming   Phys Ed = Physical Education

S = Supper   Blanks = Free time   Chem = Chemistry   Biz = Business

Important Points about a Weekly Study Schedule

You are now ready to look over the master weekly schedule, shown here, that Emily prepared to gain control of her time. You should then read carefully the points that follow; all are important in planning an effective weekly schedule. Note that you will be asked to refer to Emily's schedule to answer questions that accompany some of the points.

Point 1: Plan, at first, at least one hour of study time for each hour of class time. Depending on the course, the grade you want, and your own study efficiency, you may have to schedule more time later. A difficult course, for example, may require three hours or more of study time for each course hour. Remember that learning is what counts, not the time it takes you to learn. Be prepared to schedule as much time as you need to gain control of a course.

- How many class hours, excluding lab and phys ed, does Emily have? __15__
- How many study hours has she scheduled? __23__

Point 2: Schedule regular study time. To succeed in your college work, you need to establish definite study hours. If you do not set aside and stick to such hours on a daily or almost daily basis, you are probably going to fail at time control. Jot down in the following spaces the free hours each day that you would use as regular study time. The first column shows Emily's free hours on Monday.

For Emily		*Your Possible Study Hours*						
Mon.	*Mon.*	*Tues.*	*Wed.*	*Thurs.*	*Fri.*	*Sat.*	*Sun.*	
9-10	____	____	____	____	____	____	____	
11-12	____	____	____	____	____	____	____	
2-4	____	____	____	____	____	____	____	

There are many benefits to setting aside regular study hours. First of all, they help make studying a habit. Study times will be programmed into your daily schedule as automatically as, say, watching a favorite television program. You will not have to remind yourself to study, nor will you waste large amounts of time and energy trying to avoid studying; you will simply do it. Another value of regular study time is that you will be better able to stay up to date on work in your courses. You are not likely to find yourself several days before a test with three textbook chapters to read or five weeks of classroom notes to organize and study. Finally, regular study takes advantage of the proven fact that a series of study sessions is more effective than a single long "cram" session.

- How many separate blocks of study time has Emily built into her weekly schedule?

  14

- How many benefits of regular study hours are described in the preceding paragraph? (*Hint:* Word signals such as "First of all" are clues to each separate value.)

  Three

Point 3: Plan blocks of study time at least one hour long. If you schedule less than one hour, your study period may be over just when you are fully warmed up and working hard.

- What is the largest single block of study time that Emily has during the week? (Write down the day and the number of hours.)

  Sunday—three hours (7 to 10 P.M.)

- What is the largest single block of study time available to you each week?

  _____

Point 4: Reward yourself for using study time effectively. Research shows that people work better if they get an immediate reward for their efforts. So if your schedule permits, try to set up a reward system. Allow yourself to telephone a friend or watch a television show or eat a snack after a period of efficient study. On Emily's schedule, for example, nine to ten o'clock on Tuesday night is free for watching television as a reward for working well in the two-hour study slot before. When you are studying over a several-hour period, you can also give yourself "mini-rewards" of five to ten minutes of free time for every hour or so of study time.

Your reward system won't work if you "cheat," so deprive yourself of such pleasures as television shows when you have not studied honestly.

- Locate the other spots where Emily has built reward time into her schedule after study periods and indicate the hours here: Monday (4-5 P.M.),

  Tuesday (9-10 A.M.), Wednesday (10 P.M.-bedtime), Thursday (3-4 P.M.),

  Sunday 10 P.M.-bedtime)

  _____

- Do you think it is a good idea for Emily to reward herself with one day in the week (Saturday) free from study? Why or why not? _____

  Answers will vary.

  _____

  _____

Point 5: Try to schedule study periods before and after classes.

Ideally, you should read a textbook chapter before an instructor covers it; what you hear in class will then be a "second exposure," so the ideas are likely to be a good deal more meaningful to you. You should also look over your notes from the preceding class in case the instructor discusses the material further. Similarly, if you take a few minutes to review your notes as soon after class as possible, you will be able to organize and clarify the material while it is still fresh in your mind.

- If a new textbook chapter is to be covered in Emily's psychology class on Thursday, where in her schedule should she plan to read it?
  Thursday from 10-12, 1-3, or 4-5

Point 6: Work on your most difficult subjects when you are most alert.

Save routine work for times you are most likely to be tired. You might, for example, study a new and difficult mathematics chapter at 8 P.M. if you are naturally alert then, and review vocabulary words for a Spanish class at 11 P.M., when you may be a little tired.

- Assuming that Emily is most naturally alert early in the day and that chemistry is her most difficult subject, in what time slots should she schedule her work on that subject? Morning study hours
- At what time of day do you consider yourself most alert? _____

Point 7: Balance your activities.

Allow free time in your schedule for family, friends, sports, television, and so on. Note that there is a good deal of free time (empty space) in Emily's schedule, even with her classes, work, and study hours.

- Where is the biggest block of free time in Emily's schedule? Saturday evening
- Where do *you* plan to have a substantial block of free time? _____

Point 8: Keep your schedule flexible.

When unexpected events occur, trade times on your weekly timetable. Do not simply do away with study hours. If you find that your schedule requires constant adjustment, revise it. (Your instructor may be able to give you extra copies of the following schedule.) After two or three revisions, you will have a realistic, practical weekly schedule that you can follow honestly.

- If Emily went to a family reunion on Sunday at 1 P.M. and didn't get back until eight o'clock that evening, where in her schedule could she make up the missed hour of study time? Sunday morning or later Sunday evening

Your Weekly Schedule

	Mon.	Tues.	Wed.	Thurs.	Fri.	Sat.	Sun.	
6:00 A.M.								6:00 A.M.
7:00								7:00
8:00								8:00
9:00								9:00
10:00								10:00
11:00								11:00
12:00								12:00
1:00 P.M.								1:00 P.M.
2:00								2:00
3:00								3:00
4:00								4:00
5:00								5:00
6:00								6:00
7:00								7:00
8:00								8:00
9:00								9:00
10:00								10:00
11:00								11:00
12:00								12:00
1:00 A.M.								1:00 A.M.
2:00								2:00

Activity

Keeping the preceding points in mind, use the form provided here to make up your own realistic weekly study schedule. Write in your class and lab periods first; next, add in your hours for job and meals; and then fill in the study hours that you need in order to do well in your courses. At the bottom of your schedule, make up a key that explains the symbols you have used in the schedule. Also, add up and circle the total number of study hours you realistically plan to set aside each day.

A Daily or Weekly "To Do" List

How to Make a "To Do" List

A "to do" list is simply a list of things a person wants to accomplish within a limited period. Many successful people make the "to do" list a habit, considering it an essential step in making the most efficient use of their time each day. A "to do" list, made up daily or weekly, may be one of the most important single study habits you will ever acquire.

Emily's "To Do" List

<u>To Do</u>   <u>Monday</u>

1. Make up outline for English research paper
2. Read Chapter 6 of business text
3. Review notes for chemistry test on Wednesday
4. Reserve time in computer lab to type psych report
5. Return videos
6. Buy cat food!!
7. Find article on Internet booksellers for business class
8. Buy gym shorts
9. Call Jen; get English notes from class missed Friday
10. Do laundry
11. Answer Dan's e-mail
12. Make lunch date with Kate and Melanie
13. Review chemistry notes again before bed

Important Notes about the "To Do" List

Point 1: Carry the list with you throughout the day.
A small notebook can be kept in a purse, and a four- by six-inch slip of paper in a pocket or wallet.

You may also want to keep your to-list in a *daily planner* (also called a *datebook* or *time organizer*). A daily planner is an inexpensive purchase at any bookstore or office supply store. It combines a calendar with space for a daily "to do" list. If you actively use the planner—carrying it with you every day and consulting it and adding or crossing out items on a regular basis—it will definitely help you organize your time.

Point 2: Decide on priorities.
Making the best use of your time means focusing on top-priority items—things that will really have a negative impact if they're not done—rather than spending hours on low-priority activities. When in doubt about what to do at any time in the day, ask yourself, "What are the highest priority items on my list?" and choose one of them.

- Look at Emily's list and label each of the items *A, B,* or *C* to indicate what you think is a reasonable priority level for it.
  Answers will vary, but items 1, 2, 3, 4, 6, and 13 should be labeled "A."

Point 3: Cross out items as you finish them.
Don't worry unnecessarily about completing your list; what is not done can often be moved to the next day's list. What is important is that you make the best possible use of your time each day. Focus on top-priority activities!

Activity

Use this space to make up your own "to do" list for tomorrow. If you cannot think of at least seven items, then put down as well things that you want to do over the rest of the week. Label each item as *A, B,* or *C* in priority.

Your "To Do" List

_To Do_

Concentration

A monthly calendar, a weekly study schedule, and a "to do" list are essential methods of organizing your study time. Unfortunately, though, all your effort in creating them is useless if you waste the study time you have set aside. Unless you master the art of *concentrating* on your work, you will learn very little.

Is concentrating difficult? The answer is both *yes* and *no*. The skill of concentration somewhat resembles a beating heart. When it works, we take it for granted and are hardly aware of it; any malfunction, however, is painfully obvious. For example, you probably find it very easy to concentrate on something you are extremely interested in—a suspenseful movie, a sporting event, a conversation with a friend. But concentration may seem impossible when you are studying a biology chapter or mathematics problems.

Answers to activities in the remainder of this chapter will vary.

- Name an activity on which you can easily concentrate: _____

- Name an activity on which you can concentrate only with great difficulty:

_____

Why People Can't Concentrate

Why is it often so difficult to concentrate on studying? There are several reasons; one or more of them may apply to you.

You equate studying with punishment. If you have a history of doing poorly in school, or if you have often received poor grades even though you tried to study, you will naturally have a negative reaction every time you sit down with your books. After all, you may think, the work is hard and probably not worthwhile. You are conditioned to see studying as torture. All your negative experiences have created a study block that hinders your ability to concentrate.

- Do you think you have a block about studying because of past school experiences? _____
- If so, are you ready to break through your block by applying the study skills in this book? _____

You put everything off until the last minute. The Procrastinators Club holds its Christmas party in February. However, putting off your studies until the last minute is not as harmless and amusing as the Procrastinators' social schedule.

Trying to study ten hours for an exam tomorrow or starting at nine o'clock in the morning to write a paper that is due by three o'clock in the afternoon is like trying to work with a gun at your head: Concentration is difficult at best.

- Are you a procrastinator? _____
- If so, what do you do to avoid studying? _____
- Does procrastination make you feel anxious and guilty, as it does for most people? _____

You don't feel comfortable or settled. You're dying of thirst. The chair you're sitting in is sending shooting pains up your spine. Your head is pounding or your eyes are drooping. Your body feels so exhausted that it seems impossible to remain upright any longer. At the same time, dozens of other thoughts may crowd into your mind: next weekend's trip, the argument you had with your mother, the dirty laundry piling up in your closet. Such physical and mental distractions will soon overwhelm any concentration you may have been able to achieve.

- Of the three reasons for not concentrating just listed, which one applies most in your case? _____

Ways to Concentrate

When you can't concentrate, you can take either of two courses. You can give in to defeat by rationalizing your failures. You can tell yourself, for example, "Nobody could understand this textbook" or "I hate this course anyway and I don't care if I fail" or "I don't know why I'm in school" or "I'll really concentrate next time." The better route to take is to decide that you will do everything you can to aid concentration. Here are practical hints that will help you fix your attention on the studying you have to do.

Hint 1: Work on Having a Positive Attitude.
It is a rare student who has a deep interest in every one of his or her college courses. Most students find that at least some of the studying they have to do involves uninteresting material. In such cases, it is essential to examine your priorities and goals. Don't let some less-than-stimulating courses block your route to the college degree you want. Decide that you will do the studying because, someday, the course will be forgotten, but your college education and degree will be benefiting your life.

- What are the most unpleasant study tasks you will have this semester?

_____

- Is your college degree important enough for you to do these unpleasant tasks?

_____

Hint 2: Prepare to Work by Setting Specific Study Goals.

Hint 2: Prepare to Work by Setting Specific Study Goals. Don't stare at a foot-high pile of thick textbooks and wonder how you'll ever make it through the semester. Instead, go over your assignments and jot down a list of practical goals for the period of study time you have available. These will be the study items on your day's "to do" list. This technique helps you get organized; it also breaks your large, overwhelming study task into manageable units that you can accomplish one at a time. Here are typical study items from one student's daily "to do" list:

Read pages 125–137 in history text.
Do Internet research on possible topics for psych paper.
Memorize three chemistry formulas.
Review notes for English quiz.

You may want to work first on the assignments that seem easiest, or least painful, to you. It's a good feeling to cross something off your list; knowing you've finished at least *one* thing can often give you the confidence you need to continue.

- Jot down four specific assignments you must complete in the next school week.

_____

_____

_____

_____

Hint 3: Keep Track of Your Lapses of Concentration.

Hint 3: Keep Track of Your Lapses of Concentration. When you start studying, jot down the time (for example, "7:15") at the bottom of your "to do" list of study items. When you find yourself losing interest or thinking about something else, put the time (for example, "7:35") on that same piece of paper. Catching yourself like this can help train your mind to concentrate for longer and longer periods. You should soon find that you can study for a longer span of time before the first notation appears. The notations, too, should become fewer and fewer.

- Record the time here whenever you have a lapse in concentration while reading the rest of this chapter.

_____

Hint 4: Create a Good Study Environment.
Choose a room that is, first of all, quiet and well-lighted. To avoid glare, make sure that light comes from above or over your shoulder, not from in front of you. Also, you should have more than one light source in the room. For example, you might use a ceiling light in addition to a pole lamp behind your chair.

- Do you think that the place where you study is well-lighted? _____

- If not, what might you do to improve the lighting? _____

_____

Second, you should have a comfortable place to sit. Do not, however, try to study in a completely relaxed position. Slight muscular tension promotes the concentration needed for study. So sit on an upright chair or sit in a cross-legged position on your bed with a pillow behind you. Keep in mind, also, that you do not have to study while sitting down. Many students stay alert and focused by walking back and forth across the room as they test themselves on material they must learn.

- What is your usual position when you study? _____

_____

- Are your muscles slightly tense in this position, or are they completely relaxed?

_____

Make sure you have all the materials you will need: ballpoint pens, highlighter pens, pencils, loose-leaf or typing paper, and a small memo pad. It would be ideal (though not essential) to have a typewriter or computer and a calculator as well.

Finally, to avoid interruptions in your study place, ask your family and friends to please keep away during study hours. Tell them that you will return telephone calls after you finish studying. Preparing a good environment in advance ensures that when you do achieve concentration, nothing will interrupt you.

If you do not have a room where you can study, use a secluded spot in the library or student center, or find some other quiet spot. If you have one particular place where you usually do most of your studying, you will almost automatically shift into gear and begin studying when you go to that place.

Hint 5: Stay in Good Physical Condition.
You do not want to tire easily or have frequent illnesses. Eat nourishing meals, starting with breakfast—your most important meal of the day. For some students, breakfast is simply coffee and doughnuts or a soda and cookies from a vending machine. But a solid breakfast is not merely a combination of caffeine and sugar. It is, instead, protein, as in milk, yogurt, or a whole-grain cereal. Protein will supply the steady flow of blood sugar needed to keep you mentally alert through the entire day.

Try to get an average of eight hours of sleep a night unless your system can manage with less. Also, try to exercise on a regular basis. A short workout in the morning (if only five minutes of running in place) will help sustain your energy flow during the day. Finally, do not hesitate to take a fifteen- to thirty-minute nap at some point during the day. Research findings show that such a nap can provide a helpful energy boost.

- What is your typical breakfast? How could you realistically improve it?

  _____

- What other steps do you take—or should you take—to stay in good physical

  condition?_____

Hint 6: Vary Your Study Activities. Study sessions need not be four-hour marathons devoted to one subject. When you cannot concentrate anymore, don't waste time staring unproductively at, say, a mathematics problem. Switch over to your English paper or biology report. The change in subject matter and type of assignment can ease mental strain by stimulating a different part of your brain— verbal ability, for instance—while the other part (mathematical ability) rests. By varying your activities, you will stay fresh and alert longer than you would if you hammered away at one subject for hours.

Hint 7: Practice the Study Skills in This Book. Many students can't concentrate on their studies because they don't know *how* to study. They look at the brief notes they took during a class lecture and wonder what to do with them. They start reading a textbook as casually as if they were reading the sports page of the newspaper, and then they wonder why they get so little out of it. They have perhaps been told that taking good notes and then reciting those notes are keys to effective study, but they are not sure how to apply these skills. Learning and practicing study skills will help you become deeply involved in your assignments. Before you know it, you are concentrating.

- Of all the study skills in this book, which are the three most important for you

  to practice? _____   _____   _____

Hint 8: Use Outside Help When Needed. Some people find that studying with a friend or friends helps concentration. Others, however, find it more of a distraction than an aid because they spend more time chatting than studying cooperatively. Use the technique of team study only if you think it will be of real value to you. Also, find out if your school has a tutoring service. If so, do not hesitate to use the service to get help in a particular subject or subjects. Having a good tutor could make a significant difference in your grade for a course. And determine if your school, like many schools, has a learning center where you may work on developing skills in writing, reading, study, mathematics, and computers. Finally, learn the office hours of your instructors and find out whether you can see them if you need additional help.

- Does your school have a tutoring service? _____
- Does your school have a learning center? _____
- If so, where is each located? _____

Some Final Thoughts

You now have several practical means of gaining control of your time: a course outline, a monthly calendar, a master study schedule, and a "to do" list. In addition, you have learned useful hints for aiding concentration. Use whatever combination of techniques is best for you. These tools, combined with your own determination to apply them, can reduce the disorder of everyday life, where time slips quickly and silently away. Through time planning, you can achieve the consistency in your work that is absolutely vital for success in school. And through time control and steady concentration, you can take command of your life and accomplish more work than you have ever done before.

Practice in Time Control and Concentration

Activity 1

Several time-control skills and study and concentration habits are listed below. Evaluate yourself by putting a check mark beside each of the skills or habits that you already practice. Then put a check mark beside those steps that you plan to practice. Leave a space blank if you do not plan to follow a particular strategy.

Now Plan
Do   to Do

____ ____   • Use course outlines.

____ ____   • Use a large monthly calendar.

____ ____   • Use a weekly study schedule.

____ ____   • Use a daily or weekly "to do" list.

____ ____   • Have regular study hours.

Now Do	Plan to Do	
____	____	• Schedule as many hours as needed for a particular course.
____	____	• Have rewards for using study time effectively.
____	____	• Work on difficult subjects at times when you are most alert.
____	____	• Balance activities.
____	____	• Try to have a positive attitude about each course.
____	____	• Set goals before starting work.
____	____	• Create a good study environment (comfortable but nondistracting).
____	____	• Stay in good physical condition.
____	____	• Vary your study activities.
____	____	• Use outside help when needed.

Activity 2

Several weeks into the semester, your instructor will ask you to hand in copies of the following:

- One month from your monthly calendar.
- Your weekly study schedule.
- Your most recent daily or weekly "to do" list.

Do not simply pass in copies of the materials you have prepared while doing this chapter; instead, pass in recent and updated materials. And be honest; if you are not using one or more of these methods of time control, don't pretend you are. Instead, write a short essay explaining why you have decided not to use one or more of the time-control methods in this chapter.

Activity 3

Write a short paper about some aspect of concentration skills. Here are some suggestions.

Option 1: Write a paragraph about the problems you've had concentrating in one particular class. Describe the reasons you may not have concentrated effectively. For example, you might have had a poor attitude about school in general or this subject in particular; you might have procrastinated a good deal; you might have lacked certain study skills; you might have had a poor study environment. Use specific details to give a clear picture of your study habits in that class.

Option 2: Write a narrative paragraph about your last study session. Be specific about how well *or* how poorly you concentrated and why.

Option 3: Write a paragraph detailing three specific changes you are planning to make in the place where you study.

Option 4: Write a paragraph on the mistakes the students you see around you make when they study. Note, for example, where you see students studying, the conditions under which they are trying to study, how they are going about studying, and so on.

The PRWR Study Method

This chapter will show you how to study a textbook chapter by:

- Previewing the chapter
- Reading the chapter
- Taking notes on the chapter
- Studying your notes

Textbook Study: In Real Life

Read the profile that follows. Then ask yourself these questions:

- How did Ryan expect to feel about his college textbooks? How was he surprised?
- What techniques does Ryan use to study his textbooks?
- Which of Ryan's textbook study techniques sound most helpful to me?

Student Profile: Ryan Klootwyk

Ryan Klootwyk didn't go straight from high school to college.

He took what he now refers to as "a tiny fourteen-year break" first.

The thirty-four-year-old graduate of Grand Valley State University in Allentown, Michigan, had spent his last three years of high school "bouncing between the normal school and the alternative school for troubled kids. Usually I didn't go to either of them; I hung out at the library, reading."

Ryan had grown up amid a chaos of heroin addiction, drinking, and abuse at the hands of his mother's vicious boyfriend. He kept his grades

Continued

93

high through most of it, but when he was a teenager, the strain became too much. Turning his back on school, Ryan embraced a life of drink, drugs, and petty crime. After barely earning his high school degree, he went to work as a manual laborer. Days of backbreaking, low-paying work might have deadened his mind except for one thing: he'd never stopped reading. He found himself drawn to historical accounts of soldiers and prisoners of war, people who'd battled their way out of mental or physical prisons and emerged stronger men. Finally, at age twenty-nine, Ryan was ready to break out of his own self-imposed captivity. He enrolled for his first class at Muskegon Community College.

Although he knew going back to school at his age would be difficult, Ryan also brought a certain cockiness to the endeavor. "I went into college thinking this'd be a piece of cake," he admits today. "I'd always thought of myself as having more on the ball than the average guy. I was a great reader; I knew my comprehension was excellent, so I'd just whip through this stuff, right?"

Wrong. When Ryan got his first look at college textbooks, he was floored. "They were wordy and highfalutin, and they seemed to convey a message that was over my head. I consider myself an intelligent person, but they were just plain *frustrating.*" Fortunately, Ryan's momentum carried him through this initial discouragement. He began to seek out help—help from tutors, help from his instructors. "I got into the habit of taking my books to them and saying, 'What *is* this?'"

Gradually, thanks to the help from those outside sources and his own drive to succeed, Ryan worked out effective methods of dealing with the intimidating texts. He begins the process as soon as he gets a new book.

"First, I find some quiet time and place to look through the whole thing," he says. "I don't try to plow in and read it. I get the big picture first. I leaf through it, look at the illustrations, the captions, the headings, the titles, and try to get a sense of the book as a whole."

Continued

After he's gotten acquainted with the textbook, Ryan begins studying with highlighter in hand, marking key words and phrases—but the important word here is *key*. "I highlight *very restrictively,*" he says emphatically. "Before I touch the highlighter to the page, I search out the absolutely most essential ideas. Textbooks tend to overload you with tiny details, and if you treat them all as equally important, you'll drive yourself crazy." When Ryan saves money by buying used textbooks, he is amazed to see how much of the text the previous user has highlighted. "Sometimes there is more material highlighted than not," he says. "Highlighting like that would be of absolutely no help to me."

Another of Ryan's habits is to make notes in the margins of his textbooks as he studies. "I jot down main ideas, key words, paraphrases of the most important themes," he says. "In a pinch, if I'm running short of time to study for an exam, I can just read the highlighted material and my margin notes and be in decent shape."

A final trick of Ryan's is to keep his textbook open during class lectures. As his instructor presents ideas that are related to textbook material, Ryan jots down notes right there on the textbook page. "That way, I don't forget the relationship between the lecture and the book, the way I might if I just wrote the notes in my notebook."

Each of Ryan's textbook-study techniques is designed with the same goal in mind: to help him thoroughly understand main concepts, rather than mindlessly memorize less important details. "I don't want to overload my poor old middle-aged brain," Ryan says with a laugh. "I'd rather know five things well than sort of know ten."

Ryan must be choosing the right things to "know well." With solidly good grades, he has graduated from Grand Valley with a degree in secondary education. He now has a job teaching high school history. Like those prisoners of war Ryan read about so long ago, he has freed himself from the chains that bound him.

Using Your Textbook: A Caution

To begin this chapter on textbook study, let me share an experience with you. When I first began teaching, I was still studying for my advanced degree in reading at a nearby state college. I remember especially a class in statistics I had every Monday night. I would travel to the college after a long day of teaching. I'd be exhausted, and I'd have to sit through a class that was hardly my favorite subject.

There was a textbook, but I didn't understand much of it. I remember looking through it when I bought it and thinking, "Good grief! How in the world am I going to survive this?"

As it turned out, the instructor didn't require us to do anything with the textbook. I wasn't too surprised at that, because in many of my undergraduate courses, although we had to buy a textbook, most of the learning actually took place in the classroom. The instructor's attitude seemed to be, "Here is the textbook as a resource. But I'm going to present to you in class the most important ideas."

My statistics instructor did a lot of presenting in class. I remember sitting next to another student whose name was John also. We were a study in contrasts: he was very active in class, constantly asking questions and volunteering answers. In fact, he was so active that he didn't take many notes except to write down what the instructor put on the board. I said very little because I was so tired and neither my heart nor my head was in the subject. I did little but sit there and take lots of notes. I wrote down not just everything the instructor put on the board but also the connections between those ideas. As the instructor explained things, I didn't just listen; I wrote it all down. My attitude was, "I can't understand any of this stuff now, but later—when I don't feel turned off and brain-dead—I'll be able to go through it and try to make sense of it."

When I began to prepare for my midsemester exam, I was surprised to see that I had written some ideas down three or even four times. The instructor had repeated them, and I, getting everything down on paper, had repeated them as well. I had so many notes that I was able to make sense of the material. The instructor had done his job: He had used class time to help us understand a difficult subject. His explanations were very clear, and I had gotten them all down on paper. All I needed to study for that exam was right there in my notes. I didn't even open the textbook.

Do you want to guess who got the higher score in the midsemester exam—the other John or me? I got an 86; the other John got a 74. He saw my paper and felt, I think, a little chagrined. If he had asked me my secret, I would have said, "Take lots of notes."

The point of my story is this: *Don't underestimate the importance of taking class notes in doing well in a course.* If the truth be told, in a number of courses, good class notes will be enough to earn you a decent grade. In many courses, the textbook is only a secondary source of information for the ideas you need to know on exams.

Some students fail to take many notes in class because they think, "I'll get what else I need by reading the textbook." Whatever you do, don't make that mistake. An idea you can get down in five minutes in class might take you two hours to get out of a textbook—if it's there at all! Learn how to use the textbook, but don't *ever* make the mistake of trying to use it as a substitute for classroom note-taking.

- In a chapter on textbook study, do you think so much space should be devoted to a story about classroom note-taking? _____

PRWR: A Textbook Study Method

To become a better reader—of a textbook or any other material—you should systematically develop a whole series of important reading skills, presented in Part Four. This chapter will give you a plan of attack for dealing with a textbook assignment. It explains four steps needed for studying a chapter. The two chapters that follow give you practice in applying these four steps.

The four-step study method is known as PRWR, and variations of it (the most familiar is known as SQ3R) are taught by many reading instructors. The letters stand for the four steps in the process: (1) Preview, (2) Read, (3) Write, and (4) Recite.

Step 1: Preview

A *preview* is a rapid survey that gives you a bird's-eye view of what you are reading. It involves taking several minutes to look through an entire chapter before you begin reading it closely.

Here is how to preview a selection:

- Study the *title*. The title gives you in a few words the shortest possible summary of the whole chapter. Without reading a line of text, you can learn in a general way what the material is about. For example, if the assigned chapter in a psychology text is titled "Stress and Coping with Stress," you know that everything in the chapter is going to concern stress and how to deal with it.

- Quickly read over the *first and last several paragraphs*. These paragraphs may introduce and summarize some of the main ideas covered in the chapter.

- Then page through the chapter and look at the different levels of *headings*. Are there two levels of headings? Three levels? More? Are any relationships obvious among these headings? (For more detail on this, see "Recognizing Headings and Subheadings" in Part Four of this book.)

- Look briefly at words marked in **boldface** and *italics* and in color; such words may be set off because they are important terms. (For more on this, see "Recognizing Definitions and Examples" in Part Four.)

- Glance at *pictures, charts, and boxed material* in the chapter.

Many students have never been taught to preview. They plunge right into a chapter rather than taking a minute or two to do a survey. But remember that it can help to get the "lay of the land" before beginning to read.

Activity 1

Answer the following questions.
Answers will vary.

1. Were you taught to preview as part of your reading instruction in school? _____

2. Do you think that previewing seems like a good idea? _____

3. What part of the preview do you think might be most helpful for you?

_____

Activity 2

Take about two minutes to preview the following textbook selection; then answer the questions that follow it.

Alternatives to Conflict

The conflict process may operate at so great a cost that people often seek to avoid it. Conflict is often avoided through some form of three other processes: *accommodation, assimilation,* and *amalgamation.*

Accommodation

It threw me when my folks got a divorce right after I graduated. I guess I took them for granted. Our home always seemed to me about like most others. At graduation, Dad took me aside and said that he and Mom were calling it quits. He said that they had bugged each other for years, but now that I would be on my own, they were going to separate.

The above story, adapted from a student's life history, is an example of accommodation, a process of developing temporary working agreements between conflicting individuals or groups. It develops when persons or groups find it necessary to work together despite their hostilities and differences. In accommodations, no real settlement of issues is reached; each group retains its own goals and viewpoints but arrives at an "agreement to disagree" without fighting. Two forms of accommodation are described below.

Displacement. Displacement is the process of suspending one conflict by replacing it with another. A classic example is the threat of war to end internal conflicts and bring national unity.

Finding a scapegoat is a favorite displacement technique. The term refers to an ancient Hebrew ceremony in which the sins of the people were symbolically heaped upon a goat that was then driven into the wilderness. Unpopular minorities often become scapegoats. For example, in newly independent countries, all problems may be blamed upon the remaining "colonial influences."

Toleration. In some conflicts, victory is impossible and compromise undesirable. Toleration is an agreement to disagree peaceably. Religious conflict is a classic example of this situation. In Europe at the time of the Reformation, both Protestants and Catholics were positive that they had the "true" version of the Christian faith. Neither group was willing to compromise, and in spite of severe conflict, neither group could destroy the other. Adjustment was made on the basis of toleration; each church ceased to persecute other churches while continuing to hold that these other churches were in error.

Assimilation

Whenever groups meet, some mutual interchange or diffusion of culture takes place. This two-way process by which persons and groups come to share a common culture is called assimilation. Assimilation reduces group conflicts by blending different groups into larger, culturally homogeneous groups. The bitter riots against the Irish and the discrimination against the Scandinavians in the United States disappeared as assimilation erased group differences and blurred the sense of a separate group identity.

Amalgamation

Amalgamation is the biological interbreeding of two groups until they become one. For instance, wholesale amalgamation ended the conflicts of the Anglo-Saxons with the Norman invaders of England. An incomplete amalgamation, however, generally creates a status- and conflict-filled system where status is measured by blood "purity" as in Central America and parts of South America.

1. What is the selection about? (This question can be answered by studying the title.) _alternatives to conflict_

2. What are the three alternatives to conflict? (This question can be answered by looking at the relationship between the title and the main headings.)

   a. _accommodation_   b. _assimilation_   c. _amalgamation_

3. What are the two forms of accommodation? (This question can be answered by looking at the relationship between the heading "Accommodation" and the two subheadings under it.)

   a. _displacement_   b. _toleration_

The purpose of this activity is probably clear to you: Often a preview alone can help you key in on important ideas in a selection.

Step 2: Read

Read the chapter straight through. In this first reading, don't worry about under-standing everything. There will be so much new information that it will be impos-sible to really comprehend it all right away. You just want to get a good initial sense of the chapter. If you hit snags—parts that you don't understand at all—just keep reading. After you have gotten an overall impression of the chapter by reading everything once, you can go back to reread parts that you did not at first understand.

Read the chapter with a pen in hand. Look for and mark off what seem to be important ideas and details. In particular, mark off the following:

- *Definitions* of terms—underline definitions.
- *Examples* of those definitions—put an *Ex* in the margin.
- Items in major *lists* (also called *enumerations*)—number the items *1, 2, 3,* and so on.
- What seem to be other *important ideas*—use a star or *Imp* in the margin.

(For more detail, see the chapters in Part Four on recognizing definitions and examples, enumerations, and main ideas.)

Notes about Marking: The purpose of marking is to set off points so that you can easily return to them later when you take study notes. Material can be marked with a pen or pencil, or it can be highlighted with a felt-tip pen.

Here is a list of useful marking symbols:

Symbol	*Explanation*
————	Set off a definition by underlining it.
Ex	Set off helpful examples by writing *Ex* in the margin. Do not underline examples.
1, 2, 3	Use numbers to mark enumerations (items in a list).
☆ *Imp*	Use a star or *Imp* to set off important ideas.
|	Put a vertical line in the margin to set off important material that is several lines in length. Do not underline these longer sections, because the page will end up being so cluttered that you'll find it difficult to make any sense of the markings.
✓	Use a check to mark off any item that *may* be important.
?	Use a question mark to show material you do not understand and may need to reread later.

Marking should be a *selective* process. Some students make the mistake of marking almost everything. You have probably seen textbooks, for example, in which almost every line has been highlighted. But setting off too much material is no better than setting off too little.

Activity 1

Answer the following questions.

1. Why should you mark off definitions, examples, and enumerations when reading? *These are among the most important ideas in a selection.*

2. Why do you think you should *not* underline examples? *You need to distinguish examples from definitions.*

Activity 2

Go back and read and mark the textbook selection you previewed in Activity 2 on pages 98–99. Remember to be selective. Mark only the most important points: definitions, key examples, enumerations, and what seem to be other important ideas.

Step 3: Write

I can still remember the time when I really learned how to study. I was taking an introductory history course. For our first test, we were responsible for three chapters in the textbook plus an abundance of classroom notes. I spent about two hours reading the first chapter—about thirty pages—and then I started to "study." My "studying" consisted of rereading a page and then looking away and reciting it to myself. After a half hour or so, I was still on the first page! "This is not going to work," I muttered. "I need a faster way to do this."

Here's what I did. I went through the first chapter, rereading and thinking about the material and making decisions about what were the most important points. I then wrote those points down on separate sheets of paper. In a nutshell, I went through a large amount of information and reduced it to the most important points. The very act of deciding what was most important and writing that material down was a valuable step in understanding the material. It took me a couple of hours to prepare my study sheets. Then I was able to close the book and just concentrate on studying those sheets.

I used that study technique successfully through college and graduate school. And when I began my own professional work in reading and study skills, I discovered that almost all successful students use some variation of the same basic strategy.

The third step, then, is to *write*. Following are specific directions for taking good notes.

What to Write

1   Write the *title* of the chapter at the top of your first sheet of paper. Then write down each *heading* in the chapter. Under each heading, take notes on what seem to be the important points.

2   Rewrite headings as *basic questions* to help you locate important points. For example, if a heading is "One-Parent Families," you might convert it to the question, "How many one-parent families are there?" Then write down the answer to that question if it appears in the text. If a heading is "Choosing a Mate," you could ask "How do we choose a mate?" and write down the answer to that question.

3   Look for *definitions of key terms,* usually set off in color, **boldface,** or *italics.* Write down each term and its definition.

4   Look for *examples* of definitions. The examples will help make those definitions clear and understandable. Write down one good, clear example for each definition.

5   Look for *major items in a list* (enumerations). Write them down and number them *1, 2, 3,* and so on. For example, suppose the heading "Agents of Socialization" in a textbook is followed by four subheads, "The Family," "Peers," "School," and "The Mass Media." Write down the heading. Then write the four subheads under it and number them *1, 2, 3,* and *4.*

6   Remember that your goal is to take a large amount of information in a chapter and reduce it down to the most important points. Try not to take too many notes. Instead, use headings, definitions, examples, and enumerations in the chapter to help you focus on what is most important.

How to Write

1   Write your notes on letter-size sheets of paper (8½ by 11 inches). By using such paper (rather than smaller note cards), you will be able to see *relationships* among ideas more easily, because more ideas will fit on a single page.

2   Make sure your handwriting is clear and easy to read. Later, when you study your notes, you don't want to have to spend time trying to decipher them.

3   Leave space in the left-hand margin and top margin of your study sheet so that you can write down key words to help you study the material. Key words will be described on page 105 of this chapter.

4   Don't overuse outlining symbols when you take notes. To show enumerations, use a simple sequence of numbers (1, 2, 3, and so on) or letters (a, b, c, and so on). Often, indenting a line or skipping a space is enough to help show relationships among parts of the material. Notice, for example, that very few outlining symbols are used in the sample study sheet on page 104, yet the organization is very clear.

5 Summarize material whenever you can. In other words, reduce it to the fewest words possible while still keeping the ideas complete and clear. For instance, in the sample study sheet, the example for "accommodation" has been summarized so that it reads simply, "Parents agree to wait until child graduates before separating."

Activity 1

Answer the following questions.

1. When you are taking notes on a chapter, how many of the headings in the chapter should you write down? _All of them._ _____

_____

2. What are enumerations? _Enumerations are items in a list._ _____

_____

3. In "What to Write" on page 102, what do you consider the three most helpful guidelines?

   a. _Answers will vary._ _____

   _____

   b. _____

   _____

   c. _____

   _____

4. In "How to Write" on page 102, what do you consider the three most helpful tips?

   a. _Answers will vary._ _____

   _____

   b. _____

   _____

   c. _____

   _____

Activity 2

A sample study sheet for the selection "Alternatives to Conflict" appears on the next page. Refer to the selection (on pages 98–99) to fill in the notes that are missing.

Sociology, Chapter 14: "Social Processes"

Three Alternatives to Conflict

1. Accommodation—process of developing temporary working agreements between conflicting individuals or groups.

    Ex.—Parents agree to wait until child graduates before separating.

Two forms of accommodation:

    a. Displacement—process of suspending one conflict by replacing it with another.

        Ex.— threat of war to end internal conflicts and bring national unity

    Favorite displacement technique: find a scapegoat.

        Ex.—blame problems of new nation on "colonial influences."

    b. Toleration—agreement to disagree peaceably.

        Ex.—Protestants and Catholics during Reformation came to tolerate rather than persecute each other.

2. Assimilation— two-way process by which people and groups come to share a common culture

    Ex.—riots against Irish in the United States ceased as they were assimilated.

3. Amalgamation— biological interbreeding of two groups until they become one

    Ex.—Anglo-Saxon and Norman invaders of England became one, ending conflicts.

Step 4: Recite

Let's review what you need to do to study a textbook chapter. First you *preview* the chapter. Then you *read* it through once, marking off what appear to be important ideas. Third, you reread it, decide on the important ideas, and *write* study notes. Fourth, you need to learn your notes. How can you do this?

To learn your notes, you *recite* the material to yourself. Using key words and phrases—also known as *recall words*—will help you do this. Write the recall words in the margins of your notes. For example, look at the recall words in the margin of the following notes:

3 alternatives to conflict	Three Alternatives to Conflict
	1. Accommodation—process of developing temporary
Def + ex of accommodation	working agreements between conflicting individuals
	or groups.
	Ex.—Parents agree to wait until child graduates
	before separating.
2 forms of accommodation	Two forms of accommodation:

After you have written the recall words, use them to study your notes. To do so, turn each recall word into a question and go over the material until you can answer the question without looking at the page. For example, look at the recall words "3 alternatives to conflict" and see if you can recite those three alternatives to yourself without looking at the material. You'll find out immediately whether or not you know the material. Go back and reread the items if necessary. Then look away again and try once more to recite the material. Next, look at "Def + ex of accommodation" and see if you can say the definition and give an example of accommodation without looking at the page.

After you finish a section, go back and review previous sections. For instance, after you can recite to yourself the definition and example of accommodation, go back and make sure you can also recite the three alternatives to conflict. Continue like this—studying, reciting, and reviewing—as you move through all the material.

You will discover that recitation helps you pay attention. There is simply no way you can sleepwalk your way through it. Either you do it or you don't. Recitation is, in fact, a surefire way of mastering the material you need to learn. More information about recitation is given in the chapter "Building a Powerful Memory" (page 207).

Activity

Answer the following questions.

1. In the past, have you studied material mainly by reading and rereading it or mainly by reading and reciting? *Answers will vary.*

2. A number of experiments have found that students who spend 25 percent of their time reading and 75 percent reciting remember much more than students who spend all their time reading. Will this fact make you spend more of your study time reciting? *Answers will vary.*

3. Suppose you learn a group of four definitions until you can say them without looking at them. Then you go on and learn a group of several more definitions. What should you do after learning the second group of definitions?
   Go back and make sure you can still recite the first four definitions.

4. What are recall words? *Key words and phrases that help you remember what is in your notes*

5. Where should you write recall words? *In the margins of your notes*

Learning to Use PRWR

The following activities will give you practice in the four steps of PRWR: previewing, reading, writing notes, and reciting.

Activity 1: A Short Passage from a Speech Text

Preview: Take about thirty seconds to preview the following short textbook passage. The title tells you that the passage is about *types of noise*. How many terms are set off in *italics* within the passage? *four*

Noise

A person's ability to interpret, understand, or respond to symbols is often hurt by noise. *Noise* is any stimulus that gets in the way of sharing meaning. Much of your success as a communicator depends on how you cope with external, internal, and semantic noises.

External noises are the sights, sounds, and other stimuli that draw people's attention away from intended meaning. For instance, during a student's explanation of how a food processor works, your attention may be drawn to the sound of an airplane overhead. The airplane sound is external noise. External noise does not have to be a sound. Perhaps during the explanation, a particularly attractive classmate glances toward you, and for a moment your attention turns to that person. Such visual distraction to your attention is also external noise.

Internal noises are the thoughts and feelings that interfere with meaning. Have you ever found yourself daydreaming when someone was trying to tell you something? Perhaps you let your mind wander to thoughts of the good time you had at a dance club last night or to the argument you had with someone this morning. If you have tuned out the words of your friend and tuned in a daydream or a past conversation, then you have created internal noise.

Semantic noises are those alternative meanings aroused by certain symbols that inhibit meaning. Suppose that a student mentioned that the salesman who sells food processors at the department store seemed like a "gay fellow." If you think of "gay" as a word for *homosexual,* you would miss the student's meaning entirely. Since meaning depends on your own experience, others may at times decode a word or phrase differently from the way you intended. When this happens, you have semantic noise.

Read (and Mark): Read the passage straight through, underlining the four definitions you will find. Also, number the three kinds of noises as 1, 2, and 3 respectively. Put an *Ex* in the margin beside each example of a definition.

Write: Complete the following notes about the passage "Noise":

Noise— any stimulus that gets in the way of sharing meaning

Kinds of noises:
1. External— stimuli that draw people's attention away from intended meaning

   Ex.— sound of airplane overhead
2. Internal— thoughts and feelings that interfere with meaning

   Ex.— daydream
3. Semantic— alternative meanings aroused by certain symbols that inhibit meaning

   Ex.— a "gay fellow" interpreted as "a homosexual"

Note that the keys to the main idea here are an enumeration and definitions.

Recite: What recall words could you write in the margin to help you study this
passage? _Def of noise; def + ex of external noise, internal noise, semantic noise_

After you can recite to yourself the definition of *noise,* you should study until
you can say to yourself the definition and an example of *external noises.* What
should you then do? _See if you can say to yourself the definition of noise._

Activity 2: A Short Passage from a Sociology Text

Preview: Take about thirty seconds to preview the following short textbook
passage. The title tells you that the passage is about _____the crowd_____. How
many terms are set off in **boldface** within the passage? _____four_____

The Crowd

The crowd is one of the most familiar and at times spectacular forms of
collective behavior. It is a temporary, relatively unorganized gathering of
people who are in close physical proximity. Since a wide range of behavior is
encompassed by the concept, the sociologist Herbert Blumer distinguishes
among four basic types of crowd behavior. The first, a **casual crowd,** is a
collection of people who have little in common except that they may be par-
ticipating in a common event, such as looking through a department-store
window. The second, a **conventional crowd,** is a number of people who have
assembled for some specific purpose and who typically act in accordance with
established norms, such as people attending a baseball game or concert. The
third, an **expressive crowd,** is an aggregation of people who have gotten
together for self-stimulation and personal gratification, such as at a religious
revival or a rock festival. And fourth, an **acting crowd** is an excited, volatile
collection of people who are engaged in rioting, looting, or other forms of
aggressive behavior in which established norms carry little weight.

Read (and Mark): Read the passage straight through, underlining the five definitions you will find. Number the types of crowd behavior 1, 2, 3, and 4.

Write: Complete the following notes about the passage "The Crowd":

Crowd—_a temporary, relatively unorganized gathering of people who are_
close together

Types of crowd behavior:

1. Casual crowd—_participating in a common event_

2. Conventional crowd— *assembled for a specific purpose and acting according to established norms*

3. Expressive crowd— *gotten together for self-stimulation and personal gratification*

4. Acting crowd— *engaged in rioting, looting, or other forms of aggressive behavior*

Recite: To help you study this passage, you could write "crowd" in the margin as one recall word and *"types of crowd behavior"* as the other recall words.

Activity 3: A Short Passage from a Psychology Text

Preview: Take about thirty seconds to preview the following short textbook passage. The title tells you that the passage is about ____*types of ESP*____. How many terms are set off in *italics* within the passage? ____*four*____

Four Types of ESP

Parapsychologists (psychologists who study claims of more-than-normal happenings) have proposed four types of extrasensory perception, or ESP, each of which is said to occur without using the physical senses. *Telepathy* is one person's sending thoughts to another. For example, in an experiment, one person may look at a picture and try to "send" this picture to a "receiver" in another room. *Clairvoyance* is perceiving distant events, such as sensing that one's child has just been in a car accident. *Precognition* is "preknowing" (foretelling) future events, such as the assassination of a political leader. *Psychokinesis* is "mind over matter"—for example, levitating a table or, in an experiment, influencing the roll of a die by concentrating on a particular number.

Read (and Mark): Read the passage straight through, underlining the four definitions you will find. Number them 1, 2, 3, and 4 respectively. Put an *Ex* in the margin beside each example of a definition.

Write: Complete the following notes about the passage "Four Types of ESP":

1. Telepathy— *one person's sending thoughts to another*
   Ex.— *looking at picture and trying to "send" it to someone in another room*

2. Clairvoyance— *perceiving distant events*
   Ex.— *sensing one's child has been in a car accident*

3. <u>Precognition—preknowing future events</u>

   Ex.— <u>predicting the assassination of a political leader</u>

4. <u>Psychokinesis—"mind over matter"</u>

   Ex.— <u>levitating a table</u>

Recite: What recall words could you write in the margin to help you study this passage? <u>def and ex of ESP; four types of ESP</u>

After you can recite to yourself the definition and an example of *telepathy,* you should then study until you can say to yourself the definition and an example of *clairvoyance.* What should you then do? <u>See if you can say to yourself the</u> <u>definition and an example of telepathy.</u>

Activity 4: A Short Passage from a Social Psychology Text

Preview: Take about thirty seconds to preview the following short textbook passage. The title tells you that the passage is about <u>seeing ourselves favorably</u>. What words are set off in *italics* within the passage? <u>"self-serving bias"</u>

Seeing Ourselves Favorably

It is widely believed that most of us suffer from low self-esteem: the "I'm not OK—you're OK" problem. For example, the counseling psychologist Carl Rogers concluded that most people he has known "despise themselves, regard themselves as worthless and unlovable." As the comedian Groucho Marx put it, "I'd never join any club that would accept a person like me." The evidence, however, indicates that the writer William Saroyan was closer to the truth: "Every man is a good man in a bad world—as he himself knows." Although social psychologists are debating the reason for this *"self-serving bias"*—that is, the tendency to perceive oneself favorably—there is general agreement regarding its reality, its prevalence, and its potency.

Experiments have found that people readily accept credit when told they have succeeded (attributing the success to their ability and effort), yet often attribute failure to such external factors as bad luck or a problem's inherent "impossibility." Similarly, in explaining their victories, athletes commonly credit themselves; but they are more likely to attribute losses to something else: bad breaks, bad officiating, the other team's super effort.

And how much responsibility do you suppose car drivers tend to accept for their accidents? On insurance forms, drivers have described their accidents in words like these: "An invisible car came out of nowhere, struck my car and vanished." "As I reached an intersection, a hedge sprang up, obscuring my vision, and I did not see the other car." "A pedestrian hit me and went under my car." Situations that combine skill and chance (for example, games, exams, job applications) are especially prone to the phenomenon: Winners can easily attribute their successes to their skill, while losers can attribute their losses to chance. When I win at Scrabble, it's because of my verbal dexterity; when I lose, it's because "Who could get anywhere with a Q but no U?"

Read (and Mark): Read the passage through, underlining the one definition you will find. Put *Ex* in the margin beside an example of the definition.

Write: Complete these notes about "Seeing Ourselves Favorably" by filling in the definition and then *summarizing* one example in your own words. Summarizing the example will help you understand it and reduce it in size.

Self-serving bias— the tendency to perceive oneself favorably

Ex.— Scrabble player thinks he wins because of verbal skill, but thinks he loses because the game has a high element of chance.

Recite: After you can say the definition without looking at it, make sure that you can say the _____ example _____ without looking at it.

Activity 5: A Short Passage from a Business Text

Preview: Take about thirty seconds to preview the following short textbook passage. The title tells you that the passage is about _____ factors of production _____.
How many words are set off in *italics* within the passage? _____ four _____

Factors of Production

A society's resources are referred to by economists as the factors of production. One factor of production, *land,* includes not only the real estate on the earth's surface but also the minerals, timber, and water below. The second, *labor,* consists of the human resources used to produce goods and services. The third factor of production is *capital,* the machines, tools, and buildings used to produce goods and services, as well as the money that buys other resources. A fourth factor of production is embodied in people called *entrepreneurs.* They are the ones who develop new ways to use the other economic resources more efficiently. They acquire materials, employ workers, invest in capital goods, and engage in marketing activities. In some societies, entrepreneurs risk losing only their reputations or their positions if they fail. In our society, they also risk losing their own personal resources. On the other hand, our entrepreneurs reap the benefits if they succeed; this possibility is what motivates them to take the risk of trying something new.

Read (and Mark): Read the passage straight through. As you do, underline the five definitions you will find. Also, number as 1, 2, 3, and 4 the four definitions that fit into a group with one another.

Write: Complete the following notes about the passage "Factors of Production":

Factors of production— *a society's resources*

   1. Land— *real estate, minerals, timber, and water*

   2. Labor— *human resources used to produce goods and services*

   3. Capital— *machines, tools, and buildings used to produce goods and services, as well as money that buys other resources*

   4. Entrepreneurs— *the ones who develop new ways to use the other resources more efficiently*

Recite: Simply putting the three recall words *"factors of production"* in the margin would be enough to help you study your notes. Seeing those recall words, you would try to recite to yourself the definition of *factors of production* as well as the "four factors of production" and their definitions.

Using PRWR

This chapter will help improve your textbook study by:

- Explaining two helpful memory techniques
- Providing note-taking practice on a series of textbook passages
- Presenting hints and comments on good note-taking

This chapter will provide further practice in the PRWR study system explained in "Textbook Study I." You'll use PRWR with ten readings, longer than the readings in "Textbook Study I" and with more varied activities. Readings 1 to 5 will give you guided practice: Each of these passages appears on a left-hand page, with activities and comments on the opposite right-hand page. Readings 6 to 10 will give you more independent practice: these are still longer passages with introductory hints, for which you'll do note-taking on your own.

Before you start on the readings, you should master two valuable memory techniques that will help you recite and learn your notes after you have read and taken notes on a passage. *Catchwords* and *catchphrases* will therefore be explained briefly here. (They are also described in detail on pages 212–216, in the chapter "Building a Powerful Memory.")

Two Memory Aids for PRWR

Catchwords

In "Textbook Study I," you took notes on four kinds of crowds (page 108): (1) casual, (2) conventional, (3) expressive, (4) acting. Chances are that you might forget at least one of these four types. To help ensure that you remember all four types, you could create a catchword.

A *catchword* is a word that is made up of the first letters of several words you want to remember. For example, the first letters of the terms for the four kinds of crowds are

C (casual)

C (conventional)

E (expressive)

A (acting)

Use these letters to form an easily recalled catchword, rearranging them if necessary. The catchword can be a real word, or it can be a made-up word. For example, you might remember the letters C, C, E, A with the made-up word CACE.

After you create a catchword, test yourself until you are sure that each letter stands for a key word in your mind. For these types of words, you'd make sure that C stands for *casual,* A for *acting,* C for *conventional,* and E for *expressive.* In each case, the first letter serves as a "hook" to help you pull an entire idea into your memory.

This memory device is a proven method for remembering a group of items. Learn to use and apply it!

- "In Textbook Study I," you also took notes on the four factors of production (page 111). The first letters of these four factors are L (land), L (labor), C (capital), and E (entrepreneurs). Make up a catchword that would help you remember these four factors.

  Catchword: _____CELL_____

  Answers may vary.

Catchphrases

Sometimes you can't easily make up a catchword. In such cases, create a catch-phrase instead. A *catchphrase* is a series of words, each beginning with the first letter of a word you want to remember.

Look at the passage on noise in "Textbook Study I" (pages 106–107). The first letters of the three kinds of noise are

E   (external)

I   (internal)

S   (semantic)

You might not be able to make a good catchword out of E, I, and S, but you could create an easily remembered catchphrase.

For example, I have a friend named Ed, and I quickly came up with the catch-phrase, "I shot Ed." This is an outrageous sentence, since I do not expect to shoot Ed or anyone, or even put a gun in my hand. The point is that because I created the sentence and because it is outrageous, I would automatically remember it. That's what you want to do: Create a sentence you'll be sure to remember. The catchphrase does not have to be a model of grammar or make perfect sense. It can be so outrageous that you would not want anyone else to know what it is. All that matters is creating a line that will stick in your memory.

The purpose of the catchphrase is to give you the first letters of the words you want to remember. After you create a phrase, test yourself until you are sure each letter stands for the right word in your mind. If you were studying the kinds of noise and used the catchphrase "I shot Ed," you'd make sure that *I* helped you recall *internal,* *S* helped you recall *semantic,* and *E* helped you recall *external.*

If you were then given a test question asking you to list and describe the three kinds of noise, you would think immediately, "I shot Ed." You would have the first letters *I, S,* and *E.* The letter *I* would be a memory hook to help you remember that one kind of noise is *internal, S* would help you remember that another kind of noise is *semantic,* and *E* would help you remember that the third kind of noise is *external.*

- In "Textbook Study I," you took notes on the four kinds of ESP (page 109). The first letters of these four types are T (telepathy), C (clairvoyance), P (precogni-tion), and P (psychokinesis). Make up a catchphrase that would help you remember the letters T-C-P-P. (Note that you can put the letters in any order when creating your sentence.)

  Catchphrase: Ted's cat purrs powerfully. (Answers will vary.)

Guided Practice in PRWR

Reading 1: A Passage from a Marketing Text

Stages of the Business Cycle

The traditional business cycle goes through four stages: prosperity, recession, depression, and recovery. However, economic strategies adopted by the federal government have averted the depression stage in the United States for about sixty years. Consequently, today we think of a three-stage **business cycle**—prosperity, recession, and recovery—then returning full cycle to prosperity. Marketing executives need to know which stage of the business cycle the economy currently is in, because a company's marketing program usually must be changed from one stage of the business cycle to another.

Prosperity is a period of economic growth. During this stage, organizations tend to expand their marketing program as they add new products and enter new markets.

A *recession* is a period of retrenchment for consumers and businesses—we tighten our economic belts. People can become discouraged, scared, and angry. Naturally, these feelings affect our buying behavior, which, in turn, has major marketing implications for companies, often leading to economic losses. In a recession, consumers cut back on eating out and entertainment outside the home. As a result, firms catering to these needs face serious marketing challenges.

For some companies, though, a recession can present profitable marketing opportunities. For example, during the recession in 1991, Campbell Soups spotted a trend away from the more expensive, ready-to-serve soups and toward lower-priced cook-at-home products. The company took its new cream of broccoli soup out of the higher-priced Gold Label can, cut the price, and put it in Campbell's familiar red-and-white can. Furthermore, the label included recipes for using the soup as a base for homemade meals. The result: It became the first new soup since 1935 to be among the top ten Campbell best-sellers.

Recovery is the period when the economy is moving from recession to prosperity. The marketers' challenge is to determine how quickly prosperity will return and to what level. As unemployment declines and disposable income increases, companies expand their marketing efforts to improve sales and profits.

Source: Michael J. Etzel, Bruce J. Walker, and William J. Stanton. *Marketing*, 11th ed. (New York: Irwin/McGraw-Hill).

Activity for Reading 1

Preview: Take about thirty seconds to preview Reading 1 on the previous page. The title tells you that the passage is about _stages of the business cycle_____. How many other headings are in the passage? _none__ How many terms are set off in **boldface** in the passage? _one___ How many terms are set off in *italics?* _three_

Read and Mark: Read the passage straight through. As you do, underline the definitions you find. Mark with an *Ex* in the margin an example that makes each definition clear for you. Also, number the items in an enumeration that you'll find in the passage.

Write: On separate paper, take notes on "Stages of the Business Cycle":

1. Write down the definitions of the three stages of today's business cycle.
2. Also, add details of note by answering these questions:
   a. What emotional effects does a recession typically have on consumers?
   b. What challenge faces marketers during a period of recovery?
   c. When it repackaged its broccoli soup, what stage in the business cycle was Campbell Soups taking advantage of?
   d. How do organizations typically respond to a period of prosperity?

   The notes required are apparent in the text itself.

Recite: To remember the three stages of today's business cycle, create a *catch-phrase,* a short sentence made up of the first letters of the three stages: P for *prosperity,* R for *recession,* and R for *recovery:* _Pick red roses._
(Answers will vary.)

Comments on Reading 1: After you have created a catchphrase, use those first letters as "hooks" to help you pull into memory the words they stand for. Test yourself, then, to make sure that P stands in your head for *prosperity,* R stands in your head for *recession,* and R stands in your head for *recovery.*

Reading 2: A Passage from a Psychology Text

Anger

Anger is indeed an unpleasant emotion. Think of the last time you felt angry with yourself or someone else. Anger usually is aroused by *frustration,* a feeling that results whenever you cannot reach a desired goal. For example, assume you had a long, hard day at work and are anxious to get home at a reasonable hour. Your car engine will not turn over. You have no idea what is wrong, and there is nothing you can do about it. You feel frustrated, and your frustration leads to anger. Frustration occurs whenever you cannot reach a desired goal. Psychologists have found that frustration often results in some form of anger or resentment. If you become irritated and kick the car, your behavior is fairly normal.

There are many possible reasons why you cannot reach a desired goal. Sometimes you simply lack the ability. For example, in the case of your car's failing to start, you were unable to diagnose the problem and correct it. In addition to feeling irritation toward the car, you may have been annoyed with yourself for not learning ways to troubleshoot engine problems. Often people aspire to goals far beyond their abilities. A shy man may wish to be a supersalesman, or a woman with limited finances and intelligence may wish to become a nuclear physicist.

Frustration can also result from confusion about goals. Sometimes people feel pulls in more than one direction. Kurt Lewin specified three types of goal confusion or conflict that people experience. Each of these three types of conflicts leads to a feeling of frustration.

Approach-Approach Conflicts Of the three types of conflicts, these are the least frustrating. An *approach-approach* conflict is one that results from having to choose between two desirable goals. You cannot possibly reach both of them at the same time. Maybe there are two good parties in different parts of town at the exact same time on the same night. You must miss one, but which one? Or assume a rich aunt hands you $50,000 to buy yourself a new car. Both a Mercedes and a Porsche look appealing. You must make a choice, but indeed it is a pleasant dilemma. In an approach-approach conflict, you always win, even if you must lose another appealing alternative. As a result, approach-approach conflicts are only mildly frustrating.

Avoidance-Avoidance Conflicts These are the most frustrating of the three types of conflicts. Here the conflict results from being forced to choose between two undesirable goals. Did your mother ever tell you to clean your messy closet or go to bed? Assuming you disliked cleaning closets and were not tired, you experienced an *avoidance-avoidance* conflict. The thought of wasting hours cleaning a cluttered closet was dreadful, but the notion of suffering hours of boredom was also unappealing. The usual reaction to an avoidance-avoidance conflict is to attempt to escape. Perhaps you threatened to run away from home. When no escape is possible, facing the conflict is inevitable. The result is being forced to make an unpleasant choice. The choice is accompanied by intense frustration and anger.

Approach-Avoidance Conflicts These are the most common of the three types of conflicts. The conflict results from weighing the positive and negative aspects of a single goal. Eating a piece of chocolate fudge will provide a delicious taste. But it will also cause tooth decay and, perhaps, unwanted pounds. Studying for an exam will result in a better grade, but it will require an evening away from friends.

Source: Virginia Nichols Quinn, *Applying Psychology,* 2nd ed. (New York: McGraw-Hill).

Activity for Reading 2

Preview: Take about thirty seconds to preview Reading 2 on the previous page. The title tells you that the passage is about _____*anger*_____. How many other headings are in the passage? *three* How many terms are set off in *italics?* *three*

Read and Mark: Read the passage straight through. As you do, underline the definitions you find. Mark with an *Ex* in the margin an example that makes each definition clear for you. Also, number the items in an enumeration that you'll find. And note what seem to be important details.

Write: On separate paper, take notes on "Anger":

1. Write down the definition of *frustration.*
2. Write down the definitions and examples of the three types of conflict.
3. Also, note which is the *least frustrating* conflict, the *most frustrating* conflict, and the *most common* conflict.
   The notes required are apparent in the text itself.

Recite: To remember the three kinds of conflict, you might want to create a line like the following: "At least approach Lola since it is most frustrating to avoid her."

This line will help you remember that the first kind of conflict is *approach–approach,* and that it is the least frustrating of conflicts. And it will help you remember that the second kind of conflict is *avoidance–avoidance,* and it is the most frustrating of conflicts. All that's left, then, is for the last conflict to be *approach–avoidance,* and for it to be the most common conflict.

See if you can come up with a line of your own that will help you remember the same information: *One possibility: Whenever I approach the cat, she most commonly avoids me.*

Comments on Reading 2: After you have a line that you automatically remember in order to "anchor" your study, test yourself until you can recite from memory the definition of *frustration* as well as the kinds of conflict, their definitions, examples, and an important detail about each.

Reading 3: A Passage from a Sociology Text

Norms

All societies have ways of encouraging and enforcing what they view as appropriate behavior while discouraging and punishing what they consider to be improper conduct. "Put on some clean clothes for dinner" and "Thou shalt not kill" are examples of norms found in American culture, just as respect for older people is a norm in Japanese culture. *Norms* are established standards of behavior maintained by a society.

In order for a norm to become significant, it must be widely shared and understood. For example, when Americans go to the movies, we typically expect that people will be quiet while the film is showing. Because of this norm, an usher can tell a member of the audience to stop talking so loudly. Of course, the application of this norm can vary, depending on the particular film and type of audience. People attending a serious artistic or political film will be more likely to insist on the norm of silence than those attending a slapstick comedy or horror movie.

Types of Norms Sociologists distinguish between norms in two ways. First, norms are classified as either formal or informal. *Formal norms* have generally been written down and involve strict rules for punishment of violators. In American society, we often formalize norms into laws, which must be very precise in defining proper and improper behavior. In a political sense, *law* is the "body of rules, made by government for society, interpreted by the courts, and backed by the power of the state." Laws are an example of formal norms, although not the only type. The requirements for a college major and the rules of a card game are also considered formal norms.

By contrast, *informal norms* are generally understood but are not precisely recorded. Standards of proper dress are a common example of informal norms. Our society has no specific punishment or sanction for a person who comes to school or to college dressed quite differently from everyone else. Making fun of nonconforming students for their unusual choice of clothing is the most likely response.

Norms are also classified by their relative importance to society. When classified in this way, they are known as *mores* and *folkways.*

Mores (pronounced "MOR-ays") are norms deemed highly necessary to the welfare of a society, often because they embody the most cherished principles of a people. Each society demands obedience to its mores; violation can lead to severe penalties. Thus, American society has strong mores against murder, treason, and child abuse that have been institutionalized into formal norms. *Folkways* are norms governing everyday behavior whose violation raises comparatively little concern. For example, walking up a "down" escalator in a department store challenges our standards of appropriate behavior, but it will not result in a fine or a jail sentence. Society is more likely to formalize mores than it is folkways. Nevertheless, folkways play an important role in shaping the daily behavior of members of a culture.

Source: Richard T. Schaefer and Robert P. Lamm, *Sociology,* 4th ed. (New York: McGraw-Hill).

Activity for Reading 3

Preview: Take about thirty seconds to preview the textbook passage on the opposite page. The title tells you that the passage is about _____*norms*_____. How many other headings are in the passage? __*one*__ How many terms are set off in **boldface** in the passage? __*six*__

Read and Mark: Read the passage straight through. As you do, underline the definitions you find. Write *Ex* in the margin beside an example that makes each definition clear for you. Also, number the items in the two enumerations that you'll find.

Write: On separate paper, take notes on "Norms."

1. Write down the definition of *norms* and an example of a norm.
2. Write down and number the two ways in which sociologists distinguish between types of norms. Include definitions and examples.

   The notes required are apparent in the text itself.

Recite: To remember the four norms, create a *catchphrase:* a short sentence made up of the first letters of the four norms: *f* for *formal, i* for *informal, m* for *mores,* and *f* for *folkways:*

   Your sentence: *F*__*Fred*__ *I*__*is*__ *M*__*my*__ *F*__*friend*__
   (Answers will vary.)

Comments on Reading 3: After you can say the definition and an example of *norm* to yourself without looking at them, go on and see if you can say the four norms to yourself. Doing this should be easy because you will have created a catchphrase that will automatically give you the first letters (F, I, M, F) of those four norms. You can then use the first letters as "hooks" to help you pull the words themselves into memory. Test yourself, then, to make sure that the first *F* stands in your head for *formal, I* stands for *informal, M* stands for *mores,* and the second *F* stands for *folkways.*

Reading 4: A Passage from a Health Text

Illnesses Associated with Long-Term Alcohol Use

Alcohol is linked with many serious illnesses that can destroy the body's most important organs and sometimes result in death.

Gastrointestinal Disorders Alcohol stimulates secretion of digestive acid throughout the gastrointestinal system, irritating the lining of the drinker's stomach and the linings of the esophagus and intestines. It is not unusual for alcoholics to develop bleeding ulcers in the stomach and intestines, and sometimes lesions in the esophagus. Alcohol can give "binge drinkers" diarrhea. It may inhibit the pancreas's production of enzymes that are crucial for the digestion of food. When heavily abused, it can also lead to **pancreatitis** (inflammation of the pancreas).

Malnutrition A common myth holds that alcohol, being made from fruit or grain, is food. It is not. Worse, alcohol actually starves the body of essential nutrients. It does consist of calories, so it produces energy, but it does not contain any of the chemical substances the body needs to build and repair tissue. Alcohol abuse has been reported as the most common cause of vitamin deficiency in this country. An alcoholic may undereat; or, because the digestive system is disrupted, he or she may be unable to process properly the nutrients that are eaten. Alcoholics may also suffer nutritional imbalances because of diarrhea, loss of appetite, and vomiting. In short, alcoholism can be a form of slow starvation.

Liver Damage The liver is one of the organs most vulnerable to alcohol abuse. Alcohol changes the way the liver processes important substances; it can also contribute to infections and other disorders. If the liver is disturbed or infected, the body's immune system and ability to flush out poisons are affected. Damage to the liver can also harm other organs, because the liver is essential to the production and modification of many substances the body needs.

Many alcoholics suffer **cirrhosis of the liver,** a chronic inflammatory disease of this organ in which healthy liver cells are replaced by scar tissue. Cirrhosis of the liver caused more than 27,000 deaths in 1983; it was the ninth leading cause of death that year. Drinking can also cause **alcoholic hepatitis,** in which the liver becomes swollen and inflamed. It may also lead to a "fatty liver" condition by changing the way the liver processes fats.

Glandular (Endocrine) Disorders Excessive drinking can damage the body's glandular system, which regulates such important functions as moods and sexuality. Men who drink too much may suffer impotence and reduced levels of the hormone testosterone; in one study, researchers found that the second most frequent reason for impotence among men was excessive drinking. Women may also throw their hormonal system out of balance through heavy drinking; recent studies indicate that alcohol abuse can lead to early menopause.

Source: Marvin R. Levy, Mark Dignan, and Janet H. Shirreffs, *Essentials of Health,* 5th ed. (New York: McGraw-Hill).

Activity for Reading 4

Preview: Take about thirty seconds to preview Reading 4 on the previous page. The title tells you that the passage is about _____*illness*_____. How many other headings are in the passage? __*four*__ How many terms are set off in **boldface** in the passage? __*three*__

Read and Mark: Read the passage straight through. As you do, underline the definitions you find. Notice that each of the headings under the title is part of an enumeration, so number those headings. Also, place a check beside details that seem important under each heading.

To decide what is important, turn each heading into a basic question and read to find details that answer it. For example, turn the heading "Gastrointestinal disorders" into the question, "What are examples of gastrointestinal disorders?" Turn the heading "Malnutrition" into the question, "How does alcohol cause malnutrition?" Turn the heading "Liver Damage" into the questions, "How is the liver damaged?" and "What are the kinds of liver damage?"

The technique of turning headings into basic questions starting with words like *What, How, When,* and *In what ways* is a good way to locate and focus on important details within a section.

Write: On separate paper, take notes on "Illnesses Associated with Long-Term Alcohol Use":

1. Write down the four illnesses associated with long-term alcohol use, along with important details about each illness.

2. Be sure to include the definitions of *pancreatitis, cirrhosis of the liver,* and *alcoholic hepatitis.*

   The notes required are apparent in the text itself.

Recite: To remember the four kinds of long-term alcohol-related illness, create a *catchphrase,* a short sentence made up of the first letters of the four kinds of illness: G for *gastrointestinal,* M for *malnutrition,* L for *liver,* and G for *glandular (endocrine) disorders.*

Your four-word sentence with the letters G, M, L, and G (in any order):

Mice greatly love garbage. (Answers will vary).

Comments on Reading 4: In a passage such as this one, there are an enumeration and some definitions. At the same time, you must turn headings into questions to help yourself focus on the major points presented in each section. Asking questions that are based on headings can be an excellent way to get inside a block of material. The questions help you understand the material and pick out what might be most important.

Reading 5: A Passage from a Biology Text

Building Blocks of All Matter

Two basic principles of chemistry emerged from the work of the French chemist Antoine Lavoisier, the English chemist John Dalton, and others in the late 1700s and early 1800s.

- All matter, living and nonliving, is made up of **elements,** substances that cannot be decomposed by chemical processes into simpler substances. There are ninety-two chemical elements in nature, and thirteen more have been created in the laboratory. Some examples of elements are hydrogen (symbolized H), oxygen (O), sulfur (S), gold (Au), iron (Fe), and carbon (C).

- Each element is composed of identical particles called **atoms,** the smallest units of matter that still display the characteristic properties of the element. All the atoms in a brick of pure gold, for example, are identical to one another but different from all the atoms in a lump of carbon, an ingot of iron, or a sample of other elements. The properties of an element, such as the dense, shiny, metallic nature of gold or the dull black quality of carbon, are based on the structure of its individual atoms, as we shall see.

The Elements of Life A natural question arose from the pioneering work of Lavoisier and Dalton: Are living things made up of the same elements as rocks, planets, and stars, or is our chemical makeup different? Living things, it turns out, display a special subset of the ninety-two naturally occurring elements in the earth's crust, but the elements occur in very different proportions. Fully 98 percent of the atoms in the earth's crust are the elements oxygen, silicon (Si), aluminum (Al), iron, calcium (Ca), sodium (Na), potassium (K), and magnesium (Mg), with the first three predominating. In a typical organism, however, 99 percent of the atoms are the markedly different subset carbon, hydrogen, nitrogen (N), and oxygen, with sodium, calcium, phosphorus (P), and sulfur making up most of the remaining 1 percent, plus a few other elements present in trace amounts.

Biologists are not certain why the chemical subsets of living and nonliving things are so different, but they do know that atomic architecture determines the physical properties of elements and, in turn, the properties of living organisms.

Atomic Structure Atoms are extremely small: about three million atoms sitting side by side would probably cover the period at the end of this sentence. The physicist Gerald Feinberg once calculated that there are more atoms in the human body than there are stars in the known universe. Although minuscule in size, each atom is made up of three types of subatomic particles: protons, neutrons, and electrons. **Protons** have a positive (+) charge; **neutrons** have no electrical charge (they are neutral); and **electrons** have a negative (–) charge. Since these subatomic particles are only parts of atoms, none of them displays properties of elements. The protons and neutrons are clustered in a small dense body at the center of the atom called the *nucleus* (the diameter of an atom is about 100,000 times larger than that of the nucleus). The outer limits of the atom are defined by the paths of its electrons, which continuously race about the nucleus in cloudlike orbits. Electrons, protons, and neutrons are themselves made up of a dozen or more smaller subatomic particles held together by special forces.

Source: Janet L. Hopson and Norman K. Wessells, *Essentials of Biology* (New York: McGraw-Hill).

Activity for Reading 5

Preview: Take about thirty seconds to preview Reading 5 on the previous page. The title tells you that the passage is about _____*matter*_____. How many other headings are in the passage? __*two*__ How many words are set off in **boldface** in the passage? __*five*__ What word is set off in *italics?* __*nucleus*__

Read and Mark: Read the passage straight through. As you do, underline the definitions you find. Where appropriate, set off an example of a definition with an *Ex* in the margin. Also, number the items in the two enumerations. Finally, jot down what seem to be important details within the passage.

Write: On separate paper, take notes on "Building Blocks of All Matter":
1. Write down the two basic principles of chemistry.
2. Write down examples of elements and atoms.
3. Note whether living things are made up of the same elements as nonliving things.
4. Note the size of atoms.
5. Note the definitions of the three types of subatomic particles and of the nucleus.
   The notes required are apparent in the text itself.

Recite: Write here key words that you might put in the margin of your notes to help you study the material:

def. and ex. of elements; def. and ex. of atoms; 3 types of subatomic

particles; def. of nucleus

After you can recite the first scientific principle (involving elements) without looking at it, study until you can say to yourself the second scientific principle (involving atoms) without looking at it. Then go back and review the first principle. Remember that constant review is a key to effective study.

Comments on Reading 5: Remember that a good way of taking notes is to write down all the headings and then place notes under those headings. Textbook authors carefully organize their information through a series of major and minor headings. By writing those headings down, you help organize your own notes.

Like most scientific materials, this passage is densely packed with information. But once again, you have seen how a combination of headings, definitions, and enumerations can help you get down the important information in a textbook selection.

Independent Practice in PRWR

Following are several longer textbook passages. Apply the PRWR method—preview, read, write, recite—to study the material in each passage. Use your own paper to take study notes. Hints for note-taking are provided at the start of each selection.

Reading 6: A Passage from a Psychology Text

Hints: Definitions, examples, and answers to questions provided by the authors are the keys to important ideas in this selection.

Remember that a good way of taking notes is to write down all the headings and then place notes under those headings. Textbook authors carefully organize their information through a series of major and minor headings. By writing those headings down, you help organize your own notes.

Development of Social Attachments

"I don't believe you. I know that a baby can't do much more than cry, eat, and sleep. You're saying that your baby recognizes your face. A baby's brain isn't big enough to do that." The neighbor had finished talking and stood there with her arms crossed, looking down at the ten-week-old infant. The mother smiled, "OK, I'll show you. You stand on the left side of the crib and I'll stand on the right. Then we'll play peekaboo. If the baby spends more time looking at me, it means that she recognizes my face. If she spends more time looking at you, it means that she doesn't." The mother took her place on the right and the neighbor walked over and stood on the left side of the crib. The neighbor and the mother alternately played peekaboo. There was little doubt about the results. The baby spent more time looking at her mother's face. The neighbor was shaking her head from side to side. "Could be a coincidence. I still don't believe that tiny Kim really recognizes your face."

Whom would you believe, the mother or the neighbor? In a study similar to the peekaboo game played by the mother and the neighbor, Tiffany Field and her associates reported that four-day-old infants initially spent more time looking at their mother's face than a stranger's. Field concluded that even newborns can learn some distinctive features of their mother's face.

Lewis Lipsitt says that until recently, parents were told that their infants were mostly blind at birth and could not taste, smell, feel pain, learn, or remember. Now we know that newborns can see, taste, feel pain, detect their mother's odor, and show taste and flavor preferences. Even more remarkable, Lipsitt has shown that infants can learn and remember. The first time Kim hears a new sound, her heart accelerates briefly. But after the sound is present a number of times, her heart no longer accelerates. This indicates that she "remembers" or recognizes the sound, a process called *habituation.* Lipsitt has also shown that newborn Kim can learn to turn her head at the sound of a tone but not a buzzer to get a taste of sugar water. This is an example of *associative learning.* All these studies indicate that newborn Kim's senses and brain are functioning to a remarkable degree. One way that researchers could assess normal brain development is by analyzing Kim's crying to see whether it fits a normal or abnormal pattern. If her brain development is normal, within months she will develop further sensory and cognitive functions and form attachments to her parents.

Forming Attachments

Between four and six weeks, rhythmically moving stimuli, such as the nodding head of a puppet or a rotating mobile, will cause Kim to smile. Then gradually, between the ages of two and three months, a human face becomes the most effective stimulus for eliciting a smile. Because this smile is directed toward another person, it is called **social smiling.** Psychologists believe that Kim's social smiling may be increased by parental reinforcement. But her social smiling also serves a very important social function, that of communication. The emergence of social smiling is thought to mark the beginning of a period during which the infant forms social attachments with caretakers.

By six months, Kim will recognize her parents' faces. Soon she will begin to give them happy greetings when they reappear after a short absence. When Kim's father comes home from work, she may smile and gurgle, bounce up and down in her highchair, and hold out her arms to him. In a few more months, when Kim is able to crawl, she will begin to follow her parents wherever they go. At the same time, Kim will begin to show distress whenever her mother and father temporarily leave her in the care of someone else. This reaction, called **separation anxiety,** may include loud protests, crying, and agitation, as well as despair and depression when the separation is very long. Both separation anxiety and joyous greetings on reunion are signs that Kim is developing strong affectional bonds toward her parents, bonds called **social attachments.** A social attachment will form toward whoever is a child's primary caretaker—whether mother, father, grandparent, or any other caring adult.

By studying the reactions of infants to being separated from and reunited with their mothers, Mary Ainsworth found that infant–mother attachments vary greatly in quality. When placed in an unfamiliar room containing many interesting toys, a **securely attached** infant tends to explore freely as long as the mother looks on. If the mother leaves, most of these babies cry and become upset. But when mother returns, they greet her happily and are very easily soothed. In contrast, an **anxiously attached** infant does not respond positively when the mother comes back to the room. Some show great ambivalence toward her, one minute clinging and wanting to be held, and the next minute squirming and pushing away. Other anxiously attached infants simply avoid the mother upon her return; they turn their heads in another direction or move away from her.

There is some relationship between the security of the infant–caretaker attachment and the child's later behaviors. For example, the more secure the infant–caretaker attachment, the less dependence the child later shows and the better he or she copes with the stress of attending kindergarten. The development of the infant–caretaker attachment is important because it establishes an initial pattern of trust and understanding in the infant's life.

Why does the quality of infant–caretaker attachments vary so greatly? The answer lies in a complex interaction between traits of the parent, traits of the baby, and the kind of environment in which they both live. For instance, researchers have found that mothers of securely attached infants tend to be more sensitive to their baby's needs than mothers of anxiously attached infants. When the child is crying and upset, these mothers usually respond quickly and offer comfort until the baby is soothed. This style of mothering is called *sensitive care*. Mothers of anxiously attached infants, in contrast, are less likely to respond right away when their baby is distressed and are more apt to let the infant "cry it out." These women may also have more negative feelings toward motherhood and are more tense and irritable toward their child.

At the same time, many infants who become insecurely attached start life with certain characteristics that make them harder for an adult to respond to. For example, anxiously attached infants in general have been found to be less active, less alert, and less socially engaging as newborns. Outside conditions may also enter into the development of an insecure attachment. When a woman with a difficult baby has many additional stresses in her life and little emotional support from others, the relationship between mother and child may get off to a bad start. The development of attachments is a very complex process that involves many interacting factors.

Although psychologists have long studied the infant–mother attachment, they have only recently studied the infant–father attachment. Researchers found that mothers were more likely to interact with their infants during routine caretaking, such as feeding or bathing, and to pick up their infants at these times. In contrast, fathers were more likely to interact with their infants for the sole purpose of play. The researchers concluded that infants become attached to their fathers as well as to their mothers, and that fathers provide different kinds of stimulation and activities from mothers.

As you can see, the kind of attachment a child develops with a mother, a father, or another adult depends on a complex interaction among a host of factors. When this interaction goes very badly, the result can be tragic, as in the development of child abuse.

Source: Rod Plotnik, *Introduction to Psychology,* 2nd ed. (New York: McGraw-Hill).

Reading 7: A Passage from a Speech Text

Hints: Enumerations, headings, and subheadings are the keys to important ideas here. Notice that each heading under "How to Become a Better Listener" is part of an enumeration. When you take notes, number these headings. You will also find another enumeration in this passage that is formed from *subheadings* (headings that fit under a larger heading); be sure to number these subheadings.

How to Become a Better Listener

Take Listening Seriously

The first step to improvement is always self-awareness. Analyze your shortcomings as a listener and commit yourself to overcoming them. Good listeners are not born that way. They have *worked* at learning how to listen effectively. Good listening does not go hand in hand with intelligence, education, or social standing. Like any other skill, it comes from practice and self-discipline.

You should begin to think of listening as an active process. So many aspects of modern life encourage us to listen passively. We "listen" to the radio while studying or "listen" to the television while moving about from room to room. This type of passive listening is a habit—but so is active listening. We can learn to identify those situations in which active listening is important. If you work seriously at becoming a more efficient listener, you will reap the rewards in your schoolwork, in your personal and family relations, and in your career.

Resist Distractions

In an ideal world, we could eliminate all physical and mental distractions. In the real world, however, this is not possible. Because we think so much faster than a speaker can talk, it's easy to let our attention wander while we listen. Sometimes it's very easy—when the room is too hot, when construction machinery is operating right outside the window, when the speaker is tedious. But our attention can stray even in the best of circumstances—if for no other reason than a failure to stay alert and make ourselves concentrate.

Whenever you find this happening, make a conscious effort to pull your mind back to what the speaker is saying. Then force it to stay there. One way to do this is to think a little ahead of the speaker—try to anticipate what will come next. This is not the same as jumping to conclusions. When you jump to conclusions, you put words into the speaker's mouth and don't actually listen to what is said. In this case you *will* listen—and measure what the speaker says against what you had anticipated.

Another way to keep your mind on a speech is to review mentally what the speaker has already said and make sure you understand it. Yet another is to listen between the lines and assess what a speaker implies verbally or says nonverbally with body language. Suppose a politician is running for reelection.

During a campaign speech to her constituents she makes this statement: "Just last week I had lunch with the President, and he assured me that he has a special concern for the people of our state." The careful listener would hear this implied message: "If you vote for me, there's a good chance more tax money will flow into the state."

To take another example, suppose a speaker is introducing someone to the audience. The speaker says, "It gives me great pleasure to present to you my very dear friend, Nadine Zussman." But the speaker doesn't shake hands with Nadine. He doesn't even look at her—just turns his back and leaves the podium. Is Nadine really his "very dear friend"? Certainly not.

Attentive listeners can pick up all kinds of clues to a speaker's real message. At first you may find it difficult to listen so intently. If you work at it, however, your concentration is bound to improve.

Don't Be Diverted by Appearance or Delivery

If you had attended Abraham Lincoln's momentous Cooper Union speech of 1860, this is what you would have seen:

> The long, ungainly figure upon which hung clothes that, while new for this trip, were evidently the work of an unskilled tailor; the large feet and clumsy hands, of which, at the outset, at least, the orator seemed to be unduly conscious; the long, gaunt head, capped by a shock of hair that seemed not to have been thoroughly brushed out, made a picture which did not fit in with New York's conception of a finished statesman.

But although he seemed awkward and uncultivated, Lincoln had a powerful message about the moral evils of slavery. Fortunately, the audience at Cooper Union did not let his appearance stand in the way of his words.

Similarly, you must be willing to set aside preconceived judgments based on a person's looks or manner of speech. Gandhi was a very unimpressive-looking man who often spoke dressed in a simple white cotton cloth. Helen Keller, deaf and blind from earliest childhood, always had trouble articulating words distinctly. The renowned physicist Stephen Hawking is severely disabled and can speak only with the aid of a voice synthesizer. Yet imagine if no one had listened to them. Even though it may tax your tolerance, patience, and concentration, don't let negative feelings about a speaker's appearance or delivery keep you from listening to the message.

On the other hand, try not to be misled if the speaker has an unusually attractive appearance. It's all too easy to assume that because someone is good-looking and has a polished delivery, he or she is speaking eloquently. Some of the most unscrupulous speakers in history have been handsome people with hypnotic delivery skills. Again, be sure you respond to the message, not to the package it comes in.

Suspend Judgment

Unless we listen only to people who think exactly as we do, we are going to hear things with which we disagree. When this happens, our natural inclination is to argue mentally with the speaker or to dismiss everything she or he says, but neither response is fair—to the speaker or to ourselves. In both cases we blot out any chance of learning or being persuaded.

Does this mean you must agree with everything you hear? Not at all. It means you should hear people out *before* reaching a final judgment. Try to understand their point of view. Listen to their ideas, examine their evidence, assess their reasoning. *Then* make up your mind. If you're sure of your beliefs, you need not fear listening to opposing views. If you're not sure, you have every reason to listen carefully. It has been said more than once that a closed mind is an empty mind.

Focus Your Listening

As we have seen, skilled listeners do not try to absorb a speaker's every word. Rather, they focus on specific things in a speech. Here are three suggestions to help you focus your listening.

Listen for Main Points. Most speeches contain from two to four main points. Here, for example, are the main points of a speech delivered by Bill Clinton on the challenges facing the United Nations in the twenty-first century.

1.   The first challenge facing the U.N. is to use the benefits of global prosperity to combat poverty and disease in developing nations.
2.   The second challenge facing the U.N. is to prevent ethnic cleansing and other incidents of mass killing and displacement.
3.   The third challenge facing the U.N. is to ensure that nuclear, chemical, and biological weapons will never be used again.

These three points are the heart of Clinton's message. As with any speech, they are the most important things to listen for.

Unless a speaker is terribly scatterbrained, you should be able to detect his or her main points with little difficulty. Often a speaker will give some idea at the outset of the main points to be discussed in the speech. For example, at the end of his introduction, Clinton said he was going to offer "three resolutions for the new millennium." Noticing this, a sharp listener would have been prepared for a speech with three main points, each dealing with a different resolution. As the speech progressed, Clinton enumerated each main point to help his listeners keep track of them. He also summarized them in his conclusion. After this, only the most inattentive of listeners could have been in the dark about Clinton's main points.

Listen for Evidence. Identifying a speaker's main points, however, is not enough. You must also listen for supporting evidence. By themselves, Clinton's main points are only assertions. You may be inclined to believe them just because they were stated by the President of the United States. Yet a careful listener will be concerned about evidence no matter who is speaking. Had you been listening to Clinton's speech, you would have heard him support his claim about the need to combat poverty and disease with a mass of verifiable evidence. Here is an excerpt:

> We are still squandering the potential of far too many: 1.3 billion people still live on less than a dollar a day. More than half the population of many countries have no access to safe water. A person in South Asia is 700 times less likely to use the Internet than someone in the United States. And 40 million people each year still die of hunger—almost as many as the total number killed in World War II. . . . Over the next ten years in Africa, AIDS is expected to kill more people and orphan more children than all the wars of the twentieth century combined.

There are four basic questions to ask about a speaker's evidence:

Is it *accurate*?
Is it taken from *objective* sources?
Is it *relevant* to the speaker's claims?
Is it *sufficient* to support the speaker's point?

In Clinton's case, the answer to each question is yes. His figures about economic conditions, water quality, Internet use, hunger, and the AIDS epidemic in Africa are well established in the public record and can be verified by independent sources. The figures are clearly relevant to Clinton's claim about the problems of poverty and disease in developing nations, and they are sufficient to support that claim. If Clinton's evidence were inaccurate, biased, irrelevant, or insufficient, you should be wary of accepting his claim.

Listen for Technique. We said earlier that you should not let a speaker's delivery distract you from the message, and this is true. However, if you want to become an effective speaker, you should study the methods other people use to speak effectively. When you listen to speeches—in class and out—focus above all on the content of a speaker's message; but also pay attention to the techniques the speaker uses to get the message across.

Analyze the introduction: What methods does the speaker use to gain attention, to relate to the audience, to establish credibility and goodwill? Assess the organization of the speech: Is it clear and easy to follow? Can you pick out the speaker's main points? Can you follow when the speaker moves from one point to another?

Study the speaker's language. Is it accurate, clear, vivid, appropriate? Does the speaker adapt well to the audience and occasion? Finally, diagnose the speaker's delivery: Is it fluent, dynamic, convincing? Does it strengthen or weaken the impact of the speaker's ideas? How well does the speaker use eye contact, gestures, and visual aids?

As you listen, focus on the speaker's strengths and weaknesses. If the speaker is not effective, try to determine why. If he or she is effective, try to pick out techniques you can use in your own speeches. If you listen in this way, you will be surprised how much you can learn about successful speaking.

Source: Stephen E. Lucas, *The Art of Public Speaking,* 7th ed. (New York: McGraw-Hill).

Reading 8: A Passage from a Communications Text

Hints: Definitions, examples, enumerations, and headings and subheadings are all keys to important ideas in this selection.

Remember that a good way of taking notes is to write down all the headings and then to place notes under those headings. Textbook authors carefully organize their information through a series of major and minor headings. By writing those headings down, you help organize your own notes.

Verbal Forms of Information

As you conduct research, you'll be looking for both factual statements and expert opinions. **Factual statements** are those that can be verified. "A recent study confirms that preschoolers watch an average of twenty-eight hours of television a week," "The Macintosh Performa comes with a CD-ROM port," and "Johannes Gutenberg invented printing from movable type in the 1400s" are all statements of fact that can be verified. **Expert opinions** are interpretations and judgments made by authorities in a particular area. "Watching twenty-eight hours of television a week is far too much for young children," "Having a CD-ROM port on your computer is a necessity," and "The invention of printing from movable type was for all intents and purposes the start of mass communication" are all *opinions* based on the previous factual statements. Factual information and expert opinions may be presented in the form of examples and illustrations, statistics, anecdotes and narratives, comparisons and contrasts, and quotable explanations and opinions.

Examples and Illustrations. **Examples** are specific instances that illustrate or explain a general factual statement. The generalization "American cars are beginning to rival the quality of Japanese cars," for instance, may be illustrated or explained with the following specific example: "The frequency-of-repair records for Dodge Intrepid and Buick Regal in the past year are much closer than in previous years to those of the Nissan Maxima and Toyota Camry." Examples are useful because they provide concrete detail that makes a general statement more meaningful to the audience.

You may also find a good example cast in illustration form. An illustration is an example that has been developed with added detail. The following segment shows the difference between casting the same information in example form and in illustration form.

> **Generalization:** Most people want to accomplish an objective with the least amount of effort.
> **Example:** When entering a building, people will wait for an open door rather than use the energy to open a closed door.
> **Illustration:** "I remember watching the entrance of a large office building. There were five doors. The one on the far left was open, the rest closed. Almost everybody used the open door, even waiting for people to come out before they could enter just because the door was easier than the effort of pushing another door open. This is true of much of life."

Now let us consider guidelines for selecting and using examples. First, the examples should be specific enough to create a clear picture for the audience. If you exemplified the generalization "American cars are beginning to rival the quality of Japanese cars" with the statement "Some American cars are quite reliable," the audience would still not have a clear idea of the degree of reliability. But if you gave the example, "The 1997 Dodge Intrepid reliability record, as shown in the April 1998 issue of *Consumer Reports,* is virtually the same as that of the 1997 Toyota Camry," the point would be clear and specific.

Second, the examples you use should not be misleading. For instance, if the Ford Taurus was the only American car whose frequency-of-repair record was anything like the records of Japanese cars, it would be unethical to start with the generalization "American cars are beginning to rival the quality of Japanese cars."

Third, examples should relate to the generalization. If you say "American cars are beginning to rival the quality of Japanese cars" and then give the example "Chrysler Corporation has run a series of commercials showing the beauty of their leather interiors," the example may concern quality, but it does not show how Chrysler Corporation cars compare with Japanese cars.

Because specifics both clarify and substantiate, it's a good idea to follow this rule of thumb in preparing your speeches: Never let a generalization stand without at least one example.

Statistics. **Statistics** are numerical facts. Statistical statements, such as "Seven out of every ten local citizens voted in the last election" or "The cost of living rose 2.5 percent in 1997," enable you to pack a great deal of information into a small package. Statistics can provide impressive support for a point, but when they are poorly used in the speech, they may be boring and, in some instances, downright deceiving. Following are some guidelines on using statistics effectively.

1. Taking statistics from only the most reliable source and double-checking any startling statistics with another source will guard against the use of faulty statistics. For example, it is important to double-check statistics that you find in such sources as paid advertisements or publications distributed by special-interest groups. Be especially wary if your source does not itself provide documentation for the statistics it reports.

2. Record only recent statistics so that your audience will not be misled. For example, if you find the statistic that only two of one hundred members of the Senate, or 2 percent, are women (true in 1992), you would be misleading your audience if you used that statistic in a speech. If you want to make a point about the number of women in the Senate, find the most recent statistics. Check for both the year and the range of years to which the statistics apply.

3. Look for statistics that are used comparatively. By themselves, statistics are hard to interpret, but when used comparatively, they have much greater impact.

   In a speech on chemical waste, Donald Baeder points out that whereas in the past chemicals were measured in parts per million, today they are measured in parts per billion or even parts per trillion. Had he stopped at that point, the audience would have had little sense of the immensity of the figures. Notice how he goes on to use comparisons to put the meaning of the statistics in perspective: "One part per billion is the equivalent of one drop—one drop!—of vermouth in two 36,000-gallon tanks of gin, and that would be a very dry martini even by San Francisco standards! One part per trillion is the equivalent of one drop in two thousand tank cars."

4. Do not overuse statistics. Although statistics may be an excellent way to present a great deal of material quickly, be careful not to overuse them. A few pertinent numbers are far more effective than a battery of statistics. When you believe you must use many statistics, try preparing a visual aid, perhaps a chart, to help your audience visualize them.

Ancedotes and Narratives. Ancedotes are brief, often amusing stories; **narratives** are tales, accounts, personal experiences, or lengthier stories. Each presents material in story form. Because holding the audience's interest is so important in a speech and because the audience's attention is likely to be captured by a story, anecdotes and narratives are worth looking for, creating, and using. For a two-minute speech, you have little time to tell a detailed story, so one or two anecdotes or a very short narrative would be preferable.

The key to using stories is to make sure that the point of the story states or reinforces the point you make in your speech. In his speech about telecommunication, Randall Tobias, vice chairman of AT&T, uses a story to make a point about the promise and the threat of technology:

A lighthearted story I heard from a scientist-colleague illustrates the point.

A theologian asked the most powerful supercomputer, "Is there a God?" The computer said it lacked the processing power to know. It asked to be connected to all the other supercomputers in the world. Still, it was not enough power. So the computer was hooked up to all the mainframes in the world, then all the minicomputers, and then all the personal computers. The theologian asked for the final time, "Is there a God?" And the computer replied: "There is now."

Comparisons and Contrasts. One of the best ways to give meaning to new ideas is through comparison and contrast. **Comparisons** illuminate a point by showing similarities. Although you can easily create comparisons using information you have found, you should still keep your eye open for creative comparisons developed by the authors of the books and articles you have found.

Comparisons make ideas not only clearer but also more vivid. Notice how Stephen Joel Trachtenberg, in a speech to the Newington High School Scholars' Breakfast, uses figurative comparison to demonstrate the importance of being willing to take risks, even in the face of danger.

The eagle flying high always risks being shot at by some harebrained human with a rifle. But eagles and young eagles like you still prefer the view from that risky height to what is available flying with the turkeys far, far, below.

Whereas comparisons show similarities, **contrasts** show differences. Notice how this humorous contrast dramatizes the difference between "participation" and "commitment":

If this morning you had bacon and eggs for breakfast, I think it illustrates the difference. The eggs represent "participation" on the part of the chicken. The bacon represents "total commitment" on the part of the pig!

Quotations. When you find an explanation, an opinion, or a brief anecdote that seems to be exactly what you are looking for, you may quote it directly in your speech. Because audiences want to listen to your ideas and arguments, they do not want to hear a string of long quotations. However, a well-selected **quotation** might be perfect in one or two key places.

Quotations can both explain and vivify. Look for quotations that make a point in a particularly clear or vivid way. For example, in her speech "The Dynamics of Discovery," Catherine Ahles, vice president for College Relations at Macomb Community College, used the following quotation from Helen Keller to show the detrimental effects of pessimism: "No pessimist ever discovered the secrets of the stars . . . or sailed to an uncharted land . . . or opened a new heaven to the human spirit."

Keep in mind that when you use a direct quotation, it is necessary to credit the person who formulated it. Using any quotation or close paraphrase without crediting its source is plagiarism.

Source: Rudolph F. Verderber, *Communicate!* 9th ed. (New York: Wadsworth).

Reading 9: A Passage from a Business Text

Hints: Definitions, examples, enumerations, headings, and subheadings are all keys to important ideas in this selection.

Remember that a good way of taking notes is to write down all the headings and then to place notes under those headings. Textbook authors carefully organize their information through a series of major and minor headings. By writing those headings down, you help organize your own notes.

Consumer Products

Consumer products can be subdivided into four groups on the basis of how people buy them: (1) convenience products, (2) shopping products, (3) specialty products, and (4) unsought products.

Convenience Products

Convenience products are items that consumers want to buy with the least possible shopping effort. There are three types of convenience products: staples, impulse items, and emergency products.

Staple Items. These are convenience products for which consumers usually do some planning. Food items are good examples. For instance, though consumers don't seek much information about milk, they do buy it often, and they plan to buy it when preparing to go to the grocery store.

Impulse Items. These are purchased not because of planning but because of a strongly felt immediate need. Thus, distribution is an important factor in marketing impulse products. If they are not located conveniently, exchange will not take place. Shoppers tend to react by impulse in deciding to buy, say, *People* magazine.

Emergency Products. These are items that are needed to solve an immediate crisis. Price and quality are not of primary importance, although the product obviously has to be of sufficient quality to meet the emergency. Thus, while the price of an adhesive bandage means little when one is needed, it *does* have to stick.

Shopping Products

Consumers visit several stores to compare prices and quality before buying *shopping products.* Even before going into the store to examine such products, consumers may study magazines like *Consumer Reports,* ask friends for their opinions about certain products, or study advertisements. In other words, before buying shopping products, consumers seek information that will allow them to compare two or more brands or substitute products.

Shopping products can be divided into groups, depending on how consumers perceive them. *Homogeneous products* are perceived as being essentially similar (canned food items and home insurance policies are examples), whereas *heterogeneous products* are seen as essentially different (furniture, draperies, automobiles, and repair services are examples). With heterogeneous products the different styles and aesthetic features are important, while price is less important. But homogeneous products pose problems for marketers, because they are similar and must be differentiated in consumers' minds.

For instance, there are many smoke detectors on the market, and they all serve the same essential function; all are warning devices. From the marketing viewpoint, however, the similarity ends there. Each brand of smoke detector is technically different, performs somewhat differently, and sells for a different price. It is up to the marketers of a particular smoke detector to differentiate their product in the marketplace. Generally, they will try through advertising to show that their product is different from competing brands, and sometimes price will be used to distinguish one product from another. Homogeneous shopping products put demands on consumers because information is needed in order to sort the similar products and make a buying decision. For the same reason, such products require much attention from marketers.

Specialty Products

Specialty products are items for which there are no acceptable substitutes in the consumer's mind. Consumers are willing to search long and hard until they find them. Usually, the buyers of specialty products have investigated the products available and have decided which one they want to buy. And they are willing to search for an outlet for that particular product.

With specialty products, the brand name is extremely important. In fact, that may be most of what consumers are buying. Designer fashions are a good example. People go out of their way to find a store that carries clothes designed by Halston, Anne Klein, or Bill Blass. Such designers attempt to generate demand for their clothing so that people will search for their products and buy nothing else. A similar situation exists with specialty services like dental and medical care. People do not want to accept substitute goods and services.

Unsought Products

Unsought products are items that consumers do not readily realize they want or need. Most new products fall into this category, until marketers promote their benefits and the needs they satisfy. Not so long ago the trash compacter was an unsought product, because people didn't know they had a need for one. But as the compacter was developed and promoted, the need for it came to be recognized.

Hospitals, convalescent homes, and cemetery plots are other examples of unsought products. Consumers do not shop for such things until a need arises. But when the need is recognized, the products are sought.

Source: Charles D. Schewe and Reuben M. Smith, *Marketing* (New York: McGraw-Hill).

Reading 10: A Passage from a Chemistry Text

Hints: Definitions, examples, enumerations, and headings are all keys to important ideas in this densely packed passage from a science text.

Remember that a good way of taking notes is to write down all the headings and then to place notes under those headings. Textbook authors carefully organize their information through a series of major and minor headings. By writing those headings down, you help organize your own notes.

States of Matter

All matter on earth exists in three physical states: **solid, liquid,** and **gaseous.** Various physical properties distinguish the three states of matter. The properties most often considered are shape, volume, average density, structure, viscosity, and compressibility. Shape, volume, and density have been discussed previously; the last two properties require some explanation.

Viscosity is a measure of the resistance to flow. Substances with high viscosities do not flow readily, whereas substances with low viscosities flow more readily. If we are told that water is more fluid than motor oil, we know that the viscosity of water is less than that of motor oil. **Compressibility** is the measure of the decrease in volume of a substance with an applied pressure. A substance is deemed compressible if a force exerted on its surface (a pressure) results in a compacting of the substance.

Let's consider each physical state individually, starting with the solid state and proceeding to the liquid and gaseous states. The physical state of a substance depends on its temperature and pressure. Unless otherwise noted, room conditions of 25°C (298 K) and normal atmospheric pressure are assumed. Atmospheric pressure is measured in atmospheres, the atmosphere being a unit of gas pressure. Normal atmospheric pressure is equivalent to one atmosphere.

Solids

Solids have fixed shapes that are independent of their container. The volume of a solid is also fixed and does not change when a pressure is exerted. Solids are almost completely incompressible. Those that seem to be compressible, such as foams or corrugated paper, actually are solids that contain holes, or empty regions, throughout their volume. When these are "compressed," the solid structure fills into the empty regions: the solid itself is not compressed.

Of the three states of matter, solids have the highest average density. Densities in excess of 1 g/cm^3 are the norm for solids. Such is not the case for most liquids and gases. A high average density reflects the fact that the particles within solids are usually packed closer than those in liquids or gases. The

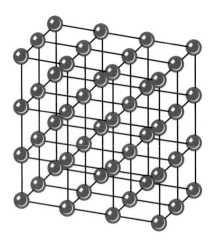

Most solids are composed of a regular array of closely packed particles. Particles within solids are usually more organized and packed more tightly than are the particles within liquids and gases.

tightly packed particles of solids are also highly organized (see the figure above). The regular patterns of particles found in solids are not detected in either liquids or gases.

Solids have practically no ability to flow because the particles that compose a solid are very tightly bonded. Stated in another way: Solids have very high viscosities.

Liquids

Liquids are quite different from solids in many respects, but the two share some characteristics. Like solids, liquids are essentially incompressible; pressure exerted on liquids generally produces little, if any, change in their volumes. When placed in a container, liquids assume the shape of the container to the level they fill (see the figure below).

As previously mentioned, the average density of liquids is less than that of solids but greater than that of gases. Liquid particles are not bonded as strongly as those in solids, and they are less orderly—more randomly distributed. Both of these factors tend to increase the average volume of liquids relative to that of solids. Thus, for equal masses of an average solid and liquid, the volume of the liquid is usually larger than that of the solid, which results in a lower density.

A liquid completely fills and takes the shape of the bottom of its container.

Viscosities of liquids vary over a broad range. Liquids have much lower viscosities than solids; i.e., they are significantly more fluid than solids. However, the viscosities of liquids are greater than those of gases. The gaseous state is the most fluid state of matter.

Gases

Gases bear little resemblance to the more-condensed states of matter, solids and liquids. To a degree, the properties of gases are the opposite of those of solids. Gases completely fill the volume of their containers, are compressible, have a completely disorganized structure, possess the lowest average density of the three states, and have the lowest viscosities.

Matter can change from one physical state to another. For example, solids, when heated, change to liquids. The characteristic temperature at which a particular solid changes to a liquid is called its **melting point.** At the melting point, the solid and liquid states of the substance coexist. Liquids, in turn, change to solids as they are cooled. The temperature at which a liquid becomes a solid is called the **freezing point.** Freezing and melting occur at the same temperature. In one case, the solid changes into a liquid—it melts. Moving in the other direction, a liquid changes into a solid—it freezes.

$$\text{Solids} \underset{\text{freezing}}{\overset{\text{melting}}{\rightleftharpoons}} \text{liquid}$$

For example, water freezes or melts at 0.0°C.

$$\text{Liquid} \underset{\text{condensation}}{\overset{\text{boiling}}{\rightleftharpoons}} \text{liquid}$$

Numerous solids change directly to their vapors without going through the liquid state. This state change is called **sublimation.** At the temperature and pressure at which a substance sublimes, the solid and vapor states coexist.

$$\text{Solid} \overset{\text{sublimation}}{\longrightarrow} \text{Vapor}$$

A good example of a solid that sublimes is "dry ice," or solid carbon dioxide. At −78°C (195 K), solid carbon dioxide and gaseous carbon dioxide coexist.

Source: Drew H. Wolfe, *Introduction to College Chemistry,* 2nd ed. (New York: McGraw-Hill).

Checking Your Mastery of PRWR: Quizzes

After you study each of the readings in this chapter, you can use the following quizzes to test your understanding of the material. It may take you too much time to study each passage as fully as you would if you were taking a test in a course. However, the very act of reading the material, making decisions on what is important, taking notes, and applying some memory techniques should give you a good basic sense of the material. That is what will be tested in the quizzes that follow.

■ Quiz on Reading 1

1. Into how many stages is today's business cycle divided?
   a. One
   b. Two
   (c.) Three
   d. Four

2. Which of the following can happen during a recession?
   a. People eat in restaurants less frequently.
   b. Companies often suffer economic losses.
   c. People can become frightened and angry.
   (d) All of the above.

3. *True or false?* __F__ Organizations are most likely to add new products during the beginning of the recovery period.

4. According to the passage, sales of Campbell's cream of broccoli soup increased when the company
   a. packaged it in a Gold Label can.
   (b) packaged it in a red-and-white can with recipes on the label.
   c. advertised it as ready to serve.
   d. announced that it was on the Campbell best-sellers list.

■ Quiz on Reading 2

1. Frustration is caused by
   (a) not being able to reach a desired goal.
   b. confusion about goals.
   c. both of the above.
   d. neither of the above.

2. The most frustrating type of conflict is the

   a.   approach-approach conflict.

   (b.) avoidance-avoidance conflict.

   c.   approach-avoidance conflict.

   d.   anger-frustration conflict.

3. The most common type of conflict is the

   a.   approach-approach conflict.

   b.   avoidance-avoidance conflict.

   (c.) approach-avoidance conflict.

   d.   anger-frustration conflict.

4. An example of an approach-approach conflict is

   (a.) having to choose between a Mercedes and a Porsche.

   b.   having to choose between cleaning a closet and going to bed.

   c.   weighing the advantages and disadvantages of eating chocolate fudge.

   d.   kicking your car when the engine will not turn over.

■ Quiz on Reading 3

1. A society's laws are examples of

   a.   folkways.

   b.   mores.

   c.   informal norms.

   (d.) formal norms.

2. *True or false?* __F__ Folkways are norms considered highly necessary to the welfare of society.

3. *True or false?* __F__ Walking up a "down" escalator is a violation of a more.

4. Standards of dress are examples of

   a.   folkways.

   b.   mores.

   (c.) informal norms.

   d.   formal norms.

■ Quiz on Reading 4

1. The four types of illnesses resulting from long-term alcohol use are gastrointestinal disorders, malnutrition, glandular disorders, and
   a. infections.
   b. cirrhosis of the liver.
   c. liver damage.
   d. chronic inflammatory diseases.

2. *True or false?* __F__ Because alcohol provides calories, it can be considered a food.

3. In alcoholic hepatitis,
   a. the pancreas is inflamed.
   b. bleeding ulcers occur.
   c. hormones are disturbed.
   d. the liver becomes swollen and inflamed.

4. Excessive drinking can cause impotence because of damage to the
   a. liver.
   b. pancreas.
   c. glandular system.
   d. digestive system.

■ Quiz on Reading 5

1. *True or false?* __T__ Chemical processes cannot break elements down into simpler substances.

2. The smallest units of matter that are still characteristic of an element are
   a. atoms.
   b. protons.
   c. neutrons.
   d. orbits.

3. One of the three subatomic particles is called a(n)
   a. element.
   b. atom.
   c. electron.
   d. orbit.

4. The small dense body at the center of an atom is called a(n)

   a.   proton.

   b.   element.

   c.   neutron.

   (d.) nucleus.

■ Quiz on Reading 6

1. An infant's getting used to a sound that at first made his or her heart beat rapidly is an example of

   (a.) habituation.

   b.   associative learning.

   c.   social attachment.

   d.   sensitive care.

2. In social smiling, a baby's smile is always directed toward

   a.   a neighbor.

   b.   a nodding puppet head.

   c.   a mobile.

   (d.) another person.

3. Separation anxiety is seen when a baby shows distress or great discomfort at

   a.   loud buzzing noises.

   (b.) being left in the care of someone other than the mother or father.

   c.   being in an unfamiliar room.

   d.   the return of the mother to an unfamiliar room.

4. *True or false?* __T__ The more secure the infant–caretaker attachment, the better the child's adjustment in kindergarten.

■ Quiz on Reading 7

1. The author has divided his advice on how to become a better listener into how many main suggestions?

   a.   Three.

   b.   Four.

   (c.) Five.

   d.   Six.

2. According to the author, listening between the lines is a way to

    a.   review mentally what the speaker has already said.

    (b.) resist distractions.

    c.   agree with what you hear.

    d.   listen for main points.

3. To focus your listening, pay attention to main points, evidence, and

    (a.) technique.

    b.   conclusions.

    c.   problems raised by the speaker.

    d.   anecdotes.

4. To judge a speaker's evidence, pay attention to its accuracy, objectivity, relevance, and

    a.   main points.

    b.   technique.

    c.   efficiency.

    (d.) sufficiency.

■ **Quiz on Reading 8**

1. The author defines *statistics* as

    a.   brief, often amusing stories.

    (b.) numerical facts.

    c.   specific instances that illustrate a statement.

    d.   a statement showing how two things are similar.

2. *True or false?* __F__ If you paraphrase a quotation, it is unnecessary to credit the person who formulated it.

3. The passage concerning the theologian who asked a computer if God existed was an example of

    a.   a comparison.

    (b.) an anecdote.

    c.   statistics.

    d.   quotations.

4. *True or false?* __F__ The author defines *factual statements* as interpretations and judgments made by authorities in a particular area.

■ Quiz on Reading 9

1. The author classifies consumer products according to
   a. cost.
   b. need.
   c. how they are bought.
   d. how important they are.

2. The four groups of consumer products are convenience products, specialty products, unsought products, and
   a. staple items.
   b. impulse items.
   c. shopping products.
   d. brand-name products.

3. *People* magazine is an example of products that tend to be
   a. staple items.
   b. impulse items.
   c. homogeneous products.
   d. unsought products.

4. *True or false?* ___F___ According to the author, emergency products are a type of specialty product.

■ Quiz on Reading 10

1. How many states of matter are there?
   a. Two.
   b. Three.
   c. Four.
   d. Five.

2. Particles are usually most tightly packed in
   a. solids.
   b. liquids.
   c. gases.
   d. oils.

3. A melting point is the characteristic temperature at which a
    a.   gas becomes liquid.
    b.   liquid becomes solid.
    c.   liquid changes to a gas.
    (d) solid changes to a liquid.
4. Dry ice is an example of substances that
    a.   are easily compressed.
    b.   never change their physical state.
    c.   have a melting point.
    (d) undergo sublimation.

Applying PRWR to a Textbook Chapter

This chapter will help improve your textbook study by:

- Reviewing the PRWR study method
- Providing note-taking practice on an entire textbook chapter
- Presenting hints and comments on good note-taking

To make your practice at textbook study as realistic as possible, you are now going to apply the PRWR method to an entire chapter from a college textbook. The book, *Sociology: An Introduction,* by Richard J. Gelles and Ann Levine, was published in a sixth edition in 1999. This McGraw-Hill book is widely used in colleges throughout the country.

You will read and take notes on the entire chapter by completing the "activities and comments" pages placed at five different spots within the chapter. The work you do will help show you just how the enormous amount of information presented within a chapter can be reduced to a limited number of notes. You will also become aware of the techniques that authors use to help communicate their ideas in an organized way.

Ideally, before studying this chapter, you should work through all the reading skills in Part Four of this book. If you have practiced individual skills such as locating definitions, enumerations, and main ideas, you will be better able to take on an entire textbook chapter. On the other hand, if you need practical guidance right away in how to read and study a textbook, you may want to proceed now with the sample chapter.

A Review of PRWR

To read and study this or any textbook chapter, apply the four steps in the PRWR study method. Following is a summary of those steps.

Step 1: Previewing the Chapter

Note the title and reflect for a moment on the fact that this entire chapter is going to be about "The Family." Then skim the chapter (which goes to page 203) to answer the following questions:

- How many major heads are in the chapter? (You'll note that major heads are set off in large boldface letters.) __6__
- Look at the major head on page 188: **Divorce.** How many subheads (which are set off in boldface capital and lowercase letters) appear under this main head? __4__
- What is the first term that is set off in **boldface italicized** print in Section 1 of the text? __family__
- What is the first idea that is set off in *italicized* print in Section 1 of the text? __regulation of sexual activity__
- How many tables, figures, and photographs are in the chapter? __23__
- How many boxes with related added material are in the chapter? __3__
- Does the chapter have an introduction? __yes__
- Does the chapter have a summary? __yes__
- Is there a list of key terms that are central to understanding the chapter? __yes__

Step 2: The First Reading

Read the chapter all the way through once. As you do so, mark off as a minimum the following: *definitions* (underline them), *examples* (put an *Ex* in the margin), *major enumerations* (number them 1, 2, 3, and so on), and what seem to be *important ideas* (put a check in the margin).

Remember that while you mark, you should not worry about understanding everything completely. Understanding is a process that will come gradually while you continue to work with the text. Bit by bit, as you reread the text, take notes on it, and study the notes, you will increase your understanding of the material.

Step 3: Writing Notes on the Chapter

As you proceed, write down all the major and minor headings in the chapter. The authors have used these headings to organize their material, and you can use the same headings to help organize your notes. Under the headings, write down definitions, examples, enumerations, and main ideas. (You will be shown just how to take such notes.)

Use common sense when taking textbook notes for your actual courses. Write down only what adds to ideas you have learned in class. Have your class notes in front of you while taking textbook notes. If a good definition of a term has been given to you by the instructor, there may be no need to write down a definition that appears in the textbook.

Step 4: Reciting Your Notes

Use the key words you have placed in the margin of your notes to go over the material repeatedly until you have mastered it.

Studying the Sample Chapter

How to Proceed

Preview, read, and take notes on the textbook chapter that follows. While previewing, you will see that five sets of "activities and comments" appear within the chapter. All the notes you need for the chapter will go on those "activities and comments" pages. Doing the activities will give you a solid, realistic grounding in the skills needed to read and study textbook material.

Chapter

Eleven

The Family

Marriage is certainly a *transformed* institution, and it plays a smaller role than ever before in organizing social and personal life. . . . Although fewer women stay single all their lives than in 1900, a higher proportion of women than ever before experience a period of independent living and employment before marriage. Women's expectations of both marriage and work are unlikely to ever be the same as in the past.

—*The Way We Really Are* (Coontz, 1997, p. 31)

Shouldn't we do more to protect and strengthen the American family? The American family is at the heart of our society. It is through the family that we learn values like responsibility, morality, commitment, and faith. Today it seems the family is under attack from all sides—from the media, from the educational establishment, from big government.

Our Family Responsibility Act is pro-family because it recognizes the value of families. We will strengthen the rights of parents to protect their children against education programs that undermine the values taught in the home. We will crack down on deadbeat parents who avoid child support payments. Pay up, or be forced to work by the state.

—*Contract with America* (Republican National Committee, 1994, p. 79)

Merle, 14, lives north of Boston with her mother Molly, and her mother's partner, Laura. Over the years she has learned to ignore the name-calling . . . from kids who know her mother is a lesbian and assume she must be one, too (as far as she knows she isn't). And there are other painful memories. . . . One day in sixth-grade health class, the teacher asked for examples of different kinds of families. When Merle raised her hand and said "lesbian," the teacher responded: "This is such a nice town. There wouldn't be any lesbians living here." (*Newsweek,* November 4, 1996, p. 52)

By what they say and sometimes even more importantly, by the information they omit, [college textbooks on marriage and family] repeatedly suggest that marriage is more of a problem than a solution. . . . The potential costs of marriage to adults, particularly women, often receive exaggerated treatment, while the benefits of marriage, both to individuals and to society, are frequently downplayed or ignored.

—*Institute on American Values' Council on Families* (in Lewin, 1997)

Everyone pays allegiance to "family values," but there is little agreement as to what kinds of families they mean. Lesbian and gay families, single-parent families, and blended families are just three of the many contemporary family forms.

As we approach the year 2000, the family is yet again at the center of a storm of controversy. On the one hand are those who applaud the diversity of "postmodern" families as healthy, ingenious, even courageous adaptations to the economic and social/cultural uncertainties of our times (Stacey, 1996). On the other hand are those who see the "breakdown" of conventional, stable families as a serious threat to the welfare of our nation's children and even to the future of our society (Blankenhorn, 1995). Families are held responsible for all manner of social problems, from declining educational standards to violent crime. At the same time, families are being called upon to solve those problems. For example, supporters of welfare reform argued that the only way to reduce poverty in the United States was "to end welfare politics that discourage marriage and reward irresponsible behavior" (California Governor Pete Wilson, State of the State Address, January 1996). Gay and lesbian parents, who have children from previous heterosexual partnerships or who start new families by adopting or through artificial insemination or surrogate mothers, are cautiously coming out of the closet. Leaders as far apart as Pat Robertson, founder of the Christian Coalition, and Louis Farrakhan, head of the Nation of Islam (or Black Muslims), call on their male followers to take back their rights and responsibilities as "head of their households." Feminists suggest that with men becoming part-time, sometimes absentee fathers, "The Family of Man"—a phrase that once stood for all humankind—is becoming "The Family of Woman." Politicians of every stripe proclaim their allegiance to "family values." But

for some this phrase means communities and kin playing an active role in bringing up related (and unrelated) children, as in Hillary Rodham Clinton's book, It Takes a Village (1996); for others it connotes rejection of recent advances in racial and ethnic, women's, and gay rights. Even college textbooks are drawn into the fray. No one disputes that American families are struggling or that they are changing; but there is little consensus over whether this is good, bad, or neutral—simply "the way we really are" (Coontz, 1997).

Concern about the family dates back at least as far as the Greek philosopher Plato, who thought the family was too weak to be entrusted with the socialization of children. Bright young people, Plato argued, should be made wards of the state and trained and educated in schools. In the early 1800s, Auguste Comte, one of the founders of sociology, worried that the social disorganization created by the French Revolution would break the patriarchal backbone of the family, undermining commitment to lifelong monogamy. In twentieth-century America, the argument has shifted from whether traditional three-generation households were enriching or stifling, to whether the independent nuclear family promoted togetherness or neurosis, and, most recently, to whether the family as a social institution is coming apart at the seams.

The intensity of the debate over the family illustrates how social institutions shape our values; affect and are affected by other major institutions (politics, economics, education, and religion); and influence the most ordinary and intimate details of our lives.

Key Questions

1. *How do families vary across cultures?*
2. *How have American families changed?*
3. *How do contemporary Americans choose a partner, decide to get married, and balance work and family?*
4. *How do sociologists explain family violence?*
5. *What are the causes and consequences of today's high divorce rate?*
6. *What will the family look like in the future?*

[Section 1 begins.]

Cross-Cultural Similarities and Differences

The *family* is a social group, and social institution, with an identifiable structure based on positions (breadwinners, child rearer, decision maker, nurturer) and interaction among people who occupy those positions. Typically, the family carries out specialized functions (such as child rearing), involves both biological and social kinship, and shares a residence (Gelles, 1995, p. 10). The family, as a social institution, is universal; every known society has families. But what form the family takes and what functions it performs vary widely over time and among societies.

In traditional Navajo society, for example, a wife and husband never live under the same roof. Rather, she lives with her mother, sisters, and their children; he lives in a communal men's house. Their "conjugal relations" are limited to discreet visits. The Maasai of east Africa consider it normal and proper for a man to ask permission to sleep with a good friend's wife. For either the husband or his wife to refuse "sexual hospitality" is considered rude. There are even societies where parents do not have final authority over their children. In Samoa, children are considered members of an extended family and wander from one relative's house to another, deciding for themselves where to live. In the United States and other western societies, we expect individuals to choose their own marriage partners and to marry for love. In India, China, and other societies, marriages are arranged by the bride's and groom's parents on the basis of what

they consider best for their respective lineages. In many ways, the marriage of Britain's Prince Charles and the late Diana Spencer was arranged.

Family Structure

To most Americans, the word "marriage" is synonymous with **monogamy**—marriage involving only one woman and one man. Although we recognize that such unions may not last, we assume that monogamy is the ideal in most societies and cultures. Not so. According to the *World Ethnographic Survey* (Murdock, 1957)—a survey of all societies known to social scientists through history, exploration, and anthropology—monogamy is the preferred form of marriage in only 25 percent of societies.

In 75 percent, the *preferred* arrangement is **polygamy**—marriage involving more than one wife or husband at the same time. Most often this takes the form of **polygyny**, marriage of one man to two or more women. Polygyny was practiced in ancient China, hardly a small, primitive society. It is part of Judeo-Christian cultural history: the ancient Hebrews (including Kings David and Solomon) were polygynists. Up until 1890, so were the Mormons of Utah. Islam, the second-largest religion in the world today, allows a man four wives (providing he treats each wife equally). Only four known societies have practiced **polyandry**—marriage of one woman to two or more men.

Group marriage—marriage of two or more men to two or more women at the same time—is the rarest family type. Indeed, there has been some debate about whether this arrangement exists at all (Linton, 1936). Group marriage is most likely in a society where polyandry is the cultural ideal, but if the first wife proves infertile, a second wife joins the marriage to provide children.

Most of the men in the societies that permit polygyny do not actually practice it, for the simple reason that there aren't enough women to go around. Even if there were an excess of women, most men could not afford the cost of marrying and maintaining several wives. In practice, polygyny is a privilege that accompanies wealth, power, status, and, in most societies, old age. As a result, monogamy is the most commonly *practiced* form of marriage in the world.

Ironically, it may be more common for a person to have more than one spouse in the United States and other "monogamous" societies than in societies that permit polygamy. The only difference—and one we consider crucial—is that a person must divorce (or outlive) one spouse before acquiring another. More than half of first marriages in America end in divorce today (Bumpass, Sweet, and Martin, 1990). Most divorced people remarry, however, and even when second marriages end in divorce, most of these people try a third time. Thus, some Americans practice *serial monogamy:* one exclusive, legally sanctioned, but relatively short-lived marriage after another (M. Mead, 1970).

Family Functions

Family functions, like family structures, vary widely. In most traditional, preindustrial societies, the family performs four central functions (Murdock, 1949). The first is the *regulation of sexual activity.* No society leaves people free to engage in sexual behavior whenever they want, with whomever they want. Some societies place a strict ban on sexual intimacy before marriage; others require that a woman demonstrate that she is fertile by becoming pregnant before she marries. All societies place a taboo on incest, though which family members are included in this taboo varies.

The second function of the family (which follows from the first) is *reproduction.* The family perpetuates itself by having children to carry on their lineage, replace members of society who have died or emigrated, and thus keep society "alive" from generation to generation.

The third function is the *socialization of children.* It is not enough simply to produce children; they must be given physical care and trained for adult roles. The family bears primary responsibility for teaching children the language, values, norms, beliefs, technology, and skills of their culture.

The fourth function of the family is *economic maintenance.* The family bears primary responsibility for providing food, shelter, protection, health care, and other necessities for its members, including those who are too young, too old, or otherwise unable to provide for themselves.

In modern, industrial societies, some of these traditional functions have either changed or been taken over in part by other institutions. For example, with effective birth control and safe, legal abortions, the regulation of sexual activity became less urgent. During the so-called sexual revolution of the 1960s and early 1970s, "sex lost not only its biological connection to reproduction but also its normative connection to marriage" (Skolnick, 1991, p. 89). It became an accepted—and even expected—part of dating and premarital relationships. But although most Americans consider sex before marriage permissible, the great majority disapprove of sex outside marriage (extramarital sex) (Smith, 1996).

The family's role in socialization has changed significantly. In traditional societies, family members teach young people all they need to know for a life that will resemble their parents' lives. The emphasis is on well-defined traditional social roles and skills. Education is continuous and largely informal, woven into the fabric of everyday life. In modern societies like our own, a child's future occupation is unpredictable. Furthermore, technical skills and even knowledge quickly become obsolete. Schools (including colleges and universities) have taken over responsibility for preparing young people for occupational roles. Day care centers now expose children to "professional socialization" at a younger age than ever before (see Chapter 4). The mass media also have a powerful impact on young people. Much of the debate over "family values" concerns whether the schools and the media have usurped the family's authority over children. For example, should the family or the school be responsible for sex education? Should the family, the media, or the government be responsible for deciding what kinds of shows young people watch on television? what information they have access to on the Internet?

Government also has taken over some of the family's former economic functions—for example, the care and financial support of the elderly through Medicare and Social Security. When one of their members is injured or sick, families turn to the medical establishment (physicians, hospitals, insurance companies, and most recently health maintenance organizations, or HMOs).

The overall trend is for functions that were previously matters of personal care within the family to be taken over by (1) professional experts, (2) large-scale markets, and/or (3) bureaucratic formal organizations.

In traditional societies, such as the Uygur of western China, families teach children all they need to know. In modern societies, schools and day care centers have taken over much of the educational function.

While many of the family's functions have diminished, one that has become increasingly important is emotional gratification. Although schools teach children skills, the family still provides "nurturant socialization" or emotional support and caring. Children are not the only ones to receive emotional gratification from the family. For most of us, the family is the group we count on to satisfy emotional needs on a continuing basis. In one poll, three out of four participants defined the family as "a group of people who love and care for one another" (*Newsweek*, 1990, in Stacey, 1996). We expect—or feel we have a right to expect—to find understanding, companionship, and affection at home. In the words of poet Robert Frost,

> Home is the place where, when you have to go there,
> They have to take you in.

The more depersonalized our work and school lives become, the more we come to depend on the family. The modern family is an "intimate environment" (Skolnick, 1996), distinguished from other social groups by the erotic attachment between husband and wife and the affectionate attachment of parents and children. Ideally, the family is a safe, secure, nurturant "haven in a heartless world"—the world of capitalism, careers, and competition (Lasch, 1977).

[Section 1 ends.]

[Section 2 begins.]

The American Family in Historical Perspective

When considering other social institutions—education, politics, the economy—we often equate change with progress. We look for new and better ways of teaching science, delivering health care, or boosting the economy. Change in the family, however, is more often viewed as a sign of decay and decline. Rather than look forward, we look back to the "good old days," when families were stable, self-sufficient, and caring—or so we like to imagine. But our image of the past is based more on fiction than on fact (Coontz, 1992, 1997). Moreover, cultural notions of the ideal family change. In the 1950s and 1960s, Americans saw the extended family as ideal; today the emphasis is on the nuclear family.

The Extended Family

In the 1950s and early 1960s, when those couples who could afford to were flocking to the suburbs and single-family homes, many Americans mourned the death of the big, multigenerational families of the past, where grandparents were the heads of the household, everyone worked together, and children grew up respecting their elders. This is

Studying Section 1

Activities for Section 1

Before starting Section 1, notice that the title page of the chapter lists all the main heads and subheads within the chapter. The title page shows that the family is examined in six different ways, starting with "Cross-Cultural Similarities and Differences" and ending with "The Future of the Family."

The notes below begin with the first heading. Next there is a main idea presented under that heading, as well as an example of that idea. Complete the notes, which are on the first three pages of the text (page 155 to the bottom of page 157). You will have to add a series of definitions, three examples, and four items in enumeration.

(Chapter 11: The Family)
Cross-Cultural Similarities and Differences

What form the family takes and the functions it performs vary widely over time and among societies.

Ex.— One tribe in East Africa considers it normal for a man to ask permission to sleep with a good friend's wife. (Other examples are possible.)

Family Structure:

1. Monogamy— marriage involving only one woman and one man

2. Polygamy— marriage involving more than one wife or husband at the same time

Polygamy is the preferred arrangement in 75 percent of human societies! Kinds of polygamy:

a. Polygyny— marriage of one man to two or more women

Ex.— up to 1890, the Mormons of Utah

b. Polyandry— marriage of one woman to two or more men

Polyandry has been found to be the norm in only four societies.

c. Group marriage— marriage of two or more men to two or more women at the same time—rarest family type

3. Serial monogamy— *one exclusive, legally sanctioned, but relatively short-lived marriage after another*

Family Functions in Traditional, Preindustrial Societies:

1. *Regulation of sexual activity*

2. *Reproduction*

3. *Socialization of children*

4. *Providing for the physical needs of both young and old members*

Changes in Traditional Family Functions in Modern, Industrial Societies:

1. *Birth control and abortion now make regulation of sexual activity less urgent.*

2. *Sex before marriage now considered permissible by most Americans.*

3. *Schools and day care centers now provide socialization and preparation for occupations: mass media also a factor.*

4. *Government and medical establishment have taken over some of the former economic functions of family, such as care for sick and elderly.*

A function that has become important in modern society— *emotional gratification*

Comments on Section 1:

- The idea that "[w]hat form the family takes and the functions it performs vary widely over time and among societies" is included in these notes because it is central to the section and is immediately followed by three examples. In your notes, all you generally need to include is one example for a particular idea or concept.

- As a general rule, take notes on a chapter by first writing down a given main heading or subheading. Then write down whatever seem to be the most important ideas under that heading. This is an extremely important guideline to keep in mind when taking notes on a chapter. *In a nutshell, write down headings, definitions, examples, enumerations, and what seem to be other important ideas.*

- Complete the following: Almost all the notes above consist of headings, definitions, _____examples_____, and enumerations. This kind of note-taking is typical with introductory textbooks, where you are often learning the special vocabulary of a subject.

- Add details that seem noteworthy. The above notes include the surprising detail that polygamy is the preferred arrangement in _____75%_____ of human societies. Such a startling and significant detail is almost a sure bet to be included in a multiple-choice exam.

- When taking notes, don't use any more symbols than you need to. When you do use symbols, make sure they really mean something. In the notes above, the symbols "1," "2," and "3" show the three kinds of family structure. The "a," "b," and "c" show that polygyny, polyandry, and group marriages are the three kinds of polygamy. Also, the symbols "1," "2," "3," and "4" make clear the four functions of the family. *Many students overuse and misuse note-taking symbols. Keep your notes simple!*

what sociologists call an *extended family:* members of three or more generations, related by blood or marriage, who live together or in close proximity.

There were always plenty of children down on Grandpa's farm and plenty of adults to look after them. No one was lonely or idle. The family produced and preserved its own food, repaired its own equipment, educated its young in vocational skills (namely, being a farmer or a farmer's wife), settled its own disputes, and cared for its own sick, disturbed, and elderly members. Births out of wedlock and divorce were unheard of. Family pride rested on self-sufficiency. The head of the household was stern but fair, and everyone in the family knew his or her place. Furthermore, the extended family was part of a close-knit community in which doors were left unlocked, neighbors came and went, and everyone minded everyone else's business. Life may sometimes have been hard, but it was secure.

The problem with this image of the extended family is that it seldom existed. As William Goode wrote, this was the "classical family of Western nostalgia" (1963, p. 6). Multigenerational families have never been the norm in the United States; at most they accounted for 20 percent of households (Coontz, 1992). A century ago most people lived in one-room cottages, not in big houses. Few farms were large or diversified enough to be self-sufficient. In order to scrape by, families depended on child labor. Many children did not have shoes, and most did not attend school regularly—if at all.

Death was a constant presence in the extended families of old (Skolnick, 1991; Whitehead, 1993). Women frequently died during childbirth; perhaps half of all children died before reaching adulthood; and few of the survivors lived beyond age 50. Because of early death, only one-third of marriages lasted more than ten years, and a quarter of the children born in 1900 lost at least one parent before reaching age 15. Some children lived with a widowed parent and other relatives; others were sent to orphanages or foster homes.

Family Networks

Ironically, the generations that mourned the death of the large, multigenerational family in the 1950s and 1960s may have had longer and closer relationships with their extended families than did Americans at the turn of the century. In a classic study of middle-class urban families in the 1950s, Marvin Sussman (1959) found that over 90 percent received some kind of aid from extended-family members. Direct financial aid (say, the down payment for a house), indirect financial aid (a gift of a major appliance or a savings account for grandchildren), help during illness, and baby-sitting were all cited. In most cases aid flowed from parents to children, but adult children also helped their parents and one another. It did not seem to matter how far apart members of the family lived; they came to one another's aid when the need arose.

Family ties remain strong. Indeed, the special relationship between grandparents and grandchildren, which leaps a generation, may be growing stronger (Cherlin and Furstenberg, 1986). More people live long enough to become grandparents (and even great-grandparents) today than in the past. Moreover, many of today's grandparents have more time and money to devote to their grandchildren, and advances in transportation and communication make it easier for them to keep in touch, even though they probably do not live together.

The result is the *modified extended family:* a network of relatives who live in separate residences, often miles apart, but maintain ties (Litwak, 1960). These interlocking families often provide significant aid to one another. But their feeling of being connected does not depend on living near one another, working together, or falling under the authority of a strong parent, as in classical extended families. Participation in the modified extended family is voluntary, not obligatory; some individuals do "drop out." Kinship has become more like friendship (Skolnick, 1996).

The Nuclear Family

Today when people talk of the golden age of families, they usually are referring to the 1950s, known affectionately as the "Ozzie and Harriet" decade. The ideal family type in this era was the *nuclear family,* consisting of a husband, his wife, and their dependent children living in a home of their own. In the ideal nuclear family, the husband/father was the sole breadwinner (an element of the "good-provider" role; see Chapter 10). Each morning he went off to work for a corporation or branch of government (not, as in generations past, for a family-owned enterprise). Although still the head of his household, he worked for somebody else. The wife/mother was a full-time homemaker. Although she had a variety of labor-saving devices (the more the better), it was assumed that she delighted in baking brownies and sewing Halloween costumes for the children herself.

"A new standard of family security and stability was established in postwar America," writes Barbara Whitehead of the Institute for American Values (1993, p. 50). At first glance, the statistics support this view (Coontz, 1992). In the 1950s rates of divorce and out-of-wedlock births were half what they are today; the family was seen as the core social institution, the heart and soul of society; nine out of ten Americans told pollsters that getting married and raising a family were the most important goals in life; many couples married in their late teens or early twenties; and the average couple had at least two and sometimes three, four, or more children. The "only child" was an object of pity and concern. During this era, America often was described as a "child-centered" society.

In discussions of family values, we tend to use the nuclear family of the 1950s as the baseline, and find contemporary families wanting. But the Ozzie

The cast of Leave It to Beaver, *which, like other TV series of the time, reflected the ideal type of American nuclear family in the 1950s: breadwinner husband and father, full-time homemaker wife and mother, and two or three children.*

and Harriet standard is misleading, for a number of reasons. The 1950s was a unique period in American family history. The early marriages and large families of the postwar period were exceptions to a trend of later marriage and smaller-size families that had begun at the turn of the century. For more than fifty years, the ages at which women married and bore their first child had been increasing, the gender gap in education narrowing, and the divorce rate rising. In the 1950s—and only the 1950s—these trends reversed. Far from exemplifying traditional family values, the nuclear family of the 1950s was a break with a long-term pattern of social change. Moreover, our image of the families of this period is based more on media portrayals than on real life (see *Sociology and the Media:* Prime-Time Families).

The 1950s also was a decade of unparalleled prosperity for Americans. Never before had so many people had money to spare after meeting basic needs. By 1960, 62 percent of American families owned their homes, 75 percent had a car in the garage, and 87 percent had purchased a television set (Coontz, 1992). Middle- and working-class wives could be full-time homemakers because their husbands earned enough to support the family in comfort.

Not all families participated in the postwar economic boom, however. In the mid-1950s, 25 percent of the population—40 to 50 million people—lived in poverty. Two out of three Americans age 65 or older subsisted on incomes of less than $1,000 a year. But poverty was "socially invisible": most people did not know, or want to know, about the poor (Harrington, 1963). African Americans were systematically excluded from the American family dream through legally sanctioned segregation and socially accepted terrorism in the south as well as discrimination and harassment in the north. During this "golden age of the family," 50 percent of two-parent black families lived in poverty, and 40 percent of mothers in these families with small children worked outside their homes (Coontz, 1992).

A distant dream for some women, the full-time homemaker role was a nightmare for others. The ideal nuclear family depended on the wife's subordinating her needs and aspirations to those of her husband and children. "Rosie the Riveter" was forced out of the challenging, relatively high-paying job she had filled during World War II and either sent home or, if she had to work, demoted to a lower-paid, less interesting "female job." Even

SOCIOLOGY & THE MEDIA

Prime-Time Families

The changing image of the family on television provides insights into changing attitudes toward the family in society. This is not to say that portrayals of the family on TV sit-coms mirror reality; they do not. But television speaks to our collective desires, our shared worries and concerns, our wish to improve or repair our own lives (E. Taylor, 1989)—and to our stereotypes (Butsch, 1992).

The 1950s and 1960s were the decades of the happy TV family. The family that viewers saw on prime-time television, for the most part, was an intact, white, comfortable (though not conspicuously wealthy), middle-class, suburban, nuclear family—as presented on *Father Knows Best, Ozzie and Harriet,* and *Leave It to Beaver.* Parents on these shows had an endless supply of time, energy, and wisdom, which they devoted to guiding their children toward adult lives that presumably would resemble their own. Blessed with all the modern conveniences, these families also were firmly grounded in traditional values. The outside world of public issues rarely, if ever, intruded on this contented domestic circle.

Other prime-time shows from this period appealed to the dream of professional success, a beautifully decorated suburban home, and an affluent middle-to upper-middle-class lifestyle, often with servants (Butsch, 1992). Writers, with no other apparent source of income, appeared well-off (*The Dick Van Dyke Show, My World and Welcome to It,* and *The Debbie Reynolds Show,* featuring Ms. Reynolds as a magazine reporter); the father in *Life with Father* was not just a banker but a Wall Street banker; on an architect's income, *The Brady Bunch* had a housekeeper. On these shows, Mom and Dad were intelligent, mature, successful "superparents." On the rare sit-coms featuring working-

> . . . the way we never were.

class characters, family life was chaotic and gender roles were reversed, with the husband playing a lovable but incompetent buffoon whose wife always knows best. Thus on *The Honeymooners* (still popular in reruns), bus driver Ralph Cramden engages in endless, hair-brained get-rich-quick schemes, while his wife Alice waits to tell him, once again, "I told you so."

Many family sit-coms of the 1970s focused on change. One of the most popular shows of this decade was *All in the Family,* the story of a white, middle-aged, working-class couple, living in a soon-to-be-integrated neighborhood in Queens, New York. The show was a battle of the generations, which pitted unrepentant bigot Archie Bunker, with his constant stream of racial and ethnic slurs, against his muddleheaded but kindly wife Edith, his feminist daughter Gloria, and her Polish American husband Michael, who was studying to become a sociologist. Social problems that had been taboo for the situation comedies of the 1960s were "lined up like ducks in a shooting range and argued back and forth in a contest between tradition and modernity," between the political conservatism of the 1950s and the liberalism of the post-Vietnam years (E. Taylor, 1989, p. 69). The gender-role reversal of *The Honeymooners* was replaced by a generation-role reversal, in which "children know best." The husband's moral authority was also questioned on *The Bob Newhart Show,* which featured an indecisive, self-doubting psychologist; *The Jeffersons,* in which George provides a middle-class standard of living but fails miserably to acquire middle-class man-

continued

ners; and *Maude,* where an outspoken feminist (and one of the first "older" women to star in prime time) exasperates her husband, their daughter, and their friends.

Prime-time soap operas in which superrich families were divided against themselves (*Dallas* and *Dynasty*) made their first appearance in the 1970s. Two of the only popular shows with happy, "intact" families—*The Waltons* and *Little House on the Prairie*—were set in the past.

The 1980s was a decade of reorganization for TV families. Alternative family forms—single parents, all-female and all-male households, mixed-race families—were treated as (almost) normal. But by far the most popular program about families was *The Cosby Show.* In many ways the Huxtables resembled the happy prime-time families of the 1950s and 1960s. Despite high-powered careers (Claire was a lawyer and Cliff, a physician), the Huxtables always had plenty of "quality time" to devote to their children. "There is no dissent, no real difference of opinion or belief, only vaguely malicious banter that quickly dissolves into sweet agreement— all part of the busy daily manufacture of consensus" (E. Taylor,

1989, p. 161). Almost all the action took place within the Huxtables' elegant brownstone; the outside world did not intrude on this charmed family circle.

Why was *The Cosby Show* so popular? With his impish grin and affluent lifestyle, Bill Cosby implicitly reassured the audience that the American system is fair to everyone, black or white. "Look!" he seemed to be saying, "even I can have it all!" (M. C. Miller, 1988, p. 71). The difficulty of combining two careers and family life, as well as the ongoing racial tensions in our society, were swept aside. *The Cosby Show* appealed to our nostalgia for "the way we never were" (Coontz, 1992).

In the early 1990s, the portrayal of a variety of family types continued, but with a new touch of cynicism. All but one of the lead characters on *Murphy Brown* were single: the news team functioned as a substitute family, and Murphy Brown, a famous, affluent single parent, struggled to disavow maternal feelings. *Cybil,* a mother of almost-adult children and a would-be actress who can't quite get her career together, was Murphy Brown's mirror image.

Roseanne was the story of an intact working-class family, in

which the heavy-set, brash, tough-talking wife leads a one-woman crusade against middle-class hypocrisy. Dan, her husband, is loving, sensible, and respected by his children. The fact that they were working-class helped make the idea that they were not superparents with all the answers, but a couple whose life did not revolve around their children, more acceptable. At the same time, however, *The Simpsons* brought back the incompetent working-class father in cartoon form. Homer, who can't even afford a TV, demonstrates fatherly love by waving to his son and thereby causing an accident at a nuclear power plant. Though his wife, Marge, is somewhat more level-headed, son Bart and even baby Lisa are clearly smarter. *Married with Children*—featuring a domineering, do-nothing wife, a blustery, incompetent husband, a stereotypical "blonde bimbo" daughter, and a nerdy son—was designed to insult everyone. The overall message seemed to be that conventional families don't work very well but neither do the alternatives.

continued

Prime-Time Families *(concluded)*

As the 1990s draw to a close, families—even dysfunctional families—are disappearing from prime-time television. *Roseanne* and her blue-collar family live on only in reruns; the last episode of *Married with Children* ran in 1997. To be sure, families appear here and there: On *Mad about You,* Jamie and Paul have a new baby; Raymond Romano copes with his wife, daughter, and twin sons, as well as his parents and divorced brother, who live across the street, in *Everybody Loves Raymond.* But, for the most part, prime-time television focuses on relationships, as in *Seinfeld* (now discontinued) and *Friends.* If TV sit-coms reflect our dreams and fears, the family is something we want to tune out when we tune in.

The cast of Everybody Loves Raymond.

(perhaps especially) women college graduates were expected to seek fulfillment in the family and to base their identity on it. For many wives, the suburban nuclear family spelled isolation and boredom. By the end of the decade, the women's magazines that once glorified the happy housewife were printing stories about runaway wives. Physicians were among the first to notice the mounting discontent among middle-class housewives. Their solution? Tranquilizers (Coontz, 1992).

Finally, the happy, smiling Ozzie and Harriet families on television concealed a host of problems, from alcoholism and mental illness to wife battering and sexual abuse of children. In the 1950s, such problems were largely unrecognized, unreported, and untreated. The family of the fifties kept up appearances at all costs. Problems were swept under the rug. Only in the plays of Tennessee Williams, Eugene O'Neill, Arthur Miller, and Edward Albee did we glimpse loveless marriages and families torn by drug addiction, madness, incest, and unrealistic expectations.

The 1950s were not all bad, of course; many people cherish happy family memories from this time. But in some ways the nuclear family contained the seeds of its own destruction (Coontz, 1992). Women who "played dumb" to catch a husband ended up resenting him for not living up to the fantasy of male superiority. Early marriage and family planning left women with time on their hands after their children left home. And the ethic of family closeness fostered a search for authenticity and a sensitivity to hypocrisy that fueled the student ("hippie") rebellion of the 1960s and 1970s— a rebellion that turned family values inside out. Most student rebels had grown up in Ozzie and Harriet families.

Contemporary Families

Americans continue to see family ties as their main source of happiness and meaning in life (Skolnick, 1996). But social and economic conditions have

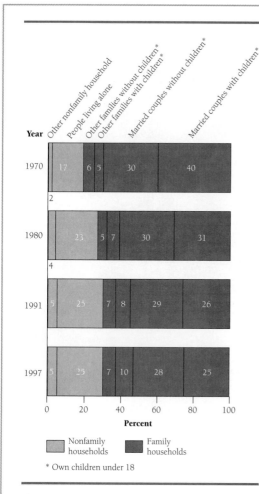

Year — Other nonfamily household — People living alone — Other families without children* — Other families with children* — Married couples without children* — Married couples with children*

1970 | 17 | 6 | 5 | 30 | 40
2
1980 | 23 | 5 | 7 | 30 | 31
4
1991 | 5 | 25 | 7 | 8 | 29 | 26
1997 | 5 | 25 | 7 | 10 | 28 | 25

0   20   40   60   80   100
Percent

Nonfamily households | Family households

* Own children under 18

Figure II-I   *Today's Changing Family*

There is no one, typical family type in the United States today. Furthermore, most people will live within several different types of family over the course of their lifetimes.

Sources: Current Population Reports, series P-20, no. 468, December 1992, p. 3, fig. 1; U.S. Census Bureau, *Current Population Survey,* March 1997.

changed dramatically since the 1950s. So have families.

Today's families are characterized not by one dominant family type but, rather, by variation (see Figure 11-1). Less than one in four households in the United States today consists of a husband, a wife, and their children at home. The numbers of single people living alone, single parents, married

couples with no children (or no children living at home), and unmarried couples living together have grown steadily. Furthermore, nuclear families have changed. Most two-parent families today have two or fewer children; very likely, the mother is employed outside the home; and the odds are about 50/50 that the parents will divorce before the children grow up (Ahlburg and De Vita, 1992). Single-mother families outnumber families with a married, stay-at-home mom by more than two to one (Stacey, 1996).

Singlehood

One reason for the changing composition of American households is that more people remain single for longer periods of time. In 1960, only 28 percent of American women age 20 to 24 had not yet married; today more than 66 percent of women in this age group are single (*Statistical Abstract,* 1996). The main reason for this increase is that more young adults are postponing marriage, not that a significant number are deciding never to marry. A larger proportion are going to college and to graduate or professional school, which tends to delay marriage. Marriage is no longer a prerequisite for a satisfying sex life, for women or men; nor is marriage a prerequisite for parenthood.

The category "single" is a diverse group, however. Some single people are students or young adults who have not yet found "Mr. or Ms. Right." Others are cohabiting couples, individuals "between marriages," people who have chosen not to marry, or elderly widows or widowers. Some live alone, some with roommates, and others with their parents, grown children, or other family members. The rising cost of housing, slow wage growth, and the increased cost of higher education (and repayment of student loans) have made it increasingly difficult for young people to establish an independent household. More than half (53 percent) of 18- to 24-year-olds still live at home with their parents (up from 47 percent in 1970). So do 12 percent of 25- to 34-year-olds (up from just 8 percent in 1970) (*Statistical Abstract,* 1996).

Singlehood changes over the life cycle. Often young adults in their twenties try out different lifestyles and make provisional choices but delay full commitments. They can have a good deal of company in this stage. The early thirties tend to be a period of reevaluation, when individuals weigh the possibilities of changing careers and/or living arrangements. People who are married may consider the alternatives; those who are single may feel increased internal and external pressure to marry. The number of single people declines in this stage. Among persons 30 to 34 years old, 28 percent of men and 19 percent of women have never married (*Statistical Abstract,* 1996). But the never-married single people are joined by those who are newly divorced. The middle years reveal a different pattern. Only 8 percent of men and 6 percent of women age 45 to 54 have never married. The ratio of unmarried men to unmarried women also changes over the life cycle. In their twenties and thirties, more men than women are single; from age 40 on, more women than men are likely to be divorced or widowed.

Given current patterns of marriage, divorce, and widowhood, the United States' single population seems likely to continue growing in the future.

Families without Children

Thirty-five percent of today's families consist of married couples without children at home (*Statistical Abstract,* 1996). This category, too, includes several distinct groups. Some of these couples are "preparents": they plan to have children, but not in the immediate future. Others are "empty-nesters," couples whose children have grown up and moved out of the family home. Still others are "nonparents," couples who either decided not to have children or were unable to have children because of infertility.

Voluntary childlessness is the exception to the rule. Although many young couples see parenthood as an option, not an obligation, most want to, and plan to, have children. A survey by the U.S. Census Bureau found that more than half of married women under age 35 still plan to have a child someday (O'Connell, 1991). Among married women in their twenties, the proportion rises to 80 percent.

Most studies of childless couples suggest that few decide never to have children before they get married or in the early years of their marriage (L. S. Gilbert, 1988; Houseknecht, 1987; Neal, Groat, and Wicks, 1989; Jacobson and Heaton, 1991). Rather, they decide to postpone parenthood until one or both complete school, until they are established in their careers and can afford to buy a home, or until they feel financially secure. This decision may escalate into a series of "temporary" postponements. In a small percentage of marriages, the couple make a conscious decision never to have children. The main reasons such couples give are freedom from responsibility, greater opportunity for self-fulfillment and career development, and a happier marital relationship. More often, couples drift into childlessness. Adoption and new technologies to combat infertility make it possible for older women (40 and over) to have children. But postponers may decide that they are too old to keep up with a small child and to support him or her into adulthood, when they themselves would be entering or past retirement age.

Single-Parent Families

In the last two decades, the number of single-parent families nearly doubled, reaching 15 million in 1995 (*Statistical Abstract,* 1996). This figure represents only the number of *current* single-parent families; the number of people who at some time will live in this type of family is much larger. At present, about 27 percent of children live in one-parent families (*Statistical Abstract,* 1996). But estimates are that 50 percent of all American children (and 80 percent of African American children) will spend time in a single-parent family before reaching age 18 (Bumpass, 1990).

The great majority of single parents (about 88 percent) are mothers. Single mothers usually have lower incomes than single fathers, mainly because men earn more than women (Cherlin, 1996). Whether unmarried, separated, or divorced, single mothers bear most of the cost of raising their children alone. More than half of single mothers (56 percent) are awarded child-support, but only 37 percent receive full or partial payment (an average of slightly more than $3,000 a year) (U.S. Department of Health and Human Services, 1997). A majority of single mothers (51 percent) do not receive any help from the father, either because they do not seek child support, the noncustodial father is unable to pay, or he simply does not pay.

Since 1960, births to unmarried mothers have climbed steadily. Almost one-third of all births in the United States today are to single women (*Statistical Abstract,* 1996) Unwed mothers have come to symbolize the supposed decline in family values in America today. People who supported the federal welfare reform legislation of 1996, which allows states to deny aid to children born to unmarried teenagers and to unmarried women already receiving aid for other "illegitimate" children, viewed aid to single mothers as a cause, not a consequence, of out-of-wedlock births, poverty, and

The great majority of single parents are mothers, and single mothers usually have lower incomes than single fathers.

related social problems. The popular stereotype of unwed mothers is a poor, minority, teenage high school dropout.

A profile of actual unwed mothers suggests the reality is more complex (Figure 11-2). The majority of never-married women who bear children outside marriage are poor or working class: 60 percent had annual family incomes of less than $25,000, of whom 43 percent lived on less than $10,000 a year. Many are poorly educated: 47 percent are high school dropouts; 30 percent are high school graduates; only 6 percent are college graduates. Although the number of out-of-wedlock births is higher for white mothers, the rates are higher for minorities. More than two out of three African American babies were born to unmarried mothers in 1992, compared with slightly more than one in five (23 percent) of white babies. Finally, teenagers account for less than one-third of all births outside marriage, and black teenagers for less than 12 percent. The rate of out-of-wedlock births has been growing fastest among women in their twenties (the age that our culture considers appropriate for women to become mothers), who now account for seven out of ten such births.

There is little evidence that increasing numbers of women *want* to become single parents or that more men want to become absentee fathers (Usdansky, 1996). Almost nine in ten unwed mothers report that their pregnancies were accidental (either unwanted or mistimed). Moreover, unwed motherhood is often a temporary state. One-quarter of single women who give birth have been married in the

past, but were divorced, separated, or widowed when they conceived. Four out of ten women whose first birth occurs outside wedlock marry within five years. One in four is currently living with a man (often, but not always, the child's father).

Polls consistently show that the overwhelming majority (90 to 95 percent) of young adults want and expect to marry, consider a good marriage and family life quite important, and think children are better off when raised within marriage (National Opinion Research Center, in Usdansky, 1996). Why, then, are births to single mothers increasing?

Part of the reason is cultural. Much of the stigma attached to "illegitimate births" has disappeared: bearing a child out of wedlock is no longer a cause for lifelong shame. Given high divorce rates, as many as half of married mothers become single parents before their children grow up, so unmarried mothers "have company"; they are not as conspicuous or isolated as their counterparts were in the past. So-called shotgun weddings (hastily arranged after the woman becomes pregnant but before she gives birth), unwed mothers' giving babies up for adoption, and abortion have all declined (Usdansky, 1996).

Part of the reason for births outside marriage is economic. Our culture holds that a man who wants to marry should be able to support a family, but this standard is becoming more difficult to meet, especially for young men without a college degree. For non-college-educated youth, a "family wage" has become a goal that fewer and fewer expect to achieve. As sociologist Andrew Cherlin told *The New*

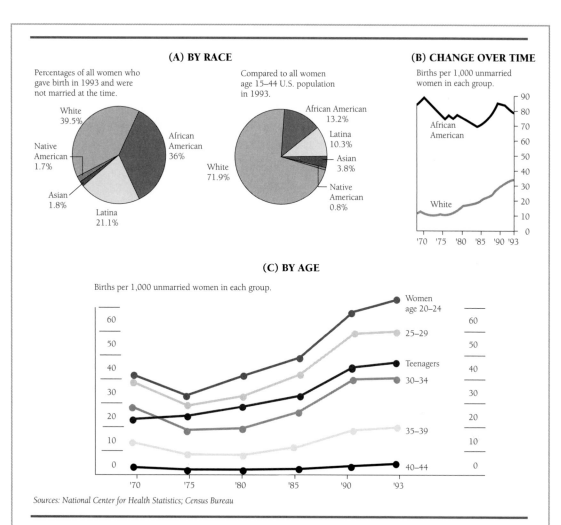

(A) BY RACE

Percentages of all women who gave birth in 1993 and were not married at the time.

White 39.5%

Native American 1.7%

Asian 1.8%

Latina 21.1%

African American 36%

Compared to all women age 15–44 U.S. population in 1993.

African American 13.2%

Latina 10.3%

Asian 3.8%

White 71.9%

Native American 0.8%

(B) CHANGE OVER TIME

Births per 1,000 unmarried women in each group.

African American

White

'70 '75 '80 '85 '90 '93

(C) BY AGE

Births per 1,000 unmarried women in each group.

Women age 20–24

25–29

Teenagers

30–34

35–39

40–44

'70   '75   '80   '85   '90   '93

Sources: National Center for Health Statistics; Census Bureau

Figure 11-2   *A Demographic Portrait of Single Mothers*

"Single mothers" is not a homogeneous category but includes women of different ages, races, and ethnic groups.

Source: M. L. Usdansky, "Single Motherhood: Stereotypes vs. Statistics," *The New York Times,* Feb. 11, 1996, p. E4.

York Times, "Marriage is still highly valued, but people don't think it's a realistic possibility" (Usdansky, 1996, p. E4). But babies "happen": the rate of unwanted or mistimed pregnancies in the United States (40 percent for married women, 88 percent for unmarried women) is much higher than in Europe.

The United States also has the highest rate of *teenage* pregnancy of any western nation, even though teenagers in Canada and Europe have as high or

higher rates of sexual activity (Pittman, 1993). Each year more than a million American teenagers become pregnant. In 1993, 501,000 teenagers gave birth. (See Figure 11-3.) The teenagers most at risk for unmarried pregnancy become sexually active at a young age, are African American or Latina, live in poor neighborhoods, attend segregated schools, and perform poorly in school (Pittman, 1993). Although the rate of pregnancy is higher for inner-city, minority teenagers, two

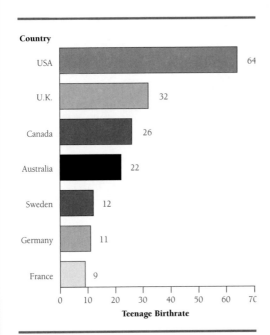

Country

Teenage Birthrate

Country	
USA	64
U.K.	32
Canada	26
Australia	22
Sweden	12
Germany	11
France	9

Figure 11-3   *Births to Teenage Mothers in International Perspective*

American teenagers are no more likely to be sexually active than are Canadian or European teenagers. Why, then, are teenage birthrates much lower in other countries? Many believe the reason is that Canadian and European nations have mandatory sex education programs and their schools provide teens with free birth control.

Source: U. Bronfenbrenner, P. McClelland, E. Wethington, P. Moen, and Stephen J. Ceci, *The State of Americas,* New York: Simon and Schuster, 1996, p. 117.

out of three teen births are to white teenagers who live in rural areas and small cities. Moreover, the birthrate for white teenagers is growing, while that for minority teenagers has leveled off. When one adjusts for income and academic skills, the difference between whites and minorities disappears. Regardless of race or ethnicity, one in five young women who come from poor families and are doing badly in school becomes an unwed mother—compared with only one in twenty young women who are better off, financially and academically (Pittman, 1993). This, in turn, suggests that teenagers who grow up surrounded by poverty and have limited opportunities, either to break out of poverty themselves or to find a husband who is a "good provider" (since most young men they know are unemployed), may feel they have little to lose by becoming teenage mothers. Indeed, they may feel they have something to gain. Realistically or unrealistically, low-income teenage girls may believe that having a baby will affirm their adult status, make the father stay in their lives, and provide love and affection.

In addition to financial problems, single mothers report less satisfaction with their lives and higher levels of stress than do single women with no children. Single mothers also report poorer relations with their children than do married mothers (McLanahan and Booth, 1989). Children in single families are worse off, on average, than children who live with both of their parents regardless of the parents' race or educational background, whether the parents were married when the child was born, and whether the parent with whom the child lives remarried (McLanahan and Sandefur, 1994). Children of single mothers are more likely to have low educational goals, to drop out of high school, to get into trouble with the law, to abuse alcohol and drugs, to marry and bear children at an early age, to get divorced, and to remain poor into adulthood.

The New Extended Family

In recent years, extended or multigeneration households are making a comeback. The high cost of housing, particularly in urban areas, combined with flat or declining wages has made it increasingly difficult for young people to establish independent households. More single adults return to their parents' households after completing school or after a divorce than in past generations. Some single parents (16.2 percent) live with their parents; some, with other relatives (U.S. Bureau of the Census, 1996). Even two-parent families are "doubling up." In the early 1990s, less than half of adults under age 35 were the head (or married to the head) of an independent family household (Ahlburg and De Vita, 1992). These households constitute the *new extended family.*

Ethnic and Racial Variations

Ethnic and racial variations add to the diversity of family life in America. A group's history, cultural ideals, and economic circumstances all affect family structure and experience.

African American Families

African American families tend to be young; they most often live in cities or in southern states; and they are more likely than other families to be headed by a woman (*Statistical Abstract,* 1996). The so-called matrifocal (mother-centered) African American family has been the subject of ongoing debate. Some observers view female-headed families as the cause of poverty and other problems African Americans endure, while others see female-headed families as a consequence of the legacy of slavery, racism, and economic inequality. This debate tends to obscure both the diversity and strengths of African American families.

African American families may be affluent professionals, working-class, or poor (Willie, 1988). Contrary to stereotypes, almost half (47 percent) of these families include two parents, and seven out of ten of the adult men work to support their households (*Statistical Abstract,* 1996). At the same time, two-thirds of African American children are born to single mothers, and four out of five will live in a female-headed household at some time in their childhood. One reason is that African Americans have a higher risk of divorce than white Americans, partly as a function of economic disadvantage. A second reason is a shortage of black men; among African Americans, because of the high rate of homicide among teenagers and premature death due to illness, women outnumber men at every age past childhood.

The outstanding feature of African American families is strong extended-family ties. They are far more likely than whites to live in three-generation or "classical" extended families (Beck and Beck, 1989). Even if they do not live together, members of extended families frequently "pool" or share economic resources and provide one another with other various kinds of assistance and support (such as child care). Strong kin and friendship networks act as a buffer against discrimination as well as economic insecurity.

Latino Families

The category "Latino" includes a range of Spanish-speaking ethnic groups (see Chapter 9), but some generalizations are possible. Latino families, like African American families, tend to be young and to experience high levels of poverty. Latino families are distinguished by their high birthrates, compared with other groups, and by their strong sense of familism. Many Latinos see *la familia* as the center of their lives; they maintain close kinship ties and live near their extended kin (Queen, Haberstein, and Quadango, 1988). The family plays a key role in assisting kin to immigrate to the United States and find employment (Wilson, 1991a). Latino familism may be part of the Latino cultural heritage or an adaptation to minority-group status and economic disadvantage, or both.

Asian American Families

Asian Americans and Pacific Islanders are an even more diverse group than Latinos in terms of place of origin, time of arrival in the United States, circumstances of their arrival, and family structure (see Chapter 9). Some migrants are single individuals, forced by war or economic hardship to leave their families behind; some are intact nuclear families; and some are incomplete extended families, composed of a couple, their children, grandparents, and other relatives (Tran, 1988).

Despite their varied origins, traditional Asian American families have some common features. They tend to be strictly patriarchal: men are the wage earners, decision makers, and disciplinarians. Even when Asian American women work, as many do, they assume near-total responsibility for housework and child rearing. Children are raised to be cooperative, obedient, and loyal and to defer to their parents' wishes (Kitano and Daniels, 1988). Marriage rates for Asian Americans are very high, and divorce rates lower than average (*Statistical Abstract,* 1996).

Minority families and new immigrants add to the variety of family experiences people encounter over the life cycle. One team of demographers has compared the American family to "a patchwork quilt—composed of many patterns yet durable and enduring even when it becomes frayed around the edges" (Ahlburg and De Vita, 1992, p. 38).

[Section 2 ends.]   *[Section 3 begins.]*

Courtship, Marriage, and Children

Despite changes in the family, the great majority of Americans get married and become parents. Women, in particular, wait somewhat longer to get

Studying Section 2

Activities for Section 2

Continue your note-taking on the sample chapter by completing the partial notes below. These notes cover the marked part of page __157__ to the marked part of page __171__.

The American Family in Historical Perspective

The Extended Family:

members of three or more generations, related by blood or marriage, who live

together or near one another

—This "good-old-days" family seldom existed in reality! About a century ago, most people lived in cottages too small for extended families and struggled on their own. Many died too young to create extended families.

The Modified Extended Family:

networks of relatives that establish separate residences but maintain ties

The Nuclear Family:

a husband, wife, and their dependent children living in a home of their own

—The image of the 1950s nuclear family is a misleading idealization for various reasons: (a) That family was an exception to family trends, not typical of it. (b) Despite unparalleled prosperity, many families lived in poverty. (c) The ideal wife was not so happy. (d) Various problems, from alcoholism to violence, were largely unrecognized and untreated.

Contemporary Families:

1. Nuclear family of husband, wife, and children—has changed greatly since the 1950s: less than one-fourth of today's households, two or fewer children, mother employed outside home, 50–50 chance of divorce.

2. Singlehood: More people remain single for longer periods of time—to go to school and because marriage is no longer needed for satisfying sex life or parenthood.

—Single people include (a) students or young adults looking for the right partner, (b) cohabiting couples, (c) people between marriages, (d) those who have chosen not to marry, and (e) elderly widows and widowers.

—Changes over life span: 20s try out, 30s reevaluate, by mid-40s to mid-50s most have married; before 50, more men are single than women, and after 40, more women are divorced or widowed.

3. Families without children at home: 35 percent of families.

—Couples without children may be (a) preparents, who have postponed childbearing; (b) empty-nesters, whose children have grown up and moved out; and (c) nonparents, who have decided not to have children or are unable to have them.

4. Single-parent families: Have nearly doubled in the last ____20____ years.

—Most single parents (88 percent) are women.

    —Financial problems

    —Less satisfaction with their lives and more stress

    —More problems with children

—Almost one-third of births in the United States are to single women. Factors contributing to high rate of births to unmarried women: (1) cultural—less stigma attached to out-of-wedlock births; (2) economic—non-college-educated men are less likely to be able to support family.

5. The new extended family: Multigeneration households are making a comeback.

—Reasons: (a) high cost of housing, (b) flat or declining wages.

Ethnic and Racial Variations:

1. African American families: tend to be young, urban or southern, and headed by women (though almost half are two-parent families), and to maintain strong extended family ties.

2. Latino families (a range of Spanish-speaking ethnic groups): tend to be young, to experience high levels of poverty and high birthrates, and to put strong emphasis on family.

3. Asian American families: _patriarchal; men earn money, make decisions, discipline children; women do housework, raise children; children taught to be cooperative and obedient; high rate of marriage; low rate of divorce_

Comments on Section 2:

- The notes above, which cover almost __12__ pages, are based on definitions, enumerations, and key details. The terms being defined are obvious because the authors set off the terms in (*fill in the missing word*) ___boldface___ type in the text.

- The key to major enumerations is subheadings provided by the author. One example is the series of subheadings that appear under "Comtemporary Families." These subheadings—"Singlehood" on page __166__; "Families without Children," on page __167__; "Single-Parent Families," on page __167__; and "The New Extended Family" on page __170__ —represent alternative forms to the changed nuclear family mentioned in the first paragraph about new families. It would have helped if the authors had used the heading "Contemporary Families: Many Forms."

The next main heading, "Ethnic and Racial Variations," is followed by three sub-headings, "African American Families," "Latino Families," and "Asian American Families." The point to remember here is that when a heading is fol-lowed by subheadings, *it is beneficial to figure out the relationship between the heading and the subheadings!* Doing so is probably going to help you under-stand and take notes on the material.

- Note that under each form of the family, you can add details that seem impor-tant. There's no need to number each detail: instead, just set it off with a dash, as shown in the notes above. Minor enumerations can be included here, such as the one under the second point of the above notes that provides a list (*a–e*) of types of (*fill in the missing word*): ___single___ people.

Table 11-1   *Median Age of First Marriage, 1900–1994*

Year	Men	Women
1900	25.9	21.9
1910	25.1	21.6
1920	24.6	21.2
1930	24.3	21.3
1940	24.3	21.5
1950	22.8	20.3
1960	22.8	20.3
1970	23.2	20.8
1980	24.7	22.0
1990	26.1	23.9
1995	26.9	24.5

Source: Adapted from U.S. Bureau of the Census, "Marital Status and Living Arrangements: March 1994," *Current Population Reports,* series P-20, no. 484, Washington , DC: GPO, 1994, p. vii, table B; Statistical Abstract, 1996, Table 149, p. 105.

In some developing countries, such as India, marriages are arranged when the bride and groom are still children. The two families participate in the wedding ceremony, but the husband and wife do not live together until they are older.

married than they did in the past (Table 11-1). But every year millions get married (2.3 million marriages in 1994). Over 95 percent marry at least once in their lives. Indeed, the United States has one of the highest marriage rates in the world (Ahlburg and De Vita, 1992). Why do people get married? Who marries whom? How do contemporary couples combine work and family?

Choosing a Mate

Why do people get married? Most Americans think the overarching reason is—or should be—"for love." This is not a universal view. Nearly all societies recognize that, on occasion, a man and a woman may develop a "violent emotional attachment" to each other—what we call love (Linton, 1936). But few societies consider this attachment desirable, much less a basis for marriage. In most societies marriages are arranged by older relatives, with an eye to expanding their network of kin. The most important criteria in mate selection are economic security and family background, not mutual attraction.

The notion of arranged marriages strikes most westerners as barbaric. Yet research suggests that in arranged marriages, the couples' romantic attachment to one another grows over the years, whereas couples who married for love report that their attraction to one another dropped precipitously after the first two to five years of marriage (Gupta and Singh, 1982). (See Figure 11-4.)

Analysis of marriage patterns shows that even in our own society, Cupid's dart is highly selective. In principle, we are free to marry anyone we like. In practice, however, our choices are limited by social forces—the same social forces that influence the neighborhood in which we live, the school we attend, and the people we meet. In sociological terms, we practice **homogamy**: the tendency to marry someone who is like ourselves in the social attributes our society considers important. Thus most Americans (95 percent) marry someone of the same race, social class, age, and educational level. Each of these criteria reduces an individual's "pool of eligibles" (see Figure 11-5).

In the past, religion played a major role in defining a person's pool of eligibles: most Americans did not marry outside their religion (whether Protestant, Catholic, or Jewish). However, to some degree educational criteria are beginning to replace religion

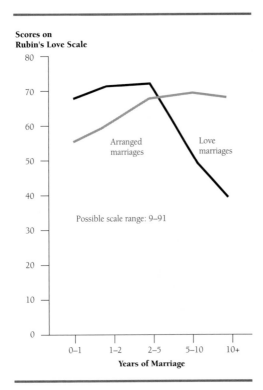

**Scores on
Rubin's Love Scale**

Arranged
marriages

Love
marriages

Possible scale range: 9–91

Years of Marriage

Figure 11-4   *Love and Marriage*

A study of romantic and arranged marriages in India found that love and marriage do go together but not necessarily in that order. Couples who marry for love may become disillusioned when the romance fades.

Source: V. Gupta and P. Singh, 1982, in D. G. Meyers, *Social Psychology,* 4th ed., New York: McGraw-Hill, 1993, p. 495, fig. 13-7.

tance on obedience in child rearing. They are likely to hold similar moral and political views and to enjoy similar leisure-time pursuits. Finally, young people spend more time in school today than in the past, and so they have more opportunities to meet and date other students. College graduates often meet their future spouses in school (Mare, 1991). As more and more people postpone marriage, however, new ways of meeting potential mates are emerging, including newspaper personal columns, singles clubs and outings (often designed around special interests), and even e-mail computer networks (Hanson, 1993, personal communication).

By one means or another, a person may meet dozens of people who fit his or her basic criteria for a future mate; how does the person choose among them? Exchange theory is a middle-range theory that holds that mate selection is the result of a series of conscious or unconscious calculations (Murstein, 1986). Each of us has an image of our value on the dating market, based on cultural standards and previous experience. In deciding whether to approach a member of the opposite sex, we compare the other person's assets to our own. If the other person has a much higher value, the potential risk of being rejected outweighs the possibility that he or she may be interested. We do not ask for a date. (To simplify, a man who considers himself successful but not good-looking might approach a woman who is good-looking but not high on the career ladder or a woman who is successful but not strikingly attractive. He would be less likely to approach someone who is both beautiful and successful.) Thus self-esteem plays as important a role in courtship as does physical attraction.

After the initial attraction and beginning of the relationship, couples spend much of their time comparing values. He asks what she thought of the party where they met; she asks what he usually does on weekends; the conversation may turn to elections, sports, religion, or food. The couple are most likely to develop a strong liking for one another if their values are similar. Values are the goals people hold in life; roles can be seen as the means to those goals.

Progress beyond attraction and liking depends on role fit. If both like to play a nurturant role (the one to whom others turn for comfort), they are less likely to get together than if one sees himself or herself as supportive and the other sees himself or her-

in the choice of mates (Kalmijn, 1991). Intermarriage between people of different religions has increased, while intermarriage between people with different levels of education has decreased. Why? First, education plays a major role in determining people's future earning potential and hence their social class and lifestyle. Second, level of education has a strong impact on the values people hold with regard to marriage and family. Whatever their class background, Americans with college educations tend to be more liberal in their attitudes toward sex roles, to have more permissive attitudes toward sex, to want fewer children, and to place less impor-

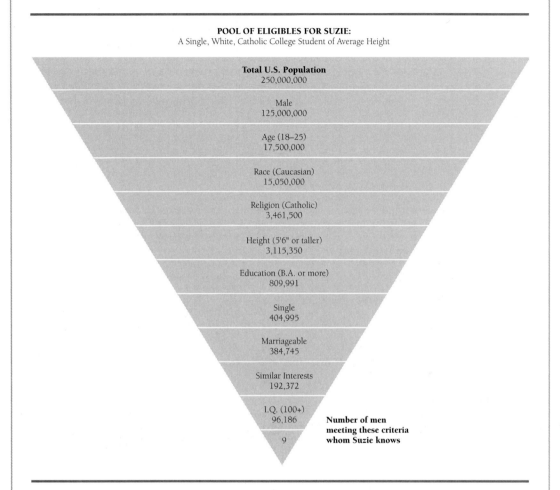

POOL OF ELIGIBLES FOR SUZIE:
A Single, White, Catholic College Student of Average Height

Total U.S. Population
250,000,000

Male
125,000,000

Age (18–25)
17,500,000

Race (Caucasian)
15,050,000

Religion (Catholic)
3,461,500

Height (5'6" or taller)
3,115,350

Education (B.A. or more)
809,991

Single
404,995

Marriageable
384,745

Similar Interests
192,372

I.Q. (100+)
96,186

Number of men meeting these criteria whom Suzie knows

9

Figure 11-5   *The Dating Game*
Who marries whom?

self as needy and dependent. Thus similarity may "heat up" a relationship in the dating stage but "cool it down" in the decision stage. Moreover, each measures the other against the image of an ideal mate. If the fit is close enough, they may become engaged or—almost as likely—try living together.

Living Together

The number of unmarried couples who live together has increased sixfold since 1970, reaching 3.6 million in 1995 (*Statistical Abstract,* 1996). (Note that this figure represents opposite-sex couples only, or, to use the Census Bureau's term, "POSSLQ's": "persons of the opposite sex sharing living quarters"). Most cohabitors (60 percent) are under age 35; a majority (58 percent) have never been married; one-third are divorced; 4 percent are widowed; and the remainder are married but living with someone other than their spouses. About one-third have children under age 15 living in their households.

Only a small percentage of couples see cohabitation as a substitute for, or alternative to, marriage. For most it has become a stage en route to marriage, somewhat like engagement, a time that allows a couple to find out whether they are compatible before getting married. At least one partner expects to get married in 90 percent of cohabitations (Bumpass, 1990). Within a year and a half of moving in together, most couples either get married (about 60 percent) or break up (about 40 percent) (Bumpass, Sweet, and Cherlin, 1991).

One might expect that couples who "look before they leap" are more likely to stay together after marriage. In fact, a national survey of married people found the reverse (Booth and Johnson, 1988). Those who had lived with their spouses before they were married reported that they argued more and spent less time together than did couples who married before living together. They also were more likely to separate or divorce. Does this mean that cohabitation has a negative effect on marriage? Not necessarily. Cohabitors may be "poor marriage risks" before they marry, either because one or both had personal problems (such as unemployment or drug use) or because they had different ideas about marriage (such as how much time and energy to invest in their careers or whether and when to have children).

Work and Families

One of the major issues confronting married couples in the 1990s is how to combine work and family life. A majority (61 percent) of married women are employed today, including 63 percent of mothers with children under age 6 and 76 percent of mothers with children age 6 to 17 (*Statistical Abstract*, 1996). Women's earnings play an important role in family income. In 1993, the median income of married-couple families in which the wife worked was $50,798 compared with $28,799 when the wife did not work and $16,000 for female-headed households (*Statistical Abstract,* 1996). Even though women still earn less than men, on average, the wife's income can lift a family out of poverty or enable a family to remain in the middle class. In polls, most women say they work to support themselves or their family (Yorburg, 1993). But 85 percent say they would continue working even if they did not need the money because they enjoy the

sense of accomplishment and the social contacts (Eggebeen and Hawkins, 1990).

Working women are not a modern phenomenon. On the contrary, in most societies and times women have played a critical role in providing for their families. American families of the 1950s and 1960s, in which most husbands were the sole providers and most wives were full-time homemakers and mothers, were not a "natural" arrangement but an unusual one (Skolnick, 1996). Nevertheless, there are two distinctive features about women's reentry into the labor market in recent times. The first is that work nearly always requires that a woman be away from her home and children; the second is that the sharp distinction between men's and women's jobs found in most earlier societies has faded.

When asked to name the major problems in a two-job marriage, men chose "time for each other" first, followed by child care and housework; women chose housework first, followed by time for each other and child care (Vannoy-Hiller and Philliber, 1989).

Housework

Regardless of whether they have a full-time job or not and no matter how much they earn, wives devote significantly more time to housework than husbands do (Ferree, 1991). Almost 80 percent of all household chores are performed by women (Berardo, Shehan, and Leslie, 1987).

Not only do women do more work around the house but they do different work (Blair and Lichter, 1991) (Figure 11-6). Women are more likely to perform the dull, routine tasks that lock them into rigid daily schedules, such as vacuuming, bed making, diapering babies, and cooking and cleaning up after meals. Women also do more of the undesirable jobs (scrubbing the bathroom or ironing). Men typically take responsibility for such nonroutine tasks as household repairs, auto maintenance, lawn mowing, snow shoveling, and disciplining children. These jobs do not require tight daily schedules; moreover, for some men, home and auto repair may be enjoyable hobbies, and yardwork allows a husband to be out of doors.

Child Care

In 1995, 21 million American children under age 6 had mothers who were employed outside their homes. Who is minding the kids? About 40 per-

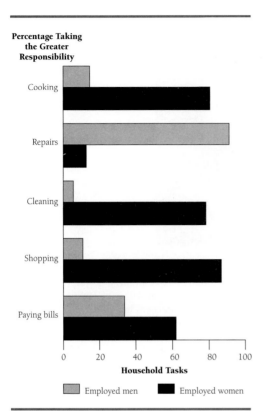

Percentage Taking the Greater Responsibility

Cooking

Repairs

Cleaning

Shopping

Paying bills

0   20   40   60   80   100

Household Tasks

☐ Employed men   ■ Employed women

Figure II-6   *A Woman's Work*

A comparison of women and men in dual-earner families shows that, except for repairs, women assume far more responsibility for household tasks.

Source: Families and Work Institute, *The New York Times*, Sept. 19, 1993, p. F21.

cent of preschoolers are cared for in their homes by a parent (often with the mother and father alternating "shifts"); 31 percent go to day care centers; 18 percent are in family day care (a nonrelative who may care for several children in her own home); 21 percent are cared for by a relative in the relative's or the child's home (*Statistical Abstract,* 1996). Employed mothers are increasingly choosing day care centers for their youngest preschool child (31 percent in 1995, compared with only 6 percent in 1960). Of children age 6 to 13 whose mothers are employed, about 18 percent go to a family or day care center after school, about 10 percent take lessons, roughly 5 percent go home to a parent, and most of the others go to a relative's or neighbor's home. Only about 2 percent are "latchkey" children, who are at home alone after school (Hoffreth et al., 1991).

More than nine out of ten parents in this survey said they were either "satisfied" or "very satisfied" with their child care arrangements. But one-quarter said they would prefer another arrangement or a combination of settings. At the same time, many found their arrangements less than totally reliable. Overall, employed mothers miss about one and a half days of work each month because of breakdowns in their child care arrangements. Low-income mothers are particularly hard hit because their child care arrangements tend to be less reliable; thus they miss more time at work, and may not be paid for time off.

In terms of sharing, today's fathers get better reports for child care than for housework. A national survey found that fathers and mothers generally agree that they share child care equally (Chapman, 1987). Fathers also share some of the worry and guilt about leaving their children in someone else's care.

How much time fathers devote to child care depends on several factors. One is the wife's schedule: the more hours the mother works, the more the father pitches in. Another factor is the *mother's* gender-role attitudes: if the mother believes the husband is competent at child care, the father is likely to be more involved (though which is cause and which is effect is difficult to say). The father's relationship with his own father is also a factor: fathers who were dissatisfied with their own fathers are likely to devote more time to their children than are fathers with happier memories. Finally, fathers are more likely to take part in child care if the child is a boy.

The Impact of Work on Families

In the not-too-distant past, the impact on the family of women working was almost universally viewed as negative. But attitudes have changed. What does research show?

Do young children suffer when their mothers work? Most contemporary researchers agree that the real issue is not so much who cares for a child but whether the child gets *good-quality care* (APA

How much time fathers spend caring for their children depends on the mother's work schedule, the mother's gender-role attitudes, the father's relationship with his own father, and the sex of the child.

Task Force, 1993). The most appropriate care for infants and toddlers is either a single caregiver or a small group (no more than four children per caregiver), where the small child can receive individual attention. In general, when the mother works, parents prefer care by a relative, especially the father or grandmother, for children up to age 3. Older preschoolers, age 3 to 5, can benefit from group care, especially if the caregivers are trained in early childhood education and if they interact verbally with each child, provide a safe environment but are not overly restrictive or punitive, and offer both continuity and new experiences. Parents often choose day care centers or nursery schools for their 4- to 5-year-olds. In addition to the caretakers' training and experience, parents also consider convenience and reliability, the attractions of the physical environment, agreement on cultural and religious values, discipline, and cost.

Care by others does not mean that children forgo maternal love and attention. Working women (especially college graduates) spend almost as much time in direct interaction with children (talking, reading stories, baking cookies) as do full-time homemakers. These career women sacrifice sleep and leisure time rather than time with their children (Hoffman, 1987).

In general, studies of school-age children show that maternal employment, by itself, has little effect (Hoffman, 1989). Children whose mothers work do as well in school as children whose mothers stay at home, and perhaps slightly better (Moore and Sawhill, 1984). In particular, daughters of working mothers tend to develop more flexible sex-role attitudes and to have higher career aspirations than do other girls (Hoffman, 1984; Lamb, 1984; Moore and Sawhill, 1984). Some studies also find that children of employed mothers are somewhat more responsible and independent than children with mothers at home (Hoffman, 1984; Moore and Sawhill, 1984). Maternal employment is most likely to have positive effects if the father is involved in family tasks (housework and child care) and the husband and wife agree about the wife's work (Lerner, 1993).

Does working improve or undermine a couple's relationship? The answer depends on a number of factors. One is the nature of the wife's job. Long hours, frequent travel, or a demanding boss can spill over into family stress (Spitze, 1988). A second factor is attitudes toward gender roles, whether traditional, egalitarian, or transitional (Hochschild, 1989). Employed wives tend to be happier and healthier than full-time homemakers, particularly when they and their husbands approve of women working; married women are most likely to be depressed when they are at home full-time but would like to be working (Ulrich, 1988). Not surprisingly, marital satisfaction tends to be highest among working wives with high levels of education who work out of choice, enjoy their jobs, and receive help from their husbands; marital satisfaction tends to be lower among women who have low incomes from undesirable jobs (Voydanoff, 1989). Time together is a problem for most working couples (Kingston and Nock, 1987). The less time they spend together, the less likely they are to be satisfied with their marriage.

The risk of divorce is higher when the wife works, particularly if she works in an unconventional (traditionally male) occupation, such as medicine, law, architecture, or engineering (Bumpass, Martin, and Sweet, 1991). This does not mean that female employment, by itself, causes divorce. Rather, women who work have greater opportunity and choice in both marriage and divorce (Spitze, 1988). Women in high-paying occupations, in particular, do not have to consider potential earning power when choosing a spouse; nor do they have to choose between an unhappy marriage and downward mobility or poverty.

[Section 3 ends.]   *[Section 4 begins.]*

Behind Closed Doors: Violence in the Family

"And they lived happily ever after." Hundreds of stories about marriages and families end with this line. Loved ones are reunited, obstacles to marriage overcome, problems with children resolved. Indeed, the very idea of living happily ever after is linked, in our minds, with the special warmth of the family. Yet if we look behind the closed doors of many American households, we discover that all is not peace and harmony.

Myths and Realities

With the exception of the police and the military, the family is the most violent social group in American society (and most other contemporary societies). The home is a more dangerous place than a dark alley. A person is more likely to be assaulted or murdered in his or her home, by a member of the family, than by anyone else, anywhere else, in society.

Thirty years ago, few Americans would have believed these statements. But things have changed. The sad case of Lisa Steinberg, a young girl killed in New York City in 1987, galvanized public attention around the issue of child abuse and neglect. Hedda

Nussbaum, who acted as Lisa's "mother,"[1] clearly was a battered wife and evoked mixed reactions: yes, she was a victim, but even so, why didn't she protect the child under her care? At that time, violence against women had not captured the interest of the public or policy makers.

The brutal murders of Nicole Brown Simpson and her friend Ron Goldman in June 1994 broke the wall of selective inattention to battered wives. Nicole Brown's ex-husband, former football star O. J. Simpson, was accused of the crime. His arrest and criminal trial galvanized public attention for nearly three years; five years later this case is still the focus of numerous books, talk shows, and articles. O. J. Simpson was an authentic American hero: a child of the ghetto who became a multimillionaire on the strength of his athletic talents; an African American, best known to the public through his ads for Hertz Rent-a-Car, who has seemingly escaped racial classifications. His marriage to Nicole Brown, a glamorous blonde, their luxurious home in Brentwood, an elite neighborhood in Los Angeles, and two beautiful children added to their allure. They were a couple who "had it all." Yet even before the trials began, the media released tapes of Brown's frantic calls to 911, suggesting a pattern of spousal threats and abuse. O. J. Simpson was found "not guilty" of the murders, in part because his defense team revealed a pattern of racism among the police who investigated the crime. But the image of the dark underside of a "perfect marriage" lingers.

Two months after the murders, Congress passed the Violence Against Women Act as part of the crime bill. The act defined "violence inspired by gender" as a violation of civil rights, created an office for domestic violence within the U.S. Justice Department, and provided funds for a national hotline and for innovative state programs to reduce domestic violence and protect victims (Gelles, 1997). Up for reauthorization in 1998, there is little doubt that it will be renewed. Innumerable state laws were enacted. If domestic violence suffered from selective inattention in the 1980s, the reverse is true at the end of the 1990s. Yet myths about family violence abound.[2]

---

[1] Lisa Steinberg had not been legally adopted: Hedda Nussbaum was neither her biological nor adoptive mother.
[2] Unless otherwise noted, the data and conclusions in this section are from Gelles and Straus, 1988, and Straus and Gelles, 1990.

Studying Section 3

Activities for Section 3

Continue your note-taking on the sample chapter by completing the partial notes below. These notes cover the marked part of page ___171___ to the marked part of page ___181___.

Courtship, Marriage, and Children

Choosing a Mate:

In most societies, marriages are ___arranged___.

Why do we marry? Because of the principle of homogamy—_the tendency to_ _marry someone who is like ourselves in the social attributes our society_ _considers important._

—Factors involved include race, social class, age, educational level, self-esteem, values, and role fit.

Living Together—A new stage in courtship:

—The number of unmarried opposite-sex couples who live together has increased sixfold since 1970; about a third live with children under 15.

—Cohabitors feel living together is a step toward marriage—either they get married or they break up within a year and a half of moving in together.

Work and Families: Major issues for couples who work

1. Housework: Women do 80 percent and are more likely to do the dull routine jobs.
2. Child Care: (*add important point here*) _In 1995, 21 million American children_ _under age 6 had mothers who worked outside the home. Result: more_ _children cared for by relatives or day care._

    —Parents tend to share child care equally, but the father is influenced by several factors: his wife's schedule, the mother's gender role attitudes, his relationships with his own father, the gender of the child.
3. The impact of work on families:
    —Impact on children:
        —The most appropriate caregiver for infants and toddlers is either _a single caregiver or a small group_

—Working women spend almost as much time in direct interaction with children as full-time homemakers.

—Impact on couple's relationship:

—Depends on various factors: nature of wife's job, attitudes toward gender roles, level of wife's education.

Comments on Section 3:

- Enumerations and important details are the keys to important ideas in this stretch of the text.

- Being aware that paragraphs may center on a main idea (often stated in the first or second sentence) can help you read and understand material. It's to be hoped that the authors of your textbooks, like the authors of this chapter, will write clearly organized paragraphs that center on main ideas.

   It is not realistic to expect, though, that every paragraph will include a clearly stated main idea. For example, a paragraph might contain an idea that is implied rather than directly stated, might have more than one idea, might be simply a short transitional paragraph, or might just be poorly written—or there may be some other reason why a main idea is missing.

- It can be helpful to indent points in your notes. Notice that some of the information in the notes about the impact of work on families is indented. At a glance you can see that the first indented information is about the "impact on children" and the second indented material is about the "impact on couple's relationship."

Myth 1: Family violence is rare or epidemic. Public attention to family violence has led some people to believe we are in the midst of an epidemic. Others have concluded that all this attention is "hype." Both are wrong. Family violence is not a modern phenomenon; it has existed in virtually all societies and times. Experts may disagree about whether family violence is increasing or decreasing, but all agree that it is a serious problem that will not go away by itself.

Myth 2: Abusers are mentally ill. When we read a description of family violence, we would like to believe that only someone who is "sick" could beat up a pregnant woman or torture a child. Health workers often find that abusers are disturbed. But whether they committed a violent act because they were disturbed or whether they became disturbed after the act is impossible to say. Only about 10 per-

cent of abusers are clinically diagnosed as mentally ill.

Myth 3: Abuse occurs only in poor, minority families. Rates of abuse are higher in poor and minority households, but violence occurs in families at all socioeconomic levels. One reason that the poor and nonwhites are greatly overrepresented in official statistics is that they are more likely to be labeled as "abusers" or "victims." Sociologists Patrick Turbett and Richard O'Toole (1980) gave groups of physicians and nurses a file describing an injured child and the child's parents. These professionals were more likely to conclude the child was a victim of abuse when they were told the father was a janitor than when they were told he was a teacher and when they were told the child was black as opposed to white. Except for these social markers, which were varied at random, the files were identical.

Myth 4: The real causes of family violence are alcohol and drugs. A news report might highlight the fact that a man who murdered his family was a "crack addict." Victims of family violence often say, "He only did it when he was drunk." Does this mean drugs cause abuse? No. Cross-cultural studies show that the effects of alcohol vary from society to society. In some, people become quiet and withdrawn when they drink; in others, they become loud and aggressive. Our society is one of the latter. We define being drunk as a "time-out" from normal rules of behavior, when a person can claim "I didn't know what I was doing." As a result, both abusers and victims often cite alcohol as the excuse for violence. In one study half the men arrested for beating their wives claimed that they had been drunk, but only 20 percent had enough alcohol in their blood to be considered legally intoxicated (Bard and Zacker, 1974). Frequent drunks (and nondrinkers) are less likely than occasional drinkers to become violent. Much less is known about the effects of illegal drugs on behavior. The only drug that has been conclusively linked with increased aggression (in studies with monkeys) is amphetamine.

Myth 5: Children who are abused grow up to be abusers. Children who are victims of family violence are more likely to be abusive as adults than are children who did not experience family violence. But this does not mean that all abused children become abusive parents. Studies of the intergenerational transmission of family violence are difficult to eval-

Public-service announcements like this one have helped to redefine family violence as a social problem, not a private matter. Until recently, few people considered verbal abuse a form of violence—one that could be as harmful as physical abuse.

uate because they usually rely on self-reports of events that occurred years earlier. The best estimate is that about 30 percent of adults who were abused as children treat their own children the same way (Gelles and Conte, 1990). A follow-up study of children who were abused or neglected twenty years ago found that they did have higher rates of juvenile delinquency, adult criminality, and violence than a matched group of controls (Widom, 1989). But this does not mean that all violent adults were abused as children, or that all abused children grow up to be violent. Abuse makes children more vulnerable to a host of social and emotional problems, but it does not determine how they will behave as adults.

Myth 6: Battered women provoke their offenders, and/or the solution is for them to leave their partners. Most people are angered and saddened by reports of battered children but puzzled by reports of battered wives. After all, the woman is an adult; if her husband beats her, why doesn't she leave him? Abused wives are often assumed to be masochists or, worse, to have provoked their husbands to violence ("She asked for it!"). Anyone who has been through a divorce knows that there is more to ending a marriage than simply walking out the door. In most cases, violence is not an everyday event. It may be easier to talk oneself into believing it will not happen again than to face the world on one's own, with little money, credit, or experience—and perhaps with children to care for as well. Where can the battered wife go? Because our society has mixed feelings about battered wives, we have been slow to build shelters.

If you reread this list of myths, you will see a common theme: Only people *other than* us assault their loved ones. Assigning family abusers to deviant categories (mentally disturbed, poor, drunk) allows us to avoid thinking that it could happen to us. These myths also blind us to the structural characteristics of the family that promote or at least allow violence.

Sociological Explanations

The potential for violence is built into the family. Many of the characteristics we cherish most about families also make us most vulnerable within the family. One is *intimacy*. Family members are intensely involved with one another. They know the private details of one another's lives and what makes the others feel proud or ashamed. When quarrels break out or problems arise, the stakes are higher than in other social groups. For example, a man who is amused by the behavior of a female colleague who is drunk may become enraged if his wife were to have a little too much to drink. A politician who has been an active supporter of gay rights, at some risk to her career, may be appalled to discover that her own child is homosexual. Why? Because we perceive the behavior of a member of our family as a direct reflection on ourselves. The intensity of family relationships tends to magnify the most trivial things, such as a burned dinner or a whining child. When did you last hear of someone beating up the cook in a restaurant for preparing an unacceptable meal? But minor offenses and small oversights often spark violent family fights.

A second factor contributing to violence in the home is *privacy*. Because family affairs are regarded as private, there are few outside restraints on violence. When a family quarrel threatens to become a fight, there are no bystanders to break it up, as there might be on the street or in some other public place. The shift from extended to nuclear families, the move to detached single-family houses in the suburbs, and the trend toward having fewer children have all increased the potential for family violence, simply because there are fewer people around to observe (and try to stop) abuse. Children in isolated single-parent families are at high risk (Gelles, 1989).

A third factor is *inequality*. Few social groups routinely include members of both sexes and different ages. In school, for example, we are segregated by age; at work we are often segregated by sex—for example, men doing heavy labor, women doing clerical work. Because men are usually bigger and stronger than women, and women bigger and stronger than children, they can get away with violent behavior that would provoke retaliation from someone their own size and strength. Moreover, the costs of leaving an abusive family—of becoming a runaway child or a single mother—may seem higher to some family members than to others.

From a feminist perspective, violence toward women in the home is an extension of male dominance in society as a whole. Acts of violence are one of many ways men control their wives, including intimidation, isolation, emotional abuse, economic

1992). Early studies found that female violence toward men they love (or had loved) was almost as common as the reverse. Closer analysis found that female violence often occurs as self-defense; that women inflict less injury than men do, whether because of size and strength or of cultural constraints; and that women rarely engage in a pattern of violent abuse. Anecdotal evidence and case studies suggest that men are more likely to stalk and kill their victims (often spouses who left them); more likely to kill their wives after a long period of physical and emotional abuse; and far more likely to kill their wives and children, in acts of familicide.

Other "Loved Ones"

Family violence is not limited to spouses and lovers or to parents who abuse their children. Children also abuse their parents. Although elder abuse is difficult to measure, estimates are that 5 percent of people age 65 or older are victims of physical abuse, verbal aggression, financial exploitation, and/or neglect at the hands of their grown sons and daughters or grandchildren (Wolf, 1995). Data on parents who are victimized by children are even more elusive, in large part because parents are reluctant to seek help for fear of being blamed for the violence. Estimates suggest that between 750,000 and 1 million American parents are assaulted by their teenage children each year (Cornell and Gelles, 1982).

"Everybody knows" that brothers and sisters fight; physical fights between siblings are by far the most common form of family violence (Straus, Gelles, and Steinmetz, 1980). For the most part, parents, physicians, and social workers consider "sibling rivalry" normal. But violence between siblings often goes far beyond so-called normal violence: each year, almost 110,000 use guns or knives to "settle their differences."

In short, no one is immune to violence by the people he or she loves (or are supposed to love). As a nation, we tend to pay more attention to violence on the street and violence on TV than to what is happening in our own homes. In part because we expect so much from our family, guard our privacy (and respect other people's), view family problems as personal failures, and learn from our parents and siblings to use force to settle disputes, we take out frustrations on those to whom we are closest.

[Section 4 ends.]

Physical fights between siblings are by far the most common form of family violence. Although most experts consider sibling rivalry to be normal, it often escalates into abusive violence.

[Section 5 begins.]

Divorce

Marriages end every day, for all sorts of reasons—of which violence is one, cited in 20 to 40 percent of divorce suits. Indeed, divorce is becoming an accepted part of our way of life, or so it appears. What can sociology reveal about divorce?

Understanding Divorce Statistics

Raw data can be deceptive, as statistics on divorce make quite clear. In 1994 there were about 2.3 million marriages in America. The same year, 1.19 million marriages ended in divorce (*Statistical Abstract,* 1996). This means that half of today's marriages end in divorce—right? Not necessarily. Direct comparisons of marriage and divorce rates for a given year are based on a fallacy. The pool of men and women eligible for marriage in a year is relatively small. It consists primarily of single people about 18 to 30 years old, plus some younger and older single people, widows, and divorced people. The pool of men and women "eligible" for divorce, in contrast, includes everyone who is currently married, whether the wedding took place yesterday or fifty years ago. That is, the "divorce pool" includes most of the adult population. Thus, measuring the

Studying Section 4

Activities for Section 4

Continue taking notes. Enumerations will help you take notes and understand this stretch of the material, which covers the marked part of page 181 to the marked part of page 188.

Behind Closed Doors: Violence in the Family

Myths and Realities:

1. Myth 1—Family violence is rare or epidemic.

   Fact—A serious problem that has existed in all families at all times.

2. Myth 2—Abusers are mentally ill.

   Fact—Only about 20 percent of abusers are clinically diagnosed as mentally ill.

3. Myth 3—Abuse occurs only in poor, minority families.

   Fact—Abuse occurs in families at all socioeconomic levels.

4. Myth 4—The real causes of family violence are alcohol and drugs.

   Fact—Only one illegal drug has been linked with increased aggression: alcohol does not itself cause abuse but is often used as an excuse for violence.

   (*Note: The authors of the text lose their focus a bit here; they should more clearly make the point that alcohol is not the cause as such for much family violence.*)

5. Myth 5—Children who are abused grow up to be abusers.

   Fact—They are more likely to be abusive, but this does not mean that all violent adults were abused as children, or that all abused children grow up to be violent.

6. Myth 6—Battered women provoke their offenders, and/or the solution is for them to leave their partners.

   Fact—It is not easy for a battered wife to simply walk out the door; we've been slow to build shelters for them.

Sociological Explanations:

Five factors contribute to violence in the family:

1. Intimacy— Family members are intensely involved with one another; when quarrels break out, the stakes are higher than in other social groups.

2. Privacy—Because family affairs are regarded as private, there are few outside restraints on violence and often few people around to observe and try to stop abuse.

3. Inequality—Within a family, men are usually stronger than women and women stronger than children; they can get away with violence that persons of equal strength would resist.

4. Social and cultural support for the use of physical force in family. A marriage license in our society is a license to hit—not just children, but spouses.

5. Socialization—we learn to associate violence with the family; our first experience of force nearly always takes place at home.

Intimate Violence: The Victims

— Infants and young children _____ are at greatest risk of abuse.

—Women are more likely to be murdered by an intimate than are men.

—Other forms of "intimate violence" are aimed against elders and siblings.

Comments on Section 4:

- Notice how the headings here help you take notes. When you see a heading like "Intimate Violence: The Victims," you should change it into the question "Who are the victims of intimate violence?"
- While there were no definitions in this part of the chapter, what helped you take notes were the following: headings, questions about the headings, and enumerations.

marriage rate against the divorce rate for a given year is highly misleading. Comparing the number of divorces issued this year with the number issued five or ten years ago is also misleading, for the population is growing and changing.

The **divorce rate** is the number of divorces per 1,000 married women (or men) age 15 or older in a given year. For example, in 1960 there were 42.6 million married women in the United States; 393,000 got divorced that year. Thus the divorce rate for 1960 was 9.2 divorces per 1,000 married women. The divorce rate climbed steadily during the 1970s, reaching a peak of almost 23 divorces per 1,000 married women in 1979–1980; it then leveled off and dropped somewhat in the 1980s. The rate for 1994 was 20.5 (*Statistical Abstract, 1996*). Today—as in much of the past—the United States has the highest divorce rate in the industrial world (see Table 11-2).

Who Gets Divorced and Why

At current rates, scholars estimate that at least half of marriages formed today are likely to end in divorce (Cherlin, 1992). But all marriages do not have an equal chance of success or failure; some segments of our population are more prone to divorce than others.

The likelihood of divorce depends, first, on *age at first marriage*. Couples who get married in their teens are twice as likely to get divorced as are couples who marry in their twenties (L. K. White,

Table 11-2   *Divorce Rates for Selected Countries, 1960–1994*

Divorces per 1,000 Married Women					
Country	1960	1970	1980	1990	1994
United States	9.2	14.9	22.6	21	21
Canada	1.8	6.3	10.8	12.6	11
France	2.9	3.3	6.3	8	N/A
Germany	3.6	5.1	6.1	8	7*
Japan	3.6	3.9	4.8	5	6*
Sweden	5.0	6.8	11.4	11.4	12*
United Kingdom	2.0	4.7	12.0	13	13*

*1993 data.

Sources: *Statistical Abstract, 1991*, in Dennis A. Ahlburg and Carol J. De Vita, "New Realities of the American Family," *Population Bulletin* 46(2), 1992, p. 15, table 3; U.S. Bureau of the Census, *Statistical Abstract, 1996*, Washington, DC: GPO, p. 833, table 1329.

1990). Not only are young marrieds more emotionally immature; they are more likely to be poor, and they are more likely to have rushed into marriage because of an unhappy family life or because of a premarital pregnancy.

Socioeconomic status is also correlated with divorce. Divorce rates are highest in lower socioeconomic groups, and they decline as one moves up the socioeconomic ladder (L. K. White, 1990). Presumably this is because poor families experience more stress than do families who are better off. Also, higher-income couples have more to lose (the house, the cars, and so on). But divorce may be a cause of low income, rather than a consequence. Women with children nearly always experience a decline in standard of living after a divorce, and many slip into poverty.

Race is another factor in divorce. Most studies report that African American couples are more likely to separate or divorce than are white couples (L. K. White, 1990). The main reason is that black men and women are more likely to be young and poor when they marry. African Americans who own their own homes and have the same incomes and the same-size families as white Americans have a divorce rate 6 percent lower than whites in similar circumstances.

A fourth factor in divorce is *religion*. In general, divorce rates for Protestants are higher than those for Catholics, although separation rates are higher for Catholics. The more often a person attends religious services, the less likely he or she is to be divorced, no matter which religion. And interfaith marriages tend to be less stable than same-faith marriages—whether because such couples are more unconventional to begin with or their families oppose the marriage, or for other reasons.

A fifth factor is *children*. The birth of a first child reduces the chances of divorce to almost zero for the year following birth, but subsequent births have little effect (L. K. White, 1990). Older children may slow the pace of divorce but do not stop it altogether. At the same time, childlessness is associated both with higher rates of divorce and with speedier divorces.

Other factors that influence divorce include premarital births (which increase the chances of divorce), cohabitation (which reduces the chances that a marriage will last), the length of time the couple knew each other before marriage (two years appears to be optimal), the divorce of their own parents, and the influence of their friends and family. When a couple's "nearest and dearest" approve of the marriage and view their own marriages as stable, the new marriage has a greater chance of survival (Gelles, 1995).

Why did divorce rates rise steadily in the late 1960s and the 1970s and then stabilize at relatively high levels in the 1980s? There is no simple explanation for high divorce rates, but several contributing factors stand out (Cherlin, 1992; L. K. White, 1990). One was changes in the divorce laws: no-fault divorce made it easier and faster to end a marriage. The movement of women into the labor force was another factor—in part because jobs made women feel freer to divorce and in part because two-worker families may experience more role conflicts than breadwinner-housewife families. At the same time, men's position in the labor force was weakened: middle-class men struggled to maintain the relatively high standard of living their parents enjoyed; increasing numbers of working-class men experienced layoffs and long spells of unemployment; and poor men found it harder and harder to break into the working class.

A third factor in changes in the divorce rate is cultural: a general shift from faith in institutions to concern with individual fulfillment. One study compared interviews with men and women who divorced in the late 1940s (Goode, 1956) with similar interviews of men and women who divorced in the 1980s (Bloom, Niles, and Tatcher, 1985). In the earlier interviews, the main reasons given for divorce were failure to live up to instrumental family roles (nonsupport, lack of interest in the home, excessive drinking and gambling). In the more recent interviews, the main reasons given for divorce were related to personal fulfillment and growth (problems in communication, conflicts over values, boredom, sexual incompatibility). Thus our definitions of a successful marriage have changed from living up to social responsibilities to finding individual happiness (Price and McKenry, 1988). Many couples want both togetherness and individual freedom—a difficult balance to achieve.

In addition, formal marriage may have lost some of its cultural significance (L. K. White, 1990). The distinctions between cohabitation and marriage and between premarital and marital childbirth are becoming increasingly blurred. One seldom hears the terms "living in sin" or "illegitimate child" anymore. But changes in attitude often follow changes in behavior (rather than precede them), as people try to explain their new and unexpected life situations.

Sociologist Andrew Cherlin (1992) put recent changes in historical perspective. When you compare divorce rates in the 1960s and 1970s with rates in the 1950s, it looks as if the family is falling apart. When you look further back in history, however, a somewhat different picture emerges (see Figure 11-9). Divorce rates have been climbing more or less steadily since the late nineteenth century. The 1950s were an exception to this trend. Perhaps in reaction to the instability of the Great Depression and World War II, Americans placed an unusually high value on family life in this decade. In the 1970s the pendulum swung the other way. Comparing these two exceptional decades creates the false impression of a divorce "boom." How divorce rates might change in the future is impossible to predict. But most indicators suggest that divorce rates have peaked and may decline somewhat.

Children and Divorce

Each year about 1 million children—almost 2 percent of all children in the United States—are involved in a divorce (Ahlburg and De Vita, 1992). But this is only a fraction of the number of children who have been or will be directly affected by divorce. Estimates are that as many as two-thirds of all children, including one-third of white children and two-thirds of African American children, will see their parents divorce before they reach age 18 (Bumpass, 1990). The number of children involved in a divorce soared in the 1960s and 1970s, then dropped slightly. Even so, a child's odds of seeing his or her parents divorce are twice as high today as they were a generation ago.

In the 1950s and 1960s, parents were admonished to stay together "for the sake of the children." In the 1970s, opinion shifted and parents were told that an unhappy family was worse for children than divorce. Current research suggests that the impact of divorce on children is more complicated than either of these recommendations suggests.

Andrew Cherlin and his colleagues followed national samples of American and British children for four to five years (Cherlin et al., 1991). At the end of the study, the children were divided into two groups: those whose parents had divorced and

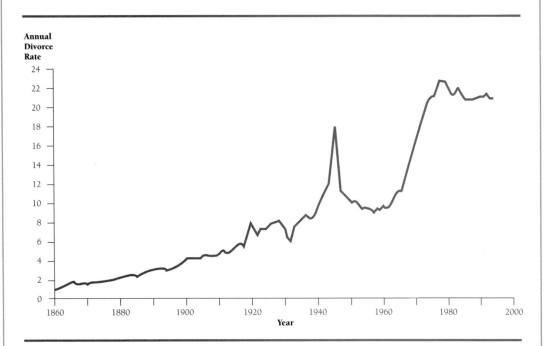

Figure II-9   *Annual Divorce Rate, United States, 1860–1994*

U.S. divorce rates have been rising more or less steadily since the mid-nineteenth century, with two exceptions: the Great Depression of the 1930s and the "family boom" of the 1950s and early 1960.

Sources: 1860–1920: Paul H. Jacobson, *American Marriage and Divorce*, New York: Rinehart, 1959, table 42; 1920–1967: U.S. National Center for Health Statistics, *100 Years of Marriage and Divorce Statistics*, series 21, no. 24, 1973, table 4; 1968–1987: U.S. National Center for Health Statistics, *Monthly Vital Statistics Report* 38(12), suppl. 2, "Advance Report of Final Divorce Statistics," 1987, table 1; 1988: ibid., (13), "Annual Summary of Births, Marriages, Divorces, and Deaths: United States, 1989," 1989; from Andrew J. Cherlin, *Marriage, Divorce, and Remarriage*, rev. ed., Cambridge, MA: Harvard University Press, 1992, p. 21, figs. 1–5.

those whose parents had stayed together. As expected, the children whose parents had divorced showed more behavior problems and scored lower on reading and mathematics tests than did the children whose parents were still married. But when the researchers looked back at records from the beginning of the study, they found that the children whose parents would later divorce *already* showed more problems. This suggests that conflict between parents and the process of divorce affects children before parents actually split up.

Psychologists Judith Wallerstein and Joan Kelly conducted an in-depth study of 131 children from 60 families in which the parents had recently divorced (J. B. Kelly and Wallerstein, 1976; J. S. Wallerstein and Kelly, 1976). All the subjects were middle-class, suburban families, and the children, by and large, were happy, healthy youngsters. Wallerstein and Kelly made this selection deliberately to eliminate the effects of poverty, urban living, and preexisting emotional disturbance on families, thus highlighting the impact of divorce.

The researchers found that divorce hit almost all children like a bolt of lightning. None of the children were prepared for divorce, no matter how much their parents had fought; many reacted to the news with stunned silence. The children's short-term reactions varied by age. The youngest children were frightened and bewildered. Some pretended that their families were not really breaking up; many worried that the parent who moved out (usually the father) would forget them. Older children

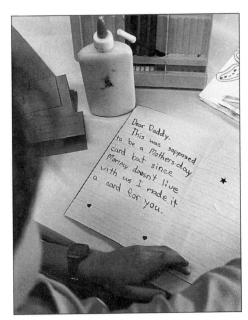

Divorce means adjustment in every area of life, for the children as well as the couple involved.

reacted with shame and anger. They took the divorce personally, as a rejection of themselves, and were embarrassed that their families were breaking up and ashamed of their parents' behavior. Adolescents were more likely than younger children to understand why their parents divorced and also more likely to worry about the impact on their own futures.

Follow-up interviews, conducted five years after the divorce, produced a mixed picture. Some of the children (29 percent) were doing reasonably well. Others (39 percent) were either moderately or severely depressed. Their most frequent complaint was loneliness. Still others (34 percent) appeared to be thriving. Surviving the divorce seemed to have strengthened them.

Interviews conducted ten years after the divorce (J. S. Wallerstein and Blakeslee, 1989) painted a more pessimistic picture. The older males (age 19 to 29 at the time of these interviews) were generally found to be lonely and unhappy; few had been able to establish lasting relationships with the opposite sex. Many of the young women who had appeared

well adjusted at the five-year mark seemed to be suffering delayed reactions to their parents' earlier divorce—in what Wallerstein and her coauthor Sandra Blakeslee called "sleeper effects." At age 19 to 23, they reported intense fear and anxiety about making an emotional commitment to a man.

Although Wallerstein's studies contain illuminating case histories, they cannot be generalized to all children of divorce. First, the sample was small and select. Second, she did not compare the subjects with a control group of children whose parents did not break up, and so it is impossible to know how common or uncommon their problems are in the population at large. Third, the subjects were referred to her clinic for short-term therapy by lawyers, clergy, and the courts. Many of the parents had suffered mental health problems in the past, including "disabling neuroses and addictions" and "chronic depression." Wallerstein did not consider how the parents' personal problems affected their children (Cherlin and Furstenburg, 1989). Given these histories, the surprise is that 60 percent of the younger children and 40 percent of the older subjects were doing so well (Cherlin, 1992).

Looking at nationally representative samples of children whose parents divorced, Andrew Cherlin (1992) concluded that most children suffer intense emotional upset at the time their parents separate, that most recover within a year or two, but that a minority suffer long-term, sometimes severe psychological problems as a result of their parents' breakup. Cherlin suggests two conditions that foster healthy recovery. First, children do better when the custodial parent (usually the mother) is able to maintain orderly household routines in the aftermath of a divorce. Second, children do better when their divorced parents are able to communicate and cooperate on child rearing and when they do not use the children as pawns or urge them to take sides. But Cherlin added, "I think it is clear that most children do not benefit from divorce" (1992, p. 88).

Remarriage and Blended Families

For most Americans, divorce and single parenthood are temporary. Divorce seems to be a rejection of a specific, unsuccessful relationship, not a rejection of the idea of marriage and family (Spanier, 1989). Put another way, people may give up on a particular marriage, but they have not given up on the institution of marriage. About two out of three divorced women and three out of four divorced men remarry, usually after cohabiting with their new partners (Cherlin, 1992). But Americans are not returning to the altar as quickly as they did in the past. In 1970 the average interval between divorce and remarriages was two and a half years; today it is three and a half to four years (B. F. Wilson and Clarke, 1992). The sharp decline in the rate of remarriage over the past two decades means that more children spend more years in single-parent homes (Bronfenbrenner et al., 1996).

The likelihood of remarriage varies among social categories. Although African Americans are more likely to separate or divorce than white Americans, the latter are more likely to remarry. Despite their tendency to say they are not interested in marriage, men are more likely to remarry than women. Social class has different effects on divorced men and women. The more education a man has and the higher his income, the more likely he is to remarry. The reverse is true for women—either because women who are better off feel less need to remarry than do women with little education and low-paying jobs or because they have more trouble finding a mate who is their educational and occupational equal.

About 24 percent of remarriages are between a divorced woman and a single man; 24 percent, between a divorced man and a single woman; and about 42 percent, between two divorced persons (B. F. Wilson and Clarke, 1992). In general, remarried couples report levels of marital satisfaction that are as high as those for couples who are in their first marriage. Yet the divorce rate for remarried couples is as high as or higher than the rate for first-time marriages (Cherlin, 1992; Furstenberg, 1990). The reason is not necessarily that certain individuals are divorce-prone but that second marriages face special problems, particularly when one or both partners have children from a previous marriage.

About eight in ten remarriages involve children. As a result, more than 7 million children live with a stepparent today. Estimates are that one-third of all children will participate in a blended family before they reach age 18. *Blended families* take different forms: a mother, her children from a previous marriage, and a stepfather; a father, his children from a previous marriage, and a stepmother; a mother, father, and children from both of their previous marriages; any of the above combinations and a new child from the current marriage. The children of previous marriages may live with the couple full-time or part-time, or one spouse's children may live with the couple and the other spouse's children may visit.

Blended families are not simply new families. They differ from other families in a number of ways. First, some members of the family have recently experienced a disruption in a close relationship (with a parent, a child, and/or a spouse), an experience that shapes their attitudes toward the new family. Second, the relationship between the parent and child predates that between the new husband and wife. The parent and child have a longer history together and may know one another better than the new spouse does. Third, the children usually belong to more than one household, for they have another parent living elsewhere. The couple may not have exclusive control over the child; comparisons between the two homes are perhaps inevitable. Fourth, there is no legal tie between the stepparent and stepchild. Neither has legal rights and responsibilities toward the other.

These special characteristics create special problems. The couple may have unrealistic expectations of righting past wrongs and solving everyone's problems with the new marriage. A spouse who has never had children may have fantasies of instant parenthood and see herself or himself as "coming to the rescue." These fantasies soon collide with unanticipated realities. The new spouse may have underestimated the amount of time and attention the parent is accustomed to giving his or her children. The couple may find that they have established very different styles of being a parent with their respective children. For small children, the new marriage may mean giving up a secret dream that their parents will get back together. For older children, the new marriage may mean giving up the position as second in command and special friend to their custodial parent. Within a year or two of the remarriage, about half of the children living in blended families are faced with a new baby. Although parents may hope that a new baby will bring the family closer together, it may have the opposite effect of making older children feel like outsiders. All blended families go through a period of adjustment. Many settle

Beyond the Nuclear Family: The Case of Sweden

In his book *Disturbing the Nest* (1988), David Popenoe warned that the family was in danger of disappearing in Europe's social democracies, especially Sweden. Marriage rates have declined more rapidly, and more dramatically, in Sweden than in any other nation. To a large degree, Sweden has moved beyond the traditional nuclear family. The only lasting family tie is between a mother and her child(ren). The family as an institution, he argued, is "losing social power and functions, losing influence over behavior and opinion, and generally becoming less important in [Swedish] life" (p. xii).

Popenoe cited three main indicators of family change in Sweden. The first is the declining marriage rate. Sweden today has the lowest marriage rate in the industrial world. Swedes also postpone marriage longer. (The mean age of first marriage for men is 30 and for women, 27.) According to one estimate, more than one-third of Swedish women born in 1955 will never have married by the time they reach age 50. Only 75 percent of Swedish men ever marry (compared with 95 percent of men in the United States). The first generation of Sweden's unmarried mothers are now becoming grandmothers.

The second measure of change is the rise in nonmarital cohabitation. Most single mothers in Sweden are living with the father, at least when the child is born; they just don't see

> The family as an institution . . . is losing influence over behavior and opinion.

the point of marrying him. Swedes view living together as a couple not just as a prelude to marriage but as an *alternative* to marriage. When asked, they tend to say marriage is "just a piece of paper." Marriage—the formal, public commitment to live together in an exclusive sexual union and to rear one's offspring together—has not disappeared in Sweden. Rather, it has

become a matter of personal choice. Half of all births in Sweden are to unmarried parents.

The third indicator is family breakup, or dissolution. Even though the marriage rate has dropped and nonmarital cohabitation has increased, the divorce rate in Sweden is as high as ever. If one assumes that as many unmarried as married couples break up, this means that a large majority of Swedes do not spend their adult lives with the same partner and that a majority of Swedish children do not live with both of their biological parents throughout their childhood.

In large part, the Swedish government had taken over the role of breadwinner and extended family. The government provides all parents and children with extensive support, including parental leave at 90 percent of salary, free day care, child support payments and housing subsidies (at a higher level for single than married parents), free medical and dental care, and free education to

down into comfortable patterns after a year or two, but a relatively high proportion fall apart.

[Section 5 ends.]   *[Section 6 begins.]*

The Future of the Family

No one disputes the fact that American families are changing. The question is what do these changes mean? Do the variety of household arrangements in the United States today mean that the family, as a social institution, is doomed? Or are these changes a sign that the family, as a social institution, is adapting and developing (and perhaps experiencing "growth pains")?

Some sociologists, such as David Popenoe (1993), are pessimistic. Popenoe makes three the university level. Materially, Swedish children undoubtedly are better off today than in the past. Parents do not have to worry about the cost of quality day care or whether they will be able to send their children to college. Never-married or divorced mothers are not plunged into poverty, and no child grows up hungry, unsupervised, or undereducated.

Nevertheless, in Popenoe's view the nonmaterial costs outweigh the benefits. Popenoe laments the decline of *familism:* "the belief in a strong sense of family identification and loyalty, mutual assistance among family members, and a concern for the perpetuation of the family unit" (1988, p. 212). In mother-only families, children have fewer (if any) sibling companions and adult role models. Even if fathers live with or maintain contact with their children, the parents and children do fewer things together as a family; they have less time to develop family-centered routines and traditions. Also, children lack the security of knowing their parents will try to stay together and provide the continuing love, understanding, guidance, and protection that every child needs. Couples may not need marriage certificates, says Popenoe, but children need parents.

In the decade since Popenoe issued his warning, the trend toward mother-only families has spread from Scandinavia to France, England, Austria, and Germany and is increasing in other countries (Bogert, 1997). (See Map 11-1.) Increasingly, marriage is viewed as unnecessary and single motherhood as normal. Almost one in three babies in France and England is born to unmarried parents, and women in the first large generation of single mothers in Scandinavia are becoming grandmothers. Even Ireland, long a bastion of Roman Catholicism, is changing. Divorce was legally recognized in 1997 (though abortion is still illegal), and the number of unmarried mothers is growing. "The feeling is, why bother to live with [men] and wash their socks?" says Noreen Byrne of Ireland's National Women's Council.

Although some European countries are facing severe cuts in government spending, reducing family subsidies is last on the list. Given years of falling birthrates (and fears that pension plans similar to Social Security in the United States—indeed, national economies—would crash for lack of young workers), European governments have actively promoted childbirth. Billboards proclaim, "Every baby is welcome in France." Motherhood (whether within marriage or not) is politically untouchable. Yet some European social scientists are beginning to worry that high rates of unemployment among single mothers promote other social problems. Whether the revolution against marriage and family will provoke a counterrevolution remains to be seen.

points. First, the American family is not simply "changing"; it is becoming weaker. Second, the disintegration of the family is behind many of our most urgent personal and social problems, including delinquency and crime, drug and alcohol abuse, suicide, depression, and long-term poverty. Third, "the heart of the problem lies in the steady breakup of the two-parent home" (1993, p. A48). The main victims of the weakening of the family, according to Popenoe, are children: "Across society, children's needs are often placed behind those of adults" (1993, p. A48). Popenoe adds that the United States is not alone (see *A Global View:* Beyond the Nuclear Family: The Case of Sweden).

Other social scientists are cautiously optimistic, including Stephanie Coontz (1997), Arlene

Beyond the Nuclear Family:
The Case of Sweden (concluded)

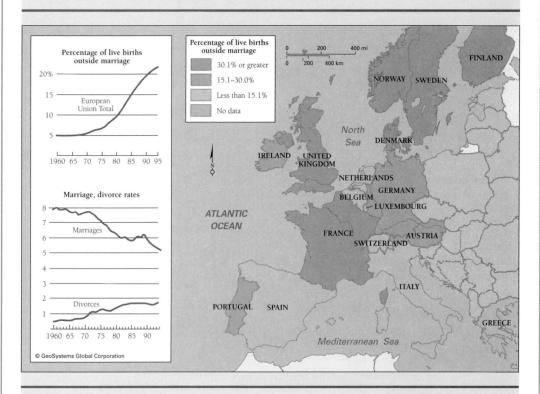

Map II-I   *Where Wedding Bells Aren't Ringing*

Source: Newsweek (International Edition), Jan. 11, 1997, p. 43.

Skolnick (1996), and Judith Stacey (1996). They maintain, first, that the idea that contemporary American families are in crisis is based on a misreading of history. In "days gone by," as many families were disrupted by death as are disrupted by divorce today, and the children often were sent to orphanages. The Ozzie and Harriet decade of two-parent families with a home of their own and a white picket fence was a unique period in American family history. Moreover, many families could not

live up to the Ozzie and Harriet ideal, and many who did found the arrangement less than ideal.

Second, to blame society's ills on families is to "blame the victim." Laments over the family divert attention from the social sources of many "private troubles" (declining wages, unequal pay for women, cutbacks in public spending for housing and social services, and so on). Many parents cannot afford a "lifestyle" choice regarding the neighborhood in which they live, the type of job at which they work, and the number of times they have to take off to attend to family matters. Cherlin (1992) recommends that instead of bemoaning the changes that have taken place in American families, we should seek to change other institutions (such as the workplace) to reduce the social, psychological, and financial costs of family change.

Third, whether one is optimistic or pessimistic depends in part on how one defines the family (Gelles, 1995). If one sees the family as "primarily a social instrument for child rearing," as Popenoe does (1988, p. viii), one is likely to be pessimistic. However, if one sees the family as primarily an institution for providing intimacy and companionship, one might be more optimistic (Skolnick, 1996). In one survey three out of four respondents defined the family as "a group of people who love and care for one another." Although a majority of those surveyed said they thought that the quality of American family life in general was declining, 71 percent said they were "at least very satisfied" with their own family lives (*Newsweek,* 1990, in Stacey, 1996, p. 9).

But even the optimists are concerned. They are concerned, first and foremost, about children. In every racial group, more children live in poverty than was true a decade ago. And these children are at significant risk for disease, violence, and other threats. The optimists are also concerned that the gains women made in the workplace in the 1970s and 1980s have produced a "backlash" (Faludi,

1991) and that the increase in the number of "good (involved) dads" has been counterbalanced by an increase in "bad dads" (who walk out on their children, emotionally and financially) (Furstenberg, 1988). They are concerned about the "stalled revolution" in the family division of labor, which allows women to pursue careers but still allows men to avoid housework (Hochschild, 1989). And they are concerned about the unknowns (Gelles, 1995).

- Will the proportion of single-parent families increase, and children continue to suffer adverse consequences?
- Will our society, the last industrial society on earth without a government-funded child care program, develop a national day care policy and program? If not, what will be the consequences for families and children? Given the work requirements of the new welfare law, who will care for children of poor mothers?
- When the time limits for welfare run out, what will happen to families and children?
- What new forms might families take, and what will this mean for adults and especially for children?

Arlene Skolnick calls the family an "embattled paradise," a seeming contradiction in terms. But this phrase captures the ambivalence most people feel toward family. "For better or worse," writes Skolnick, "family life, and an idealized image of what the family should be, remain at the source of our greatest joys, our deepest worries, and our most painful hurts" (1991, p. 220).

[Section 6 ends.]

Summary

1. **How do families vary across cultures?** Every known society has families. But the structure of the family (the number of spouses a man or woman may have and household composition) varies from culture to culture, and the functions the family performs have changed over time. In postindustrial societies, the family's main function has become providing intimacy and emotional gratification.

2. **How have American families changed?** Images of the "traditional" family tend to be based more on ideals than on realities. Today nostalgia for the *extended family* (several generations in one household) has been largely

replaced by nostalgia for the *nuclear family* of the 1950s (a husband, wife, and their children, living in a home of their own). In fact neither family type was universal, and both had weaknesses as well as strengths. The biggest change in the family has been the increase in the variety of family arrangements, including singles, single parents, and childless couples.

3. **How do contemporary Americans choose a partner, decide to get married, and balance work and family?** Most Americans say they marry for love, but sociological research shows that love is highly selective. Most people marry someone with similar social characteristics (the

Studying Sections 5 and 6

Activities for Sections 5 and 6

Continue taking notes. This stretch of material covers page 188 to page 199.

Divorce

Understanding Divorce Statistics:

Divorce rate— _Number of divorces per 1,000 married women (or men) in a_

given year.

    Ex.— _In 1994, the rate was 20.5 per 1,000 married women._

Who Gets Divorced and Why:

At least half of marriages formed today are likely to end in divorce.

Main factors affecting likelihood of divorce:

1. _Age at first marriage—couples who married in teens are much more likely to divorce than couples in their twenties._

2. _Socioeconomic groups—divorce rates are highest in the lower socioeconomic groups._

3. _Race—African-American couples (more likely to be young and poor when they marry) have higher rate than white couples._

4. _Religion—in general, the more often a person attends religious services, the less likely he or she is to divorce._

5. _Children—couples without children have the highest divorce rate._

Contributing factors in social institutions to high divorce rates include (a) no-fault divorce laws, (b) women's increased and men's decreased roles in the workforce, (c) general shift from faith in institutions to concern with individual fulfillment, and (d) the fact that formal marriage may be losing some of its cultural significance.

Children and Divorce:

Almost 2 percent of children involved in divorce every year; two-thirds of children will have divorced parents by age eighteen.

Andrew Cherlin concludes that most children recover from upset of a divorce after a year or two.

—Two conditions that can help: (a) the maintenance of orderly household routines by custodial parent and (b) cooperation and communication between divorced parents on child rearing.

Remarriage and Blended Families:

Most divorced people remarry, whites more so than African Americans, and men more so than women.

The divorce rate for second marriages is as high as, if not higher than, the rate for first marriages.

About eight in ten remarriages involve children.

Blended families involve different forms and have special characteristics that create special problems.

The Future of the Family:

The problems of the family in the modern world are directly linked to the problems of society.

The sociologist Popenoe (like others) is pessimistic about the family: Its disintegration is behind many of our social problems and will mainly hurt children.

Others are optimistic: The family is no worse off than in most previous times; family is the victim of society's ills; family is not an instrument for child rearing but an institution for intimacy and companionship.

—Issue is how "family" is defined.

—Even optimists are concerned about various risks for children, and also women's gains in workplace and at home, HIV, and abortion.

Comments on Sections 5 and 6:

- Once again, the keys to important ideas are a definition, an example, and enumerations. In addition, notes include major details under the headings.

- The chapter closes with a summary and a list of key terms. Just as the preview has given you an overview of the chapter, the summary can also provide such an overview. These opening and closing overviews help ensure that you do not lose sight of the forest for the trees. And in the list of key terms, the authors themselves underscore how important *definitions* are in learning the chapter. Always use a summary and a list of key terms—or other end-of-chapter study aids—as a check to make sure you have not missed some important ideas.

SOCIOLOGY ON THE WEB

Children at Risk?

The chapter notes that family structure is undergoing rapid change, as couples find new ways to form families, balance work and home, and care for children. How are children affected by rapid social change? Socially and economically, are children better or worse off than they were in more traditional families? What proportion of children live in poverty in your state, and how does that compare with the national average? How many mothers work outside the home, and who is taking care of their children? What government programs support parents' need for quality child care? Are rates of child abuse and neglect rising or falling?

Pick one of these questions, or one of your own, and begin to look for answers by exploring the following sites and the many others you will find that provide information and data about children's issues:

http://ericps.ed.uiuc.edu/nccic/nccichome.html
The web site of the National Child Care Information Center provides state child care profiles and demographic information on children, families, and child care in each state.

http://www.aecf.org/aeckids.htm
The Annie E. Casey Foundation maintains the Kids Count project, which tracks child welfare throughout the United States. The foundation's web site provides a wealth of demographic data on children and families. For example, you can compare a number of criteria of child well-being between 1985 and 1994 on a state-by-state basis. You can also obtain data on such factors as teen birthrates, immunization rates, health insurance, poverty rates, and school attendance by year and by state.

http://www.childrensdefense.org/
The Children's Defense Fund's web site gives information on lobbying and current political initiatives on behalf of children, as well as discussions of current issues, such as day care and immunizations.

http://www.acf.dhhs.gov/programs/cb/stats/ncands/
At this site, you can find state-by-state data on rates of child abuse and neglect, as well as information about victims and perpetrators. For example, did you think that most child abuse was perpetrated by strangers lurking near the playground? Think again.

---

principle of *homogamy*). Exchange theory portrays courtship as an exchange of assets and liabilities in which people weigh the costs and benefits of a potential partner. With wives working, the daily routine may become more hectic, but there is little evidence that two careers either harm or improve the quality of family life.

4. **How do sociologists explain family violence?** All families do not live happily ever after: violence in American families at all socioeconomic levels is surprisingly common. Intimacy, privacy, cultural support for the use of force, and socialization all contribute to this social problem.

5. **What are the causes and consequences of today's high divorce rate?** The *divorce rate* reached an all-time high in the United States in 1979, and the number of divorces involving children has grown. Studies find that virtually all children are upset by a divorce; most recover in a few years, but some suffer lasting and/or serious problems. The high rate of remarriage after divorce and the number of *blended families* indicate that people believe as strongly in the institution of marriage as they ever did.

6. **What will the family look like in the future?** Some social scientists see the breakup of the two-parent family as a major social problem and as the cause of other problems. Others see

changes in American families as adaptations to changing social circumstances, and they view many of the problems these families face as the result of uneven changes in other institutions.

Key Terms

blended family

divorce rate

extended family

family

group marriage

homogamy

modified extended family

monogamy

new extended family

nuclear family

polyandry

polygamy

polygyny

serial monogamy

Recommended Readings

Blankenhorn, David, Bayme, Steven, & Elshtain, Jean Bethke (Eds.). (1990). *Rebuilding the Nest: A New Commitment to the American Family*. Milwaukee, WI: Family Service America.

Cherlin, Andrew J. (1992). *Marriage, Divorce, Remarriage*. Cambridge, MA: Harvard University Press.

Coontz, Stephanie. (1992). *The Way We Never Were: American Families and the Nostalgia Trap*. New York: Basic Books.

Furstenberg, Frank F., Jr., & Cherlin, Andrew J. (1991). *Divided Families: What Happens to Children When Parents Part*. Cambridge, MA: Harvard University Press.

Gelles, Richard J. (1997). *Intimate Violence in Families,* 3d ed. Thousand Oaks, CA: Sage Publications.

Gutman, Herbert G. (1976). *The Black Family in Slavery and Freedom: 1750–1925*. New York: Pantheon.

Hochschild, Arlie, with Machung, Anne. (1989). *The Second Shift*. New York: Viking Penguin.

McAdoo, Harriette Pipes (Eds.). (1993). *Family Ethnicity: Strength in Diversity*. Thousand Oaks, CA: Sage Publications.

Popenoe, David. (1988). *Disturbing the Nest: Family Change and Decline in Modern Societies*. New York: Aldine DeGruyter.

Rubin, Lillian. (1994). *Families on the Fault Line: America's Working Class Speaks about the Family, Economy, Race, and Ethnicity*. New York: HarperCollins.

Skolnick, Arlene. (1991). *Embattled Paradise: The American Family in the Age of Uncertainty*. New York: Basic Books.

Wallerstein, Judith S., & Blakeslee, Sandra. (1990). *Second Chances: Men, Women, and Children a Decade after Divorce*. New York: Ticknor & Fields.

Closing Comments

In the process of taking notes, you have reduced almost forty pages of material to five pages! These five pages provide an anchor for your understanding of the chapter. Keep in mind that if your instructor intends to test you on just this chapter, you may need to have a very detailed knowledge of the material and may want to do more rereading and add even more notes. On the other hand, if your instructor intends to test you on this and two other chapters, plus several weeks of classroom notes, it may well be that the five pages of notes are more than enough. You will quickly develop skill at making a good judgment call about just how much you need to learn.

• Complete the following description of the final stage of textbook study:

After taking as many notes as you need, your final step is to study the notes. To do so, put ____key (or recall)____ words in the margin. For instance, the words "family structure" and "family functions" would help you learn the material on the first page of your notes. Your purpose would be to study until you could _____recite_____ to yourself the family structures and family functions without looking at them. You could then go on to study the other four pages of notes. After completing each page of notes, you should go back and _____review_____ the previous pages. Through this process of repeated self-testing, you will effectively learn the material.

Checking Your Mastery:
A Quiz on the Sample Chapter

After you have completed taking notes on the sample chapter, you or your instructor may decide that you should spend some time studying the notes. You can then use the following quiz to see how well you have learned the material.

■ Quiz on "The Family"

1. *True or false?*___F___ Monogamy is the *preferred* arrangement in most human societies.

2. The specific term for the marriage of one man to two or more women at the same time is
   a. polygamy.
   (b.) polygyny.
   c. polyandry.
   d. serial monogamy.

3. The nuclear family consists of
   a. a single mother and her children.
   (b.) a husband, a wife, and their children.
   c. a husband and wife without children.
   d. a remarried couple and their stepchildren.

4. *True or false?*___F___ Today, people are getting married at younger and younger ages.

5. Multigeneration households are becoming more common because of
   a. the high cost of housing.
   b. poor wages.
   (c.) both of the above.
   d. neither of the above.

6. In most societies, marriages are
   a. based on love.
   (b.) arranged by older relatives.
   c. the result of kidnapping.
   d. becoming outdated.

7. Homogamy is the tendency to marry someone
   a.   our own age.
   (b.) like ourselves in important ways.
   c.   we've lived with.
   d.   who is rich.

8. *True or false?*___F___ The real causes of family violence are alcohol and drugs.

9. According to the authors, one factor influencing whether a couple gets divorced is
   a.   health.
   b.   age at high school graduation.
   (c.) socioeconomic status.
   d.   difference in age between spouses.

10. Optimists about the family define it as an institution for
    a.   child rearing.
    b.   marriage and divorce.
    (c.) intimacy and companionship.
    d.   risk.

Building a Powerful Memory

Building a Powerful Memory: In Real Life

Read the profile that follows. Then ask yourself these questions:

- How does Joe combine using a highlighter and using index cards as he memorizes?
- Why does Joe read his notes aloud to himself?

Student Profile: Joe Davis

Joe Davis wants to make one thing clear: He has a lousy memory. "It's bad across the board," he admits. "Facts, dates, names, faces. If I work with you and see you every day, I'm fine. But if I meet you today and see you again in a week, I have to ask your name again. That's embarrassed me more than once." He envies people who memorize things easily. "What an advantage a good memory is!" he explains. "You learn more quickly, you test better, you work more efficiently. But I've got to work with what I've got."

Continued

What Joe's got has gotten him pretty far. A recent graduate student at the University of Pennsylvania, Joe has just earned his master's degree in social work. He works as a therapist at the John F. Kennedy  Mental Health Center in Philadelphia. He is also coordinator of Think First, a program at Magee Rehabilitation Hospital. Think First sends speakers who have suffered spinal-cord and head injuries into local schools. There they share their personal stories, making their audiences aware of the consequences of high-risk behavior.

The story Joe shares with Think First audiences involves years of drug use and crime, behavior that finally resulted in his being on the receiving end of a .22 bullet. The shooting left Joe paralyzed from the chest down. After a long and rocky rehabilitation, marked by continued drug use and an eventual suicide attempt, Joe took a good look at his life and was sickened by what he saw. He enrolled in a vocational rehabilitation program and got his first real job. Then he signed up for a university math class. He didn't do well. Refusing to give up, he enrolled in basic math and English courses at a local community college. Bit by bit, inch by inch, week by week, he struggled to acquire the academic skills he'd never cared about before.

"It was *hard*. It still *is* hard," Joe says today. "But it's worth the work."

As he works to memorize the material he studies, Joe says he'd be lost without two things: his highlighter and a stack of 3- by 5-inch cards. Reading slowly through his textbooks, he highlights definitions, examples, and "anything brand-new; anything that I haven't heard or seen before." Grabbing a pen, he'll scrawl notes to himself in the margin: "Look this up" or "Definition?" Then he'll read through the material yet again, this time copying whatever he's highlighted onto his 3-by-5 cards. Later, he'll read those cards out loud to himself. If they include terms he's not familiar with, he'll look the terms up, then talk about

Continued

them to a colleague or instructor. "I want to know for sure how to pronounce them and how to use them correctly," he says. "I remember the embarrassment back in college when I mixed up the words 'stigma,' which means a mark of disgrace, and 'astigmatism,' which is an eye disorder. Now I look everything up, and I ask questions."

Joe finds that the combination of writing down new material and speaking it aloud works. "When it's time for me to remember that material, in a discussion or on a test, I can call up that recent memory. I can *see* myself writing it down or *hear* my voice saying it out loud. Studying just by reading the material silently is not nearly as effective for me."

Perhaps you think that memorizing material for a test is a waste of time; you may be convinced that you will forget what you memorize as soon as a test is over. Moreover, because some instructors believe that memorization and learning are incompatible, they may tell you that you shouldn't *memorize* material; rather, you should *understand* it.

Memorization, however, can be an important aid to understanding—and not just in situations where basic, uncomplicated material is involved. Effective memorizing requires that you organize and repeatedly test yourself on the material to be learned. As you do this, you are sure to enlarge your comprehension of the material and notice relationships you have not seen before. In short, memorization and understanding *reinforce* one another. Together, they help you learn—and learning is the goal of education. What you need, then, is a series of strategies, or steps, to help you memorize effectively. The following pages present seven such steps:

1 Organize the material to be learned.
2 Intend to remember.
3 Test yourself repeatedly on the material to be memorized.
4 Use several memory techniques.
5 Space memory work over several sessions.
6 Overlearn the material.
7 Use as a study period the time just before going to bed.

Step 1: Organize the Material to Be Learned

The first key to effective remembering is to organize in some meaningful way the material to be learned.

For example, imagine that your instructor has given you and your fellow students the assigment of memorizing each others' names. In such a situation, students typically begin by introducing themselves in isolated pairs. This doesn't work well for learning all the names, however, and someone usually suggests that the introductions be done in an organized manner. What usually happens then is that, one by one, people take turns giving their names to the entire class. Some students even jot down a rough seating chart (a further organizational device) to help them remember all the names. The point is that some meaningful kind of *organization* is a vital first step in the memorization process. The following two examples should also show how organizing material will aid memory.

Example A: Suppose that you had to memorize these numbers in any sequence:

1, 10, 7, 12, 22, 28, 20

You could eventually memorize the numbers by sheer mechanical repetition. However, you could learn them far more quickly, and remember them far longer, by grouping them in a meaningful and logical way:

$$10 + 12 = 22$$
$$1 + 7 + 20 = 28$$

Example B: Suppose that before you left for school or work, you were asked to look at a shopping list attached to the refrigerator door and to pick up the items later, at the store. To save the time of writing down the items, and to exercise your memory, you look over the list:

Tide
Bic razors
spaghetti
ChapStick
garlic bread
Parmesan cheese
Dawn
Windex
hair gel

Memorizing the items at random would be difficult. So you organize them into meaningful groupings:

Dinner	Cleaning Items	Personal-Care Items
spaghetti	Tide	Bic razors
garlic bread	Dawn	hair gel
Parmesan cheese	Windex	ChapStick

The three groups of related items are far easier to study and remember than the nine random items.

To be an effective student, you must learn how to organize the material in classroom lectures and reading assignments. It is easier to remember ideas and details that are related to one another than ideas that are isolated, unorganized, and unrelated. In this book, "Taking Classroom Notes" will help you learn how to organize the material in classroom lectures, and the three chapters on textbook study (pages 93–206) will help you tie together ideas and details in reading assignments. You will then be ready to memorize any of the information that is necessary for you to remember.

- Material in your class notes and textbooks should be ___*organized*___ in some meaningful way before you attempt to memorize it.

Step 2: Intend to Remember

An important aid to memory is *deciding* to remember. This advice appears to be so obvious that many people overlook it. But if you have made the decision to remember something and you then work at mastering it, you *will* remember. Anyone can improve his or her memory by working at it.

When assigned the task of memorizing classmates' names, students are often surprised at their ability to learn the names so quickly and completely. A main reason for their success is that they have decided to learn—for it might be embarrassing if they were the only ones not to have mastered the names when the instructor returns. The lesson here is that *your attitude is crucial in effective memorization.* You must begin by saying, "I am going to master this."

- Do you ever have trouble, as many people do, in remembering the names of persons you are introduced to? _____ Yes   _____ No

- If you do, the reason is probably that you did not consciously decide to remember their names. Suppose you were introduced to a person who was going to borrow money from you. Is it safe to say you would make it a point to

  remember (and so *would* remember) that person's name? _____ Yes _____ No

Step 3: Test Yourself Repeatedly on the Material to Be Learned

After you have organized the material you intend to learn, memorize it through repeated self-testing. Look at the first item in your notes; then look away and try to repeat it to yourself. When you can repeat the first item, look at the next item; look away and try to repeat it. When you can repeat the second item, *go back* without looking at your notes and repeat the first *and* second items. After you can recall the first two items without referring to your notes, go on to the third item, and so on. In short, follow this procedure: *After you learn each new item, go back and test yourself on all the previous items. This constant review is at the heart of self-testing and is the key to effective memorization.*

- If you were memorizing a list of ten definitions, what would you do after you mastered the second definition? The sixth? The tenth?

  You would go back and test yourself on the ones you had memorized so far.

Step 4: Use Several Memory Techniques

The following techniques will help you in the self-testing process:

- Use several senses.
- Use key words.
- Use catchwords.
- Use catchphrases.

Catch words and catchphrases are sometimes called *mnemonic* (nĭ mŏn′ĭk) devices. (The term is derived from the Greek word for *memory.*) All four techniques are explained and illustrated on the pages ahead.

Use Several Senses

Use several senses in the self-testing process. Research has shown that most people understand and retain information more effectively when several senses are involved in learning the material. Do not, then, merely recite the information silently to yourself. Also repeat it out loud so that you *hear* it, and write it down so that you both *see* and, as it were, *touch* it. These steps will help you learn more than you would if you only repeated the information silently to yourself.

• What senses do you use in studying material? _____

_____

Use Key Words

Key words can be used as "hooks" to help you remember ideas. A *key word* stands for an idea and is so central to the idea that if you remember the word, you are almost sure to remember the entire concept that goes with the word.

Here is an illustration of how key words may function as hooks to help you recall ideas. Assume that your biology instructor has announced that the class will be tested on a textbook chapter dealing with the ecology of urban life. This is one important paragraph taken from that chapter.

> Urban planners who want to replace living plants with plastic ones seem to think that the city does not need to have living plants in it. Actually, plants do many useful things in a city even if they are not producing food for people. Plants improve the quality of the air by giving off oxygen and woodsy-smelling compounds, such as those emitted by pine trees. Smog contains some gases that, in low concentrations, can be used as nutrients by plants. Thus plants can absorb some air pollutants. Evaporation of water from plants cools the air; also, the leaves of plants catch falling dust particles. Trees and shrubs muffle the noise of what otherwise could be the deafening sound of street traffic and construction work. Finally, the roots of plants—even weeds on vacant lots—help to hold earth in place and reduce the number of soil particles blown into the air and washed into sewers.

Since you want to learn this information, you would first prepare study notes that might look something like this:

Uses of Plants in City
1. Give off oxygen (and pleasant smell)
2. Absorb air pollutants (gases used as nutrients)
3. Cool the air (evaporation from leaves)
4. Catch dust particles
5. Muffle noises (traffic, construction)
6. Hold earth in place

It is now necessary for you to memorize the study notes, and to do that you will need a technique.

One way to memorize these study notes is to use key words as hooks. What you do is circle a key word from each of the listed items. The word you select should help you pull into memory the entire idea that it represents. Write each of the words, one after the other, under the study notes. Here is how your notes would look.

Uses of Plants in City
1. Give off oxygen (and pleasant smell)
2. Absorb air pollutants (gases used as nutrients)
3. Cool the air (evaporation from leaves)
4. Catch dust particles
5. Muffle noises (traffic, construction)
6. Hold earth in place

Key words: oxygen, pollutants, cool, dust, muffle, earth

After you pick out key words, the next step would be to test yourself repeatedly until you remember each of the six key words *and* the concepts they stand for.

- Take five minutes to study your six key words for the uses of plants in the city. Test yourself until you can recite from memory all the words and the ideas they stand for. Your instructor may then ask you to write from memory the six words and concepts on a sheet of paper.

Use Catchwords

Sometimes people who use key words to pull central ideas into memory can't remember one of the key words, and so they forget the entire concept the word represents. Using catchwords is one way to ensure that you remember an entire series of key words and so the ideas they stand for. *Catchwords* are words made up of the first letters of other words. (See also page 114.)

Follow these guidelines when you create catchwords. First, circle the key words in your study notes. Then write down the first letter of each key word. Here are the first letters for the key words in the paragraph about city plants: O (oxygen), P (pollutants), C (cool), D (dust), M (muffle), and E (earth). Now, if necessary, rearrange the letters to form an easily recalled catchword. It can be a real word or a made-up word. For example, you might remember the letters O-P-C-D-M-E with the made-up word MEDCOP.

What matters is that you create a word that you can automatically remember and that the letters in the word help you recall the key words (and so the ideas the key words represent).

After you create a catchword, test yourself until you are sure each letter stands for a key word in your mind. Here is how you might use the catchword MEDCOP to pull into memory the textbook paragraph about city plants:

MEDCOP
M ≈ muffle
E ≈ earth
D ≈ dust
C ≈ cool
O ≈ oxygen
P ≈ pollutants

Cover the key words (*muffle, earth,* etc.) with a sheet of paper, leaving only the first letter exposed. Look at the letter M and see if you can recall the key word *muffle* and the idea that plants muffle noise. Next, look at the letter E and see if you remember the key word *earth* and the idea that plant roots hold the earth in place. Then do the same for the other four letters. In each case, the letter serves as a hook to pull into memory the key word and then the whole idea.

Here is an illustration of how first letters and key words help you remember ideas. As shown here, the first letter helps you remember the key word, which helps you pull the entire idea into memory.

First Letter	*Key Word*	*Entire Idea*
M ⟶	muffle ⟶	muffle noise of traffic and construction
E ⟶	earth ⟶	hold earth in place
D ⟶	dust ⟶	catch dust particles
C ⟶	cool ⟶	cool the air
O ⟶	oxygen ⟶	give off oxygen
P ⟶	pollutants ⟶	absorb air pollutants

- An instructor in a psychology class described the following four techniques used in behavior therapy: (1) extinction, (2) imitation, (3) reinforcement, and (4) desensitization. Make up a catchword that will help you remember the four techniques, and write the word here: <u>DIRE or RIDE (Answers may vary.)</u>

Use Catchphrases

Another way to remember key words is to form some easily recalled *catchphrase*. Each word in a catchphrase begins with the first letter of a different key word. For example, suppose you had to remember the six uses of city plants in the exact order in which they are presented in the textbook paragraph (*oxygen, pollutants, cool, dust, muffle, earth*). You would write a six-word phrase with the first word beginning with *O,* the second with *P,* the third with *C,* and so on. Here is a catchphrase you might create to help remember the order of the six letters and the key words they stand for:

Our **p**arents **c**ook **d**inner **m**ost **e**venings.

Your catchphrase does not have to be perfect grammatically; it does not even have to make perfect sense. It simply needs to be a phrase that will stick in your memory and that you will automatically remember.

Once you create a catchphrase, follow the testing process already described above in the section on catchwords. Note that the first letter of each word in the catchphrase pulls into memory a key word and the key word recalls an entire idea. For example, the *O* in *Our* recalls the key word *oxygen* and the idea that plants give off oxygen, the *P* in *parents* helps you remember the key word *pollutants* and the idea that plants absorb air pollutants, and so on.

- Suppose an instructor wants you to learn the following five influences on a child's personality. The influences are listed in order of importance.

Influences on Children

One: Parents

Two: Siblings (brothers and sisters)

Three: Friends

Four: Close relatives

Five: Teachers

Make up a catchphrase that will help you remember in sequence the five influences on children and write the phrase here:

Answers will vary. One catchphrase might be: Paul sanded Fran's rough table.

Step 5: Space Memory Work Over Several Sessions

If you try to do a great deal of self-testing at any one time, you may have trouble absorbing the material. Always try to spread out your memory work. For instance, three two-hour sessions will be more effective than one six-hour session.

Spacing memory work over several time periods gives you a chance to review and lock in material you have studied in an earlier session but have begun to forget. Research shows that we forget a good deal of information right after studying it. However, review within a day reduces much of this memory loss. So try to review new material within twenty-four hours after you first study it. Then, if possible, several days later review again to make a third impression or "imprint" of the material in your memory. If you work consistently to retain ideas and details, they are not likely to escape you when you need them during an exam.

- Do you typically try to study the material for a test "all at once," or do you spread out your study over several sessions?

  _____

  _____

- How might you spread out six hours of memory work that you need to do for a biology exam?

  _____

  _____

Step 6: Overlearn the Material

If you study a subject beyond the time needed for perfect recall, you will increase the length of time that you will remember it. You can apply the principle of overlearning by going over several times a lesson you have already learned perfectly. The method of repeated self-testing is so effective partly because it forces you to overlearn. After you study each new idea, the method requires that you go back and recite all the previous ideas you have studied.

Another way to apply the principle of overlearning is to devote some time in each session to review. Go back to restudy—and overlearn—important material that you have studied in the past. Doing so will help ensure that you will not "push out" of memory old ideas at the time you are learning new ones.

- If you memorize a list of ten definitions using the process of repeated self-testing, how many times, at a minimum, will you have tested yourself on the first definition? _ten_

Step 7: Study before Going to Bed

Study thoroughly the material to be learned. Then go right to sleep without watching a late movie or allowing other activities to interfere with your new learning. Your mind will work through and absorb much of this material during the night. Set your clock a half hour earlier than usual so that you will have time to go over the material as soon as you get up. The morning review will complete the process of solidly fixing the material in your memory.

- Have you ever used this technique and found it to be helpful? _____

  _____

- Do you think you should practice the technique daily or use it more as a study aid in the review period before an exam? _____

Practice in Building a Powerful Memory

Activity 1

1. An instructor in a criminal justice class describes the four traditional goals of punishment. Make up a catchword that will help you remember all four goals.
   One possibility: DIRR

   Retribution
   Deterrence
   Incapacitation
   Rehabilitation

2. An instructor in a psychology class writes on the board the following five characteristics of schizophrenia. Make up a catchword that will help you remember these five characteristics.
   One possibility: PILED

Language-thought disturbances

Delusions

Perceptual disorders

Emotional disturbances

Isolation

3. The following six avoidance tactics often used by students were described on pages 17–18 of this book. Circle the first letter of a key word in each of these tactics and then create a catchphrase to help remember the six key words. The key words, in turn, will help you remember the six avoidance tactics.

One possibility: Carol bought two lovely baby hamsters.

I can't do it.

I'm too busy.

I'm too tired.

I'll do it later.

I'm bored with the subject.

I'm here, and that's what counts.

4. You have memorized three groups of items individually. Now take ten to fifteen minutes to prepare for a quiz in which you will be asked to write from memory the four goals of legal punishment, the five characteristics of schizophrenia, and the six avoidance tactics.

Activity 2

1. A psychology text explains Abraham Maslow's theory of basic human needs. The five needs, in order of importance, follow. Use a catchphrase to memorize them *in sequence.*

One possibility: Bob's Siamese cat eats salmon.

Basic Human Needs

First: Biological needs

Second: Safety needs

Third: Need for companionship

Fourth: Esteem needs

Fifth: Need for self-actualization

2. Many articles and textbooks refer to Holmes and Rohe's scale of specific life experiences that result in stress. Use a catchphrase to memorize *in sequence* the first six experiences on that scale as well as the point value assigned to each.

(D)eath of spouse   100

(D)ivorce   73

(M)arital separation   65   *One possible catchphrase: Don't*

(J)ail term   63   *drive my Jeep downtown, Paul.*

(D)eath of close family member   63

(P)ersonal injury or illness   53

3. A sociology text describes the following seven steps that are taken in scientific research. Use a catchphrase to memorize the seven steps *in sequence.*

First: (D)efine the problem.

Second: (R)eview the literature.

Third: (F)ormulate the hypotheses.   *One possible catchphrase:*

Fourth: (P)lan the research design.   *Driving Ray's Ford, Pete clipped*

Fifth: (C)ollect the data.   *a Datsun.*

Sixth: (A)nalyze the data.

Seventh: (D)raw conclusions.

4. You have memorized three groups of items individually. Now take ten to fifteen minutes to prepare for a quiz in which you will be asked to write from memory, and *in sequence,* the five human needs, the six sources of stress, and the seven steps in scientific research.

Activity 3

1. Read over the following selection from a text on public speaking. Then look over the study notes on the selection.

Analyzing the Audience

A number of factors about the audience should be kept in mind when you are planning your speech. First, how large is the audience? If the group is very small, you can get away with speaking quite informally. But the larger the audience, the more polished and formal your delivery should be. Second, how much interest does your audience have in your topic? Especially if you are addressing a "captive audience" of students, you should take pains to adjust your topic so as to involve your listeners. In addition, how much does your audience already know about your topic? If the audience members are already well-informed, you can speak at a sophisticated level. But if they know little about the topic, you will have to speak in elementary terms. Next, what is the audience's attitude toward the topic? If you are speaking on the subject of abortion rights, for example, and your audience is largely antiabortion, you will need to take a different approach from the one you would take if the audience shared your view. Finally, how does the audience perceive you, the speaker? If the audience members see you as well prepared and well informed, they'll listen to what you have to say more favorably than if they see you as unprepared, ill-informed, or otherwise unbelievable.

Study Notes

Analyzing the Audience

One possible catchword: PALIK or LIKAP
One possible catchphrase: Larry King prepares all interviews.

One: How large is the audience?

Two: How much interest does the audience have in the topic?

Three: How much knowledge does the audience have?

Four: What is the audience's attitude toward the topic?

Five: How does the audience perceive the speaker?

Pick out a key word for each of the five tips for analyzing an audience, and then use a catchword or catchphrase to memorize the tips.

2. Read the following selection taken from a psychology textbook. Then look over the study notes on the selection.

Personal Space

In addition to what you wear and how you stand, where you stand can communicate your attitude. One researcher, E. Hall, identified four types of personal zones or spaces. The first type of personal space is intimate distance (from body contact to one foot away). This space is reserved for a limited few, including lovers, parents, children, and close friends. In addition, health professionals, such as doctors, nurses, and dentists, are allowed to enter this space. If anyone else got this close, you would feel very uncomfortable. The second zone is personal distance (one to four feet away). This zone is used for personal conversations with close friends. If you are sitting in a half-empty theater or bus, and someone takes the seat next to you, you will probably feel annoyed. A stranger in our personal zone makes us feel ill at ease. If people must be packed together—as on a crowded bus—they often avoid eye contact as a way of protecting their personal space. The third zone is social distance (four to ten feet). This zone is used for social and casual conversations or for business transactions. The final zone is public distance (ten feet and beyond). Communication within a large lecture hall, or the relationship of an audience to a sports event or performance, takes place at public distance. Often, in these situations, we consider private behavior or comments inappropriate.

Study Notes

Personal zones

One: (I)ntimate distance (body contact to one foot away)

Two: (P)ersonal distance (one to four feet)   *Catchword:* SIPP

Three: (S)ocial distance (four to ten feet)   *Catchphrase:* I prefer Spanish

Four: (P)ublic distance (ten feet and beyond)   *people.*

Pick out a key word for each of the four personal zones and then use a catchword or catchphrase to memorize the four zones.

3. You have memorized two groups of items individually. Now take ten to fifteen minutes to prepare for a quiz in which you will be asked to write from memory the five tips for analyzing an audience and the four personal zones.

Activity 4

Use catchwords to memorize this outline of a selection on job hunting.

Four Stages in Getting a Job

A. Make (c)ontact through:

    1. College (p)lacement bureau

    2. Want (a)ds and employment agencies

    3. (T)elephone calls

    4. Personal (c)onnections

B. Prepare essential (w)ritten materials

    1. (R)ésumé

    2. (C)over letter

C. Go out on (i)nterview

    1. Interview (e)tiquette

    2. Prepare (r)esponses to some typical questions

        a. "Why are you (i)nterested in this job?"

        b. "What are your greatest (s)trengths and weaknesses?"

A catchword for the four stages in getting a job (make contact, written materials, interview, thank-you note) might be CWIT.

A catchword for the four ways to make contact (placement bureau, want ads, telephone calls, and personal connections) might be PACT.

A catchphrase for the two types of written materials (résumé, cover letter) might be Robbers creep.

A catchword for three interview guidelines (etiquette, responses to questions, come across as a competent person) might be REC.

   c.   "Tell me about yourself."
   d.   "Why should we hire you?"
   3.   Come across as a competent person
   D.   Follow up on interview with thank-you note

A catchword for the four typical interview questions (why are you interested, what are your greatest strengths and weaknesses, tell me about yourself, why should we hire you) might be YISH.

Activity 5   Answers will vary.

This activity will help you apply memory techniques to different kinds of lecture and text-book notes. Use catchwords or catchphrases to do one or more of the following:

- Learn the four steps in writing a paper (pages 67–69).
- Learn the concentration hints (pages 86–90).
- Learn the two forms of water pollution (page 371).
- Learn the five ways of becoming a better listener (pages 129–133).

Activity 6   Answers will vary.

From one of your course textbooks or from the class notes for one of your courses, select a list of important items that you will need to remember. Then do these three things and turn in a copy of your work to your instructor.

1. Write the full list on a sheet of paper.
2. Circle key words that will help you remember each item on the list.
3. Make up a catchword or catchphrase for the first letters of the key words.

Activity 7   Answers will vary.

Select four lists of important items to remember from the sample textbook chapter on pages 152–203. Then do the three things listed in Activity 6.

Taking Objective Exams

This chapter will show you how to:

- Prepare for and take tests in general
- Prepare for objective exams
- Take objective exams
- Cram when you have no other choice

Taking Objective Exams: In Real Life

Read the profile that follows. Then ask yourself these questions:

- When Katie knows that a test is coming up, how does she adjust her week's schedule?
- What is one way that Katie eliminates possible answers for a multiple-choice item?

Student Profile: Katie Peacock

Katie Peacock had been home-schooled throughout her high school years, and making the transition to college required certain adjustments for her. No longer could she attend class in her pajamas. No longer could she put off classes until after lunch. And no longer could she avoid taking tests.

Test-taking, then, was a skill that Katie had to learn, and learn quickly. She took advantage of the information provided in her developmental reading course and came up with a strategy that has worked for her.

Katie's strategy for preparing for an objective test includes the following steps:

- She takes careful notes in her classes and reviews them before an exam.
- If her textbook includes end-of-chapter review questions or mastery tests, she makes sure she can complete them successfully.

Continued

- She is sure to attend any review sessions offered by her instructors before exams.
- When she knows a test is coming up, she takes that into account as she schedules her week's work. "I get my other assignments out of the way so that I really have time before the test to study for it," she says. "I want to go into the test well-prepared, with the information fresh in my mind."

- She pays attention to an instructor's hints that certain material may be on the test. "Sometimes an instructor will say directly, 'You'll be tested on this,'" Katie says. "But in other cases, I'll just notice when she spends an especially long time talking about a certain point. I'll put a big star beside that material in my notes."

Here are some of Katie's tips for actually taking the test:

- "I don't start filling in answers right away. I look over the entire test first. Then I go back, quickly answer the questions I know for sure, and use the rest of the time to work on the more difficult items."
- "As I look at multiple-choice items, I eliminate answers in a couple of ways. First, the longest answer is often the right one. Of course I have to read it carefully to make sure it makes sense. Also, you can often eliminate answers with words like 'always' and 'never' in them. Answers that include 'often' or 'much of the time' are more likely to be correct."
- "True-and-false questions are often hard for me. They're often written in a way that I find really tricky. I have to take extra time to read them carefully before I answer them."

Katie's mastery of test-taking skills is helping her to do well in all her courses. She expects to graduate from Delaware County Community College with an associate's degree in business management, and then to transfer to Cabrini College, also in Pennsylvania, to earn a bachelor's degree.

Avoiding Exam Panic

A familiar complaint of students is, "I'm always afraid I'll panic during an exam. I'll know a lot of the material, but when I sit down and start looking at the questions, I forget things that I know. I'll never get good grades as long as this happens. How can I avoid it?" The answer is that if you are *well prepared,* you are not likely to block or panic on exams.

"How, then," you might ask, "should a person go about preparing for exams?" The answer is plain: You must go to class consistently, read the textbook and any other assigned material, take class and textbook notes, and study and at times memorize your notes. In short, you must start preparing for exams in the first class of the semester. The pages that follow offer a series of practical suggestions to help you use your study time efficiently.

Note: Many of the suggestions offered in this chapter assume that you know how to take effective classroom and textbook notes and that you know how to memorize such notes. If you have not developed these essential skills, refer to the appropriate chapters.

- *Complete the following sentence:* You are unlikely to forget material during exams if you are <u>well prepared.</u>

What to Study

You will not always know beforehand if a scheduled exam will be an objective test or an essay test (or a combination of both). To be prepared for whichever kind is given, you should, throughout the course, pay attention to the following.

Key Terms: Look for key terms, their definitions, and examples that clarify the meaning of the terms (see also page 361). Look for this material in your class and textbook notes. If your textbook notes are not complete, go back to the original reading material to locate key terms. This information is often set off in *italic* or **boldface** type.

- Which of the courses you are now taking contains a number of new terms you will probably have to know for exams? <u>Answers will vary.</u>

Enumerations: Look for enumerations (lists of items) in your class and textbook notes (see also page 368). Enumerations are often the basis of essay questions.

Items in a list will probably have a descriptive heading—for example, characteristics of living things, major schools of contemporary psychology, or primary consequences of the Industrial Revolution—and the items may be numbered. Be sure to learn the heading that describes the list as well as the items in the list.

Points Emphasized: Look for points emphasized in class or in the text. Often phrases such as *the most significant, of special importance, the chief reason,* and so on (see page 391) are used to call attention to important points in a book or a lecture. When you take notes on such material, mark these significant points with an *imp,* an asterisk (*), or some other mark.

Also, as you go through your class notes, concentrate on areas the instructor spent a good deal of time discussing. For example, if the instructor spent a week talking about present-day changes in the traditional family structure, you can reasonably expect to get a question on the emphasized area. Similarly, review your textbook. If many pages in a chapter deal with one area, you may be sure that this subject is important, and you should expect a question about it on an exam.

- Write down here the name of one of your courses and an area that your instructor has spent a good deal of time discussing in the course.

Course: _Answers will vary._____

Area: _Answers will vary._____

Topics Identified by the Instructor: Pay attention to areas your instructors have advised you to study. Some instructors conduct in-class reviews during which they tell students what material to emphasize when they study. Always write down these pointers; your instructors have often made up the test or are making it up at the time of the review and are likely to give valuable hints about the exam. Other instructors indicate the probable emphasis in their exams when they distribute reviews or study guides. You should, of course, consider these aids very carefully.

- One study-skills instructor has said, "I sometimes sit in on classes, and time and again I have heard instructors tell students point-blank that something is to be on an exam. Some students quickly jot down this information; others sit there in a fog." Which group of students do you belong to?
  _Answers will vary._____

- What are some specific study aids instructors have given to help you prepare for tests? _Answers will vary._____

_____

Questions on Earlier Tests: Pay attention to questions on past quizzes and reviews as well as tests at the end of textbook chapters.

If you follow these suggestions, you will have identified most, if not all, of the key concepts in the course.

The following hints will help you make the most of your time before a test.

Hint 1: Spend the night before an exam making a final review of your notes. Then go right to bed without watching television or otherwise interfering with the material you have learned. Your mind will tend to work through and absorb the material during the night. To further lock in your learning, get up a half hour earlier than usual the next morning and review your notes.

- Do you already review material on the morning of an exam? _Answers will vary._

  If so, have you found it to be very helpful? _Answers will vary._

Hint 2: Make sure you take with you any materials (pen, paper, eraser, dictionary, and other aids allowed) you will need during the exam.

Hint 3: Be on time for the exam. Arriving late sets you up to do poorly.

Hint 4: Sit in a quiet spot. Some people are very talkative and noisy before an exam. Since you don't want anything to interfere with your learning, you are better off not talking with others during the few minutes before the exam starts. You might want to use those minutes to make one final review of your notes.

- How do you typically spend the minutes in class right before an exam?
  Answers will vary.

Hint 5: Read over carefully *all* the directions on the exam before you begin. Many students don't take this important step and end up losing points because they fail to do what is required. Make sure you understand how you are expected to respond to each item, how many points each section is worth, and how many questions you must answer. Also, listen carefully to any oral directions or hints the instructor may give. Many students wreck their chances at the start because they do not understand or follow directions. Don't let this happen to you.

- Do you already have the habit of reading all the directions on an exam carefully before you begin? _Answers will vary._

Hint 6: Budget your time. Take a few seconds to figure out roughly how much time you can spend on each section of the test. Write the number of minutes in the margin of your exam paper or on a scratch sheet. Then stick to that schedule. Be sure to have a watch or to sit where you can see a clock.

Exactly *how* you budget your time depends on what kinds of questions you are good at answering (and so can do more quickly) and the point value of different sections of the test. Keep in mind that the reason for budgeting your time is to prevent you from ending up with ten minutes left and a fifty-point essay still to write or thirty multiple-choice questions to answer.

Activity 1

This activity will check your skill at following written directions.

A Test in Following Directions: First read all ten directions carefully. Then follow them.

_____   _____
          Langan, John (written)   Langan, John (printed)

1. Print your full name, last name first, on the line at the right above.

2. Write your full name, first name last, under the line at the left above.

3. Count the number of *e*'s in this sentence and write out the total number in the margin to the right of this line. twelve (written out, not in figures).

4. Fold this page in half, side to side; then open it again. A lot of people fold the page, and only afterwards see instruction 6.

5. Read the following question carefully and answer it in the space provided. "A plane crashes on the United States–Canadian border. On which side are the survivors buried?" ____Survivors are not buried.____

6. Disregard the fourth instruction.

7. If Kurt and Gail each have $100, how much would Kurt have to give Gail for her to have $10 more than he has? __$5__

8. How many birthdays does the average hippopotamus have? One birthday a year, like everyone else.

9. Block out the three-letter words, circle the four-letter words, and underline the five-letter words in this sentence. Then indicate in the space that follows the number of words left unmarked. Seven (a 7) Many people include the second sentence as well as the first.

10. If Glug zorted the rochenelle and hochwinded a swattorg, what fortig dorts Glug? The moral of this question is: If you don't understand a question, ask the instructor to clarify it. The correct response for this question is for the student to raise his or her hand and say, "What does number 10 mean?" or "I don't understand number 10."

Note on Activity 1:
I always challenge students when they do the short activity above. I explain that no student has ever gotten all ten of the "following directions" questions correct, but that if anyone does, I will on the spot give him/her an A for the course, and he/she may leave the classroom and not come back for the rest of the semester.

Activity 2

Here is an activity that will check your skill at budgeting time. Suppose that you had two hours for a test made up of the following sections:

Part 1: 10 true–false questions worth 10 points   (_____ minutes)

Part 2: 40 multiple-choice questions worth 40 points   (_____ minutes)

Part 3: 2 essay questions worth 50 points   (_____ minutes)

In the spaces provided, write how much time you would spend on each part.

One possible division of time is to spend an hour on the first two parts (about ten minutes on the true–false questions and fifty minutes on the multiple-choice questions) and a half hour on each essay question. Because the essay questions are worth half the points on the test, you want at least an hour to work on them.

Preparing for and Taking Objective Exams

Objective exams may include multiple-choice, true–false, fill-in, and matching questions. Perhaps you feel that objective tests do not require as much study time as essay exams do. A well-constructed objective test, however, can evaluate your understanding of major concepts and can demand just as sophisticated a level of thinking as an essay exam. In short, do not cut short your study time just because you know you will be given an objective test.

To do well on objective tests, you must know how to read test items carefully. The pages that follow describe a number of strategies you can use to deal with the special problems posed by objective tests.

Getting Ready for Objective Exams

Hint 1: Be prepared to memorize material when studying for an objective test. The test may include short-answer questions. For example, the instructor may give several technical terms and ask you to define them. Or the instructor may include headings such as "Three Values of the Social Security Act" and expect you to list the values underneath. He or she may include fill-in questions such as "An important leader of the stimulus-response school of psychology has been

_____."

Even objective tests made up only of multiple-choice and true–false questions can include such fine distinctions that memorization may be necessary. In addition, memorization helps keep your study honest: It forces you to truly *understand* the material you are learning.

There is one difference worth noting between the kind of memorizing needed for essay exams and the kind needed for objective tests. In an essay test, you are actually expected to *recall course material.* For example, an essay test might ask you to list and explain three kinds of defense mechanisms. In an objective test, you are expected to *recognize the correctness of course material.* For instance, an objective test might give you a defense mechanism followed by a definition and ask you whether that definition is true or false. In either kind of test, however, memory is required.

- Describe the specific kinds of objective exams that your instructors give:

    Answers will vary.

Hint 2: Ask your instructor what kind of items will be on the test. Not all instructors will provide this information. However, finding out beforehand that an exam will include, let's say, fifty multiple-choice and fill-in items relieves you of some anxiety. At least you know what to expect.

Hint 3: Try to find a test that is similar to the one you will be taking. Some instructors distribute past exams to help students review. Also, some departments keep on file exams given in earlier semesters. Looking at these exams closely can familiarize you with the requirements, format, and items you may reasonably expect on your exam.

Hint 4: Be sure to review carefully all the main points presented in the course. These were detailed in "What to Study" on pages 227–228. To sharpen your understanding of the key material, apply the techniques of repeated self-testing (page 212) to the recall words written in the margin of your class and textbook notes (pages 51 and 105).

Hint 5: Make up practice test items when you study. That way you will be getting into the rhythm of taking the test, and you may even be able to predict some of the questions the instructor will ask.

Taking Objective Exams

Hint 1: Answer all the easier questions first. Don't lose valuable time stalling over hard questions. You may end up running out of time and not even getting a chance to answer the questions you can do easily. Instead, put a light check mark (✓) beside difficult questions and continue working through the entire test, answering all the items you can do right away. You will find that this strategy will help give you the momentum you need to go confidently through the rest of the exam.

Hint 2: Go back and spend the remaining time with the difficult questions you have marked. Often you will find that while you are answering the easier questions, your unconscious mind has been working on questions you at first found very difficult. Or later items may provide just the extra bit of information you need to answer earlier items you found difficult. Once you answer a question, add a mark to the check you have already made (✗) to show you have completed that item.

Hint 3: Answer *all* questions unless the instructor has said that extra points will be deducted for wrong answers. Guess if you must; by doing so, you are bound to pick up at least a few points.

Hint 4: Ask the instructor to explain any item that isn't clear. Not all instructors will provide this explanation, but probably many will. Most experienced instructors realize that test questions may seem clear and unambiguous to them as they make up the exam but that students may interpret certain questions in other and equally valid ways. In short, you can't lose anything by asking to have an item clarified.

Hint 5: Put yourself in the instructor's shoes when you try to figure out the meaning of a confusing item. In light of what was covered in the course, which answer do you think the instructor would say is correct? If a test item is worded so ambiguously that no single response seems correct, you may—in special situations—use the margin of your test paper to explain to the instructor what you feel the answer should be. Obviously, use this technique only when absolutely necessary.

Hint 6: Circle or underline the key words in difficult questions. This strategy can help you untangle complicated questions and focus on the central point in the item.

Hint 7: Express difficult questions in your own words. Rephrasing an item in simpler terms and then writing it down or even saying it to yourself can help you cut through the confusion and get to the core of the question. Be sure, however, not to change the original meaning of the item.

Hint 8: Take advantage of the full time given and go over the exam carefully for possible mistakes. People used to say that it is not a good idea to change the first answer you put down. However, as long as you have a good reason, you *should* change your earlier answers if they seem incorrect. At the same time, be on guard against last-minute anxiety that prompts you to change, without good reason, *many* of your original answers. You should control any tendency you may have to make widespread revisions.

Activity

Write here what you think are the three most important of the preceding hints to remember in taking objective exams.

1. _Answers will vary._ _____

2. _____

3. _____

Specific Hints for Answering Multiple-Choice Questions

1 Remember that in multiple-choice exams, a perfect answer to every question may not be provided. You must choose the best answer *available.*

2 Cross out answers you know are incorrect. Eliminating wrong answers is helpful because it focuses your attention on the most reasonable options. If you think all options are incorrect, the correct answer may be "none of the above"—if that choice is given.

3 Be sure to read all the possible answers to a question, especially when the first answer seems correct. Remember that the other options could also be correct. In this case, "all of the above" would be the correct response—if that choice is given.

4 Minimize the risk of guessing the answer to difficult items by doing either of the following:

a Read the question and then the first possible answer. Next, read the question again and the second possible answer, and so on until you have read the question with each separate answer. Breaking the items down this way will often help you identify the option that most logically answers the question.

b When you return to difficult items, try not to look at the answers. Instead, read the question, supply your own answer, and then look for the option on the test that is closest to your response.

5 Use the following clues, which may signal correct answers, *only* when you have no idea of the answer and must guess.

a The longest answer is often correct.

- *Use this clue to answer the following question:* The key reason students who are well-prepared still don't do well on exams is that they (a) are late to the test, (b) don't have all their materials, (c) forget to jot down catchphrases, (d) haven't studied enough, (e) don't read all the directions before they begin the test.

  The correct answer is *e,* the longest answer.

b The most complete and inclusive answer is often correct.

- *Use this clue to answer the following question:* If you have to cram for a test, which of these items should receive most of your attention? (a) The instructor's tests from other years; (b) important ideas in the class and text notes, including such things as key terms, their definitions, and clarifying examples; (c) the textbook; (d) class notes; (e) textbook notes.

  The correct answer is *b,* the most complete and inclusive choice. Note that the most complete answer is often also the longest.

c An answer in the middle, especially if it is longest, is often correct.

- *Use this clue to answer the following question:* Many students have trouble with objective tests because they (a) guess when they're not sure, (b) run out of time, (c) think objective exams are easier than essay tests and so do not study enough, (d) forget to double-check their answers, (e) leave difficult questions to the end.

  The correct answer is *c,* which is in the middle and is longest.

d If two answers have opposite meanings, one of them is probably correct.

- *Use this clue to answer the following question:* Before an exam starts, you should (a) sit in a quiet spot, (b) join a group of friends and talk about the test, (c) review the textbook one last time, (d) read a book and relax, (e) study any notes you didn't have time for previously.

  The correct answer is *a.* Note that *a* and *b* are roughly opposite.

e Answers with qualifiers, such as *generally, probably, most, often, some, sometimes,* and *usually,* are frequently correct.

- *Use this clue to answer the following question:* In multiple-choice questions, the most complete and inclusive answer is (a) never correct, (b) often correct, (c) always correct, (d) all of the above, (e) none of the above.

  The correct answer is *b,* the choice with the qualifying word *often.* Note also that answers with absolute words, such as *all, always, everyone, everybody, never, no one, nobody, none,* and *only,* are usually incorrect.

- *Use this clue to answer the following question:* In multiple-choice questions, the answer in the middle with the most words is (a) always correct, (b) always incorrect, (c) frequently correct, (d) never wrong, (e) never right.

  The correct answer is *c;* all the other answers use absolute words and are incorrect.

Activity

Write here what you think are the three most helpful clues for you to remember when you are guessing the answer to a multiple-choice question.

1. Answers will vary. _____

2. _____

3. _____

Specific Hints for Answering True–False Questions

1 Simplify questions with double negatives by crossing out both negatives and then determining the correct answer.

- *Use this hint to answer the following question: True or false?* _____ You won't be unprepared for essay exams if you anticipate several questions and prepare your answers for those questions.

  The statement is true. It can be reworded to read, "You will be prepared for essay exams if you anticipate several questions and prepare your answers to those questions."

2 Remember that answers with qualifiers such as *generally, probably, most, often, some, sometimes,* and *usually* are frequently true.

- *Use this hint to answer the following question: True or false?* _____ Some instructors will tell students what kinds of items to expect on an exam.

  The statement, which contains the qualifier *Some,* is true.

3 Remember that answers with absolute words such as *all, always, everyone, never, no one, nobody, none,* and *only* are usually false.

- *Use this hint to answer the following question: True or false?* _____ You should never review your notes on the morning of an essay exam.

  The statement, which contains the absolute word *never,* is false.

Specific Hints for Answering Fill-In Questions

1 Read the questions to yourself so you can actually hear what is being asked. If more than one response comes to mind, write both responses lightly in the margin. Then, when you review your answers later, choose the answer that feels most right to you.

2 Make sure each answer you provide fits logically and grammatically into its slot in the sentence. For example: An _____ lists ideas in a sequence.

The correct answer is *enumeration.* Note that the word *an* signals that the correct answer begins with a vowel.

3 Remember that not all fill-in answers require only one word. If you feel that several words are needed to complete an answer, write in all the words unless the instructor or the directions indicate that only single-word responses will be accepted.

Specific Hints for Answering Matching Questions

1 Don't start matching items until you read both columns and get a sense of the choices. Often, there's an extra item or two in one column. This means that not all items can be paired. Some will be left over. For example:

1. Sentence-skills mistakes _____	a.	compare, explain, analyze
2. Absolute words _____	b.	often, usually, most
3. Connecting words _____	c.	from, over, in, with
4. Qualifying words _____	d.	misspelled and omitted words
5. Direction words in instructions _____	e.	all, never, only
	f.	first, second, next, also

The correct answers are 1-*d,* 2-*e,* 3-*f,* 4-*b,* and 5-*a.* Item *c* is extra.

2 Start with the easiest items. One by one, focus on each item in one column and look for its match in the other column. Cross out items as you use them.

A Final Note: How to Cram When You Have No Other Choice

Students who consistently cram for tests are not likely to be successful; they often have to cram because they have not managed their time well. However, even organized students may sometimes need to cram because they run into problems that disrupt their regular study routine. If you're ever in this situation, the following steps may help you do some quick but effective studying.

1   Accept the fact that, in the limited time you have, you are not going to be able to study everything in your class notes and textbook. You may even have to exclude your textbook if you know that your instructor tends to base most of a test on class material.

2   Read through your class notes (and, if you have them, your textbook notes) and mark off those ideas that are most important. Use as a guide any review or study sheets that your instructor has provided. Your purpose is to try to guess correctly many of the ideas your instructor will put in the test.

Important ideas often include definitions, enumerations (lists of items), points marked by emphasis words, and answers to basic questions made out of titles and headings. See also "What to Study" on pages 227–228.

3   Write the ideas you have selected on sheets of paper, using one side of a page only. Perhaps you will wind up with three or four "cram sheets" full of important points to study.

4   Prepare catchwords or catchphrases to recall the material and then memorize the points using the method of repeated self-testing described on page 212.

5   Go back, if time remains, and review all your notes. If you do not have textbook notes, you might skim your textbook. Do not use this time to learn new concepts. Instead, try to broaden as much as possible your understanding of the points you have already studied.

Practice in Test-Taking

Activity 1

Evaluate your present test-preparation and test-taking skills. Put a check mark beside each of the following steps that you already practice. Then put a check mark beside those steps that you plan to practice. Be honest; leave a blank space if you do not plan to follow a particular point.

Now   Plan
Do   to Do   *What to Study*

_____ _____   Key terms, definitions, and examples.

_____ _____   Enumerations (lists of items).

_____ _____   Points emphasized in class.

_____ _____   Reviews and study guides.

_____ _____   Questions in past quizzes and textbook chapters.

Now   Plan
Do   to Do

General Tips before an Exam

____ ____   1. Study right before sleep.

____ ____   2. Take materials needed to the exam.

____ ____   3. Be on time for the exam.

____ ____   4. Sit in a quiet spot.

____ ____   5. Read all directions carefully.

____ ____   6. Budget your time.

Getting Ready for Objective Exams

____ ____   1. Memorize as necessary.

____ ____   2. Ask instructor about makeup of test.

____ ____   3. Look at similar tests.

____ ____   4. Review carefully all main points of course.

____ ____   5. Make up practice test items.

Taking Objective Exams

____ ____   1. Answer all easier questions first.

____ ____   2. Do difficult questions in time remaining.

____ ____   3. Answer all questions.

____ ____   4. Ask instructor to explain unclear items.

____ ____   5. For difficult questions, think of the instructor's point of view.

____ ____   6. Mark key words in difficult questions.

____ ____   7. State difficult questions in your own words.

____ ____   8. Use all the time given.

____ ____   9. Use the specific hints given for multiple-choice, true–false, fill-in, and matching questions.

Activity 2

All the questions that follow have been taken from actual college tests. Answer the questions by using the specific hints for answering multiple-choice and true–false questions that follow. Also, in the space provided, give the letter of the hint or hints used to determine the correct answer.

Hints for Test Taking

a The longest multiple-choice answer is often correct.

b The most complete and inclusive multiple-choice answer is often correct.

c A multiple-choice answer in the middle, especially one with the most words, is often correct.

d If two multiple-choice answers have the opposite meaning, one of them is probably correct.

e Answers with qualifiers, such as *generally, usually, probably, most, often, some, may,* and *sometimes,* are usually correct.

f Answers with absolute words, such as *all, always, everyone, everybody, never, no one, nobody, none,* and *only,* are usually incorrect.

Hint __F__   1. *True or false?* __F__ Denial and intellectualization always reduce anxiety.

Hint __A and C__   2. Newton's third law of motion is

    a. $x = 2y$.

    b.   "force equals mass times acceleration."

    (c.) "for every force there is an opposing force of equal value."

    d.   a measure of inertia.

Hint __D__   3. With a policy of exclusive market coverage, a manufacturer

    a.   expands the availability of a product.

    (b.) restricts the availability of a product.

    c.   seeks multiple retail outlets.

    d.   advertises in low-circulation magazines.

Hint __E__   4. *True or false?* __T__ Too much thyroxin can often result in tenseness and agitation.

Hint __A and C__   5. Charismatic authority is based on

    a.   law.

    b.   established behavior.

    (c.) belief in the extraordinary personal qualities of the ruler.

    d.   religious beliefs.

Hint _E and F_   6. Schizophrenics labeled *paranoid*
   a. always display "waxy flexibility."
   (b) usually fear that they are being persecuted.
   c. are invariably the children of schizophrenics.
   d. always display multiple personalities.

Hint _A_   7. Prohibition
   a. was supported mainly by urban dwellers.
   b. caused a decrease in crime.
   c. was an unqualified success.
   (d) failed because of widespread violations, an upsurge in crime, and inadequate enforcement.

Hint _E_   8. *True or false?* _T_ A charged cloud may cause an induced charge in the earth below it.

Hint _A_   9. A covalent bond is
   (a) a bond between two atoms made up of a shared pair of electrons.
   b. impossible in organic compounds.
   c. an extremely unstable chemical bond.
   d. the basis of all inorganic compounds.

Hint _F_   10. *True or false?* _F_ The only factors influencing the decision of the United States to enter World War I were economic ones.

Taking Essay Exams

Taking Essay Exams: In Real Life

Read the profile that follows. Then ask yourself these questions:

- When Rod first started college, what did he consistently do that caused him to lose points on tests?
- According to Rod, there is a question that a student should keep in mind throughout a course in order to prepare for essay exams. What is that question?

Student Profile: Rod Sutton

By the time he was permanently expelled from his junior high school in Newark, New Jersey, Rod Sutton had been suspended fifty-two times. His troubled public-school career ended when the 190-pound youngster got into a shoving match with a teacher who was encouraging him to move along to class.

Amazingly, Rod is now a committed seventh-grade teacher at an inner-city school in Philadelphia. In his previous position as an elementary teacher in Camden, New Jersey, he designed an exciting program which provided positive direction to at-risk boys. He is married, a graduate student, a homeowner, and the father of two treasured children.

The road that led Rod from expulsion to a career as a respected educator took him to St. Benedict's School, a Catholic boys' school in Newark, and on to Franklin and Marshall College in Lancaster, Pennsylvania. It was not a straight path: two weeks after enrolling at St. Benedict's, he got into a violent chair-throwing fight with another student

Continued

that shattered windows and, Rod believed, his chances for remaining at the school. But the compassionate response from the headmaster—he handed Rod a broom and dustpan, told him to clean up the mess, and never mentioned the incident again—had a powerful effect on Rod. He determined that he was going to succeed in school.

And succeeded he has. Since then—first as a student, next as a teacher, and now as a mentor to less experienced instructors—Rod has learned more about *how* to learn than most of us will ever know.

Rod talks about taking essay exams with the same passion that he brings to all subjects concerning education. He is eager to share his hard-earned knowledge with those it will benefit. "There are two keys to taking essay exams," he says. "The first sounds obvious, but it trips up many students. I know it tripped me up. That is the need to read the questions *carefully,* to understand *exactly* what is being asked. When I was first in college, I was constantly getting tests back with points off and comments like, 'You answered only part of the question,' or 'Good point, but that's not really what was asked.' I slowly, painfully realized that all my wonderful ideas didn't matter if I didn't answer precisely what had been asked."

Key number two, says Rod, "is to anticipate just what *is* going to be asked, so that you can focus your preparation for the exam." If that sounds like mind reading, Rod points out that the task isn't really that mysterious. The way he explains it, it's all a matter of putting yourself in the instructor's shoes. "People don't become teachers just because they want to follow a curriculum," he says. "They become teachers because they want to pass on a particular worldview, a particular way of looking at things. The trick is to identify that worldview. As you take the course, keep asking yourself, 'What are the *major ideas* this instructor wants us to take away from this class?' Chances are those ideas will be the focus of the essay questions."

Continued

For example, Rod describes two European history courses he took in college. "In one, the professor constantly referred to the competition between Spain, England, and France. For every event that occurred, he'd point out how those three countries were struggling for the upper hand. It became obvious that if we took nothing else away from that course, the instructor wanted us to understand the importance of that competition. It would have been amazing if that theme *hadn't* been the focus of the final essay exam—and it was.

"In the other history course, the focus was entirely different. The instructor looked at every event from the point of view of 'What was the effect on the common person?' And *that* was the focus of the final essay test."

Anticipate the probable questions. Read the questions carefully. It's part of the technique that has carried Rod Sutton on his long journey from school failure to outstanding success.

Essay exams are perhaps the most common type of writing you will do in school. They include one or more questions to which you must respond in detail, writing your answers in a clear, well-organized manner. Many students have trouble with essay exams because they do not realize there is a sequence to follow that will help them do well on such tests. Here are five steps you should master if you want to write effective exam essays:

1 Anticipate probable questions.
2 Prepare and memorize an informal outline answer for each question.
3 Look at the exam carefully and do several things.
4 Prepare a brief, informal outline before answering an essay question.
5 Write a clear, well-organized essay.

Each step will be explained and illustrated on the pages that follow.

Step 1: Anticipate Probable Questions

Because exam time is limited, the instructor can give you only a few questions to answer. He or she will reasonably focus on questions dealing with the most important areas of the subject. You can probably guess most of them.

Go through your class notes with a colored pen and mark those areas where your instructor has spent a good deal of time. The more time spent on any one area, the better the chance you'll get an essay question on it. If the instructor spent a week talking about the importance of the carbon molecule, about the advantages of capitalism, or about key early figures in the development of psychology as a science, you can reasonably expect that you will get a question on the emphasized area.

In both your class notes and your textbooks, pay special attention to definitions and examples and to basic lists of items (enumerations). Enumerations in particular are often the key to essay questions. For instance, if your instructor spoke at length about the causes of the Great Depression, or about the long-range effects of water pollution, or about the advantages of capitalism, you should probably expect a question such as "What were the causes of the Great Depression?" or "What are the wide-range effects of water pollution?" or "What are the advantages of capitalism?"

If your instructor has given you study guides, look for probable essay questions there. (Some instructors choose their essay questions from among those listed in a study guide.) For clues to essay questions, look at any short quizzes that you may have been given. Finally, consider very carefully any review that the instructor provides. Always write down such reviews—your instructor has often made up the test or is making it up at the time of the review and is likely to give you valuable hints about the test. Take advantage of them! Note also that if the instructor does not offer to provide a review, do not hesitate to *ask* for one in a friendly way. Essay questions are likely to come from areas the instructor may mention.

- *Complete the following sentence:* Very often you can predict essay questions,

  for they usually concern the most ___*important*___ areas of a subject.

Step 2: Prepare and Memorize an Informal Outline Answer for Each Question

Write out each question you have made up and, under it, list the main points to be discussed. Put important supporting information in parentheses after each main point. You now have an informal outline that you can go on to memorize.

If you have spelling problems, make up a list of words you might have to spell in writing your answers. For example, if you are having a psychology test on the principles of learning, you might want to study such terms as *conditioning, reinforcement, Pavlov, reflex, stimulus,* and so on.

An Illustration of Step 2: One class was given a day to prepare for an essay exam on the note-taking hints on pages 43–51. The students were told that the question would be, "Describe seven helpful hints for taking classroom notes." One student, Tony, made up the following outline answer for the question:

Hints to remember when taking class notes:

1   *Read [text] in advance (understand more, take better notes)*
2   *[Signals of] importance (defs. + enumerations, emphasis words, repeats, tone of voice, blackboard)*
3   *Write [connections] between ideas (need for full understanding; also, previews + reviews)*
4   *Written [record] of class (80% forgetting in 2 weeks)*
5   *[Outline] form (main points at margin, skip line)*
6   *[Discussion] notes (may not cover later main ideas that arise)*
7   *[Review] soon after class (gaps, organization)*

TSCRODR (Tom Smothers's cat ran outside dressing room)

Activity

Complete this explanation of what Tony did to prepare for the essay question.

First, Tony wrote down the heading and then numbered the seven hints under it. Also, in parentheses beside each point he added ___*supporting material*___. Then he picked out and circled a key ___*word*___ in each hint, and underneath his outline he wrote down the first ___*letter*___ of each key word. Tony then used the first letter in each key word to make up a catchphrase that he could easily remember. Finally, he ___*tested*___ himself over and over until he could recall all seven of the words that the first letters stood for. He also made sure that each word he remembered truly stood for an ___*idea*___ in his mind and that he recalled much of the supporting material that went with each idea.

Step 3: Look at the Exam Carefully and Do Several Things

1 Get an overview of the exam by reading *all* the questions on the test.

2 Note the direction words (*compare, illustrate, list,* and so on) for each question. Be sure to write the kind of answer that each question requires. For example, if a question says "illustrate," do not "compare." The list on the following page will help clarify the distinctions among various direction words. Notice that, ordinarily, you are not asked for your opinion. Instead, essay questions ask you to give back information you have learned about a given topic.

3 Budget your time. Write in the margin the number of minutes you should spend for each essay. For example, if you have three essays worth an equal number of points and a one-hour time limit, figure twenty minutes for each one. Make sure you are not left with only a couple of minutes to do a major essay.

4 Start with the easiest question. Getting a good answer down on paper will help build up your confidence and momentum. Number your answers plainly so that your instructor will know which question you answered first.

An Illustration of Step 3: When Tony received the exam, he circled the direction word *describe,* which meant that he should explain in detail each of the seven hints. He also jotted a 30 in the margin when the instructor said that students would have a half hour to write the answer.

Activity

Complete the short matching quiz below. It will help you review the meanings of some of the direction words shown in the box.

1. List __b__   a. Tell in detail about something.

2. Contrast __d__   b. Give a series of points and number them 1, 2, 3 . . .

3. Define __e__   c. State briefly the important points.

4. Summarize __c__   d. Show differences between two things.

5. Describe __a__   e. Give the formal meaning of a term.

Direction Words Used in Essay Questions

Compare	Show similarities between things.
Contrast	Show differences between things.
Criticize	Give the positive and negative points of a subject as well as evidence for these positions.
Define	Give the formal meaning of a term.
Describe	Tell in detail about something.
Diagram	Make a drawing and label it.
Discuss	Give details and, if relevant, the positive and negative points of a subject as well as evidence for these positions.
Enumerate	List points and number them 1, 2, 3 . . .
Evaluate	Give the positive and negative points of a subject as well as your judgment about which outweighs the other and why.
Illustrate	Explain by giving examples.
Interpret	Explain the meaning of something.
Justify	Give reasons for something.
List	Give a series of points and number them 1, 2, 3 . . .
Outline	Give the main points and important secondary points. Put main points at the margin and indent secondary points under the main points. Relationships may also be described with symbols, as follows:

    1. _____

        a. _____

        b. _____

    2. _____

Prove	Show to be true by giving facts or reasons.
Relate	Show connections among things.
State	Give the main points.
Summarize	Give a condensed account of the main points.
Trace	Describe the development or history of a subject.

Step 4: Prepare a Brief, Informal Outline before Answering an Essay Question

Use the margin of the examination or a separate piece of scratch paper to jot down quickly, as they occur to you, the main points you want to discuss in each answer. Then decide in what order you want to present these points in your response. Put *1* in front of the first item, *2* beside the second item, and so on. You now have an informal outline to guide you as you answer your essay question.

If there is a question on the exam that is similar to the questions you anticipated and outlined at home, quickly write down the catchphrase that calls back the content of the outline. Below the catchphrase, write the key words represented by each letter in the catchphrase. The key words, in turn, will remind you of the concepts they represent. If you have prepared properly, this step will take only a minute or so, and you will have before you the guide you need to write a focused, supported, organized answer.

An Illustration of Step 4: Tony immediately wrote down his catchphrase "Tom Smothers's cat ran outside dressing room." He next jotted down the first letters in his catchphrase and then the key words that went with each letter. He then filled in several key details. At that point, he was ready to write his actual essay answer.

Here is what Tony's brief outline looked like:

Tom Smothers's cat ran outside dressing room

T Text—read in advance

S Signals (defs. + enumerations, repeats, voice, emphasis words)

C Connections between ideas

R Record of the class (80% forgotten in 2 weeks)

O Outline

D Discussion notes

R Review after class

Step 5: Write A Clear, Well-Organized Essay

If you have followed the suggestions to this point, you have done all the preliminary work needed to write an effective essay. Be sure not to wreck your chances of getting a good grade by writing carelessly. Instead, as you prepare your response, keep in mind the principles of good writing: unity, support, organization, and clear, error-free sentences.

First, start your essay with a sentence that clearly states what it will be about. Then make sure that everything in your essay relates to your opening statement.

Second, though you must obviously take time limitations into account, provide as much support as possible for each of your main points.

Third, use transitions to guide your reader through your answer. Words such as *first, next, then, however,* and *finally* make it easy for the reader to follow your train of thought.

Last, leave time to proofread your essay for sentence-skills mistakes you may have made while you concentrated on writing your answer. Look for illegible words; for words omitted, miswritten, or misspelled (if possible, bring a dictionary with you); for awkward phrasings or misplaced punctuation marks; for whatever else may prevent the reader from understanding your thoughts. Cross out any mistakes and make your corrections neatly above the errors. If you want to change or add to some point, insert an asterisk at the appropriate spot, put another asterisk at the bottom of the page, and add the corrected or additional material there.

An Illustration of Step 5: Read through Tony's answer, on the following page, and then do the activity below.

Activity

The following sentences comment on Tony's essay. Fill in the missing word or words in each case.

1. Tony begins with a sentence that clearly signals what his paper _is about_. Always begin with such a clear signal!

2. Notice the various _corrections_ that Tony made when writing and proofreading his paper. He crossed out awkward phrasings and miswritten words; he used his _dictionary_ after he had finished the essay to correct misspelled words; he used insertion signs (∧) to add omitted words; and he used an asterisk to add omitted details.

3. The transition words that Tony used to guide his reader, and himself, through the seven points of his answer include

First	Also	Second
Next	A fourth hint	Another hint
A sixth hint	Finally	

The seven hints that follow are helpful to remember when taking classroom notes. ~~he~~ First, read the textbook in advance. This way you should understand more of the material given in class. Also, you may be able to organize your notes better. ~~A~~ Second, be ready for signals of importance. These ~~un~~ include definitions and enumerations, emphasis words ("the chief cause . . ."), the teacher's tone of voice.* Next, write down the connections between ideas so that you will be able to tie together and fully understand your ideas later. Write down any ~~previous~~ previews or reviews the teacher gives as well. A fourth hint is ~~a written~~ to make sure you get a written record of the class. This must be done because in only ~~too~~ two weeks we forget 80% of what we hear. In added time we ~~about~~ forget just about everything. Another hint is to try to outline notes when you can. Keep the main points at the margin and indent supporting ~~info below~~ information under main points. Also use white space to show when the instructor has moved from one topic to another. A sixth hint is to keep taking notes during discussion periods. Important ideas may come up here that the instructor will not come back to later. Finally, review your notes soon after class, when you still remember enough to add to the ~~matri~~ material. You can also make the organization clearer to yourself, if necessary.

*and everything the instructor puts on the board.

Practice in Preparing for and Taking Essay Exams

Activity 1

Evaluate your present skills in preparing for and taking essay tests. Put a check mark beside each of the following steps that you already practice. Then put a check mark beside those steps that you plan to practice. Leave a space blank if you do not plan to follow a particular point.

Answers will vary.

Now   Plan
Do   to Do

____ ____   1. List ten or so probable questions.

____ ____   2. Prepare a good outline answer for each question and memorize the outline.

3. Look at the exam carefully and do the following:

____ ____   a.   Read *all* the questions.

____ ____   b.   Note direction words.

____ ____   c.   Start with the easiest question.

____ ____   4. Outline an answer before writing it.

5. Write a well-organized answer by doing the following:

____ ____   a.   Have a main-idea sentence.

____ ____   b.   Use transitions throughout the answer.

____ ____   c.   Write complete sentences.

____ ____   d.   Proofread the paper for omitted words, miswritten words, unclear phrasing, punctuation problems, and misspellings.

Activity 2

The student paragraph that follows was written in response to the essay question "Describe seven helpful hints to remember when taking classroom notes." On separate paper, rewrite the paragraph, expanding and correcting it. Begin with a clear opening statement, use transitions throughout your answer, and make sure that each point and the supporting details for that point are clearly presented.

An expanded version of this paragraph appears in the Instructor's Manual.

	One of the first things is to be in class. Attending class is often the chief to
	doing well in a course. Read your text book to help notetaking. Always write
	down examples they are good for you and can help you very much. Remember
	that forgetting sets it almost immediate. In two week we forget 80% of what
	we hear. Always try to review your notes after class still fresh in your mind.
	Next, the connections between ideas—label PREVIEW or REVIEW. Last,
	notes at the end of a class are important.

Activity 3

Spend a half hour getting ready to write a one-paragraph essay on the question "Describe seven steps you can take to improve your memory." (Refer to pages 210–218.) Prepare for the test by following the advice given in step 2 on page 246.

Activity 4

Prepare five questions you might be expected to answer on an essay exam in one of your courses. Make up an outline answer for each of the five questions. Memorize one of the outlines, using the technique of repeated self-testing (see page 212). Finally, write a full essay answer, in complete sentences, to one of the questions. Your instructor may ask you to hand in your five outlines and the essay.

Using the Library
and the Internet

This chapter will show you how to use the library and its:

- Main desk
- Catalog
- Book stacks
- Periodicals indexes
- Periodicals area
- Online databases

In addition, this chapter will teach you how to use the Internet to:

- Find books on your subject
- Find articles on your subject

Using the Library and the Internet: In Real Life

Read the profile that follows. Then ask yourself these questions:

- What lesson did Shannon learn when she typed the search term "drugs" into an Internet search engine?
- For what purpose does Shannon use her college library, rather than the Internet?

Student Profile: Shannon Moore

As a middle-school student in Indiana, Shannon Moore was introduced to the personal computer. It was a source of fun for her. "We played games like 'Oregon Trail' on it," she remembers.

Continued

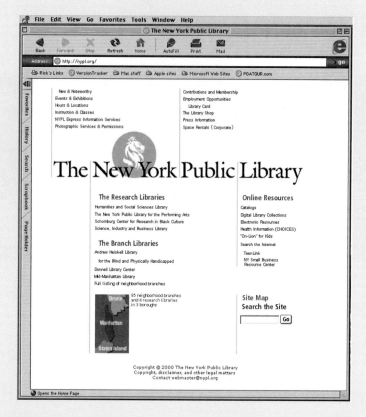

In high school, Shannon enjoyed the computer as well. She used it to send e-mail to her friends, goof around in America Online chat rooms, and keep up with the plotlines of her favorite TV shows.

Gradually Shannon's use of the computer deepened. When she became friends with a student from India, she began using the computer to learn more about that country. A lifelong desire to visit Ireland led her to read about it online.

When Shannon was a senior in high school, she began to see the computer as a serious research tool. "I wanted to write a paper about drug use in America," she recalls, "so I thought I'd do some of my research on the Internet instead of in the library."

Her first research attempts were discouraging. "I went to Yahoo! (a popular Internet search engine) and typed in the search terms 'drugs' and 'drugs in America.' I got about 90 million hits in return. I was overwhelmed! How was I going to know what to use?

Continued

"But gradually I figured out how to narrow my topic. For instance, if I typed in 'cocaine use in America' or 'statistics about alcohol abuse' I got back a more manageable number of results."

Shannon, now a sophomore majoring in psychology at Middle Tennessee State University, has become a more sophisticated Internet researcher. She has also figured out how to use the Internet to complement her traditional library research.

"I use the library to research books that I might want to use," says Shannon. "The library catalog is online, so I can actually do most of that from my computer too, and then go to the library knowing exactly what I'm looking for. But for looking up statistics or magazine or journal articles, I find the Internet faster to use and more up-to-date than the college library."

The two great challenges of using the Internet, says Shannon, are these:

"One—there's just *too much* information available," she says. "It's hard to narrow down your search to a manageable size.

"And the second problem is reliability. Is the information you read on the Internet for real? You have to realize that a ten-year-old can sit down and create a website. You can't necessarily trust information you read online in the same way you can trust something you read in the newspaper."

This chapter provides the basic information you need to use your college library with confidence. It also describes the basic steps you should follow in researching a topic. You will learn that for most research topics there are two basic steps you should take:

1 Find books on your topic.
2 Find articles on your topic.

You will learn, too, that while using the library is the traditional way of doing such research, a home computer with an online service and Internet access now enables you to investigate any topic quickly and easily.

Most students seem to know that libraries provide study space, word-processing facilities, and copying machines. They are also aware of a library's reading area, which contains recent magazines and newspapers. But the true heart of a library is the following: a *main desk,* the library's *catalog or catalogs of holdings, book stacks,* and the *periodicals storage area.* Each of these will be discussed on the pages that follow. Next you will learn about computer online databases. Doing research on the Internet will then be described in a separate section.

Using the Library

Main Desk

The main desk is usually located in a central spot. Check at the main desk to see if there is a brochure that describes the layout and services of the library. You might also ask if the library staff provides tours of the library. If not, explore your library to find each of the areas described below.

Activity   Answers will vary.

Make up a floor plan of your college library. Label the main desk, catalog or catalogs, book stacks, and periodicals area.

Library Catalog

The *library catalog* will be your starting point for almost any research project. A *catalog* is a list of all the holdings in the library. It may still be an actual card catalog: a file of cards alphabetically arranged in drawers. But most libraries have computerized their book files. You can access a computerized book file on computer terminals located at different spots in the library. Many local and college libraries now make their book files available online, so you may be able to check their book holdings on your home computer.

Finding a Book—Author, Title, and Subject:
Whether you search through an actual file of cards, use a computer terminal, or visit your library's holdings online, it is important for you to know that there are three ways to look up a book. You can look it up according to *author, title,* or *subject.* For example, suppose you wanted to see if the library has the book *Raising Cain: Protecting the Emotional Life of Boys*, by Dan Kindlon and Michael Thompson. You could check for the book in any of three ways:

1 You could do a *title* search and look it up under *R* for *Raising.* Note that you always look up a book under the first word in the title, excluding the words *A, An,* or *The.*

2 You could do an *author* search and look it up under *K* for *Kindlon.* An author is always listed under his or her last name. When a book has two or more authors, look for the name of the author listed first.

3 If you know the subject that the book deals with—in this case, "boys, psychology"—you could do a *subject* search and look it up under *b* for *boys.* Then, within the listings for *boys*, you'd look under *p* for *psychology.*

In most libraries, card catalogs have been replaced with computerized book files. If you want to look for the author of a book, the computer may instruct you to type "A=" (for "Author") and then the name of the author you wish to find—in this case, "Dan Kindlon." You may have to press the Enter/Return key for the computer to begin its search.

After a second or two, a screen may appear showing a numbered list of all the books written by that author. You may have to type the number that matches the title you are looking for and then press the Enter/Return key. Something like the following may then appear on your screen.

Author:	Kindlon, Daniel J., Michael Thompson.
Title:	Raising Cain: Protecting the Emotional Life of Boys
Publisher:	New York: Ballantine Books, 2000
Subjects:	1. Boys—Psychology. 2. Emotions in children. 3. Emotions in adolescence. 4. Sex roles in children. 5. Masculinity.
Call Number:	305.23 K577
Material:	Book
Location:	Glenside Public Library
Status:	Checked Out

In addition to telling you the publisher (Ballantine Books) and year of publication (2000), the entry also gives you the *call number*—where to find the book in the library.

A computer will give you the same basic information that is available on a catalog card, but it can do more as well. For instance, if the computerized catalog is part of a network of libraries, you may learn which branch or location has the book. You may find out if the book is checked out or available. If the book is not at your library but is available at another location, you can probably ask a librarian to arrange for an interlibrary loan.

Using Subject Headings to Research a Topic: Generally, if you are looking for a particular book, it is easier to search by *author* or *title*. But if you want to find more than one book about the same topic, you should search by *subject*. Searching by subject has these advantages:

1 It will give you a list of books on a particular topic. For example, if you typed "S" (for *Subject*) and then "boys," a screen might come up showing twelve different titles.

2 In addition, it may list other headings under which you might find related books about the topic.

3 The *Subjects* section will also give you specific subject headings within your topic, making it easier for you to narrow your topic.

• In the catalog card shown above, how many subject headings are listed that might help you find books that are specifically about emotions? _____2_____

The *Subjects* section, then, can be extremely helpful when you are researching a topic. There are three points to remember here: (1) Start researching a topic by using the subjects section of the catalog. (2) Look at the book titles as well; they sometimes suggest specific directions in which you might develop a paper. (3) Keep trying to narrow your topic. Chances are that you will be asked to do a paper of about five to fifteen pages. You do not want to choose a topic so broad that covering it would require writing an entire book. Instead, you want to come up with a limited topic that can be dealt with adequately in a relatively short paper.

Activity

Part A: Answer the following questions about your library's catalog.

1. Is your library's catalog an actual file of cards in a drawer, or is it computerized?
   Answers will vary.

2. What are the three ways of looking up a book in the library?
   a. By author   b. By title   c. By subject

3. Which type of catalog search will help you research and limit a topic?
   By subject

Part B: Use your library's catalog to answer the following questions.

1. What is the title of one book by Alan Keyes?
   Answers will vary. One example: Our Character, Our Future: Reclaiming America's Moral Destiny.

2. What is the title of one book by Julia Alvarez?
   Answers will vary. One example, How the Garcia Girls Lost Their Accents.

3. Who is the author of *The Cider House Rules*? (Remember to look up the title under *Cider*, not *The*.)
   John Irving

4. Who is the author of *Ordinary People*?

   Judith Guest

5. List two books dealing with the subject of water pollution, and note their authors.

   a. _Answers will vary. Examples: Acid Rain, Sally Morgan;_

   b. _The Late, Great Lakes: An Environmental History, William Ashworth._

6. List two books dealing with the subject of Fidel Castro, and note their authors.

   a. _Answers will vary. Examples: Fidel: A Critical Portrait, Tad Szulc;_

   b. _Guerrilla Prince: The Untold Story of Fidel Castro, Georgie Anne Geyer._

7. Look up a book titled *How It Feels to Be Adopted* or *The Elements of Style* or *The Greatest Generation* and give the following information: Answers will vary.

	Examples:	Adopted	Style	Generation
a.	Author	Jill Krementz	William Strunk and E. B. White	Tom Brokaw
b.	Publisher	Knopf	Macmillan	Random House
c.	Date of publication	1982	1999 (4/e)*	1998
d.	Call number	362.7 KRE	808 STR	940.548 B
e.	Subject headings	Adoption	English language-Rhetoric	World War II

   *Earlier editions: 1959, 1972, 1979

8. Look up a book written by Dr. Laura Schlessinger or Calvin Trillin or Stephen Hawking and give the following information: Answers will vary. Examples:

		Schlessinger	Trillin	Hawking
a.	Author	How Could You Do That?	Family Man	A Brief History of Time
b.	Publisher	HarperCollins	Farrar Straus Giroux	Bantam
c.	Date of publication	1996	1998	1988
d.	Call number	170.44 S	814 T	523.1 H
e.	Subject headings	Character, Courage, Conscience	Child rearing, Family life	Cosmology

   Note: Dewey Decimal call numbers are shown.

Book Stacks

Book stacks are library shelves where books are arranged according to their call numbers. The *call number* identifies one specific book, just as a social security number helps identify one specific person. It always appears in the catalog entry for any book. It is also printed on the spine of the book.

If your library has *open stacks* (ones that you are permitted to enter), follow these steps to find a book. Suppose you are looking for the book *The Autobiography of Malcolm X*, which has the call number E185 / 97 / 15 / A3 in the Library of Congress system. (Libraries using the Dewey Decimal system have call letters made up entirely of numbers rather than letters and numbers. However, you use the same basic method to locate a book.) First you go to the section of the stacks that holds the E's. After that, you look for the 185s. After that, you look for E185 / 97 / 15 / A3, and you have the book.

If your library has *closed stacks* (ones you are not permitted to enter), you will have to write down the title, author, and call number on a slip of paper called a request form. You'll then give the form to a library staff person, who will locate the book and bring it to you.

Activity

Use the book stacks to answer one of the following sets of questions. Choose the questions that relate to the system of classifying books used by your library.

Library of Congress System (Letters and Numbers)

1. Books in the BF21–BF204 area deal with
    a. biology.
    b. sociology.
    c. psychology.
    d. theology.

2. Books in the GC1–GC1581 area deal with
    a. folklore.
    b. oceanography.
    c. archeology.
    d. recreation.

3. Books in the PR502–PR610 area deal with
    a. poetry.
    b. drama.
    c. novels.
    d. essays.

4. Books in the LC37–LC44 area deal with
    a. home schooling.
    b. boarding schools.
    c. history of education.
    d. kindergartens.

Dewey Decimal System (Numbers)

1. Books in the 615 area deal with
   a. music.
   b. medicine.
   c. sports.
   d. sewing.

2. Books in the 799 area deal with
   a. hunting.
   b. skiing.
   c. fishing.
   d. tennis.

3. Books in the 929.1 area deal with
   a. genealogy.
   b. astronomy.
   c. language.
   d. pets.

4. Books in the 331.4 area deal with
   a. computer systems.
   b. religious groups.
   c. ancient Greece.
   d. working women.

Periodicals

Periodicals (from the word *periodic*, which means "at regular intervals") are magazines, journals, and newspapers. Periodicals often contain more recent or more specialized information about a subject than you will find in a book. It is important, then, to check periodicals as well as books when you are doing research.

The library's catalog lists the periodicals that it holds, as well as its books. To find articles in these periodicals, however, you will need to use a *periodicals index*. Three indexes widely used in libraries are *Readers' Guide to Periodical Literature*, *Magazine Index Plus*, and *EBSCOhost*.

Readers' Guide to Periodical Literature: The old-fashioned way to do research is to use the familiar green volumes of the *Readers' Guide*, found in just about every library. They list articles published in more than two hundred popular magazines, such as *Newsweek, Sports Illustrated, People Weekly, Ebony, Psychology Today, Working Woman,* and *Popular Science.* Articles appear alphabetically under both subject and author. For example, if you wanted to find articles published on the subject of AIDS within a certain time span, you would look under the heading "AIDS."

Here is a typical entry from the *Guide:*

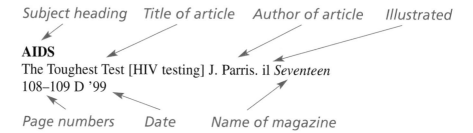

Note the sequence in which information is given about the article:

1 The subject heading—in this case, AIDS.

2 The title of the article—"The Toughest Test." In some cases, there will be bracketed words [like these] after the title that help make clear just what the article is about—in this case, HIV testing.

3 The author (if it is a signed article)—here, J. Parris. The author's first name is always abbreviated.

4 Whether the article has a bibliography (*bibl*) or is illustrated with pictures (*il*). Other abbreviations sometimes used are shown in the front of the *Readers' Guide.*

5 The name of the magazine. A short title like *Seventeen* is not abbreviated, but longer titles are. For example, the magazine *Popular Science* is abbreviated *Pop Sci.* Refer to the list of magazines in the front of the index to identify abbreviations.

6 The page numbers on which the article appears.

7 The date when the article appeared. Dates are abbreviated: for example, *Mr* stands for *March, Ag* for *August, O* for *October.* Other abbreviations are shown in the front of the *Guide.*

Readers' Guide is published in monthly supplements. At the end of a year, a volume is published covering the entire year. You will see in your library large green volumes that say, for instance, *Readers' Guide 1999* or *Readers' Guide 2000.* You will also see the small monthly supplements for the current year.

The drawback of *Readers' Guide* is that it gives you only a list of articles. You must still go to the library's catalog to see if the library actually had copies of the magazines containing those articles. If it does, you must locate the relevant issue of the magazine and then read and take notes on each article or make a copy of it.

Readers' Guide is also available in a much more useful form on CD-ROM (compact disk, read-only memory). Using a computer terminal that accesses the CD-ROM, you can quickly search for articles on a given subject. You do this by typing into a box provided a keyword or phrase (for example, *HIV testing*) that will enable the computer to search for articles on your topic.

Magazine Index Plus: *Magazine Index Plus* is a computerized file that lists articles published over the last several years in about four hundred general-interest magazines. Once again, by sitting at a computer terminal and typing in a keyword or phrase for your subject, you can rapidly locate relevant articles.

EBSCOhost and Others: Many libraries now provide an online computer search service such as *InfoTrac, Dialog,* or *EBSCOhost*. Sitting at a terminal and using *EBSCOhost*, for instance, you will be able to use keywords to quickly search many hundreds of periodicals for full-text articles on your subject. When you find articles that are relevant, you can either print them, using a library printer (libraries may charge you about ten cents a page), or you can e-mail the articles to your home computer and print them at home.

Obviously, online search services and CD-ROM databases are quicker and easier to use than *Readers' Guide to Periodical Literature*. If they are available to you, you should certainly use them to conduct your research.

Activity 1

At this point, you know the two basic steps in researching a topic in the library. What are those steps?

1. Find books on your topic.

2. Find articles on your topic.

Activity 2   *Answers will vary.*

1. Look up a recent article on gambling using one of your library's periodicals indexes, and fill in the following information:

    a.   Name of the index you used_____

    b.   Article title _____

    c.   Author (if given) _____

    d.   Name of magazine _____

    e.   Pages on which article appears _____ Date _____

2. Look up a recent article on home schooling, using one of your library's periodicals indexes, and fill in the following information:

    a.   Name of the index you used_____

    b.   Article title _____

    c.   Author (if given) _____

    d.   Name of magazine _____

    e.   Pages on which article appears _____ Date _____

Specialized Indexes: Once you know how to use the *Readers' Guide* and other general periodical indexes—either in book form, on CD-ROM, or through online databases—you will find it easy to use some of the more specialized indexes in most libraries. Your instructors may expect you to consult one or more of these indexes to obtain more specialized and professional information on a given subject. Here are some helpful ones:

*   *New York Times Index.* This is an index to articles published in the *New York Times*, one of the most respected newspapers in the country. After you look up a subject, you'll find a list of articles published on that topic, with a short summary of each one.

*   *Business Periodicals Index.* The articles here are from over three hundred publications that generally treat a subject in more detail than it would receive in the popular magazines indexed in the *Readers' Guide*. At the same time, the articles are usually not too technical or too hard to read.

*   *Social Sciences Index.* This is an index to articles published by journals in anthropology, environmental science, psychology, and sociology.

*   Other specialized indexes that your library may have include the following:

General

Biography Index

Humanities Index

Speech Index

Art and literature

Art Index

Book Review Index

MLA Index

Music Index

New York Times Book Review Index

Education

Education Index

ERIC

History and political science

Historical Abstracts

Public Affairs Information Service

Philosophy and religion

Religion Index

Sciences

Applied Science and Technology Index

Biological Abstracts

Environment Index

Women's and ethnic studies

Hispanic American Periodicals Index

Index to Periodical Articles by and about Blacks

Women's Resources International

A Note on Other Reference Materials: Every library has a reference area, often close to the place where the *Readers' Guide* (in book form) is located, in which additional reference materials can be found. These include dictionaries, encyclopedias, atlases, yearbooks, almanacs, a subject guide to books in print (this can help in locating books on a particular subject), anthologies of quotations, and the like.

You may also find in the reference area a series of file cabinets called the *pamphlet file*. These cabinets are full of pamphlets, booklets, and newsletters on a multitude of topics. I looked in the *A* drawer of the pamphlet file in my library and found booklets about subjects including abortion, adoption, and animal rights, along with many other topics starting with *A*. At my library, a booklet called "Pamphlet File Subject Headings" lies on top of the file cabinets. If a similar booklet is available in your library, it will quickly tell you if the file includes material on your subject of interest.

Periodicals Area: Unless you have located your articles online, you'll need to go to the periodicals themselves. Libraries keep their periodicals in a special *periodicals area*, sometimes called the *magazine area* or *magazine storage area*. The periodicals indexes may be kept there as well.

Here, you will often find slips of paper called *periodical request forms*. As you locate each magazine and journal article that you would like to look at, fill out a slip, writing down the name and date of this periodical. Include the article title and pages so you'll know where to start reading. Then give the slips to a library staff person working nearby. (Don't hesitate to do this: Helping you obtain the articles you want is part of his or her job.)

Here's what will probably happen next:

- If a magazine that you want is very recent, it may be on the open shelves in the library. The staff member will tell you, and you can find it yourself.

- If the magazine you want is a little older—up to a year or so—it may be kept in a closed area. The staff person will find it and bring it to you.

- Sometimes you'll ask to see an article in a magazine that the library does not carry. You'll then have to plan to use other articles, or go to a larger library. However, most college libraries or large public libraries should have what you need. (Somewhere in this area is probably a list of all the magazines your library subscribes to. Ask a staff person if you would like to see this list.)

- In many cases, especially with older issues, the magazine will be on microfilm or on microfiche. (*Microfilm* is a roll of film on which the articles have been reproduced in greatly reduced size; *microfiche —fiche* is pronounced "feesh"— is the same thing, but it is on easily handled sheets of film rather than on a roll. In both cases, the film is viewed on a special machine.) The staff person will bring you the film or fiche. If you ask, he or she will show you how to load this material onto the machine nearby.

Activity   Answers will vary.

1. Put a check mark next to each of the following periodicals indexes that your library has available:

___ *Readers' Guide* (in book form)

___ *Readers' Guide* (on CD-ROM)

___ *Magazine Index Plus*

___ *InfoTrac*

___ *Dialog*

___ *EBSCOhost*

___ *Social Sciences Index* (in book form)

___ *Social Sciences Index* (CD-ROM)

2. What are three other periodicals indexes in your library besides the ones mentioned in question 1?

_____

3. Use the *Readers' Guide* or another general periodicals index to find an article about the Supreme Court that was published in the last three months. Write down the name of the magazine and the date on a slip of paper and give it to a library staff person.

    Is the article available in the actual magazine? _____ If so, is it on an open shelf, or is it in a closed area where a staff person must bring it to you?

_____

4. Use the *Readers' Guide* or another general magazine index to find an article on the Supreme Court that was published more than one year ago. Write down the name of the magazine and the date on a slip of paper and give it to a library staff person. Is the article available in the actual magazine, or is it available on microfiche or microfilm?

_____

5. Check off what your library has:

    ___ Microfiche machine   ___ with a print option

    ___ Microfilm machine   ___ with a print option

Using the Internet

Few modern developments have affected our daily lives as much as the computer revolution. One dramatic part of that revolution is the *Internet*—a giant network that connects computers at tens of thousands of educational, scientific, government, and commercial agencies around the world. Existing within the Internet is the *World Wide Web* (usually called just "the Web"), a global information system which got its name because countless individual websites contain *links* to other sites, forming a kind of web.

To use the Internet, you need a personal computer with a *modem*—a device that sends and receives electronic data over a telephone line for the cost of a local telephone call. You also need to subscribe to an online service provider such as America Online or Earthlink. If you have an online service as well as a printer for your computer, you can do a good deal of your research for a paper at home. As you would in a library, you should proceed by searching for books and articles on your topic.

Before you begin searching the Internet on your own, though, take the time to learn if your local or school library is online. If it is, visit its online address to find out exactly what sources and databases it has available. You may be able to do all your research using the online resources available through your library. But if your library's resources are limited, you can turn on your own to the Internet to search for material on any topic, as explained on the pages that follow.

Find Books on Your Topic

To find current books on your topic, go online and type the address of one of the large commercial online booksellers:

Amazon at *www.amazon.com*
Barnes and Noble at *www.bn.com*

The search facilities of both Amazon and Barnes and Noble are free and easy to use, and you are under no obligation to buy books from them.

In some cases, you may not have to type *www.* (for *World Wide Web*); the program you are using will provide it for you. Note, by the way, that *.com* in the three addresses above is an abbreviation for *commercial*, referring to a business. Other common abbreviations you'll see at the end of Internet addresses (known as URLs) are *.edu*, which indicates an educational institution; *.org*, a nonprofit organization; *.gov*, for government agencies; and *.net*, for Internet service providers and some businesses.

Use the "Browse Subjects" Box: Once you go to an online book site, use the "Browse Subjects" box to locate categories where you might find books on your general subject. (If you first arrive at a general "Welcome" page, click on "Books" to begin your search). For example, if your assignment, like Shannon's at the beginning of the chapter, is to find books on the topic of drug abuse, you would notice that one of the subject listings within Amazon.com is "Health, Mind and Body." Click on that, and you would get a list of subcategories, including "Recovery." If you then clicked on that subcategory, you would see even smaller and more specialized categories, one of which is "Substance Abuse." Click on that, and a list of recent books on substance abuse appears, with a brief description of the contents of each book. You could then click on each title for information about that book, often including helpful reviewers' comments. All this browsing and searching could be done very quickly and would help you decide which books were worth reading.

Use the "Keyword" Box: If you were assigned, for example, a paper on some aspect of the Vietnam War, you would type in the words "Vietnam War" in the key-word search box provided on the opening screen. You would then get a list of books on that subject. Just looking at the list could help you narrow your subject and decide on a specific topic to develop. For instance, one student typed in the keywords "Vietnam War" and got back a list of 1,800 books on the subject. Browsing through that list gave her the idea of writing about the antiwar movement. She typed "Vietnam antiwar movement" and got back a list of nine titles. After looking at information about those books, she was able to decide on a limited topic for her paper.

A Note on the Library of Congress: To find additional books on your topic, you can also visit the Library of Congress website (*www.loc.gov*). The Library of Congress, in Washington, D. C., has copies of all books published in the United States. Its online catalog contains about twelve million entries. You can browse this catalog by subject or search by keywords. The search form permits you to check just those books that interest you and then print the list or e-mail it to yourself. Clicking on "Full Record" provides a book's publication information and call numbers. You can then try to find the book in your college library or through an interlibrary loan.

A Few Other Points to Note: Remember that at any point, you can use your printer to quickly print out information presented on the screen. (The student planning a paper on the Vietnam War could, for example, print out a list of the nine books on the antiwar movement, along with sheets of information about individual books.) You could then take those printouts to the library and use them as a "shopping list" for the books you want to borrow. You may even be able to visit your library online to find out in advance whether it owns the books you want. Also, if you have time and money and some of the books are in paperback, you may want to purchase them from the online bookstore. Such stores typically ship books in just two or three days.

Find Articles on Your Topic

There are many online sources that will help you find articles on your subject. Following are descriptions of some of them.

A Resource for Magazines and Newspaper Articles:

A very helpful online research resource that you can use at home is Electric Library, available at *www.elibrary.com.* You may get a free thirty-day trial subscription, or you'll be able to enroll on a monthly basis at a limited cost. Electric Library contains millions of newspaper and magazine articles as well as many thousands of book chapters and television and radio transcripts. After typing in one or more keywords, you'll get long lists of articles that may relate to your subject. When you then click on a given title, the full text of the article appears. If it fits your needs, you can print it out right away on your printer. Very easily, then, you can research a full range of magazine and newspaper articles.

For example, one student using Electric Library knew he wanted to write something about whales. He typed in the keyword "whales" and indicated that he wanted to see thirty documents. He also indicated he wanted to see results from books, magazines, and newspapers. (In Electric Library, the user can choose the number of results he or she wishes to see, as well as the sources of those results.) Browsing through the thirty documents he received helped him to narrow his topic. He decided to write on efforts to save the whale from extinction. Unsure which keywords to use, he first typed in "save the whales" and then "whales and extinction." Both key phrases worked: he received a variety of newspaper and magazine articles and book excerpts that dealt specifically with whales in danger of extinction and the efforts to save them.

Search Engines:

A *search engine* is a tool that combs the Web looking for sites or articles that match your research needs. You start a search by typing in one or more keywords that tell the engine what to look for and then clicking a "search" button. The search engine then provides you with a list of "hits," or links, to web-sites or articles containing your keywords. Links typically show up as an underlined word or phrase that is different in color from the other type on the page. When you click on a link, you are automatically transported to that related site or article.

One search engine that is excellent and particularly easy to use is Google, at *www.google.com,* whose opening screen is shown below.

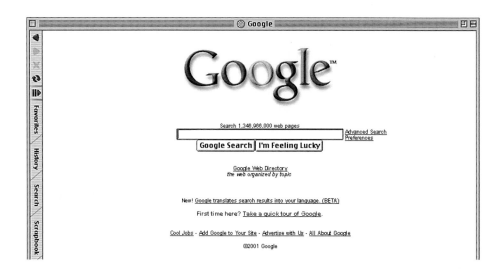

Other good search engines are AltaVista, at *www.altavista.com*; Excite, at *www.excite.com*; and Northern Light, at *www.northernlight.com.*

When the student doing a paper on saving whales from extinction, for example, first typed the word "whales" into the Google search box, he got back a list of 394,000 hits! He realized he had to narrow his search, so he typed "whales and extinction" and got back 15,900 matches. When he added "save" and "efforts" to his keywords, he got 2,090 matches.

Challenges in Searching: As you have seen from the experience of the students in our examples, the challenge with searches is usually getting too much information rather than too little. Most search engines include a *help* feature that will provide you with suggestions on ways to limit your search. Also, be aware that search engines vary widely in the quality of the results they produce. The Web now consists of more than a billion pages, and even the best search engine has catalogued only a fraction of those. It's a good idea to try the same search on several engines. You are likely to find one that produces more useful results than the others.

A word of caution: The fact that you find a document on the Internet does not necessarily mean that it is reliable. Remember that anyone with a bit of computer know-how can post information there. The person whose page you have accessed could easily be a junior-high-school student, someone selling a product, or even a crackpot. As you do research on the Internet, make sure the author of any document you use has credentials that qualify him or her to provide unbiased information on the topic.

Search Directories: *Yahoo!* is one of most popular and user-friendly search resources on the Web. Its address is *www.yahoo.com.* Like Google, AltaVista, Lycos, and Northern Light, Yahoo! provides a search engine. But it may be even more valuable to you as a *search directory*, for it organizes websites by category.

If, for instance, you wanted to do a research paper on some aspect of television, you could click on the category "News and Media" on the opening page (also called the *home page*) of Yahoo! Doing so would bring up several dozen subcategories, including "Magazines," "Newspapers," "Photojournalism," and "Television." Clicking on "Television" brings you a long list of subcategories beginning with "Actors and Actresses" and ending with "Web Directories," with titles including "Cable TV," "History," "Nielsen Ratings" and "Theme Songs" in between. A search directory like Yahoo! is a great place to start your research. It excels in helping you move from a broad, general idea of what you want to research to a narrow, specific topic.

Also worth checking out is Refdesk.com (*www.Refdesk.com),* whose name is its address. In a clear, easy-to-use format, Refdesk.com links you to daily newspapers from all over the world as well as online versions of many popular magazines. It also offers access to encyclopedias, dictionaries, and many specialized research tools, as well as links to several hundred online search engines.

A Final Note—Saving Your Favorite Places: When you find an online site that you like and will want to visit again, you should *bookmark* it. A bookmark allows you to return to the site with one click of the mouse, rather than having to remember and type in its address. America Online users click on a small red heart appearing in the upper right-hand corner of the screen, which adds the site to their Favorite Places list. Other online services have similar methods for bookmarking favorite sites.

Practice in Using the Library and the Internet

Activity

Use your library or the Internet to research a subject that interests you. Select one of the following areas, or (with your instructor's permission) an area of your own choice:

Parkinson's disease	Computer viruses
Adoptions by gay couples	Credit-card scams
Best job prospects today	Animals nearing extinction
Book banning in schools	Animal rights movement

Home schooling	Hate crimes
Greenhouse effect	Drug treatment programs for adolescents
Animal cloning	
Pro-choice movement today	Fertility drugs
Pro-life movement today	Witchcraft today
Attention deficit disorder	New treatments for AIDS
Pollution of drinking water	Mind-body medicine
Foster parent system	Habitat for Humanity
Cremation	Fathers' rights movement
Road rage	Drug treatment programs
Prenatal care	New research in spinal-cord injuries
Acid rain	Nongraded schools
Video games and violence	Buying versus leasing a car
New remedies for allergies	Ethical aspects of hunting
Censorship on the Internet	Low-carbohydrates diets
New prison reforms	Recent consumer frauds
Teenage fathers	Stress reduction in the workplace
Keeping schools safe	Global warming
New treatments for insomnia	Everyday addictions
Organ donation	Toxic waste disposal
Child abuse	Self-help groups
School uniforms	Drug testing in the workplace
Maintaining a good credit rating	Date rape
Alzheimer's disease	Heroes for today
Holistic healing	Preserving wilderness areas
Adoptions: Open records or closed?	Surrogate mothers
Crack-addicted babies	

Research the topic first through a subject search in your library's catalog or that of an online source. Then research the topic through a periodicals index (print or online) or an online search engine or search directory. On a separate sheet of paper, provide the following information:

Answers will vary.

1. The topic

2. Three books that either cover the topic directly or at least in some way touch on the topic. Include these items:

Author

Title

Place of publication

Publisher

Date of publication

3. Three articles on the topic published in 1998 or later. Include these items:

Title of article

Author (if given)

Title of magazine

Date

Page(s) (if given)

4. Finally, include a paragraph describing just how you went about researching your topic. In addition, include a photocopy or printout of one of the three articles.

Writing A Research Paper

This chapter divides the process of writing a research paper into seven steps:

1 Select your topic.
2 Limit your topic.
3 Take notes on your topic.
4 Plan your paper.
5 Keep a record of your sources.
6 Write your paper.
7 Document your sources.

We'll look at each of those steps and then consider a sample paper.

Steps in Writing a Research Paper

Step 1: Select Your Topic

Select a topic that you can readily research. First of all, determine whether there are at least three books available on your general subject. You can find out by doing a *subject* search of your library's catalog, as described on page 259, and seeing what's available. If you have access to a computer with online service, visit one of the major online bookstores, as described on page 270, and do the same.

For example, when Charles Rivera, author of the sample paper "Birth Order," began his research, he knew he wanted to write something about children's personalities. He decided to start browsing at an online bookstore, amazon.com.

"First I went to 'search books' and tried searching by subject," Charles said, "but when I typed in the subject 'personality,' I got back more than 4,000 titles! That was a bit discouraging. But then I noticed Amazon had an option called 'browse by subject.' Clicking on that brought up a bunch of categories, including one called 'Parenting and Families.' Within that were a lot of subcategories, including 'Family Relationships.' That sounded like a good bet, so I clicked on it and got a long list of books, including many about why children grow up the way they do. Another category, 'Health, Mind, and Fitness,' also had lots of books about psychology, child development, and other topics I was interested in. When I'd find a book that sounded good, I'd click on the title and get specific information about it. What was really helpful was the comments about the book from reviewers or ordinary people who'd read it. Those saved me a lot of time—by reading them, I knew whether or not the book would be of interest to me."

Charles then took a "shopping list" of books he was interested in to his local library. He found that four of them were available on the shelves there. When he discovered that one title he particularly wanted was not in the library, a librarian told him she could get it for him through an interlibrary loan. In addition, he purchased a paperback edition of one book through the online store.

To find articles on your topic, go to the *Readers' Guide* or another periodicals index, an online search service, or a CD-ROM database available at your library, as described on page 265, to see if you find five or more articles on your subject. Using the CD-ROM index *Magazine Index Plus*, Charles typed in the search term "children's personalities" and found more than 300 recent articles on his topic. The online search service Electric Library also yielded plenty of newspaper, magazine, and journal articles on children's personalities.

If, like Charles, you find that both books and articles are at hand, you are ready to begin. Otherwise, you may have to choose another topic. You cannot write a paper on a topic for which research materials are not readily available.

Step 2: Limit Your Topic

As you read books and articles about your topic, consider how you can limit that topic. A successful research paper is one that develops a *limited* topic. Your topic should be narrow and deep rather than broad and shallow.

Charles, for instance, soon realized that "children's personalities" was far too broad a topic to try to tackle in a brief research paper. He spent several days skimming through the material he'd found in order to refine his topic. As he read, he considered a number of narrow topics: children with attention deficit disorder, children with autism, and children growing up with gay parents. Finally, though, he settled on his narrow topic: the effects of birth order on children's personalities.

Also as you read, think about what the *purpose* of your paper will be. Most papers have one of two purposes. In the first kind, you try to make and defend a point of some kind. Charles, for instance, wanted to make the point that birth order has certain predictable effects on children. Another student might present evidence that playing violent video games makes children more violent in real life. A second purpose might be to simply present information about a particular subject. For example, you might be asked to do a paper about the latest findings about how memories are created and stored.

Do not expect to decide instantly on your limited topic or purpose. Chances are good that you won't discover either of those until you've done quite a bit of reading.

Step 3: Take Notes on Your Topic

Take notes as you continue to read about your topic. Take notes on whatever seems relevant to or significant for your limited topic. Write your notes on sheets of loose-leaf paper, on 4- by 6-inch or 5- by 8-inch note cards, or in a computer file. Your notes can be in the form of *direct quotations* or *summaries in your own words*, or a *combination* of the two.

Here is a copy of notes that one student took while doing a paper on diet and cholesterol:

Dr. Anderson's oat-bran experiment
James Anderson, M.D., U. of Kentucky School of Medicine. Began eating oat-bran porridge for breakfast. "My blood cholesterol level plummeted 110 points in five weeks, from 285 to 175. I was the first human as far as I know to eat oat bran to lower cholesterol. . . . This is what we need to fight heart disease."

Carper, 40.

Keep the following points in mind when taking notes:

- Write on only one side of a sheet or card, so that it will be easy to refer to your notes as you are writing your paper.
- Put only one kind of information, from one source, on any one sheet or card or in any one file. For example, the preceding sample has information on only one idea from one source (a book by Jean Carper).
- Identify the source and page number under your notes.
- Put quotation marks around all material which you take word for word from any source.
- Include at the top of the sheet, card, or file a heading that summarizes the content of the notes. This heading will help you organize the different kinds of information that you gather on your topic.

A Note on Plagiarism: If you do not document information that is not your own, you will be stealing. The formal term is *plagiarizing*—using someone else's work as your own, whether you borrow a single idea, a sentence, or an entire essay. Plagiarism is a direct violation of the academic code; if you pass someone else's work off as your own, you risk being failed or even expelled. Also, plagiarism undermines the money, time, and energy you have spent in school, cheating you out of an education.

With the accessibility of the Internet—especially websites targeting students—come new temptations to plagiarize. But remember that those sites are just as accessible to your instructor as they are to you. Many writing instructors are aware of these Internet "resources" and can spot "recycled" work.

If you use another person's material, *you must acknowledge your source.* When you cite a source properly, you give credit where it is due, you provide your readers with a way to locate the original material on their own, and you demonstrate that your work is carefully researched.

Step 4: Plan Your Paper

Plan the paper, making clear your point and your support for the point. As you take notes, think constantly about the specific content and organization of your paper. Begin making decisions about the exact information you will present and the arrangement of that information. Prepare a basic outline of your paper that shows both its point and the areas of support for that point.

Point: _____

Support: (1) _____

         (2) _____

         (3) _____

See if you can divide your support into at least three different areas.

Step 5: Keep a Record of Your Sources

Keep a written record of all your sources. On a sheet of paper or in a computer file, record the information below about every source. You will need this information later, because you are expected to place at the end of your paper a list of all the sources you consulted.

For Books	*For Magazines*
Author	Author (if given)
Title	Title of article
Place of publication	Title of magazine
Publisher	Volume number (if available)
Date of publication	Page numbers
Call number	Date

For Online Sources

URL (online address)—for example:
  http://www.time.com/time/magazine/articles/0,3266,48109,00.html

Author

Title of document

Title of the periodical

Volume number, issue number, or other identifying information

Date of publication

Date you accessed the material

Note: Some online sources will provide all the above information; others will not. Write down as much of the information as is available.

Step 6: Write Your Paper

After you have finished your reading and note-taking, you should be ready to proceed with the writing of your paper. Make a final outline and use it as a guide to write the first draft of your paper. Your paper should have five basic parts:

- *Title page*, which should contain the title of the paper, your name, and the date. Center all these on the sheet.

- *Opening page*, which should include an introductory paragraph that (1) attracts the reader's interest, (2) states the point of the paper, and (3) gives the plan of development that the paper will follow.

- *Body* of the paper, which will develop all the areas of support for your point.

- *Concluding paragraph*, which may consist of a summary, a final thought, or both. Note that your final thought might be in the form of a recommendation.

- *Final page*, with an alphabetical list of "Works Cited," which should include all the sources you have used.

The sample paper beginning on page 285 includes explanatory labels that show how one student handled the above requirements.

Step 7: Document Your Sources

Within your paper, you must cite your sources. Following are instructions to follow as you do your own citations. In addition, the sample paper that begins on page 285 includes citations that you may refer to as models.

Citations within a Paper: When you cite a source, you must mention the name of the author and the relevant page number. If you name the author within your sentence, provide only the page number in parentheses following the sentence. If you do not name the author, however, provide both the author's last name and the page number in parentheses. Here are two examples:

Author Named within the Sentence

A writer for Redbook magazine, Andrea Thompson, says something similar. "It's often amazing to parents of twosomes how their children, living in the same house, breathing the same air, seem to come from separate planets" (177).

Author Not Named within the Sentence

Of the first twenty-three American astronauts sent into outer space, twenty-one were firstborns and the other two were only children (Leman 17).

If you are using more than one work by the same author, include a shortened version of the title inside the parentheses. For example, suppose you were citing two books written by Kevin Leman: *Bringing Up Kids Without Tearing Them Down* and *The New Birth Order Book*. This is how you would cite those two books:

(Leman, Kids, 57).
(Leman, Birth Order, 125).

Use the abbreviation *qtd. in* when citing a quotation from another source. For example, a quotation from Lorie M. Sutter on page 2 of the paper is from an article not by Sutter but by Cynthia Burns. The citation is handled this way:

In the online magazine <u>Kids</u>, the researcher Lorie M. Sutter of Ohio State University says that "middle children are good mediators and have superior cooperation skills. Since they don't have their parents all to themselves or get their own way, they learn to negotiate and compromise. Middle children often make excellent managers and leaders because of these skills" (qtd. in Burns).

Citations at the End of a Paper: The final page of your paper should be a list of "Works Cited." In that list, you include all the sources you actually used in the paper. (Don't list any other sources, no matter how many you read.) Look at the "Works Cited" page after the model research paper (page 292) and note the following points:

• The list is organized alphabetically, according to the authors' last names.
• Entries are double-spaced, with no extra space between entries.
• After the first line of each entry, there is a half-inch indentation for each additional line.

Model Entries for a List of "Works Cited": Here is a list of some of the most common sources cited in student research papers. Use these entries as a guide when you prepare your own list.

Book by One Author
Preston, Diana. <u>The Boxer Rebellion</u>. New York: Walker, 2000.

Two or More Entries by Same Author
—. <u>A First Rate Tragedy</u>. New York: Houghton Mifflin, 1998.

If you cite two or more books by the same author (in the example above, a second book by Diana Preston is cited), do not repeat the author's name. Instead, begin the line with three hyphens followed by a period. Arrange works by the same author alphabetically by title. Ignore the words *A*, *An*, and *The* as you alphabetize.

Book by Two or More Authors
Piven, Joshua, and David Borgenicht. <u>The Worst-Case Scenario Survival Handbook</u>. San Francisco: Chronicle Books, 1999.

For a book with two or more authors, give all the authors' names but reverse only the first name.

Magazine Article

Gray, Paul. "Coming of Age in Chaos." <u>Time</u> 10 July 2000: 104.

Write the date of the issue as follows: day, month, and year. The final number or numbers refer to the page or pages on which the article appears.

Newspaper Article

"Foster Parents Soon May Spank." <u>Washington Times</u> 3 July 2000: C1.

If an article is signed, begin the entry with the author's name, listed last name first, as you would for a book. If it is unsigned, begin with the article's title. The final letter and number refer to section C, page 1.

Online Source in a Reference Database

"Cloning." <u>Compton's Encyclopedia Online</u>. Vers. 3.0 1998. 15 Feb. 1999 <http://www.comptons.com/ceo99-cgi/article?'fastweb?getdoc+ view comptons+A+2055+2++Cloning'>.

The first date tells when the material was electronically published, updated, or posted (if that date is available). The second date refers to when the student researcher accessed the material.

Online Article

Cummins, H.J. "Rethinking Ritalin." <u>Minneapolis Tribune</u> 11 Jan. 1999. 3 March 1999. <http://www.elibrary.com/getdoc.cgi?id=168925987x127y 65202w0&Form=EN&Button=MEM&OIDS=0Q001D009&pubname= Minneapolis_Star_Tribune&puburl=http~C~~S~~S~www.startribune.com &querydocid=879930@library_i&dtype=0 ~0&dinst=>.

The first date refers to the issue of the publication in which the article appeared; the second date refers to the day when the student researcher accessed the material.

Sample Research Paper

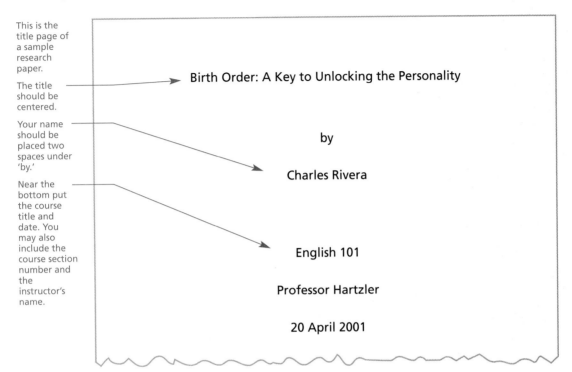

This is the title page of a sample research paper.

The title should be centered.

Your name should be placed two spaces under 'by.'

Near the bottom put the course title and date. You may also include the course section number and the instructor's name.

Birth Order: A Key to Unlocking the Personality

by

Charles Rivera

English 101

Professor Hartzler

20 April 2001

Rivera 1

Three spaces

Three-paragraph introduction, ending in a thesis statement

Double-space between lines of text. Leave a one-inch margin all the way around the page. Your name and page number should be typed one-half inch from the top of the page.

Birth Order: A Key to Unlocking the Personality

In most households in which there are two or more children, this kind of thing happens occasionally. A mother stares at her children and wonders: How can one be so peaceful while the other loves to argue? Why does one want meat at every meal while the other one is a vegetarian? The parent finally says, "I give up. You two can't be related. There must have been a mix-up at the hospital."

Rivera 2

A writer for <u>Redbook</u> magazine, Andrea Thompson, says something similar: "It's often amazing to parents of twosomes how their children, living in the same house, breathing the same air, seem to come from separate planets" (177).

It's puzzling how kids who are closely related and grow up together can be so different from each other. But according to a number of researchers, there is an answer. That answer is the order in which the children were born. Cynthia Burns, writing for the online magazine <u>Kids</u>, says, "Birth order may offer clues about why your children—and you—tend to be the way they are. Through your position in the family, you develop a pattern of behavior, a way of thinking and an emotional response." Meri Wallace, author of <u>Birth Order Blues: How Parents Can Help Their Children Meet the Challenges of Birth Order</u>, says that "birth order is, in fact, one major aspect of a child's experience that has a powerful impact upon his emotions and his development" (7).

Actually, people have always assumed that birth order had some effect on people's personality. Wallace points out, "In the Bible, Cain, who was a firstborn son, was so jealous because his younger brother Abel was the preferred child that he actually killed him. Joseph's older brothers were so tormented by the fact that their father, Jacob, gave their younger brother the famous coat of many colors and generally seemed to favor him that they planned to kill him; instead, they later ended up selling him into slavery." (6).

But now modern researchers are trying to figure out exactly how birth order affects us. This paper will look at three positions within the family: the firstborn, the middle child (any child between the first and the last), and the lastborn. It will also discuss "functional firstborns,"

Because the author is named in the text, her name does not appear in the parentheses.

No page number given, since it is an online source.

The first time you mention an author, provide his or her full name and the title of the work you are citing.

Rivera 3

children who were not actually born first in the family but who act as if they were. This can happen, for instance, if a child's older siblings died young, leaving the younger child to fill the firstborn position.

Firstborn children seem to share a number of characteristics. Here are some statistics about them. Kevin Leman, author of <u>The New Birth Order Book: Why You Are the Way You Are</u>, points out that of the first forty-one U.S. presidents, twenty-three of them—56 percent—were firstborns or functional firstborns (16). Frank J. Sulloway, author of <u>Born to Rebel: Birth Order, Family Dynamics, and Creative Lives</u>, makes a similar point. He writes that firstborns "are overrepresented among political leaders, including American presidents and British prime ministers" (69). Firstborn children stand out in other fields as well. Of the first twenty-three American astronauts sent into outer space, twenty-one were firstborns and the other two were only children (Leman 17). Jobs requiring high levels of motivation and ambition, such as the sciences, medicine, and the law, attract many firstborns.

It seems that firstborns "have special affinity for power and success," says an article in the <u>Independent</u> of Bangladesh. Leman, a therapist who uses birth order theories to counsel his clients, says that firstborns "tend to be conscientious, well-organized, serious, goal oriented, achieving, people pleasers, and believers in authority. And when you add other signs of firstborns and onlies, such as perfectionist, reliable, list maker, critical, scholarly, self-sacrificing, conservative, supporter of law and order, legalistic, and self-reliant, you can see why firstborns usually get more ink in the write-ups of life. Firstborns are often the achievers because they are driven toward success and stardom in their given fields" (78).

No page number given, since read online.

Rivera 4

So firstborns tend to be confident, self-disciplined people who work hard to succeed. They like jobs where they can work on their own, instead of as part of a team. They tend to follow the rules, instead of wanting to change traditional ways of doing things. Why do firstborns develop like this? The answer seems to be the firstborns' relationship with their parents. Parents pay a great deal of attention to their first baby. After younger children are born, parents often treat the oldest child almost as a third parent instead of as a child. As they grow up, children look at the next oldest people in the family for their examples of how to behave. Firstborn children look at the parents. Leman says, "With only parents (and maybe grandparents, aunts, and uncles) for role models, they [firstborns] naturally take on more grown-up characteristics. That is why firstborns are often serious and not much for surprises. They prefer to know what's happening and when: they thrive on being in control, on time, and organized—all characteristics that stand adults in good stead" (88). Sulloway also says, "It is natural for firstborns to identify more strongly with power and authority [than later-born children do]. They arrive first within the family and employ their superior size and strength to defend their special status. Relative to their younger siblings, firstborns are more assertive, socially dominant, ambitious, jealous of their status, and defensive" (xiv).

The words "jealous" and "defensive" show that not everything about being a firstborn is good. While they are hardworking and ambitious, firstborns can also be bossy, hard to get along with, and full of "anger and vengefulness" (Sulloway 70). Because they grow up feeling a strong need to satisfy their parents' expectations, firstborns can be anxious people who worry that they are never

The word in brackets indicates that that word did not appear in the original text. The author of the paper inserted it in order to clarify the meaning of the sentence.

Rivera 5

good enough. Leman calls them "discouraged perfectionists" (94). They can develop unrealistic expectations for themselves and others, and that can cause problems for them. "Only children suffer the most from this problem," he writes, "but first borns are not far behind" (137).

What are middle children, the ones born somewhere between the first child and the baby, like? "Middle children," according to a 1998 Newsday article, "are flexible, diplomatic, generous, social and competitive. They often function as peacemakers" (Burby). In the online magazine Kids, researcher Lorie M. Sutter of the Ohio State University says that "middle children are good mediators and have superior cooperation skills. Since they don't have their parents all to themselves or get their own way, they learn to negotiate and compromise. Middle children often make excellent managers and leaders because of these skills" (qtd. in Burns).

Middle children are very different from firstborns. According to Kevin Leman, the middle child looks at the firstborn in the family and "branches off" (151) in another direction. As a result, the middle child is most difficult to describe. He or she cannot be really understood without knowing what the firstborn child is like. "A general conclusion of all research studies done on birth order is that second borns will probably be somewhat the opposite of first borns." (152)

Many middle children complain that they are overlooked, even "neglected" (Burns). According to a study cited by Burns, they really do have the fewest pictures in the family photo albums. They're the ones who wear mostly hand-me-downs. As a result, middle children can feel left out within the family. Because their parents don't draw them out as they do the oldest child, says Leman, middle children often have a hard

No page number is given, since the source is a one-page article.

Rivera 6

time sharing their emotions (162). They are the most likely to hang out with a group of friends instead of their families, because they feel a sense of belonging with their friends that they don't have at home. As adults, they are the most likely to move far away from the family home (Leman 153–154). But being a middle child has its advantages too. Because parents aren't putting so much pressure on them, middle children can grow up more relaxed and less anxious than firstborns. Middle children can feel more free to just be themselves than live up to family expecations. They typically have more friends than firstborns and have the lowest rate of divorce (Leman 154). Middle children may be the most well-adjusted of all birth orders. In the words of Cynthia Burns, "A good description of middle children is balanced."

People have lots of opinions about "the baby's" position in the family. Everyone's heard remarks like these: "Youngest children are spoiled." "They're brats." "They go through life expecting to get their own way." "They're irresponsible." These sayings have some truth in them, according to birth order research. But they don't tell the whole story about youngest children.

Like firstborn children, lastborns do get special treatment in the family. Their older brothers and sisters act as extra "parents," giving them extra attention and praising their cute baby ways. They also tend to help the "baby" out a lot, even when their help isn't really needed. Lastborns realize that being "little" and "helpless" gets them lots of family attention, so they may hang on to those behaviors longer than necessary.

According to Kevin Leman, who is the baby of his own family, lastborns are "outgoing charmers" who can also be "rebellious, temperamental, manipulative, spoiled, impatient, and impetuous"

Common knowledge is not documented.

Rivera 7

Cited material extends from one page to another, so both page numbers are given.

(168–169). Lastborns often grow up to be the family entertainer. Leman points out that many well-known comedians are lastborns, including Eddie Murphy, Goldie Hawn, Billy Crystal, Joan Rivers, Leslie Nielsen, Danny DeVito, Drew Carey, Jim Carrey, Steve Martin, and Chevy Chase. (18)

Youngest children often make the best salespeople because they are so people-oriented. They are "outgoing and great at motivating other people" (Sutter, qtd. in Burns). All in all, research shows that lastborns are entertaining, affectionate, and lovable but can also tend to be self-centered, undisciplined, and too emotional.

Conclusion

People's personalities are influenced by more than their birth order. But birth order is a powerful influence that helps explain what makes people tick. Every position in the family has its strengths and its challenges. Understanding our position in our own families can help us understand our place in the larger world.

Works cited
should be
double-
spaced. Titles
of books,
magazines,
and the like
should be
underlined.
Titles of
articles should
be enclosed in
quotation
marks.

Works Cited

Burby, Liza N. "Birth Order: Should the Theories Make a Difference in

the Way You Parent?" Newsday 17 Jan. 1998, B1.

Burne, Jerome. "Relative Rebels." Independent [Bangladesh] 5 June

1996, E6-7. 17 April 2000 <http://www.elibrary.com/getdoc.cgi?id

=162866805x127y53725w0&OIDS=0Q006D001&Form=RL&pub

name=Independent&puburl=http~c~~s~~s~wor.independent>.

Burns, Cynthia. "Parenting by Birth Order." Kids 17 April 2000

<http://family.go.com/Features/family_1998_07/kids/kids78order/k

ids78order.html> N. pag.

Leman, Kevin. The New Birth Order Book: Why You Are the Way You

Are. Grand Rapids: Fleming H. Revell, 1998.

Sulloway, Frank J. Born to Rebel: Birth Order, Family Dynamics, and

Creative Lives. New York: Pantheon, 1996.

Thompson, Andrea. "How Many Kids Should You Have?" Redbook

Sept. 1997: 177–178.

Wallace, Meri. Birth Order Blues: How Parents Can Help Their Children

Meet the Challenges of Birth Order. New York: Owl, 1999.

If a
publication
date for the
online source
is available,
list it
immediately
after the
source's title.
Then list the
date you
accessed it
online. If a
publication
date is not
available, as in
this case, still
provide the
date you
accessed it.

'N.pag.'
indicates that
no page
numbers were
available.

Part Three

A Brief Guide to Important Word Skills

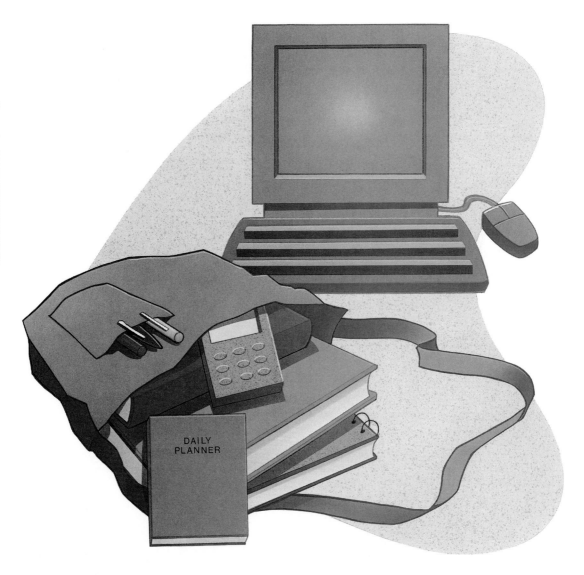

Preview

In Part Three, the chapter "Understanding Word Parts" will help you review sixty of the most common word parts used in forming English words. The explanations and activities in "Using the Dictionary" will explain the most important kinds of information about words that a good dictionary provides. "Word Pronunciation" describes several basic rules you can use to pronounce unfamiliar words, including the specialized terms you will meet in your different college subjects. "Spelling Improvement" suggests techniques and provides spelling rules and a word list to make you a better speller. Finally, "Vocabulary Development" explains three approaches that can increase your word power.

An Important Note

Part Three provides a concise review of important word skills, some of which you may remember from earlier school years. All these skills can be supplemented by the extensive materials usually available in college learning centers. With the basic information in Part Three, you can quickly brush up on word skills or refer to them when needed. You can also discover which skills you may want to work on at greater length in your school learning center.

Understanding
Word Parts

This chapter will help you recognize and spell:

- Twenty common prefixes
- Twenty common suffixes
- Twenty common roots

One way to improve your pronunciation and spelling of words is to increase your understanding of common word parts. These word parts—also known as *prefixes, suffixes,* and *roots*—are building blocks used in forming many English words. The activities in this section will give you practice with sixty of the most common word parts. Working with them will help your spelling, for you will realize how many words are made up of short, often-recurring, easily spelled parts. Increasing your awareness of basic word parts will also help you to pronounce many unfamiliar words and, at times, to unlock their meanings.

Prefixes

A *prefix* is a word part added to the beginning of a word. The prefix changes the meaning of some words to their opposites. For example, when the prefix *in-* is added to *justice,* the result is *injustice;* when the prefix *mis-* is added to *understanding,* the result is *misunderstanding.* A prefix need not change a word to its opposite, but it will alter the meaning of the word in some way. For instance, when the prefix *re-* (meaning *again*) is added to *view,* the result is *review,* which means *to view again.* When the prefix *mal-* (meaning *bad*) is added to *practice,* the result is *malpractice,* which means *bad* or *improper practice.*

Activity

In the following activities, look carefully at the meanings of the two prefixes presented. Then add the appropriate prefix to the base word (the word in *italics*) in each of the five sentences *a* to *e.* Write your word in the space provided. You will know which prefix to choose in each case if you consider both its meaning and the general meaning of the sentence. Next, you'll see two groups of words separated by a slash line (/). In the spaces provided, write a sentence using one word from the first group and a sentence using one word from the second group.

1   mono   alone, one
2   trans   across, over, beyond

    Example: After the full moon rose, Lawrence Talbott was (. . . *formed*) _transformed_ into the Wolfman.

a.   The interpreter (. . . *lated*) _translated_ the speech into sign language.

b.   She hates the student in her psychology course who tries to (. . . *polize*) _monopolize_ the class discussion time.

c.   As soon as they (. . . *ported*) _transported_ the stolen cigarettes across the state line, they were guilty of a federal offense.

d.   A (. . . *poly*) _monopoly_ occurs when one person or group exerts unfair control over others.

e.   Some people use yoga or other Eastern disciplines to try to (. . . *cend*) _transcend_ everyday cares and difficulties.

Now write a sentence using one of the words before the slash line and a sentence using one of the words that appear after the slash.

monologue   monotony   mononucleosis / transplant   transition   transparent
Answers will vary.

3   dis   apart, away
4   pre   before

a.   She (. . . *cards*) _discards_ friends the way some people throw away clothing they no longer want.

b.   I would be frightened to go to a fortune-teller if he or she truly had the ability to (. . . *dict*) _predict_ the future.

c.   The speaker was (. . . *composed*) _discomposed_ by the conversations that went on during his talk.

d.   I sometimes have a tendency to (. . . *judge*) _prejudge_ people; only when I meet them do I find out how biased I've been.

e.   I worry about germs taking over the house if I don't (. . . *infect*) _disinfect_ the bathroom once a week.

disorient dispassionate dissatisfied / presume preliminary prevention

Answers will vary.

_____

_____

5 inter between, among
6 sub   under, below

a. During the halftime (. . . *val*) _____interval_____ at the football game, I ran out to get a pizza.

b. Cold medicines will (. . . *due*) _____subdue_____ a cold, but they won't cure it.

c. She has the bad habit of (. . . *rupting*) _____interrupting_____ people when they are in the midst of making a point.

d. Seeing whether and how (. . . *heads*) _____subheads_____ relate to main heads in a text is an important reading skill.

e. My mother would constantly (. . . *fere*) _____interfere_____ in my relationship with my first girlfriend, who lived next door to us.

interact   interject   intercom   /   subdivide   subvert   submerged

Answers will vary.

_____

_____

7 ex   out
8 mis   badly, wrong

a. In grade school I shunned the pursuit of grades and majored in (. . . *conduct*) _____misconduct_____.

b. Snakes are often (. . . *represented*) _____misrepresented_____ as slimy; in fact, they feel pleasantly dry and cool.

c. If a football player doesn't learn how to (. . . *ecute*) _____execute_____, or carry out, a play properly, he will soon lose his job.

d. One day Mel suddenly realized that he had (. . . *treated*) _____mistreated_____ his children in the same way his father had been unfair to him.

e. When Raid wasn't enough, I called in an (. . . *terminator*) _____exterminator_____ to battle the roaches.

exorcist exhaust exclamation / misspelling mismatch misunderstanding

Answers will vary.

_____

_____

9 con   together, with
10 post   after, following, later

a.   A (. . . *mortem*) _____postmortem_____ examination was not needed to reveal the obvious cause of death: a wooden stake through the heart.

b.   He could hardly walk across the attic floor because of the (. . . *glomeration*) _____conglomeration_____ of items piled there.

c.   His (. . . *operative*) _____postoperative_____ condition was poor, and so he was put in the intensive care unit.

d.   Part of me often wants to (. . . *form*) _____conform_____ to the group; the other part of me wants to follow the beat of my own drummer.

e.   She feels persecuted and believes that everyone is (. . . *spiring*) _____conspiring_____ against her.

congested   concur   conflict   /   postnasal   postpone   postscript

Answers will vary. _____

_____

11 anti   against
12 pro   before; for (in favor of)

a.   The (. . . *posal*) _____proposal_____ to legalize gambling was placed on the state ballot.

b.   Because I had forgotten to put in (. . . *freeze*) _____antifreeze_____, my car's radiator turned into a block of ice one frigid winter morning.

c.   The main purpose of marriage, according to some religions, is (. . . *creation*) _____procreation_____—that is, having children.

d.   Even though the new cold remedy was no more effective than others on the market, millions of dollars were spent to (. . . *mote*) _____promote_____ it.

e.   If an (. . . *dote*) _____antidote_____ is not given within minutes after the bite of a cobra, death is almost a certainty.

antiseptic   antipathy   antithesis   /   proponent   promise   progress

Answers will vary. _____

_____

13 un   not, reverse
14 ad   to, toward

a. The (. . . *hesive*) ____adhesive____ tape stuck to his fingers more than it stuck to the package.

b. Because she finds it difficult to tolerate (. . . *certainty*) ____uncertainty____, she quickly closes her mind on many issues.

c. (. . . *diction*) ____Addiction____ to alcohol or other drugs is a major problem in our country.

d. The dog continued to run around the neighborhood (. . . *restrained*) ____unrestrained____, and so someone decided to call the police.

e. People who feel very depressed are likely to have (. . . *productive*) ____unproductive____ workdays.

unreasonable   unfamiliar   uncompromising   /   address   advise   advocate

Answers will vary.

_____

15 in   not, within
16 extra   more than

a. The school principal showed (. . . *ordinary*) ____extraordinary____ composure when the first grader threw a rock at him.

b. Students who do well in (. . . *curricular*) ____extracurricular____ activities but earn poor grades are mistaking the sideshow for the main event.

c. Because of (. . . *adequate*) ____inadequate____ funds, the school athletic program was canceled.

d. The old father in the play was driven mad by the (. . . *gratitude*) ____ingratitude____ of his daughters.

e. The instructor explained that the class would be run in an (. . . *formal*) ____informal____ way, for she wanted students to be relaxed.

incompetent   inaudible   insatiable   /   extrasensory   extravagance   extramarital

Answers will vary.

_____

17 re   again, back
18 mal   bad

a. In many poor families in Appalachia, you will find children and adults suffering from (. . . *nutrition*) ___malnutrition___ .

b. After her (. . . *covery*) ___recovery___ from a pulled leg muscle, the tennis pro went on to have a great year.

c. The politician was convicted of (. . . *feasance*) ___malfeasance___ in office and was sentenced to a one-week jail term.

d. Most students agree that they should (. . . *view*) ___review___ their notes right after class, but few take the time to do so.

e. Psychologists advise parents to give children (. . . *inforcement*) ___reinforcement___ —compliments and rewards for doing well.

relapse   recount   reflect   /   malpractice   malfunction   maladjusted

___Answers will vary.___

19 com   with, together with
20 de   down, from

a. (. . . *munal*) ___Communal___ living is difficult for someone who feels a strong need for privacy.

b. An entire block of houses had been (. . . *molished*) ___demolished___ in order to build the shopping center.

c. The man who stopped to help us change our flat tire (. . . *meaned*) ___demeaned___ himself afterward by asking for $5.

d. If I did not (. . . *ply*) ___comply___ with my parents' household rules, I would be punished.

e. Homes (. . . *preciated*) ___depreciated___ in value as soon as plans for a nearby airport were publicized.

compatible   combine   companion   /   descend   deplore   detract

___Answers will vary.___

Suffixes

A *suffix* is a word part added to the end of a word. While a suffix may affect a word's meaning slightly, it is more likely to affect how the word is used in a sentence. For instance, when the suffix *-ment* is added to the verb *measure,* the result is the noun *measurement.* When the suffix *-less* is added to *measure,* the result is the adjective *measureless.* Very often, one of several suffixes can be added to a single word. Understanding common suffixes is especially helpful when you are learning new words. If you note the suffixes that can be added to a new word, you will learn not just a single word but perhaps three or four other forms of the word as well.

Activity

In the following activities, decide from the context which suffix in each pair should be added to the base word (the word in *italics*) in sentences *a* to *e.* Then write the entire word in the space provided. Alternative forms of some suffixes are shown in parentheses, but you will not have to use alternative forms to complete the spelling of any of the base words. Next, you'll find two groups of words separated by a slash line (/). In the spaces provided, write a sentence using one word from the first group and a sentence using one word from the second group.

1   ion (tion)
2   less

a. Heartburn and a knotted feeling in the stomach often develop when people are

under a lot of (*tens* . . .) _____tension_____ .

b. The panhandler who everyone thought was (*penni* . . .) _____penniless_____ turned out to have a $50,000 bank account.

c. The dealer I bought the junk car from is a master in the art of (*persuas* . . .)

_____persuasion_____ .

d. One type of (*care* . . .) _____careless_____ driver is the person who neglects to signal before making a turn.

e. The squirrel sat (*motion* . . .) _____motionless_____ on the tree trunk, as if made of stone.

Now write a sentence using one of the words before the slash line and a sentence using one of the words that appear after the slash.

corruption   election   confusion   /   worthless   speechless   restless

_____Answers will vary._____

_____

3   ant (ent)
4   ness

a. Men seem to have more difficulty admitting vulnerability and (*sad* . . .)
    _____sadness_____ than women do.

b. Popeye was (*reluct* . . .) _____reluctant_____ to swallow the spinach, for he
    wanted to give his opponent a fighting chance.

c. He refuses to use (*deodor* . . .) _____deodorant_____ because he believes that
    sweating is a natural process.

d. The storm broke with such (*sudden* . . .) _____suddenness_____ that the floors
    were wet before we had time to shut all the windows.

e. (*Abund* . . .) _____Abundant_____ practice is the best way of mastering a skill.

    apparent   convenient   dependent   /   togetherness   happiness   loneliness
    _____Answers will vary._____

    _____

5   en
6   ize (ise)

a. Some people do not know how to (*memor* . . .) _____memorize_____ material
    efficiently.

b. He saw her eyes (*soft* . . .) _____soften_____ as she greeted him, and he
    realized that she loved him.

c. To (*strength* . . .) _____strengthen_____ and tone her muscles, she began doing
    the Royal Canadian Air Force exercises.

d. The sky began to (*dark* . . .) _____darken_____, the wind picked up, and the
    rain hurtled down.

e. For some people, having children is a way to (*immortal* . . .)
    _____immortalize_____ themselves.

    fasten   weaken   risen   /   theorize   materialize   compromise
    _____Answers will vary._____

    _____

7 age
8 ist

a. Approximately one week after their (*marri . . .*) ___marriage___, they realized they had made a mistake.

b. At one time in this country, people lost their jobs if they were accused of belonging to the (*Commun . . .*) ___Communist___ Party.

c. He was reluctant to go to a medical (*special . . .*) ___specialist___, for he was afraid of the expense.

d. Because the bathtub was not caulked, there was water (*leak . . .*) ___leakage___ onto the floor below.

e. His favorite things to read in the newspaper are the sports and Abby, the advice (*column . . .*) ___columnist___.

overage   breakage   mileage   /   tourist   capitalist   pharmacist
___Answers will vary.___

9 ment
10 ful

a. Many people are demanding reforms in the tax system of our (*govern . . .*) ___government___.

b. My (*forget . . .*) ___forgetful___ brother did not leave me the key to the house, and I was locked out.

c. She felt both nervousness and (*excite . . .*) ___excitement___ when she took her driver's test; her face was flushed and her knees trembled.

d. The ten-year-old girl felt (*grate . . .*) ___grateful___ to her uncle, who spoke to her as though she were an adult, not a little child.

e. As he saw the (*improve . . .*) ___improvement___ in his grades, he began to study more; success bred success.

replacement   establishment   movement   /   helpful   useful   hopeful
___Answers will vary.___

11 ship
12 able (ible)

a. People who are part of an assembly line seldom have pride in their (*workman* . . .) __workmanship__.

b. She is not (*comfort* . . .) __comfortable__ until she takes off her working shoes and clothes and puts on slippers and a bathrobe.

c. Many persons describe their first goal in life as achievement in their work; their second goal is love and (*friend* . . .) __friendship__.

d. More and more companies put their products in plastic bottles, even though plastic is not always (*recycl* . . .) __recyclable__.

e. She never forgot the poverty and (*hard* . . .) __hardship__ her family went through when she was a little girl.

membership apprenticeship leadership / capable noticeable changeable

Answers will vary.

13 ence (ance)
14 ify (fy)

a. She attempted to achieve (*excell* . . .) __excellence__ in whatever she did.

b. He was cooperative and courteous to his demanding boss because he wanted to use him later as a (*refer* . . .) __reference__.

c. Many students are afraid to ask questions to (*clar* . . .) __clarify__ an instructor's point.

d. The landlord was not able to (*just* . . .) __justify__ his neglect of the slum properties that he owned.

e. An animal's (*depend* . . .) __dependence__ on its mother for survival varies from several days to several years.

continuance   acquaintance   assistance   /   verify   notify   rectify

Answers will vary.

15 ate
16 ly

a. There was not enough good topsoil on their lawn for them to (*cultiv . . .*) _____cultivate_____ a healthy crop of grass.

b. I ate my meal too (*quick . . .*) _____quickly_____, and my stomach suffered as a consequence.

c. Education is one means of breaking the vicious circle in which slums (*perpetu . . .*) _____perpetuate_____ more slums.

d. The restaurant waiter (*final . . .*) _____finally_____ served their dinner, but they were so angry about waiting so long that they decided to leave.

e. The television show did not (*gener . . .*) _____generate_____ enough interest to keep him awake.

fortunate   populate   aggravate   /   obviously   apparently   carefully

Answers will vary.

_____

_____

17 ious (ous)
18 or (er)

a. They went to a marriage (*counsel . . .*) _____counselor_____ to try to improve their relationship.

b. He had a troubling dream in which he saw a (*myster . . .*) _____mysterious_____ stranger in a dark robe standing by a lake.

c. The fact that many students don't follow test directions is an example of how we often overlook the (*obv . . .*) _____obvious_____.

d. Ben Franklin was an (*invent . . .*) _____inventor_____, a statesman, a philosopher, and a businessman.

e. After three years as an unemployed (*act . . .*) _____actor_____, I decided on another career.

dangerous   jealous   glamorous   /   builder   teacher   employer

Answers will vary.

_____

_____

19 ism
20 ery (ary)

a. Her (*tomfool* . . .) _____*tomfoolery*_____ in grade school classes kept her from getting good marks.

b. Some people believe that (*terror* . . .) _____*terrorism*_____ in the form of kidnapping deserves the death penalty.

c. For a long time, (*alcohol* . . .) _____*alcoholism*_____ was regarded as a vice rather than a physical disease.

d. It was cold in the (*cemet* . . .) _____*cemetery*_____, so Dracula decided to move his coffin to a Howard Johnson motel.

e. The instructor stopped assigning research projects when she realized that most of her students resorted to (*plagiar* . . .) _____*plagiarism*_____, or stealing, to do their papers.

realism   socialism   baptism   /   imaginary   dictionary   library

Answers will vary.
_____

_____

Roots

A *root* is a basic word part to which prefixes, suffixes, or both are added. For example, to the root word *port* (meaning *carry*), the prefix *trans-* (meaning *across*) could be added; the resulting word, *transport,* means *to carry across.* Various suffixes could also be added, among them *-ed* (*transported*), *-able* (*transportable*), and *-ation* (*transportation*).

Activity

In the following activities, decide from the context which root in each pair should be added to the word part or parts in italics in sentences *a* to *e*. Then write the entire word in the space provided. Some common roots at times change their spelling slightly, especially in the last one or two letters. Alternative spellings of such roots are shown in parentheses. Note, however, that you will not have to use the alternative spellings to complete any of the following sentences.

Next, you'll find two groups of words separated by a slash line (/). In the spaces provided, write a sentence using one word from the first group and a sentence using one word from the second group.

1   duc (duct)   take, lead
2   mit (miss)   send, let go

a. The preface at the beginning of a book often serves as an (*intro . . . tion*) _introduction_, or lead-in, to a subject.

b. Copper wire is an excellent (*con . . . tor*) _conductor_ of electricity.

c. The collection agency warned me that if I did not (*re . . .*) _remit_ my payment, I would be harassed day and night.

d. News is instantly (*trans . . . ted*) _transmitted_ over the Internet.

e. The only decision that the (*com . . . tee*) _committee_ made during the meeting was to call another meeting.

Now write a sentence using one of the words before the slash line and a sentence using one of the words that appear after the slash.

reduce   abduct   conducive   /   submit   missile   commission

Answers will vary.

3   port   carry
4   voc (vok)   call

a. He decided that his (*. . . ation*) _vocation_ in life was to be a plumber, but his guidance counselor wanted him to apply to law school.

b. She is an (*ad . . . ate*) _advocate_ of the death penalty; her husband is not.

c. I am going to buy a (*. . . able*) _portable_ television that I can carry from the living room to the bedroom.

d. (*Re . . . ers*) _Reporters_ channel the news from its source to the general public.

e. She began reading faster when she learned the difference between main ideas and (*sup . . . ing*) _supporting_ details.

export   supporter   transport   /   vocal   revoke   avocation

Answers will vary.

5   tract (trac)   draw
6   auto   self

a. He wore his leather jacket and tight pants, for he wanted to (*at . . .*)
    _____attract_____ girls at the dance.

b. The television, stereo, and phone in her room are such strong (*dis . . . ions*)
    _____distractions_____ that they pull her away from her studies.

c. He loves to read (. . . *biographies*) _____autobiographies_____, for he is curious about
    what other people write about themselves.

d. The Mediterranean design of the console (*de . . . s*) _____detracts_____ from
    the country style in the rest of the room.

e. Because the thirteen American colonies wanted to form their own (. . . *nomous*)
    _____autonomous_____ government, they rebelled against British rule.

attraction   traction   retract   /   automobile   automation   autograph
_____Answers will vary._____

_____

7   path   feeling
8   cept (capt)   take, seize

a. The audience felt an embarrassed (*sym . . . y*) _____sympathy_____ for the
    young comedian who had to continue his performance even though no one
    was laughing.

b. Both political candidates seemed so inferior that many voters were completely
    (*a . . . etic*) _____apathetic_____ about the election.

c. Everyone (*ex . . .*) _____except_____ me seemed to understand the directions
    for the test, so I was afraid to ask the instructor to clarify them.

d. The bad cowboys had a (*re . . . ion*) _____reception_____ waiting for the good
    cowboys—a hail of bullets.

e. The parents were gratified that their own children quickly (*ac . . . ed*)
    _____accepted_____ the foster child they had decided to adopt.

pathos   telepathy   pathetic   /   deception   interception   except
_____Answers will vary._____

_____

9 dict (dic)   say, tell, speak
10 script (scrib)   write

a. The article's vivid (*de . . . ion*) ___description___ of the beauties of Switzerland made her want to visit there.

b. They bought the magazine because it contained an astrologer's (*pre . . . ions*) ___predictions___ for the coming year.

c. The (*manu . . .*) ___manuscript___ was damaged in the mail; fortunately, she had made a Xerox copy.

d. One does not (*contra . . .*) ___contradict___ him, or he will blow up entirely.

e. The (*in . . . ion*) ___inscription___ on the tombstone of Henry David Thoreau is simply "Henry."

diction   indicate   dictator   /   postscript   scripture   subscribe

___Answers will vary.___

_____

11 vers (vert)   turn
12 tang (tact)   touch

a. Children's ideas often get (*. . . led*) ___tangled___ together, and they try to say several things at once.

b. She is a (*. . . atile*) ___versatile___ athlete, able to perform in different sports with ease.

c. The judge dismissed the case for lack of (*. . . ible*) ___tangible___ evidence; everything was hearsay.

d. He had been down on his luck for so long that he felt he deserved a (*re . . . al*) ___reversal___ of fortune.

e. While spending ten hours as a security guard in a lonely warehouse, he does crossword puzzles for (*di . . . ion*) ___diversion___.

reversal   subversive   introvert   /   tangent   tactless   tactics

___Answers will vary.___

_____

13 cess (ced)   go, move, yield
14 sist   stand

a. Almost more than any other quality, (*per . . . ence*) _____persistence_____ is needed for college success.

b. When the infamous Dr. Frankenstein was killed, his (*as . . . ant*) _____assistant_____, Igor, got a job as a medical lab technician.

c. The only part of her grade school days that she enjoyed was (*re . . .*) _____recess_____.

d. With the help of a police escort, the long funeral (*pro . . . ion*) _____procession_____ was able to proceed (*suc . . . fully*) _____successfully_____ through the midday traffic.

e. An expensive paint is likely to be more weather-(*re . . . ant*) _____resistant_____ than a cheap paint would be.

precede   intercession   concede   /   consistent   subsistence   insist

_____Answers will vary._____

_____

15 gress   go
16 pend (pens)   hang, weigh

a. To succeed in many businesses, you must be highly (*ag . . . ive*) _____aggressive_____.

b. The ruby (*. . . ant*) _____pendant_____ around her neck was her mother's.

c. Our instructor has a tendency to go off on (*di . . . ions*) _____digressions_____ from his topic that are interesting but not helpful to us.

d. Because of the (*im . . . ing*) _____impending_____ divorce trial, he was unable to sleep at night.

e. He is thirty-two years old but is still entirely (*de . . . ent*) _____dependent_____ on his mother.

progress   transgress   regression   /   appendix   suspend   pending

_____Answers will vary._____

_____

17 psych   mind
18 vid (vis)   see

a. It was (*e . . . ent*) _____*evident*_____ from the instant replay that the umpire's call had been correct.

b. When she began hearing voices inside her head, she realized she was suffering from a severe (*. . . osis*) _____*psychosis*_____.

c. The teenagers in our family spend much of their time watching the music (*. . . eo*) _____*video*_____ television channel.

d. A neighbor of mine who claims to have (*. . . ic*) _____*psychic*_____ powers has predicted the end of the world on two occasions.

e. Some people try to use pills for body pains that are (*. . . osomatic*) _____*psychosomatic*_____ in origin.

psychology   psychotherapy   psychedelic   /   visual   vision   visibility

Answers will vary.

_____

19 spec (spic)   look
20 graph   write

a. In (*retro . . . t*) _____*retrospect*_____, he realized that his decision to go to college right after high school had been a mistake.

b. She hated her job as a stocking (*in . . . tor*) _____*inspector*_____ at the knitting mill.

c. She believes that (*re . . . t*) _____*respect*_____ is something you buy with money rather than earn with deeds.

d. Some companies insist on giving regular (*poly . . .*) _____*polygraph*_____ tests to check on their employees' honesty.

e. The two essential steps in writing an effective (*para . . .*) _____*paragraph*_____ are to make a point and to support that point.

perspective   spectator   respectable   /   photography   biography   stenographer

Answers will vary.

_____

Practice in Understanding Word Parts

Activity 1

Draw a single line under the prefix and a double line under the suffix in each of the following words:

transparent   antiseptic   replacement

disorient   preliminary   subdivision

exclamation   malpractice   extrasensory

compatible   confusion   conductive

deceptive   reversal   interpretation

Activity 2

Your instructor will give you a spelling test on all the words used in the prefix activities on pages 295–300. You will be expected to spell the *prefix part of the word* correctly and to do your best with the spelling of the rest of the word. (The word will be marked wrong only if the prefix is spelled incorrectly.) Study carefully, then, the spelling of the twenty prefix parts. You will find that knowing the spelling of a prefix will help you considerably in the spelling of an entire word.

Activity 3

The same instructions apply that were given for Activity 2, except that the test will be on the twenty suffixes on pages 301–306.

Activity 4

The same instructions apply that were given for Activity 2, except that the test will be on the twenty roots on pages 306–311.

Using the Dictionary

This chapter will help you use the dictionary to:

- Look up the spelling of words
- Find the syllable divisions in a word
- Pronounce an unfamiliar word
- Obtain other information about words

The dictionary is a valuable tool. To take advantage of it, you need to understand the main kinds of information that a dictionary gives about a word. Look at the information provided for the word *disdain* in the following entry from *The American Heritage Dictionary,* paperback edition.*

Spelling and syllabication   *Pronunciation*   *Parts of speech*

dis•dain (dĭs•dān′) *v.* 1. To show contempt for. 2. To refuse aloofly. —*n.* Mild contempt and aloofness. [< Lat. *dedignari.*] —**dis•dain′ful** *adj.* —**dis•dain′ful•ly** *adv.*

Meanings

Other forms of the word

Spelling

The first bit of information, in the **boldface** (heavy-type) entry itself, is the spelling of *disdain*. At times you may have trouble looking up words that you cannot spell. Be sure to pronounce each syllable in the word carefully and write it down the way you think it is spelled. If you still cannot find it, proceed as follows:

1 Try other vowels. For example, if you think the vowel is *e,* try *a, o, i, u,* and *y.*

2 Try doubling consonants. If you think the letter is one *c,* try *cc;* if one *m,* try *mm;* if one *t,* try *tt;* and so on. On the other hand, if you think the word has double letters, try a single letter.

---

* Dictionary excerpts in this chapter and in the Mastery Tests © 1994 by Houghton Mifflin Company. Reprinted by permission from *The American Heritage Dictionary of the English Language,* Third Paperback Edition.

3 If you think a word has the letter or letter combination in the first column of each group that follows but you can't find the word in the dictionary, try looking at the letter or letters in the second column of each group.

c	k, s	g, j	j, g	s	c, z, sh
er, re	re, er	ie, ei	ei, ie	sh, ch	ch, sh
f	v, ph	k	c, ch	shun	tion, sion
		oo	u	y	i, e

Use your dictionary and the preceding hints to correct the spelling of the following words.

guidence	_guidance_	acomplish	_accomplish_
writting	_writing_	acsept	_accept_
agresive	_aggressive_	enviroment	_environment_
plesent	_pleasant_	particuler	_particular_
akomodate	_accommodate_	conscous	_conscious_
progrem	_program_	artical	_article_
disese	_disease_	nesessary	_necessary_
begining	_beginning_	chalenge	_challenge_

Syllabication

The second bit of information that the dictionary gives, also in the boldface entry, is the syllabication of *disdain*. Note that a dot separates each syllable (or part) in the word. The syllable divisions help you pronounce a word and also show you where to hyphenate a word as needed when writing a paper.

Use your dictionary to mark the syllable divisions in the following words. Also, indicate how many syllables are in each word.

s p a r|k l e   (_2_ syllables)

h y p|n o|t i z e   (_3_ syllables)

e x|o r|c i|s m   (_4_ syllables)

o p|p o r|t u|n i s|t i c   (_5_ syllables)

Pronunciation

The third bit of information in the dictionary entry is the pronunciation of *disdain:* (dĭs-dān′). You may already know how to pronounce *disdain,* but if you didn't, the information within the parentheses would serve as your guide. Use your dictionary to complete the following exercises that relate to pronunciation.

Vowel Sounds

You will probably use the pronunciation key in your dictionary mainly as a guide to pronouncing different vowel sounds (vowels are the letters *a, e, i, o,* and *u*). Here is a pronunciation key similar to the one that appears in the paperback *American Heritage Dictionary:*

> ă pat ā pay â care ä father ĕ pet ē be ĭ pit ī tie î pier ŏ pot ō toe ô paw, for oi noise oo took o͞o boot ou out th thin *th* this ŭ cut û urge yo͞o abuse zh vision ə about, item, edible, gallop, circus

The key tells you, for example, that the sound of the short *a* is pronounced like the *a* in *pat,* the sound of the long *a* is like the *a* in *pay,* the sound of the short *i* is like the *i* in *pit,* and so on.

Now look at the pronunciation key in your dictionary. The key is probably located in the front of the dictionary or at the bottom of every page. What common word in the key tells you how to pronounce each of the following sounds?

Answers will vary.

ĕ	pet	ō	toe
ī	tie	ŭ	cut
ŏ	pot	o͞o	boot

(Note that the long vowel always has the sound of its own name.)

The Schwa (ə)

The symbol ə looks like an upside-down *e.* It is called a *schwa,* and it stands for the unaccented sound in such words as *ago, item, edible, gallop,* and *circus.* More approximately, it stands for the sound *uh*—like the *uh* speakers may make when they hesitate. Perhaps it would help to remember that *uh,* as well as ə, could often be used to represent the schwa sound.

Here are some of the many words in which the sound appears: *recollect* (rĕk′ə-lĕkt′ *or* rĕk′uh-lĕkt′); *hesitate* (hĕz′ə-tāt *or* hĕz′uh-tāt); *courtesy* (kûr′tə-sē *or* kûr′tuh-sē). Open your dictionary to any page, and you will almost surely be able to find three words that make use of the schwa in the pronunciation that appears in parentheses after the main entry. Write each of the three words and their pronunciations in the following spaces:

1. _Answers will vary._____   (_____)

2. _____   (_____)

3. _____   (_____)

Accent Marks

Some words contain both a primary accent, shown by a heavy stroke (′), and a secondary accent, shown by a lighter stroke (′). For example, in the word *discriminate* (dĭs krĭm′ə-nāt′), the stress, or accent, goes chiefly on the second syllable (krĭm′) and to a lesser extent on the last syllable (nāt′).

Use your dictionary to add accent marks to the following words:

connote (kə nōt′)

admonish (ăd mŏn′ĭsh)

behemoth (bĭ hē′məth)

reciprocal (rĭ sĭp′rə kəl)

extravaganza (ĕk străv′ə găn′zə)

polyunsaturated (pŏl′ē ŭn săch′ə rā tĭd)

Full Pronunciation

Here are ten pronunciations of familiar words. See if you can figure out the correct word in each case. Confirm your answers by checking your dictionary. One is done for you as an example.

kwĭz	_quiz_	kwĕs′chən	_question_
tĭk′əl	_tickle_	ĕg′zĭt	_exit_
wûr′ē	_worry_	kē′bôrd′	_keyboard_
dĭ-zurt′	_dessert_	fĭk-tĭsh′əs	_fictitious_
mēt′bôl′	_meatball_	lŭg′zhə-rē	_luxury_

Now use your dictionary to write out the full pronunciation (the information given in parentheses) for each of the following words:

1. cogent	kō′ jənt	6. lucrative	loo′ krə tĭv	
2. fiasco	fē ăs kō	7. nemesis	něm′ ə sĭs	
3. rationale	răsh ə năl′	8. deprecate	děp′ rĭ kāt	
4. atrophy	ăt′ rə fē	9. lethargy	lěth′ ər jē	
5. trenchant	trěn′ shənt	10. rapacious	rə pā′ shəs	

Now practice *pronouncing* each word. Use the pronunciation key in your dictionary as an aid to sounding out each syllable. Do *not* try to pronounce a word all at once; instead, work on mastering *one syllable at a time.* When you can pronounce each of the syllables in a word successfully, say them in sequence, add the accent, and pronounce the entire word.

Other Information about Words

Parts of Speech

The next bit of information that the dictionary gives about *disdain* is *v.* This label, as the key in the front of your dictionary explains, indicates the *part of speech* and is one of the abbreviations given in the dictionary.

Fill in any meanings that are missing for the following abbreviations:

v.   =   verb

n.   =   _____noun_____

adj. =   adjective

pl.   =   _____plural_____

sing. =   _____singular_____

Principal Parts of Irregular Verbs

Disdain is a regular verb and forms its principal parts by adding *-ed, -ed,* and *-ing* to the stem of the verb. When a verb is irregular, the dictionary lists its principal parts. For example, with *write* the present tense comes first (the entry itself, *write*). Next comes the past tense (*wrote*) and then the past participle (*written*), the form of the verb used with such helping words as *have, had,* and *was.* Then comes the present participle (*writing*)—the *-ing* form of the verb.

Look up the parts of the following irregular verbs and write them in the spaces provided. The first one has been done for you.

Present	*Past*	*Past Participle*	*Present Participle*
write	wrote	written	writing
begin	began	begun	beginning
steal	stole	stolen	stealing
eat	ate	eaten	eating

Plural Forms of Irregular Nouns

The dictionary supplies the plural forms of all irregular nouns (regular nouns form the plural by adding *-s* or *-es*). Give the plurals of the following nouns. If two forms are shown, write both.

apology	apologies
wife	wives
hypothesis	hypotheses
formula	formulas or formulae
passer-by	passers-by

Meanings

When a word has more than one meaning, its meanings are numbered in the dictionary, as with *disdain*. In many dictionaries, the most common meanings are presented first. The introductory pages of your dictionary will explain the order in which meanings are presented.

Use the context to try to explain the meaning of the italicized word in each of the following sentences. Write your definition in the space provided. Then look up and record the dictionary meaning of the word. Be sure you pick out the meaning that fits the word as it is used in the sentence.

1. *Effervescent* drinks like soda appeal to children; they enjoy the bubbles that burst below their noses.

   Your definition: Answers will vary.

   Dictionary definition: containing many small bubbles of gas

2. The actress's *effervescent* personality saved the show from being a disaster.

   Your definition: Answers will vary.

   Dictionary definition: sparkling, high-spirited

3. The small border skirmish was merely a *prelude* to the full-scale war that followed.

   Your definition: Answers will vary.

   Dictionary definition: preliminary action

4. The pianist began the *prelude* in a hesitant manner; then he relaxed and gained confidence.

   Your definition: Answers will vary.

   Dictionary definition: short composition serving as an introduction

Etymology

Etymology refers to the history of a word. Many words have origins in foreign languages, such as Greek (Gk) or Latin (L). Such information is usually enclosed in brackets and is more likely to be present in a hardbound desk dictionary than in a paperback one. Good desk dictionaries include the following:

American Heritage Dictionary   *Webster's New Collegiate Dictionary*

Random House College Dictionary   *Webster's New World Dictionary*

A good desk dictionary will tell you, for example, that *maverick* derives from the name of a Texas rancher who refused to brand his calves. The word is now a general term used to describe someone who does not conform or "follow the herd."

See whether your dictionary gives the origins of the following words:

sandwich sandwich—from the first Earl of Sandwich, who had "sandwiches" of bread and beef brought to him so he would not have to leave the gambling table for meals.

breakfast breakfast—from the Middle English word brekefast, meaning "to break one's fast," usually by eating in the morning.

Usage Labels

As a general rule, use only standard English words in your writing. If a word is not standard English, your dictionary may give it a usage label such as *informal*, *nonstandard*, or *slang*. Look up the following words and record how your dictionary labels them. Note that a recent hardbound desk dictionary will be the best source of information about usage.

rough (meaning *difficult*)	*informal*
finagle	*informal*
hang-up (meaning *inhibition*)	*informal*
ain't	*nonstandard*
cool (meaning *composure*)	*slang*

Practice in Using the Dictionary

Activity 1

Use your dictionary to write the full pronunciation for the following words.

1. encomium *ĕn kō′ mē əm*
2. caustic *kô′ stĭk*
3. conjecture *kən jĕk′ shər*
4. pernicious *pər nĭsh′ əs*
5. Roquefort *rōk′ fərt*

6. verbatim *vər bā′ tĭm*
7. amorphous *ə môr′ fəs*
8. primeval *prī mē′ vəl*
9. machination *măk′ ĭ nā′ shən*
10. disingenuous *dĭs′ ĭn jĕn′ yo͞o əs*

Activity 2

Refer to the excerpt on the facing page from the paperback *American Heritage Dictionary* to answer the questions that follow.

1. How many syllables are in the word *expostulate?* *four*
2. Where is the primary accent in the word *exposition?* *third syllable (zĭsh)*
3. Where is the primary accent in the word *exposé?* *last syllable (zā)*
4. What word in the pronunciation key tells you how to pronounce the *a* in *ex post facto?* *pat*
5. In the word *exponent,* the *o* is pronounced like the *o* in
   - a. boot.
   - b. hot.
   - c. drop.
   - (d) toe.
6. In the word *expiate,* the *i* is pronounced like a
   - a. long *i.*
   - b. short *i.*
   - c. schwa.
   - (d) long *e.*

expertise/exposure

ex·per·tise (ex′spər-tez′) *n.* Expert skill or knowledge. [< OFr.]

ex·pi·ate (ĕk′spē-āt′) *v.* **at·ed, -at·ing.** To atone or make amends for. [< Lat. *expiare.*]—**ex·pi·a·tion** *n.* —**ex·pi·a·tor** *n.* —**ex·pi·a·to′ry** (-ə-tôr′ē, -tōr′ē) *adj.*

ex·pire (ĭk-spīr′) *v.* **-pired, -pir·ing. 1.** To come to an end; terminate. **2.** To die. **3.** To breathe out; exhale. [< Lat. *exspirare.*] —**ex′·pi·ra′tion** *n.*

ex·plain (ĭk-splān′) *v.* **1.** To make plain or comprehensible. **2.** To offer reasons for; account for. [< Lat. *explanare.*] —**ex·plain′·a·ble** *adj.* —**ex·plain′er** *n.* —**ex′pla·na′tion** *n.* **ex·plan′a·to′ri·ly** *adv.* —**ex·plan′a·to·ry** (-splăn′-ə-tôr′ē, -tōr′ē) *adj.*

ex·ple·tive (ĕks′plĭ-tĭv) *n.* An exclamation or oath. [LLat. *expletivus.*]

ex·pli·ca·ble (ĕk′splĭ-kə-bəl) *adj.* Capable of being explained.

ex·pli·cate (ĕx′splĭ-kāt′) *v.* **-cat·ed, -cat·ing.** To explain, esp. in detail. [Lat, *explicare.* to unfold.] —**ex′pli·ca′tion** *n.* —**ex′pli·ca′tive** *adj.* —**ex′pli·ca′tor** *n.*

ex·plic·it (ĭk-splĭs′it) *adj.* Clearly defined; specific; precise. [< Lat. *explicitus,* p.p. of *explicare,* to unfold.] —**ex·plic′it·ly** *adv.* —**ex·plic′it·ness** *n.*

Syns: explicit, categorical, clear-cut, decided, definite, express, positive, precise, specific, unequivocal adj.

Usage: Explicit and express both apply to something clearly stated rather than implied. *Explicit* applies more particularly to that which is carefully spelled out: *explicit instructions.* *Express* applies particularly to a clear expression of intention: *an express promise.*

ex·po·nent (ĭk-spō′nənt) *n.* **1.** One who explains, interprets, or advocates. **2.** A number or symbol, as *3* in $(x + y)^3$, placed to the right of and above another number, symbol, or expression, denoting the power to which the latter is to be raised [< Lat. *exponere,* to expound.] —**ex′po·nen′tial** (-nĕn′shəl) *adj* —**ex′po·nen′tial·ly** *adv.*

ex·port (ĭk spôrt′, -spōrt′, ĕk′spôrt′, -spōrt′) *v.* To send or carry abroad, esp. for sale or trade —*n.* (ĕk′spôrt, -spōrt′). **1.** The act of exporting. **2.** Something exported. [Lat. *exportare.*] —**ex·port′a·ble** *adj.* —**ex′por·ta′tion** *n.*—**ex·port′er** *n.*

ex·pose (ĭk-spōz′) *v.* **-posed, -pos·ing. 1.** To uncover; lay bare. **2.** To lay open or subject, as to a force, influence, etc. **3.** To make visible or known; reveal. **4.** To subject (a photographic film or plate) to the action of light [< Lat. *exponere.*] —**ex·pos′er** *n.*

ex·po·sé (ĕk′spō-zā′) *n.* A public revelation of something discreditable. [Fr.]

ex·po·si·tion (ĕk′spə-zĭsh′ən) *n.* **1.** A setting forth of meaning or intent. **2.** The presentation of information in clear, precise form. **3.** A public exhibition of broad scope. —**ex·pos′i·tor** *n.* —**ex·pos′i·to′ry** (-tôr′ē, -tōr′ē) *adj.*

ex post fac·to (ĕks′ pōst făk′tō) *adj.* Formulated, enacted, or operating retroactively [Med. Lat., from what is done afterwards.]

ex·pos·tu·late (ĭk-spŏs′chə-lāt′) *v.* **-lat·ed, -lat·ing.** To reason earnestly with someone, esp. to dissuade. [Lat. *expostulare,* to demand strongly.] —**ex·pos′tu·la′tion** *n.* —**ex·pos′tu·la·tor** *n.*—**ex·pos′tu·la·to′ry** *adj.*

ex·po·sure (ĭk-spō′zhər) *n.* **1.** An act or example of exposing. **2.** The condition of being exposed. **3.** A position in relation to direction of weather conditions. **4. a.** The act or time of exposing a photographic film or plate. **b.** A film or plate so exposed.

ă pat ā pay â care ä father ĕ pet   ē be ĭ pit ī tie î pier ŏ pot ō toe ô paw, for oi noise o͞o took o͞o boot ou out th thin *th* this ŭ cut û urge yoo abuse zh vision ə about, item, edible, gallop, circus

7. In the word *explicate,* the a is pronounced like a

(a) long *a.*   c.   schwa.

b.   long *i.*   d.   short *a.*

8. *True or false?* ___F___ The word *exposé* is a verb.

9. *True or false?* ___T___ *Exponent* is a word with a specific meaning in mathematics.

10. Which word in the excerpt is followed by a list of synonyms and a note on usage? ___explicit___

11. In the sentence "Our free pass to the movie theater will *expire* if we do not use it within the next month," which meaning of *expire* applies?
    (a) Meaning 1
    b. Meaning 2
    c. Meaning 3

12. In the sentence "I don't quite understand how a kernel of corn pops into popcorn. Can you *explain* it to me?" which meaning of *explain* applies?
    a. Meaning 1
    (b) Meaning 2

13. In the sentence "People in other countries learn about the United States through one of our major *exports:* movies," which meaning of *export* applies?
    a. Noun meaning 1
    (b) Noun meaning 2

14. In the sentence "In the agricultural *exposition* at our state fair, I saw a purple cabbage that weighed fifty pounds," which meaning of *exposition* applies?
    a. Meaning 1
    b. Meaning 2
    (c) Meaning 3

Word
Pronunciation

This chapter will help you:

- Review the two major rules for dividing words into syllables
- Apply the two rules to specialized terms in different subjects
- Review other rules relating to word division and pronunciation

Why You Need to Learn Pronunciation

You will meet many specialized terms in your various academic subjects. Knowing how to *pronounce* the terms will help you master their meanings. You can often locate difficult-to-pronounce words in the dictionary. But in other cases the words may be too technical to appear in a desk dictionary—or you will simply not have the time to look up every pronunciation.

Another problem related to word pronunciation is that there are probably more words in your *listening* vocabulary than in your *sight* vocabulary. That is, you probably recognize more spoken words than written ones. Learning how to sound out and pronounce unfamiliar words will help narrow any gap between your listening and sight vocabularies.

Using the two major rules provided in this section, you should be able to divide most unfamiliar words into syllables—and so pronounce them without having to refer to the dictionary. The rules hold true most of the time; with them, you will never be far from correct word pronunciation.

Background Information

Before looking at the rules, be sure you understand the necessary background information that follows. First of all, remember that the vowels are *a, e, i, o, u,* and sometimes *y;* the consonants are all the other letters.

It is also important to remember that each syllable is a different general sound in a word. If a word has two syllables, it has two sounds; three syllables, three sounds; and so on. For example, in the word *impacted* (as in "impacted wisdom tooth"), there are three syllables (im pact ed) and three sounds. How many syllables (and sounds) are there in the following words?

nostril   (__2__ syllables)

Frankenstein   (__3__ syllables)

contemporary   (__5__ syllables)

After you use the rules below to divide a word into syllables, work on pronouncing *one syllable at a time*. Only when you can pronounce each syllable in a word separately should you put the sounds together in succession. Then, when you can correctly pronounce all the sounds in the word in succession, you should add the accent (stress) where it sounds right. If the word doesn't "sound right," or if it is hard or awkward to say, change the accent or the pronunciation (or both) slightly until it does sound right to your ear. Remember that the rules given below will get you close to the correct pronunciation, but they are not always exact. You may have to make final adjustments.

Two Major Rules for Dividing Words into Syllables

Rule 1: Divide between Double Consonants

Here are examples of rule 1:

mes/sage   dis/tance   fun/gus

In each case the division is between the double consonants: the *ss* in *message,* the *st* in *distance,* and the *ng* in *fungus.*

At times, the division will occur between a consonant and a *consonant blend*—two or more consonants that blend together to form one sound. Here are examples:

mor/phine   con/struct   sub/stance

The syllable division in *morphine* is between the consonant *r* and the consonant blend *ph;* in *construct,* between the consonant *n* and the consonant blend *str;* in *substance,* between the consonant *b* and the consonant blend *st.*

Activity

Use a slash line to divide the following words into syllables at the point where double consonants occur.

1. cen|ter
2. pol|len
3. hor|rid
4. twit|ter
5. pres|sure

6. um|ber
7. ac|rid
8. ger|mane
9. sten|cil
10. tur|bid

11. fer|vent
12. spec|tral
13. grem|lin
14. vis|cous
15. trans|ves|tite

Pronunciation Hint: The vowel before double consonants usually has a short sound. For example, the *u* in *umber* has a short sound, like the *u* in *cut*.

Rule 2: Divide before a Single Consonant

Here are examples of rule 2:

lo/cal   vi/per   bla/tant

In each case, the syllable division is before the single consonant: before the *c* in *local*, before the *p* in *viper*, and before the first *t* in *blatant*.

At times, the division will occur before a consonant blend. For example, in the word *preclude*, the division occurs before the consonant blend *cl: pre/clude*.

Activity

Use a slash line to divide the following words into syllables before single consonants.

1. co|gent
2. e|voke
3. hu|mid
4. le|thal
5. sa|vor

6. su|ture
7. i|rate
8. so|lace
9. pa|thos
10. fru|gal

11. de|claim
12. mi|mo|sa
13. lu|mi|nous
14. ma|tron
15. cre|ma|tion

Pronunciation Hint: The vowel before a division at a single consonant usually has a long sound. For example, the *o* in *cogent* has a long sound, like the *o* in *go*.

■ **Review Test**

Divide these words into syllables by applying either or both of the two rules.

1. ad|vo|cate
2. de|sist
3. con|do|lence
4. fes|ti|val
5. non|par|ti|san

6. si|ne|cure
7. rep|ri|mand
8. pa|tel|la
9. in|con|clu|sive
10. las|si|tude

11. cur|so|ry
12. scru|ti|nize
13. co|los|to|my
14. in|con|tro|ver|ti|ble
15. phe|no|bar|bi|tal

Other Helpful Rules for Dividing Words into Syllables

Rule 3: Always Divide Compound Words between the Words That Form the Compound

Divide the following words:

straight|forward   ever|green   strong|hold
whole|sale   monkey|shine   news|print

Rule 4: Divide between Prefixes and Suffixes

Common prefixes include *anti, trans, non, re, post, con, mis, ex, de, inter, sub, ad, dis, ante, ultra, bi, syn, ab, tri, in, pre.* Common suffixes include *en, ize, ess, ism, able, ible, ward, ment, ry, ic, ist, less, ship, ance, age, ful, ness, ier, ious, ition, ion, ing.*
Divide the following words at prefix or suffix divisions:

head|ing   ex|hume   syn|drome
spine|less   dis|con|tent   sub|merge
state|ment   re|vers|able   anti|biot|ics

Rule 5: Two Vowels Together May Represent Separate Sounds and Be in Separate Syllables

Use this rule to divide and pronounce the following words:

ne|on   co|op|er|ate   du|o|de|num
ob|vi|ous   ve|ne|re|al   ac|tu|a|ry

Note: Only some vowel pairs divide into separate syllables. There are many vowel pairs in English that are in one syllable, usually with the first vowel long and the second vowel silent. For example: *please, chain, road,* and *dream.*

Practice in Word Pronunciation

Activity 1

Divide the words listed below into syllables. When you have done so, you should be able to sound out and pronounce each separate syllable and then the whole word.

Remember that the chief rules for syllable division are to (1) divide between double consonants and (2) divide before a single consonant.

Example: dis/con/so/late
(The word has four syllables. The first two divisions are between double consonants—*sc* and *ns;* the third division is before the single consonant.)

1. de|ter|gent
2. vo|ra|cious
3. bul|wark
4. prog|nos|ti|cate
5. ful|some
6. fur|tive
7. vi|cis|si|tude
8. con|sum|mate
9. fab|ri|cate
10. ca|jo|lé
11. nu|ance
12. sal|i|ent
13. em|bel|lish
14. in|ad|ver|tent
15. re|pu|di|ate
16. post|pran|di|al
17. al|lac|ri|ty
18. a|bor|tive
19. pug|na|cious
20. pro|mul|gate
21. cas|ti|gate
22. oc|to|ge|nar|i|an
23. ab|ste|mi|ous
24. scur|ri|lous
25. as|pi|rant

Note: After you divide a word into syllables, place the stress, or accent, on the syllable that makes the word easier to pronounce. The stress that sounds the most natural is generally the correct one. For instance, the word *disconsolate* is most easily emphasized on the second syllable—*dis **con** so late*—and that accent is the correct one.

Activity 2

The following lists are made up of specialized terms you can expect to encounter in your various content courses. You should be able to divide the words into syllables and pronounce them correctly (or come close to the correct pronunciation) using chiefly the two basic rules for syllable division.

Terms from Psychology

1. en|gram
2. sen|so|ry
3. ger|mi|nal
4. pre|na|tal
5. a|ver|sive

6. sib|ling
7. li|bi|do
8. vis|ce|ral
9. ol|fac|to|ry
10. sub|li|ma|tion

Terms from Sociology

1. mar|gi|nal
2. dis|sent|er
3. ac|com|mo|da|tion
4. kib|butz
5. a|mal|ga|ma|tion

6. de|mog|ra|phy
7. hal|lu|ci|no|gen
8. ge|sell|schaft
9. hos|pice
10. com|part|men|tal|i|za|tion

Terms from Biology and Other Sciences

1. cor|tex
2. mi|to|sis
3. ru|bel|la
4. pep|tide
5. his|ta|mine

6. in|su|lin
7. es|tro|gen
8. der|ma|ti|tis
9. he|ma|to|ma
10. pla|cen|ta

Terms from Business and Economics

1. sur|tax
2. fis|cal
3. mer|can|tile
4. con|ver|gence
5. in|den|ture

6. con|sump|tion
7. mer|ger
8. ag|gre|gate
9. Mal|thu|si|an
10. de|cen|tra|li|za|tion

Spelling
Improvement

This chapter will show you how to improve your spelling by using:

- A dictionary
- Electronic aids
- A personal spelling list
- Lists of specialized words
- A list of common English words
- Four basic spelling rules

Poor spelling often results from bad habits developed in early school years. With work, such habits can be corrected. If you can write your name without misspelling it, there is no reason why you can't do the same with almost any word in the English language. The six steps that you can follow to improve your spelling are discussed below.

Using the Dictionary

Get into the habit of using the dictionary. When you write a paper, allow yourself time to look up all those words whose spelling you are unsure about. Do not overlook the value of this step just because it is such a simple one. Through using the dictionary, you will probably improve your spelling 95 percent almost immediately.

Using Electronic Aids

There are three electronic aids that may help your spelling. First, many *electronic typewriters* can be set to beep automatically when you misspell a word. They include built-in dictionaries that will then give you the correct spelling. Second, *electronic spell-checkers* are pocket-size devices that look much like the pocket calculators you may use in math class. Electronic spellers can be found in almost any electronics store. The checker includes a tiny keyboard. You type out the word the way you think it is spelled, and the checker quickly provides you with the correct spelling of related words. Finally, *a computer with a spell-checker* as part of its word processing program will identify incorrect words and suggest correct spellings. If you know how to write on the computer, you will have little trouble learning how to use the spell-check feature.

Keeping a Personal Spelling List

Either in a separate notebook for spelling or in a specific section in your English or reading and study skills notebook, keep a list of words that you misspell.

To master such words, do the following:

1 Look at the first word, say it, and spell it. Then look away and try to spell it. When you can, go on and work on the next word until you can spell it without looking at it. Then go back and test yourself on the first word. After learning each new word, go back and review all the preceding ones. *This review and repeated self-testing are the keys to effective learning.*

2 As a reinforcement, you may want to write out difficult words several times or "air-write" them with your finger in large, exaggerated motions. Also, you may want to capitalize the letters you confuse in a word when you write it out. For example, if you tend to spell *resources* as *resorces,* you might want to write *resOURces.*

3 With long words, divide the word into syllables and try to spell the syllables. For example, *misdemeanor* can be spelled easily if you can hear and spell in turn its four syllables: *mis de mean or.* Again, the word *formidable* can be spelled easily if you hear and spell in turn its four syllables: *for mi da ble.* Even a very long word like *antidisestablishmentarianism* becomes simple if you first break it down into syllables: *an ti dis es tab lish men tar i an is m.* Remember, then: Try to see, hear, and spell long words in terms of their syllable parts.

Activity

Use the space that follows as a starter for words that you misspell. As you accumulate additional words, you may want to jot them down on a back page of this book or your English or reading notebook.

Incorrect Spelling	Correct Spelling	Points to Remember
alot	a lot	two words
writting	writing	one "t"
alright	all right	two words

Learning Key Words in Major Subjects

Make up lists of words central to the vocabulary of your major subjects. For example, a list of key words in business might include *economics, management, resources, scarcity, capitalism, decentralization, productivity, enterprise,* and so on; in psychology: *behavior, investigation, experimentation, frustration, cognition, stimulus, response, organism,* and so on. Set aside a specific portion of your various course notebooks to be used only for such lists and study them using the methods for learning words described on pages 350–354.

Activity

Write in the space below the name of one of your subjects and fifteen repeatedly used terms which you should learn to spell for that subject.

Subject _Answers will vary._

1. _____

2. _____

3. _____

4. _____

5. _____

6. _____

7. _____

8. _____

9. _____

10. _____

11. _____

12. _____

13. _____

14. _____

15. _____

Studying a Basic Word List

Master the spellings of the words in the following list. They are some of the most often used words in English. Your instructor may assign twenty-five or fifty words for you to study at a time and give you a series of quizzes until you have mastered the list.

ability	against	animal	awful
absent	all right	another	awkward
accept	almost	answer	back
accident	a lot	anxious	balance
across	also	apply 25	bargain
address	always	approve	beautiful
advertise	although	argue	because
advice	among	around	become
after	amount	attempt	been
again	angry	attention	before

begin	direction 75	house	mountain
being	distance	however	much
believe	does	hundred	needle
between	doubt	hungry	neither
bottom	dozen	instead	newspaper
brake	during	intelligence	noise
breathe	each	interest	none
building	early	interfere	nothing 150
business	earth	kindergarten	number
came 50	easy	kitchen	ocean
careful	education	knowledge	offer
careless	either	labor	often
cereal	English	language	omit
certain	enough	laugh	only
change	entrance	learn	operate
cheap	everything	length	opportunity
chief	examine	lesson 125	original
children	exercise	letter	ought
church	expect	listen	pain
cigarette	family	loneliness	paper
clothing	flower	making	peace
collect	foreign	marry	pencil
color	friend	match	people
comfortable	from	matter	perfect
company	garden	measure	period
condition	general 100	medicine	person
conversation	grocery	middle	picture
daily	guess	might	place
danger	handkerchief	million	pocket
daughter	happy	minute	possible
death	heard	mistake	potato
deposit	heavy	money	president
describe	himself	month	pretty 175
different	holiday	morning	promise

psychology	sentence	than	upon
public	several	there	usual
quick	should	thing	value
quiet	since	thought	vegetable
quite	sleep 200	thousand	view
raise	smoke	through	visitor
ready	something	ticket	voice
really	soul	tired	warning
reason	state	today	weather
receive	straight	together	whole
recognize	street	tomorrow 225	window
remember	strong	tonight	without
repeat	student	tongue	would
restaurant	studying	touch	writing
ridiculous	suffer	travel	written
right	summer	truly	yesterday
said	sweet	under	your 250
same	teach	understand	
sandwich	telephone	until	

Learning Basic Spelling Rules

A final way to improve your spelling is to learn and practice the four often-used rules that follow. While the rules have exceptions, they usually hold true.

Rule 1: *I* before *E*

Use *i* before *e* except after *c*. For example:

believe	deceive	yield
chief	receive	receipt
field	perceive	piece
grief	ceiling	priest
cashier	conceited	deceit

Activity

Fill in *ie* or *ei* in each of the following words:

1. fr__*ie*__nd
2. c__*ei*__ling
3. br__*ie*__f
4. misch__*ie*__f
5. retr__*ie*__ve
6. rel__*ie*__ve
7. rec__*ei*__ve
8. th__*ie*__f
9. ach__*ie*__ve
10. hyg__*ie*__ne

Note: Here are some exceptions to rule 1: *height, either, leisure, seize, weird, neighbor, efficient, science.*

Rule 2: Final *E*

Drop a final *e* when adding a suffix that begins with a vowel. Keep the final *e* when adding a suffix that begins with a consonant. Some background information will help make this rule clear to you.

- There are two kinds of letters in the alphabet: vowels (*a, e, i, o, u,* and sometimes *y*) and consonants (all the other letters).
- Suffixes are common endings on many English words. Here are some suffixes that begin with vowels: *en, ize, ess, ism, able, ible, ic, ist, ance, age, ier, ation, ition, ion, ing, ed.* Here are some suffixes that begin with consonants: *ward, ment, ry, ship, ful, ness.*
- In the following examples, the final *e* is dropped before a suffix beginning with a *vowel:*

hope   + ing = hoping   sense + ible = sensible
excite + ed   = excited   create + ive = creative
believe + able = believable   fine   + est = finest

- In the following examples, the final *e* is retained before a suffix beginning with a *consonant*:

hope	+ less	= hopeless
excite	+ ment	= excitement
extreme	+ ly	= extremely

use	+ ful	= useful
life	+ like	= lifelike
apprentice	+ ship	= apprenticeship

Activity

Use the final *e* rule with the following words:

1. describe + ing = _describing_
2. lone + er = _loner_
3. care + ing = _caring_
4. immense + ly = _immensely_
5. like + ness = _likeness_
6. arrive + al = _arrival_
7. use + able = _usable_
8. peace + ful = _peaceful_
9. service + ing = _servicing_
10. retire + ment = _retirement_

Rule 3: *Y* to *I*

When a word ends in a consonant plus *y*, change the *y* to *i* when you add a suffix. Here are some examples:

reply	+ es	= replies
angry	+ ly	= angrily
lazy	+ ness	= laziness
happy	+ er	= happier

carry	+ age	= carriage
marry	+ es	= marries
defy	+ ed	= defied
penny	+ less	= penniless

- *Complete this sentence:* The letter before *y* in all the preceding examples is a _consonant_. Therefore, you change the _y_ to _i_ before adding the suffix.

Activity

Use the *y*-to-*i* rule with the following words:

1. fly   + es   = _____ flies _____
2. hurry + ed   = _____ hurried _____
3. empty + ness = _____ emptiness _____
4. easy   + er   = _____ easier _____
5. try   + ed   = _____ tried _____
6. worry + es   = _____ worries _____
7. ready + ness = _____ readiness _____
8. baby   + es   = _____ babies _____
9. pretty + er   = _____ prettier _____
10. beauty + ful = _____ beautiful _____

Note: Do not worry about the following exceptions. They are here simply to make the rule complete. One exception is that you do not change the *y* when you add *ing*. For example, *play + ing = playing*. A second exception is that you do not change the *y* when a word ends in a vowel plus *y* (rather than a consonant plus *y*). For example, *employ + ed = employed.*

Rule 4: Doubling

Double the final consonant of a word when all of the following apply:

1 The word is one syllable or is accented on the last syllable.
2 The word ends with a consonant preceded by a vowel.
3 The suffix you are adding begins with a vowel.

Here are some examples:

• If you are adding *-ing* to *drop,* you double the final consonant because

Drop is one syllable.
Drop ends with a consonant preceded by a vowel.
The suffix (*ing*) being added begins with a vowel.

- If you are adding -*able* to *control,* you double the final consonant because

  Control is accented on the last syllable.
  Control ends with a consonant preceded by a vowel.
  The suffix (*able*) being added begins with a vowel.

- If you are adding -*ed* to *happen,* you do *not* double the final consonant, because *happen* is accented on the first rather than the last syllable.

Activity

Use the doubling rule with the following words.

1. big   + er   = _____bigger_____
2. shop   + ed   = _____shopped_____
3. swim   + ing   = _____swimming_____
4. compel   + ed   = _____compelled_____
5. begin   + ing   = _____beginning_____
6. forget   + ful   = _____forgetful_____
7. equip   + ed   = _____equipped_____
8. repel   + ent   = _____repellent_____
9. commit   + ed   = _____committed_____
10. ship   + ment = _____shipment_____

■ Final Activity

Use the four rules to spell the following words.

1. regret + ing = _____regretting_____
2. sip   + ed = _____sipped_____
3. dec__ei__t
4. study + es = _____studies_____
5. mere   + ly = _____merely_____
6. rely   + ed = _____relied_____
7. rob   + ery = _____robbery_____

8. rec_ei_pt

9. forgot + en = ___forgotten___

10. nerve + ous = ___nervous___

On the lines below, explain which rule you applied to spell each word.

1. Rule 4—Doubling

2. Rule 4—Doubling

3. Rule 1—I before E

4. Rule 3—Y to I

5. Rule 2—Final E

6. Rule 3—Y to I

7. Rule 4—Doubling

8. Rule 1—I before E

9. Rule 4—Doubling

10. Rule 2—Final E

Vocabulary Development

This chapter will explain how you can develop your vocabulary by:

- Regular reading
- Using context clues
- Systematically learning new words

A good vocabulary is a vital part of effective communication. A command of many words will make you a better writer, speaker, listener, and reader. In contrast, a poor vocabulary can seriously slow your reading speed and limit your comprehension. Studies have shown that students with a strong vocabulary and students who work to improve a limited vocabulary are more successful in school. And one research study found that *a good vocabulary, more than any other factor, was common to people enjoying successful careers.*

The question, then, is not whether vocabulary development is helpful but what the best ways are of going about it. This section will describe three related approaches you can take to increase your word power. Remember from the start, however, that none of the approaches will help unless you truly decide in your own mind that vocabulary development is an important goal. Only when you have this attitude can you begin doing the sustained work needed to improve your word power.

- *Complete the following sentence:* Most people who enjoy successful careers have in common a _good vocabulary_____.

Regular Reading

The best way to learn words is by experiencing them a number of times in a variety of sentences. Repeated exposure to a word will eventually make it a part of your working language. This method of learning words requires that *you make reading a habit.* You should, first of all, read a daily newspaper. You do not have to read it from first page to last. Instead, you should read the features that interest you. You might, for instance, read the movie and television pages, the sports section, columns on consumer tips, and any news articles or features that catch your eye. Second, you should subscribe to one or more weekly magazines such as *Newsweek, Time,* or *People,* as well as monthly magazines suited to your interests. Among monthlies, you might choose from such magazines as *Sports Illustrated, Cosmopolitan, Science Digest, Consumer Reports, Ladies' Home Journal, Oprah, Personal Computing, Glamour, Redbook,* and many others.

Finally, you should, if possible, try to fit reading for pleasure into your schedule. A number of interesting books are included in the selected list on page 621. You may find such reading especially difficult when you also have textbooks to read. Try, however, to redirect a half hour to an hour of your recreational time to reading books on a regular basis instead of watching television, listening to music, or the like. By doing so, you may eventually reap the rewards of an improved vocabulary *and* discover that reading can be truly enjoyable.

- *Complete the following sentence:* The best way to learn a word is by seeing it

  in several different <u>contexts</u>   .

- Put a check next to each step that you can realistically take to make reading a part of your life.

  Answers to these items will vary.

  _____ Begin a subscription to a daily newspaper. What newspaper would be a good

  choice for you? _____

  _____ Begin a subscription to a weekly magazine. What magazine might you want to

  subscribe to? _____

  _____ Go to the library or bookstore and pick out a book you will read for pleasure. (You may want to look at the list of recommended books starting on page 621.) What book might you want to try first?

  _____

  _____ Find a time and place that will be suitable for quiet reading. (I, for example, read in bed for a half hour or so before I go to sleep. That's an ideal quiet time for me.) What is one possibility?

  _____

Activity 1

Read through a daily newspaper. Record below the name and date of the paper and the titles and authors (when their names are given) of five different features or articles that you found interesting to read.

Name of newspaper: _Answers will vary._____ Date: _____
Articles read:

1. _____
2. _____
3. _____
4. _____
5. _____

    Bring one of the articles to class and give a three-minute talk on it to a small group of other students. Do not read the article to them. Instead, explain what you felt was the main point of the article (the title will often provide a clue). Also, express in your own words some of the details used to support or develop the main point.

Activity 2

Go through a weekly or monthly magazine and read at least five articles that seem interesting to you. Record the following information:

Name of magazine: _Answers will vary._____ Date: _____
Articles read (title and author):

1. _____
2. _____
3. _____
4. _____
5. _____

    Prepare a three-minute report on one of the articles, to be presented to a small group of students.

In your report for Activity 2, do the following:

- Explain briefly the main point of the article (again, the title often provides a clue to the author's main idea).
- Then present to the group the chief details that are used to support or develop that point.
- As you provide details, quote several sentences (no more than three) from the article.

Activity 3

Obtain one of the books listed on pages 621–626. Fill in the following information about the book:

Title: _____ Author: _____

Place of publication: _____ Publisher: _____ Year: _____

Read a minimum of fifty pages in the book. Prepare a ten-minute oral report on these pages for a small group of your peers. Your purpose in this report is to give them a good sense of the flavor of the book. To do this, you should explain and summarize in your own words how the book begins, who the main characters are, and what specific problems or conflicts are developed. Read at least two passages you like from the book as part of your report. The passages you read should be no more than 20 percent of your entire report.

Alternatively, prepare a written report that you will hand in to your instructor. Follow the same instructions that were given for the oral report. Set off quoted passages longer than three sentences by single-spacing them and by indenting them ten spaces in from the left margin of your paper.

Some Final Thoughts about Regular Reading

Keep in mind that you cannot expect to make an instant habit of reading newspapers, magazines, and books. Also, you should not expect such reading to be an instant source of pleasure. You may have to work at becoming a regular reader, particularly if you have done little reading in the past. You may have to keep reminding yourself of the enormous value that regular reading can have in developing your language, thinking, and communication power. Remember that if you are determined and if you persist, reading can become a rewarding and enjoyable activity.

Using Context Clues

When asked how they should deal with an unknown word they meet in reading, many people answer, "Use the dictionary." But stopping in midsentence to pull out a dictionary and look up a word is seldom a practical—or necessary—solution. You can often determine the meaning of an unknown word by considering the context in which the word appears. The surrounding words and sentences frequently provide clues to the meaning of the word. Notice the italicized word in the following selection:

> A poll showed that the senator's *candor* was appreciated even by the voters who did not agree with him. "I don't go along with some of his views," one voter said. "But it's refreshing to have a politician tell you exactly what he believes."

Even if you do not know the meaning of *candor,* the context helps you realize that it means *openness,* or *honesty.* Much of the time, such context clues in surrounding words or sentences will help you make sense of unknown words in your reading.

If you are a regular reader, you will use context clues on repeated occasions to determine the meaning of a word. Perhaps another time you will read:

> Tony appreciated Lola's *candid* remark that his pants were baggy. And he was pleased with himself for not getting upset when faced with an unflattering truth.

Again, context helps you understand and learn the word. And through repeated use of such context clues to understand an unfamiliar word, you will make that word a natural part of your working vocabulary.

In combination with regular reading, the use of context clues is an excellent way to improve your vocabulary. Unfamiliar words, encountered often enough in context, eventually become part of one's natural working vocabulary. If you develop the habits of reading regularly and using context clues to guess the meanings of unknown words, you will turn many unfamiliar words into familiar ones.

- *Complete the following sentence:* Instead of using a dictionary, you can often determine the meaning of an unknown word by looking at _____

  the context in which the word appears.

Activity 1

Read each of the following sentences carefully. Then decide which of the four choices provided comes closest in meaning to the word in *italic* type. Circle the letter of your choice.

1. As a *naive* little boy, I thought elbow grease was something you bought in a store.
    a. Careless
    b. Serious
    c. Unknowing
    d. Easygoing

    (The misinterpretation of elbow grease is not a matter of carelessness; it is simply a matter of not knowing.)

2. The billionaire J. Paul Getty was so *frugal* that he had a pay telephone for the guests in his home.
    a. Honest
    b. Generous
    c. Sensitive
    d. Thrifty

3. Sue *affected* to like him only until she found a better-looking boyfriend.
    a. Decided
    b. Bothered
    c. Pretended
    d. Agreed

4. My Corvette's *voracious* appetite for gasoline made me decide to trade it in for an economy car, the Chevette.
    a. Huge
    b. Tiny
    c. Finicky
    d. Sensational

5. When I was called on to give an on-the-spot speech in class, I was so surprised that I stood up and recited nothing but *gibberish*.
    a. Stories
    b. Jokes
    c. Nonsense
    d. Lies

6. My neighbors are hardly *gregarious;* they keep their blinds drawn and have put a high fence around their property.

   a. Hostile

   b. Lonely

   c. Strange

   (d) Friendly

7. Ted is a *masochist;* he encourages people to criticize and hurt him.

   a. One who likes pleasure

   (b) One who likes pain

   c. One who agrees with others

   d. One who feels angry

8. School council members often complain about the *apathy* of the student body; they ignore the fact that students have interests other than school government.

   a. Hostility

   b. Loneliness

   c. Discourtesy

   (d) Indifference

9. I felt *vindictive* toward the sales clerk who rudely ignored me, so I decided to complain to the store manager.

   a. Apologetic

   b. Jealous

   c. Sorry

   (d) Inclined to revenge

10. The instructor said my term paper had no *contemporary* references; I should have cited some up-to-date research on my topic.

   (a) Recent   (The context clue here is in the second part of the sentence:

   b. Scholarly   "I should have cited some *up-to-date* research on my topic.")

   c. Local

   d. Clear

Activity 2

Use the context to try to explain the italicized word in each of the following sentences. Then check your answers in a dictionary.

1. Sometimes I have *ambivalent* feelings toward my husband; I both love him and hate him.

   Your definition: _____Answers will vary._____

   Dictionary definition: _____conflicting_____

2. I tried to *emulate* my sister's success in school by studying as hard as she did.

   Your definition: _____Answers will vary._____

   Dictionary definition: _____equal or surpass_____

3. The doctor gave a *placebo* to the overworried patient who imagined that she was not taking enough pills for her arthritis.

   Your definition: _____Answers will vary._____

   Dictionary definition: _____harmless substance given to humor a patient_____

4. I have never met anyone who has not made *disparaging* comments about certain national politicians.

   Your definition: _____Answers will vary._____

   Dictionary definition: _____disrespectful; belittling_____

5. My paper was so *redundant* that my instructor asked me to reduce its number of words by half.

   Your definition: _____Answers will vary._____

   Dictionary definition: _____repetitive; wordy_____

Activity 3

The sentences on the following pages are taken from widely used college textbooks. They should dramatize how context clues are a practical tool for helping you identify the meanings of words you may not know in your college work. Read each sentence carefully. Circle the letter of the choice that comes closest in meaning to the italicized word.

1. The move from stage to stage is not automatic, and Greeley indicates that *regression* to an earlier stage is always a possibility.

   a. Progress

   b. Advance

   c. Expansion

   (d.) Return

2. The *fallacy* of this approach is that it overlooks the extent to which every large organization is a network of small primary groups.

   a. Incorrectness *(The word overlooks is a context clue that helps you understand that fallacy means "incorrectness.")*

   b. Value

   c. Cause

   d. Result

3. Most of us are *deferential* toward those whose social position we believe to be above ours and look down on those whom we consider socially below us.

   a. Open

   b. Impolite

   c. Bitter

   d. Respectful

4. Like reward, punishment serves two major functions in discipline. It *deters* the repetition of socially undesirable acts, and it shows the adolescent what the social group considers wrong.

   a. Encourages

   b. Discourages

   c. Permits

   d. Organizes

5. The first stage is denial. The patient refuses to accept the *prognosis,* typically believing that it is a mistake, and consults other doctors or even faith healers.

   a. Medical forecast

   b. Therapy

   c. Medicine

   d. Bill

6. America has been called the "*affluent* society" because of its abundance of goods and services.

   a. Divided

   b. Middle-class

   c. Prosperous

   d. Anxious

7. For four years, Hitler had concentrated on making northern France the most *impregnable* wall of his fortress.

   a. Expensive

   b. Unconquerable

   c. Inconspicuous

   d. Interesting

8. Competition functions as one method of *allocating* scarce rewards. Other methods are possible. We might ration goods on some basis such as need, age, or social status. We might distribute scarce goods by lottery or even divide them equally among all people.

(a.) Distributing   (*The context clues here include ration, distribute, and*
   b. Disputing   *divide them equally.*)
   c. Collecting
   d. Taxing

9. As artificial parts *proliferate,* the need for transplants lessens.

(a.) Increase
   b. Become more expensive
   c. Decrease
   d. Break down

10. Catholic Democrats who were *adamant* that federal aid should go to parochial schools and Republicans who were *adamant* that aid not go to any school were locked in a stalemate that ended hopes for the passage of any bill.

(a.) Set in a belief
   b. Flexible in a belief
   c. Reluctant
   d. Agreeable

Systematically Learning New Words

Learning Technical Words

Some of the most important words you must learn and remember are the technical terms used in specific subjects. In a psychology course, for instance, you need to understand such terms as *behaviorism, stimulus, regression, cognition, neurosis, perception,* and so on. With an introductory course in particular, you must spend a good deal of time learning the specialized vocabulary of the subject. Mastering the language of the subject will be, in fact, a major part of mastering the subject.

Textbook authors often define a technical word at the same time they introduce it to you. Here are several examples:

Catharsis, the release of tension and anxieties by acting out the appropriate emotions, has long been recognized as helpful to one's health.

A *capitalist,* then, is an individual who invests money or other assets in a business, hoping to make a profit.

The word *ulcer* is used to designate an open sore in the skin or in the alimentary canal.

If you should come upon a technical word that is not explained, look for its definition in the glossary of words that may appear in the back of the book. Or look for the word in the index that will probably be included in the back of the book. Once introduced and explained, many technical words may then recur frequently in a book. If you do not learn such words when they are first presented, it may be impossible for you to understand later passages where the words are used again. To escape being overwhelmed by a rising flood of unfamiliar terms, you should mark off and master important technical words as soon as they appear.

Your instructor may be your best source of information about important technical terms. He or she will probably introduce a number of these terms to you during class discussions and provide definitions. You should write down each definition and clearly set it off in your notes by underlining the term and perhaps putting *def* beside it in the margin. If you are responsible for textbook material, you should mark off and then write down definitions and other important ideas, as described on page 361. (If an instructor's definition of a term differs in wording from a text definition of the same term, you should study the one that is clearer for you.)

Some students find it helpful not only to set off definitions in their class and text notes but also to keep a list of such definitions at the back of their course notebooks. What is crucial is that you realize the importance of noting and mastering the definitions of key words in a subject. If you do not do this, you cannot expect to understand fully and master the subject.

The activities on pages 362–367 will give you practice in locating and writing down definitions of technical terms.

- *Complete the following sentences:*

Courses such as sociology, psychology, and biology have their own specialized ___vocabularies___.

Technical terms are often ___defined___ when they are first introduced; they may also be defined in a ___glossary___ or an ___index___ at the back of a textbook.

You may find it helpful to keep a list of important definitions at the back of ___your course notebook___.

Learning General-Interest Words

General-interest words are not technical terms but words you might come upon in your everyday reading. Perhaps while reading a magazine you encounter the italicized word in the following sentence: "People who vacation in resort towns often have good reason to feel *exploited*." You may be able to guess the meaning of *exploited* from the context and so feel no need to consider the word any further. However, perhaps it is a word you have seen and been slightly puzzled about before, and a word you think it would be useful for you to master. You should have an organized method of learning words such as *exploited* so that you can not only recognize them but also use them in speaking and writing.

A Method of Learning New Words: To build your vocabulary, first mark off in your reading words that you want to learn thoroughly. If you are reading a newspaper or magazine, tear out the page on which the word appears and put the page in a file folder. If you are reading a book, jot down the word and the page number on a slip of paper which you have tucked into the book for that purpose. Then, every so often, sit down with a dictionary and look up basic information about each word. Put this information on a vocabulary word sheet like the one that follows.

Vocabulary Word Sheet

1   Word: ___*exploit*___ Pronunciation: ___*(eks ploit′)*___

Meanings: ___*v. 1 To take advantage of*___

___*2 To make use of selfishly*___

Other forms of the word: *exploiter   exploitable   exploitative*

Use of the word in context: *People who vacation in resort towns often have good reason to feel exploited.*

Your own sentence using the word: *I tried to exploit the fact that my boss was my father-in-law by asking for a raise.*

2   . . .

Study each word as follows:

- First, make sure you can correctly pronounce the word and its derivations. (Page 315 explains the dictionary pronunciation key that will help you pronounce each word properly.)
- Second, study the main meanings of the word until you can say them without looking at them.
- Finally, spend a moment looking at the example of the word in context.

You should then go on to follow the same process with the second word. Then, after testing yourself on the first and the second words, go on to the third word. Continue going back and testing yourself on all the words you have studied after you learn each new word. Such repeated self-testing is the key to effective learning.

An Alternative Method of Accumulating Words: Some people can effectively use three- by five-inch cards, rather than the word sheet shown before, to accumulate words. In this method, you prepare a card for each word, using the following format.

1 *Front of the card:* word; pronunciation; part of speech; forms of the word; example of the word in context.

exploit   (eks ploit') v.

exploiter   exploitable   exploitative

People who vacation in resort towns often have good reason to feel exploited.

2 *Back of the card:* different meanings of the word; check (✔) beside the meaning that fits the context in which you found the word; sentence using the word.

> ✔ 1 To take advantage of
>
> 2 To make use of selfishly
>
> I tried to exploit the fact that my boss was my father-in-law by asking for a raise.

An advantage of this method is that the cards can be shuffled and the words can be studied in any order. A drawback of the method is that some people do not find it practical or convenient to keep handy a pack of vocabulary cards. Use whichever method you think will work for you.

Activity

Locate five words in your reading that you would like to master. Enter them on your vocabulary word sheet and fill in all the needed information. Your instructor may then check your word sheet and perhaps give you a quick oral quiz on selected words.

You may receive a standing assignment to add five words a week to a word sheet and to study the words. Note that you can create your own word sheets using loose-leaf paper, or your instructor may give you copies of the word sheet that follows.

Answers will vary.

1. Word: _____ Pronunciation: _____

   Meanings: _____

   _____

   _____

   _____

   Other forms of the word: _____

   Use of the word in context: _____

   _____

2. Word: _____ Pronunciation: _____

Meanings: _____

_____

_____

_____

Other forms of the word: _____

Use of the word in context: _____

_____

3. Word: _____ Pronunciation: _____

Meanings: _____

_____

_____

_____

Other forms of the word: _____

Use of the word in context: _____

_____

4. Word: _____ Pronunciation: _____

Meanings: _____

_____

_____

_____

Other forms of the word: _____

Use of the word in context: _____

_____

5. Word: _____ Pronunciation: _____

Meanings: _____

_____

_____

_____

Other forms of the word: _____

Use of the word in context: _____

Learning through Vocabulary Study Books

A final systematic way of learning new words is to use vocabulary study books. The most helpful of these books present words in more than one sentence context and then provide several reinforcement activities for each word. The more you work with a given word in actual sentence situations, the better your chances of making it part of your permanent word base.

There may also be materials in your college learning center that take a "word in context" approach. The regular use of vocabulary study books and materials, combined with regular reading and with your own ongoing vocabulary word sheets, is a solid way to improve your vocabulary.

Part Four

Reading Comprehension Skills

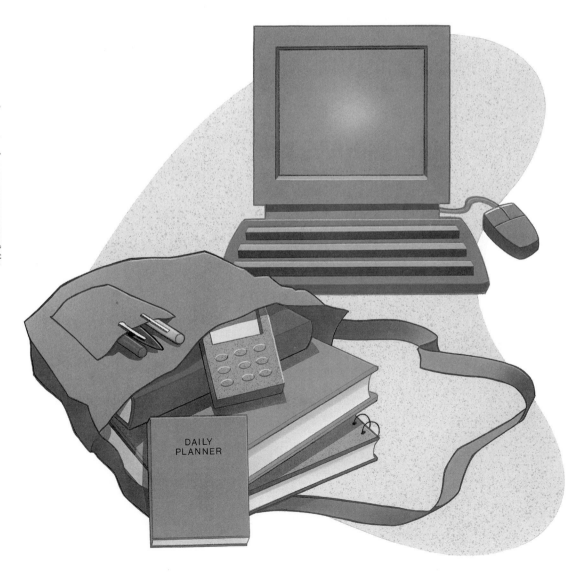

DAILY PLANNER

Preview

Part Four explains and offers practice in eight key reading comprehension skills. All these skills will help you read and take notes on your textbooks and other college materials. The first five skills involve the ability to recognize and use (1) definitions and examples of definitions, (2) enumerations and their headings, (3) the relationship of headings to subheadings, (4) emphasis words and other signal words, and (5) main ideas in paragraphs and short selections. The sixth and seventh skills involve the ability to outline and to summarize material you have read. And the last skill involves the ability to understand graphs and tables.

Introduction

One misleading idea that some students have about reading is that comprehension should happen all at once. They believe that a single reading of a textbook selection should result in a satisfactory understanding of that selection. But what such students do not realize is that good comprehension is usually a *process*. Very often, comprehension is achieved gradually, as you move from a general feeling about what something means to a deeper level of understanding.

Eight Key Skills

The purpose of Part Four is to help you learn eight key skills that will increase your understanding of what you read. The first five skills include the ability to recognize and use important elements of written material; the next two skills are techniques that will help you take effective study notes; and the last skill will assist you in interpreting and understanding the material presented in graphs and tables.

1 Recognizing definitions and examples
2 Recognizing enumerations
3 Recognizing headings and subheadings
4 Recognizing signal words
5 Recognizing main ideas in paragraphs and short selections
6 Knowing how to outline
7 Knowing how to summarize
8 Understanding graphs and tables

Your mastery of the eight basic skills will enable you to read and understand the important ideas in articles and textbook chapters.

- *Complete the following statements:*
  Good comprehension seldom happens all at once but is usually a
  <u>process</u>.

  There are eight skills you can learn to improve your
  <u>understanding of what you read</u>

Comprehension and Rapid Reading

Another misleading idea that students sometimes have about reading is that an increase in reading *rate*—the purpose of the much-advertised speed-reading courses—means an automatic increase in reading comprehension. Speed-reading courses *may* increase the number of words your eyes take in and "read" per minute. And comprehension may improve because you tend to concentrate more as you read faster. However, with difficult material, understanding is likely to fall as the rate rises. The surest way to achieve reading speed *and* comprehension is to develop reading comprehension skills. Speed will automatically follow as you learn how to identify main ideas and then go quickly over lesser points and supporting details. Speed will also result as you learn how to vary your reading rate according to the nature of the material and your purpose in reading. In summary, by emphasizing comprehension rather than sacrificing it, you will make yourself a more efficient reader, and therefore a faster reader.

- What are two misleading ideas that students sometimes have about reading?

  1. Comprehension is something that should happen all at once.

  2. An increase in reading rate means an automatic increase in reading comprehension.

- What is the drawback of speed-reading courses?

  With difficult material, understanding is likely to fall as the rate rises.

- What is the surest way to develop reading speed *and* comprehension?

  Develop reading comprehension skills.

Skill 1: Recognizing Definitions and Examples

Definitions are often among the most important ideas in a selection. They are particularly significant in introductory courses, where much of your time is spent mastering the specialized vocabulary of the subject. You are, in a sense, learning the "language" of sociology or biology or whatever the subject might be.

Most definitions are abstract, and so they are usually followed by one or more examples that help clarify their meaning. Always select and mark off at least one example that helps make an abstract definition clear for you.

In the following passage from a sociology textbook, underline the definition. Also, locate the two examples and write *ex* in the left-hand margin beside each of them.

Intuition

Galen, a famous Greek physician of the second century, prepared an elaborate chart of the human body showing exactly where it might be pierced without fatal injury. How did he know the vulnerable spots? He just *knew* them. True, he had learned a good deal of human anatomy through his observations and those of his associates, but beyond this, he relied upon his intuition to tell him which zones were fatal. *Intuition* is any flash of insight (true or mistaken) whose source the receiver cannot fully identify or explain. Hitler relied heavily upon his intuition, much to the distress of his generals. His intuition told him that France would not fight for the Rhineland, that England would not fight for Czechoslovakia, that England and France would not fight for Poland, and that England and France would quit when he attacked Russia. He was right on the first two insights and wrong on the last two.

You may have realized that the first lines of the passage are not the definition of intuition but an example. The definition ("Intuition is any flash of insight") is found midway through the paragraph. The examples (of Galen and Hitler) are found at the beginning and end of the paragraph. Underlining the definition and putting *ex* in the margin beside the examples will be helpful later when you are taking study notes on the passage.

- How should you mark off definitions? *Underline them.*
- Why should you mark off examples? *Examples help clarify abstract definitions.*
- If a text gives several examples of a definition, which one should you mark off, write down, or both? *An example that makes sense and "works" for you.*

Activity 1

Read quickly through the following selections, underlining each definition and writing *ex* in the left-hand margin beside an example of the definition. Some definitions will have several examples, but you need mark off only the example that makes the definition clear for you.

Note that textbook authors often call attention to terms they are defining by setting them off in *italic* or **boldface** type.

1. *Territoriality* refers to persons' assumptions that they have exclusive rights to certain geographic areas, even if these areas are not theirs by legal right. To take a common example: By the end of the first week of class most
ex.   students consider a particular seat to be their territory and will show signs of distress or irritation if someone else sits in that seat. What is interesting, even for the simple example we cited, is the subtle ways in which strangers observe certain implicit territorial rights and the emotional mechanisms that regulate this behavior.

   Personal space refers not to a geographic area but to the space surrounding our body, a space that moves with us. Persons regard that space as private
ex.   and try to prevent others from entering it. For example, persons sitting in a public reading room definitely seek to have at least one empty seat between themselves and the next reader. The phenomenon is also evident in less formal settings.

2. We should not yield to the **allness fallacy**—the attitude that what we know or say about someone or something is all there is to know and say. The more we delve into some subjects, the more we realize there is so much more to learn and to consider. Even authorities on certain subjects humbly admit they don't know all the answers. Though they sometimes disagree among

themselves on various topics, they continue to study all available facts. So do conscientious, open-minded business executives, government leaders, educators, students. Unfortunately, it is true of some people that "the less they know, the more sure they are that they know it all." Perhaps you have

ex. worked with such persons. A conspicuous example is that of the high school sophomore chatting casually with a man who (unknown to the student) was a distinguished scientist devoting his lifetime to studying botany. The smug sophomore commented, "Oh, botany? I finished studying all about that stuff last semester." As Bertrand Russell stated, "One's certainty varies inversely with one's knowledge."

3.   Matter can be said to have both potential and kinetic energy. <u>Potential energy is stored-up energy or energy an object possesses due to its relative position.</u> For example, a ball located twenty feet above the ground has more

ex. potential energy than another ball located ten feet above the ground and will bounce higher when allowed to fall. Water backed up behind a dam rep-

ex. resents potential energy that can be converted into useful work in the form of electrical energy. Gasoline represents a source of stored-up chemical potential energy that can be released during combustion.

<u>Kinetic energy is the energy that matter possesses due to its motion.</u> When the water behind the dam is released and allowed to flow, its potential

ex. energy is changed into kinetic energy, which may be used to drive generators and produce electricity. All moving bodies possess kinetic energy. The pressure exerted by a confined gas is due to the kinetic energy of rapidly moving gas particles. We all know the results when two moving vehicles collide—their kinetic energy is expended in the "crash" that occurs.

4.   The fact that you have been going to school for so many years indicates society's faith that you will transfer your training from classroom situations to everyday life situations. There are two fundamentally different types of transfer: positive and negative. Suppose I have learned that in order to keep the

ex. attention of my class in introductory psychology, I must tell a joke every ten minutes or so. It seems to be a reasonably successful device, so I try it in my class in personality psychology, and it works there too. This is an example of *positive transfer:* <u>What I have learned to do in one situation applies equally well in another situation.</u> But suppose that I try to carry it one step further and

ex. use the technique in a talk that I give at the faculty club. Here I discover that my jokes fall flat and the talk is a failure. This is an example of *negative transfer:* <u>What works in one situation is not applicable to another situation.</u>

Activity 2

Mark off definitions and examples in the following selections. In addition, take brief study notes on each selection on separate paper. Your study notes should consist of the definition or definitions plus one example that makes the definition or definitions clear to you. In each case, try to summarize your example—that is, condense it into the fewest words possible that are still complete and clear. One selection is done for you as an example.

Example

Edwin Sutherland, who popularized the differential association theory discussed earlier, noted that certain crimes are committed by affluent, "respectable" individuals in the course of their daily business activities. Sutherland referred to such offenses as *white-collar* crimes. More recently, the term *white-collar crime* has been widened to include offenses by businesses and corporations as well as by individuals. A wide variety of offenses are included in this classification, such as income tax evasion, stock manipulation, consumer fraud, bribery and extracting "kickbacks," embezzlement, and misrepresentation in advertising.

White-collar crime—offenses by businesses and corporations as well as by "respectable" business individuals
  Ex.—Income tax evasion

1. The effort to completely exterminate a people by killing all of them is called *annihilation.* It is ironic that the greatest annihilation in recorded history was conducted by a highly civilized Christian state. Between 1933 and
ex. 1945, the German Nazis killed about 4.5 million European Jews, marching many of them into gas chambers with a systematic bureaucratic efficiency. Other cataclysms in history may have produced more deaths, but we have no comparable example of such a deliberate, premeditated mass slaughter carried out as a government policy. Several instances of mass slaughter have occurred since then, perhaps the greatest of which accompanied the Hindu-
ex. Moslem clashes in India and Pakistan in 1948. Others include the slaughter of
ex. the Ibos in northern and western Nigeria in 1966 and of the Communists in Indonesia after their unsuccessful attempt to seize power in 1965.

2. Often, when faced with a conflict, we engage in the kind of behavior called vacillation—the tendency to be drawn first toward one possible resolution of the conflict, then toward another. Torn between studying and work-
ex. ing and going out with friends, we may change our minds several times. At one moment we may lean strongly toward studying, at the next moment toward going out. In an extreme case of vacillation, we may take so long making up our minds that we wind up with very little time left for either of the possibilities.

3.   Behavior therapists have applied their knowledge of operant conditioning to large groups of hospitalized patients. The basic premise in this work is
that patients should be treated as normal people capable of learning normal
behavior if they are appropriately rewarded. Normal people are paid money
for doing a job. They also receive attention and affection when they interact
with other people. If they were not paid, they would not work; if they were
ignored, they would not respond socially to others.
            In the treatment method known as the **token economy,** hospitalized psy-
chiatric patients receive rewards for performing "normal" behaviors. For

ex. example, one patient's job is to work in the hospital laundry each day. He
receives fifty "tokens," usually in the form of poker chips, for each day's
work. He can then trade in his tokens for his meals, a more comfortable bed
than the hospital's standard equipment, weekend passes to leave the hospital, magazines, cigarettes, and so on.

ex. 4.   Throw a stone into a lake: water waves move outward from the splash.
ex. Clap your hands: sound waves carry the noise all around. Switch on a lamp:
ex. light waves illuminate the room. Water waves, sound waves, and light waves
are very different from one another in important respects, but all have in common the basic properties of wave motion. A wave is a periodic disturbance—
a back-and-forth change of some kind (of water height in the case of water
waves, of air pressure in the case of sound waves, of electric and magnetic
fields in the case of light waves)—that spreads out from a source and carries
energy as it goes. Information, too, can be carried by waves; this is how sights
and sounds reach us.

Activity 3

Working with a chapter or chapters in one of your textbooks, find five definitions
and examples. Choose only definitions for which there are examples. Also, make
sure each example is one that helps make a definition clear to you. Use separate
paper for this activity. Include the number of the page on which you find each definition and example, in case your instructor wants to refer to the text in reviewing
your answers.
            Here is a model for Activity 3:

Textbook _Understanding Psychology_   Author(s): _Feldman_
Definition: _Personal stressors—major life events that have immediate_
negative consequences that generally fade with time.
Example: _Death of a family member_

■ Review Test

Read these selections, noting definitions and examples of the definitions. In the space provided, write the number of the sentence that contains a definition. Then write the number of the *first* sentence that gives an example of the definition.

1.   ¹Rumors are both a form of collective behavior and an important element in other types of collective behavior. ²A rumor is a difficult-to-verify piece of information that people transmit to one another in relatively rapid fashion. ³Although many rumors are false, some are accurate, or contain a measure of truth (for instance, a local plant will close or a product will be discontinued). ⁴Rumors typically arise in times of tension and sagging economic conditions in which we lack information or distrust official sources of information. ⁵They are a substitute for hard news. ⁶Rumors regarding alleged contamination and conspiracy are quite common. ⁷Unfounded rumors have hurt the sales of some of the nation's largest corporations. ⁸For instance, McDonald's and Wendy's have had to fight rumors that they put earthworms in hamburgers (perhaps suggested by the fact that raw hamburger resembles red worms). ⁹Some people have seen a Communist connection in the bent-elbow, clenched-fist symbol of Arm & Hammer, the baking soda. ¹⁰And Procter & Gamble removed its 135-year-old moon-and-stars trademark from its products when it was unable to dispel the rumor that the symbol is a sign of devil worship.

Definition: __2__   Example: __3__

2.   ¹You know what happens if you set out a pan of water: In time, the water will "disappear." ²The water did not boil. ³So what did happen? ⁴Remember, particles of matter are always in motion. ⁵Therefore, at the surface of a liquid, some particles will have enough kinetic energy to leave the liquid. ⁶It makes no difference what the temperature is. ⁷The particles that leave the surface are replaced by other particles. ⁸Some of these have enough kinetic energy to leave the surface. ⁹The process continues to go on. ¹⁰Finally, there is no liquid left. ¹¹This change from liquid to vapor (gas) is called *evaporation.*

Definition: __11__   Example: __1__

3.   ¹Phobias are fears that are out of proportion to the actual danger involved in a situation. ²Some people will not use elevators. ³Yes, the cable could break, the ventilation could fail, you could be stuck in midair awaiting repairs. ⁴But these problems are infrequent, and it would be foolhardy to walk forty flights twice daily to avoid them. ⁵Other people will not receive injections, even

when quite ill. [6]Injections can be painful, but these people would tolerate an even more painful pinch. [7]Phobias can seriously interfere with our lives. [8]People may know that a phobia is irrational yet still experience fear.

Definition: ___1___   Example: ___2___

4.   [1]Making up excuses or false attributions for potential failures is especially common when we think we might fail at something. [2]For example, a student fails to get enough sleep before an exam, an employee drinks too much at lunch with his boss, an investor says that he never has any luck in the stock market. [3]According to Edward Jones and Steven Berglas, these individuals are making up excuses so that they can blame some external thing if they fail. [4]The student can blame lack of sleep if she does poorly on the exam, the employee can blame drinking too much if he does not get his raise, and the investor can blame a run of bad luck if he loses money on the stock market. [5]Researchers Jones and Berglas call this tendency to make up an excuse for one's potential failure the use of a **self-handicapping strategy**. [6]By attributing to yourself all kinds of handicaps (missing sleep, drinking, bad luck), you can fail without having failure seem to be your own fault.

Definition: ___5___   Example: ___2___

Skill 2: Recognizing Enumerations

Like definitions, enumerations are keys to important ideas. Enumerations are lists of items that may actually be numbered in the text. More often, however, a list of items is signaled by such words as *first of all, second, moreover, next, also, finally,* and others. Typical phrases that introduce enumerations are: "There are three reasons why . . . "; "The two causes of . . . "; "Five characteristics of . . . "; "There are several ways to . . . "; and so on.

Activity

In the following selection, number *1, 2,* and *3* the guidelines for constructive criticism. Note that each of the guidelines will be indicated by a signal word.

> At times people need help so they can perform better. A necessary and yet far too often misused response is constructive criticism. *Constructive criticism* is evaluation of behavior—usually negative—given to help a person identify or correct a fault. Because criticism is such an abused skill, we offer several guidelines that will help you compose criticism that is both constructive and beneficial. First, make sure that the person is interested in hearing the criticism. The safest rule to follow is to withhold any criticism until it is asked for. It will be of no value if a person is not interested in hearing it. Another guideline is make the criticism as specific as possible. The more detailed the criticism, the more effectively the person will be able to deal with the information. Finally, show the person you are criticizing what can be improved. Don't limit your comments to what a person has done wrong. Tell him or her how what was done could have been done better.

You should have put a *1* in front of "make sure that the person is interested in hearing the criticism" (signaled by *First*), a *2* in front of "make the criticism as specific as possible" (signaled by *Another guideline*), and a *3* in front of "show the person you are criticizing what can be improved" (signaled by *Finally*). Develop the habit of looking for and numbering all the enumerations in a chapter.

When you take study notes on enumerations, be sure to include a heading that explains what a list is about. For example, because the following list does not have a descriptive heading, the notes are not as clear:

1. Make sure the person is interested in hearing the criticism
2. Make the criticism as specific as possible
3. Show the person you are criticizing what can be improved

Your notes will be clear and helpful if they include, as the following notes do, a heading describing what the list is about:

Guidelines for Constructive Criticism
1. Make sure the person is interested in hearing the criticism
2. Make the criticism as specific as possible
3. Show the person you are criticizing what can be improved

• Why should you look for and number enumerations? They are often keys to important ideas.

• What do phrases such as *Two effects of, Three important results are, Five factors to note* tell you? They tell you that an enumeration is coming (and help you write the heading that describes what the list is about).

The activities that follow will give you practice in the skill of locating and marking off enumerations.

Activity 1

In the selections that follow, number *1, 2, 3,* and so on, the items in each list or enumeration. Remember that words such as *first, another, also,* and *finally* often signal an enumeration. Also, in the space provided, write a heading that explains what each list is about. Look first at the example and the hints.

Example

Heading: Rewards of Schooling

In strictly pragmatic terms, schooling yields three rewards, and the amount of each reward increases in proportion to the amount of schooling. First, the individual who is well-schooled stands the [1]best chance of getting any job, other things being equal. Thus, the chance of unemployment is reduced. Second, the individual with a good background is the [2]one chosen for advancement and promotion; this enables him or her to earn more over the long run. Third, because of rewards one and two, the educated individual has [3]more personal freedom. Such a person will have more job opportunities from which to choose, is less threatened with unemployment, and can be freer economically because of his or her higher earning power. The decision in favor of further schooling needs to be encouraged if only for the above listed pragmatic reasons.

Hints

a   A selection often contains a phrase that introduces the enumeration. The introductory phrase in the preceding passage is "schooling yields three rewards." Look for such introductory phrases; they will help you write your heading.

b   Every heading that you write should begin with a word that ends in *s,* as in "Reward*s* of Schooling." As a reminder, the *s* has been added to each of the heading spaces that follow.

1. Heading: _____ Type *s* of Income _____

An American worker can be said to earn several types of income.[1] Money income is the amount a person receives in actual cash or checks for wages, salaries, rents, interest, and dividends.[2] Real income is what the money income will buy in goods and services; it is purchasing power. If a person's money income rises 5 percent in one year but the cost of purchases increases 8 percent on the average, then real income decreases about 3 percent.[3] Psychic income is an intangible but highly important income factor related to comfortable climate, a satisfying neighborhood, enjoyment of one's job, and so on. Some people prefer to take less real income so they can live in a part of the country with a fine climate and recreation opportunities—greater psychic income.

2. Heading: _____ Element*s* in Networking _____

Networking is the way people find out about jobs that aren't advertised in the newspaper; it is the way they learn about valuable new developments in their field before the crowd does. There are three main elements in networking. The first is[1] *visibility,* making your presence known. The more people meet you, the more are likely to remember you. The second element is[2] *familiarity,* letting people get to know you. It takes courage to expose your skills, attitudes, and opinions, but people are more likely to deal with you if they have some idea of how to think and react. The third element,[3] *image,* means giving people the impression that you are competent and pleasant to deal with. An optimistic, enthusiastic approach to business—and to life—is magnetic.

3. Heading: _____ Forms of Water Pollution _____

Water pollution takes two forms. The first occurs when[1]garbage and chemicals are thrown into the water. These waste materials upset the natural environment and often prove dangerous to the fish and other life in the water. To prevent further deterioration of our waters, business is now treating its wastes before putting them into the water or is looking for other, safer ways to dispose of them.

A second common problem is[2]thermal, or warm-water, pollution. Hydroelectric power plants, in particular, tend to cause this type of pollution. In creating electricity, utilities take water from a nearby lake or river, convert it to steam for turning the plant's turbine engines, change the steam back to water, and then return it to the original lake or river. The problem is that the water is often returned at five to ten degrees above the original temperature. This causes a change in the environment of the lake or river and can be harmful to the aquatic life there.

4. Heading: _____ Reasons for the Existence of Stereotypes _____

Three reasons for the existence of stereotypes will be noted. First, they [1]simplify explanations of human behavior. The crudest way to explain a phenomenon is to classify it. Aristotle was asked, for example, "Why do stones fall to Earth?" He answered that stones belong to the class Earth, and objects yearn to return to the class to which they belong. The explanation seems rather foolish in the light of modern physics. However, if you saw someone behaving oddly in a mental hospital, you might inquire of a psychiatrist, "Why does he behave that way?" The psychiatrist might answer, "He is a schizophrenic." You would probably be satisfied. But the answer is no explanation at all. Why is he diagnosed as a schizophrenic? The answer to this question is: Because he acts oddly—in ways characteristic of schizophrenic patients. Explanations by classification all have this quality of circularity. Nonetheless, explanations by classification often put curiosity to rest. Therefore, stereotypes are sometimes comforting pseudo-explanations.

Second, stereotypes often[2]provide a scapegoat for aggression. A scapegoat is a target for abuse. Scapegoats may actually be innocent, but because they can't fight back, they have all sorts of abuse heaped upon them. Minority groups are often unable to fight back, and they serve as an easy target for angry feelings that may have their real roots in other sources. A man who is angry at his boss may pick a fight with his wife; she becomes the scapegoat for his hostile feelings toward his boss. In the same way, it has been argued that the Nazis offered the Jew as a scapegoat to the German people. Prior to World War II, Germany had numerous economic problems. There was widespread frustration and latent anger. The Jew was blamed for Germany's problems.

Third, stereotypes [3] give members of a dominant group a sense of superiority. The members of the larger group can look at the members of the minority group and say to themselves, "I'm better than they are." These thoughts help individuals compensate for any dominant feelings of inferiority they themselves may possess. To illustrate, poor white Southern sharecroppers, feeling inadequate and incompetent in many ways, can look at black people and feed their egos by thinking, "We're white and they're black."

From the three reasons postulated for the creation of stereotypes, it seems clear that stereotypes exist for very real reasons. They meet human needs for explanation, aggression, and superiority.

Activity 2

In the following selections, number *1, 2, 3,* and so on the items in each list and underline the words that introduce the list. In addition, take brief study notes on each selection on separate paper. Your notes should consist of a numbered list of items and an accurate heading for that list. Try to summarize the items in each list—that is, condense them to the fewest words possible that are still complete and clear. One selection is done for you as an example.

Example

Studies have indicated <u>a number of values to reading and reciting</u>, as opposed to just reading. For one thing, when you read something with the knowledge that you must soon recite what you have read, you are [1] more likely to be motivated to remember and less likely to become inattentive. Moreover, recitation provides [2] immediate knowledge of results, so that you can see how well you are doing and adjust and modify your responses accordingly. Finally, recitation provides [3] active practice in recalling the material you wish ultimately to retain.

Values of Reading and Reciting

1. More motivation to remember
2. Immediate knowledge of results
3. Active practice in recalling material

1.   <u>Private property serves two important functions</u> in capitalism. First, it [1] places in the hands of individuals power over the use of productive resources. Economic activity cannot occur unless someone makes decisions about which goods are to be produced and when and how they are to be produced. The more complex the method of production, the more crucial is the decision-making process. The owners of resources may delegate part of their powers to others, but for there to be capitalism, the owners must have the final say

as to how resources are used. Second, private property[2] serves as an incentive for the accumulation of wealth. This incentive is necessary if the stock of capital in the economy is to grow. The right of property owners to benefit from the use of their property in the productive process encourages them to save and invest in capital goods.

2.   Physical punishment is a less efficient means of shaping behavior than is reinforcement. Spanking a child for hitting another child may have negative results. First, the child's main[1] response to the spanking may be anger and frustration—reactions that are incompatible with learning other, more socially acceptable responses. Second, the feelings aroused by the spanking [2] may lead to aggressive acts against "safe," nonpunishing objects in the environment. Third, the punishment effects[3] may extend only to behavior in the presence of the parents: Children may refrain from hitting while their parents are with them, but as soon as the parents are out of sight, the children will do what they want.

3.   It's likely that you respond to criticism in one of three ways. Perhaps you are one of those people who[1] withdraw when judged negatively by others. Sometimes this withdrawal takes the form of accepting the attack silently, even though you don't agree with or appreciate it. In other cases the withdrawal is physical: you might leave the presence of the critic temporarily or even permanently if the criticism is harsh enough. Although such a response does maintain peace and quiet, it takes a toll on your self-respect, for in addition to silently accepting the other's judgment of your behavior, you now must also suffer from the loss of self-esteem that comes from failing to stand up for your rights.

A second possible response to criticism is to[2] justify yourself. While this alternative has the advantage of at least maintaining your self-respect, it has two drawbacks. First, the criticism you are resisting may be valid. Compulsive justifiers will defend against any attack and in so doing fail to learn much valuable information about themselves. A second shortcoming of justification is that the critic seldom accepts your explanation. "You can defend yourself all day long," the other might seem to say, "but I still think you're wrong." In such cases justification is hardly worth the effort.

A third typical response to criticism is to[3] counterattack—to reduce the pressure on yourself—by pointing out some fault of the speaker. Although this strategy often shifts the spotlight away from your faults, it also has the undesirable consequence of generating ill will between you and the critic, thus weakening the relationship. In this sense counterattacking can sometimes result in your winning a battle and losing a friendship.

4.   We have defined directed thinking as being aimed at the solution to a specific problem, and logical thinking as one method of getting to such a solution. But in concrete terms, what are the actual steps we go through when we have a complex problem to solve?

It is first necessary to ^{1}*identify* the problem—to know that it exists and then to pinpoint and delineate it in order to see how you will direct your thinking to solve it. You first become aware of a problem as an obstacle or frustration—not always an unpleasant one, certainly, or sports and puzzles would not exist. Say you have just made a date to play tennis. After hanging up the phone, you realize that you have a dental appointment for exactly the same time. The problem is now identified—you are committed to being at two different places at one-thirty tomorrow afternoon.

After this, you begin to ^{2}*search* for possible solutions. With some problems this search can be as simple as random trial and error, like fitting one key after another into a lock until you find the one that works. If you stumble upon the right solution by the trial-and-error method, of course, you need go no further. But many problems do not yield to such a mechanical solution, and trying every possible alternative is not a very economical approach. Still, to some extent trial and error probably does enter into your search for a solution. First you start restricting your alternatives. Can you simply not turn up at the dentist's? No. Not show up at the tennis court? Not a good idea, either. Perhaps you had better call your friend back. Next, you ^{3}*analyze* the situation: If you explain to your friend what the difficulty is, maybe you can work out another time for the tennis game.

You then move to the ^{4}*attack* itself. You telephone your friend, and you agree to meet on the courts at four o'clock instead of one-thirty. You no longer have to be in two places at once, and your problem is solved.

Sometimes, of course, the interval between the appearance of a problem and its solution is short enough that you think of it as all having happened in a single step. What has really happened is that these four steps have occurred so rapidly that the solution seemed to come instantaneously. Other times—if the problem is a very complicated one, such as finding a cure for cancer—the single problem must be broken down into many parts, and the steps must be gone through, over and over, by many people.

Activity 3

Using one of your textbooks, find and record five separate enumerations. Write a heading for each list. There should be at least three items under each heading.

At the top of the first sheet of paper on which you do this activity, give the name of the textbook you are using and the authors. Also include the number of the page on which you find each enumeration, in case your instructor wants to refer to the text in reviewing your answers. A model follows.

Model

Textbook: _Alive and Well_   Authors: _A. & H. Eisenburg_

Heading: _Problems of the Elderly_   Pages: _542-544_

(1) Retirement

(2) Health

(3) Finances

■ **Review Test**

Locate and number the enumeration in each selection that follows. Then, in the space provided, summarize the points in each enumeration. Also, write a heading that accurately describes what the enumeration is about.

1.   There are at present three approaches to treating the allergic patient. One approach is to[1] control the environment by removing the offending substances. Such control could be achieved, for example, by keeping the home—especially the bedroom—free of carpeting, upholstery, clutter, and other dust collectors. Another approach to treating the allergic patient is to[2] use drug therapy or chemotherapy. Antihistamine drugs are the most widely used of all allergy drugs. Most effective for nasal allergies, they are often useful in skin and other allergies as well. Corticosteroids, used since 1949 for asthmatic attacks, have many adverse effects and are usually recommended only for life-threatening attacks and for short-term use. Finally, when environmental control and antihistamines fail to bring relief, the physician may consider [3]"desensitizing" the patient. This is accomplished by a series of injections of the allergen in increasing amounts. Unfortunately, even a successful hyposensitization may wear off with time and need to be repeated.

Heading: _Approaches to Treating the Allergic Patient_

(1) _Control the environment_

(2) _Use drug therapy or chemotherapy_

(3) _"Desensitize" the patient_

2.   There are several reasons why children involved in the divorce situation often live disrupted lives. First, they[1] must deal with the trauma of their parents' separation and of one parent's leaving home. "I remember it was near my birthday when I was going to be six that Dad said at lunch he was leaving," one eight-year-old recalled. "I tried to say, 'No, Dad, don't do it,' but I couldn't get my voice out. I was much too shocked." In addition, the child of divorce now [2]has only one parent to turn to on a day-to-day basis, and that parent—usually

the mother—may often be too busy with work, housekeeping, or finding a social life to offer sufficient support and guidance to the child. Children of divorce[3] must also often deal with the continuing conflict between warring parents. This conflict is especially traumatic in cases of child custody battles, in which the parents vie with each other for custody of the child while the child awaits the outcome.

Heading: _Why Children of Divorce Often Live Disrupted Lives_

(1) _Must deal with trauma of parents' separation_

(2) _Have only one parent to turn to on daily basis_

(3) _Must deal with continuing conflict between parents_

3.   Human beings are biological organisms. They possess the ability to respond to stimulation, to move, to regulate inputs and outputs of energy, and to reproduce. They proceed physically through the process of development (that is, over time, they move from simple to complex levels of organization). In the [1] embryonic stage (the first two months after conception) the organism increases in size from about 0.14 millimeter in diameter to about 1½ inches. Cell layers that become the nervous, circulatory, skeletal, muscular, digestive, and glandular systems are formed and continue to develop. During the [2] fetal stage (third month after conception until birth), the organism continues developing in such a manner that it has all the biological equipment necessary to survive at birth. During the [3] neonatal stage (roughly the first four weeks after birth), the organism "breaks in" its biological equipment. It begins to breath, to digest, to circulate blood, and so on. By the beginning of [4] infancy (about the first two or three years of life), the organism is well designed for sleeping, eating, and eliminating. It is during infancy that the organism truly begins to become human. The process of maturation defines the blank tablet so that experience may imprint a unique identity on it.

Heading: _Stages of Human Development_

(1) _Embryonic—first two months after conception_

(2) _Fetal—third month to birth_

(3) _Neonatal—first four weeks after birth_

(4) _Infancy—first two or three years of life_

4.   Most warfare is confined within the tribe itself and is part of a series of forms of patterned violence. At the lowest level is the [1] chest-pounding duel. This occurs between villages that are in alliance and occurs in response to accusations of cowardice or excessive demands for food or women. Here a

man represents his village at feasts and offers his chest to be beaten upon. Someone from the "insulting" village takes up the challenge. "Fierce fighters will take as many as four blows before demanding to hit the opponent. The recipient of the blows has a chance to hit the first man as many times as he was hit, unless he knocks him unconscious before delivering all the blows." Serious injury or unconsciousness terminates the matter, and the disputants usually patch up the quarrel. This, then, is legal violence. The second form of patterned violence is the club fights that occur between and within villages over adultery and theft of food. Here the offended party takes a long pole (club) and insults his opponent, who then comes with his own pole, and they alternately strike each other in the head. At the first sight of blood these often turn into a free-for-all with other men joining both sides. Theoretically, the village headman, armed with bow and arrows, will shoot anyone deliberately trying to kill his opponent or escalating the violence level. Often, however, a village may split into permanent factions over this, or the different villages will terminate their alliance. The club fight is regulated combat. The final violence level, that of the raid, is actual warfare. It takes place between unrelated villages and those who have broken their alliances. Here a war party practices throwing spears into a grass dummy representing the enemy, and before leaving, the members of the war party "psych" themselves up by singing their war song ("I am a meat-hungry buzzard"). They attack early in the morning, trying to pick off and kill some one individual and then retreat back to their home territory without being detected.

Heading: *Forms of patterned violence within the tribe*

(1) *Chest-pounding duels (legal violence)*

(2) *Club fights (regulated warfare)*

(3) *Raid (actual warfare)*

Skill 3: Recognizing Headings and Subheadings

Headings and subheadings are important visual aids that give you a quick idea of how the information in a chapter is organized. The model below shows a typical use of heads in a selection.

CHAPTER TITLE

The chapter title is set off in the largest print in the chapter. The title represents the shortest possible summary of what the entire chapter is about.

THIS IS A MAIN HEADING

Appearing under the chapter title are a series of main headings. Main heads may be centered or may start at the left margin; they are often set off with capital letters and, sometimes, a different color of ink. They represent a breakdown of the main topics covered in the chapter.

This Is a Subheading

Set off under the main headings are subheadings. They are in smaller type; sometimes they are underlined, italicized, or set in from the left margin. The subheadings represent a breakdown of the different ideas that are explained under the main headings.

Activity

1. Look at the first chapter of this book (pages 11–19).

   How many main heads are there in the chapter? __2__

   How many subheads are there? __9__

   How do the main heads differ from the subheads? _____

   Main heads are set in larger type than subheads.

   _____

   _____

2. Look at the excerpt from a textbook chapter on pages 171–181. The main head is "Courtship, Marriage, and Children."

   How many subheads fit under that main head? __3__

   One of the subheads is "Work and Families." How many subsubheads fit under it? __3__

   How do the subsubheads differ from the subheads? _____

   Subsubheads are italicized.

   _____

   _____

3. Look at a chapter in one of your other textbooks. Answers will vary.

   How many main heads are there in the chapter? _____

   How many subheads are there? _____

   How do the subheads differ from the main heads? _____

   _____

   _____

   _____

Using Headings to Locate Important Ideas

There are two methods for using headings to locate key ideas. Each method is explained and illustrated on the following pages.

Method 1: Change Headings into Basic Questions

Change a heading into one or more basic questions. A basic question can be general, starting with the word *What, Why,* or *How.* Or it can be specific, starting with the word *When, Where,* or *Who.* Use whatever words seem to make sense in terms of the heading and the passage that follows it. Consider, for example, the following textbook selection:

Decline of the Puritan Work Ethic

The Puritan concept of work as necessary for survival and as a duty and virtue in and of itself long dominated our culture. Work, obedience, thrift, and the delay of gratification were valued highly, and people's righteousness was often judged according to how hard they worked and how much they accomplished.

These views have changed, however, at an accelerated pace. Today's workers, particularly young workers, demand much more of themselves and their jobs than simply "filling a slot" and earning a living. The search for a meaningful, fulfilling job has become crucial. Workers increasingly desire to have responsibility and autonomy, to have a voice, and to demand not merely good physical working conditions but also good psychological working conditions. Rigid, authoritarian work structures are increasingly rejected as workers look to their jobs as a significant source of creative self-expression.

- What are two questions that could be made out of the heading "Decline of the Puritan Work Ethic"?

_____

_____

The title could be changed into the two basic questions: "What is the Puritan work ethic?" "Why has the Puritan work ethic declined?" The answer to the second question especially (the Puritan work ethic has declined because today's workers want meaningful, personally fulfilling jobs) forms the main idea of the passage. This technique of turning headings into basic questions often helps you cut through a mass of words to get to the heart of the matter. Develop the habit of using such questions.

Method 2: See How Subheads Relate to Main Heads

If subheads follow a main head, determine how they are related to the main head. For example, suppose you noted the following main head and subheads spaced out over three pages of a business text:

ADVANTAGES OF THE PRIVATE ENTERPRISE SYSTEM

Freedom of Choice by Consumers
Decentralized Decision Making
High Productivity

Without having read a word of the text, you will have found one of the main ideas: The private enterprise system has three advantages—(1) freedom of choice, (2) decentralized decision making, and (3) high productivity.

Often the relationship between headings and subheads will be as clear and direct as in this example. Sometimes, however, you must read or think a bit to see how a heading and its subheads are related. For instance, in the excerpt from a speech text on page 129, following the main head "How to Become a Better Listener" are the subheads "Take Listening Seriously," "Resist Distractions," and so on. When you realize that the subheads are a list of the different ways to become a better listener, you have found one of the most important ideas on those pages—without having read even a word of the text. Sometimes there will be no clear relationship between the heading and the subheads. You want to be ready, though, to take advantage of a relationship when it is present.

• Why should you change headings into a basic question or questions?
  Doing so is a way of getting at the main idea.

• Why should you check to see how subheads relate to the main heads?
  The relationship between the main head and subheads may express a main idea in a selection.

• Look at the excerpt from the speech text starting on page 129. How many sub-subheads appear under the subhead "Focus Your Listening"? _____3_____
  What is the relationship between "Focus Your Listening" and the three sub-subheads?
  The subsubheads are a list of ways to focus your listening.

• Look at the excerpt from the business text starting on page 137. How many sub-heads appear under the heading "Convenience Products"? _____3_____
  What is the relationship between "Convenience Products" and the subheads?
  The subheads are types of convenience products.

Activity 1

Read the following selections to find the answer or answers to the basic question or questions asked. Write your answer or answers in the space provided.

1. *Question:* What is an important difference between writing and talking?

An Important Difference between Writing and Talking

In everyday conversation, you make all kinds of points or assertions. You say, "I'm not going out with him anymore," or "She's really generous," or "I hate my job," or "That was a tremendous party." The people you are talking to don't always challenge you to give reasons for your statements. They may know why you feel as you do, or may already agree with you, or may simply not want to put you on the spot, so they don't always ask "Why?" But the people who *read* what you write may not know you, agree with you, or feel in any way obligated to you. So if you want to communicate effectively with them, you must provide solid evidence for any point that you make. In writing, any idea that you advance must be supported with specific reasons or details.

Answer: <u>In writing, any idea that you advance must be supported with solid</u>
<u>reasons or details.</u>

2. *Questions:* What is selfish learning? What is an example of selfish learning?

Selfish Learning

How can one explain the star football player who knows fifty plays by heart and the individual movements of all eleven players for most of the plays yet seems incapable of remembering a simple verb conjugation? Then there is the boy who hears the lesson instructions repeated four times yet fails to do the lesson correctly even though he can remember the pretty girl's phone number that he heard only once. At least some of the answers to the problems posed rest in what the author terms "selfish learning." In its simplest form, selfish learning refers to learning that the student accomplishes only for himself or herself—for his or her own ends with little or no regard for extrinsic, or external, reasons (requirements, grades) for the learning. The boy who knows fifty football plays by heart yet cannot conjugate a verb does not suffer from some impairment of his learning process, nor will general learning theory explain this apparent paradox. The explanation is to be found in those factors that activate or bring learning processes into action, namely, motivation, attention, and personal meaningfulness of the material once it is studied.

Answer: <u>Learning the student accomplishes for his own ends with little or</u>
<u>no regard for extrinsic reasons for learning. Example: Boy who knows 50</u>
<u>football plays by heart yet cannot conjugate a verb.</u>

3. *Question:* In what ways can job boredom be overcome?

Overcoming Job Boredom

A major problem in the production process is the fact of job boredom. We know from research in industry that many people are bored with their jobs. For example, assembly line workers who spend their entire day doing the same operation over and over complain that the work is painfully dull and unrewarding. Many of them have no pride in their jobs. On the other hand, without this division of labor in which everyone performs a simple task, industry could never achieve high production. How can the workers and the work be brought together in a meaningful way? Today a number of methods are being tried, including job enlargement and job enrichment. *Job enlargement* involves giving the workers added duties, such as having them perform more operations or move from job to job on an assembly line. By making the work less routine, the company tries to break down the boredom factor. *Job enrichment* involves changing the jobs so as to build into them things that motivate the workers. These include increased responsibility, challenging work, opportunity for advancement and growth, and a greater feeling of personal achievement.

Answer: Job boredom can be overcome through job enlargement and job enrichment.

4. *Questions:* How many people work in service jobs? Which services predominate?

Service Industries in the United States

The United States is the world leader in service industries. It is estimated that more than 65 percent of the labor force in this country is engaged in providing services. Services are provided by government workers such as police officers, firefighters, post office clerks, public school teachers, and state office employees. Services are also provided by those in the nonprofit private sector, such as employees in hospitals, museums, charities, churches, private schools, and private colleges. But the largest employment in service occupations is seen in profit-oriented and marketing-oriented businesses: airlines, banks, hotels and motels, consulting firms, restaurants, real estate agencies, insurance companies, beauty salons, amusements, caterers, and so on. And that listing continues to expand and increase.

Answer: More than 65 percent of the labor force. Profit-oriented and marketing-oriented businesses.

Activity 2

Following are chapter and section headings taken from a variety of college texts. Change each into a *meaningful* basic question or questions, using words like *what, why, who, which, when, in what ways, how.* Note the example.

Example: **Alternatives to**
Conflict

a. *What are alternatives to conflict?*

b. *Which is the best alternative?*

Sociology

Possible questions:

1. **Primary and Secondary Groups**

a. *What is a primary group?*

b. *What is a secondary group?*

2. **Prison Abuses and the Reform Movement**

a. *What are some prison abuses?*

b. *How does the reform movement work?*

3. **Barriers to Social Knowledge**

a. *What is social knowledge?*

b. *What are some barriers to social knowledge?*

4. **Beneficial and Negative Impacts of Cities**

a. *What are the beneficial impacts of cities?*

b. *What are the negative impacts of cities?*

Psychology

5. **Loneliness in Modern Life**

a. *What causes loneliness in modern life?*

b. *Who is affected by this loneliness?*

6. **The Social Dropouts**

a. *Who are social dropouts?*

b. *Why do they drop out?*

7. **Coping with Frustration**

a. *What are some ways of coping with frustration?*

b. *What are the results of not coping?*

8. **The Mentally Retarded**

a. *What is mental retardation?*

b. *What are some causes of retardation?*

History and Political Science

9. **The Dark Ages and the Glimmer of Light**

a. *What were the Dark Ages?*

b. *What was the glimmer of light?*

10. **The Two Terms of Theodore Roosevelt**

a. *When did Roosevelt serve two terms?*

b. *What did Roosevelt accomplish?*

11. The Fourteenth Amendment
   a. *What is the Fourteenth Amendment?*
   b. *When was it passed?*

12. The War of 1812
   a. *What caused the War of 1812?*
   b. *What countries were involved?*

Business and Economics

13. Types of Economic Systems
   a. *What are the types of economic systems?*
   b. *What are their advantages and disadvantages?*

14. Pollution and Business
   a. *How does business contribute to pollution?*
   b. *How can pollution by business be controlled?*

15. Taft-Hartley Act
   a. *What was the Taft-Hartley act?*
   b. *What were its values and drawbacks?*

16. Regulation of Business
   a. *How is business regulated?*
   b. *Should business be regulated?*

Biology and Other Sciences

17. Characteristics of Living Things
   a. *What are the characteristics of living things?*
   b. *What is the most basic characteristic?*

18. Cell Development
   a. *In what ways do cells develop?*
   b. *What interferes with cell development?*

19. Energy
   a. *How is energy defined?*
   b. *What are different forms of energy?*

20. Heart Disease
   a. *What is heart disease?*
   b. *How can heart disease be prevented?*

Activity 3

Using a chapter from one of your textbooks, change five headings into basic questions. Then read the sections under the headings to find concise, accurate answers to the questions.

On a separate sheet of paper, indicate the headings, the questions you ask about the headings, and the answers to the questions. At the top of the first sheet on which you do this activity, give the name of the textbook, the author or authors, and the pages. Turn this activity in to your instructor.

Activity 4

Scrambled together in the list that follows are five textbook headings and four subheadings for each of them. Write the headings in the lettered blanks (A, B, C, D,
E) and write the appropriate subheadings in the numbered blanks (1, 2, 3, 4).

Note: The order of the lettered sections may vary.

Conquest of the Plains	The Cattle Kingdom	Frontier Farmers
Cells	Tissues	Freewriting
Preparing a Scratch Outline	Heart and Artery Disease	Organ Systems
Urban Problems	Pollution	Kinds of Body Units
The Sheepherders	Brainstorming	Crowding
Organs	Arthritis	Diabetes
Noncommunicable Diseases	Making a List	Prospectors and Ranchers
Techniques in the Writing Process	Strikes	Slums
	Cancer	

A. _Urban problems_

   1. _Pollution_

   2. _Strikes_

   3. _Crowding_

   4. _Slums_

B. _Conquest of the Plains_

   1. _The Sheepherders_

   2. _The Cattle Kingdom_

   3. _Frontier Farmers_

   4. _Prospectors and Ranchers_

C. _Techniques in the Writing Process_

   1. _Preparing a Scratch Outline_

   2. _Brainstorming_

   3. _Making a List_

   4. _Freewriting_

D. Kinds of Body Units
    1. Cells
    2. Tissues
    3. Organs
    4. Organ Systems
E. Noncommunicable Diseases
    1. Heart and Artery Disease
    2. Arthritis
    3. Cancer
    4. Diabetes

Activity 5

Using one of your textbooks, find five sets of main heads and subheads that have a clear relationship to each other. Be sure to number the subheads and to find a minimum of two subheads in each case. Also, include the numbers of the pages on which you find your main heads and subheads, in case your instructor wants to refer to the text in reviewing your answers. A model follows.

Example

Textbook: *Business Today*   Authors: Rachman and others

Heading: The Marketing Mix   Pages: 298–301

    1. Product   3. Place

    2. Price   4. Promotion

Following the main head "The Marketing Mix" are four subheads—titles in smaller print under the main heading. Each subhead, it is clear, is one of the ingredients in a marketing mix. By recognizing the relationship between the main head and the subheads, the reader has found an important idea—without having yet read a word of the text!

■ **Review Test**

Part A: Answer the basic questions that are asked about the selections below.

1. *Questions:* How much of a problem is teenage drinking? Who are the teenage drinkers?

    Note: Wording of answers may vary.

    ### Teenage Drinking

    Drinking patterns are often set in high school. Thus the growing use of alcohol by adolescents and even preadolescents and the high rate of misuse and abuse are of increasing concern. An estimated 1.3 million teenagers and preteens drink to excess. Though casual drinking is found among all groups of teenagers, problem drinking is found more often among students who also engage in other types of deviant behavior, who value and expect achievement less and esteem independence more than nondrinkers, and who are more tolerant of deviant behavior in others. Girls with drinking problems are likely to have parent problems.

    Answers: Estimated 1.3 million teens and preteens drink to excess. Problem drinkers often engage in other deviant behavior, value independence more than achievement, tolerate deviant behavior in others. Girls often have parent problems.

2. *Questions:* What is the myth of acceptance? Why is it a myth?

    ### The Myth of Acceptance

    The myth of acceptance states that the way to judge the worth of one's actions is by the approval they bring. Communicators who subscribe to this belief go to incredible lengths to seek acceptance from people who are significant to them, even when they must sacrifice their own principles and happiness to do so. Adherence to this irrational myth can lead to some ludicrous situations:

Remaining silent in a theater when others are disturbing the show for fear of "creating a scene"

Buying unwanted articles so that the salespeople won't think you have wasted their time or think you are cheap

In addition to the obvious dissatisfaction that comes from denying your own principles and needs, the myth of acceptance is irrational because it implies that others will respect and like you more if you go out of your way to please them. Often this simply isn't true. How is it possible to respect people who have compromised important values only to gain acceptance? How is it possible to think highly of people who repeatedly deny their own needs as a means of buying approval? While others may find it tempting to use these people to suit their ends or amusing to be around them, genuine affection and respect are hardly due such characters.

Answers: Myth states that the worth of one's actions is judged by the approval they bring. It's a myth because it isn't true, and acting on it causes one to lose the affection and respect he or she wants.

Part B: Using words such as *what, why, who, which, in what ways,* and *how,* write two meaningful questions for each textbook head that follows.

Possible questions:

Our Changing Life Span
- a. What is our life span today?
- b. What factors are causing it to change?

Children of Divorce
- a. How many children of divorce are there?
- b. How does divorce affect children?

Corporate Cover-Ups
- a. Which corporations have been involved in cover-ups?
- b. How were those cover-ups discovered?

Industrial Revolution
- a. When did the Industrial Revolution occur?
- b. What were the effects of the Industrial Revolution?

Part C: Scrambled together in the list that follows are three textbook headings and three subheadings for each of the headings. Write the headings in the lettered blanks (A, B, C) and write the appropriate subheadings in the numbered blanks (1, 2, 3).

Advertising Media	Drug Abuse	Hypnosis
Sleep	Problems of Adolescence	Juvenile Delinquency
Dropping Out of School	Meditation	Altered States of Consciousness
Television	Direct Mail	
	Magazines	

Note: The order of the lettered sections may vary.

A. Advertising Media

1. Television

2. Direct Mail

3. Magazines

B. Problems of Adolescence

1. Dropping Out of School

2. Drug Abuse

3. Juvenile Delinquency

C. Altered States of Consciousness

1. Sleep

2. Meditation

3. Hypnosis

Skill 4: Recognizing Signal Words

Signal words help you, the reader, follow the direction of a writer's thought. They are like signposts on the road that guide the traveler. Common signal words show emphasis, addition, comparison or contrast, illustration, and cause and effect.

Emphasis Words

Among the most valuable signals for you to know are *emphasis words,* through which the writer tells you directly that a particular idea or detail is especially important. Think of such words as red flags that the author is using to make sure you pay attention to an idea. Look over the following list, which contains some typical words showing emphasis.

important to note	especially valuable	the chief factor
most of all	most noteworthy	a vital force
a significant factor	remember that	above all
a primary concern	a major event	a central issue
the most substantial issue	the chief outcome	a distinctive quality
a key feature	the principal item	especially relevant
the main value	pay particular attention to	should be noted

Activity

Circle the one emphasis signal in each of these selections. Note the example.

Example

The safest and most effective solution to the various approaches to sex education is obviously a course of compromise. Certain sexual needs should be permitted expression; unadorned information about the physiological and psychological aspects of sex should be presented to all; and the Judeo-Christian traditions within which we live must be understood and dealt with sensibly in the framework of present-day society.

1.   Although the resources of our world are limited, the wants of people are not. Indeed, one of the most important assumptions of economics is that total human wants can never be satisfied. No matter how much we have, we seem to want more. As people's incomes increase, so does their desire for more and better goods and services.

2.   Chronic air pollution is expensive to the American public, costing us dearly in terms of both money and health. Air pollution causes buildings and automobiles to deteriorate. Our poisoned air damages crops, livestock, roads, and metals and forces huge cleaning bills for everything from dusty draperies to soot-blackened buildings. It is especially in terms of health, however, that pollution hurts. It is estimated that breathing the air of New York City is the equivalent of smoking two packs of cigarettes a day.

3.   To be happy, adolescents must be realistic about the achievements they are capable of, about the social acceptance they can expect to receive, and about the kind and amount of affection they will receive. Of the three, social acceptance is the most crucial. Well-accepted adolescents will automatically receive affection from those who accept them, and their achievements will win approval if not acclaim.

4.   In practice, a deficiency of just one nutrient, such as protein, is not generally seen. More likely, a combination of protein and calorie malnutrition will occur. Protein and calorie deficiency go hand in hand so often that public health officials have given a name to the whole spectrum of disease conditions that range between the two—*protein-calorie malnutrition* (PCM). This is the world's most widespread malnutrition problem, killing millions of children every year.

Addition Words

Addition words tell you that the writer's thought is going to continue in the same direction. He or she is going to add on more points or details of the same kind. Addition words are typically used to signal enumerations, as described on pages 368–377.

Look over the following addition words.

also	first of all	last of all	and
another	for one thing	likewise	second
finally	furthermore	moreover	the third reason
first	in addition	next	

Activity

Read the selections that follow. Circle the *three* major addition words in the first passage and the *five* major addition words in the second passage.

1.   Despite favorable surface conditions, there were throughout the 1920s defects in the American economy. First, some major industries did not experience the general prosperity which characterized most of the economy. Meager farm income meant that farmers lacked purchasing power to buy their share of the increasing output of goods and services. Coal, textiles, and shoes were among other industries that suffered from low profit margins. Moreover, while employment rose during the 1920s, the biggest gains were in the low-paid service trades rather than in those industries where earnings were high. Furthermore, the condition of American foreign trade was not as healthy as it appeared.

2.   Here are ways to take some of the danger out of smoking. First of all, choose a cigarette with less tar and nicotine. The difference between brands (including those with filters) can be as much as two to one, even more. See how much you can reduce your tar and nicotine intake by switching. Also, don't smoke your cigarette all the way down. You get the most tar and nicotine from the last few puffs because the tobacco itself acts as a filter. Smoke halfway and you get only about 40 percent of the total tar and nicotine. The last half of the cigarette will give you 60 percent. Another help is to take fewer draws on each cigarette. Just reduce the number of times you puff on each cigarette and you'll cut down on your smoking without really missing it. In addition, you should reduce your inhaling. Remember, you're not standing on a mountain gulping in fresh air, so don't welcome it with open lungs. Don't inhale as deeply; take short shallow drags. Practice on a big cigar. Finally, you should smoke fewer cigarettes each day. For some people this is easy, but for others it may be the most difficult step of all. Don't think of it as cutting down; think of it as postponing. It's always easier to postpone a cigarette if you know you'll be having one later. Carry your cigarettes in a different pocket; at work, keep them in a desk drawer or a locker—any place where you can't reach for one automatically. The trick is to change your habit patterns.

Comparison or Contrast Words

Comparison words signal that the author is pointing out a similarity between two subjects. They tell you that the second idea is like the first one in some way. Look over the following comparison words.

like	just as	in the same way	similarly
likewise	in like manner	alike	equally
just like	in a similar fashion	similarity	as

Contrast words signal a change in the direction of the writer's thought. They tell you that the author is pointing out a difference between two subjects or statements. Look over the following contrast words.

but	yet	variation	on the other hand
however	differ	still	conversely
in contrast	difference	on the contrary	otherwise

Activity

Circle the *one* comparison and the *one* contrast signal in each passage.

1. Sleep has always been a fascinating topic. We spend about one-third of our adult life sleeping. Most animals sleep in a similar fashion—they collapse and relax their muscles. In contrast, birds and horses sleep upright, with their antigravity muscles at work.

2. Between 1860 and 1910, some 23 million foreigners migrated to America. Just as before the Civil War, most of them came in search of better economic opportunities. But there were new forces at work in the United States and Europe that interacted to attract ever-increasing numbers of immigrants.

3. Premarital sex does not always result from a desire for intimacy. Peer pressure also seems to be an important factor. For young males, sexual intercourse is often considered a way to prove their manliness. In like manner, young females believe that sexual intimacy will prove they are sexy and desirable. Several studies have found that young women with a poor self-image sometimes use sex as a way to feel better about themselves. On the other hand, females who plan to attend college are less likely to be sexually intimate than females who do not plan to go to college.

4. The steadily increasing flow of women into the labor force was caused, then, by a number of economic factors. And just as these economic changes were occurring, attitudes were changing as well. Many women no longer felt that being a full-time homemaker was providing them with an adequate sense of fulfillment and self-worth. Still, many career ladders have remained frustratingly difficult for women to climb.

Illustration Words

Illustration words tell you that an example or illustration will be given to make an idea clear. Such words are typically used in textbooks that present a number of definitions and examples of those definitions (see pages 361–367). Look over the following illustration words.

for example	specifically	for instance
to illustrate	once	such as

Activity

Circle the one illustration signal in each selection below.

1. One purpose for incorporating sexual themes or pictorial material into advertisements is to attract consumers' attention to the ad. However, evidence suggests that use of such material may not always have an easily predictable or desired effect. For example, one study found nonsexual and sexual-romantic themes to have a greater influence on consumers' attention than did nudity.

2. An interesting point about role playing is the way middle-years and adolescent youngsters play the role of being their age. One eight-year-old boy, for instance, avidly collected baseball cards and kept track of games and team standings in the sports pages in accordance with the mores of his neighborhood, even though he had never seen a baseball game or expressed the slightest interest in attending one.

3. Many problems, of course, do not lend themselves to straightforward strategies but rely more on the use of flexible and original thinking. Psychologists sometimes refer to this type of thinking as *divergent* thinking, in contrast to *convergent* thinking. A problem such as a math problem requires convergent thinking—it has only one solution or very few solutions. Problems that have no single correct solution and require a flexible, inventive approach call for divergent thinking.

4. Short-term memory is like your attention span. If you're distracted, you'll forget whatever is in short-term memory. This can be a nuisance sometimes, but it helps to preserve sanity. Suppose that you remembered every trivial transaction you were involved in all day long. Such information would interfere with your ability to go on with other activities and to take in new material. To illustrate, if you were waiting on tables and could not put the orders of the previous ten customers out of your mind after they had left the restaurant, you would have a hard time remembering the orders of your current customers.

Cause-and-Effect Words

Cause-and-effect words signal that the author is going to describe results or effects. Look over the following cause-and-effect words.

because	reason	since
therefore	effect	as a result
so that	thus	if . . . then
cause	consequently	result in

Activity

Circle the *one* instance of a cause-and-effect word or words in each of the following passages.

1.   One study of the criminal justice system found that in one year over 800,000 felonies were committed in the city. About 104,000 people were arrested and only 1,000 were imprisoned. The great majority got off "scot free" because many victims refused to testify. When people call the police, they often do so to frighten the offender and show their anger; they cool off when it comes to giving testimony that will send the person to prison.

2.   Thirty years ago, coal miners and workers in cotton mills accepted cancer of the lung as part of life. In a vague way they knew that longtime workers got short of breath and coughed up blood, and they wrote folk songs about brown lung disease. But as a result of a new awareness about occupational diseases and a social movement against cotton dust and coal dust, an accepted fact of life was transformed into an unacceptable illness.

3.   "The hamburger end of the fast-food industry is facing the long-awaited problem of saturation," says analyst Michael Culp at the brokerage firm of Bache Halsey Stuart Shields. "It's increasingly difficult to open more restaurants, and it's harder to sell more hamburgers." Thus, to maintain their growth momentum, the industry's big names are moving aggressively to steal each other's customers, enlarge their menus, and spawn new fast-food concepts.

4.   There are several possible explanations why retail prices are set to end on certain odd or even numbers. The practice is supposed to have started many years ago when retailers priced products so that clerks were forced to record the sale and make change. This discouraged the clerks from pocketing the money from sales. Some people believe that the practice of odd–even pricing continues today because consumers view these prices as bargains. If the price of the shirt is only $14.95, then they are able to spend "less than $15 for a shirt."

Practice in Recognizing Signal Words

Activity 1

Below are some of the signal words that are most often used by writers. Place each word under its proper heading.

for example	in addition
therefore	for instance
moreover	just as
most important	consequently
but	most significant
also	however
differ	such as
alike	similarly
as a result	especially valuable

Emphasis

most important

most significant

especially valuable

Addition

moreover

also

in addition

Comparison

alike

just as

similarly

Contrast

but

differ

however

Illustration

for example

for instance

such as

Cause and Effect

therefore

as a result

consequently

Activity 2

Circle the signal words in the selections that follow. The number and kind of signal words you should look for are indicated at the start of each selection.

1. One cause-and-effect signal; one contrast signal.

    Many of the restless and dissatisfied sons and daughters of these middle-, upper-middle-, and upper-class homes had never known want or poverty. Consequently, they could not understand their parents' emphasis upon money, status, and work. Parents, on the other hand, could not understand how some of their children could be indifferent, even hostile, to formal education and preparation for work.

2. One emphasis signal; one illustration signal; one contrast signal; one addition signal.

    One of the most persistent desires of human beings has been to indulge in mood-changing and pleasure-giving practices. For instance, diverse cultures have engaged in the drinking of alcoholic beverages of all descriptions. But as with most pleasures, overindulgence can be harmful to oneself and others. Also, not everyone agrees that drinking or using other mood modifiers should be an accepted pleasure.

3. One emphasis signal; one contrast signal; one cause-and-effect signal.

    The greatest value of play technique is in the study of personality. Children often cannot or will not explain themselves in the first person. However, they may reveal much of their inner lives in play. The child who will not tell about his or her own fears and conflicts may readily project these feelings onto dolls. Feelings of rejection, insecurity, mixed attitudes about parents, repressed hatred, fears, and aggressions may all be freely revealed in play. As a result, the play technique, when properly handled, offers opportunities for understanding the child that are otherwise difficult to create.

4. Two cause-and-effect signals; four addition signals; one contrast signal.

    As you are well aware, bureaucracies, while designed for maximal efficiency, are notorious for their inefficiencies. In practice, Weber's ideal form of bureaucracy is not achieved, for a number of reasons. First, human beings do not exist just for organizations. People track all sorts of mud from the rest of their lives with them into bureaucratic arrangements, and they have a great many interests that are independent of the organization. Second, bureaucracies are not immune to social change. When such changes are frequent and rapid, the pat answers supplied by bureaucratic regulations and rules interfere with a bureaucracy's rational operation. Third, bureaucracies are designed for the "average" person. However, in real life people vary in intelligence, energy, zeal, and dedication so that they are not in fact interchangeable in the day-to-day functioning of organizations. And fourth, in a bureaucracy each person considers anything that falls outside his or her province to be someone else's problem. Consequently, bureaucrats find it easy to evade responsibility.

■ **Review Test**

Signal words have been removed from each of the following textbook excerpts and placed above it. Fill in the missing signal word or words in the answer spaces provided.

Note that you will have to read each passage carefully to see which words logically fit in each answer space.

1. *In addition   most vital   Yet   however   for instance*

   We take plants for granted. The carpet of greenery that blankets the earth is, to us, an ordinary and everyday thing. Plants, _____*however*_____, are the only living things on earth capable of producing life-sustaining oxygen. _____*In addition*_____, plants release moisture into the atmosphere, which contributes to the climate conditions we know today. Unfortunately, human beings continue to destroy this _____*most vital*_____ element of their environment. In the Amazon jungle, _____*for instance*_____, vast tracts of rain forest are being leveled; without the moisture-producing plants, the climate there is already undergoing dangerous changes. People are constantly learning more about the delicate interrelation of life on this planet. _____*Yet*_____ they persist in these suicidal actions.

2. *important   Consequently   However   For example*

   Many Americans view gambling, prostitution, public drunkenness, and use of marijuana as victimless crimes in which there is no "victim" other than the offender. _____*Consequently*_____, there has been pressure from some groups to decriminalize certain activities. Such groups believe that decriminalization is an _____*important*_____ step to freeing up the resources of the overburdened criminal justice system. _____*However*_____, opponents of decriminalization insist that such offenses do indeed bring harm to innocent victims. _____*For example*_____, a person with a drinking problem can become abusive to a spouse or children; a compulsive gambler may steal in order to pursue this obsession.

3. *One   For example   Because   Finally   Another   important*

   In an ideal world, we could eliminate all physical and mental distractions. In the real world, however, this is not possible. _____*Because*_____ we think so much faster than a speaker can talk, it's easy to let our attention wander while we listen. Whenever you find this happening, it is _____*important*_____ that you make a conscious effort to pull your mind back to what the speaker is saying. Then force it to stay there. _____One_____ way to do this is to think a little ahead of the speaker— try to anticipate what will come next. _____Another_____ way to keep your mind on a speech is to review mentally what the speaker has already said and make sure you understand it. _____Finally_____, listen between the lines and assess what a speaker implies verbally or says nonverbally with body language. _____For example_____, suppose a speaker is introducing someone to an audience. The speaker says, "It gives me great pleasure to present to you my very dear friend, Mrs. Smith." But the speaker doesn't shake hands with Mrs. Smith. He doesn't even look at her—just turns his back and leaves the podium. Is Mrs. Smith really his "very dear friend"? Certainly not.

4. *Still   But   As a result   Yet   Second   First*

Adolf Hitler was a short, dark man who believed that the tall, blond "Aryan" race was infinitely superior to all others and had to maintain its purity. _____Yet_____ his view neglected some uncomfortable facts. _____First_____, there is no such thing as a "pure" race, and certainly no such thing as an "Aryan" race. _____Second_____, it is a matter of scientific fact that interbreeding between different human populations is apt to produce offspring that are healthier than either parental stock. _____Still_____, Hitler's theories fired Germany with a sense of national identity—and led to gas chambers and concentration camps, to the murder of up to six million Jews, and to a global war. _____As a result_____, racist ideology was made utterly disreputable, and few people or governments today, whatever their private attitudes, dare to openly endorse a racist attitude. _____But_____ it is worth noting that the United States fought Hitler with a racially segregated army and that German prisoners of war ate in canteens in which black American soldiers were refused service.

Skill 5: Recognizing Main Ideas in Paragraphs and Short Selections

The Two Basic Parts of a Paragraph

Almost every effective communication of ideas consists of two basic parts: (1) a point is made, and (2) evidence is provided to support that point. The purpose of textbooks is to communicate ideas, and they typically do so by using the same basic structure: A point is advanced and then supported with specific reasons, details, and facts. You will become a better reader by learning to look for and take advantage of this basic structure used in textbooks.

Activity

To make sure that you understand the concept of two basic parts in the communication of ideas, take a few minutes to do the following. Make a point about anything at all and then provide at least two bits of specific evidence to support that point. Here are examples.

Point: I dislike the fast-food restaurant in my town.

Support: 1. The roast beef sandwiches have a chemical taste.

            2. Prices are high—for example, 80 cents for a small soda.

Point: My neighbors are inconsiderate.

Support: 1. They allow their children to play on my lawn.

            2. They often have their stereo on loud late at night.

Point: There are many inexpensive ways to save energy.

Support: 1. Install a water-saver plug in your showerhead.

            2. Turn down the thermostat of your hot water heater to 120 degrees.

Point: Marijuana should not be legalized.

Support: 1. Some people who don't use it now will begin using it because of its availability.

                2. Legalization will give a stamp of social approval that no mind-altering drug deserves.

                Now write your own point and support for that point:

Point: Answers will vary. _____

Support: 1. _____

                _____

                2. _____

                _____

        Many textbook paragraphs that you read will be made up of the same two basic parts. The point is usually expressed in one sentence called a *main-idea*, or *topic, sentence*. The other sentences in the paragraph contain specific details that support or develop the main-idea sentence. Learning how to recognize these two basic parts quickly is sure to increase your reading comprehension.

Activity

Read the following textbook paragraph and see if you can identify the two major parts. Underline the main idea and put numbers in front of each reason that supports the main idea.

        Changes are occurring in the traditional nine-to-five workday. Many employers are exploring new options, such as flextime, compressed workweeks, and job sharing. With flextime, employees have a choice of starting and stopping times for their workdays. As long as they are present during a midday core period of six hours, they can choose to arrive any time between 7 and 9 A.M. and leave any time between 3 and 5 P.M. Compressed workweeks are another option. In this scheme, employees work longer shifts but fewer days. In one bank's computer department, employees work three twelve-hour days, at the end of which they have a four-day "weekend." Shared jobs are also becoming more popular. Two employees split the hours, work, and benefits of a single full-time job—a situation ideal for parents of young children and others who do not want a full-time job. Alternatives such as these may soon help solve the problems of rush-hour commuting and child care as well as increase employees' morale.

The main idea is expressed in the first sentence, and the supporting ideas follow. The outline that follows shows clearly the two basic parts of the paragraph:

Changes are occurring in the traditional nine-to-five workday.

(1) Flextime

(2) Compressed workweeks

(3) Job sharing

The Value of Finding the Main Idea

Finding the main idea is a key to understanding a paragraph or short selection. Once you identify the main idea or general point that an author is making, everything else in the paragraph should click into place. You will know what point is being made and what evidence is being provided to support that point. You will see the parts (the supporting material in the paragraph) in relation to the whole (the main idea).

If the main idea is difficult and abstract, you may want to read all the supporting details carefully to help increase your comprehension. If the main idea is easily understood, you may be able to skip the supporting details or read them over quickly, since they are not needed to comprehend the point.

The main idea is often located in the first sentence of a paragraph. You should thus pay special attention to that sentence when reading a paragraph. However, the main-idea sentence may also be at the end, in the middle, or any other place in the paragraph. On occasion, the main idea of a paragraph may appear in slightly different words in two or more sentences in the paragraph—for example, in the first and last sentences. In other cases, the main idea in one paragraph will serve as the central thought for several paragraphs that follow or precede it. Finally, at times the main idea will not be stated directly at all, and the reader will have to provide it by combining parts of several sentences or by looking closely at the evidence presented.

- *Complete the following sentences:* One way to help yourself understand a paragraph or short selection is to look for two basic parts: (1) _a main idea_ and (2) _reasons or details that develop the idea._

  The main idea most often appears in the _first_ sentence of a paragraph.

Practice in Finding the Main Idea

Activity 1

Locate and underline the main idea in each of the paragraphs that follow. The paragraphs are taken from a variety of articles and college textbooks.

To find the main idea, look for a general statement. Then ask yourself, *"Does most of the material in the paragraph support or develop the idea in this statement?"* Get into the habit of using this question as a test for a main idea.

1.   During the Depression, money shortages produced important changes in the daily lives of people. Car owners often ran their automobiles until they simply defied repair. Children's college education was postponed because parents could not pay even modest tuition charges of less than $100 in state-supported institutions. Trips to the doctor and dentist were delayed until a major emergency forced a family to seek medical attention. Even with federal food distribution after 1933, millions of families had an inadequate diet. What made the lack of money and the resulting poverty tolerable was that the condition was so widespread.

2.   The very idea of a fire in a crowded building is enough to frighten most people. And with good reason: all too often, the cry of "Fire!" causes people to stampede to the nearest exit, trampling each other on the way. Fear seems to break down normal rational behavior. The result is unnecessary injury. Research studies have duplicated this panic behavior. In one experiment several people were given strings to hold, each of which was attached to a spool inside a bottle. The bottleneck was only large enough for one spool at a time to be removed. Told to get the spools out before the bottle filled with water, everyone tried to remove his or her spool at the same time. The resulting traffic jam kept *everyone* from getting the spool out in time. Even worse jams were produced when the experimenters threatened their subjects with electric shocks if they did not get their spools out before the bottle filled.

3.   In our society a person who wishes to marry cannot completely disregard the customary patterns of courtship. If a man saw a woman on the street and decided he wanted to marry her, he could conceivably choose a quicker and more direct form of action than the usual dating procedure. He could get on a horse, ride to the woman's home, snatch her up in his arms, and gallop away with her. In Sicily, until recently, such a couple would have been considered legally "married," even if the woman had never met the man before or had no intention of marrying. But in the United States any man who acted in such a fashion would be arrested and jailed for kidnapping and would probably have his sanity seriously challenged. Such behavior would not be acceptable in our society; therefore, it could not be considered cultural.

Note: The first sentence provides the definition of integrity, but it is not the main idea of the selection. If it were the main idea, the selection would consist of a number of examples of integrity. In fact, the selection is devoted to showing how "being honest is not always easy."

4. The term *integrity* essentially refers to being honest with oneself and others. But even on a simple level, being honest is not always easy. Suppose your friend asks you if you like her new hairstyle. Even though you may not think it becoming, it may not be very diplomatic to say, "If you really want to know, I think it looks awful." For such a statement would be far from reassuring and would be of little positive value. Perhaps a more diplomatic and supportive answer would be simply, "I would like to get used to it before I render an opinion." If your opinion remains negative, you can tell her your true feelings at a later time—perhaps suggesting an alternative hairstyle that you think would be more attractive. But even here, the answer is not easy; for the moment a person evades the truth, he or she tends to initiate a process of deception that may make a satisfying relationship impossible.

Activity 2

Following each paragraph below are four general statements. Circle the letter of the statement that best expresses the main idea of the paragraph. The statement you choose should be supported by all or most of the material in the paragraph.

1. Leaving no stone unturned in their search for the killer of two boys in the early 1980s, the Atlanta police turned to psychics. But after hundreds of psychic visions had been scrutinized, the murderer remained at large until, later, the case was solved through tireless police work. Las Vegas casinos skim off only 1.4 percent of money bet at the tables. So a psychic who could beat chance by even 3 percent could make as much profit from the game as the house normally does. But casino owners who, in a sense, perform ESP experiments every night of the week, worry little about people who can predict or influence the roll of the dice. The casinos continue to operate, showing, as always, the expected return. Is there, in all the world, a single psychic who can discern the contents of a sealed envelope, move remote objects, or read others' minds? If so, magician James Randi will be surprised—and poorer. For nearly twenty years, he has been offering $10,000 to anyone who can perform just one such feat. To date, nearly six hundred would-be psychics have inquired, fifty-seven of whom submitted to a test. All have failed.

    a. Psychics who perform for profit are fakes.
    b. The use of psychics in police investigations has a history of failure.
    c. Scientists refuse to believe in the existence of ESP.
    d. Little scientific evidence exists to support a belief in ESP.

2. It has been estimated that over 98 percent of American households have at least one television set, and more than half have several. The average American household has the television turned on over six and three-quarters

hours a day, or almost half of our waking day. Americans spend more time watching television than doing anything else except sleeping. For some, the time spent watching television equals or surpasses the time spent working. According to media personality and critic Robert MacNeil, "If you fit the statistical averages, by the age of twenty you will have been exposed to something like twenty thousand hours of television. You can add ten thousand hours for each decade you have lived after the age of twenty." By the time you are sixty-five, it is predicted that you will have spent about nine years of your life watching television. Sleeping habits are changed because of TV, mealtimes are altered because of TV, and leisure time is consumed. In fact, one study demonstrated that more than 40 percent of the leisure time we have available to us is spent watching television; that is almost three times the time we spend using all the other mass media.

a.   Most American households have at least one TV set.

b.   Some people actually watch TV for more hours than they work.

c.   TV alters sleeping and eating habits.

(d)   To a great degree, TV has affected the structure and makeup of daily life.

3.   What kind of illness would civilized people find so repulsive that they would reject the sufferers in the most barbaric fashion and brand them with a stigma that would remain even if a cure were achieved? These unfortunates—the mentally ill—used to be scorned and burned, but in more enlightened times we have built backwoods fortresses for them, presumably to protect ourselves from contagion. They have been executed as witches, subjected to exorcisms, chained, or thrown into gatehouses and prisons to furnish horrible diversion for the other prisoners. In some countries they were gathered together and placed on a "ship of fools" and shipped off to uninhabited lands where they were left to wander on their own. The methods recommended by Celsus, a first-century Roman scholar, established the pattern of treatment for the years to come: "When he [the mentally ill person] has said or done anything wrong, he must be chastised by hunger, chains, and fetters." In line with that approach, throughout human history the mentally ill have been subjected to misguided, cruel, sadistic, and fear-based treatment ranging from burning at the stake to banishment from society.

a.   Mentally ill people are now treated in a humane way.

b.   The Romans began the pattern of mistreating the mentally ill.

c.   Mental illness is only now beginning to be understood.

(d)   The mentally ill have been mistreated throughout history.

4.   Some scientists consider hostility to represent a biological trait that makes aggressive behavior as inevitable a part of the human condition as fighting over territories is for baboons and other animals. Others, probably a majority, believe that hostility is learned and that it stems from the fact that the child cannot have everything he wants. Some of his desires are bound to be frustrated by the rules of society and by the conflicting desires of other people. He cannot always eat when he wants to. He has to learn to control his drive for elimination except when he is in the bathroom. He cannot have the toy that another child owns and is playing with. His mother cannot spend all her time catering to his whims. Other children, bigger than he, push him around.

a.   Aggressive behavior is an inevitable part of the human condition.

(b)   Some scientists believe that hostility is biological, but many believe that it is learned.

c.   A child cannot always have everything he wants.

d.   Hostility is learned.

Activity 3

Do one or both of the following assignments, as directed by your instructor.

1.   In the sample textbook chapter on pages 152–203, locate four paragraphs in which the main idea is clearly expressed in one sentence. On a separate sheet of paper, write down the page of this book on which each paragraph appears, the first five words of each paragraph you have chosen, and the full sentence within the paragraph that expresses the main idea.

2.   In an article or textbook, locate four paragraphs in which the main idea is clearly expressed in one sentence. Make copies of the paragraphs (using the copying machine in your library), underline the main-idea sentences, and hand in the paragraphs to your instructor.

■ Review Test

Locate and underline the main-idea sentence in each selection. Then put the number of each main-idea sentence in the space provided at the left.

_____1_____   1.   ¹Little in American society remained untouched by World War II. ²Family ties loosened as millions of men left their homes for military duty and women moved from the household to the factory. ³The housing shortage became critical in many areas, especially near military installations. ⁴Gasoline rationing sharply reduced travel in private automobiles. ⁵As one observer remarked, "You could have fired a bazooka down any Main Street in the country without hitting a vehicle." [6]Colleges and universities were deeply affected. [7]Faculty members joined the armed services; student enrollments dropped sharply as only women and young or physically disqualified men remained. [8]The government used college and university facilities for some training programs. [9]Higher education suffered because of the war, but religion flourished. [10]Churches were filled with worshipers, and between 1940 and 1946 membership in all religious bodies rose by some six million. [11]Moreover, religion became more personal and emotional as wives and parents prayed for their loved ones abroad.

____2____ 2.   [1]Education for handicapped children has come a long way since the family of Helen Keller, who was deaf and blind, had to travel to distant cities and eventually hire a private tutor for their daughter. [2]<u>But many children with disabilities still are not receiving the education that could help them to become fully functioning members of society.</u> [3]It has been estimated that about half the nation's seven million disabled youngsters are not being educated adequately. [4]These children—about 10 percent of the school-aged population—are deaf, blind, mentally retarded, physically deformed, emotionally disturbed, speech-impaired, or afflicted with other problems. [5]Some do not attend school at all because their local districts are unable or unwilling to meet their needs. [6]Some are placed in regular classes where they cannot keep up or are channeled into the wrong kind of special classes.

____5____ 3.   [1]The clearest single statement we can make is that women who smoke during pregnancy are likely to have infants with lower birth weight. [2]This finding has been reported again and again and seems to be reliable. [3]In addition, there are some indications from studies of smoking during pregnancy that women who smoke are more likely to have infants with some kind of malformation or stillborn infants. [4]Some recent research also points to long-term consequences for the infants: in three different studies seven- to eleven-year-old children whose mothers smoked during pregnancy had more difficulties in school and were more likely to be hyperactive. [5]<u>It seems pretty clear that smoking is harmful not only to the smoker but also to the fetus.</u>

____6____ 4.   [1]You have probably had the experience of trying to obtain directions to a particular place in an unfamiliar neighborhood. [2]When you think you are at least in the right area, you stop a pedestrian and ask, "How do you get to the stadium from here?" [3]If he or she says, "Go three blocks north, turn to the right, and it's down a block or two on the left-hand side," you can probably process the information easily enough and will reach your destination with little difficulty. [4]But suppose you ask for directions and the local character says to you, "Well, let's see, go three blocks north, turn right at the diner, go five blocks until you come to a Texaco station, turn left until you hit the third stop sign, turn left again . . . " [5]If you are like most people, you will probably go part of the way, wonder where you are, and then seek new directions. [6]<u>Regardless of how well you listen, you can be overloaded with details.</u>

Skill 6:
Knowing How
to Outline

The five skills already discussed will help you locate and understand the main ideas in your textbooks. Outlining is another skill that will improve your reading comprehension as well as provide additional benefits. Outlining is an organizational skill that develops your ability to think clearly and logically. It will help as you prepare textbook and classroom notes. It will also help as you plan speeches that you have to give or papers that you have to write. You have already learned a good deal about outlining in marking enumerations, noting relationships between heads and subheads, and identifying main ideas in paragraphs. You will now practice this important skill directly.

A Sample Outline

In an outline, you reduce the material in a selection to its main and supporting points and details. Special symbols are used to show how the points and details relate to one another.

To understand the outlining process, read the selection below and study the outline of the selection. Then look carefully at the comments that follow.

All homeowners can take action if they are serious about saving on energy costs. Those with more than a hundred dollars to spend should consider any of the following steps. First, the sidewalls and especially the ceiling should be fully insulated. Proper insulation can save 30 percent or more of a heating or cooling bill. Next, storm windows and doors should be installed. They provide an insulating area of still air that may reduce energy loss by 10 percent or more. Finally, a homeowner might consider installing a high-efficiency gas furnace, especially if the existing heating system is an older one.

Homeowners with less than a hundred dollars to spend can take many energy-saving steps as well. To begin with, two kinds of inexpensive sealers can be used to reduce energy leaks around the house. Caulking will seal cracks around outside windows and door frames, and at corners of the house. Weather stripping can be applied to provide a weather-tight seal between the frame and moving parts of doors and windows. Another inexpensive step is to check that a home heating or cooling system is clean. A dirty or clogged filter, for example, can make a furnace or an air conditioner work much harder to heat or cool a house. Next, a "low-flow" shower head can be used to reduce hot water use. A special shower head can be purchased or a small plastic insert available at a hardware store can be added to a regular head to limit water flow. Finally, blinds and curtains can be used to advantage throughout the year. In winter they can be closed at night to reduce heat loss. In summer they can be closed during the day to keep the house cooler. These and other relatively inexpensive steps can produce large savings.

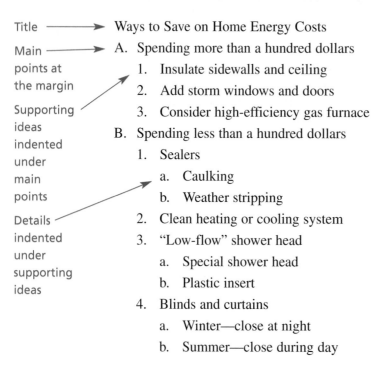

Title ⟶ Ways to Save on Home Energy Costs

Main points at the margin ⟶
A. Spending more than a hundred dollars

Supporting ideas indented under main points
   1. Insulate sidewalls and ceiling
   2. Add storm windows and doors
   3. Consider high-efficiency gas furnace

B. Spending less than a hundred dollars
   1. Sealers

Details indented under supporting ideas
     a. Caulking
     b. Weather stripping
   2. Clean heating or cooling system
   3. "Low-flow" shower head
     a. Special shower head
     b. Plastic insert
   4. Blinds and curtains
     a. Winter—close at night
     b. Summer—close during day

Points to Note about Outlining

First: The purpose of an outline is both to summarize material and to show the relationships between different parts of the material. An outline is a summary in which letters and numbers are used to mark the main and supporting points and details.

In outlining, a sequence of symbols is used for the different levels of notes. In the outline above, capital letters (A and B) are used for the first level, numbers (1, 2, 3 . . .) for the second level, and small letters (a, b, c . . .) for the third level.

Second: Put all the headings at each particular level at the same point in relation to the margin. In the outline above, A and B are both at the margin; 1, 2, and 3 are all indented an equal amount of space from the margin; and a, b, and c are all indented an equal, greater amount of space from the margin.

Third: Most outlines do not need more than two or three levels of symbols. In textbook note-taking, two levels will often do. Use a sequence like the following, with subpoints indented under main points.

    1. _____
        a. _____
        b. _____
        c. _____
        d. _____
    2. _____
    3. _____
        a. _____
        b. _____
        c. _____
    4. _____
        a. _____
        b. _____

Fourth: Every outline should have a title (such as "Ways to Save on Home Energy Costs") that summarizes the information in the outline.

Activity

To check your understanding of outlining, answer question 1 and complete the statements in items 2 and 3.

1. Why do you think you should always begin main ideas at the margin?

    To make them visually clear, so you can see them at a glance

    _____

    _____

    _____

2. Supporting ideas must always be *consistently indented under* main ideas.

3. The material that appears in an outline is summarized in its *title* .

    _____.

Diagramming

Many students find it helpful at times to use *diagramming* (also known as *mapping* or *clustering*) rather than outlining. In diagramming, you create a visual outline of shapes as well as words. Diagrams usually use circles or boxes that enclose major ideas and supporting details. The shapes are connected with lines to show the connections between ideas.

Following are two diagrams of the selection "Ways to Save on Home Energy Costs."

Notice that in the balloon diagram, the main idea is written in the large circle that anchors the entire outline. Each supporting idea occupies one of the balloons attached to the main idea. In the box diagram, the main idea is written in the long box at the top. Below the long box are smaller boxes that contain the supporting ideas.

Activities in this chapter will ask you to use diagrams as well as outlines to make relationships between ideas visually clear. Then, in your own note-taking, you will be able to use either diagrams or outlines, whichever you find more helpful.

Balloon Diagram

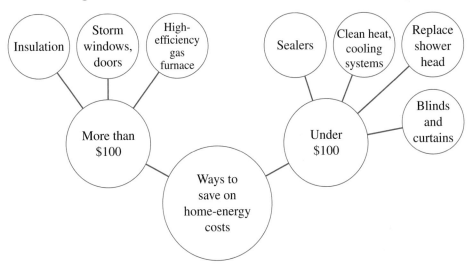

Box Diagram

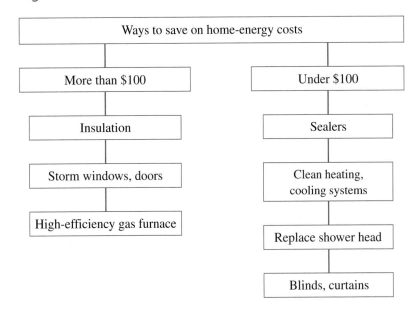

Practice in Outlining and Diagramming

The following pages provide a series of exercises that will develop your ability to outline and diagram effectively.

Activity 1:
Completing Outlines

Read each of the following selections. Then complete the outline that comes after each selection. Certain items in some outlines have already been added.

Note: In the chapter "Recognizing Enumerations," you practiced making one-level outlines. Here you will practice making two-or-more-level outlines as well.

Selection 1

Population in the South, which totaled about eleven million on the eve of the Civil War, fell into rather distinct social and economic classes. At the top of the scale stood the small aristocracy of large planters. In 1860 there were 2,292 planters who owned more than a hundred slaves and 10,658 who held over fifty. However, the wealth of this small group gave them social prestige and political power far beyond their numbers. Slightly below the large planters in social and economic status were the lesser planters who had fewer slaves and farmed less land; in 1860 there were 35,616 planters who had twenty to fifty slaves. Professionals and the few business and industrial leaders were also in this general class. Most of the people in the old South were in the middle or lower middle class and were mainly yeoman farmers, skilled mechanics, and tradespeople. The so-called plain people of the old South owned very few slaves, in many cases none at all. They raised a wide variety of crops and livestock and were largely self-sufficient. Below the yeoman farmers were the poor whites and free blacks. And at the bottom of the southern class structure stood the slaves.

Social and Economic Classes in the South

1. Aristocracy of large planters

2. Lesser planters, professionals, business and industrial leaders

3. Middle and lower-middle class; yeoman farmers, skilled mechanics, tradespeople

4. Poor whites and free blacks

5. Slaves

Selection 2

The purchase price of a house is not the only cost that buyers must consider. Buying a house is a major transaction that involves a title search, closing costs, property insurance, and special assessments. A title search is done by a title guaranty company in order to see if a piece of property has any encumbrances. When a title search is done, the history of the property is traced back to the original owners to find out if anyone else has a claim to the property. For example, a power company may have obtained the right to place poles on the property. Any restrictions like this are called encumbrances. Closing costs occur when settlement is made on a piece of property. Costs may include lawyers' fees, the commission due a real estate agent, certain taxes that must be paid in advance, and the expenses in filing records. Property insurance is also essential in purchasing a house. Insurance policies are available for flood, fire, and burglary protection. Insurance is also needed to protect the homeowner against lawsuits, especially if someone is injured on the property. Finally, home buyers may have special assessments that will be charged at settlement. They may have to pay for such services as sewers, sidewalks, and community parks.

Special Costs in Buying a House

1. Title search
2. Closing costs
   a. Lawyers' fees
   b. Real estate agent's commission
   c. Taxes paid in advance
   d. Expenses of filing records
3. Property insurance
   a. Flood
   b. Fire
   c. Burglary
   d. Protection against lawsuits
4. Special assessments at settlement
   a. Sewers
   b. Sidewalks
   c. Community parks

Selection 3

When you are deciding to go to a professional for psychological help, there are several steps you can take. Begin by asking for recommendations. Talk with your instructor; also, confer with someone in your school's counseling service. Other good sources for recommendations are physicians and members of the clergy. After you have one or two names, try to check out reputations through the professional sources available to you. For instance, if your priest gives you a name, you might check it out with your school counselor. Next, call the professionals and ask about their training, degrees, and experience; a good therapist will not hesitate to give you this information. You might also want to find out what approach they follow and what goals they aim for in treating people. Finally, make your first visit to the professional an exploratory one: learn as much as you can about how he or she does therapy and how your own problems might be dealt with. If you aren't satisfied, go to someone else. One visit to a professional doesn't commit you to further visits. This approach to selecting a professional, while initially somewhat time-consuming, will be well worth it in terms of the quality of help you receive.

Getting Psychological Help

1. Ask for recommendations

    a. Instructor

    b. School counseling service

    c. Physicians

    d. Clergy

2. Check out reputations

3. Call the professionals

    a. Ask about training, degree, experience

    b. Ask about approaches and goals

4. Exploratory visit

Activity 2:
Completing Diagrams

Read each of the following selections. Then complete the diagram that comes after each selection.

Selection 1

There are several easy ways to lose weight without feeling deprived. If you drink three cups of coffee a day, simply eliminating milk and sugar from the coffee will save approximately two hundred calories a day. If you cut out two hundred calories a day, you'll lose seventeen pounds in a year! Another way to avoid unnecessary calories is to use nonstick pots and pans. You can melt a large pat of butter to cook your eggs, thereby adding one hundred calories. Or you can use a nonstick pan and eliminate those calories. Avoiding calorie-laden salad dressings is another easy way to lose weight. One small spoonful of creamy Russian or blue cheese dressing adds as much as one hundred calories. And how many of us are content with just one small spoonful? That "low-calorie" salad can quickly turn into a diet disaster. Substituting diet dressings, or a dash of lemon and pepper, is an easy way to slash calorie intake. One final way to avoid calories is to substitute broiling or baking for frying. The oil used in frying is absorbed by the food, and oil is high in calories. Broiled or baked chicken, for example, is as delicious as fried chicken, and the saving in calories is enormous.

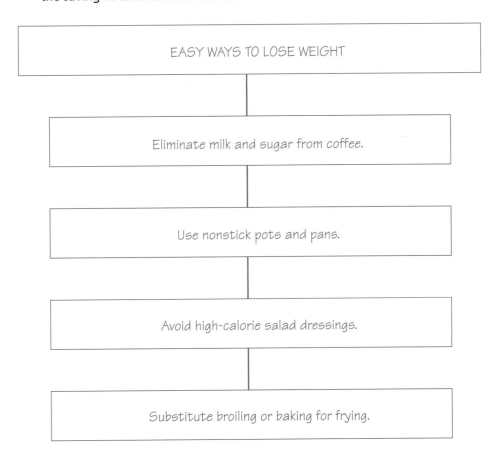

EASY WAYS TO LOSE WEIGHT

Eliminate milk and sugar from coffee.

Use nonstick pots and pans.

Avoid high-calorie salad dressings.

Substitute broiling or baking for frying.

Selection 2

Research psychologists have identified three kinds of depression. Few of us have not at some time experienced "the blues" because of crises in our lives. This is *normal depression.* Such depression usually clears up by itself in a very short time. But an estimated ten million Americans react to life's problems— most often a loss, disappointment, change, frustration, or threat to identity— with depression deep enough or long-lasting enough to interfere with their functioning. This is *neurotic depression.* Symptoms usually disappear when stress is lifted.

Another six to eight million have medically triggered depression that appears out of the blue, apparently unrelated to life's problems. It may be caused by hereditary factors, hormonal or chemical imbalance, dietary defi- ciency, or drug or allergic reaction. This *psychotic depression* is more serious and more complex. It is usually divided into two main types: (1) *bipolar depres- sive disease,* also known as manic-depressive psychosis, in which the individual swings from deep depression to unexplained "highs," during which he or she feels all-powerful and all-wise and becomes difficult to control; (2) *unipolar depressive disease,* in which the patient has bouts of depression and is severely withdrawn and uncommunicative or behaves in an extremely agitated fashion.

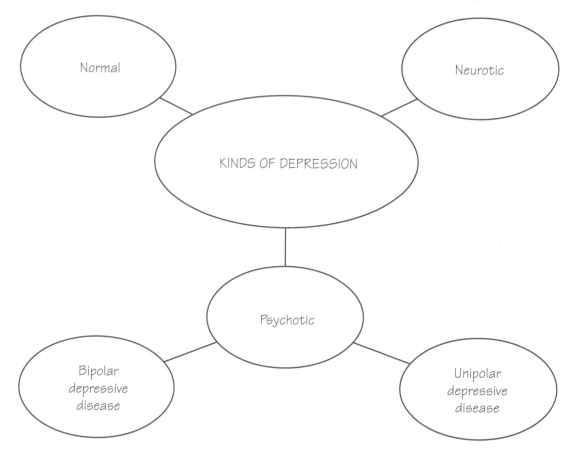

Selection 3

Because alcohol abuse is such a common problem, it is important to recognize the danger signals of alcoholism. Progression from a "social drinker" to a problem drinker to an alcoholic is often subtle. In the *initial phase,* the social drinker begins to turn more frequently to alcohol to relieve tension or to feel good. There are four danger signals in this period that signal excessive dependence on alcohol. The first is increasing consumption. The person drinks more and more and may begin to worry about drinking. The second is morning drinking. Morning drinking is a dangerous sign, particularly when it is used to combat a hangover or to "get through the day." Next is regretted behavior. The person engages in extreme behavior while drunk that leaves him or her feeling guilty or embarrassed. Finally, there are blackouts. Excessive drinking may be accompanied by an inability to remember what happened during intoxication. The *crucial phase* begins when the person begins to lose control over drinking. At this stage there is usually control over when and where a first drink is taken, but one drink starts a chain reaction leading to a second and a third, and so on. In the *chronic phase,* the alcoholic drinks compulsively and continuously. He or she eats infrequently, becomes intoxicated from far less alcohol than before, and feels a powerful need for alcohol when deprived of it. Work, family ties, and social life all deteriorate. Self-drugging is usually so compulsive that when there is a choice, the bottle comes before friends, relatives, employment, and self-esteem. The drinker is now an addict.

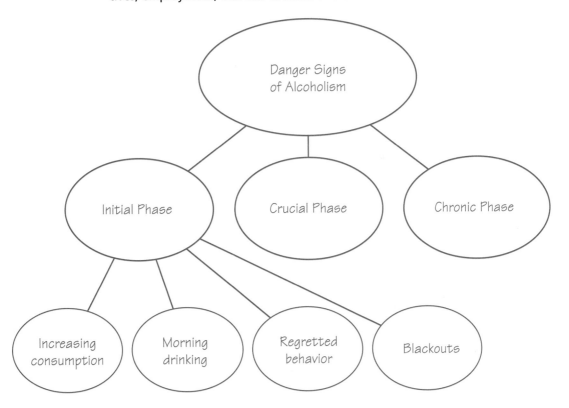

■ **Review Test**

Complete the diagram or outline for each of the following selections.

Selection 1

By the time students reach junior high school (their eighth or ninth year of formal education), they are usually well-entrenched in a world of their peers. Parents and teachers assume a secondary place as a source of significant values. What is important is what one's crowd thinks. At this age and on through high school, the crowd is primarily fellow students. Burton R. Clark identifies three types of subcultures; almost every junior and senior high school student belongs to one of them. First is the so-called *fun subculture,* which places utmost emphasis on having a good time. In this subculture, one must have a "good personality" and *savoir-faire* about clothes, automobiles, hangouts, and sports. Books and learning represent drudgery and low status. The second subculture is the *academic,* which places value on being a good student, discussing serious questions and interests of the day, and high educational achievement. This subculture is considerably less popular than the fun subculture in most secondary schools. The least popular but most publicized student subculture is the *delinquent.* Members of this group have contempt for the school and its faculty in addition to a defiant attitude toward any form of regulation and toward anybody not approved by their crowd.

Subcultures of High School Students

1. Fun subculture

2. Academic subculture

3. Delinquent subculture

Selection 2

Nonasserters pay in several ways for not expressing themselves. The most obvious costs are social. Shy people make few new acquaintances and have a hard time building friendships with those people they do meet. Even when they do mingle with others, nonexpressive people are often misunderstood.

Nonassertiveness also takes a psychological toll on its victims. Three attitudes often develop in people who are not able to express the full range of their feelings. Some simply withdraw from any kind of meaningful contract with others, taking refuge in impersonal activities such as watching TV for hours at a time or distracting themselves with liquor or other drugs. Other people deal with their inept communications by becoming cynics, claiming that people aren't worth caring about anyway. A third group of nonasserters react to the condition with despair at themselves and at an imperfect world where life is not worth living.

Besides social and psychological consequences, nonassertion also has physiological costs, in the form, first of all, of psychosomatic illnesses. Such illnesses are real, differing in no physical way from organically caused illnesses. Nonassertive people often develop stress-related diseases as well as psychosomatic disorders. Hypertension, or high blood pressure, often has its roots in chronic stress.

Costs of Being Nonassertive

1. Social costs

2. Psychological costs

    a. Withdrawal

    b. Becoming cynical

    c. Despair

3. Physiological costs

    a. Psychosomatic illnesses

    b. Stress-related diseases

Selection 3

There are two types of smog. The first is a *combination of smoke and fog.* Such combinations occur in cities that burn lots of coal. The droplets of fog combine with the smoke particles. The fog acts like a giant sponge in creating this type of smog. The second type of smog is more common. It is properly called *photochemical smog* and is caused by sunlight reacting with certain pollutants. The chemicals in the exhaust of automobile engines are the biggest troublemakers. One of these chemical pollutants is carbon monoxide. In concentrated form, this odorless, colorless gas is a deadly poison. Another pollutant is nitrogen dioxide, a yellow-brown gas that gives photochemical smog its color. Nitrogen dioxide has a sharp odor that is described as "sweetish." Ozone is the other pollutant that results from the photochemical process. Ozone is colorless, but it has a sharp odor. You may have smelled ozone during an electrical storm or when a piece of electrical equipment short-circuited.

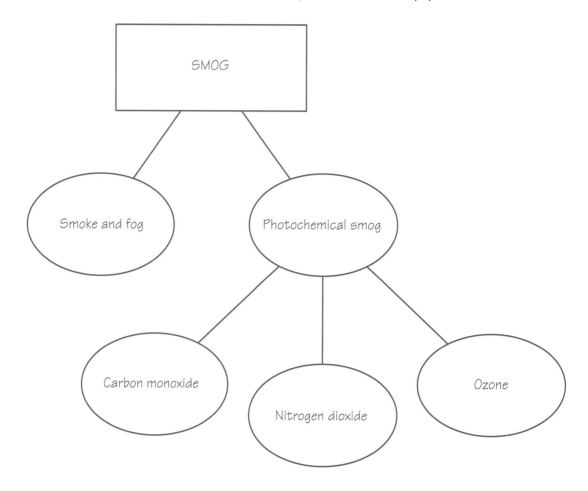

Selection 4

In some ways, there is bound to be some physical decline or slowing down during the years of middle age. A number of signs of aging can be identified. The bone structure, for one thing, stiffens and even shrinks a bit during the course of adulthood. This is the reason why some people may be shorter at their fortieth high school reunion than they were when they were students. Another sign of aging is that skin and muscles begin to lose some elasticity so that, for example, areas of the face and jaws begin to sag. Another sign is the tendency to accumulate more subcutaneous fat, especially in certain areas such as the midriff. There are more sensory defects during the adult years, too. Vision tends to be constant from adolescence to the forties or early fifties, when visual acuity may begin to show signs of decline. However, near-sighted people often are able to see better in middle age than they could as young adults. There is an increased incidence of hearing problems during mid-adulthood, especially hearing loss in the upper frequencies. Long-term exposure to high levels of noise increases the likelihood of hearing loss. Therefore, some factory workers and many city dwellers may be particularly prone to hearing problems in later years.

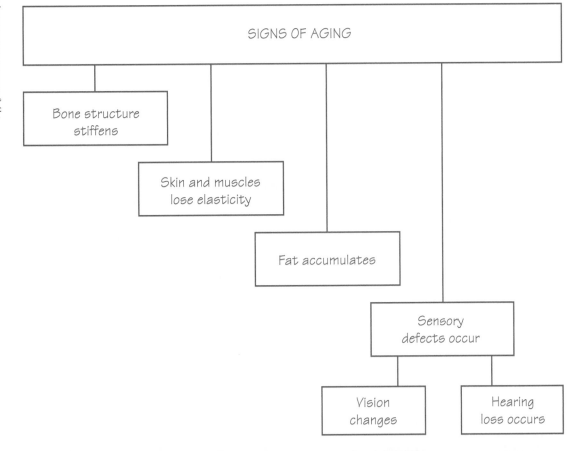

Skill 7: Knowing How to Summarize

To understand the summarizing process, first read the following selection and summary. Then study the points about summarizing that follow.

> In another kind of coping behavior, *rationalization,* an acceptable motive is substituted for an unacceptable one. Put another way, we "make excuses"—we give a different reason from the real one for what we are doing. Rationalization is a common defense mechanism for avoiding the anxiety connected with an unacceptable motive. A student who has sacrificed studying to have a good time may blame his or her failing grades on bad teaching, unfair examinations, or too heavy a workload. A father may beat his child just because he is angry but rationalize it by saying that he is acting for the child's good.

Summary

> Rationalization—a kind of coping behavior in which an acceptable motive is substituted for an unacceptable one.
>   Ex.—father rationalizes beating child by saying it's for child's good.

Points to Note about Summarizing

1 A *summary,* like an outline, is a reduction of a large quantity of information to the most important points. Unlike an outline, however, a summary does not use symbols such as A, 1, a, and so on, to indicate the relationships among parts of the original material. The preceding summary includes the most important points—the definition of *rationalization* and an example that makes the definition clear—but the other material is omitted.

2 Summarizing is helpful because it requires that you thoroughly *understand* the material you are reading. You must "get inside" the material and realize fully what is being said before you can reduce it to a few words. Work in summarizing material will help build your comprehension power. It will also markedly improve your ability to take effective classroom and textbook notes.

3 The length of a summary depends on your *purpose* in summarizing. The shortest possible summary is a title. If your purpose requires more information than that, a one-sentence summary might be enough. Longer passages and different

purposes might require longer summaries. For example, in writing a report on an article or book, you might often want to have a summary that is a paragraph or more in length.

In the following practice activities you will be writing title summaries, single- and several-sentence summaries, and one-paragraph summaries. After such varied practice, you should be prepared to write whatever kind of summary you might need to.

- *Complete the following sentences:* A summary _____*reduces*_____ a large quantity of material to the most important points. Unless you fully _____*understand*_____ the material you are reading, you will not be able to summarize it.

Practice in Summarizing

Activity 1

This activity will give you practice in choosing title summaries and one-sentence summaries. In each case, circle the letter of the title and then of the sentence that best summarize each selection. Your choices should be ones that best answer the question, "What is this about?" Your choices should be as specific and descriptive as possible and at the same time account for all the material in each selection.

Selection A

It is commonly believed that the poor are lazy people who could work if they were willing. In fact, over 60 percent of the poor consist of children under age fourteen, elderly people over age sixty-four, and people of working age who are ill or in school. Another quarter work but do not earn enough to rise above the poverty line. This leaves less than 15 percent of the poor of working age who do not work, and the vast majority of those are mothers of young children. When it comes to work, the poor do not look as bad as their reputation, for most of them are too old, too young, too sick, or too busy caring for children to work.

1. What would be an accurate title for this selection?
   a. Poor Children
   b. Who Are the Poor?
   c. The Working Poor

2. Which sentence best summarizes the selection?

    a.   Most of the poor are too young or too old to work.

    b.   Many people believe that the poor are lazy people who could work if they really wanted to.

    (c.) A great majority of the poor either don't work for a good reason or work but are poorly paid.

Selection B

Depending on weather conditions, we may or may not worry about drought in any particular year, but regardless of temporary weather conditions, our nation is using water much faster than the supply is being replenished. One-fourth of the water used in America comes from a system of aquifers—underground areas of porous soils in which water has accumulated through the ages. In some cases, such aquifers are covered by hardpan or rock, through which water penetrates only slowly, even during years of abundant rain. Consequently, although our "bank account" of water is very large, it is being overdrawn. In 1950, the nation pumped 21 trillion gallons from underground; now it pumps more than twice that much each year. In fact, each day, 21 billion more gallons are pumped out than enter the underground aquifers. One water planner notes that the rate of depletion in the Midwest differs from place to place but adds, "Some people project that eventually there will be parts of Nebraska with their water supplies so depleted that farming may never return."

3. What would be an accurate title for this selection?

    (a.) Our Vanishing Water Supply

    b.   The Coming Drought in the Midwest

    c.   Sources of Our Water Supply

4. Which sentence best summarizes the selection?

    a.   Weather conditions may lead to temporary droughts.

    (b.) We are using up our water supply faster than it is being replenished.

    c.   Eventually it may no longer be possible to farm in Nebraska.

Selection C

Trichinosis is a disease caused by eating pork infested with the larvae (developmental stage) of a worm called the trichina. From the intestinal tract of the human body, the worm larvae enter the blood, reach the muscles, and burrow into them. Muscular pain and fever may develop about seven days after eating the pork; the fever may last for several weeks. Even after these early symptoms have subsided, however, the larvae may lie dormant in the muscles for years. In fact, some of the aches and pains of rheumatism may be caused by trichina larvae in the muscles. The government does not inspect pork for the larvae, and there is no effective treatment for the disease. Therefore, as a precaution, pork and pork products (such as sausage) should always be cooked until they are well-done; thorough cooking will kill any worms that are present.

5. What would be an accurate title for this selection?

   a.   Cooking Pork

   b.   The Trichina Worm

   c.   Trichinosis and Its Prevention

6. Which sentence best summarizes the selection?

   a.   Trichinosis, an illness with short- and long-term effects, is caused by a worm in pork that can be killed by thorough cooking.

   b.   Trichinosis may last for several weeks and then lie dormant for years.

   c.   Entering the body from the intestinal tract, the trichina worm eventually burrows into muscles, causing an illness that may last for several weeks.

Selection D

Did you ever have someone's name on the tip of your tongue, and yet you were unable to recall it? When this happens again, don't try to recall it. Do something else for a few minutes, and the name may pop into your head. The name is there, since you have met this person and learned his or her name. It only has to be dug out. The initial effort to recall *primes* the mind, but it is the subconscious activities that go to work to pry up a dim memory. *Forcing* yourself to recall almost never helps because it doesn't loosen your memory; it only tightens it. Students find the *priming method* helpful on examinations. They read over the questions before trying to answer any of them. Then they answer first the ones of which they are most confident. Meanwhile, deeper mental activities in the subconscious mind are taking place; work is being done on the more difficult questions. By the time the easier questions are answered, answers to the more difficult ones will usually begin to come into consciousness. It is often just a question of *waiting* for recall to be loosened up.

7. What would be an accurate title for this selection?

   a.   Memory Techniques

   b.   The Priming Method of Memory

   c.   Success in Exams

8. Which sentence best summarizes the selection?

   a.   The priming method can be very useful to students when taking exams.

   (b) In the priming method, the subconscious brings up a memory in response to an initial conscious effort to recall it.

   c.   When you have someone's name on the tip of your tongue but can't recall it, trying to force yourself to remember may make it harder to do so.

Activity 2

This activity will give you practice in writing title summaries and one-sentence summaries. Each title and sentence should condense into a few words the essential thoughts of each selection. A good way to proceed is to try the find the fewest words that will answer the question, "What is this about?"

Note when you write the titles that you will be doing exactly the kind of summarizing that textbook authors do when they write headings and subheadings for their work. The experience of "writing labels" should help you appreciate—and take advantage of—the headings given by textbook authors.

Selection A

Instead of letting your mind wander or preparing what you are going to say when you have a chance, you can practice and use active listening skills. *Active listening* includes repeating important details to yourself; questioning; paraphrasing; distinguishing among governing idea, main points, and detail; and, in some situations, note-taking. Active listening involves you in the process of determining meaning. Too often people think of the listening experience as a passive situation in which what they remember is largely a matter of chance. In reality, good listening is hard work that requires concentration and willingness to mull over and, at times, verbalize what is said. Good listening requires using mental energy. If you really listen to an entire fifty-minute lecture, for instance, when the lecture is over you will feel tired because you will have put as much energy into listening as the lecturer put into talking.

Heading: _Active Listening_____

One-sentence summary: _Active listening is hard work, for it requires the_ _listener to concentrate on, think about, and sometimes repeat what is_ _being said._____

Selection B

When Captain Cook asked the chiefs in Tahiti why they always ate apart and alone, they replied, "Because it is right." If we ask Americans why they eat with knives and forks, or why their men wear pants instead of skirts, or why they may be married to only one person at a time, we are likely to get similar and very uninformative answers: "Because it's right." "Because that's the way it's done." "Because it's the custom." Or even "I don't know." The reason for these and countless other patterns of social behavior is that they are controlled by *social norms*—shared rules or guidelines which prescribe the behavior that is appropriate in a given situation. Norms define how people "ought" to behave under particular circumstances in a particular society. We conform to norms so readily that we are hardly aware they exist. In fact, we are much more likely to notice departures from norms than conformity to them. You would not be surprised if a stranger tried to shake hands when you were introduced, but you might be a little startled if he or she bowed, curtsied, started to stroke you, or kissed you on both cheeks. Yet each of these other forms of greeting is appropriate in other parts of the world. When we visit another society whose norms are different, we quickly become aware that things we do this way, they do that way.

Heading: <u>Social Norms</u>

One-sentence summary: <u>Patterns of social behavior are controlled by social norms—shared rules or guidelines which prescribe the behavior that is appropriate in a given situation.</u>

Selection C

On the American plains, buffalo were once so numerous that they were counted in the millions. A herd of buffalo could cover the prairie as far as the eye could see. The hoofbeats of an approaching buffalo herd could be heard several miles away. Amazingly, within only a few decades, the vast numbers of buffalo would be reduced to a mere handful by the white man. After railroads reached the plains area, bringing more and more whites, the buffalo were doomed. Special trains would carry passengers into buffalo country; passengers armed with rifles would shoot into the herd from the train window. The "hunters" did not even collect the buffalo carcasses. Thousands of pounds of buffalo meat and hide were left to rot in the sun. Occasionally the buffalo tongue, a delicacy, would be retrieved. After the carcasses had rotted, local farmers would collect wagonloads of bones, in order to sell them as fertilizer at $5 a ton. The buffalo slaughter was so enormous that one hunter, after witnessing the destruction of a herd, wrote, "A man could have walked twenty miles on their carcasses." By the end of the nineteenth century, this wanton waste had made the buffalo practically extinct.

Heading: _The Slaughter of the Buffalo_

One-sentence summary: _In the nineteenth century, vast herds of American buffalo were reduced to a mere handful by the white man's wanton slaughter._

Selection D

The British approach to heroin addiction (heroin maintenance) is fundamentally different from the American approach. The object of the American model is to get addicts "off" heroin by drying up their supplies and imprisoning the addicts. Narcotics control, under this plan, is placed under the jurisdiction of law enforcement authorities. The British plan, in sharp contrast, places control in the hands of medical authorities. Instead of treating addicts as criminals, the British allow doctors to administer drugs to addicts under two conditions: when their complete withdrawal cannot be accomplished and when they can perform satisfactorily if given a controlled dosage. The doctors must notify the British Home Office of all patients under this treatment. When properly registered, those addicts are entitled to receive maintenance doses of heroin; however, if an addict commits a crime, then he or she is treated the same as any other offender. Moreover, if not registered but in possession of opiates, the individual is prosecuted for illegal possession of a dangerous drug.

Heading: _British Approach to Heroin Addiction_

One-sentence summary: _The British treat heroin addicts very differently from Americans, putting them in the hands of medical authorities rather than law enforcement officials._

Activity 3

Read the textbook selection "Defense Mechanisms" on pages 466–469 and then summarize it by answering the questions that follow.

1. Circle the letter of the statement that best summarizes paragraph 1.
   a. Defense mechanisms are methods used to protect one's self-esteem against the many challenges to it.
   b. Getting a new blemish or wrinkle and receiving a low grade are challenges to your self-esteem.
   c. There are numerous ways in which your self-esteem is challenged.

2. Circle the letter of the statement that best summarizes paragraphs 2 and 3.

   a. Going to a movie is a good way to avoid thinking about an argument.

   b. Scarlett O'Hara's line "I'll think about it tomorrow" illustrates the defense mechanism of suppression.

   (c.) Suppression, useful only for minor problems, is a conscious effort to avoid stressful thoughts.

3. Circle the letter of the statement that best summarizes paragraphs 4 and 5.

   (a.) Repression is the unconscious forgetting of painful thoughts, which can be "remembered" through only dreams or hypnosis.

   b. Repression of a friend's departure may be the reason you forget to contribute money for a going-away gift.

   c. It is common for people to push thoughts out of the conscious mind.

4. Circle the letter of the statement that best summarizes paragraphs 6–8.

   (a.) Other unconscious defense mechanisms include withdrawal, or avoidance, a response to fear or frustration that can be positive or negative, depending on its use.

   b. Many famous, likable people have suffered from shyness, a common result of the fear of rejection.

   c. Withdrawal can lead to negative actions, such as quitting jobs, dropping out of school, separating, and divorcing.

5. Circle the letter of the statement that best summarizes paragraph 9.

   a. If used excessively, daydreaming can become an unhealthy substitute for activity.

   (b.) Escaping and relaxing through fantasy—for example, through daydreaming or reading a novel—can be healthy if used in moderation and not as a substitute for activity.

   c. A person can live in a fantasy world in which he or she is always accepted, admired, and loved.

6. Circle the letter of the statement that best summarizes paragraph 10.

   a. Regression is what occurs when a new baby arrives and an older child returns to previous methods of gaining attention.

   b. People who behave in a childlike way are likely to do such things as burst into tears, suck their thumbs, throw things, scream, or have a tantrum.

   (c.) Regression is a return to earlier ways of handling problems, a response to being deeply upset and unable to handle a problem maturely.

7. Circle the letter of the statement that best summarizes paragraphs 11 and 12.

    a.   Most people are not aware that they rationalize often.

    (b)   Rationalization, a common defense mechanism, is a distortion of the truth to maintain self-esteem.

    c.   Richard Nixon rationalized his loss of the 1960 presidential election by commenting that he would have more time to devote to his family.

8. Circle the letter of the statement that best summarizes paragraph 13.

    a.   Projection may explain why a woman who flirts complains that it is the males who are flirting with her.

    b.   Psychological tests may use projection to uncover problems.

    (c)   Projection is accusing someone else of your own weaknesses.

9. Circle the letter of the statement that best summarizes paragraph 14.

    (a)   Displacement is responding to a problem by victimizing someone else.

    b.   Husbands and wives should avoid controversial topics after either one has had a bad day.

    c.   Using displacement, the rejected person in the cartoon might ridicule and chastise the bartender.

10. Circle the letter of the statement that best summarizes paragraph 15.

    a.   Someone may make up for being a poor student by seeking popularity with clever jokes.

    b.   Compensation generally leads to a healthy adjustment to an inadequacy.

    (c)   Compensation is making up for an inadequacy by doing well in another area, generally a healthy response.

11. Circle the letter of the statement that best summarizes paragraph 16.

    (a)   Sublimation is channeling unacceptable urges into constructive or creative efforts.

    b.   Some of the finest creative works have resulted from the sublimation of members of oppressed groups.

    c.   Sublimation is a very positive type of defense mechanism.

Activity 4

Read the following article and then write a one-paragraph summary of 100 to 125 words. Here are some guidelines for summarizing an article:

a   Think about the title for a minute or so. The title often summarizes what the article is about.

b   Consider any subtitle that may appear. The subtitle, a caption, or other words in large print under or next to the title often provide a quick insight into the meaning of an article.

c   Note any subheadings that appear in the article. Subheadings provide clues to the article's main points and give an immediate sense of the content of each section.

d   Make an outline of the article before beginning to write.

e   Express the author's ideas in your own words—not in the words of the article itself.

f   Do not write an overly detailed summary. Remember that the purpose of a summary is to reduce the original material to its main ideas and essential supporting points.

g   Do not begin your sentences with expressions like "the author says"; equally important, do not introduce your own opinions into the summary with comments like "another good point made by the author." Instead, concentrate on presenting directly and briefly the author's main points.

Note: Summary appears in Instructor's Manual.

When Kids Come Home to an Empty House

Experts Worry about the Effects of "Latchkeyism" and Suggest Some Countermeasures.

Wearing the front-door key on a chain around his neck, eleven-year-old Jeremy Cavin comes home from school each day to an empty house.

"Lonely is the word for it," says Jeremy, an only child who is not allowed to have friends over while his parents are at work.

Says Jeremy's father, Bob: "I don't like the situation. I don't think any parent does." But with no suitable after-school programs in their area of North Carolina, the Cavins feel they have no choice. For as long as both of his parents work, Jeremy will be a so-called *latchkey child.*

The label has been around since the nineteenth century, but the number of latchkey kids between the ages of seven and thirteen has burgeoned in recent years. Because of the dramatic increases in one-parent and two-paycheck families, there are now more than two million children who fend for themselves for part of every workday. And with two out of every three mothers expected to work outside the home by the end of this decade, the latchkey legion can only grow larger still.

Until recently, little was known about this phenomenon. Now research is under way, "survival" courses geared to latchkey kids are being offered, and some communities are beginning to come up with attractive alternatives.

Some Real Problems

One of the new studies reveals that some latchkey children face very real emotional problems. Dr. Thomas Long, professor of education at the Catholic University of America, and his wife, Dr. Lynette Long, assistant professor of education at Loyola University, interviewed more than fifty latchkey kids in Washington, D.C. One child who lost her key recalled crying on the front porch for hours until her mother returned from work. Another told of climbing into a chair and clutching her shoe as a possible weapon when she heard suspicious noises outside.

Latchkey children can also suffer from being bored, isolated, and confined, the Longs believe. "Where is play for these kids?" asks Thomas Long. "For years these children are denied a social life at a critical time in their development." Kids left alone at home watched up to seven hours of television a day, according to the Longs' study.

But beyond marathon TV watching, the Longs worry about the possible long-term effects of "latchkeyism": feelings of alienation leading to academic failure, violence, vandalism, and experimentation with drugs and alcohol. Thomas Long says police in his area are seeing more and more latchkey kids in trouble. But he and other experts concede that any conclusive link between latchkey children and delinquency remains hypothetical.

What Can Be Done

What can worried latchkey parents do to minimize the risks? Long suggests that parents help structure empty hours by assigning chores and suggesting a schedule to follow, and by trying to arrange for some after-school activities—scouting, dance lessons, recreation programs—to vary their kids' solo routines. From the comments of children in his study, he also believes that pets can help by providing comfort and companionship in an empty house. Above all, Long suggests that once parents return home, they should put off household duties and "make an extended effort to get into their child's world."

Another study now in progress by Dr. Hyman Rodman, director of the Family Research Center at the University of North Carolina at Greensboro, reveals how nearly twelve hundred latchkey mothers are trying to make the arrangement as *safe* as possible. The women said they worry about fires, forgotten keys, and other frightening possibilities. But most stay in close touch with their children by phone, have a neighbor to turn to in emergencies, and have rules for the kids to follow. Among the most common rules:

- No one is allowed in the house, even friends, without prior special permission.
- The door is not to be opened when someone knocks unless the child is told beforehand that certain persons can be let in or unless it is someone well known to the family.
- Children are given specific tasks that they are expected to do while they care for themselves.
- No use of the stove or other electrical appliances, except the TV, radio, or record player, is allowed.
- No one who calls on the telephone is to be told by the children that they are alone.

Most latchkey mothers who have these rules told Dr. Rodman they were satisfied, if not happy, with the arrangement. Many believed that their children were learning responsibility and self-reliance.

Activity 5

Write a one-paragraph summary of an article in a weekly or monthly magazine. Identify at the start of the summary the title and author of the work. Also, include in parentheses the date of publication. For example, "In an article titled 'Where We Go from Here' (*Time,* November 20, 2000), Christopher Buckley states . . . "

Then, in your own words, summarize the main point of the article and the key details used to support or develop that point.

Finally, be sure to clip or make a copy of the article and attach it to your summary.

Activity 6

Watch a television show of special interest to you. Then prepare a one-paragraph summary of the show. In your first sentence, give basic information about the show by using a format such as the following: "The September 9, 2001, broadcast of CBS's *60 Minutes* examined . . . "

Activity 7

Write a one-paragraph summary of an important concept from one of your textbooks. Try to choose a general-interest subject such as psychology or sociology rather than a highly specialized field such as anatomy or electronics.

In your summary, first provide the necessary identifying information. For example, "In the chapter 'The Family and Intimate Relations' in *Sociology* (McGraw-Hill, 2000), Richard T. Schaefer explains . . . " Then present the important idea in the chapter, along with key details that support or develop the idea.

■ **Review Test**

Part A: Circle the letter of the title and then of the sentence that best summarize each of the following two selections. Remember that the title should be as specific and descriptive as possible and at the same time account for all the material in the selection.

> Sacrifice is a rather widespread ritual. It is generally based on the hope that if an individual gives up something of value to honor a supreme being, he or she will receive a divine blessing. A common sacrificial custom within industrial societies is making a contribution to a religious institution, as in the practice of tithing (giving one-tenth of one's income to a church). Other examples of religious sacrifice include fasting on holy days (such as Yom Kippur, the Day of Atonement for Jews) and giving up worldly pleasures (as Christians do for Lent). The most ancient form of sacrifice—still commonly found throughout the world in the 1980s—is the burial of goods with a corpse. Such artifacts as food, clothing, money, and weapons are intended to provide the soul of the deceased with whatever will be needed during an afterlife. In American society, the provision of comfortable coffins for well-dressed corpses and the regular placement of flowers near a grave are forms of sacrifice offered in a similar spirit.

1. What would be an accurate title for this selection?
   a. Tithing
   b. Religious Rituals
   (c.) Rituals of Sacrifice

2. What sentence best summarizes the selection?
   a. In industrial societies, a common form of sacrifice is making a contribution to a religious institution.
   (b.) Sacrifice, a widespread ritual, is based on the hope of gaining a blessing by giving up something in honor of a supreme being.
   c. The oldest form of sacrifice, the burial of goods with a corpse, was still common throughout the world in the 1980s.

> During the post–Civil War years students entered schools at all levels in ever-increasing numbers. Between 1870 and 1910, public school enrollment rose from 6.9 to 17.8 million. Most of this growth occurred in the first eight grades, but the number attending public high schools increased from 80,000 to 915,000. Private schools taught thousands more. College enrollments revealed comparable gains, rising from only 52,000 in 1870 to 355,000 forty

years later. Compulsory school attendance, typically for children between eight and fourteen, was an important factor in the growing enrollments. By 1898 thirty-one states and territories had laws setting minimum attendance requirements; unfortunately, these statutes were often poorly enforced. With more children in school, expenditures for education jumped sharply. The cost of public elementary and secondary education in the United States rose from $63.4 million in 1870 to $426 million in 1910.

3. What would be an accurate title for this selection?

a. The Post–Civil War Years

(b) Education in America after the Civil War

c. Public Schools: 1870–1910

4. Which sentence best summarizes the selection?

a. Between 1870 and 1910, enrollment in public schools rose from 6.9 to 17.8 million.

b. Between 1870 and 1910, the cost of public elementary education in the United States grew enormously.

(c) During the post–Civil War years, enrollment in schools and expenditures for education increased greatly.

Part B: Circle the letter of the title that best summarizes each of the following two selections. Then write a one-sentence summary of each. If there is a summary sentence in a paragraph, you may use it; one paragraph has such a sentence.

Sheer proximity is perhaps the most decisive factor in determining who will become friends. Our friends are likely to live nearby. Although it is said that absence makes the heart grow fonder, it also causes friendships to fade. While relationships may be maintained in absentia by correspondence, they usually have to be reinforced by periodic visits, or they dissolve. Several researchers decided to investigate the effects of proximity on friendships. They chose an apartment complex made up of two-story buildings with five apartments to a floor. People moved into the project at random, so previous social attachments did not influence the results of the study. In interviewing the residents of the apartment complex, the researchers found that 44 percent said they were most friendly with their next-door neighbors, 22 percent saw the people who lived two doors away the most often socially, and only 10 percent said that their best friends lived as far away as down the hall. People were even less likely to be friendly with those who lived upstairs or downstairs from them.

5. What would be an accurate title for this selection?

    a.   Proximity

    b.   Factors in Determining Friendships

    (c.) Proximity as a Factor in Friendships

6. Summary sentence: _Sheer proximity is perhaps the most decisive_

    factor in determining who will become friends.

The institutional care we give our older people is a good reflection of the overall attitude of our society toward the aged. In the past few years, nursing homes have received wide attention as boring, meaningless places where people often have little else to do but wait for the end of their lives. Senility wards in mental hospitals are even worse. One of the shocking things about nursing homes has been the unwillingness of people on the outside to show real concern for what happens in these institutions. Even people who are entrusting a parent to the care of a home rarely ask about the nurse–patient ratio, about the kind of creative facilities or physical therapy equipment available, or even about the frequency of doctors' visits. And the government has provided federal money without enforcing high standards of care. In fact, federal standards were lowered in 1974; therefore, in some sense our concern for the aged seems to be moving backward, not forward.

7. What would be an accurate title for this selection?

    (a.) Institutional Care for the Elderly: A National Disgrace

    b.   The Elderly

    c.   Government Support of Nursing Homes

8. Summary sentence: _The care given elderly people in institutions is_

    inadequate and poorly regulated.

Skill 8: Understanding Graphs and Tables

Sometimes, being a skillful reader means more than just having the ability to read words. It can also mean being able to read the visual information presented in graphs and tables. As a student, you will probably encounter many graphs and tables in your textbooks. Such visual material can help you understand important ideas and details as you read. Knowing graphics will probably also help in your career work as well, for occupations in our computerized age increasingly rely on graphics to convey information.

Graphs and tables present information by using lines, images, or numbers as well as words. They often compare quantities or show how things change over a period of time. Reading a graph or table involves four steps:

- *Step 1: Read the title and any subtitles.* This important first step gives you a concise summary of all the information in the graph or table.

- *Step 2: Read any information at the top, at the bottom, and along the sides.* Such information may include an explanatory key to the material presented. It may also include a series of years, percentages, or figures.

- *Step 3: Ask yourself the purpose of the graph or table.* Usually, the title can be turned into a question beginning with *What, How much* or *many,* or *How.* The purpose of the graph or table is to answer that question.

- *Step 4: Read the graph or table.* As you read, keep in mind the purpose of the material.

Using these four steps, let us analyze the sample graph and table that follow.

Sample Graph

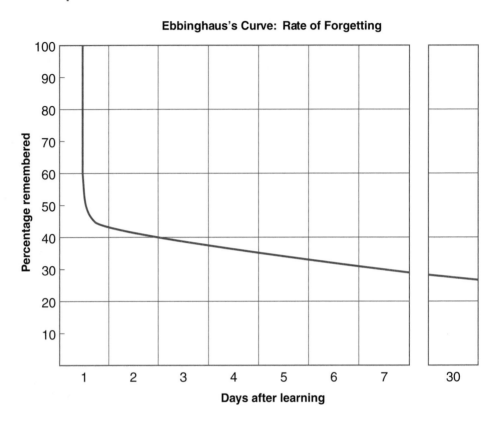

Step 1: The title of the graph is "Ebbinghaus's Curve: Rate of Forgetting." Therefore, the information in the graph will show the rate at which people forget material.

Step 2: On one side of the graph is a series of numbers, ranging from 10 to 100 and labeled "Percentage remembered"—this refers to the percentage of material. Along the bottom of the graph is a series of numbers labeled "Days after learning." The numbers are in sequence from 1 to 7; then there is a gap on the graph followed by the number 30. The curved line on the graph will show what percentage of material is remembered on day 1, day 2, and so on—up to day 30.

Step 3: We can turn the title of the graph into the question "What is the rate at which people forget material?" The purpose of the graph is to answer that question. The graph will show us what percentage of material people remembered as days passed.

Step 4: Read the graph and try to answer the following questions. Put your answers in the spaces provided.

1. What was the percentage of material remembered *by the end of* day 1? _____

2. What percentage of material did people remember on day 3? _____

3. On what day did the percentage of material remembered drop to approximately 30 percent? _____

4. *True or false?* _____ The percentage of material remembered dropped drastically between day 7 and day 30.

On day 1, the percentage of material remembered dropped from 100 percent to approximately 50 percent; therefore, people remembered only 50 percent of the material by the end of the day. On day 3, people remembered approximately 40 percent of the material they had learned. (By moving *up* the graph on the line labeled "Day 3" to the heavy black graph line and then moving *across* the graph to the left-hand column, you will arrive at "40": the percentage remembered.) On day 7, the percentage of material remembered dropped to approximately 30 percent. (By locating "30" in the left-hand column, moving across the graph to the point where the heavy line appears, and then moving down to the series of numbers on the base of the graph, you arrive at day 7.) The percentage of material did not drop drastically between days 7 and 30.

Sample Table

Sound Levels and Human Responses

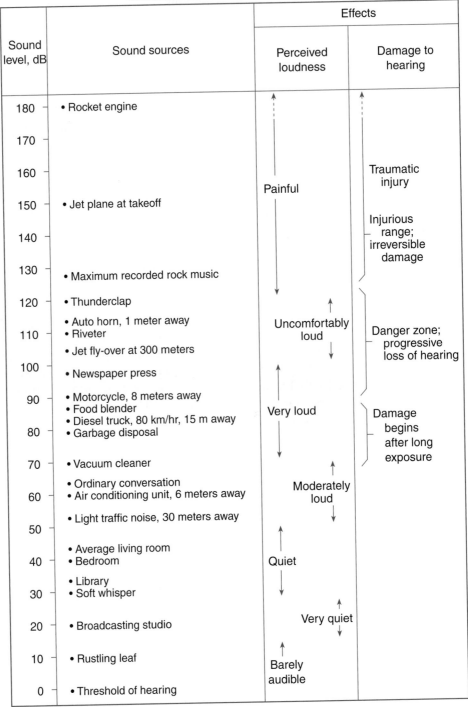

Follow the four reading steps listed on page 439, and then try to answer the following questions about the sample table. Put your answers in the spaces provided.

1. What is the title of the table?

_____

2. What is the decibel (dB) level of a vacuum cleaner? _____

3. List two sounds that are described as "Uncomfortably loud":

_____

_____

4. List one item that can lead to hearing damage after long exposure:

_____

Since the title of the table is "Sound Levels and Human Responses," the table will answer the question "What are the human responses to various levels of sound?" By reading the information along the top and side of the table, we can locate the answers to the next three questions. We can locate "vacuum cleaner" by looking down the column labeled "Sound sources." In the column to the left, we find the decibel (dB) level of a vacuum cleaner: 70 dB. Looking below the column head "Perceived loudness," we find "Uncomfortably loud." The arrow shows that several items on the column to the left fit this description: thunderclap, auto horn that is one meter away, riveter, and jet fly-over at three hundred meters. Looking down the column labeled "Damage to Hearing," we find the heading "Damage begins after long exposure." Listed to the left of it are the items "food blender," "diesel truck," "garbage disposal," and "vacuum cleaner."

Practice in Reading Graphs and Tables

Activity 1

1. Follow the four reading steps listed on page 439, and then try to answer the questions about the following graph.

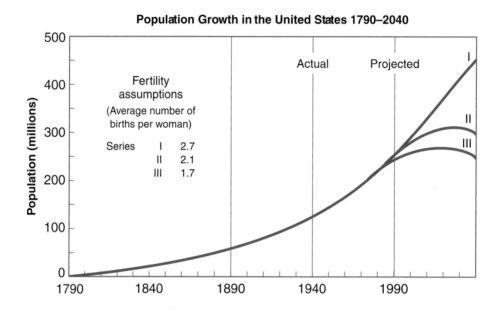

Population Growth in the United States 1790–2040

a. What is the purpose of this graph? _To show U. S. population growth from 1790 to 2040._

b. What (approximately) was the population of the United States in 1940?
   125 million

c. What (approximately) was the population of the United States in 1990?
   225 million

d. If we assume that each woman gives birth to 2.7 children between now and 2040, what will the U.S. population be (approximately) in 2040?
   450 million

e. What will the U.S. population be in 2040 if the projected Series III actually occurs?
   250 million

2. Follow the four reading steps listed on page 439, and then try to answer the questions about the following table.

Average Estimated Electrical Energy Use per Year for Typical Household Appliances

Appliance	Power (W)	Average hours used per year	Approximate energy used (kWh/year)
Clock	2	8,760	17
Clothes dryer	4,600	228	1,049
Hair dryer	1,000	60	60
Lightbulb	100	1,080	108
Compact fluorescent	18	1,080	19
Television	350	1,440	504
Water heater (150 L)	4,500	1,044	4,698
Energy-efficient model	2,800	1,044	2,900
Toaster	1,150	48	552
Washing machine	700	144	1,008
Refrigerator	360	6,000	2,160
Energy-efficient model	180	6,000	1,100

a. What is the purpose of this table? _To show how much energy appliances_
 use per year.

b. Which appliance is used for the least hours per year? _Toaster_
 For the most hours per year? _Clock_

c. Which appliance uses the most energy per year? _Water heater_
 The least energy per year? _Clock_

d. Which appliance uses more energy per year, a washing machine or a clothes dryer? _Clothes dryer_

e. Which appliance is used more, a television or a water heater?
 Television

f. About how much energy is saved per year by using an energy-efficient refrigerator instead of a regular model?

 ____ 100 kW/h   ____ 500 kW/h   ✓ 1000 kW/h   ____ 2000 kW/h

g. Fill in the blank: A compact fluorescent lightbulb uses as little energy as a *(clock, hair dryer, toaster, regular light bulb)* _clock_

Activity 2

1. Follow the four reading steps listed on page 439, and then try to answer the questions about the following graph.

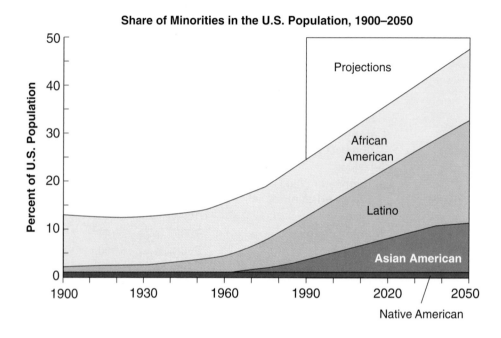

Share of Minorities in the U.S. Population, 1900–2050

a. What is the purpose of the graph? _To show the share of minorities in_
   the U. S. population between 1900 and 2050.

b. In 1990, approximately what percentage of the United States population was made up of minorities?

   _✓_ 12 percent   ____ 20 percent   ____ 30 percent   ____ 50 percent

c. By 2050, approximately what percentage of the United States population will be made up of minorities?

   ____ 12 percent   ____ 20 percent   ____ 30 percent   _✓_ 50 percent

d. Which minority group will be the largest percentage of the United States population in 2050?

_____ African American   ✓ Latino

_____ Asian American   _____ Native American

e. Which group will be the smallest percentage of the United States population in 2050?

_____ African American   _____ Latino

_____ Asian American   ✓ Native American

f. Which group was not a statistically significant percentage of the United States population before 1960?

_____ African American   _____ Latino

✓ Asian American   _____ Native American

g. Which *two* groups' shares of the population have remained about the same since 1900?

✓ African American   _____ Latino

_____ Asian American   ✓ Native American

2. Follow the four reading steps listed on page 439, and then try to answer the questions about the following table.

How Different Do Men and Women Think the Sexes Are?

Question: Now I want to ask about some more specific characteristics of men and women. For each one I read, please tell me whether you think it is generally more true of men or more true of women.

Fifteen characteristics most often said to describe men

Fifteen characteristics most often said to describe women

| | | Opinions of | | | | | Opinions of | |
	Total	Men	Women			Total	Men	Women
1. Aggressive	64%	68%	61%	1. Emotional	81%	79%	83%
2. Strong	61	66	57	2. Talkative	73	73	74
3. Proud	59	62	55	3. Sensitive	72	74	71
4. Disorganized	56	55	57	4. Affectionate	66	69	64
5. Courageous	54	55	53	5. Patient	64	60	68
6. Confident	54	58	49	6. Romantic	60	59	61
7. Independent	50	58	43	7. Moody	58	63	52
8. Ambitious	48	51	44	8. Cautious	57	55	59
9. Selfish	47	49	44	9. Creative	54	48	60
10. Logical	45	53	37	10. Thrifty	52	51	53
11. Easygoing	44	48	40	11. Manipulative	51	54	48
12. Demanding	43	39	46	12. Honest	42	44	41
13. Possessive	42	38	45	13. Critical	42	43	41
14. Funny	40	47	34	14. Happy	39	38	39
15. Levelheaded	39	46	34	15. Possessive	37	43	32

a. What is the purpose of the table? _To show how men and women think the sexes differ._

b. Which characteristic do 63 percent of men feel describes women?
    Moody

c. What percentage of women think that men are disorganized? _57%_

d. What is the percentage of people (both men and women) who think that creativity is a feminine characteristic? _54%_

e. What percentage of men think that men are logical? What percentage of women think that men are logical? _Men, 53%; women, 37%_

Activity 3

The following questions are based on tables and graphs in "The Family," the sample textbook chapter on pages 152–203. The table or graph you need to look at in order to answer each question is indicated in parentheses after each question, along with the page number.

1. In 1997, what percentage of families in the United States consisted of married couples without children? _____28%_____ (Figure 11–1, page 166)

2. How much did the percentage of people living alone rise from 1970 to 1997? __19% (from 6% to 25%)__ (Figure 11–1, page 166)

3. Of unmarried women who gave birth in 1993, which racial group contributed the largest percentage? __White (39.5%)__ The smallest percentage? __Native American (1.7%)__ (Figure 11–2, page 169)

4. Among teenagers, how much did the births per 1,000 unmarried women rise between 1970 and 1993? _From about 20 to about 44_ (Figure 11–2, page 169)

5. In 1900, what was the median age of first marriage among men in the United States? __25.9__ In 1960? __22.8__ In 1995? __26.9__ (Table 11–1, page 175)

6. In 1900, what was the median age of first marriage among women in the United States? __21.9__ In 1960? __20.3__ In 1995? __24.5__ (Table 11–1, page 175)

7. At the beginning of their marriages, what is the average score on Rubin's Love Scale for Indian couples who marry for love? __About 69__ What is their average score on the Love Scale after 10+ years of marriage? __About 39__ (Figure 11–4, page 176)

8. At the beginning of their marriage, what is the average score on Rubin's Love Scale for Indian couples whose marriages are arranged? __About 55__ What is their average score on the Love Scale after 10+ years of marriage? __About 68__ (Figure 11–4, page 176)

9. What is the total population of the United States? __250,000,000__ How many people does Suzie know that meet her criteria to be a mate? __9__ (Figure 11–5, page 177)

10. Next to making repairs, what is the household task most done by men in dual-earner families? __Paying bills__ (Figure 11–6, page 179)

11. During which year between 1985 and 1996 did deaths related to child abuse and neglect reach their highest point? _____1994_____ (Figure 11–7, page 187)

12. What is the current trend in the annual divorce rate in the United States? _Holding steady at about 22%_____ (Figure 11–9, page 193)

■ Review Test

1. Study the graph below, and then answer the questions about it.

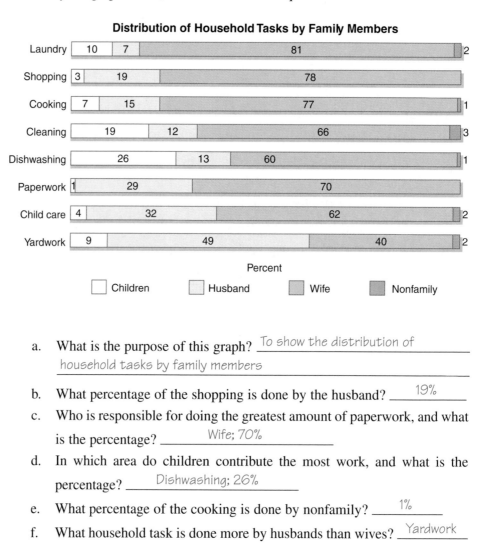

Distribution of Household Tasks by Family Members

	Children	Husband	Wife	Nonfamily
Laundry	10	7	81	2
Shopping	3	19	78	
Cooking	7	15	77	1
Cleaning	19	12	66	3
Dishwashing	26	13	60	1
Paperwork	1	29	70	
Child care	4	32	62	2
Yardwork	9	49	40	2

Percent

☐ Children   ☐ Husband   ☐ Wife   ☐ Nonfamily

a. What is the purpose of this graph? _To show the distribution of household tasks by family members_

b. What percentage of the shopping is done by the husband? _19%_

c. Who is responsible for doing the greatest amount of paperwork, and what is the percentage? _Wife; 70%_

d. In which area do children contribute the most work, and what is the percentage? _Dishwashing; 26%_

e. What percentage of the cooking is done by nonfamily? _1%_

f. What household task is done more by husbands than wives? _Yardwork_

2. Study the table below, and then answer the questions about it.

Employment and Earnings

| | All Workers | | | |
| Major Occupation or Longest Job Held | Women | | Men | |
	Number (1,000)	Median earnings	Number (1,000)	Median earnings
Executive, administrators, and managerial	6,577	$22,551	9,244	$37,010
Professional specialty	8,814	23,113	8,035	36,942
Technical and related support	2,044	20,312	2,053	28,042
Sales	8,393	7,307	7,871	22,955
Administrative support, including clerical	16,728	14,292	4,141	20,287
Precision production, craft, and repair	1,395	13,377	13,448	22,149
Machine operators, assemblers, and inspectors	3,773	10,983	5,389	19,389
Transportation and material moving	511	10,805	5,056	20,053
Handlers, equipment cleaners, helpers, and laborers	995	8,270	4,885	9,912
Service workers	11,722	5,746	7,801	10,514
Farming, forestry, and fishing	680	3,810	3,548	7,881
Total	**61,732**	**12,250**	**72,348**	**21,522**

a. What is the purpose of this table? _To compare numbers and earnings of men and women in the same occupations._

b. How many women are machine operators, assemblers, and inspectors, and what are their median earnings? _3,773,000; $10,983_

c. What are the median earnings of women who work in sales? _$7,307_

d. What are the median earnings of men who work in sales? _$22,955_

e. In what occupation do the fewest women work? _Transportation and material moving_

f. What are the total median earnings of women and the total median earnings of men? _Women: $12,250 Men: $21,522_

Part Five

Skim Reading and Comprehension

Preview

Part Five shows you how to do skimming, or selective reading. You will read quickly through a series of selections, looking for and writing down what seem to be important ideas. To locate the important ideas, you will be asked to apply several of the comprehension skills that you learned in Part Four. Each article or textbook chapter that you skim-read and take notes on will be timed, and you will check your performance by answering questions on the selections afterward. Through a progress chart, you will be able to measure both your skim-reading rate and your comprehension score for each selection.

Introduction

One of the chief myths that students believe about reading is that they must read every word. Consider, though, that the average textbook contains about six hundred pages, or more than 350,000 words. If students have several textbooks and try to read every word of every assignment, they are likely to have little time left to study what they have read—let alone to attend to the essentials of their everyday lives!

Fortunately, not every word in a book must be read, nor must every detail be learned. The purpose of this part of the book is to give you practice in *skimming,* or selective reading. In skimming, you do not read every word; instead, you go quickly and selectively through a passage, looking for and marking off important ideas but skipping secondary material. You can then go back later to read more closely and take notes on important points.

Skim reading will help you when you do not need to read every word of every assignment. Skim reading will also help make you a flexible reader, and this should be your final reading goal. Flexible readers, depending on their purpose in reading and the nature of the material, are able to practice several different kinds of reading: study reading (using the skills learned in Part Four), rapid reading (the concern of Part Six), and skim reading—the subject of this part of the book.

How to Skim-Read

To skim-read effectively, you must be able to apply several of the comprehension skills you learned in Part Four. You must know how to do the following things:

1 *Find definitions:* Remember that they are often signaled by special type, especially *italics.* Look also for one example that makes a definition clear to you.

2 *Locate enumerations:* And remember that locating a numbered series of items is helpful only if you know what *label* the series fits under. So be sure to look for a clear heading for each enumeration.

3 *Look for relationships between headings and subheadings:* Such relationships are often the key to basic enumerations. And when it seems appropriate, you will also want to *change headings into questions* and find the answers to the questions.

4 *Look for emphasis words and main ideas:* If time permits, look for points marked by emphasis words and for main ideas in what seem to be key paragraphs.

• What is one of the chief myths about reading? That every word must be read

_____

• What is often a real alternative to reading every word of a selection? _____
  Skimming (reading selectively for main ideas)

• What are three skills to practice when you are skim reading?
  1. Find definitions
  2. Locate enumerations
  3. Look for relationships between headings and subheadings

The five reading selections that follow will give you practice in skim reading. You will have a limited amount of time to (1) read and (2) take notes on each selection. At the end of a time period, you will be asked questions about important ideas in the selection, and you can use your notes to answer the questions. You should do well on the quizzes if you have been able to quickly pick out and write down main ideas.

The timed practice will have several benefits. It will teach you skim reading, improve your note-taking and handwriting efficiency, and help you solidify the comprehension skills you practiced in Part Four. By using the progress chart on page 474, you will be able to measure your performance as you move through the selections.

Selection 1

You have ten minutes to skim the following selection for its main points and to take notes on those points. Be sure to time yourself or have your instructor time you as you read and take notes on the selection.

Hint: Definitions and a major enumeration are the keys to the important points in this selection.

Visual Elements in Assertive Communication

"Actions speak louder than words" may be an overworn phrase, but it's still true. If you mean what you say, your nonverbal behavior will back up your statements. On the other hand, the most assertive words will lose their impact if expressed in a hesitant, indirect manner. All the following visual elements can be part of assertive communication.

Eye Contact

Inadequate eye contact is usually interpreted in a negative way as anxiety, dishonesty, shame, boredom, or embarrassment. Even when they are not aware of a person's insufficient eye contact, others will often react unconsciously to it by either avoiding or taking advantage of the person exhibiting it. Don't go overboard and begin to stare down everyone you meet—this will just be as distracting as the other extreme—but do be sure to keep your gaze direct.

Distance

Choosing the correct distance between yourself and another person is an important ingredient of assertion. The anthropologist Edward Hall has outlined four distinct distances used by Americans in differing situations. *Intimate distance* ranges from the surface of the skin to about eighteen inches. As its name implies, it is appropriately used for private purposes: expressions of affection, protection, and anger. *Personal distance* runs from eighteen inches to approximately four feet and is used with people we know well and feel relaxed with. As Hall states, this is the range at which we keep someone "at arm's length," suggesting that while there is relatively high involvement here, the immediacy is not as great as that which occurs within intimate distance. *Social distance* ranges from four to twelve feet and is generally appropriate in less personal settings: meeting strangers, engaging in impersonal business transactions, and so on. This is the range at which job interviews are often conducted, customers are approached by salespeople, or newcomers are introduced to us by a third party. We often accuse someone who ought to be using social distance but instead moves into our personal

457

space of being "pushy." Finally, Hall labels as *public distance* the space extending outward from twelve feet. As its name implies, public distance is used in highly impersonal settings and occasions involving larger numbers of people: classrooms, public performances, and so on. Be sure you are using the appropriate range for the message you want to express.

Facial Expression

In the typical assertiveness training group, one or two participants will express confusion as to why they have such trouble being taken seriously. They claim to use the appropriate language, keep eye contact, stand at the proper distance, and so on. When asked to demonstrate how they usually express themselves, the problem often becomes apparent: the facial expression is totally inappropriate to the message. Many communicators, for example, verbally express their dissatisfaction while smiling as if nothing were wrong. Others claim to share approval or appreciation while wearing expressions more appropriate for viewing a corpse.

Gestures and Posture

Like facial expressions, your movements and body positioning can either contribute to or detract from the immediacy of a message. Fidgeting hands, nervous shifting from one foot to another, or slumped shoulders will reduce or even contradict the impact of an assertive message. On the other hand, gestures that are appropriate to the words being spoken and a posture that suggests involvement in the subject will serve to reinforce your words. Watch an effective storyteller, an interviewer, an actor, or some other model and note the added emphasis he or she gives to a message.

Body Orientation

Another way of expressing your attitude is through the positioning of your body in relation to another person. Facing someone head-on communicates a much higher degree of immediacy than does a less direct positioning. In fact, a directly confronting stance in which the face, shoulders, hips, and feet squarely face the other is likely to be interpreted as indicating an aggressive attitude. (To verify this impression, think of the stance used by a baseball player who is furious with an umpire's decision or a Marine drill instructor facing a recruit.) Observation for assertive models will show that the most successful body orientation for most settings is a modified frontal one, in which the communicators are slightly angled away from a direct confrontation— perhaps ten to thirty degrees. This position clearly suggests a high degree of involvement, yet allows occasional freedom from total eye contact, which you have already learned is not to be desired.

When the ten minutes are up, try to answer the questions on page 475 by referring to your notes but *not* referring to the text.

Selection 2

You have ten minutes to skim the following textbook selection for its main points and to take notes on those points.

Science and the Search for Truth

A pathologist after elaborate preparation places a slide under the microscope and adjusts the lens carefully. Members of a Purari war party watch carefully as they place their canoe in the water, for unless it rocks, the raid will not be successful. A man steps from a new station wagon, cuts a forked twig, and carries it around holding it above the ground, while a well-drilling crew stands by, waiting to drill where the twig tells them water will be found. A woman in Peoria, anxious over her teenage daughter, prays to God for guidance. A physician leafs through the pages of a parasitology textbook and tries to identify a patient's puzzling skin rash. A senator scans the latest public opinion poll and wonders how to vote on the farm bill.

Each of these persons is seeking guidance. Their problems vary, and their sources of truth are different. Where shall human beings find truth? How can they know when they have found it? In the million years, more or less, of human life on this earth, people have sought truth in many places. Where are some of them?

Some Sources of Truth

Intuition. Galen, a famous Greek physician of the second century, prepared an elaborate chart of the human body, showing exactly where it might be pierced without fatal injury. How did he know the vulnerable spots? He just *knew* them. True, he had learned a good deal of human anatomy through his observations and those of his associates, but beyond this, he relied upon his intuition to tell him which zones were fatal. *Intuition is any flash of insight (true or mistaken) whose source the receiver cannot fully identify or explain.* Hitler relied heavily upon his intuition, much to the distress of his generals. His intuition told him that France would not fight for the Rhineland, that England would not fight for Czechoslovakia, that England and France would quit when he attacked Russia. He was right on the first two insights and wrong on the last two.

459

Intuition is responsible for many brilliant hypotheses, which can later be tested through other methods. Perhaps intuition's greatest value is in the forming of hypotheses.

Authority. Two thousand years ago, Galen knew more about human anatomy than any other mortal; as recently as 1800, physicians were still quoting him as an authority. Aristotle stated that a barrel of water could be added to a barrel of ashes without overflowing, and for two thousand years thereafter, a student who might suggest trying it out would be scolded for his impertinence. For many centuries, creative thought was stifled by Aristotelian authority, for since an authority is *right,* any conflicting ideas must be wrong. Authority does not discover new truths, but it can prevent new truths from being discovered or accepted.

Dangerous though authority may be, we cannot get along without it. Our accumulation of knowledge is too great for anyone to absorb, so we must rely upon specialists who have collected the reliable knowledge in a particular field. An authority is a necessary and useful source of knowledge—*in the field in which he is an authority.* Science recognizes no authorities on "things in general."

Authority is of several sorts. *Sacred* authority rests upon the faith that a certain tradition or document—the Bible, the Koran, the Vedas—is of supernatural origin. *Secular* authority arises not from divine revelation but from human perception. It is of two kinds: *secular scientific* authority, which rests upon empirical investigation, and *secular humanistic* authority, which rests upon the belief that certain "great men" have had remarkable insight into human behavior and the nature of the universe. The search for truth by consulting the "great books" is an example of the appeal to secular humanistic authority.

Tradition. Of all sources of truth, tradition is one of the most reassuring. Here is the accumulated wisdom of the ages, and one who disregards it may expect denunciation as a scoundrel or a fool. If a pattern has "worked" in the past, why not keep on using it?

Tradition, however, preserves both the accumulated wisdom and the accumulated bunkum of the ages. Tradition is society's attic, crammed with all sorts of useful customs and useless relics. A great deal of "practical experience" consists in repeating the mistakes of our ancestors. One task of social science is to sort out our folklore into the true and the merely ancient.

Common Sense. Common sense and tradition are closely interwoven, with many commonsense propositions becoming part of a people's traditional lore. If a distinction is to be drawn, it may be that traditional truths are those which have long been believed, while commonsense truths are uncritically accepted conclusions (recent or ancient) which are currently believed by one's fellows.

What often passes for common sense consists of a group's accumulation of collective guesses, hunches, and haphazard trial-and-error learning. Many commonsense propositions are sound, earthy, useful bits of knowledge. "A soft answer turneth away wrath" and "Birds of a feather flock together" are practical observations on social life. But many commonsense conclusions are based on ignorance, prejudice, and mistaken interpretation. When medieval Europeans noticed that feverish patients were free of lice while most healthy people were lousy, they made the commonsense conclusion that lice would cure fever and therefore sprinkled lice over feverish patients. Not until the fever subsided would the lice be removed. Common sense, like tradition, preserves both folk wisdom and folk nonsense, and to sort them out one from the other is a task for science.

Science. Only within the last two or three hundred years has the scientific method become a common way of seeking answers about the natural world. *Science* may be defined as a method of study whereby a body of organized scientific knowledge is discovered. Science has become a source of knowledge about the social world even more recently; yet in the brief period since human beings began to rely upon the scientific method, they have learned more about their world than they learned in the preceding ten thousand years. The spectacular explosion of knowledge in the modern world parallels the use of the scientific method. What makes the scientific method so productive? How does it differ from other methods of seeking truth?

Characteristics of Scientific Knowledge

Verifiable Evidence. Scientific knowledge is based on verifiable evidence. By *evidence* we mean concrete factual observations that other observers can see, weigh, measure, count, or check for accuracy. We may think the definition too obvious to mention; most of us have some awareness of the scientific method. Yet only a few centuries ago medieval scholars held long debates on how many teeth a horse had, without bothering to look into a horse's mouth to count them.

At this point we raise the troublesome methodological question, "What is a fact?" While the word looks deceptively simple, it is not easy to distinguish a fact from a widely shared illusion. Suppose we define a fact as a descriptive statement upon which all qualified observers are in agreement. By this definition, medieval ghosts were a fact, since all medieval observers agreed that ghosts were real. There is, therefore, no way to be *certain* that a fact is an accurate description and not a mistaken impression. Research would be easier if facts were dependable, unshakable certainties. Since they are not, the best we can do is to recognize that a fact is *a descriptive statement of reality that scientists, after careful examination and cross-checking, agree in believing to be accurate.*

Ethical Neutrality. Science is knowledge, and knowledge can be put to differing uses. Atomic fission can be used to power a city or to incinerate a nation. Every use of scientific knowledge involves a choice between values. Our values define what is most important to us. Science tells us that over-eating and cigarette smoking will shorten our life expectancy. But can science tell us which we should choose—a longer life or a more indulgent one? Science can answer questions of fact but has no way to prove that one value is better than another.

Science, then, is ethically neutral. Science seeks knowledge, while society's values determine how this knowledge is to be used. Knowledge about group organization can be used to preserve a democracy or to establish a dictatorship.

When the ten minutes are up, try to answer the questions on page 476 by using your notes but *not* referring to the text.

Selection 3

You have ten minutes to skim the following textbook selection for its main points and to take notes on those points. Be sure to time yourself or have your instructor time you as you read and take notes on the selection.

Hint: Definitions and enumerations are the keys to the important points in this selection.

The Nature of Power

Niccolò Machiavelli (1469–1527) wrote *The Prince* as a way of giving advice to Italian princes (such as Cesare Borgia) in their struggle against the pope to establish an Italian state. Machiavelli saw the power of the prince as a means for achieving the moral goal of Italian unification. In the following passage, he makes an important distinction:

> You must know, then, that there are two methods of fighting, the one by law, the other by force: the first method is that of men, the second of beasts; but as the first method is often insufficient, one must have recourse to the second. . . .
>
> Thus it is well to seem merciful, faithful, humane, sincere, religious, and also to be so; but you must have the mind so disposed that when it is needful to be otherwise you may be able to change to the opposite qualities. . . . And therefore, you must have a mind disposed to adapt itself according to the wind, and as the variations of fortune dictate, and, as I said before, not deviate from what is good if possible, but be able to do evil if constrained.

In this celebrated passage, Machiavelli is discussing power. *Power in society is the ability to control the behavior of others—against their will if necessary—by using force, authority, or influence.* As the passage indicates, there are different kinds of power. Machiavelli recognized two kinds: force and law. Contemporary sociologists, however, find it more useful to speak of three kinds of power: *force, authority,* and *influence.*

Force

Machiavelli is not a particularly popular person in Italian history, partly because of his favorable attitude toward the use of *force*. Force is *physical coercion or the threat of such coercion.* In Machiavelli's terms, it is the method "of beasts" rather than "of men." Yet he advised his prince to resort to it whenever other means of controlling people's behavior fail. The use of force is at odds with many of our fundamental values, such as equality, freedom, and the importance of the individual personality. Yet there are situations, as illustrated by the aggression of Hitler's Germany or that of a gunman on the loose, where such values are threatened by people willing to use force. Using force to counter force in such situations can protect those values, but it also conflicts with them at the same time.

Authority

A second type of power is *authority,* which may be defined as *legitimate power,* that is, power based on values and norms. Machiavelli contrasted the use of force with the rule of law, and the latter illustrates authority. Authority tends to be a much larger component of most existing power than is force. The socialization process teaches us to conform to a wide variety of norms that allow others—parents, teachers, friends, employers, and officials of all kinds—to direct our behavior.

Three Kinds of Authority: Max Weber enables us to gain some historical perspective on the nature of authority. At the same time, he distinguishes three kinds of authority: charismatic, traditional, and legal. *Charismatic authority is rule based on belief in the extraordinary personal qualities of the ruler.* Weber illustrates such authority by referring to "the magical sorcerer, the prophet, the leader of hunting and booty expeditions, the warrior chieftain, the so-called 'Caesarist' ruler." For example, we might think of Jesus Christ, Joan of Arc, Adolf Hitler, and Winston Churchill as exercising charismatic authority. They all had qualities of personality that deeply appealed to their followers.

Traditional authority is rule based on conformity to established modes of behavior. It is illustrated by the patriarchal domination of a family by the father or husband, by the rule of the lord over vassals and serfs, or by the rule of the master over slaves. By contrast, *legal authority is rule based on law or formal decrees and regulations.* It is exemplified by the authority of a president, a police officer, a member of Congress, a court official, the head of a government agency, a member of a school board, and a welfare investigator. With the development of industrial society has come a shift from traditional to legal authority. Charismatic authority has existed in the past and continues to exist in the present. It can be combined with the other two kinds of authority.

Influence

The third component of power is *influence,* which may be defined as *the ability to control the behavior of others beyond any authority to do so.* In certain situations, a leader may neither choose to exert force nor have any authority—legal, traditional, or charismatic—yet nevertheless may wish to assert power. He or she may be able to exert our third type of power, influence, simply on the basis of the "exchanges" that can be made. A teacher can influence students to develop interest in a subject by proving to be trustworthy as well as helpful. Such interest cannot be compelled on the basis of the teacher's authority.

The different aspects of power—force, authority, and influence—may be illustrated by Mohandas K. Gandhi's success in leading India toward independence from Great Britain. Gandhi was seen by his followers as a highly charismatic person. Further, his manner of living embodied such traditional ideals as humility, self-sacrifice, and spirituality. He refused to use force and, in its place, developed techniques of passive resistance. Among other things, he trained volunteers to march forward and allow themselves to be struck down by police clubs without defending themselves. Gandhi's leadership illustrates charismatic and traditional authority as well as influence. This was reflected in the title "mahatma" (great soul) that his followers bestowed on him.

Gandhi opposed his authority and influence against the force and legal authority of the British, and that opposition proved to be highly effective. For example, the British exercise of force, although perfectly legal in British terms, came to be seen as immoral not only by Indians but also by large segments of the British population.

The Gandhian approach to conflict influenced Martin Luther King to develop his own techniques of passive resistance in the struggle of American blacks against discrimination. For example, black people's boycotts of buses in Montgomery, Alabama, in 1955 (in reaction to the injustice of being forced to sit only in the backs of buses) were almost 100 percent effective. Here King, as Gandhi had done, avoided the use of force and combined charismatic and traditional authority with personal influence to undermine the legal authority of the local government.

When the ten minutes are up, try to answer the questions on page 476 by referring to your notes but *not* referring to the text.

Selection 4

You have ten minutes to skim the following textbook selection for its main points and to take notes on those points.

Defense Mechanisms

Maintaining a good self-concept and high self-esteem is not easy. Each day there are many events that could shatter your self-image. If you notice a new blemish or wrinkle on your face, receive a low grade, or are not invited to lunch by the group, you need to take action to protect your self-esteem. The methods you use to protect your self-esteem are called *defense mechanisms.*

Suppression and Repression

One way to protect your self-esteem is to avoid thinking about your problem. For example, you might intentionally go to a movie to avoid thinking about an argument. This defense mechanism, a deliberate attempt to avoid stressful thoughts, is labeled "suppression." Scarlett O'Hara in *Gone with the Wind* is among the more famous practitioners of suppression. Remember her line, "I'll think about it tomorrow"? Scarlett was suppressing her unpleasant thoughts. Have you ever felt lonely and intentionally kept yourself busy with chores, sports, or shopping to avoid thinking about your loneliness? If so, you were using suppression.

Suppression is useful only for minor problems. Usually you can pretend a problem does not exist for only a short period. Thoughts and worries tend to come back and may be even more stressful if they have been bottled up. Suppression requires a conscious and voluntary effort and has limited use as a defense mechanism.

Issues that are deeply wounding to self-esteem may be too painful to reach consciousness. You unconsciously put them out of your mind. Unconsciously motivated forgetting is called "repression." Everyone tends to push unpleasant thoughts out of the conscious mind. Since thoughts that are repressed are not conscious, people can become aware of them only through dreams or hypnosis.

Repression is the most basic defense mechanism. Most other defense mechanisms stem from repression. In its simplest form repression is unconscious forgetting. Suppose you forget to contribute money to a going-away gift for a close friend. Unconsciously you wish your friend were not leaving.

"Normally I don't let rejection bother me, but . . ."

The rejection stamped on his forehead may also become buried
in his unconscious. Time for some defense mechanisms . . .

Forgetting appointments, birthdays, weddings, and other important events
can be a sign of repression. Have you ever met someone who was rejecting
and cruel to you? If you have difficulty recalling any persons or names, you
may be repressing them! Usually thoughts and feelings that are repressed
bring on other defense mechanisms.

Other Defense Mechanisms

Assuming that the fellow in the cartoon above is deeply worried about
being rejected, he may repress the situation. As a result he could forget the
name of the woman, their entire conversation, what he was drinking, and
where he was that evening. Rather than admit his rejection and suffer, he
could also use a number of other unconscious defense mechanisms.

Withdrawal: If the man in the cartoon has trouble talking to women in
the future, it could be that he unconsciously fears rejection. *Withdrawal* usually
results when people become intensely frightened or frustrated by a situation.
People who fear rejection often avoid or withdraw from social situations.
Sometimes the result is shyness. Often people fear rejection even when it is
unlikely. Many famous and likable people have suffered from shyness.

If you have ever tried to escape from an unpleasant situation, you have used a withdrawal defense mechanism. If used cautiously, withdrawal can be a healthy defense mechanism. Often, stepping out of a situation can help you gain a better perspective. However, withdrawal can also result in quitting jobs, dropping out of school, separations, and divorces.

Fantasy: Sometimes people withdraw into a make-believe or *fantasy* world. If the rejected man in the cartoon used a fantasy defense mechanism, he might daydream about his successes with women. He could create his own dream world where he would always be accepted, admired, and loved. Used in moderation, daydreaming and fantasy can be healthy and lead to creative thinking. Everyone daydreams as a method of reducing anxiety. Fantasy can bring a healthy escape from boredom and aid mental relaxation. Reading a novel or watching a soap opera can provide fantasy escapes. However, if fantasy is used excessively, it can become an unhealthy substitute for activity.

Regression: *Regression* is withdrawal into the past. If the rejected fellow regressed in a childlike way, he would behave like a child. He might burst into tears, or pout, suck his thumb, throw things, scream, and have a tantrum. Regression requires a return to earlier ways of handling problems. It is generally used when a person is deeply upset and cannot cope in a mature manner. Young children who have been toilet-trained and taught to drink from a cup often regress and forget their training when a new baby arrives in their home. The older child does not know how to win parental affection in the new situation. Consequently the child must resort to previous methods for gaining attention and love. The result is regression.

Rationalization: *Rationalization* is a distortion of the truth to maintain self-esteem. It provides an excuse or explanation for a situation that is really unacceptable. The man in the cartoon might rationalize that the woman was not really his type and that he was delighted to be rid of her so he could arrive home at a reasonable hour. He might even rationalize that he was just having an unlucky day. Failures are often rationalized as being the result of some external factor, but success is deemed the result of personal abilities.

Most people are unaware of how often they rationalize. Although rationalization is indeed a misuse of logic, it can help to reduce anxiety. Have you ever excused yourself from a poor grade by arguing that the test was unfair or that you were feeling sick when you took the test? Rationalization can also allow you to look at the bright side. If an unpleasant event has already occurred, often little or nothing can be done to change it. After losing the 1960 presidential election, Richard Nixon reportedly commented that he would have more time to devote to his family. This was clearly a rationalization but probably aided his acceptance of a painful reality.

Projection: Projection is based on guilt. Rather than accept personal weaknesses, unacceptable features are projected onto another person. The rejected man could project his rejection onto the woman who stamped him. He would then maintain that it was she who was rejected by everyone. Projection permits you to accuse someone else of your weaknesses. Perhaps you have heard complaints from one fraternity that members of another fraternity hated them. They could easily be projecting their own feelings onto the other group. Or maybe you have known a flirt who complained that every male she met flirted with her. Psychologists often use projective tests to uncover problems. It is assumed that individuals will project their own feelings onto the pictures and illustrations in the test material.

Displacement: Displacement requires finding a target or victim for pent-up feelings. The rejected fellow at the bar might ridicule and chastise the bartender for poor drinks or slow service. The chosen victim is usually a safe person, someone who is not likely to deflate self-esteem. Spouses are often selected. As a result, husbands and wives often learn to avoid controversial topics when their mate has had a bad day.

Compensation: Compensation allows a person to make up for inadequacies by doing well in another area. Perhaps the rejected fellow at the bar could go back to work and prove himself an outstanding accountant, attorney, or automobile salesman. Compensation allows you to deemphasize your weaknesses and play up your strengths. A child who is a poor student may try learning clever jokes to become popular. Compensation is a reasonable defense mechanism and usually leads to a healthy adjustment.

Sublimation: Sublimation is the most accepted defense mechanism. Unacceptable impulses are channeled into something positive, constructive, or creative. If the man left the bar and wrote a beautiful blues song about rejection and loneliness, he would be sublimating. Some of the finest poetry and folk music have emerged from oppressed groups, an example of their sublimations.

Of the many defense mechanisms, compensation and sublimation are considered the most healthy and acceptable. Since defense mechanisms are unconscious, usually people are completely unaware of them. Think about some of your own behavior. Can you identify the defense mechanisms you choose most often?

When the ten minutes are up, try to answer the questions your instructor gives you by using your notes but *not* referring to the text.

Selection 5

You have ten minutes to skim the following article for its main points and to take notes on those points.

Hint: Definitions and enumerations are the keys to the important points in this article.

Fatigue

Fatigue is one of the most common complaints brought to doctors, friends, and relatives. You'd think that in this era of laborsaving devices and convenient transportation, few people would have reason to be so tired. But probably more people complain of fatigue today than in the days when hay was baled by hand and laundry was scrubbed on a washboard. Witness these typical complaints:

"It doesn't seem to matter how long I sleep—I'm more tired when I wake up than when I went to bed."

"Some of my friends come home from work and jog for several miles or swim laps. I don't know how they do it. I'm completely exhausted at the end of a day at the office."

"I thought I was weary because of the holidays, but now that they're over, I'm even worse. I can barely get through the week, and on the weekend I don't even have the strength to get dressed. I wonder if I'm anemic or something."

"I don't know what's wrong with me lately, but I've been so collapsed that I haven't made a proper meal for the family in weeks. We've been living on TV dinners and packaged mixes. I was finally forced to do laundry because the kids ran out of underwear."

The causes of modern-day fatigue are diverse and only rarely related to excessive physical exertion. The relatively few people who do heavy labor all day long almost never complain about being tired, perhaps because they expect to be. Today, physicians report, tiredness is more likely a consequence of underexertion than of wearing yourself down with overactivity. In fact, increased physical activity is often prescribed as a *cure* for sagging energy.

Kinds of Fatigue

There are three main categories of fatigue. These are physical fatigue, pathological fatigue, and psychological fatigue.

Physical. This is the well-known result of overworking your muscles to the point where metabolic waste products—carbon dioxide and lactic acid—accumulate in your blood and sap your strength. Your muscles can't continue to work efficiently in a bath of these chemicals. Physical fatigue is usually a pleasant tiredness, such as that which you might experience after playing a hard set of tennis, chopping wood, or climbing a mountain. The cure is simple and fast: You rest, giving your body a chance to get rid of accumulated wastes and restore muscle fuel.

Pathological. Here fatigue is a warning sign or consequence of some underlying physical disorder, perhaps the common cold or flu or something more serious like diabetes or cancer. Usually other symptoms besides fatigue are present that suggest the true cause.

Even after an illness has passed, you're likely to feel dragged out for a week or more. Take your fatigue as a signal to go slowly while your body has a chance to recover fully even if all you had was a cold. Pushing yourself to resume full activity too soon could precipitate a relapse and almost certainly will prolong your period of fatigue.

Even though illness is not a frequent cause of prolonged fatigue, it's very important that it not be overlooked. Therefore, anyone who feels drained of energy for weeks on end should have a thorough physical checkup. But even if nothing shows up as a result of the various medical tests, that doesn't mean there's nothing wrong with you.

Unfortunately too often a medical workup ends with a battery of negative test results, the patient is dismissed, and the true cause of serious fatigue goes undetected. As Dr. John Bulette, a psychiatrist at the Medical College of Pennsylvania Hospital in Philadelphia, tells it, this is what happened to a woman in Pennsylvania who had lost nearly fifty pounds and was "almost dead—so tired she could hardly lift her head up." The doctors who first examined the woman were sure she had cancer. But no matter how hard they looked, they could find no sign of malignancy or of any other disease that could account for her to be wasting away. Finally, she was brought to the college hospital, where doctors noted that she was severely depressed.

They questioned her about her life and discovered that her troubles had begun two years earlier, after her husband died. Once treated for depression, the woman quickly perked up. She gained ten pounds in just a few weeks, and then she returned home to continue her recovery with the aid of psychotherapy.

Psychological. Emotional problems and conflicts, especially depression and anxiety, are by far the most common causes of prolonged fatigue. Fatigue may represent a defense mechanism that prevents you from having to face the true cause of your depression, such as the fact that you hate your job. It is also your body's safety valve for expressing repressed emotional conflicts, such as feeling trapped in an ungratifying role or an unhappy marriage. When such feelings are not expressed openly, they often come out as physical symptoms, with fatigue as one of the most common manifestations. "Many people who are extremely fatigued don't even know they're depressed," Dr. Bulette says. "They're so busy distracting themselves or just worrying about being tired that they don't recognize their depression."

One of these situations is so common it's been given a name—tired housewife syndrome. The victims are commonly young mothers who day in and day out face the predictable tedium of caring for a home and small children, fixing meals, dealing with repair persons, and generally having no one interesting to talk to and nothing enjoyable to look forward to at the end of their boring and unrewarding day. The tired housewife may be inwardly resentful, envious of her husband's job, and guilty about her feelings. But rather than face them head-on, she becomes extremely fatigued.

Today, with nearly half the mothers of young children working outside the home, the tired housewife syndrome has taken on a new twist: that of conflicting roles and responsibilities and guilt over leaving the children, often with an overlay of genuine physical exhaustion from trying to be all things to all people.

Emotionally induced fatigue may be compounded by sleep disturbance that results from the underlying psychological conflict. A person may develop insomnia or may sleep the requisite number of hours but fitfully tossing and turning all night, having disturbing dreams, and awakening, as one woman put it, feeling as if she "had been run over by a truck."

Understanding the underlying emotional problem is the crucial first step toward curing psychological fatigue and by itself often results in considerable lessening of the tiredness. Professional psychological help or career or marriage counseling may be needed.

What You Can Do about It

There is a great deal you can do on your own to deal with both severe prolonged fatigue and periodic washed-out feelings. Vitamins and tranquilizers are almost never the right answer, sleeping pills and alcohol are counterproductive, and caffeine is at best a temporary solution that can backfire with abuse and cause life-disrupting symptoms of anxiety. Instead, you might try:

Diet. If you eat a skimpy breakfast or none at all, you're likely to experience midmorning fatigue, the result of a drop in blood sugar, which your body and brain depend on for energy. For peak energy in the morning, be sure to eat a proper breakfast, low in sugar and fairly high in protein, which will provide a steady supply of blood sugar throughout the morning. Coffee and a doughnut are almost worse than nothing, providing a brief boost and then letting you down with a thud. . . .

The same goes for the rest of the day: Frequent snacking on sweets is a false pick-me-up that soon leaves you lower than you were to begin with. Stick to regular, satisfying, well-balanced meals that help you maintain a trim figure. Extra weight is tiring both physically and psychologically. Getting your weight down to normal can go a long way toward revitalizing you. . . .

Exercise. Contrary to what you may think, exercise enhances, rather than saps, energy. Regular conditioning exercises, such as jogging, cycling, or swimming, help you to resist fatigue by increasing your body's ability to handle more of a workload. You get tired less quickly because your capability is greater.

Exercise also has a well-recognized tranquilizing effect, which helps you work in a more relaxed fashion and be less dragged down by the tensions of your day. At the end of the day exercise can relieve accumulated tensions, give you more energy in the evening, and help you sleep more restfully. . . .

Sleep. If you know you're tired because you haven't been getting enough sleep, the solution is simple: Get to bed earlier. There's no right amount of sleep for everyone, and generally sleep requirements decline with age. Find the amount that suits you best and aim for it. Insomnia and other sleep disorders should not be treated with sleeping pills, alcohol, or tranquilizers, which can actually make the problem worse. . . .

Knowing Yourself. Try to schedule your most taxing jobs for the time of day when you're at your peak. Some are "morning people" who tire by midafternoon; others do their best work in the evening. Don't overextend yourself trying to climb the ladder of success at a record pace or to meet everyone's demands or expectations. Decide what you want to do and what you can handle comfortably and learn to say no to additional requests. Recognize your energy cycles and plan accordingly. For example, many women have a low point premenstrually, during which time extra sleep may be needed and demanding activities are particularly exhausting.

Taking Breaks. No matter how interesting or demanding your work, you'll be able to do it with more vigor if now and again you stop, stretch, and change the scenery. Instead of coffee and a sweet roll on your break, try meditation, yoga, calisthenics, or a brisk walk. Even running up and down the staircase can provide refreshment from a sedentary job. If your job is physically demanding, relax in a quiet place for a while. The do-something-different rule also applies to vacations; "getting away from it all" for a week or two or longer can be highly revitalizing, helping you to put things in perspective and enabling you to take your job more in stride upon your return.

When the ten minutes are up, try to answer the questions your instructor gives you by using your notes but *not* referring to the text.

Skim-Reading Progress Chart

On the following chart are skim-reading speeds for the selections in Part Five. The term WPM refers here to the number of words *processed* per minute. (You have not been able to literally *read* every word in the limited time involved.) The reading speeds assume that you have taken one-quarter of your time to read each selection and three-quarters of your time to take notes on what you have read.

Selection	WPM	Comprehension
1 Visual Elements in Assertive Communication (731 words)	505	
2 Science and the Search for Truth (1,464 words)	525	
3 The Nature of Power (1,152 words)	460	
4 Defense Mechanisms (1,625 words)	660	
5 Fatigue (1,957 words)	783	

Note: Reading speed will vary depending on the nature and difficulty of the material. In the five preceding selections, the highest speed is for "Fatigue," an article by the popular health writer Jane Brody, taken from a newspaper. Because the four other selections, all from textbooks, contain more information to process, slightly lower skim-reading rates are suggested.

Questions on the Skim-Reading Selections

■ **Selection 1**

1. Name any four visual elements in assertive communication.

   Any four would be acceptable.

Eye contact	Facial expression	Body orientation
Distance	Gesture and posture	

2. What are the four distinct distances that are used by Americans in differing situations?

   Intimate distance

   Personal distance

   Social distance

   Public distance

Score: Number correct (_____) × 12.5 = _____%

■ Selection 2

1. What are the five sources of truth?

Intuition   Authority   Tradition

Common sense   Science

2. Define intuition. Any flash of insight whose source the receiver cannot fully
identify or explain

3. What are the two characteristics of scientific knowledge?
Verifiable evidence   Ethical neutrality

4. Define science. A method of study whereby a body of organized scientific
knowledge is discovered

5. Define a fact. A fact is a descriptive statement of reality which scientists,
after careful examination and cross-checking, agree in believing is accurate.

> **Score:** Number correct (_____) × 10 = _____%

■ Selection 3

1. What are the three kinds of power?
Force   Authority   Influence

2. What is force? Physical coercion or the threat of such coercion

3. What are the three kinds of authority?
Charismatic authority

Traditional authority

Legal authority

4. What is influence? The ability to control the behavior of others beyond any
authority to do so

> **Score:** Number correct (_____) × 12.5 = _____%

■ **Selection 4**

Your instructor will refer to the Instructor's Manual to give you the questions for Selection 4.

■ **Selection 5**

Your instructor will refer to the Instructor's Manual to give you the questions for Selection 5.

Part Six

Rapid Reading and Comprehension

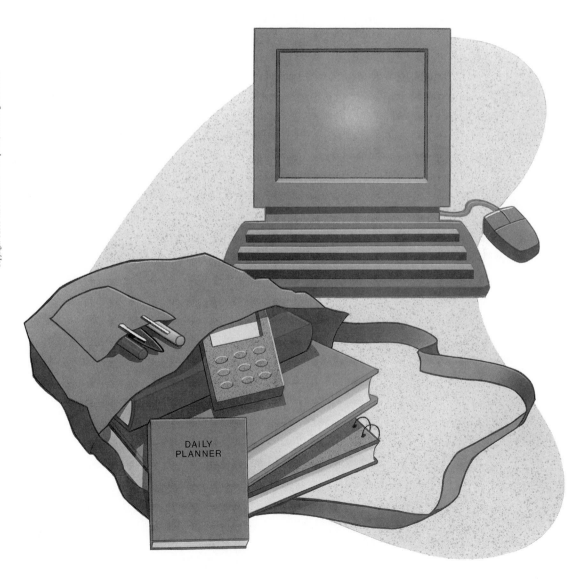

Preview

Part Six is concerned primarily with developing your comprehension but also with trying to increase the number of words that your eyes take in and "read" per minute. Poor perception habits that may slow down your reading rate are explained, and an activity is provided to show you how your eyes move when they read. You then learn how a conscious effort to increase your speed may be a key to overcoming careless perception habits and achieving a higher reading rate.

A series of ten reading selections then gives you practice in building up your comprehension and perhaps your reading speed as well. Through a progress chart, you will be able to compare your reading rate and comprehension scores as you move through the selections.

Introduction

This part of the book will give you further practice in developing comprehension skills. At the same time, it will help you discover whether you can realistically increase the number of words that your eyes take in and "read" per minute. An increase in reading speed can be valuable, though it is certainly no cure-all for reading problems.

If you feel you are reading your college assignments too slowly or ineffectively, *factors other than reading speed are probably responsible.* For example, perhaps you don't know where and how to look for main ideas and key supporting details in a textbook chapter. You may need to work on the reading comprehension and skim-reading skills presented in Parts Four and Five of this book. Also, you may need to learn more about study skills such as textbook previewing, marking, and note-taking. And you may have to learn how to read flexibly. This means that you adjust your speed and style of reading to accommodate your purpose as well as the level of difficulty of the material.

In summary, there is much more to effective reading than an increase in speed alone. It is also true, however, that some students do benefit from working to improve reading speed. If nothing else, the extra effort and concentration that it takes to increase speed can improve comprehension as well.

- *Complete the following sentence:* <u> Rapid (or speed) </u> reading is only one part of effective reading.

Poor Perception Habits

If you read material of average or less than average difficulty slowly, you can probably significantly increase your present reading speed. In all likelihood, poor perception habits are slowing down your reading. Such habits include *subvocalizing*

481

(pronouncing words silently to yourself as you read); slow and stilted *word-for-word reading;* unnecessary *regressions* (returns to words you have already read); and *visual inaccuracy* (the tendency to misread letters and words on the page). Poor concentration habits often cause this last problem.

- How many bad perception habits are mentioned in the preceding paragraph?

  <u> 4 </u>

How the Eyes Read

You will understand more clearly how the eyes work during reading when you perform the following experiment. Punch a hole with a pen or pencil through the black dot that follows this paragraph. Hold the page up for another person to see and have him or her read a paragraph or two silently. As the person reads, put your eye close to the hole and watch his or her eye movements. In the space provided here, write down your observations, including a description of how the reader's eyes moved across the lines of print.

●

Answers will vary.

In performing this activity, you probably observed that the reader's eyes did not move smoothly across the printed lines. Instead, they moved in jerks, making stop-and-go motions across the lines of print. These stops, which you may have been able to count as you peeked through the hole, are called *fixations,* and only during such fixations do you actually read. You may remember as a child trying—and failing—to catch your eyes moving as you looked in a mirror. You never saw them move because the eyes go too quickly between fixations for any clear vision. The eye must fixate, or stop, in order to see clearly. In summary, then, the eye reads by making a number of fixations or stops as it proceeds across a line of print.

In addition to the stops, you probably also noted the sweep of the eyes, like the carriage return of a typewriter, back and down to the beginning of each new line. Possibly you also noticed an occasional backward eye movement, or regression, when the eyes skipped back to reread words or phrases a second time.

Eye reading speed can be increased, in part, by reducing the number of fixations per line. Someone who makes eight stops per line is not reading as quickly as someone who makes four. To read faster, you should learn to take in several words at each stop rather than only one or two. And as this is done, the tendency to subvocalize and to read one word at a time will also be minimized. In addition, speed can be increased by reducing the duration of each pause or stop, by increasing the speed of the return sweep, and by cutting down on the number of backward eye movements or regressions. Finally, with improved concentration, the eyes can be made to read with greater accuracy as well as speed.

The Key to Rapid Reading

Eye speed can be increased and bad perception habits overcome through practice with timed passages in which you consciously *try to read faster.* As you read for speed in the situations that follow, remember that your *mind* is probably not slowing you down; your *eyes* are. The mind is an incredible computerlike instrument that can process words at an extraordinary rate of speed. What holds it back is the limited rate at which your eyes feed in words for it to process. Consciously force your eyes to move and work at ever higher and higher speeds. Your deliberate effort to "turn on" your speed through practice should yield impressive results.

On the following pages are ten selections to use in developing your reading speed. You should read only the first selection at your normal rate of speed. You can then use this rate to measure later increases in speed. As you finish each selection, get your time from your instructor—or time yourself—and record it in the space provided. Then answer the comprehension questions.

Afterward, find your reading rate with the help of the table on pages 536–538. Also, check your answers with the instructor and fill in your comprehension score in the space provided. Finally, record both your reading rate and your comprehension score in the progress chart on page 535.

- Many people have paid hundreds of dollars for speed-reading courses whose message or "secret" can be reduced to four simple words. What are the words?
  Try to read faster.

Rapid Reading and Comprehension: Final Thoughts

You are about to experiment with rapid reading—making your eyes and brain work together to process words at a high rate of speed. It is suggested that you try rapid reading for at least the first five selections that follow. If you feel after doing so that rapid reading works for you, continue it through the final five readings as well. You may then want in general to *try to read faster* as you deal with different kinds of reading material.

At the same time, be sure to keep rapid reading in perspective. It is different from slow, leisurely reading, in which your purpose is pleasure. It is different from skim reading, in which your purpose is to locate the main points in an article or chapter. It is different from the kind of slow study reading that you do to increase your understanding of a difficult selection. It is but one of the many skills of an effective reader, and it is useful at certain times for certain reading purposes.

Finally, if your comprehension drops even after repeated efforts to read quickly, you may reasonably decide that rapid reading is not for you. In that case, you may simply want to focus on developing your comprehension skills, and all ten of the readings in this section of the book will provide you with useful practice.

Selection 1

Read the *Preview* and check the *Words to Watch* below. Then read this first selection at your present comfortable rate of speed. You can use the difference in speeds between this selection and the ones that follow to measure any advances in your reading rate.

From

The Autobiography of Malcolm X

Malcolm X and Alex Haley

■ Preview

While confined to a prison cell, the inspirational African American leader Malcolm X learned to loosen the chains that imprisoned his mind. This excerpt from *The Autobiography of Malcolm X* describes how words were the key to his newfound freedom.

■ Words to Watch

riffling (line 12): flipping through

succeeding (line 29): following

inevitable (line 35): bound to happen

It was because of my letters [which Malcolm X wrote to people outside while he was in jail] that I happened to stumble upon starting to acquire some kind of a homemade education.

I became increasingly frustrated at not being able to express what I wanted to convey in letters that I wrote. . . . And every book I picked up had 5 few sentences which didn't contain anywhere from one to nearly all the words that might as well have been in Chinese. When I skipped those words, of course, I really ended up with little idea of what the book said. . . .

I saw that the best thing I could do was get hold of a dictionary—to study, to learn some words. I requested a dictionary along with some tablets and 10 pencils from the Norfolk Prison Colony school.

I spent two days just riffling uncertainly through the dictionary's pages. I'd never realized so many words existed! I didn't know *which* words I needed to learn. Finally, just to start some kind of action, I began copying.

485

In my slow, painstaking, ragged handwriting, I copied into my tablet every- 15
thing printed on that first page, down to the punctuation marks. I believe it
took me a day. Then, aloud, I read back to myself everything I'd written on
the tablet. Over and over, aloud, to myself, I read my own handwriting.

I woke up the next morning, thinking about those words—immensely
proud to realize that not only had I written so much at one time, but I'd 20
written words that I never knew were in the world. Moreover, with a little
effort, I also could remember what many of these words meant. I reviewed
the words whose meanings I didn't remember. Funny thing, from the dictionary's first page right now, that *aardvark* springs to my mind. The dictionary
had a picture of it, a long-tailed, long-eared, burrowing African mammal, 25
which lives off termites caught by sticking out its tongue as an anteater does
for ants.

I was so fascinated that I went on—I copied the dictionary's next page.
And the same experience came when I studied that. With every succeeding
page, I also learned of people and places and events from history. Actually, 30
the dictionary is like a miniature encyclopedia. Finally, the dictionary's A section had filled a whole tablet—and I went on into the B's. That was the way
I started copying what eventually became the entire dictionary. It went a lot
faster after so much practice helped me to pick up handwriting speed.

I suppose it was inevitable that as my word-base broadened, I could for 35
the first time pick up a book and read and now begin to understand what the
book was saying. Anyone who has read a great deal can imagine the new
world that opened. Let me tell you something: from then until I left the
prison, in every free moment I had, if I was not reading in the library, I was
reading on my bunk. You couldn't have gotten me out of books with a 40
wedge. Months passed without my even thinking about being imprisoned. In
fact, up to then, I never had been so truly free in my life.

Time: _____   *Reading Rate (see page 536):* _____ *WPM*

■ Reading Comprehension

1. Malcolm X had trouble writing letters and reading books because

   a.   he was not given free time.

   b.   it was too dark in his cell.

   (c)   he didn't know enough words.   *(See paragraph 2)*

   d.   he needed eyeglasses.

2. Malcolm compares the dictionary to

   a.   the Bible.

   (b) a miniature encyclopedia. *(Paragraph 7)*

   c.   a thesaurus.

   d.   an almanac.

3. How much of the dictionary did Malcolm eventually copy?

   a.   A's

   b.   A's and B's

   c.   A through P

   (d) All of it   *(Paragraph 7)*

4. Malcolm's way of learning new words was to

   (a) first copy them out on paper. *(Paragraph 5)*

   b.   open up the dictionary at random to a word he didn't know.

   c.   study them right off the dictionary page.

   d.   recite them silently to himself.

5. *True or false?* __F__ One of the first words that Malcolm studied in the dictionary was *anteater.* *(Paragraph 6)*

6. *True or false?* __T__ Only when Malcolm's vocabulary increased was he able to read and understand books. *(Last paragraph)*

7. Malcolm says that to know and imagine the new world that books opened up for him, a person would have to

   a.   read the same books he did.

   (b) read many books.   *(Last paragraph)*

   c.   be in prison.

   d.   be as ignorant as he was when he began.

8. Having books to read and knowing how to read them, Malcolm says that he

   (a) became truly free even though in prison. *(Last paragraph)*

   b.   was still bored and restless occasionally.

   c.   felt like an educated man.

   d.   gained the admiration of his fellow prisoners.

Number Wrong: _____   *Score:* _____

0 wrong = 100%	2 wrong = 75%	4 wrong = 50%	6 wrong = 25%
1 wrong = 88%	3 wrong = 63%	5 wrong = 38%	7 wrong = 13%

■ **Critical Thinking and Discussion**

1. Malcolm X knew that he wanted to increase his vocabulary. Because he didn't know how else to start, he began copying the dictionary, page by page. What are some other techniques that he might have used to learn new words?

2. What conclusions can you draw about Malcolm X from this selection? What kind of man does he seem to be? What values seem to be important to him?

3. Although he was in prison, Malcolm X says, "I never had been so truly free in my life." In what sense had he become "free"?

Selection 2

Read the *Preview* and check the *Words to Watch* below. Then read this second selection both to understand it and, in addition, *to try to increase your reading speed.*

The Fine Art of Complaining
Scott Rego

■ **Preview**

What is "good complaining"? According to this selection, it is *not* complaining that is whiny, shrill, or apologetic. Instead, it is justified, firm, and effective. Read the selection and see how *you* stack up in the complaints department.

■ **Words to Watch**

slink (line 14): sneak

disembodied (line 33): without a body

full-blown (line 56): completely developed

You waited forty-five minutes for your dinner, and when it came it was cold—and not what you ordered in the first place. You asked for a seat in the nonsmoking section, and the flight attendant put you between two chain-smokers. Your new car broke down the first month, and the dealer wouldn't honor the warranty.   5

Do these examples of life's annoyances sound familiar to you? They probably do—because things just like them happen to all of us. And when they do, most of us just sit there and take it. We eat cold meals we didn't want. We cough on secondhand smoke. We pay for repairs that were supposed to be free.   10

What we don't often do is complain effectively. We talk about standing up for our rights, but when the opportunity comes, we don't. Perhaps we make one awkward attempt at protest—"Uh, excuse me, but I don't think I ordered squid and onions. . . . " Then we give up and suffer in silence. Or slink quietly away. We're afraid to "make a scene."   15

489

The truth is, though, that complaining often works. As the old proverb says, "The squeaky wheel gets the grease." Complain about a problem and it may be solved for you. If you don't complain, nothing will be done. But complaining is an art form. In order to do it successfully, you have to know two things: how to complain, and whom to complain to.   20

How to Complain

The way to complain is to act businesslike and important. If your complaint is immediate—you got the wrong order at a restaurant or the wrong seat at a theater—make a polite but firm request to see the manager or supervisor. When the manager comes, ask his or her name, and then state your problem and what you expect to have done about it. Be polite; shouting   25
or acting rude will get you nowhere. But also be firm. Don't say, "I, uh, was sort of expecting . . . ." Say, "I expected . . . ."

Act important. This doesn't mean to puff up your chest and say, "Do you know who I am?" What it means is that people are often treated the way they expect to be treated. If you act like someone who expects a fair request   30
to be granted, chances are it will be granted.

The worst way to complain is over the telephone. You are speaking to a disembodied voice, so you can't tell how the person on the line is reacting. It is easy for that person to give you the runaround. Complaining in person or by letter is generally more effective.   35

If your complaint does not require a this-moment response, it often helps to complain by letter. If you have an appliance that doesn't work, for example, send a letter to the store that sold it, the company who made it, or both. Be businesslike and stick to the point—don't spend a paragraph on how your Uncle Joe tried to fix the problem and couldn't. Here's an outline for an effec-   40
tive letter of complaint, including a "P.S.":

Paragraph 1: Explain what the problem is. Include any facts that back up your story.

Paragraph 2: Tell how you trust the company and are confident that your reader will fix the problem. (This is to "soften up" the reader a little bit.)   45

Paragraph 3: Carefully explain what you want done (repair, replacement, refund, etc.).

P.S. (Readers always notice a "P.S.") State when you expect the problem to be solved and what you'll do if it isn't.

Notice that the P.S. says what you'll do if your problem isn't solved. In   50
other words, you make a (polite) threat. Your threat ought to be believable. A threat that you'll burn down the store if your purchase payment isn't refunded is not believable. (And if it were believed, it could get you thrown into jail.) A threat to report the store to the Better Business Bureau, on the other hand, is believable.   55

One common threat is "I'll sue!" A full-blown lawsuit, with lawyers, is more trouble than most problems are worth. But most areas have a small-claims court where suits involving relatively modest amounts of money are heard. These courts don't use complex legal language or procedures, and you don't need a lawyer to use them. A store or company will often settle with 60 you (if you have a fair claim) rather than go to small-claims court.

Whom to Complain To

One of the greatest frustrations in complaining is talking to a clerk or receptionist who can't solve your problem and whose only purpose seems to be to drive you crazy. Getting mad doesn't help, for the person you're mad at probably had nothing to do with your actual problem. 65

When complaining in person, ask for the manager or supervisor. When complaining by letter, get the name of the store manager or company president. (A librarian can help you find this information.) If you are complaining over the phone, ask for the customer-relations department. If there is none, then ask for the manager or appropriate supervisor. Or talk to the head tele- 70 phone operator, who will probably know who is responsible for solving problems.

Be persistent. One complaint may not get results. In that case, it may work to simply keep on complaining. This will "wear down" resistance on the other side. If you have a problem with a store, call the store two or three times every 75 day. Chances are someone there will get tired of you and take care of your complaint in order to be rid of you. *The squeaky wheel gets the grease.*

Time: _____   *Reading Rate (see page 536): _____ WPM*

■ Reading Comprehension

1. Which sentence best expresses the main idea of the selection?

   a.   Life is full of annoyances.

   b.   Most people don't like to complain.

   c.   It is usually most effective to complain in person or by letter.

   d.   Complaining succeeds if you know how to complain and whom to complain to.   (See paragraph 4)

2. The best way to complain is to

   a.   act rudely.

   b.   be polite but firm.   (Paragraph 5)

   c.   be loud and angry.

   d.   hire a lawyer.

3. To get results, complainers should
   a. act as if they expect their problem to be fixed. (Paragraphs 5, 6, and 8)
   b. complain only over the phone.
   c. never threaten.
   d. write long letters.

4. Successful complainers
   a. prefer complaining over the phone.
   b. become violent.
   c. complain to receptionists.
   d. are persistent. (Paragraph 13)

5. *True or false?* __T__ According to the author, companies would often rather settle with a complaining customer than go to small-claims court. (Para. 10)

6. The author implies that when you write a complaint letter, you should
   a. have a lawyer sign it.
   b. provide a list of witnesses.
   c. use professional stationery.
   d. use a little flattery. (Paragraph 8)

7. We can conclude that small-claims courts
   a. are useless.
   b. are expensive.
   c. are used by ordinary citizens. (Paragraph 10)
   d. forbid the use of lawyers.

8. From the selection, we can conclude that
   a. it's our duty to complain.
   b. the author is a lawyer.
   c. complaining takes effort. (Paragraph 4; the selection goes on to discuss letter writing, including obtaining the names of
   d. receptionists can solve complainers' problems. the appropriate people to write to, and small-claims suits, both of which involve effort.)

Number Wrong: _____

Score: _____

| 0 wrong = 100% | 2 wrong = 75% | 4 wrong = 50% | 6 wrong = 25% |
| 1 wrong = 88% | 3 wrong = 63% | 5 wrong = 38% | 7 wrong = 13% |

■ Critical Thinking and Discussion

1. According to the selection, the best way to complain is immediately and in person. The worst way is by telephone. Does your experience support these claims? Why do you think complaining in person is more effective than making a phone call?

2. If you have a complaint, the writer advises you to ask to see the manager or supervisor and to ask his or her name before explaining the problem. Why do you think you should ask the manager's name?

3. *Does* the squeaky wheel get the grease? Judging from your experience, do people who speak up when they have a complaint generally have that complaint solved satisfactorily?

Selection 3

Read the *Preview* and check the *Words to Watch* below. Then, once again, you should make a deliberate effort to read at a faster rate. You should *will* your eyes to move faster, and you should *will* your brain to process the incoming facts, ideas, and details more quickly.

If you are not already doing so, sit up straight, put your feet flat on the floor, and hold the book at a comfortable angle. Consciously force your eyes to move at a higher rate of speed. Make the decision that you are going to read faster, and do it.

Learning to Keep Your Cool during Tests
Margaret Jerrard

■ **Preview**

If the word *test* fills you with as much anxiety as a visit to the dentist, take heart: Help is available. There are effective ways to deal with test-related anxiety. This selection outlines some of the best.

■ **Words to Watch**

secreted (line 6): formed and released

peripheral sight (line 9): the ability to see beyond the edges of the line of direct sight

optimum (line 30): most favorable

keyed up (line 32): excited or tense

interspersing (line 40): doing at varying intervals

intuitive (line 53): done without reasoning

Have you ever felt so panicky during an examination that you couldn't even put down the answers you *knew?* If so, you were suffering from what is known as test anxiety.

According to the psychologist Ralph Trimble, test anxiety is a very real problem for many people. When you're worried over your performance on an exam, your heart beats faster, your pulse speeds up, hormones are secreted. These reactions trigger others: You may sweat more than you normally do or suffer from a stomachache or headache. Your field of vision narrows and becomes tunnel-like, leaving you with very little peripheral sight. Before you know it, you're having difficulty focusing.

"What I hear students say over and over again," says Dr. Trimble, who is associated with the Psychological and Counseling Center at the University of Illinois, "is, 'My mind went blank.'"

For a number of years, Dr. Trimble helped many students learn how to function better during exams and to bring up their grades. Some of these students were interested in sharing what they learned and, with Trimble's help, began holding workshops on overcoming test anxiety. For many students, just being in a workshop with other sufferers was a relief. They realized they weren't freaks, that they were not the only ones who had done poorly on tests because of tension. The workshops were so successful that they are still given.

In the workshops, students are taught that anxiety is normal. You just have to prevent it from getting the best of you. The first step is to learn to relax. If before or during an examination you start to panic, stretch as hard as you can, tensing the muscles in your arms and legs; then suddenly relax all of them. This will help relieve tension.

But keep in mind that you don't want to be too relaxed. Being completely relaxed is no better than being too tense. "If you are so calm you don't *care* how you do on an examination, you won't do well," Trimble says. "There is an optimum level of concern when you perform at your best. Some stress helps. There are people who can't take even slight stress. They have to learn that in a challenging situation, being keyed up is good and will help them to do better. But if they label it anxiety and say, `It's going to hit me again,' that will push them over the edge."

As a student you must also realize that if you leave too much studying until a day or two before the examination, you can't do the impossible and learn it all. Instead, concentrate on what you *can* do and try to think what questions are likely to be asked and what you can do in the time left for studying.

When you sit down to study, set a moderate pace and vary it by interspersing reading, writing notes, and going over any papers you have already written for the course, as well as the textbooks and notes you took in class. Review what you know. Take breaks and go to sleep in plenty of time to get a good night's rest before the exam. You should also eat a moderate breakfast or lunch, avoiding drinks with caffeine and steering clear of fellow students who get tense. Panic is contagious.

Get to the exam room a few minutes early so that you will have a chance to familiarize yourself with the surroundings and get out your supplies. When the examination is handed out, read the directions twice and underline the significant instructions, making sure you understand them. Ask the instructor or proctor to explain if you don't. First answer the easiest questions, then go back to the more difficult. If you are stumped on a multiple-choice question, first eliminate the impossible answers, then make as good an intuitive guess as possible and go on to the next.

On essay questions, instead of plunging right in, take a few minutes to 55
organize your thoughts, make a brief outline, and then start off with a summary
sentence. Keep working steadily, and even when time starts to run out, don't
speed up.

After the examination is over, don't torture yourself by thinking over all
the mistakes you made, and don't start studying immediately for another 60
exam. Instead, give yourself an hour or two of free time.

Among the students who are working now as volunteer leaders in the
workshops are a number who started out panicky and unable to function on
exams. They learned how to deal with test anxiety and are now teaching
others. It's almost as easy as ABC.   65

Time: _____   *Reading Rate (see page 536):* _____ *WPM*

■ Reading Comprehension

1. Which would be a good alternative title for this selection?
   a. How to Overcome Test Anxiety   *(See paragraph 4)*
   b. The Physical Side of Anxiety
   c. How to Get Better Grades
   d. Why Students Are Concerned about Grades

2. Which sentence best expresses the main idea of the selection?
   a. Most students suffer from test anxiety.
   b. Test anxiety can be controlled. *(Paragraph 4)*
   c. Being relaxed is essential to doing well on exams.
   d. All students should attend stress-management workshops.

3. If you start to panic during a test, you should
   a. leave the room briefly.
   b. drink a cup of coffee.
   c. stretch and then relax your arms and legs. *(Paragraph 5)*
   d. skip the essay questions.

4. The first thing to do when you receive the exam is to
   a. answer the questions you are sure of.
   b. underline the important instructions. *(Paragraph 9)*
   c. make an outline of what you know.
   d. begin timing yourself.

5. *True or false?* __T__ Anxiety can cause a well-prepared student to perform poorly on a test. (Paragraph 1)

6. From the selection we can conclude that
   a. textbooks make better study guides than class notes do.
   b. anxiety is learned behavior that can be unlearned. (Paragraph 4)
   c. students who do poorly in tests may need eyeglasses.
   d. good students are completely calm before tests.

7. Which of the following tips is *not* mentioned in the article?
   a. Do easy questions first.
   b. Organize your thoughts before starting to write an essay answer.
   c. Ask the instructor to explain unclear directions.
   d. Budget your time for each part of the test. (Paragraphs 9, 10)

8. The author implies that
   a. you should get to the exam room at the last minute in order to avoid panicky students.
   b. you should never guess on an exam.
   c. caffeine can increase anxiety. (Paragraph 8)
   d. if you have kept up with the work, there's no need to study for the test.

Number Wrong: _____   *Score:* _____

| 0 wrong = 100% | 2 wrong = 75% | 4 wrong = 50% | 6 wrong = 25% |
| 1 wrong = 88% | 3 wrong = 63% | 5 wrong = 38% | 7 wrong = 13% |

■ Critical Thinking and Discussion

1. According to the selection, what are some of the symptoms of test anxiety? What symptoms of anxiety have you most frequently observed in yourself or others?

2. Do you practice any of the anxiety-relieving techniques described in the selection? Can you recommend any others that might be helpful to your fellow students?

3. The selection advises people with test anxiety to avoid fellow students who also get tense, noting "Panic is contagious." Do you think this is true? Does it matter what kind of people surround you as you prepare for or take an exam?

Selection 4

Read the *Preview* and check the *Words to Watch* below. Then you may want to try the following technique. As you read, lightly underline each line of print with your index finger. Do not rest your hand on the page, and do not point to individual words with your finger. Hold your hand slightly above the page and use your finger as a pacer, moving it a little more quickly than your eyes can comfortably follow. Try to glide your finger smoothly across each line of print, and to make your eyes follow just as smoothly. If the technique helps you attend closely and read more quickly, use it in other selections as well.

An Electronic Fog Has Settled over America
Pete Hamill

■ ### Preview

Are we dumber than we were a generation ago? Some indicators, including nationwide SAT scores, seem to suggest that we are. What could explain the intellectual decline of a nation? The columnist Pete Hamill describes the experience of one man's family and the electronic presence that does their thinking for them.

■ ### Words to Watch

erratic (line 14): irregular

baffled (line 16): puzzled

pondered (line 17): considered carefully

distracted (line 22): had (his) attention drawn away

disconsolate (line 79): cheerless

The year his son turned fourteen, Maguire noticed that the boy was getting dumber. This was a kid who had learned to talk at fourteen months, could read when he was four, was an A student for his first six years in school. The boy was bright, active, and imaginative. And then, slowly, the boy's brain began to deteriorate.

"He started to slur words," Maguire told me. "He couldn't finish sentences. He usually didn't hear me when I talked to him and couldn't answer me clearly when he did. In school, the A's became B's, and the B's became C's.

5

I thought maybe it was something physical, and I had a doctor check him out. He was perfectly normal. Then the C's started to become D's. Finally, he started failing everything. Worse, the two younger kids were repeating the pattern. From bright to dumb in a few short years." 10

Maguire was then an account executive in a major advertising agency; his hours were erratic, and the pace of his business life was often frantic. But when he would get home at night and talk to his wife about the kids, she would shake her head in a baffled way and explain that she was doing her best. Hustling from the office of one account to another, Maguire pondered the creeping stupidity of his children. Then he took an afternoon off from work and visited his oldest boy's school. 15

"They told me he just wasn't doing much work," Maguire said. "He owed them four book reports. He never said a word in social studies. His mind wandered, he was distracted, he asked to leave the room a lot. But the teacher told me he wasn't much different from all the other kids. In some ways, he was better. He at least did some work. Most of them, she told me, didn't do any work at all." 20

25

Maguire asked the teacher if she had any theories about why the kids behaved this way.

"Of course," she said. "Television."

Television? Maguire was staggered. He made his living off television. Often, he would sit with the kids in the TV room and point out the commercials he had helped to create. Television had paid for his house in the suburbs, for his two cars, his clothes, his food, the pictures on the walls. It even paid for the kids' schools. 30

"What do you mean, television?" he said.

"Television rots minds," the teacher said flatly. "But most of us figure there's nothing to be done about it anymore." 35

At work the next day, Maguire told his secretary to do some special research for him. Within a week, he had some scary numbers on his desk. The Scholastic Aptitude Tests (SATs) showed that the reading scores of all American high school students had fallen in every year since 1950, the year of television's great national triumph. The mathematics scores were even worse. The average American kid spent four to six hours a day watching television and by age sixteen had witnessed eleven thousand homicides on the tube. 40

"I came home that night, and the kids were watching television with my wife," he said. "I looked at them, glued to the set. They nodded hello to me. And suddenly I got scared. I imagined these four people, their brains rotted out, suddenly adding me to the evening's homicide count because I wanted them to talk to me. I went to the bedroom, and for the first time since college, I took down *Moby-Dick* and started to read." 45

In the following week, Maguire accumulated more and more ideas about the impact of television on the lives of Americans. All classes and colors had been affected intellectually; reading requires the decoding of symbols, the 50

transforming of a word like *cat* into a cat that lives in the imagination. Television shows the cat. No active thought is required. Television even sup- 55
plies a laugh track and music to trigger the emotions the imagination will not
create or release.

"I read somewhere that the worst danger to kids who become TV addicts
is that while they are watching TV, they're not doing anything else," Maguire
said. "They're not down in the schoolyard playing ball, or falling in love, or
getting into fights, or learning to compromise. They're alone, with a box that 60
doesn't hear them if they want to talk back. They don't have to think, because
everything is done for them. They don't have to question, because what's the
point if you can't challenge the guy on the set?"

Television had also changed politics; Maguire's kids had political opinions
based on the way candidates looked and how they projected themselves 65
theatrically. Politics, which should be based on the structure of analysis and
thought, had become dominated by the structures of drama, that is to say, by
conflict.

"I knew Reagan would win in a landslide," Maguire said. "As an actor, he
fit right into the mass culture formed by thirty years of television."   70

Maguire tried to do something. He called a family conference after dinner
one night, explained his discoveries, and suggested a voluntary limiting of
television watching or its complete elimination for three months.

"I said we could start a reading program together," he told me. "All read
the same book and discuss it at night. I told them we'd come closer together, 75
that I'd even change my job so I could be home more and not work on television commercials anymore."

After ten minutes, the kids began to squirm and yawn, as if expecting a
commercial. Maguire's wife dazed out, her disconsolate face an unblinking
mask. He gave up. Now, when he goes home, Maguire says hello, eats dinner, 80
and retreats to his bedroom. He is reading his way through Balzac.

Beyond the bedroom door, bathed in the cold light of the television set,
are the real people of his life. Their dumbness grows, filling up the room,
moving out into the quiet suburban town, joining the great gray fog that has
enveloped America.   85

Time: _____   *Reading Rate (see page 536):* _____ *WPM*

■ Reading Comprehension

1. Which would be a good alternative title for this selection?

   a. Why Students Dislike School

   b. Maguire's Story

   ⓒ The Dangers of Television   *(See paragraphs 4–6)*

   d. How to Cut Down on TV Watching

2. Which sentence best expresses the main idea of the selection?

    a.   Maguire's family has become dumber from watching TV.

    b.   Children must watch less TV if they want to do well in school.

    c.   Neglecting one's family life can lead to serious problems.

    (d)   By deadening thought, television has turned us into zombies.
          (Paragraphs 4–6, 9, 13, next-to-last paragraph)

3. *True or false?* ___T___ The average American child spends four to six hours a day watching television. *(Paragraph 10)*

4. Television is most dangerous to children because it makes them

    a.   bored.

    (b)   passive. *(Paragraph 13)*

    c.   violent.

    d.   depressed.

5. Maguire believes that many politicians are elected on the basis of their

    a.   experience.

    (b)   image. *(Paragraph 14)*

    c.   wealth.

    d.   conservative beliefs.

6. *True or false?* ___T___ The teacher interviewed by Maguire appeared resigned to the influence of TV on her students. *(Paragraph 9)*

7. The author implies that

    a.   Maguire's children would have been better students if Maguire had been home more.

    (b)   the Maguires' problem could be found in most of the households in America. *(Paragraph 10, last paragraph)*

    c.   President Reagan's acting abilities made him a better leader.

    d.   educational television does not rot the mind.

8. The "great gray fog" symbolizes

    a.   a decline in moral standards.

    b.   political corruption.

    (c)   growing passivity and weakening intellectual skills. *(Last paragraph)*

    d.   the use of television as a political tool and mind-control instrument.

Number Wrong: _____   *Score:* _____

0 wrong = 100%	2 wrong = 75%	4 wrong = 50%	6 wrong = 25%
1 wrong = 88%	3 wrong = 63%	5 wrong = 38%	7 wrong = 13%

■ Critical Thinking and Discussion

1. According to the selection, SAT scores of American high school students have fallen every year since TV became a common household presence. Can you think of any possible explanations, besides television, for the falling test scores?

2. All in all, do you believe that television has had a positive or a negative effect on American society? What reasons support your opinion?

3. What will be (or is) your attitude about television viewing and your own children? Will you set limits on how much TV they can watch? On what kinds of programs? Why or why not?

Selection 5

Read the *Preview* and check the *Words to Watch* below. Then read the selection that follows. Remember that it is your deliberate effort to read faster, along with extensive practice, that will make you a faster reader. Keep this fact in mind as you read the following selection.

The Scholarship Jacket
Marta Salinas

■ **Preview**

She had earned the beautiful scholarship jacket. But at the last minute, it seemed that it would be stolen away from her. Marta Salinas remembers a painful, but ultimately triumphant, experience as a young Mexican-American girl in south Texas.

■ **Words to Watch**

agile (line 14): able to move quickly

fidgeted (line 56): moved nervously

muster (line 65): bring together

mesquite (line 76): a sweet-smelling tree

gaunt (line 114): thin

adrenaline (line 131): a hormone that raises the blood pressure and stimulates the heart

The small Texas school that I attended carried out a tradition every year during the eighth grade graduation: a beautiful gold-and-green jacket, the school colors, was awarded to the class valedictorian, the student who had maintained the highest grades for eight years. The scholarship jacket had a big gold S on the left front side, and the winner's name was written in gold 5 letters on the pocket.

My oldest sister, Rosie, had won the jacket a few years back, and I fully expected to win also. I was fourteen and in the eighth grade. I had been a straight-A student since the first grade, and the last year I had looked forward to owning that jacket. My father was a farm laborer who couldn't earn 10 enough money to feed eight children, so when I was six I was given to my grandparents to raise. We couldn't participate in sports at school because there were registration fees, uniform costs, and trips out of town; so even though we were quite agile and athletic, there would never be a sports school jacket for us. This one, the scholarship jacket, was our only chance. 15

In May, close to graduation, spring fever struck, and no one paid any attention in class; instead we stared out the windows and at each other, wanting to speed up the last few weeks of school. I despaired every time I looked in the mirror. Pencil-thin, with not a curve anywhere, I was called "Beanpole" and "String Bean," and I knew that's what I looked like. A flat chest, no hips, 20 and a brain, that's what I had. That really isn't much for a fourteen-year-old to work with, I thought, as I absentmindedly wandered from my class to the gym. Another hour of sweating during basketball and displaying my toothpick legs was coming up. Then I remembered that my P.E. shorts were still in a bag under my desk where I'd forgotten them. I had to walk all the way back and 25 get them. Coach Thompson was a real bear if anyone wasn't dressed for P.E. She had said I was a good forward and once she even tried to talk Grandma into letting me join the team. Grandma, of course, said no.

I was almost back at my classroom door when I heard angry voices and arguing. I stopped. I didn't mean to eavesdrop; I just hesitated, not knowing 30 what to do. I needed those shorts and I was going to be late, but I didn't want to interrupt an argument between my teachers. I recognized the voices: Mr. Schmidt, my history teacher, and Mr. Boone, my math teacher. They seemed to be arguing about me. I couldn't believe it. I still remember the shock that rooted me flat against the wall as if I were trying to blend in with the graffiti 35 written there.

"I refuse to do it! I don't care who her father is, her grades don't even begin to compare to Martha's. I won't lie or falsify records. Martha has a straight A-plus average and you know it." That was Mr. Schmidt, and he sounded very angry. Mr. Boone's voice sounded calm and quiet. 40

"Look, Joann's father is not only on the Board, he owns the only store in town; we could say it was a close tie and—"

The pounding in my ears drowned out the rest of the words; only a word here and there filtered through. ". . .Martha is Mexican . . . .resign . . . .won't do it. . . ." Mr. Schmidt came rushing out, and luckily for me went down the 45 opposite way toward the auditorium, so he didn't see me. Shaking, I waited a few minutes and then went in and grabbed my bag and fled from the room. Mr. Boone looked up when I came in but didn't say anything. To this day I don't remember if I got into trouble in P.E. for being late or how I made it through the rest of the afternoon. I went home very sad and cried into my pillow that 50 night so Grandmother wouldn't hear me. It seemed a cruel coincidence that I had overheard that conversation.

The next day when the principal called me into his office, I knew what it would be about. He looked uncomfortable and unhappy. I decided I wasn't going to make it any easier for him, so I looked him straight in the eye. He 55 looked away and fidgeted with the papers on his desk.

"Martha," he said, "there's been a change in policy this year regarding the scholarship jacket. As you know, it has always been free." He cleared his throat and continued. "This year the Board decided to charge fifteen dollars—which still won't cover the complete cost of the jacket." 60

I stared at him in shock and a small sound of dismay escaped my throat. I hadn't expected this. He still avoided looking in my eyes.

"So if you are unable to pay the fifteen dollars for the jacket, it will be given to the next one in line."

Standing with all the dignity I could muster, I said, "I'll speak to my grand- 65 father about it, sir, and let you know tomorrow." I cried on the walk home from the bus stop. The dirt road was a quarter of a mile from the highway, so by the time I got home, my eyes were red and puffy.

"Where's Grandpa?" I asked Grandma, looking down at the floor so she wouldn't ask me why I'd been crying. She was sewing on a quilt and didn't 70 look up.

"I think he's out back working in the bean field."

I went outside and looked out at the fields. There he was. I could see him walking between the rows, his body bent over the little plants, hoe in hand. I walked slowly out to him, trying to think how I could best ask him for the 75 money. There was a cool breeze blowing and a sweet smell of mesquite in the air, but I didn't appreciate it. I kicked at a dirt clod. I wanted that jacket so much. It was more than just being a valedictorian and giving a little thank-you speech for the jacket on graduation night. It represented eight years of hard work and expectation. I knew I had to be honest with Grandpa; it was my only 80 chance. He saw me and looked up.

He waited for me to speak. I cleared my throat nervously and clasped my hands behind my back so he wouldn't see them shaking. "Grandpa, I have a big favor to ask you," I said in Spanish, the only language he knew. He still waited silently. I tried again. "Grandpa, this year the principal said the scholarship 85 jacket is not going to be free. It's going to cost fifteen dollars and I have to take the money in tomorrow; otherwise it'll be given to someone else." The last words came out in an eager rush. Grandpa straightened up tiredly and leaned his chin on the hoe handle. He looked out over the field that was filled with the tiny green bean plants. I waited, desperately hoping he'd say I could 90 have the money.

He turned to me and asked quietly, "What does a scholarship jacket mean?"

I answered quickly; maybe there was a chance. "It means you've earned it by having the highest grades for eight years and that's why they're giving 95 it to you." Too late I realized the significance of my words. Grandpa knew that I understood it was not a matter of money. It wasn't that. He went back to hoeing the weeds that sprang up between the delicate little bean plants. It was a time-consuming job; sometimes the small shoots were right next to each other. Finally he spoke again. 100

"Then if you pay for it, Marta, it's not a scholarship jacket, is it? Tell your principal I will not pay the fifteen dollars."

I walked back to the house and locked myself in the bathroom for a long time. I was angry with Grandfather even though I knew he was right, and I was angry with the Board, whoever they were. Why did they have to change   105
the rules just when it was my turn to win the jacket?

It was a very sad and withdrawn girl who dragged into the principal's office the next day. This time he did look me in the eyes.

"What did your grandfather say?"

I sat very straight in my chair.   110

"He said to tell you he won't pay the fifteen dollars."

The principal muttered something I couldn't understand under his breath and walked over to the window. He stood looking out at something outside. He looked bigger than usual when he stood up; he was a tall, gaunt man with gray hair, and I watched the back of his head while I waited for him to speak.   115

"Why?" he finally asked. "Your grandfather has the money. Doesn't he own a small bean farm?"

I looked at him, forcing my eyes to stay dry. "He said if I had to pay for it, then it wouldn't be a scholarship jacket," I said and stood up to leave. "I guess you'll just have to give it to Joann." I hadn't meant to say that; it had just   120
slipped out. I was almost to the door when he stopped me.

"Martha—wait."

I turned and looked at him, waiting. What did he want now? I could feel my heart pounding. Something bitter and vile tasting was coming up in my mouth; I was afraid I was going to be sick. I didn't need any sympathy   125
speeches. He sighed loudly and went back to his big desk. He looked at me, biting his lip, as if thinking.

"OK, damn it. We'll make an exception in your case. I'll tell the Board, you'll get your jacket."

I could hardly believe it. I spoke in a trembling rush. "Oh, thank you, sir!"   130
Suddenly I felt great. I didn't know about adrenaline in those days, but I knew something was pumping through me, making me feel as tall as the sky. I wanted to yell, jump, run the mile, do something. I ran out so I could cry in the hall where there was no one to see me. At the end of the day, Mr. Schmidt winked at me and said, "I hear you're getting the scholarship jacket this year."   135

His face looked as happy and innocent as a baby's, but I knew better. Without answering I gave him a quick hug and ran to the bus. I cried on the walk home again, but this time because I was so happy. I couldn't wait to tell Grandpa and ran straight to the field. I joined him in the row where he was working and without saying anything I crouched down and started pulling up   140
the weeds with my hands. Grandpa worked alongside me for a few minutes, but he didn't ask what had happened. After I had a little pile of weeds between the rows, I stood up and faced him.

"The principal said he's making an exception for me, Grandpa, and I'm getting the jacket after all. That's after I told him what you said."   145

Grandpa didn't say anything; he just gave me a pat on the shoulder and a smile. He pulled out the crumpled red handkerchief that he always carried in his back pocket and wiped the sweat off his forehead.

"Better go see if your grandmother needs any help with supper."

I gave him a big grin. He didn't fool me. I skipped and ran back to the   150 house whistling some silly tune.

Time: _____   *Reading Rate (see page 536):* _____ *WPM*

■ Reading Comprehension

1. Which sentence best expresses the main idea of this selection?

   a. When she went to pick up her gym clothes, Marta overheard a conversation between two teachers that shocked and saddened her.

   b. At Marta's school, the eighth-grade valedictorian was traditionally awarded a beautiful green- and gold-jacket.

   c. Although Marta had earned the scholarship jacket, she almost lost it to a less deserving student.   (*See paragraphs 2, 5, 6, 27*)

   d. Marta's older sister had won the scholarship jacket, and Marta deeply wanted to win it as well.

2. Which of the following statements is *false?*

   a. Marta was being raised by her grandparents because her parents were dead.   (*Paragraph 2*)

   b. Mr. Schmidt was angry at the attempt to give the scholarship jacket to someone less deserving than Marta.

   c. Marta's grandfather refused to give her the money for the scholarship jacket.

   d. Joann's grades were not nearly as good as Marta's.

3. Marta's grandparents supported themselves by

   a. running the only store in town.

   b. teaching high school.

   c. working on their own farm. (*Paragraph 26*)

   d. working as hired labor on other people's farms.

4. *True or false?* __F__ Marta could not look the principal in the face after he called her into his office.   (*Paragraph 8*)

5. After her second conversation with the principal, Marta felt

    a.   humiliated.

    b.   overjoyed.   *(See paragraphs 31–32, 36)*

    c.   disappointed.

    d.   confused.

6. The relationship between the two sentences below is one of

    a.   time.

    b.   contrast.

    c.   comparison.

    d.   cause-effect.

       Another hour of sweating during basketball and displaying my toothpick legs was coming up. Then I remembered that my P.E. shorts were still in a bag under my desk where I'd forgotten them.

7. The author implies that Mr. Boone

    a.   had a strong personal dislike for Marta.

    b.   knew Marta was not really as intelligent as other people thought.

    c.   felt that while Joann's grades were not as good as Marta's, Joann had more leadership ability.

    d.   was more concerned about pleasing Joann's father than being fair to Marta. *(Paragraph 6)*

8. By saying, ". . . it's not a scholarship jacket, is it?" Marta's grandfather was implying that

    a.   the jacket was not worth fifteen dollars.

    b.   a real award should not have to be bought with money. *(Paragraph 19)*

    c.   Marta did not deserve to win the scholarship jacket.

    d.   he did not understand what a scholarship jacket was.

Number Wrong: _____   *Score:* _____

0 wrong = 100%	2 wrong = 75%	4 wrong = 50%	6 wrong = 25%
1 wrong = 88%	3 wrong = 63%	5 wrong = 38%	7 wrong = 13%

■ Critical Thinking and Discussion

1. Why was winning the scholarship jacket so important to the Salinas children?

2. What difference did it make to Mr. Boone whether Marta or Joann won the scholarship jacket? What can you infer about his reasons?

3. Why do you think Marta's grandfather asked her, "What does a scholarship jacket mean?" Do you think he did not understand the meaning of the jacket himself?

Selection 6

Read the *Preview* and check the *Words to Watch* below. Then, in this selection and the four selections that follow, continue trying to read for both speed *and* understanding. Your effort to concentrate more and increase your speed is very likely to help your comprehension as well. Only if you decide at some point that the effort to improve your speed is *not* working should you return to your normal reading rate.

Dare to Think Big
Ben Carson

■ Preview

Benjamin Carson, growing up poor with his single mother in inner-city Detroit, was considered the "dummy" of his fifth-grade class. The realization that he could learn and, in fact, do brilliantly in school fueled an amazing journey that has led Dr. Carson to become one of the world's most respected surgeons. In this excerpt from his book *The Big Picture,* Dr. Carson shares a message with young people of today.

■ Words to Watch

prevalent (line 8): widespread

deplorable (line 8): deserving of scorn

dire (line 11): extreme in a negative way

cavernous (line 15): wide and empty, like a cave

graphically (line 38): vividly

gratification (line 39): satisfaction

bevy (line 44): group

perspective (line 70): point of view

I do not speak only to parent groups. I spend a lot of time with students, such as those I encountered not long ago on a memorable visit to Wendell Phillips High School, an inner-city school on Chicago's south side.

Before I spoke, the people who invited me to the Windy City held a reception in my honor. There I met and talked with school officials and local religious leaders, many of whom informed me about the troubled neighborhood where the school is located. They indicated that gang influence was prevalent, living conditions were deplorable in the surrounding public housing developments, dropout statistics were high, and SAT scores were low.

It sounded like a lot of other high schools I have visited around the country. Yet so dire were these warnings that, on the crosstown drive to the school, I could not help wondering what kind of reception I would receive from the students.

I need not have worried. When I walked into Wendell Phillips High School, its long, deserted hallways gave the building a cavernous, empty feel. The entire student body (1,500 to 2,000 strong) had already been excused from class and was assembled quietly in the school's auditorium. A school administrator, who was addressing the audience, noted my entrance through a back door and abruptly interrupted his remarks to announce, "And here's Dr. Carson now!"

All eyes turned my way. Immediately students began to applaud. Some stood. Suddenly they were all standing, clapping, and cheering. The applause continued the entire time I walked down the aisle and climbed the steps onto the auditorium stage. I couldn't remember ever receiving a warmer, more enthusiastic, or more spontaneous reception anywhere in my entire life.

I found out later that a local bank had purchased and distributed paperback copies of my autobiography, *Gifted Hands,* to every student at Wendell Phillips. A lot of those teenagers had evidently read the book and felt they already knew me. By the time I reached the microphone, the noise faded away. I felt overwhelmed by their welcome.

I did what I often do when facing such a young audience. I wanted them thinking seriously about their lives and futures. So I quickly summarized my earliest years as a child, about my own student days back at Southwestern High School in Detroit. I referred briefly to the incident when my anger nearly caused a tragedy that would have altered my life forever. I recounted my struggles with peer pressure, which sidetracked me for a time.

Then I talked about the difference between being viewed as *cool* and being classified as a lowly *nerd.* I find that serves as a graphically relevant illustration for my message on *delayed gratification*—a theme I hit almost every time I speak to young people.

The *cool* guys in every school are the ones who have earned a varsity letter in some sport—maybe several sports. They wear the latest fashions. They know all the hit tunes. They can converse about the latest blockbuster movies. They drive sharp cars and seem to collect a bevy of beautiful girlfriends.

The *nerds* are the guys always hauling around an armload of books, with more in their backpacks. They wear clean clothes—and often big, thick glasses.

They even understand the science experiments. They ride the school bus, or worse yet, their parents drive them to school. Most of the popular girls would not be caught dead speaking to them in the hallway between classes.

The years go by, and graduation draws near. Often the cool guy has not 50 done well in school, but his personality wins him a job at the local fast-food franchise, flipping hamburgers and waiting on customers. The nerd, who has won a scholarship, goes off to college.

A few more years go by. The cool guy is still flipping burgers. Maybe he has even moved up to Assistant Shift Manager by now. The girls who come in 55 to eat lunch may notice and smile at him. He is still cool.

The nerd finishes up at college and does very well. Upon graduation he accepts a job offer from a Fortune 500 company. With his first paycheck, he goes to the eye doctor, who replaces those big, old, thick glasses with a pair of contacts. He stops at the tailor and picks out a couple of nice suits to wear. 60 After saving a big chunk of his first few paychecks, he makes a down payment on a new Lexus. When he drives home to visit his parents, all the young women in the old neighborhood say, "Hey, don't I know you?" Suddenly, they do not want to talk to the guy behind the fast-food counter anymore.

The first guy—the cool guy—had everything back in high school. So what 65 did he get for all that?

The other guy was not cool at all—but he was focused. Where did he go in the long run?

"And that," I told my audience, "is how we have to learn to think about life! With a long-term view. A Big-Picture perspective!" 70

Those students at Chicago's Wendell Phillips High School could not have been more attentive as I recounted the things this former *nerd* has seen and done. They listened to me explain and illustrate the incredible potential that resides in the average human brain. They even seemed receptive to my challenge that they begin to use those brains to plan and prepare for the future. 75 So, as I wrapped up my talk by daring them to THINK BIG, I did something I had never done before, though I realized it could backfire if I had read this audience wrong. But since they had been such a responsive group, I decided to risk it.

I concluded by asking that auditorium full of high school students for a 80 show of hands. "How many of you are ready, here today, to raise your hands and say to me, to your teachers, and to your peers, 'I want to be a nerd.'"

Although many of them laughed, almost all the students of Wendell Phillips High School raised their hands as they stood and applauded and cheered even louder than when I had walked in. 85

Time: _____   *Reading Rate (see page 536):* _____ *WPM*

■ Reading Comprehension

1. Which of the following would be the best alternative title for this selection?

   a. An Inner-City School

   (b.) An Encouraging Talk   *(See paragraphs 7–19)*

   c. High School Popularity

   d. Cool Guys in High School

2. Which sentence best expresses the main idea of this selection?

   (a.) In a talk to high school students, Ben Carson encouraged them to focus on long-term goals. *(Paragraphs 7, 8, 15, 16)*

   b. The student body of a tough inner-city high school listened politely to Ben Carson's talk.

   c. Benjamin Carson, a famous surgeon, was considered a nerd in high school.

   d. Guys who earn varsity letters, know all the current music, and drive sharp cars seem to collect the most girlfriends in high school.

3. A lot of the students at Wendell Phillips High School

   (a.) had already read Ben Carson's autobiography. *(Paragraph 6)*

   b. skipped school on the day that Dr. Carson spoke.

   c. had unusually high SAT scores.

   d. worked in fast-food restaurants.

4. Peer pressure

   (a.) sidetracked Dr. Carson for a while during his teenage years. *(Para. 7)*

   b. never affected Dr. Carson during his teenage years.

   c. was less of a problem during Dr. Carson's teen years than it is now.

   d. affected Dr. Carson in positive ways during his teenage years.

5. *True or false?* __F__ Dr. Carson expected to receive a warm welcome at Wendell Phillips High School. *(Paragraph 3)*

6. *True or false?* __F__ Dr. Carson often ended his talks to high school audiences by inviting them to say, "I want to be a nerd." *(Paragraph 17)*

7. From the article, the reader might conclude that

   a. Dr. Carson was considered cool in high school.

   (b.) planning for the future can mean giving up some pleasure today. *(Paragraphs 8–13)*

   c. Dr. Carson hardly ever speaks to parent groups.

   d. The visit to Wendell Phillips High School was Dr Carson's first to Chicago.

8. Dr. Carson implies that

   a.   girls in high school aren't impressed by cool guys.

   (b)   the cool guy in high school wasn't thinking about his future.
       (Paragraphs 11–14)

   c.   the cool guy in school had a "Big Picture" perspective on his life.

   d.   when the nerd got his first paychecks, he should have saved them instead of spending them as he did.

Number Wrong: _____   *Score:* _____

| 0 wrong = 100% | 2 wrong = 75% | 4 wrong = 50% | 6 wrong = 25% |
| 1 wrong = 88% | 3 wrong = 63% | 5 wrong = 38% | 7 wrong = 13% |

■ Critical Thinking and Discussion

1. As Dr. Carson drove to Wendell Phillips High School, he worried about "what kind of reception" he would receive from the students. Why do you think he was concerned? What kind of reception do you think he imagined he might find?

2. Why do you think Dr. Carson admitted to the students that his hot temper had once nearly caused a tragedy, and that he was "sidetracked" by peer pressure for a while? Wouldn't it set a better example if he revealed only the positive parts of his life?

3. In your experience, is it true that "cool," popular guys in high school generally do less well academically than hardworking "nerds"? Do you agree with Dr. Carson that the cool guys will do less well in the long run of life?

Selection 7

Winning the Job Interview Game
Marcia Prentergast

■ **Preview**

Job interviews, like final exams, can cause self-doubts and upset stomachs. You may feel that interviews are even worse than finals since you can't prepare for them. In the reading below, however, Marcia Prentergast explains that there is much you can do to get ready for job interviews—and to make yourself stand out from the crowd of other applicants.

■ **Words to Watch**

personable (line 6): friendly

conservative (line 18): customary, traditional

flustered (line 23): nervously confused

potential (line 73): possible

Few things in everyday life are dreaded more than going to a job interview. First you have to wait in an outer room, which may be filled with other people all applying for the same job you want. You look at them and they look at you. Everyone knows that only one person is going to get the job. Then you are called into the interviewer's office, where you have to sit in front of a   5
complete stranger. You have to try to act cool and personable while you are asked all sorts of questions. The questions are highly personal, or confusing, or both. *"What are your strengths and weaknesses?"* *"Where do you see yourself in five years?"* The interview may take twenty minutes, but it may seem like two hours. Finally, when you're done, you get to go home and wait   10
a week or so to find out if you got the job.

The job-interview "game" may not be much fun, but it is a game you can win if you play it right. The name of the game is standing out of the crowd—in a positive way. If you go to the interview in a Bozo the Clown suit, you may stand out of the crowd, all right, but not in a way that is likely to get you hired.   15

A few basic hints can help you play the interview game to win:

1. **Dress as if you're in charge.** That means wearing business clothing: usually a suit and tie or a conservative dress or skirt suit. Don't dress casually or sloppily, but don't overdress—remember, you're going to a business meeting, not a social affair. Business attire will impress the interviewer. More than that, 20 it will actually help *you* to feel more businesslike, more in charge. As the old saying goes, clothes make the man (or woman).

2. **Plan to arrive early.** This will keep you from getting hurried and flustered, and also help you avoid the disaster of being late. Give yourself a few minutes to catch your breath and mentally go over your application or résumé. 25

3. **Expect to do some small talk first.** Knowing what to expect can put you ahead of the game. When the interviewer calls you in, you will probably spend a minute or so in small talk before getting down to the actual interview questions. This small talk is a good time to make a positive impression, though. Follow the interviewer's lead, and if he or she wants to discuss the 30 weather, let's say, by all means do so for a little bit.

4. **Be prepared.** Certain questions come up regularly in job interviews. *You should plan for all these questions in advance!* Here are common questions, what they really mean, and how to answer them:

"Tell me about yourself." This question is raised to see how organized you 35 are. If you give a wandering, disjointed answer, the interviewer may put you down as a scatterbrain. You might talk briefly about where you were born and raised, where your family lives now, where you went to school, what jobs you've had, and how you happen to be here now looking for the challenge of a new job. You should have planned and rehearsed your answer, so you can 40 present this basic information about yourself quickly and smoothly.

This question can also give you a chance to show that you're right for the job. If you're applying for a sales job, for example, you might want to point out that you like being around people.

"What are your weaknesses?" This question is asked to put you off your 45 guard, perhaps making you reveal things you might not want to. A good ploy is to admit a "weakness" that employers might actually like—for example, admit to being a workaholic or a perfectionist.

"Why did you leave your last job?" This can be a "killer" question, especially if you were fired, or if you quit because you hated your boss. According to the 50 experts, never badmouth anyone when asked this question. If you were fired, talk about personality conflicts, but without blaming anyone. If you hated

your boss, say you quit for some other reason—to find a position with more growth opportunities, for example.

"Why did you apply for this job?" This question is really asking how eager   55
an employee you will be. The simple answer might be "I need the money"—but that is not what job interviewers and employers want to hear. They want employees who will work hard and stay with the company. So be honest, but give a suitable response. You might say that this is the sort of work you've always wanted to do, or that you see this company as the kind of place where   60
you would like to create a career.

Other typical questions are pure softball—if you're ready. If you are asked, "Are you creative?" or "Are you a leader?" give some examples to show that you are. For instance, you may want to discuss your organizational role in one of your college clubs. Perhaps you helped recruit new members or   65
came up with ideas to increase attendance at events. If you are asked, "What are your greatest strengths?" be ready to talk about your abilities that fit the job. Perhaps you'll mention your ability to learn quickly, your talent for working with others, your skill with organizing time efficiently, or your ability to solve problems.   70

No amount of preparation is ever going to make job interviews your favorite activity. But if you go in well-prepared and with a positive attitude, your potential employer can't help thinking highly of you. And the day will come when you will be the one who wins the job.

Time: _____   *Reading Rate (see page 536):* _____ *WPM*

■ Reading Comprehension

1. Which statement best expresses the central point of the selection?
    a. Interviewers may ask some difficult and highly personal questions.
    b. When going to an interview, dress in business clothing, mentally go over your application or résumé, and go in with a positive attitude.
    c. There are several things you can do to make yourself stand out in a positive way at job interviews. *(See paragraph 2)*
    d. Employers may ask you why you left your last job.

2. What is the main point of paragraph 8 (lines 35–41)?
    a. Your answer to the question "Tell me about yourself" can demonstrate that you are well-organized.
    b. You should tell the interviewer where you were born and raised, where your family lives now, and so on.
    c. You should have planned and rehearsed your answers to common interview questions.
    d. The interviewer may put you down as scatterbrained.

3. What statement best expresses the main point of paragraph 13 (lines 62–70)?

    a.   It is a good idea to back up any mention of your college activities with specific examples of what you did.

    b.   An interviewer may ask questions such as "Are you creative?" or "Are you a leader?"

    c.   You should possess the skills of learning quickly, organizing time efficiently, and being able to solve problems.

    (d)   "Softball" questions give you the opportunity to describe your good points and how they fit the job.

4. If you were fired from your last job, the author advises you

    a.   to make sure your interviewer realizes how unfair your former boss was.

    (b)   not to blame anyone for the firing. (Paragraph 11)

    c.   not to tell the truth, but to convince the interviewer that you quit.

    d.   to tell your interviewer a lot of people were fired by the same boss.

5. According to the author, some advantages of arriving early to an interview are:

    (a)   You will not be flustered or late, and you'll have time to review your application or résumé. (Paragraph 5)

    b.   You will have time for small talk with the interviewer.

    c.   You will have time to see all the other people applying for the same job.

    d.   You will have time to check your appearance and to speak to the interviewer's secretary.

6. In the opinion of the author, what do interviewers really want to know when they ask, "Why did you apply for this job?"

    a.   How much money you want to earn.

    (b)   If you are eager to be hired and will stay with the company. (Para. 12)

    c.   If you are creative and a leader.

    d.   If you were fired from your last job and are desperate for another one.

7. In the sentence that follows, what kind of signal word is used to show the relationship of the second sentence to the first?

    (a)   Illustration

    b.   Addition

    c.   Time

    d.   Cause and effect

    If you are asked, "Are you creative?" or "Are you a leader?" give some examples to show that you are. For instance, you may want to discuss your organizational role in one of your college clubs. (Lines 62–65)

8. We can infer from paragraph 11 (lines 49–54) that

(a) if you blame someone else for your troubles at work, interviewers may think that you may be a difficult employee.

b. most people who quit a job do so because they hate the boss.

c. as long as you are telling the truth, it is all right to tell the whole story of why you were fired or quit.

d. honesty is always the best policy.

Number Wrong: _____   *Score:* _____

| 0 wrong = 100% | 2 wrong = 75% | 4 wrong = 50% | 6 wrong = 25% |
| 1 wrong = 88% | 3 wrong = 63% | 5 wrong = 38% | 7 wrong = 13% |

■ Critical Thinking and Discussion

1. What advice does Prentergast give if you are asked, "Why did you leave your last job?" If you could ask her just why she gives this advice, what do you think she might say?

2. What, according to the author, is the real purpose of "small talk" at the beginning of the interview?

3. In your experience, are job interviews usually as "dreaded" as the author suggests? What has made the difference (for you) between a pleasant interview and an awful one?

Selection 8

Flour Children

Lexine Alpert

■ Preview

Raising a child is a huge responsibility. Yet the decision to have a child is often made carelessly. One high school program gives teenagers a three-week taste of parenthood. Even though the students' "babies" do not cry, eat, or need to have their diapers changed, the "parents" often find out that they are not ready for the job.

■ Words to Watch

convene (line 8): bring together

random (line 17): using no planned pattern; without a particular method

consequence (line 19): result

circumstantial evidence (line 31): evidence that tends to prove a fact

predominantly (line 38): mainly

novelty (line 41): a new experience; newness

"Hey, Mister V., what are you doing dressed like that?" says a student as he enters the classroom at San Francisco's Mission High School. "I'm getting ready to deliver your baby," replies the sex education teacher, in surgical greens from cap to booties. "Do you have to take this thing so seriously?" asks another, laughing nervously as she watches her teacher bring out rubber gloves. "Yes, 5 babies are a serious matter," he answers. As the students settle into their seats, Robert Valverde, who has been teaching sex education for four years—and "delivering babies" for three—raises his voice to convene the class.

"Welcome to the nursery," he announces. "Please don't breathe on the babies. I just brought them from the hospital." The students' giggles quickly 10 change to moans as Valverde delivers a "baby" — a five-pound sack of flour— to each student. "You must treat your baby as if it were real twenty-four hours a day for the next three weeks," he says. "It must be brought to every class. You cannot put the baby in your locker or your backpack. It must be carried like a baby, lovingly, and carefully in your arms. Students with jobs or other 15 activities must find baby-sitters." To make sure the baby is being cared for at night and on weekends, Valverde calls his students at random. "If the baby is

519

lost or broken, you must call a funeral parlor and find what it would cost to have a funeral," he says. The consequence is a new, heavier baby—a ten-pound flour sack. 20

Valverde came up with the "flour baby" idea after hearing that some sex education classes assign students the care of an egg; he decided to try something more realistic. "A flour sack is heavier and more cumbersome—more like a real baby," Valverde says. To heighten the realism, he has the students dress their five-pound sacks in babies' clothes, complete with diaper, blanket, 25 and bottle.

"The primary goal is to teach responsibility," says Valverde. "I want those who can't do it to see that they can't, and to acknowledge that the students who can are doing something that is very difficult and embarrassing." After thirty-six classes and more than a thousand students, Valverde's project seems 30 to be having the effect he wants. "I look at all the circumstantial evidence—the kids are talking to their parents in ways they never have talked before, and for the first time in their lives, they are forced to respond to an external environment. They have to fill out forms every day saying where they'll be that night and who's taking care of the baby. If their plans change I make 35 them call me and say who's with the baby. They're forced to confront people's comments about their babies."

Lupe Tiernan, vice-principal of the predominantly Hispanic and Asian inner-city high school, believes Valverde's class has helped to maintain the low number of teenage pregnancies at her school. "His students learn that having 40 a baby is a novelty that wears off very quickly, and by three weeks, they no longer want any part of it," she says.

At the beginning of the assignment, some students' parental instincts emerge right away. During the first week, sophomore Cylenna Terry took the rules so seriously that she was kicked out of her English class for refusing to 45 take the baby off her lap and place it on the floor as instructed. "I said, 'No way am I putting my baby on the floor.'" Others, especially the boys, learn early that they can't cope with their new role. "I just couldn't carry the baby around," says Enrique Alday, fifteen. "At my age it was too embarrassing so I just threw it in my locker." He failed the class. 50

By the second week, much of the novelty has worn off and the students begin to feel the babies are intruding on their lives. "Why does it have to be so heavy?" Cylenna Terry grumbles. "It's raining out—how am I supposed to carry this baby and open up my umbrella at the same time?" She has noticed other changes as well. "There's no way a boy is even going to look at me 55 when I have this in my arms. No guys want to be involved with a girl who has a baby—they just stay clear."

Rommel Perez misses baseball practice because he can't find a baby-sitter. Duane Broussard, who has helped care for his one-year-old nephew who lives in his household, learns new respect for how hard his mother and sister work 60 at child care. "At least this baby doesn't wake me in the middle of the night," he says. Maria Salinis says, "My boyfriend was always complaining about the sack and was feeling embarrassed about having it around. I told him, 'Imagine if it was a real baby.' It made us ask important questions of one another that we had never before considered." 65

On the last day of the assignment, the temporary parents come to class dragging their feet. Valverde calls the students one by one to the front of the room to turn in their babies. Most, their paper skin now fragile from wear, are returned neatly swaddled in a clean blanket. But others have ended up broken and lying in the bottom of a trash bin; a half-dozen students wound 70 up with ten-pound babies. The students' consensus is that babies have no place in their young lives. "I know that if I had a baby it would mess up my future and hold me down." "After this class, I don't want to have a baby. I couldn't handle it," says fifteen-year-old Erla Garcia. "It was only a sack of flour that didn't cry or scream, didn't need to be fed or put to sleep, and I still 75 couldn't wait to get rid of it."

Time: _____   *Reading Rate (see page 536):* _____ *WPM*

■ Reading Comprehension

1. Which sentence best expresses the main idea of the selection?

   a. A high school in San Francisco teaches sex education in unusual ways.

   b. Students in Mr. Valverde's sex education class are required to treat sacks of flour like babies, even to the point of finding baby-sitters for them.

   c. Some students in Mr. Valverde's sex education class take very good care of their flour-sack babies, while others neglect and abuse them.

   d. A class requiring students to care for flour-sack babies makes them realize how much hard work and commitment goes into caring for a real child. (See paragraphs 1, 2, and 9.)

2. Students who break or lose their five-pound flour sack

   a. fail the class.

   b. have to admit in front of the class that they would make poor parents.

   c. have to help a fellow student care for his or her baby.

   d. are given a ten-pound flour sack.   (Paragraph 2)

3. As a result of the flour-sack experiment, Maria Salinis and her boyfriend

   a. talked together about important questions. (Paragraph 8)

   b. broke up.

   c. decided they would never have a baby.

   d. got married.

4. One student got into trouble in an English class for

   a.   throwing the baby in her locker.

   b.   leaving her baby on the floor.

   c.   coming to class without finding a baby-sitter first.

   (d)   refusing to put the baby on the floor.   (Paragraph 6)

5. *True or false?* __T__ The author suggests that in Mr. Valverde's class, boys were more likely than girls to decide that they couldn't cope with being a "parent." (Paragraph 6)

6. Which of the following ideas does *not* appear in the article?

   a.   Mr. Valverde makes random calls to students' homes to make sure they're caring for their babies.

   b.   One student missed baseball practice because he couldn't find a baby-sitter.

   c.   Students are required to dress their flour-sack babies in clothes.

   (d)   Students must get up several times each night to check on their babies.
                                                                (Paragraphs 2–3)

7. The article implies that the flour-sack program

   a.   is currently in its first year.

   b.   is frequently criticized by students' parents.

   (c)   is supported by the school administration.   (Paragraph 5)

   d.   has been discontinued.

8. From the selection, we might conclude that

   (a)   students who have taken the class have fewer teenage pregnancies than those who haven't.   (Paragraphs 4–5)

   b.   Mr. Valverde became a father himself at a very young age and doesn't want others to make the same mistake.

   c.   Most students consider the flour-sack program silly and quickly forget about it.

   d.   Having learned a great deal about caring for babies, Mr. Valverde's students are likely to have babies as soon as possible.

Number Wrong: _____   *Score:* _____

0 wrong = 100%	2 wrong = 75%	4 wrong = 50%	6 wrong = 25%
1 wrong = 88%	3 wrong = 63%	5 wrong = 38%	7 wrong = 13%

■ Critical Thinking and Discussion

1. Why, according to Robert Valverde, did he select a flour sack to represent a baby for his students? What rules does he give his students for the care of their "babies"?

2. The vice-principal of Mr. Valverde's high school says that for teenagers, "having a baby is a novelty that wears off very quickly." In what way is a baby a "novelty"? From your own observations, do you think she is right?

3. In your opinion, do sex education programs like Mr. Valverde's belong in high schools? Or should sex education be a private matter to be handled at home?

Selection 9

From Nonreading to Reading
Stacy Kelly Abbott

■ Preview

As an adult, married and a father, Stacy Abbott had to face the fact that he could not read well enough to function in society. In this selection, Abbott tells why he grew up a nonreader and describes his struggle to gain the reading skills he needed.

■ Words to Watch

reinforcement (line 30): support

peers (line 53): people of the same class, age, etc., such as classmates

taunting (line 59): insulting in a sarcastic way

jargon (line 69): the specialized vocabulary of a given field

retain (line 95): keep in mind, remember

abstractly (line 96): concerning general ideas (not specific things), theoretically

Reading is the key to success in American society. Everything our society is and does depends on that one word. In addition to the thousands of illiterates we hear about on television and in magazines, there is an unspoken and silent category of people never mentioned. This is the group of people who can read, but not quite well enough to feel comfortable or successful with it.   5
According to *Time* magazine, "There are over seventy-five million illiterate people in America. Another forty million are termed 'marginal readers.'" This is the group that I fit into. I am not totally comfortable with reading, but I am able to get by. Slowly and gradually the role of reading in my life is changing from nonexistent to partially existent to existent.   10
As early as I can remember, there were never any recreational books in our home. They just were not something that was thought to be needed—or wanted, for that matter. My wife tells me that the most important thing for preschoolers to have is exposure to reading. They need to have books to look at and "play" read. She has bought our daughter—who is only a year old—   15
an entire library. Sometimes, when I think about it, I think, "It's not fair! Why didn't my parents buy me books and read to me the way my wife reads to our daughter?" Of course, until my wife told me, I never knew books were supposed to be a part of your early childhood. I had absolutely no exposure to

any type of stories, poetry, or even picture books before I entered kinder-   20
garten. This was my very first setback in reading. It was my first step on a road
to nonreading.

I remember being excited when I entered kindergarten. In my memory, I
was not slower than or behind the other children. First grade was about the
same. I kept up fairly well, and—although I do not remember learning the   25
actual mechanics of reading—I still learned to read at the first-grade level.
The thing to remember is that this was twenty-three years ago, and school
has gotten much harder now. I probably would not be able to keep up now,
because schools give homework.

What I learned in school was the end of it. I had absolutely no reinforce-   30
ment at home of what I learned at school. It was at this point that drugs and
alcohol were entering my life. My father was an alcoholic, and my three
brothers and sisters were all teenagers at this time in my life. My two brothers
had already dropped out of school, and my sister was well on her way too.
Drugs and alcohol were not considered wrong at my house. They were an   35
everyday part of my life. I did not know that everyone else's home was not
like this. It was inevitable that I try them when they were so readily available.
This was my next step on the road to nonreading.

Second grade was where major problems began surfacing. I was held
back in second grade, and my second year I was placed in "resource" classes.   40
I could no longer fit into regular classes. I could not read past a first-grade
level. Most of my memories of early school are of second grade. It was here
that my self-esteem plummeted. I realized that I was slower than the other
children. Sometimes children can be really cruel. They teased me and told me
I was stupid.   45

School and my self-esteem continued on this downward path for several
years. During junior high, everything seemed to get worse. This is when
"resource" became an embarrassment. It was shameful to be so "stupid." It
was not so bad when I was in the resource class, because most of the others
were about on my level. Reading aloud in front of this group was sort of   50
calming. It was not bad at all. But I still had to take some regular classes. This
was where the humiliation was horrible. I could read a little, but reading in
front of this group of peers was impossible. I just stuttered along. This is how
the remainder of my school career went. Resource was satisfying, but regular
classes were awful. Somehow, though, I stuck with school and did not quit.   55

All my brothers and sisters had dropped out, but they still lived at home.
Drugs and alcohol were still readily available. I do not recall exactly when, but
sometime while I was in high school one of my brothers found out that I could
not read. He began teasing and taunting me. It was horrible. I was one of
those millions of marginal readers who graduated from high school barely   60
able to function in American society. I made sure I maintained a job where no
reading was required. Life was fine for several years, but I was still continuing
down the road to nonreading.

The beginning of the change in my life came when I became active in my church. It is common for young men in my church to serve a mission. This idea was not so bad, except that all the reading and learning required to be successful was overwhelming. My desire to get my life in order finally convinced me to serve a mission. I learned to read much better, but only on church-related subjects. It was like learning a jargon for a job. I really still did not read very well at all.

About a year after I came home from my mission, I got married. It was then that I realized what bad shape I was really in. I had accumulated several delinquent bills simply because I could not read the late notice letters. I even almost lost my home. By this time in my life, my fear of reading aloud haunted me. In school, I had more of a "don't care" attitude and really had not cared what other people thought. Now I did care what people thought of me. I did not want my wife to think any less of me because of my problem. My wife convinced me that I was OK and she could help me learn to read better.

At her urging, I began college in the summer of 1990. I had been married for a year and had a daughter who was one week old. I read on an elementary school level, and my fear of reading aloud was a nightmare. My wife assured me that she had been through four years of college and had never had to read aloud. I took her word for it. I was taking a developmental reading class, and the very first day of class the instructor called on me to read a passage aloud. Somehow I struggled through it, humiliated and all. When I told my wife what happened, she could not believe it! But she still reassured me that I could do it. I went and spoke with the instructor about my problem, and she was very understanding. All during the summer and fall my wife helped me by reading all my material on tape and making notes for me. I was quickly seeing all the benefits of reading. Those few years had started me on the path to becoming a reader.

I struggled with school and worked really hard. We discovered that the Texas Rehabilitation Commission could help with fees and tutors for reading. The commission sent me for testing, and it was discovered that I had a visual-spatial learning disability. This explained why it was so hard for me to retain information and think abstractly—two skills that are required in college. Once the problem was discovered, I found it easier to deal with. Now I knew I was not stupid; I just had to learn to get around this. Though this explained the problem, it did not solve it. I still had to learn to read at a higher level. I have received all my textbooks on tape to help me read them. I have purchased a phonics program to help me with my reading, and it is going slowly but steadily. I am making my way down the road of active reading.

As I look back over the past four years, I see all the things that have happened to make me understand how important reading is. I am not where I want to be yet, but I will be in a year or two. I can say this with confidence now. I see reading now as a key to unlocking my whole future, especially my financial future. No more will there be the fear of having to fill out an application for employment in front of someone. I will be able to fill it out with ease, because I will know how to *read*. No more will there be the fear that my daughter will ask me to read her a book and I will have to say, "Not right now." No more will there be the fear of delinquency letters because of my inability to read. Reading has truly been transformed from a totally nonexistent part of my life to an existent and very essential part. Reading has simply helped me "to be."

Time: _____   *Reading Rate (see page 536):* _____ *WPM*

■ Reading Comprehension

1. Which of the following would be the best alternative title for this selection?
   a. Stacy Abbott
   b. Illiteracy in America
   c. The Story of a Marginal Reader   *(See paragraph 1)*
   d. The Importance of Reading to Children

2. Which sentence best expresses the main idea of this selection?
   a. There were no recreational books in the author's home while he was growing up.
   b. Abbott has improved his reading by getting his textbooks on audiotape and by using a phonics program.
   c. There are forty million marginal readers in the United States.
   d. Despite coming from an unsupportive home and having a learning disability, Abbott is learning to read.

3. Abbott implies in paragraph 2 that
   a. he thinks his wife is foolish for buying books for their baby daughter.
   b. he respects his wife's judgment when she buys books for their daughter.
   c. there were not many story, poetry, or picture books published for children when he was a child.
   d. his daughter can already read.

4. Which sentence best expresses the main idea of paragraph 4?
   a. Drugs and alcohol were not considered wrong in Abbott's home.
   b. One obstacle to Abbott's reading was his family's lack of support for school and the family members' use of drugs and alcohol.
   c. Abbott's brothers dropped out of school, and his sister was on her way to doing the same.
   d. Children often imitate what they see their parents or siblings doing.

5. According to this selection, marginal readers
   a.   are completely illiterate.
   b.   are rare in the United States.
   (c) can read only enough to get by. *(Paragraph 1)*
   d.   are very comfortable with reading and often attend college.

6. *True or false?* __F__ Abbott's poor reading prevented him from serving a mission for his church. *(Paragraph 8)*

7. The sentence below expresses a relationship of
   a.   time.
   (b) addition. *(Paragraph 10)*
   c.   contrast.
   d.   illustration.

   I read on an elementary level, and my fear of reading aloud was a nightmare.

8. Abbott implies that a person with a learning disability
   a.   is unlikely to ever learn to read.
   (b) may deal better with the disability once it is fully identified. *(Para. 11)*
   c.   is probably mentally ill as well.
   d.   should not expect to go to college.

Number Wrong: _____   *Score:* _____

| 0 wrong = 100% | 2 wrong = 75% | 4 wrong = 50% | 6 wrong = 25% |
| 1 wrong = 88% | 3 wrong = 63% | 5 wrong = 38% | 7 wrong = 13% |

■ Critical Thinking and Discussion

1. What were some of the "steps along the road to nonreading" in Stacy Abbott's life? In your opinion, were some of those steps more damaging to him than others?

2. Abbott writes that realizing he had a specific learning disability made it easier for him to deal with his reading problem. Why do you think this made a difference to him?

3. "Reading is the key to success in American society." Do you think that is true? In what ways would inability to read make success in today's world difficult?

Selection 10

What You Need to Know to Succeed at Math
Paul Nolting

■ Preview

Common sense and a positive attitude go a long way toward helping students do well in most college courses. But mathematics courses have requirements all their own. In this excerpt from his textbook *Winning at Math*, Dr. Paul Nolting spells out some important hints to help college students do well in math courses.

■ Words to Watch

sequential (line 12): occurring in a necessary order

enhances (line 61): increases

kamikaze (line 78): suicidal (from the Japanese air attack corps in World War II assigned to make suicidal crashes on targets)

subjective (line 95): based on opinion

The Importance of Practice

Because mathematics courses are so unlike other college courses, they require different study procedures. Passing most of your other college courses requires only that you read and understand the subject material. However, to pass mathematics, an extra step is required: *applying* the material in order to solve problems. 5

Example: Political science courses require that you learn about politics and public service. But your instructor isn't going to make you run for governor to pass the course.

In mathematics you must not only understand the material but apply the material. 10

Sequential Learning Pattern

Another way that learning mathematics is different from learning other subjects is its sequential learning pattern. Sequential learning means that the material learned on one day is used the next day, and the next day, and so forth.

A similar sequential pattern is seen in the building of a house. A house must be built foundation first, walls second, and roof last. Math learning, too, 15 must follow a specific order. If you study Chapter One and understand it, study Chapter Two and understand it, and study Chapter Three and *do not understand it,* then you're not going to understand Chapter Four either.

This is not the case in most subjects. In a history class, if you understand Chapter One and Chapter Two, do *not* understand Chapter Three, but study 20 and understand Chapter Four, you could pass the course. Understanding Chapter Four in history is not totally based on comprehending Chapter Three.

To succeed in mathematics, you need to understand each chapter before continuing on to the next chapter.

Math as a Foreign Language

Another way to understand studying for mathematics is to consider it a 25 foreign language. Looking at mathematics as a foreign language can improve your study procedures. In the case of a foreign language, if you do not practice it, what happens? You forget it. If you do not practice mathematics, what happens? You are likely to forget it too. Students who excel in a foreign language study it and practice it *at least* every other day. The same study 30 habits apply to mathematics.

Like a foreign language, mathematics has unfamiliar vocabulary words or terms to be put in sentences called expressions or equations. Understanding and solving a mathematics equation is similar to speaking and understanding a foreign language. Mathematics sentences use symbols (which are actually 35 spoken words) such as equal ($=$), less ($-$), and unknown (a).

Learning how to speak mathematics as a language is the key to success.

Math—The Unpopular Subject

Math is not a popular topic. You do not hear the nightly news anchor on television talking in mathematics formulas. Instead, you hear him or her talking about major events to which we can relate politically, geographically, 40 and historically. Through television we learn about English, humanities, speech, social studies, and natural sciences, but rarely mathematics. Mathematics concepts are not constantly reinforced the way English and some other subject areas are reinforced in our everyday lives. Mathematics has to be learned independently. Therefore, it requires more study time. 45

Example: In basketball, the way to improve your free throw is to *see and understand* the correct shooting form and then to *practice* the shots yourself. Practicing the shots improves your free-throwing percentage. However, if you simply listened to your coach describe the correct form and saw him demonstrate it but did not practice the correct form yourself, you would not 50 improve your shooting percentage.

Math works the same way. You can go to class, listen to your instructor, watch the instructor demonstrate skills, and understand everything that is said. However, if you leave the class *and do not practice*—by working and successfully solving the problems—you will not learn math.   55

High School versus College Math

Mathematics as a college-level course is far more difficult than high school mathematics. In college, the fall and spring math class time has been cut to three hours a week. High school math gives you five hours a week. Furthermore, college courses cover twice the material in the same time frame as high school courses. What is learned in one year in high school is learned   60
in one semester (four months) in college. This enhances study problems for the college mathematics student; you are receiving less instructional time and proceeding twice as fast. The responsibility for learning mathematics has now shifted from the school to the student, and most of your learning will have to occur outside the college classroom.   65

Summer versus Fall or Spring Semesters

Mathematics courses taught in summer semesters are more difficult than courses given in the fall or spring semesters. Students in a six-week summer session must learn math two and a half times as fast as regular semester students. Though you receive the same amount of instructional classroom time, there's less time to understand the material between class sessions.   70
Summer semester classes are usually two hours a day and four days a week. If you don't understand the lecture on Monday, then you have only Monday night to learn the material before progressing to more difficult material on Tuesday. Since mathematics is a sequential learning experience where every building block must be understood, you can fall behind quickly and never   75
catch up. In fact, some students become *lost* during the first half of a math lecture and never understand the rest of the lecture. Such an accelerated course is called *kamikaze* math, since most students don't survive it.

If you *must* take a summer mathematics course, take a ten- or twelve-week session so that you have more time to process the material between   80
classes.

Course Grading System

The course grading system for college mathematics is different from that for high school mathematics. In high school, if you make a D or borderline D-F, the teacher more than likely will give you a D and you may go on to the next course. However, in some college mathematics courses, students cannot make   85
a D, or if a D is made, the course will not count toward graduation. Also, college

instructors are more likely to give an N (no grade), W (withdraw from class), or F for barely knowing the material, because the instructors know you will be unable to pass the next course.

The grading system for math courses is very precise compared with the 90 systems in English or humanities courses. In a math course, if you have a 79 percent average and 80 percent is a B, you will get a C in the course. If you made a 79 percent in English, you might be able to talk your instructor into giving you extra-credit work to earn a B. Since math is an exact science and not as subjective as English, do not expect to talk your math instructor into 95 extra work to earn a better grade.

Your First Math Test

Making a high grade on the first major math test is more important than making a high grade on the first major tests in other college subjects. The first major math test taken is the easiest and most often least prepared for.

Students feel that the first major math test is mainly review and they can 100 make a B or C without much study. These students are overlooking an excellent opportunity to make an A on the easiest major math test of the semester. At the end of the semester, these students sometimes do not pass the math course (or perhaps just miss making an A) because their first major test grade was not high enough to pull up a low test score on one of the remaining major tests. 105 Studying hard for the first major math test and obtaining an A has several advantages. A high score on this test can:

- Compensate for a low score on a more difficult fourth or fifth math test— and all major tests have equal value in the final grade calculations.
- Provide assurance that you have learned the basic skills required to pass the 110 course. This means you will not have to spend time relearning the misunderstood material covered on the first major test while learning new material for the next test.
- Motivate you to do well. Improved motivation can cause you to increase your math study time, allowing you to master the material.   115
- Raise your confidence. With more confidence you are more likely to work harder on the difficult math homework assignments, which will increase your chances of doing well in the course.

You and Your Instructor

College math instructors treat students differently from high school mathematics instructors. High school mathematics teachers warn you about your 120 grades and offer help or makeup work. But college instructors expect *you* to keep up with how well or poorly you are doing. You must take responsibility and make an appointment to seek help from your instructor.

Sometimes there are more part-time than full-time math faculty members. This problem can restrict students' and instructors' interaction. Full-time faculty members have regular office hours and are required to help students a certain number of hours per week in their office or math lab. However, part-time faculty members are only required to teach their mathematics courses; they don't have to meet students after class, even though some part-time instructors will provide this service. Since mathematics students usually need more assistance from the instructor after class than other students, having a part-time math instructor could require you to find another source of course help. *Try to select a full-time math faculty member as your instructor.*

125
130

Time: _____   *Reading Rate (see page 536):* _____ *WPM*

■ Reading Comprehension

1. Which of the following would be a good alternative title for this selection?
   a. Math: A Tough Subject
   b. Keys to Doing Well in Math   *(See paragraphs 1, 4, 8, etc.)*
   c. High School Math versus College Math
   d. Why So Many Students Fail Math

2. Which sentence best expresses the main idea of the selection?
   a. College math instructors have higher expectations for their students than high school instructors do.
   b. It is helpful to think of math as a foreign language.
   c. Math is one subject that is not reinforced in daily life as subjects like English or social studies are.
   d. Successful math students understand that math must be approached differently from other subjects. *(Paragraphs 1, 4, 8, etc.)*

3. According to the author, which of the following is *not* a way that math is different from other school subjects?
   a. Math is rarely useful in everyday life.
   b. Math must be learned in a sequential pattern.
   c. Math is forgotten if it is not practiced regularly.
   d. Math courses require that you not only understand what you've learned but apply it as well.

4. Compared with high school math teachers, college math instructors

    a.   are more likely to warn students who are in danger of failing the course.

    b.   expect students to take more responsibility for their own success.
       (Paragraphs 14, 22)

    c.   offer more office hours and other opportunities to meet with students.

    d.   prefer teaching courses in the summer, rather than in the spring or fall.

5. *True or false?* __F__ Students often do poorly on their first major math test because it is one of the most difficult tests of the semester. (Paragraph 19. They do poorly because they fail to prepare.)

6. The author compares learning math to

    a.   anchoring a news program.

    b.   running for governor.

    c.   building a house. (Paragraph 5)

    d.   doing extra credit work in English class.

7. *True or false?* __F__ If possible, you should take math classes during a six-week summer session. (Paragraphs 15–16)

8. From the selection you can conclude that

    a.   part-time instructors don't know math well enough to help students.

    b.   many students fail in math because they approach it like other courses.
       (Paragraphs 1, 2, 13)

    c.   English courses are taught through a sequential learning pattern.

    d.   learning a foreign language helps one learn math more quickly.

Number Wrong: _____   *Score:* _____

| 0 wrong = 100% | 2 wrong = 75% | 4 wrong = 50% | 6 wrong = 25% |
| 1 wrong = 88% | 3 wrong = 63% | 5 wrong = 38% | 7 wrong = 13% |

■ Critical Thinking and Discussion

1. In what way does Nolting contrast studying math with studying political science? How does he compare it with studying a foreign language?

2. Why does Nolting refer to an accelerated summer math course as *kamikaze* math? How does that term relate to his earlier comparison between studying math and building a house?

3. In what ways, according to the author, are high school and college math instructors different? Have you found these differences in your own experience?

Rapid Reading
Progress Chart

Reading Selection (shortened titles)	Speed (WPM)	Comprehension (%)
1 Malcolm X		
2 Complaining		
3 Tests		
4 TV Fog		
5 Jacket		
6 Think Big		
7 Job Interview		
8 Flour Children		
9 Nonreading		
10 Math		

Initial Reading Rate ("Malcolm X")

Speed _____ WPM; comprehension _____ %

Final Reading Rate ("Math")

Speed _____ WPM; comprehension _____ %

Reading Rate Table

You can use the following table to find the number of words you read per minute in each of the ten selections in Part Six and in the mastery test on page 593. Suppose, for example, that you read Selection 5 in three minutes thirty seconds (3:30). To locate your WPM, go across the 3:30 column until you come to column 5. The place where the two columns meet gives your WPM—in this case, 559.

Enter your WPM and your comprehension score for a selection into the progress chart on the preceding page.

Time	1 Malcolm X	2 Complaining	3 Tests	4 TV Fog	5 Jacket	6 Think Big	7 Job Interview	8 Flour Children	9 Nonreading	10 Math	Detention Camps
1:00	510	906	800	1050	1958	1041	966	998	1557	1592	770
1:10	437	777	689	905	1679	893	827	856	1335	1365	660
1:20	382	680	602	789	1472	783	724	750	1171	1197	578
1:30	340	604	533	700	1305	694	644	665	1038	1061	513
1:40	306	544	482	633	1175	627	579	601	935	959	462
1:50	278	494	437	574	1068	568	523	544	849	869	420
2:00	255	453	400	525	979	521	483	499	779	796	385
2:10	235	418	370	486	904	481	445	461	719	735	355
2:20	218	388	343	451	840	447	414	428	668	683	330
2:30	204	362	320	420	783	416	386	399	623	637	308
2:40	191	340	301	395	736	391	362	375	585	598	288
2:50	180	320	283	371	691	367	340	352	550	562	271
3:00	170	302	267	350	653	347	322	333	519	531	256
3:10	161	286	253	332	618	329	305	315	492	503	243
3:20	152	272	240	315	588	313	289	300	468	478	231
3:30	145	259	229	300	559	297	276	285	445	455	220

Time	1 Malcolm X	2 Complaining	3 Tests	4 TV Fog	5 Jacket	6 Think Big	7 Job Interview	8 Flour Children	9 Nonreading	10 Math	Detention Camps
3:40	139	247	219	287	535	284	263	273	425	435	210
3:50	133	236	209	274	511	272	252	260	406	415	200
4:00	127	227	200	263	490	260	241	250	389	398	192
4:10	122	217	192	252	470	250	231	240	374	382	184
4:20	117	209	185	242	452	240	222	230	360	368	177
4:30	113	201	178	233	435	231	214	222	346	354	171
4:40	109	194	172	225	420	223	206	214	334	342	165
4:50	105	187	166	217	405	215	199	206	322	329	159
5:00	102	181	160	210	392	208	193	200	311	318	154
5:10	98	175	155	203	379	202	186	193	301	308	149
5:20	95	170	150	197	367	195	181	187	292	299	144
5:30	92	165	145	191	356	189	175	181	283	289	140
5:40		160	141	186	346	184	170	176	275	281	135
5:50		155	137	180	336	178	165	171	267	273	132
6:00		151	133	175	326	174	161	166	260	265	128
6:10		147	130	170	318	169	156	162	253	258	124
6:20		143	126	166	309	164	152	158	246	252	121
6:30		140	123	162	301	160	148	154	240	245	118
6:40		136	120	158	294	156	144	150	234	239	115
6:50		133	117	154	287	152	141	146	228	233	112
7:00		130	114	150	280	149	138	143	222	227	110
7:10		126	112	147	273	145	134	139	217	222	107
7:20		124	109	143	267	142	131	136	212	217	105
7:30		121	107	140	261	139	128	133	208	212	102
7:40		118	104	137	256	136	126	130	203	208	100

Time	1 Malcolm X	2 Complaining	3 Tests	4 TV Fog	5 Jacket	6 Think Big	7 Job Interview	8 Flour Children	9 Nonreading	10 Math	Detention Camps
7:50		116	102	134	250	133	123	127	199	203	98
8:00		113		131	245	130	120	125	195	199	
8:10		111		127	240	127	118	122	191	195	
8:20		109		126	235	125	115	120	187	191	
8:30		107		124	230	122	113	117	183	187	
8:40		105		121	226	120	111	115	180	184	
8:50		103		119	222	118	109	113	176	180	
9:00		101		117	218	116	107	111	173	177	
9:10		99		115	214	114	105	109	170	174	
9:20				113	210	112	103	107	167	171	
9:30					206	110	101	105	164	168	
9:40					203	108	99	103	161	165	
9:50					199	106	98	101	158	162	
10:00					196	104	96	100	156	159	

Part Seven

Mastery Tests

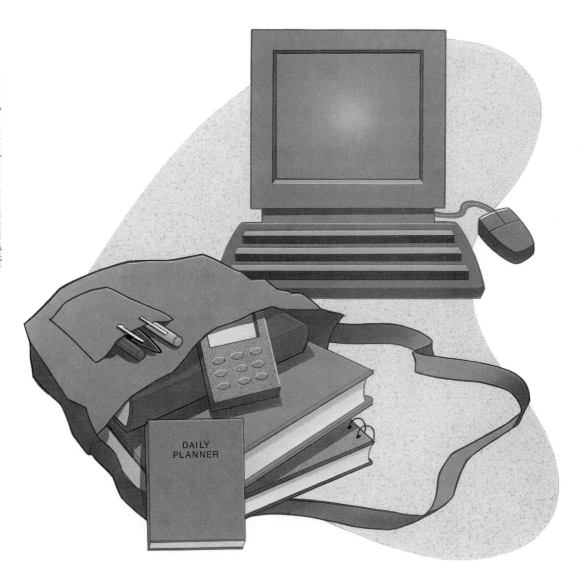

Preview

Part Seven consists of a series of mastery tests for many of the skills in the book. Such tests can be used as homework assignments, supplementary activities, in-class quizzes at the end of a section, or review tests at any point during the semester. As much as possible, the tests are designed so that they can be scored objectively, using the special box at the bottom of each test page.

Note to Instructors: Another complete set of mastery tests for use with *Reading and Study Skills* is included in the Instructor's Manual.

Motivational Skills

■ **Mastery Test**

Answer the following questions.

1. An inner commitment to doing the work that college demands
   a. is impossible when your life is confusing and difficult.
   (b.) is the most important factor in doing well in school.
   c. will help solve your personal and family problems.
   d. guarantees that you will get A and B grades.

2. To achieve a long-term career goal, a person must first set and work toward a continuing series of ___*short-term*___ goals.

3. *True or false?* __T__ One way you can begin to set a career goal is by visiting the college counseling center.

4. Career-oriented courses should be
   a. the only courses you take.
   (b.) geared toward an area with promising employment opportunities.
   c. entertaining, not boring.
   d. studied in specialized, vocational-type schools.

5. *True or false?* __F__ Because the author spent most of his first college years in the student game room, he had to drop his mathematics and chemistry courses.

6. According to Jean Coleman's recommendation, a student with a forty-hour-a-week job should take
   a. four courses.
   b. no courses.
   c. two courses.
   (d.) one course.

7. *True or false?* __T__ According to Jean Coleman, younger students are more prone to dropping out of school than older students are.

8. Jean Coleman sees two kinds of students each semester: those with a childish attitude toward school and those with a ___*mature*___ attitude.

9. Withdrawing from college
   a.   never helps.
   b.   shows a weak character.
   (c.) is sometimes the best response.
   d.   will solve your personal problems.

10. Which of the following is *not* one of the avoidance tactics described in the section about students' attitudes?
   a.   "I'll do it later."
   (b.) "I'm too disorganized."
   c.   "I can't do it."
   d.   "I'm bored with the subject."

Score: Number correct (_____) × 10 = _____%

Taking Classroom Notes

■ **Mastery Test**

Some of the questions that follow are true–false or multiple-choice questions, and some require you to write short answers.

1. To guard against forgetting, it is essential to ____*write down*____ the material that you hear in class.

2. What symbol should you use in the margin of your notes to mark examples that you have written down? ___*Ex*_____

3. To get a head start on understanding a topic to be presented in class, you should read about it in advance in your ____*textbook*____.

4. Which of the following methods might an instructor use to signal the importance of an idea?

    a. Repetition of a point

    b. Emphasis signals

    c. Tone of voice

    d. Enumerations

    (e) All of the above

5. Often the most important single step you can take to perform well in a course is to

    a. sit where the instructor can see you and listen carefully.

    b. write down definitions and examples.

    (c) be there and take effective notes.

    d. not stop taking notes during discussion periods or at the end of a class.

6. *True or false?* __*T*__ Some instructors present important ideas during discussion periods rather than in a formal lecture.

7. Circle the two methods that are effective ways of studying your classroom notes:

    a. Record them on a tape and listen to the recording after class.

    (b) Pick out key recall words on each page and write them in the margin.

    (c) Make up brief study notes on each page of notes.

    d. Rewrite the notes as neatly as possible.

8. As far as possible, take notes in outline form by starting main points at the margin and by ___indenting___ secondary points.

9. *True or false?* __T__ Taking too few rather than too many notes in class is one reason students have trouble doing well in their courses.

10. How would you abbreviate the term *self-actualization* during a fast-moving psychology lecture? __S-a (or SA)__

Score: Number correct (_____) × 10 = _____%

Time Control and Concentration

■ Mastery Test

Some of the questions that follow are true–false or multiple-choice questions, and some require you to write short answers.

1. What dates should you mark off on a large monthly calendar?

   Exam dates and paper deadlines

2. What are the four principal steps that you should take to gain control of your time?
   a.   Watch your health.
   (b.) Use a daily or weekly "to do" list.
   c.   Try to study each class day.
   (d.) Use a large monthly calendar.
   e.   Keep your schedule flexible.
   (f.) Make up a weekly study schedule.
   (g.) Consult course outlines.

3. *True or false?* ___F___ During a study session, you should try to ignore lapses of concentration.

4. You can probably study most effectively in a
   a.   very tense position.
   (b.) slightly tense position.
   c.   completely relaxed position.

5. Studying may be most effective in time blocks of
   a.   15 minutes.
   b.   30 minutes.
   (c.) 60 minutes.
   d.   120 minutes.

6. The value of regular study hours is that
   a.   you will make studying a habit.
   b.   you will stay up-to-date on courses.
   c.   you will learn more effectively by spacing your study sessions.
   (d.) all of the above will happen.

7. Where should you place your monthly calendar and weekly study schedule?

   A place where you will see them every day.

8. When you make up a "to do" list, you should

   a. schedule one-hour blocks of study time.

   b. mark down exam deadlines.

   (c.) decide on priorities.

   d. hang it on your wall.

9. *True or false?* ___F___ As a general rule, you should not reward yourself after a period of effective study time.

10. One benefit of setting specific study goals at the start of a study session is that

    a. you work on one subject during an entire study session.

    b. you keep track of your lapses of concentration.

    c. you avoid working on difficult subjects.

    (d.) your task is broken down into manageable units.

Score: Number correct (_____) × 10 = _____%

Textbook Study I

■ Mastery Test

Some of the questions that follow are true–false or multiple-choice questions, and some require you to write short answers.

1. Circle the one thing you do *not* do when previewing a selection.

   a. Study the title.

   b. Read over the first and last paragraphs.

   (c) Write down important ideas.

   d. Look for relationships between headings and subheadings.

2. *True or false?* __T__ Many students mark off too much material when reading a textbook.

3. *True or false?* __F__ Your first reading of a chapter should proceed slowly, and you should stop as often as necessary to reread material until you are sure you understand it all.

4. Examples should be

   a. underlined.

   b. circled.

   (c) labeled *ex* in the margin.

   d. underlined and labeled *ex* in the margin.

5. You should set off definitions in the text by ___underlining___ them.

6. Use ___numbers___ to mark off each point in an enumeration (list of items).

7. *True or false?* __F__ Every note that you write down should have a symbol in front of it, such as *A, B, 1, 2, a, b,* or the like.

8. To study a textbook chapter, first you *preview* the chapter. Then you ___read___ it through once, marking off what appear to be important ideas.

9. As the third step in studying a chapter, you reread, decide on the important ideas, and ___write___ study notes. Finally, you recite the material to yourself, over and over, until you have learned it.

10. Leave space in the margin of your notes so that you can write key ___words and phrases (or recall words)___ to help you study the notes.

Score: Number correct (_____) × 10 = _____%

Textbook Study II

■ **Mastery Test**

This selection is from a sociology textbook. Complete the four-step study process that follows it.

Statuses

A *status* is a position an individual occupies in a social structure. In a sense, a status is a social address. It tells people where the individual "fits" in society—as a mother, college professor, senior citizen, or prison inmate. Knowing a person's status—knowing that you are going to meet a judge or a janitor, a ten-year-old or a fifty-year-old—tells you something about how that person will behave toward you and how you are expected to behave toward him or her. Misjudging status is a frequent cause of embarrassment—as when a woman invites a man she assumes is a bachelor to an intimate dinner and discovers he is married.

Social statuses can be divided into two groups. Some social statuses are *achieved,* or attained through personal effort. For example, individuals achieve the status of senator or sanitation-man, concert pianist or soccer coach, wife or divorcee, through their own choices and behavior. The statuses of convict, junkie, and high school dropout are also achieved. Other social statuses are *ascribed,* or assigned to the individual at birth or at different stages in the life cycle. For instance, men and women, blacks and whites, occupy different statuses in American society because of "what they are," not because of anything they do. Age is another ascribed status. Children occupy one position in society, adults another, elderly people still another. Individuals at each level are expected to act their age. It is important to note that while individuals have considerable control over achieved statuses, they have little or no control over ascribed statuses. The Prince of Wales, for example, was born to his position; he is a prince whether he likes it or not; there is almost nothing he can do to change his "social address."

Step 1: *Preview.* Take about fifteen seconds to preview the passage above. The title tells you that the passage is about _____ *statuses* _____ . How many terms are set off in italics in the passage? __ *3* __

Step 2: *Read and Mark.* Read the passage straight through. As you do, underline the definitions you find. Mark with an *Ex* in the margin an example that makes each definition clear for you. Also, number the items in the basic enumeration in the passage.

Step 3: *Write.* Complete the following study notes on "Statuses":

Status— *a position an individual occupies in a social structure* _____

_____

Two kinds of _*social statuses*_ _____

Achieved _____

Ex.— *Any of the following: senator, sanitation-man, concert pianist, coach, wife, divorcee, convict, junkie, high school dropout* _____

Ascribed _____

Ex.— *gender, race, age* _____

Individuals can control achieved statuses but not ascribed ones. E.g., Prince of Wales has ascribed status from birth.

Step 4: *Recite.* Jot down in the spaces below the recall words that could help you recite the material to yourself.

Achieved status   *Ascribed status*
_____   _____

Score: Number correct (_____) × 10 = _____%

Textbook Study III

■ **Mastery Test**

This selection is from a psychology textbook. Complete the four-step study process that follows it.

Reasons for Forgetting

Forgetting can be embarrassing, inconvenient, and unpleasant. The kind of forgetting of greatest concern to psychologists is of items or events that have been stored in long-term memory and that have become difficult to retrieve. Several explanations have been given to describe why this type of retrieval problem occurs.

Repression

One possible explanation for being unable to retrieve memories is *repression*. Repression is unconsciously motivated forgetting; it is an unconscious blocking of things that are frightening or threatening. Traumatic events and anxiety-provoking people and situations can be painful if they are retrieved from long-term memory. Everyone has encountered some form of repression. Any time you refuse to talk or think about an unpleasant happening, you are experiencing a type of repression. According to Freud, it is a way of protecting yourself from remembering things that are distressing.

Suppression

Have you ever wanted to forget something? Perhaps you did something embarrassing or foolish and wanted to suppress the memory. *Suppression* is a conscious effort to avoid thinking about an event. Since you are aware of the event, suppression is different from repression.

Amnesia

Amnesia is a disorder that displays the most extreme form of repression. It is a loss of memory or a memory gap that includes forgetting personal information that would normally be recalled. Because of the dramatic effect, amnesia patients have been used as the subjects of novels, films, and soap operas. While amnesia victims forget almost all basic information, they do retain basic memories. They remember how to add, subtract, read, write, dress, and cook.

Like repression, amnesia is a limited explanation of why forgetting occurs. It is not nearly as common as the media suggest and can account for only a tiny percentage of forgetting.

Interference

Interference is the most popular explanation for why forgetting occurs. You forget because other information interferes with your memory. According to the interference description of forgetting, there are two types of obstructions to remembering: proactive interference and retroactive interference.

Proactive Interference. Proactive means "acting forward." *Proactive interference* refers to instances when previous memories block the recall of more recent learning. Suppose you meet a new psychology instructor named Professor Kassel, who reminds you of your old girlfriend, Flora Belle. You may have difficulty remembering the professor's correct name and want to call her Flora Belle. In proactive interference, earlier learning interferes with new learning.

Retroactive Interference. Retroactive means "acting backward." *Retroactive interference* refers to instances where recent learning blocks the recall of previous memories. If the next time you meet your old girlfriend Flora Belle, you have difficulty remembering her name and have an urge to call her "Professor," retroactive inhibition will be contributing to your forgetting.

Step 1: *Preview.* Take about thirty seconds to preview the passage above. The title tells you that the passage is about the reasons for forgetting. How many subheads are there in the passage? __4__ How many terms are set off in italics in the passage? __5__

Step 2: *Read and Mark.* Read the passage straight through. As you do, underline the definitions you find. Mark with an *Ex* in the margin any example that helps make a definition clear. Also, number the items in the two enumerations in the passage.

Step 3: *Write.* Complete the following study notes on "Reasons for Forgetting":

Reasons for forgetting:

Repression— unconsciously motivated forgetting

Suppression— a conscious effort to avoid thinking about an event

Amnesia— loss of memory including forgetting personal information that would normally be recalled

Interference—Forget because other information interferes with your learning.

    a. Proactive interference— *previous memories block the recall of more recent learning*

        Ex—Want to call new Professor Kassel by name of your old girlfriend Flora Belle.

    b. Retroactive interference— *recent learning blocks the recall of previous memories*

        Ex— *want to call Flora Belle "Professor"*

Step 4: *Recite.* To remember the four reasons for forgetting, create a *catchword:* a word made up of the first letters in the four reasons for forgetting. Write your catchword here:

Example: SARI

To remember the two kinds of interference, create a *catchphrase:* a two-word sentence in which the first word begins with P (for *proactive*) and the second word begins with R (for *retroactive*). Write your catchphrase here:

Example: Panthers run.

Score: Number correct (_____) × 10 = _____%

Building a Powerful Memory

- ## Mastery Test

    Some of the questions that follow are true–false or multiple-choice questions, and some require you to write short answers.

    1. The first step in effective remembering is to _____*organize*_____ the material to be learned.

    2. The best way to avoid passive studying is to
        a. study right before bed.
        b. test yourself on the material to be learned.
        c. copy several times the material to be learned.
        d. review material in the morning.

    3. *True or false?* __F__ Material is best studied in a single long session rather than spaced out over several sessions.

    4. Overlearning is
        a. unnecessary memorization.
        b. going over a lesson you already know.
        c. incompatible with learning.
        d. a way to "push out" old ideas so that you can learn new ones.

    5. If you reduce ideas to key words and memorize the key words, they will often serve as _____*hooks*_____ that will help you pull the ideas into memory.

    6. What aid to memory is illustrated by the fact that someone will always remember the name of a person who owes him or her money?
        a. Spacing memory work.
        b. Intending to learn.
        c. Using key words as hooks.
        d. Overlearning.

    7. To gain the overall understanding you need in order to learn material effectively, you should
        a. attend class lectures regularly.
        b. read textbook assignments.
        c. take classroom and textbook notes.
        d. do all of the above.

8. One memory aid is to include as a study period the time just before
   _____bed_____.

9. Write a catchword that will help you remember the first letters of the following
   kinds of defense mechanisms: *projection, repression, identification.*
   RIP (or IRP or PIR)

10. Write a catchphrase that will help you remember the following kinds of
    taxes: *self-employment, income, sales, property.* Answers will vary.
    Example: Sally is so popular.

Score: Number correct (_____) × 10 = _____%

Taking Objective Exams

■ Mastery Test

All the questions that follow have been taken from actual college tests. Answer the questions by using the specific hints for multiple-choice and true–false questions that are listed below. Also, in the space provided, give the letter of the hint used to determine the correct answer.

Test-Taking Hints

a The longest multiple-choice answer is often correct.

b A multiple-choice answer in the middle, especially one with the most words, is often correct.

c Answers with qualifiers, such as *generally, probably, most, almost, often, may, some,* and *sometimes,* are usually correct.

d Answers with absolute words, such as *all, always, everyone, everybody, never, no one, nobody, none,* and *only,* are usually incorrect.

Hint __d__   1. *True or false?* __F__ IQ tests are always reliable measures of intelligence.

Hint __c__   2. *True or false?* __T__ After June 1944, the Allies had almost completely eliminated the German submarine threat in the Atlantic.

Hint __a__   3. A good justification for establishing a new business would be

    a.   a strong personal desire to run a business.

    b.   a shrinking market.

    c.   successful businesses nearby.

    (d.) an expanding market combined with the presence of inefficient firms.

Hint __b__   4. Diabetics lack

    a.   vitamins.

    (b.) insulin, an enzyme needed to use sugar properly.

    c.   amino acids.

    d.   epinephrine.

Hint __c__   5. *True or false?* __T__ Generally, single-story buildings are preferred for most types of factory operations.

Hint _b_   6. During World War II, black Americans

   a.   achieved social equality.

   b.   lived mostly in the South.

   (c) found more job opportunities open and benefited from the movement for equality fostered by the war.

   d.   served in fully integrated service units.

Hint _d_   7. *True or false?* _F_ The only function of the hypothalamus is to activate the sympathetic nervous system.

Hint _b_   8. Affective explanations are statements intertwined with

   a.   altruistic behavior.

   b.   love and intimacy.

   (c) emotions, values, or expectations regarding self-control.

   d.   antisocial behavior.

Hint _d_   9. *True or false?* _F_ There are no gaps between scientific ideals and the realities of any actual research project.

Hint _a_   10. In an attempt to deal with unemployment, President Hoover

   a.   established the NRA.

   b.   began a welfare program.

   c.   created unemployment insurance.

   (d) established the Reconstruction Finance Corporation to make loans to businesses.

Score: Number correct (_____) × 10 = _____%

Taking Essay Exams

■ **Mastery Test**

Spend a half hour getting ready to write a one-paragraph essay on the subject "Describe eight points to remember when planning a weekly study schedule." The eight points are presented on pages 79–81.

Study Hint: First summarize each of the eight points in the spaces below. Then study the points by following the advice given in step 2 on pages 246–247.

Important Points about a Weekly Study Schedule:

1. Hour of study time for hour of class time (change later if needed)
   _____

2. Regular study time (definite study hours essential for success)
   _____

3. One-hour blocks of study time (takes while to get warmed up)
   _____

4. Reward for study (research shows rewards help—e.g., TV after study)
   _____

5. Study before and after class (preview and review)
   _____

6. Difficult subjects when most alert (do hard math if alert at 8 P.M.)
   _____

7. Balance activities (free time for friends, sports, etc. as well as work time)
   _____

8. Flexible schedule (trade, don't omit, times)
   _____

When the half hour is up, write your essay answer on the other side of this sheet.

Sample Essay Answer

There are eight points to remember when planning a weekly study schedule. First, plan one hour of study time for each hour of class time. Add or deduct more time later as needed. Secondly, have regular study time. Definite study hours are essential for success in school. Next, study in at least one-hour blocks of study time. In shorter time blocks, too much time might be spent just in getting warmed up. Another point to remember is that you should reward yourself for study. Research shows that a reward such as watching TV after work helps encourage you to study. Fifth, study before and after class. You'll get more out of a lecture if you read a textbook chapter before it, and if you review and add to your notes after the lecture. Another point is to study difficult subjects when you're most alert. For example, you should work on a hard math chapter at 8 P.M. if that's a time when you're very alert. Seventh, balance activities. Allow free time for sports, friends, and so on in your schedule as well as work time. Finally, keep your schedule flexible. Be ready to trade (but not omit) work times and free times in your schedule depending on the situation. Following the above hints will help you develop a study routine that should lead to good grades in school.

Score: Number correct (_____) $\times$ 12.5 = _____%

Taking Objective and Essay Exams

■ Mastery Test

You have five kinds of questions to answer on this quiz: following directions, matching, sentence completion, true–false, and multiple-choice.

Following Directions: Print your full name, last name first, under the line at the right-hand side below. Write your full name, first name last, on the line at the left-hand side below.

1. ___Langan, John (written)___   2. _____

                                            Langan, John (printed)

Matching: Enter the appropriate letter in the space provided next to each definition.

3. Show similarities between two things. __e__   a. Define

4. Explain by giving examples. __f__   b. Contrast

5. Give the formal meaning of a term. __a__   c. Direction words

6. Words that tell you exactly what to   d. List

   do. __c__   e. Compare

7. Give a series of points and number   f. Illustrate

   them 1, 2, 3, and so on. __d__   g. Summarize

8. Give a condensed account of the main points. __g__

Fill-Ins: Write the word or words needed to complete each of the following sentences.

9. You should ____study____ consistently in order to avoid last-minute cramming that may cause exam panic.

10. On either an objective or an essay exam, you will build up confidence and momentum if you do the easier questions ____first____.

11. Because time is limited on an essay exam, instructors can give you only a few questions to answer. They will reasonably focus on questions dealing with the __most important__ areas of the subject.

12. Before starting an objective or essay test, you should __budget (or plan)__ your time.

True or False: Write the word *true* or *false* to the left of the following statements.

True 13. Often the main reason that students choke, or block, on exams is that they are not well prepared.

True 14. When studying for an essay test, prepare a good outline answer for each question and memorize the outlines.

False 15. If you have to cram, you should try to study everything in your class notes and textbook.

False 16. You should spend the night before an exam organizing your notes.

Multiple Choice: Circle the letter of the answer that best completes each of the following statements.

17. One step that is *not* necessarily recommended in preparing for and taking an essay exam is to
   a. list ten or so probable questions.
   b. prepare an outline answer for each question.
   c. concentrate on details in your class and text notes.
   d. understand direction words.

18. When taking an objective test, remember that
   a. absolute statements are always false.
   b. absolute statements are often false.
   c. absolute statements are rarely false.
   d. absolute statements are never false.

19. When taking an essay exam, you should
   a. outline your answers before you begin to write.
   b. be direct when you write.
   c. use signal words to guide your reader through the answer.
   d. do all of the above.

20. In preparing for an objective or essay exam, pay attention to
   a. key terms and their definitions.
   b. major lists of items.
   c. points emphasized in class or in the text.
   d. all of the above.

Score: Number correct (_____) × 5 = _____%

Using the Library and the Internet

■ Mastery Test

1. In order to locate a book called *A Walk in the Woods*, what kind of search should you do?

   a.   Title search under *A*

   (b) Title search under *W for Walk*

   c.   Title search under *W for Woods*

   d. Subject search under *W for Walk*

2. *True or false?* __T__ The best way to find more than one book about the same topic is to do a search by subject.

3. To locate a book in the library stacks, you need to know its ___call number___.

4. Periodicals include

   a.   books.

   b.   card files.

   (c) magazines.

   d. all of the above.

Items 5–8: Following is an entry from the *Readers' Guide to Periodical Literature*. Answer the questions about the entry:

Health
Who'll Care for Dad? K. Springen. il *Newsweek*
   85–86 N 6, '00

5. What is the title of the article?
   "Who'll Care for Dad?"

6. What is the name of the magazine?
   Newsweek

7. On what pages of the magazine does the article appear?
   pp. 85–86

8. What is the date of the issue in which the article appeared?
   November 6, 2000

9. A good way to use the Internet to find books on a topic is to
   a.   visit an online bookstore and use its keyword search box.
   b.   visit an online bookstore and use its "Browse Subjects" box.
   c.   visit the Library of Congress website and use its search form.
   (d) do all of the above.

10. *True or false?* __T__ To narrow an Internet search to a reasonable number of entries, use more than one keyword.

Score: Number correct (_____) × 10 = _____%

Writing a Research Paper

■ Mastery Test

1. A research paper should be narrow and deep rather than broad and shallow. Which of the following topics would be most suited for a research paper of about ten pages?

   a. Crime

   b. Punishments

   c. The death penalty

   (d) Economic benefits of the death penalty

2. *True or false?* __T__ The subject headings in the book file can help you to limit the subject of a paper.

3. To find articles on your topic, which of the following sources should you go to?

   a. Periodicals index in the library (such as *Readers' Guide*)

   b. CD-ROM database in the library (such as *Magazine Index Plus*)

   c. Internet search engine

   (d) All of the above

4. The notes you take for your research paper may be in the form of either __direct quotations__ or summaries in your own words.

5. The bottom of each summary note card should

   (a) list the source and page number of the information on the card.

   b. contain the heading of the section where it will be used.

   c. contain the author's name.

   d. be blank.

6. If you use specialized information or ideas that are not your own and you do not give the author credit, you are __plagiarizing__.

7. *True or false?* __F__ While doing your research, you need to keep a written record of only the print sources you have used, not the online sources.

8. The first time you cite a source in a research paper, you must state

   a. the author's name and the title of the book or article.

   b. the author's name, the title of the book or article, and the page number.

   (c) the author's name and the page number.

   d. just the author's name.

9. The "Works Cited" section of a paper should

    a.   have numbered entries.

    b.   include all books the author of the paper has read.

    c.   not include any more than one book by the same author.

    (d.) include only the books and articles referred to in the paper.

10. Which of the following shows the correct format for a "Works Cited" entry?

    (a.) Quindlen, Anna. <u>A Short Guide to a Happy Life</u>. New York: Random House, 2000.

    b.   Anna Quindlen. <u>A Short Guide to a Happy Life</u>. New York: Random House, 2000.

    c.   <u>A Short Guide to a Happy Life</u>. Anna Quindlen. New York: Random House, 2000.

    d.   Quindlen, Anna. "A Short Guide to a Happy Life," Random House, 2000.

Score: Number correct (_____) × 10 = _____%

Understanding Word Parts

■ **Mastery Test**

Complete the italicized word in each sentence by adding the correct word part. Use the meaning of the word part and the sentence context to determine the correct answer in each case.

port—carry	*psych*—mind	*trans*—across	*mis*—badly	*in*—not
tract—draw	*tact*—touch	*inter*—between	*post*—after	*dis*—apart

1. The (. . . *ition*) _transition_ from prison to life on the "outside" can cause psychological problems.

2. To show his (. . . *content*) _discontent_ with the restaurant meal, Fred dumped his dinner onto the floor.

3. When two burly customers started to fight, the skinny bartender was afraid to (. . . *vene*) _intervene_.

4. The (*re* . . . *able*) _retractable_ ballpoint pen leaked red ink all over the inside of my purse.

5. A blind person's (. . . *ile*) _tactile_ sense is highly developed; the fingertips transmit a wealth of information.

6. Mark, enrolled in five difficult courses, felt he had been (. . . *guided*) _misguided_ by his college counselor.

7. In a (. . . *script*) _postscript_ to his will, the crazy old man left a million dollars to the Internal Revenue Service.

8. The (. . . *er*) _porter_ was told to bring a mop and a pail to the lobby; a bottle of orange juice had smashed on the floor.

9. (. . . *iatrists*) _Psychiatrists_ must qualify as medical doctors before specializing in studies of the mind.

10. The (. . . *edible*) _inedible_ pancakes oozed a sticky white batter as they lay on the plate.

Score: Number correct (_____) × 10 = _____%

Using the Dictionary

■ Mastery Test

Refer to the following excerpt from the paperback *American Heritage Dictionary* to answer the questions that follow.

---

e·merge (ĭ-mûrj′) *v.* **e·merged, e·merg·ing.** **1.** To rise up or come forth into view; appear. **2.** To come into existence. **3.** To become known or evident. [Lat. *emergere.*] —**e·mer′gence** *n.* —**e·mer′gent** *adj.*

e·mer·gen·cy (ĭ-mûr′jən-sē) *n., pl.* **-ies.** An unexpected situation or occurrence that demands immediate attention.

e·mer·i·tus (ĭ-mĕr′ĭ-təs) *adj.* Retired but retaining an honorary title: *a professor emeritus.* [Lat., p.p. of *emereri,* to earn by service.]

em·er·y (ĕm′ə-rē, ĕm′rē) *n.* A fine-grained impure corundum used for grinding and polishing. [< Gk *smuris.*]

e·met·ic (ĭ-mĕt′ĭk) *adj.* Causing vomiting. [< Gk. *emein,* to vomit.] —**e·met′ic,** *n.*

–emia *suff.* Blood: *leukemia.* [< Gk. *haima,* blood.]

em·i·grate (ĕm′ĭ-grāt′) *v.* **-grat·ed, -grat·ing.** To leave one country or region to settle in another. [Lat. *emigrare.*] —**em′i·grant** *n.* —**em′i·gra′tion** *n.*

é·mi·gré (ĕm′ĭ-grā′) *n.* An emigrant, esp. a refugee from a revolution. [Fr.]

em·i·nence (ĕm′ə-nəns) *n.* **1.** A position of great distinction or superiority. **2.** A rise or elevation of ground; hill.

em·i·nent (ĕm′ə-nənt) *adj.* **1.** Outstanding, as in reputation; distinguished. **2.** Towering above others; projecting. [< Lat. *eminēre,* to stand out.] —**em′i·nent·ly** *adv.*

em·phat·ic (ĕm-făt′ĭk) *adj.* Expressed or performed with emphasis. [< Gk. *emphatikos.*] —**em·phat′i·cal·ly** *adv.*

em·phy·se·ma (ĕm′fi-sē′mə) *n.* A disease in which the air sacs of the lungs lose their elasticity, resulting in an often severe loss of breathing ability. [< Gk. *emphusēma.*]

em·pire (ĕm′pīr′) *n.* **1.** A political unit, usu. larger than a kingdom and often comprising a number of territories or nations, ruled by a single central authority. **2.** Imperial dominion, power, or authority. [<Lat. *imperium.*]

em·pir·i·cal (ĕm-pîr′i-kəl) *adj.* Also **em·pir·ic** (-pir′ik). **1.** Based on observation or experiment. **2.** Relying on practical experience rather than theory. [<Gk. *empeirikos,* experienced.] —**em·pir′i·cal·ly** *adv.*

em·pir·i·cism (ĕm-pîr′ĭ-sĭz′əm) *n.* **1.** The view that experience, esp. of the senses, is the only source of knowledge. **2.** The employment of empirical methods, as in science.— **em·pir′i·cist** *n.*

em·place·ment (ĕm-plās′mənt) *n.* **1.** A prepared position for guns within a fortification. **2.** Placement. [Fr.]

em·ploy (ĕm-ploi′) *v.* **1.** To engage or use the services of. **2.** To put to service; use. **3.** To devote or apply (one's time or energies) to an activity. —*n.* Employment. [< Lat. *implicare,* to involve.] —**em·ploy′a·ble** *adj.*

em·ploy·ee (ĕm-ploi′ē, ĕm′ploi-ē′) *n.* Also **em·ploy·e.** One who works for another.

ă pat ā pay â care ä father ĕ pet   ē be ĭ pit ī tie î pier ŏ pot ō toe ô paw, for oi noise o͞o took o͞o boot ou out th thin *th* this ŭ cut û urge yoo abuse zh vision ə about, item, edible, gallop, circus

---

1. How many syllables are in the word *emphatic?* _____3_____

2. Where is the primary accent in the word *emphysema?* _____SE_____

3. Where is the primary accent in the word *empiricism?* _____PIR_____

4. What word in the pronunciation key tells you how to pronounce the *i* in *emeritus?* _____*pit*_____

5. What word in the pronunciation key tells you how to pronounce the *oi* sound in *employ?* _____*noise*_____

6. In the word *eminence,* the first *e* is pronounced like the *e* in
   a. heat.
   (b.) pet.
   c. trace.
   d. item.

7. In the word *empirical,* the *a* is pronounced like
   a. long *a.*
   b. short *a.*
   (c.) schwa.
   d. short *e.*

8. *True or false?* __T__ The word *emery* may be pronounced two ways.

9. In the sentence "Picasso's *eminence* in the art world is a result of talent and hard work," which meaning of *eminence* applies?
   (a.) Meaning 1
   b. Meaning 2

10. In the sentence "The instructor said, 'Martin, please *employ* your pen for taking class notes, not for letters to classmates,'" which meaning of *employ* applies?
    a. Verb meaning 1
    (b.) Verb meaning 2
    c. Verb meaning 3
    d. Noun meaning

Score: Number correct (_____) × 10 = _____%

Word Pronunciation

■ Mastery Test

Using the rules in the box, divide the following words into syllables. And for each word, write the number of the rule or rules that apply. Note the example.

> 1 Divide between two consonants.
>
> 2 Divide before a single consonant.

Example
enigma   _e-nig-ma_   _rule 2_   _rule 1_

Part A: General-Interest Words

	Syllable Division	Rule Numbers	
1. culprit	cul-prit	1	
2. rampant	ram-pant	1	
3. harbinger	har-bin-ger	1	1
4. martinet	mar-ti-net	1	2
5. subterfuge	sub-ter-fuge	1	1
6. conjecture	con-jec-ture	1	1
7. importune	im-por-tune	1	1
8. abrogate	ab-ro-gate	1	2
9. masticate	mas-ti-cate	1	2
10. cognizant	cog-ni-zant	1	2

Part B: Specialized Words

		Syllable Division	Rule Numbers			
11.	visceral	vis-ce-ral	1	2		
12.	aversive	a-ver-sive	2	1		
13.	glucose	glu-cose	2			
14.	antigen	an-ti-gen	1	2		
15.	atropine	at-ro-pine	1	2		
16.	carcinoma	car-ci-no-ma	1	2	2	
17.	charisma	cha-ris-ma	2	1		
18.	malignancy	ma-lig-nan-cy	2	1	1	
19.	compensation	com-pen-sa-tion	1	1	2	
20.	elucidative	e-lu-ci-da-tive	2	2	2	2

Score: Number correct (_____) × 5 = _____%

Spelling Improvement

■ Mastery Test

Use the four spelling rules you reviewed earlier in the book to spell the following words.

1. refer	+ ed	=	referred
2. lively	+ hood	=	livelihood
3. shr____k	(ie *or* ei)	=	shriek
4. win	+ ing	=	winning
5. city	+ es	=	cities
6. involve	+ ment	=	involvement
7. drive	+ ing	=	driving
8. safe	+ ty	=	safety
9. pity	+ ful	=	pitiful
10. n____ce	(ie *or* ei)	=	niece
11. fantasy	+ es	=	fantasies
12. rebel	+ ion	=	rebellion
13. arrange	+ ment	=	arrangement
14. lucky	+ ly	=	luckily
15. write	+ ing	=	writing
16. conc____ted	(ie *or* ei)	=	conceited
17. state	+ hood	=	statehood
18. marry	+ ed	=	married
19. admit	+ ance	=	admittance
20. achieve	+ able	=	achievable

Score: Number correct (_____) × 5 = _____%

Vocabulary Development

■ Mastery Test

Read each of the following sentences carefully. Then decide which of the four choices comes closest in meaning to the word in italic type. Circle the letter of your choice.

1. Because of the *brusque* manner of the waitress, I decided to leave no tip.
   a. Slow
   b. Courteous
   (c) Rude
   d. Passive

2. We kept our plans *tentative,* so we could quickly change them in case there were new developments.
   a. Fixed
   (b) Indefinite
   c. Superficial
   d. Honest

3. I could not tolerate an *austere* apartment like the one she lives in; I need plants, pictures, and plenty of furnishings.
   (a) Bare
   b. Lavish
   c. Expensive
   d. Small

4. She is a *tenacious* person; even though she failed her first biology tests, she kept studying and eventually passed the course.
   a. Humorous
   b. Stingy
   c. Softhearted
   (d) Persistent

5. Among the many *paradoxes* in the Bible are that the meek shall inherit the earth and the first shall be last.
   a. Famous passages
   b. Verses
   (c) Apparent contradictions
   d. Prayers

6. His clothes are neat and tasteful, but his hair, *incongruously,* is unkempt and oily.

   a. Boldly

   (b.) Inconsistently

   c. Apologetically

   d. Consistently

7. My English paper had many good details but lacked *coherence;* the instructor said I had a lot to learn about how to structure my ideas.

   a. Unity

   b. Support

   c. Sentence skills

   (d.) Organization

8. I used to be a three-letter athlete in school; now I enjoy sports in a *vicarious* way by watching them on television.

   a. Curious

   b. Dangerous

   (c.) Substitute

   d. Inexpensive

9. My progress in school was *impeded* by poor study habits and a poor attitude.

   a. Aided

   b. Increased

   (c.) Hindered

   d. Reinforced

10. The counselor listened in a *perfunctory* way as she doodled on her notepad; I felt she wasn't really interested in my problem.

    (a.) Indifferent

    b. Responsive

    c. Intense

    d. Apologetic

Score: Number correct (_____) × 10 = _____%

Definitions and Examples

■ Mastery Test

In the spaces provided, write the number of the sentence in each selection that contains a definition. Then write the number of the sentence that provides the *first* example of the definition.

1.   [1]Admittedly a good deal of our social interaction is motivated by self-interest. [2]You may offer to run an errand for a professor because you hope that he or she will take that help into account when awarding grades. [3]Or you may offer to take care of the neighbors' dog while they are away on vacation because you want them to take care of your cat when you go on vacation. [4]But if behavior that benefits others is *not* linked to personal gain, it is called **altruistic behavior.** [5]For example, many people go to considerable trouble to help a sick neighbor, take in a family left homeless by fire, or serve as hospital aides. [6]Charitable contributions are often directed at strangers and made anonymously.

Definition: ___4___   Example: ___5___

2.   [1]Generally, nurses work directly with patients. [2]However, in some instances, they function as *patients' advocates;* that is, they work indirectly on behalf of the patient or intercede for the patient. [3]For example, the nurse who lobbies in the legislature in support of programs of benefit to the consumer of health services functions as a patient advocate. [4]A few other examples are the nurse who seeks the services of other health practitioners on behalf of a patient; the nurse who intercedes for patients by helping them obtain services from various community health agencies; and the nurse who intercedes for the patients by interpreting their needs to family. [5]Nurses become patient advocates also as they plan total health care while serving as a member of the health team.

Definition: ___2___   Example: ___3___

3.   [1]Price lining is based on the fact that most retailers have more than one product to price, and a number of substitute products or brands within each product category. [2]For instance, a women's clothing store may offer a variety of wool scarves. [3]But consumers will not respond to a series of minor price differences, such as scarves at $6.50, $6.60, $6.70, $6.90, $7.00, and so on. [4]Instead, buyers prefer a *few* prices that seem to differentiate the product

into "lines" based on some attribute such as quality or prestige. [5]For instance, there may be scarves priced at $5, $8, $10, and $16. [6]These prices clearly indicate that there are scarves for the economy-minded at $5, medium-quality scarves at $8 and $10, and top-of-the-line scarves at $16. [7]Price lining means, then, that a limited number of prices are established for the products or brands within a product class.

Definition: __7__   Example: __2__

4.   [1]When teachers feel that a certain child will do well in school, that child probably will do well. [2]The *self-fulfilling prophecy,* by which people act as they are expected to, has been documented in many different situations. [3]In the "Oak School experiment," some teachers in this California school were told at the beginning of the term that some of their pupils had shown unusual potential for intellectual growth. [4]Actually, the children had been chosen at random. [5]Yet several months later many of them—especially first- and second-graders—showed unusual gains in IQ. [6]And the teachers seemed to like the "bloomers" better. [7]Their teachers do not appear to have spent more time with them than with the other children or to have treated them differently in any obvious ways. [8]Subtler influences may have been at work, possibly in the teachers' tone of voice, facial expression, touch, and posture.

Definition: __2__   Example: __3__

5.   [1]Resocialization differs from other types of adult socialization in that it points to a rapid and drastic change, usually one that is forced on the individual to some degree. [2]Military service involves resocialization, since it is a deliberate attempt to remold a person's life and personality in certain respects. [3]The recruit is stripped of previous status and gains a new status only by meeting the demands of the military. [4]A more extreme example is that of religious conversion, in which the person may feel completely reoriented— experiencing a sense of rebirth into a new personality or of having been "born again." [5]Both the recruit and the convert experience a change from an old lifestyle to a new one that is willingly accepted and not seen as abandoning old loyalties.

Definition: __1__   Example: __2__

Score: Number correct (_____) × 10 = _____%

Enumerations

■ Mastery Test

Locate and number the enumerations in the selections that follow. Then, in the space beneath each selection, summarize briefly the points in the enumeration. Note that headings have already been provided for you.

1.   Credit cards can be divided into three basic groups. One type, the easiest to obtain, is the retail credit card. These are the cards issued by department stores, boutiques, and gasoline companies. Interest is charged on an unpaid balance, but the minimum payment required per month may vary; department stores usually require the highest monthly payments. Another type of credit card is the bank card, such as MasterCard or Visa. Overall, these credit corporations issue more cards than anyone else, but a card must be obtained from a local bank. Like retail cards, bank cards require a minimum monthly payment and charge about 18 percent interest annually on the balance. Some also charge an annual membership fee. These cards may be used in a wide variety of places for items from food to clothes to college tuition payments. A third type of card is that offered by American Express, Carte Blanche, and Diners' Club. Unlike the other types, these companies expect payment in full every month. They also charge a yearly membership fee to card owners. Such cards are usually the most difficult to obtain, since these companies look for more affluent customers capable of meeting all monthly charges.

Types of Credit Cards

(1) _Retail—e.g., department store card_

(2) _Bank—e.g., Visa_

(3) _Membership charge—e.g., American Express_

2.   As you might guess, pollutants do their greatest damage to the organs of the breathing system. There are several kinds of damage that can occur. The tubes and passages of the breathing system are lined with hairlike structures called cilia. The cilia are constantly moving back and forth; they function like a broom that sweeps out foreign material inhaled from the air. Some pollutants can slow down these cilia—or stop them altogether. This leaves the lungs with one of their protective devices out of order.

    Besides the cilia, the air passages and tubes are also lined with a sticky fluid called mucus, which traps particles that have been inhaled. Mucus production greatly increases when certain pollutants are inhaled. This is a defensive response by the body. Normally, the cilia would sweep out the mucus and much of the foreign matter. But when they do not function, the mucus builds up and narrows the tubes and air passages. Coughing results, and breathing is more difficult.

Pollutants can also cause muscle spasms in the tubes of the lungs. During the spasms, the muscle contracts and gets thicker. This narrows the passageway in the tubes and makes breathing more difficult. Along with the muscle spasms, the membranes inside the tubes may swell. This results in more narrowing of the tubes and more difficulty in breathing.

Ways That Pollutants Damage the Breathing System

(1) _Slow down or stop the cilia_

(2) _Build up mucus and narrow the tubes and air passages_

(3) _Cause muscle spasms in the tubes of the lungs_

3.   There are numerous advantages associated with franchising. One of the most important is the training and guidance given by the franchisor. One of the best-known training programs is that offered by McDonald's, which sends the owner to "Hamburger U." Here the individual learns how to make hamburgers, control inventory, keep records, handle human relations problems, and manage the unit.

Another advantage is the customer appeal associated with buying a well-known name. Many franchisors advertise on television and radio and have catchy jingles that attract customers to the unit. Just think of some you have heard during this past week from Pizza Hut, Holiday Inn, and Kentucky Fried Chicken.

A third advantage is that the franchise, assuming it is an established one, is a proven idea. There is no need to worry about whether people will like the food being sold or the auto service being provided. There are many other successful franchised units selling the same goods and services.

Finally, there is the financial assistance angle. Some bankers will not be willing to lend money to get a small business started but will change their mind when they find that it is a Dairy Queen franchise, a Holiday Inn, or a Jack-in-the-Box.

Advantages of Franchising

(1) _Training and guidance given by franchisor_

(2) _Customer appeal associated with well-known name_

(3) _A proven idea_

(4) _Financial assistance likely_

Score: Number correct (_____) × 10 = _____%

Headings and Subheadings

■ Mastery Test

Part 1: Answer the questions below about the selection that follows.

Questions: What is meant by *burnout?* What are the results of burnout?

"Burnout" in the Professions

While professional-level jobs provide prestige, a relatively high income, and other benefits, they are far from perfect. Boredom and alienation are associated with certain types of professional work. Poverty-program lawyers, physicians, prison personnel, social workers, clinical psychologists, psychiatric nurses, and other professionals who work extensively with human problems often feel unable to cope continually with distress. Eventually, they may see themselves as "burned out." Behavioral scientists have found that many handled "burned-out" feelings by distancing themselves from clients and treating suffering people in detached, dehumanizing ways. As emotions grew increasingly negative, these workers experienced severe tension-related problems, including alcoholism.

Answers: 1. Professionals who work extensively with human problems often feel unable to cope continually with distress.

2. Distancing from clients; tension-related problems that include alcoholism.

Part 2: Using words such as *what, why, who, which, in what ways,* and *how,* write two meaningful questions for each of the textbook heads that follow.

1. Emotional Problems in Childhood   a. What are common emotional problems in childhood?

   b. What are the causes of these problems?

2. Reconstruction in the South   a. When did Reconstruction begin?

   b. How long did it take?

3. Infectious Diseases   a. What are the infectious diseases?

   b. Which ones are most common?

4. Our Business System: Its Expansion and Regulation   a. How does our business system expand?

   b. How is it regulated?

   Note: Other questions are possible.

Part 3: Scrambled together in the list that follows are three textbook headings and three subheadings for each of the headings. Write the headings in the lettered blanks (A, B, C) and write the appropriate subheadings in the numbered blanks (1, 2, 3). Two items have already been inserted for you.

Paranoia	The Muscular System	Sherman's March
The Siege of Petersburg	Schizophrenia	Major Events of the Civil War
Cardiac Muscle	Behavior Disorders	Skeletal Muscle
The Battle of Gettysburg	Smooth Muscle	Psychosis

(order of subheads may vary.)

A. The Muscular System

   1. Cardiac Muscle

   2. Skeletal Muscle

   3. Smooth Muscle

B. Major Events of the Civil War

   1. The Siege of Petersburg

   2. The Battle of Gettysburg

   3. Sherman's March

C. Behavior Disorders

   1. Paranoia

   2. Schizophrenia

   3. Psychosis

Score: Number correct (_____) × 5 = _____%

Signal Words

■ **Mastery Test**

In the spaces provided, write the major signal words used in the following selections. The number and kinds of signal words that you should look for are shown at the start of each selection.

Selection 1: Two contrast signals; one cause-and-effect signal; one addition signal.

The elderly age segment is a growing market that presents many opportunities for marketers. Demand will continue to rise for health care and services, books, nursing homes, travel, retirement housing, and many leisure-time activities. But people in this age group do not like to be stereotyped, and marketers must be sensitive in communicating with them. Several years ago, the H. J. Heinz Company test-marketed a line of "Senior Foods"—lamb, beef, and chicken dishes in eight-ounce containers. The products were dropped six months later; the reason was that older people did not like to see their age reflected in the product's name. On the other hand, the marketing focus of Gerber Products Company does not inhibit older consumers from purchasing and consuming (for dietary reasons) an estimated 6 percent of its baby food. Also, a study conducted by Dannon Yogurt found that 25 percent of the company's sales were made to people over age fifty-five. Clearly, the elderly have unique needs that marketers must try to satisfy.

1. _But_____

2. _reason_____

3. _On the other hand____

4. _Also_____

Selection 2: One emphasis signal; one cause-and-effect signal; two addition signals; two contrast signals.

Speed-reading courses often claim that an increase in speed will mean an automatic increase in comprehension. But this claim is simply not true. With difficult material, understanding is likely to fall as rate rises. Speed-reading courses may increase the number of words your eyes take in and "read" per minute. In addition, comprehension may improve while you take such a course. The cause for this, however, is that you tend to concentrate more as you read faster. The best way to increase reading speed *and* comprehension is to develop reading comprehension skills. Speed will come as you learn how to identify main ideas and go quickly over lesser points and supporting details. Also, speed will come as you learn how to vary your reading rate according to the nature of the material and your purpose in reading.

5. But

6. In addition

7. cause

8. however

9. best

10. Also

Score: Number correct (_____) × 10 = _____%

Main Idea

■ Mastery Test

Locate and underline the main-idea sentence in each selection that follows. Then, in the spaces provided in the margin, put the number of each sentence you underlined.

_____1_____ 1.   [1]Violence surrounds us—not only in real life but in our entertainment. [2]Films emphasize it—as those who saw *The Godfather* and its sequels know. [3]In fact, violence is big at the box office. [4]A drive-in favorite was *The Texas Chainsaw Massacre,* which graphically portrayed a series of murders perpetrated by unemployed cattle butchers. [5]Indeed, the realism with which film violence is staged is ever increasing. [6]Improved techniques allow close-ups of realistically bruised and mutilated bodies. [7]Television, in both its news reports and its entertainment, provides a steady diet of violence. [8]Riots, uprisings, wars, terrorists' raids—all are a part of our daily lives in the evening news. [9]Even children's toys can encourage aggression.

_____2_____ 2.   [1]One of childhood's saddest figures is the child who is chosen last for every team, hangs around the fringes of every group, walks home alone after school, is not invited to any of the birthday parties, and sobs in despair, "Nobody wants to play with me." [2]There are many reasons why this child and other children can be unpopular. [3]Sometimes such children are withdrawn or rebellious. [4]They are often the youngsters who walk around with a "chip on the shoulder," showing unprovoked aggression and hostility. [5]Or they may act silly and babyish, "showing off" in immature ways. [6]Or they may be anxious and uncertain, exuding such a pathetic lack of confidence that they repel other children, who don't find them any fun to be with. [7]Extremely fat or unattractive children, children who behave in any way that seems strange to the others, and slow-learning youngsters are also outcasts.

_____2_____ 3.   [1]Companies are constantly changing the packaging that covers their products. [2]At times, however, the changes backfire and reduce rather than increase customers' satisfaction with the product in question. [3]One of the most successful packages has been the Camel cigarette pack, which shows a camel, two pyramids, and three palm trees. [4]An executive at R. J. Reynolds some years ago decided that the package would be more striking if the pyramids and trees were removed. [5]The surgery was performed, but the public howled. [6]Camel sales fell off instantly, and, not surprisingly, Reynolds quickly returned the camel's props.

_____11_____   4. ^{1}Colonial farmers in America grew all their own food, with the exception of certain imported luxury items, such as coffee, tea, and sugar. ^{2}Farm animals such as sheep, pigs, and cows provided milk and meat. ^{3}Clothing was made from plant and animal sources. ^{4}The flax plant's fibers were dyed with berry juices, spun into thread, woven into cloth, and sewn into shirts and dresses. ^{5}Sheep provided wool for heavier clothing, and the hides of pigs and cows were tanned into leather. ^{6}Leather could be cut and crafted into shoes, boots, gloves, shirts, and leggings; leather was also needed for harnesses, bridles, whips, and reins. ^{7}The abundant forests of a young America were filled with timber for houses and fuel. ^{8}Colonists chopped down trees and corded wood in order to cook and to heat their homes. ^{9}Only a few necessary items, such as glass and iron, were bought by the farmers. ^{10}Luxuries such as books, china, and lace were purchased when it was possible; they were by no means considered essential items. ^{11}This self-sufficiency, or ability to provide for themselves, was a characteristic of many early American settlers.

_____6_____   5. ^{1}A bottle of cologne on a department store counter catches your eye. ^{2}It is beautifully packaged in a handsome bottle and shiny box. ^{3}You check the price tag, which reads "$37.50," and walk away wondering how two ounces of cologne can be so expensive. ^{4}After all, cologne is made from only a few pennies' worth of alcohol and essential oils mixed with a good amount of water. ^{5}How can a department store charge so much for it? ^{6}The price on the cologne box reflects not only the cost of the raw materials but a variety of additional costs. ^{7}The department store is paying the salary of the salesperson behind the counter and the cost of the space needed to store the cologne inventory. ^{8}The department store also provides services such as charge accounts; the cost of each piece of merchandise is raised accordingly. ^{9}The manufacturer of the cologne may have spent more on its fancy bottle and box than on the fragrance itself. ^{10}The packaging caught your eye, as the manufacturer wanted, but you are going to pay for it. ^{11}You'll also pay for the advertising done by the nationally known cosmetics company and the cost of the transportation used to ship the cologne to the store. ^{12}And if the cologne was made in and shipped from France, the price goes up even more!

Score: Number correct (_____) × 20 = _____%

Outlining

■ Mastery Test

Part A: Read the selection below and then complete the outline that follows.

Stress is a factor in all our lives. Learning to deal with stress in a positive, intelligent way is essential to good health. One way to combat stress is to work it off in physical activities. Anything from jogging around the neighborhood to a workout on the dance floor can relieve stress and, surprisingly, give you more energy to cope with life. Stress can also be controlled by changing your mental attitude. Learn to accept things; fighting against the unavoidable or the inevitable is useless. Learn to take one thing at a time. Rather than trying to do everything at once, deal with more important problems first, and leave the rest to another day. Learn to take your mind off yourself. Since stress is self-centered, doing something for others helps reduce it. Finally, talking about stress is important. When events in your life seem overwhelming, talk about your troubles. This can be done informally, by opening up to your family. You can also set aside special time to confide in friends. When your emotional life is severely shaken, however, formal help may be needed. Seek out a psychologist who has been recommended to you by a reliable source. Alternatively, find a professional counselor who will assess your difficulties and help you deal with them.

Ways to Deal with Stress

A. Work it off in physical activities.

B. Change your mental attitude.

　　1. Learn to accept things.

　　2. Take one thing at a time.

　　3. Learn to take your mind off yourself.

C. Talk about stress and your troubles.

　　1. Informally

　　　　a. Family

　　　　b. Friends

　　2. Formally

　　　　a. Psychologist

　　　　b. Professional counselor

Part B: Read the selection below and then complete the diagram that follows.

Credit cards have both advantages and disadvantages, depending on how the credit-card holder chooses to use them. One of the benefits of credit cards, for example, is that they can be used to obtain interest-free loans for up to two months. By purchasing goods just after the close of one billing cycle, taking advantage of the grace period of twenty-five days or so for payment, and then paying the bill in full, you have borrowed the amount of your purchase with no interest fee. Another advantage of credit cards is that they are convenient. You can buy anywhere without the hassle of carrying large amounts of money or trying to use a personal check. Credit cards, however, do have disadvantages. Occasionally, billing mix-ups occur, and customers may be overcharged or charged for items they never purchased. The major problem presented by credit cards, though, is the fact that they tempt some consumers to overspend. Such people find it easy to charge items they would probably not purchase for cash; when the bills arrive, they have trouble making the payment. Or they find themselves trapped in a cycle of making minimum payments and thereby paying high finance charges on a never-shrinking balance.

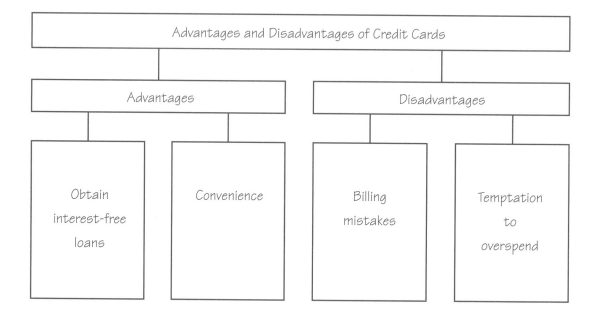

Advantages and Disadvantages of Credit Cards

Advantages

Disadvantages

Obtain interest-free loans

Convenience

Billing mistakes

Temptation to overspend

Score: Number correct (_____) × 5 = _____%

Summarizing

■ Mastery Test

Part A: Circle the letter of the title and then of the sentence that best summarizes each of the following three selections. Remember that the title and sentence should be as specific and descriptive as possible and at the same time account for all the material in the selection.

> Suppose a friend of yours has the habit of wearing absolutely atrocious clothes. You decide to go on a campaign to help reform his taste. How do you go about it? Your friend has just one outfit in which he looks great—but which he rarely wears. Every time he wears a shirt the same color as the one you like, you compliment him, and perhaps you also mention the shirt you're trying to "promote." After *that* shirt appears more frequently for a while, you "reinforce" only it—not the less attractive ones of the same color. At the same time, you try to suggest that your favorite shirt looks so good on him that he really should get more like it. And when he does, you compliment him on the new outfits. Gradually, you are "shaping his behavior," though you might not call it that.

1. Which would be an accurate title for this selection?
    a.   Helping a Friend
    (b) Shaping Behavior through Reinforcement
    c.   Differences in Taste
2. Which sentence best summarizes the selection?
    a.   If a friend wears atrocious clothing, you should try to improve his taste.
    (b) Through a careful program of compliments, you can shape someone's behavior.
    c.   When friends wear attractive clothing, you should compliment them.

Between 1862 and 1871, politics in New York City was controlled by a political machine called Tammany Hall, led by William Marcy Tweed. "Boss" Tweed and his henchmen bilked the city out of millions of dollars. They usually sold contracts for city work to corrupt companies. These companies would overcharge the city government for the job and "kick back" a fee to the political machine. Once, one of Tweed's friends billed the city for $179,729.60 for three tables and forty chairs. Of course, the Tweed Ring received a good share of that money. Gradually, the press began to take notice. Especially damaging to Tweed were the political cartoons by Thomas Nast. Nast drew cartoons showing Tweed and his men as vultures preying on the body of New York. Tweed's Ring eventually collapsed, and Tweed died in jail while awaiting trial.

3. Which would be an accurate title for this selection?
    a. Political Corruption
    b. Thomas Nast
    c. Boss Tweed and Tammany Hall
4. Which sentence best summarizes the selection?
    a. Tammany Hall, a corrupt nineteenth-century New York City political machine led by "Boss" Tweed, was defeated by the press.
    b. Tammany Hall was led by "Boss" Tweed, who cheated New York City out of millions of dollars.
    c. The cartoonist Thomas Nast depicted "Boss" Tweed and his men as vultures preying on the body of New York City.

The Leboyer method of childbirth seeks to protect a newborn's delicate senses from the shock of bright lights, harsh sounds, and rough handling. After the baby's head has begun to emerge, lights are dimmed and the delivery room is quieted. The baby is not held by the ankles and slapped to encourage the first breath; Leboyer states that since the fetus's spinal column has never been in a straight position, this kind of handling is a severe shock to the infant. Instead, the baby, with the umbilical cord still attached, is gently placed on the mother's abdomen until breathing begins naturally. At this point, the baby is rinsed in a tepid bath, rather than weighed on a cold scale. Babies born this way are usually relaxed and smiling, not tense and screaming. Some studies of Leboyer babies and standard-delivery babies have shown that Leboyer children are slightly more physically advanced and quicker to learn. Parents of Leboyer children, in general, saw the birth as a positive, exhilarating experience.

5. Which would be an accurate title for this selection?
    a. Types of Delivery Rooms
    b. A Baby's First Moments
    c. The Leboyer Method

6. Which sentence best summarizes the selection?

   a. The usual method of childbirth subjects newborns to bright lights, harsh sounds, and rough handling.

   b. In the Leboyer method of childbirth, a newborn's first breath is never encouraged by the common process of holding the infant by the ankles and slapping it.

   (c) The Leboyer method of childbirth, designed to protect a newborn's delicate senses from the shock of standard deliveries, has positive effects.

Part B: Circle the letter of the title that best summarizes each of the following two selections. Then write a one-sentence summary of each. If there is a summary sentence in a paragraph, you may use it; one paragraph has such a sentence.

> We are all familiar with a slogan spoken by a stern bear in a forest ranger's hat: "Only you can prevent forest fires!" For many years, an extensive advertising campaign has been conducted, using symbols like Smokey the Bear and Woodsy Owl, to warn the public about the dangers of forest fires. We are told that forest fires are ugly, destructive, and dangerous. However, despite the advertising campaigns, forest fires are actually beneficial to forest ecologies. First of all, they clear out underbrush and debris on the forest floor. The fire consumes this unnecessary material, and the larger, more resistant trees are spared. Without regular, small forest fires, the dry tinder of brush and fallen limbs on the forest floor builds to a high level. Then, if a fire starts, it will be intense enough to destroy every tree, large and small. Forest fires also eliminate undesirable species of trees that take root in the forest from wind-borne seeds. Some special forests are actually dependent on fire to exist. In New Jersey's Pine Barrens, seeds are liberated from tightly closed pine cones by the intense heat of a fire. The cones pop open as the fire passes, and a new generation of trees begins.

7. Which would be an accurate title for this selection?

   a. Advertising Campaigns and Forest Fires

   b. Dangers of Forest Fires

   (c) Benefits of Forest Fires

8. Summary sentence: _However, despite the advertising campaigns, forest fires are actually beneficial to forest ecologies._

The large, gleaming refrigerator is the focal point of most American kitchens. It holds enough food to last many days, and even for months in the freezer. It is cold enough to preserve that food well. It can provide ice cubes, ice chips, and ice water. Its advantages are clear. But that big refrigerator has its drawbacks as well. First of all, a large refrigerator encourages the hoarding of food and leads to obesity and other eating problems. Also, it has destroyed the pleasant custom, still common in Europe, of going to market each day. Picking out one's fresh produce daily while chatting with friends and neighbors is no longer a part of our lives. In addition, people's desire to buy huge amounts of groceries just a few times a month has encouraged the growth of supermarkets and destroyed local grocery stores. Other victims of the giant refrigerator have been small local farmers, who can't compete against the mega-producers favored by the supermarkets.

9. Which would be an accurate title for this selection?
   (a)   The Modern Refrigerator: Pluses and Minuses
   b.   The Advantages of the Modern Refrigerator
   c.   Victims of the Modern Refrigerator

10. Summary sentence: _The modern refrigerator has both advantages and_ _disadvantages._

Score: Number correct (_____) × 10 = _____%

Understanding Graphs and Tables

■ Mastery Test

1. Study the graph below, and then answer the questions about it.

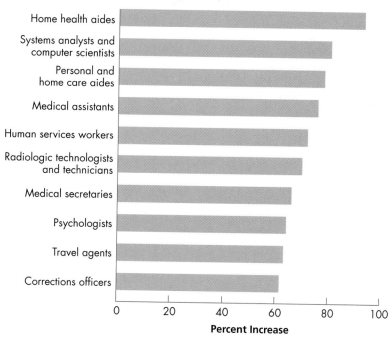

The Ten Fastest-Growing Occupations: 1990 to 2005

a. What is the purpose of this graph, and how many years does it cover?

To show the ten fastest-growing occupations from 1990 to 2005; 15 years

b. Of the professions listed, which one will grow the least?

Corrections officers

c. By approximately what percentage will human services workers grow?

75%

d. Which occupations are expected to increase by about 80 percent or more?

Home health aides, systems analysts and computer scientists, personal and home care aides

e. Which occupation will increase more, travel agents or medical assistants?
    Medical assistants

f. Approximately what is the difference in percentage points between the
    fastest- and the slowest-growing occupations? _30 percentage points_

2. Study the table below, and then answer the questions about it.

Divorce Rates for Selected Countries, 1960–1994

Country	Divorces per 1,000 Married Women				
	1960	**1970**	**1980**	**1990**	**1994**
United States	9.2	14.9	22.6	21	21
Canada	1.8	6.3	10.8	12.6	11
Germany	3.6	5.1	6.1	8	7
Japan	3.6	3.9	4.8	5	6
Sweden	5.0	6.8	11.4	11.4	12
United Kingdom	2.0	4.7	12.0	13	13

a. What is the purpose of this table? _To compare divorce rates in different_
    countries from 1960 to 1994

b. Which country on the table has consistently had the greatest number of
    divorces? _United States_

c. What has been the trend for divorce rates in the United States between
    1980 and 1994, and what was the total percentage change between those
    years? _They decreased by 1.6 percentage points._

d. In which country did the divorce rate change the least over the years
    shown? _Japan_

Score: Number correct (_____) × 10 = _____%

Skim Reading

■ **Mastery Test**

Take five minutes to skim-read the following selection and to take notes on it. Then see if you can answer the questions that follow by referring to your notes but *not* referring back to the text.

The Hospice Program
Objectives of the Hospice Program

The hospice program is a fairly new method of caring for the dying. While there is no solid definition of *hospice,* it is generally considered a program with two objectives. The first objective is to keep patients free from pain on a continuous basis. The second objective is to provide the dying with a home-like atmosphere in which to spend their final days.

How Hospices Reach Their Goals

Hospices reach their goals through one of several approaches. Some hospices work on an outpatient basis and thus have no physical facility from which to work. Outpatient hospices depend on team efforts of professionals from several institutions. An outpatient team could consist of a member of the clergy, social workers, nurses, doctors, and psychologists. A second approach some hospices have adopted is to work on an inpatient basis, using a building that is set up to have a homelike atmosphere. These buildings include some sort of sleeping quarters, eating facilities, and lounges or some other recreational area. In these inpatient facilities, the patients decide when to eat, sleep, and relax. Still other hospices use a combination of inpatient and outpatient services. Services are provided in the home when possible and in the hospice facility when necessary.

How Hospices Differ from Other Health Care Facilities

Even if a hospice operates only on an inpatient basis, it still differs from hospitals and nursing homes. Hospices differ from other health care facilities in four major ways. First, there is a lack of scheduling and structure in hospices. For one thing, there are no time schedules (with the exception of medication schedules) forced on hospice patients. This means open-ended visiting hours, mealtimes, bedtimes, and so on. Patients can adjust more easily to their condition if they are allowed to live by their own life patterns in the "no-schedule" atmosphere. Lack of structure means something else too: no restrictions on diet or activity. If a patient wants to have a favorite dessert at every meal or if a visitor brings a patient a special snack, the patient is allowed to have the food. If patients desire to try a strenuous activity one day and the activity tires them out so much that they must spend the next day in bed, so be it. The patient's schedule is what he or she wants it to be.

Another aspect of hospices that differs from other care facilities is that the facility personnel concentrate solely on the patient and don't become involved in side activities such as research and teaching. Patients' psychological needs, for example, are a main concern to hospice personnel. If a patient needs to talk over his or her feelings with someone in the middle of the night, personnel are there to listen. Personnel have time to be with patients because they have no other duties to distract or detain them.

View of pain control is another aspect of hospice care that sets it apart from care in hospitals and other facilities. In traditional health care institutions, patients may be expected to bear pain until it is unbearable. In hospices, patients are given medication as often as necessary to keep pain from surfacing at all.

Finally, unlike the philosophy of most health care facilities, the hospice theme includes the patient's family in the care cycle. Family needs are mainly psychological. Hospices provide the family members with counseling to help them accept the eventual death of their relative. Once the family member has died, hospices also provide the family with bereavement follow-up services.

Questions about the Selection

What are the two objectives of the hospice program?

1. _Keep patients free from pain on a continuous basis_

2. _Provide the dying with a homelike atmosphere in which to spend their final days_

What are three ways that hospices reach their goals?

3. _Outpatient basis_

4. _Inpatient basis_

5. _Combination of outpatient and inpatient services_

What are three ways that hospices differ from other health care facilities?

6. _Lack of scheduling and structure in hospices_

7. _Facility personnel concentrate on patient; don't become involved in research and teaching._

8. _Patients are given medication as often as necessary to keep pain from surfacing._

Also correct: Patient's family is included in care cycle.

Score: Number correct (_____) × 12.5 = _____%

Rapid Reading Passage

■ Mastery Test

Read this selection as rapidly as you can without sacrificing comprehension. Then record your time in the space provided and answer the comprehension questions that follow.

America's Detention Camps

John is a junior college English teacher. When he was three years old, the United States government sent him, and his family, to a detention camp. Howard, a newspaper publisher, spent eight months imprisoned with his wife and children in a one-room tarpaper shack. He had committed no crime; his imprisonment was legal. Jeanne, an author, was sent to a prison camp when she was seven. She spent three years there and now says: "All I knew was that we were in camp, behind barbed wire. Everything had fallen apart. No more Christmas, Thanksgiving."

John, Howard, and Jeanne had all been in America; neither they nor their families had committed, been tried for, or been convicted of a crime. They were imprisoned in "internment camps" simply because their parents or grandparents (or even great-grandparents) had come to America from Japan. They had Japanese faces.

In December 1941, the Japanese attacked Pearl Harbor and destroyed America's Pacific fleet. The rallying cry in America was "Remember Pearl Harbor!" and the country was plunged into a wave of anti-Japanese sentiment. On February 19, 1942, President Franklin Roosevelt signed Executive Order 9066. It allowed the military to move Japanese American civilians to ten relocation camps, stretching from California to Arkansas. Most Japanese Americans lived on the West Coast, and the government acted on fears that they would become saboteurs and spies for Japan.

Eventually, almost 110,000 civilians, over two-thirds of whom were American citizens, were forced to move. Laws were passed penalizing those who disobeyed military orders. Indeed, the Supreme Court ruled that the confinement of these people, based only on race, was legal; the Court also upheld rulings on curfews and travel restrictions for Japanese Americans.

Many of those who were interned left families, prosperous businesses, farms, and personal possessions behind. The resettlement was swift; money was lost in the shuffle or confiscated by the government. One California bank, in 1942, estimated the loss by Japanese Americans at $400 million. Japanese American homes were searched without warrants, and workers were fired for no reason.

The Japanese, of course, were not America's only enemies in World War II; we also fought Germans and Italians. However, none of these immigrants or their children received the treatment that the Japanese did. They were not interned or taken to "safe" locations. Strong racial prejudice against the Japanese seemed to be at work. Earl Warren (later to become Chief Justice of the United States Supreme Court) was then attorney general of California. Even Warren, who became known as a strong fighter for civil liberties, appeared to show racial bias. In 1942, he said: "We believe that when we are dealing with the Caucasian race we have methods that will test the loyalty of them . . . but when we deal with the Japanese we are in an entirely different field and we cannot form any opinion that we believe to be sound."

During the war, second-generation Japanese Americans (called Nisei) were eventually allowed to join the army; they made up a special unit, the 442nd Regimental Combat Team, that fought in the European theater, especially the Italian campaign. Many of these men came out of internment camps to fight for the country they loved, the country that had so wronged them. The Nisei won more decorations than any regiment in history and suffered an extremely high casualty rate. Senator Daniel Inouye, who served on the Watergate investigation committee, is a Nisei who lost an arm in the war.

When the war ended, the Japanese Americans were released. They went back to their homes and attempted to pick up the pieces of their lives. The Evacuation Claims Act of 1948 was to compensate them for their economic losses, but it returned only $38 million to the internees—less than 10 percent of the estimated losses.

How do Japanese Americans feel about this treatment now? One, an army sergeant, says:

> I was born in [a camp] in 1944. Living quarters were small, and they never had enough blankets. . . . The guns around the camp were always pointed into the camp, not outward. . . . My folks say they want to forget this ever happened. They lost a lot of relatives who went to Europe with the 442nd Combat Team.

Some Japanese Americans feel that a financial repayment is called for. Others feel that money is no longer important, but justice is. Since their rights were violated, since they were denied the privileges of citizens, they want an apology. One woman says: "It is the gesture, the recognition, the honor that is restored. It is the symbolic gesture of the government standing up and saying it was wrong." Since no other immigrant group has ever been singled out for such harsh and unfair treatment, this seems to be the least our government could do.

Time: _____   *Reading Rate (see page 536):* _____ *WPM*

Reading Comprehension

1. *True or false?* __F__ Japanese Americans were not allowed to fight in World War II.

2. On February 19, 1942, President Franklin Roosevelt signed Executive Order 9066, which

   a. imposed curfews.

   b. imposed travel restrictions.

   (c.) allowed the military to move Japanese Americans.

   d. confiscated the property of Japanese Americans.

3. Two-thirds of the interned Japanese Americans were

   (a.) American citizens.

   b. farm owners.

   c. from the West Coast.

   d. homeowners.

4. Economic losses of Japanese Americans were estimated at

   a. $20 million.

   b. $40 million.

   c. $200 million.

   (d.) $400 million.

5. The word *Nisei* means

   (a.) second-generation Japanese Americans.

   b. a Japanese American combat regiment.

   c. a Japanese American senator.

   d. an internment camp.

6. The Evacuation Claims Act of 1948

   a. fully restored all financial losses.

   (b.) partially restored financial losses.

   c. declared that Japanese Americans should be interned.

   d. was signed by President Roosevelt.

7. The main idea in the selection is that

   a. Japanese Americans are bitter about their treatment.

   (b.) the government's action against the Japanese was unfair and unjust.

   c. Germans and Italians should have received the same treatment as the Japanese did.

   d. Americans were hysterical during the war.

8. The government feared the Japanese Americans would
   a.   hide their money.
   b.   defect to Japan.
   c.   join the armed services.
   (d) spy for Japan.

9. The 442nd Regimental Combat Team
   a.   fought in the Pacific theater.
   (b) won more decorations than any other regiment.
   c.   had a low casualty rate.
   d.   fought the internment policy.

10. The writer suggests that Japanese Americans
   a.   were reasonably compensated for their losses.
   b.   wish to forget the detention camps.
   (c) deserve an official apology.
   d.   lacked patriotism during the war.

Score: Number correct (_____) × 10 = _____%

Part Eight

Additional Learning Skills

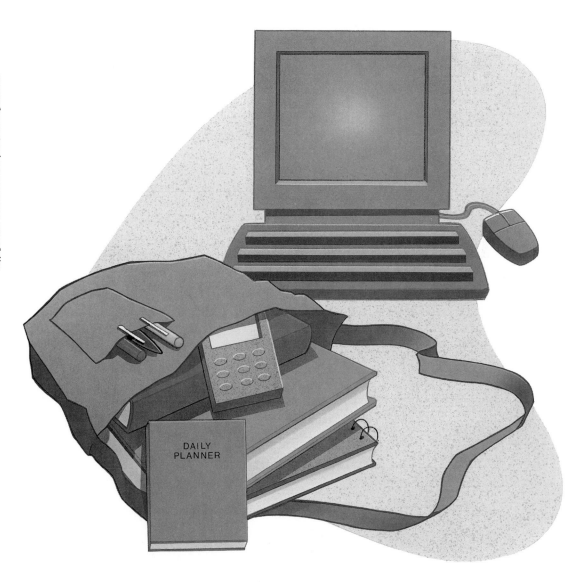

Preview

Part Eight takes up some extra learning skills that will help you get more out of your studies. In "Studying Mathematics and Science," you'll find tips that will help you deal more effectively with math and science courses. A related chapter is "Reading Literature and Making Inferences," which provides some guidelines that will better equip you to read literary works. Next, "Reading for Pleasure: A List of Interesting Books" offers short descriptions of a number of widely admired books that will give you reading practice and may provide you with some of the most pleasurable and illuminating experiences of your life. Finally, "Writing Effectively" is a brief guide that shows you how to write effective paragraphs and essays, describes relationships between writing and reading, and provides some writing assignments.

Studying Mathematics and Science

For many people, mathematics and science courses are terrifying. There are several very understandable reasons for this feeling. Many of us, first of all, come to class weak in the basics we need to know to handle such courses. A college mathematics or biology instructor, for example, may expect students to know how to handle fractions, decimals, proportions, and simple algebra. Some of the students, in contrast, have forgotten (or never learned) these skills. Without this kind of foundation, the work in the class starts out on a difficult level indeed.

Another reason students dread these courses is that there is no way to pass them without doing a great deal of hard work. Mathematics and science courses *demand* excellent attendance, complete notes, extensive homework, and intensive study sessions. Students looking for courses they can just "slide by" in are naturally wary of mathematics and science. But other students—ones who need chemistry or calculus, for example, to become medical technicians, nurses, or computer programmers—are willing to work hard; the problem is that they don't know how to deal with such courses. Their note-taking and study skills just don't seem adequate for mathematics and science.

Doing well in mathematics and science courses *is* possible. But you must be aware of the adjustments you should make when you switch to mathematics and science from your less technical subjects. The pointers that follow will help you gain control over these subjects.

- *In mathematics and science, knowledge is cumulative.* The learning that you do in mathematics and science courses is cumulative—each fact or formula you learn must rest on a basic structure of all you have learned before. You have to begin with the essentials and build your knowledge in a methodical, complete way. For this reason, *absences from class or weaknesses that are never corrected can be academically fatal.* You will not understand a simple algebra equation, for example, if you are not sure what a "variable" is. It is essential to stay current in such courses and to attack your weak points early. If you don't understand something, ask your instructor for help or visit the tutoring center. Every day you wait makes it more likely that you will do poorly in the course.

- *In mathematics and science, great emphasis is placed on specialized vocabulary, rules, and formulas.* Mathematics and science deal in precision. Everything has a specific name, and every problem can be solved with specific rules and formulas. In a way, this quality makes such courses easier because there is little fuzziness involved and few individual interpretations are required. If you know the vocabulary and have the rules down pat, you should do well.

    An important study technique for mathematics and science is the use of flash cards. These are three- by five-inch index cards that help you memorize and test yourself on terms and formulas. On one side of the card, write the term, rule, or formula you need to know (for instance, "photosynthesis," "Bohr's energy law," or "formula for weight density"). On the other side, write the information that you must memorize. Flash cards enable you to study the material conveniently and to discover quickly what you know and what exactly you are unsure of.

- *In mathematics and science, special emphasis is placed on homework.* In many mathematics and science classes, you will be given numerical problems to solve outside class. Often, these problems will not be checked by the instructor; their purpose is to give you practice in the kinds of material you will find on tests. Many students do a hurried job on—or skip completely—any work that is not graded. If you are not conscientious about this homework, however, you will be panicky before tests and unprepared for what is on them. If you want to pass your mathematics and science classes, you *must* take the responsibility for much of the necessary learning yourself by doing the problems and asking questions in class about problems that puzzle you.

- *Taking clear notes in class is crucial.* In your class notes for mathematics and science, you will often be copying problems, diagrams, formulas, and definitions from the blackboard. In addition, you will be trying to follow your instructor's train of thought as he or she explains how a problem is solved or how a process works. Such classes obviously demand intense concentration. As you copy material from the board, be sure to include in your notes any information the instructor gives that can help you see the *connections between steps or the relationship of one fact to another.* For example, if an instructor is explaining and diagramming human blood circulation patterns, you should copy the diagram; you should also be sure you have definitions ("alveoli," "aorta") and any important connecting information ("blood moves from artery to capillaries").

As soon as possible after a mathematics or science class, you should clarify and expand your notes while the material is still fresh in your mind.

- *Mathematics and science require patient, slow reading.* The information in mathematics and science tests is often densely packed; texts are filled with special terms that are often unfamiliar; blocks of text are interspersed with numerical formulas, problems to solve, charts, diagrams, and drawings. Such textbooks cannot be read quickly; for this reason, you have to keep up with the assigned reading. It is impossible to read and understand fifty pages—even ten pages— the night before a test.

    The good news about mathematics and science textbooks is that they are usually organized very clearly. They also have glossaries of terms and concise reviews at the ends of chapters. When you are reading mathematics and science books, proceed slowly. Do not skip over any unfamiliar terms; check the index or the glossary in the back of the book for the definition. With mathematics textbooks, spend time going over each sample problem. After you have gone over the sample, you might want to write out the problem on a piece of paper and then see if you remember how to solve it. With science textbooks, be sure to study the visual material that accompanies the written explanations. Study each chart or diagram until you understand it. Being able to visualize such material can be crucial when you are asked to reproduce it or write an essay on it during an exam.

    You can succeed in mathematics and science classes if you are organized, persistent, and willing to work. When passing these courses is necessary to achieve your goals, the effort must be made.

Studying a Math Excerpt

Following are the first two pages of a popular college math textbook, *Intermediate Algebra* (McGraw-Hill), by James Streeter, Donald Hutchison, and Louis Hoelzle. Read the text and study the terms and examples in the box. You will be learning the names of properties of addition patterns.

Next, work your way carefully through Example 1, which is a sample practice. To find the answers, compare each item with the examples and explanations in the box. Don't look at an answer in the Solution until you have honestly tried to state the property that applies. (Covering up the answers with a piece of paper will help keep you honest.)

Once you understand the items in Example 1, go on to do Activity 1.

Properties of the Real Numbers

OBJECTIVE
To recognize and apply the properties of the real numbers

Algebra is a system consisting of a set, together with operations that follow certain properties. The set of real numbers is the set we use most often. In this section, we discuss the properties of the operations of addition and multiplication on the set of real numbers.

For the most part, you will find that these properties are familiar from your past experience in working with numbers. As just one example, you know that

$3 + 5 = 8$

But it is also true that

$5 + 3 = 8$

Your experience tells you that the *order* in which two numbers are added does not matter. This fact is called the *commutative property of addition* and is one of the properties we consider in this section. Let's proceed now with the formal statement of these properties.

PROPERTIES OF ADDITION ON REAL NUMBERS

For any real numbers *a*, *b*, and *c*:

CLOSURE PROPERTY

$a + b$ is a real number

In words, the sum of any two real numbers is always a real number.

COMMUTATIVE PROPERTY

$a + b = b + a$

In words, the *order* in which two numbers are added does not affect the sum.

ASSOCIATIVE PROPERTY

$a + (b + c) = (a + b) + c$

In words, the *grouping* of numbers in addition does not affect the sum.

> **ADDITIVE IDENTITY**
> There exists a unique real number 0 such that
>
> $$a + 0 = 0 + a = a$$
>
> In words, 0 is the additive identity. No number loses its identity after addition with 0.
>
> **ADDITIVE INVERSE**
> There exists a unique real number $-a$ such that
>
> $$a + (-a) = (-a) + a = 0$$
>
> In words, $-a$ is the *additive inverse* of a. The sum of a number and its additive inverse is 0.

The additive inverse is also called the opposite of a.

The $\boxed{+/-}$ key on your calculator is an additive-inverse key. Pushing this key gives you the opposite of the number in the display.

Our first example illustrates the use of the properties introduced above.

Example 1

State the property used to justify each statement.

(a) $2 + (4 + 5) = (2 + 4) + 5$
(b) $-8 + 0 = -8$
(c) $(-8) + 5$ is a real number.
(d) $b + (-b) = 0$
(e) $62 + 8 = 8 + 62$

Solution

(a) Associative property of addition   The *grouping* has been changed.
(b) Additive identity
(c) Closure property of addition
(d) Additive inverse
(e) Commutative property of addition   The *order* has been changed.

CHECK YOURSELF 1

State the property (or properties) used to justify each statement.

1. $2x + y = y + 2x$
2. $3n + 0 = 3n$
3. $2x + (3x + 4y) = (2x + 3x) + 4y$
4. $7 + (-10)$ is a real number.
5. $5n + [7 + (-7)] = 5n + 0 = 5n$

Activity 1

State the property (or properties) used to justify each statement. Then read the explanations that follow.

The Property of Addition That Justifies Each Statement

(1) $2x + y = y + 2x$ _____

(2) $3n + 0 = 3n$ _____

(3) $2x + (3x + 4y) = (2x + 3x) + 4y$ _____

(4) $7 + (-10)$ is a real number. _____

(5) $5n + [7 + (-7)] = 5n + 0 = 5n$ _____

Following is an explanation of each item.

1. Note that in the equation in item (1), *the order of the numbers changes.* Checking the box above, we see that this change in order matches the definition and pattern of the commutative property. So that is the answer for this item.

2. In this equation, $3n$ does not lose its identity after addition with 0—the sum is the same: $3n$. So the answer to this item must be the additive identity. The definition for that property says, "No number loses its identity after addition with 0."

3. Note that this item contains *a change in number groupings.* The pattern and definition in the box that match and justify this equation are for the associative property.

4. The statement "$7 + (-10)$ is a real number" means that the sum of two real numbers—7 and (-10)—is another real number. This statement matches the definition and pattern given for the closure property.

5. *Two* properties justify this equation. First, it shows that adding 7 to -7 equals 0. That part of the equation is justified by the property of additive inverse: "The sum of a number and its additive inverse is 0." The sum of 7 and its additive inverse, -7, is 0.

   The last part of this equation, "$5n + 0 = 5n$," is justified by the property of additive identity: "No number loses its identity after addition with 0." When $5n$ is added to 0, it keeps its identity—the sum is $5n$.

Activity 2

Here is another opportunity to practice using the five properties of addition on real numbers. Feel free to refer to the patterns and definitions in the box on pages 602–603 if necessary. Again, state the property used to justify each statement.

The Property of Addition That Justifies Each Statement

(1) $5n + (-5n) = 0$ Additive inverse

(2) $-3 + 0 = -3$ Additive identity

(3) $5y + x = x + 5y$ Commutative property

(4) $(-1) + 2$ is a real number.   Closure property

(5) $7 + (2a + 4) = (4 + 7) + 2a$ Associative property

Studying a Science Passage

This activity will help you see how well you can actually do in science with careful study techniques. Below are guidelines and questions to help you use the PRWR method (explained in full on pages 97–105) to study a passage about immunity from the college textbook *Life and Health* (McGraw-Hill), by Marvin R. Levey, Mark Dignam, and Janet H. Shirreffs. Work your way through each of the four steps of the activity. Afterward, you can test your understanding of the material by taking a quiz.

Activity

Step 1. *Preview:* Answer the following questions about the reading below by previewing it: Check the title, read the first paragraph, and look at the headings and highlighted words.

1. The title tells you that the selection is about immunity

   _____

2. How many boldfaced terms are there to learn in the reading? eight

Immunity

Immunity is a group of mechanisms that help protect the body against specific diseases. Immunity is the body's most efficient disease-preventing weapon; it can help fight either a viral infection or a bacterial one.

The Role of Lymphocytes

In the immune mechanism, white blood cells become involved in fighting infection. The protective white blood cells are of a type known as **lymphocytes,** including two key subtypes: B and T lymphocytes.

B lymphocytes, or B cells, are believed to originate in the bone marrow (hence the letter B). When foreign or invading pathogens (disease-causing agents) are present in the body, these cells help produce substances called immunoglobulins, or **antibodies.** Antibodies react specifically to the parts of a pathogen that link up to human cells and cause damage. These parts, which are called **antigens,** are thus neutralized. If the invaders are viruses, the antibodies lock on to their antigens and prevent them from entering the target cells. If the invaders are bacteria, the antibodies lock on to them and cause them to clump together, making it easier for certain white blood cells to engulf and digest them. These bacterial-antibody clumps also activate certain bactericidal (bacteria-killing) substances in the blood. Antibodies can also lock on to bacterial toxins to make them less harmful to the body.

T lymphocytes, or T cells, named for their origin in the thymus gland, fight infection in three major ways. First, some T lymphocytes hasten the activity of those white cells that surround and eat foreign substances. Second, some help stimulate the production of antibodies by B lymphocytes. Third, some can attack foreign cells (such as cells in tissues that have been transplanted), cells that have been killed by viruses, and possibly cancer cells.

Natural Immunity

When an invading antigen enters the body, it stimulates the body to produce certain antibodies that can inactivate it. When antigens lock on to specific receptor sites on a body cell's plasma membrane, the immune response is set in motion and antibodies are produced. Antibodies work only on the specific antigens that trigger them: Measles antibodies work only on the measles virus, mumps antibodies on the mumps virus, and so on. There are over a million different specific antibodies, each capable of fighting one antigen. That means that over a million different foreign antigens can stimulate the immune system to take action.

Acquired Immunity

In the past, having a disease was the only way to develop immunity to it (natural immunity through the development of antibodies to fight the current infection and subsequent ones). Today, however, immunity may be induced artificially by means of **vaccines,** which consist of killed or weakened viruses, taken orally or by injection. Several days or weeks after an individual receives a vaccination, the body starts to produce specific antibodies, which circulate in the bloodstream, ready to attack the initiating antigen.

People who contract a disease or receive a vaccine for it usually develop **active immunity.** But what happens if a person is exposed to a serious disease and it is too dangerous to wait for the person's body to produce its own antibodies? In this instance a physician may confer **passive immunity** by giving the person antibodies from another person or an animal. These antibodies are found in certain proteins in the donor's blood that are collectively called **gamma globulin.** Gamma globulin is used to confer passive immunity against infectious hepatitis and other diseases for which an effective vaccine has not been devised.

In general, active immunity is long-term and in some cases lifelong, whereas passive immunity generally lasts only a few weeks or months. Babies have passive immunity at birth because antibodies that pass through the placental membrane become part of the fetus's immune system. Within six weeks after birth, however, passive immunity begins to weaken, and the baby will need to receive vaccinations to start the development of active immunity against certain diseases.

Step 2. Read: Read the passage straight through. As you do, mark the text, using symbols such as those shown on page 100. For example, in the first paragraph, underline the words that follow *immunity,* which explain what that word means, and in the section titled "The Role of Lymphocytes," number the two key subtypes of lymphocytes.

Read as slowly as necessary to understand the material, and don't be discouraged by new terms. You will feel more comfortable with new words as you clarify their meanings to yourself.

Step 3. *Write:* Complete the following notes on the selection.

Immunity—*a group of mechanisms that help protect the body against*
specific diseases

The Role of Lymphocytes

    Lymphocytes—Certain protective white blood cells

    Two kinds of lymphocytes and their functions:

1. B cells (believed to come from <u>b</u>one marrow) produce antibodies

    Antibodies—Substances that react to and fight antigens

    Antigens—*the parts of a pathogen that link up to human cells and*
cause damage

Pathogens—Disease-causing agents

—Ways that antibodies fight the two kinds of pathogens:

    (1) Viruses— *antibodies lock on to their antigens and prevent them from entering cells*

    (2) Bacteria—antibodies lock on to bacteria and clump them together for white blood cells to eat up

        —Can also activate bacteria-killer in blood and make bacterial toxins less harmful

2. T cells (from thymus gland) fight infection in three major ways:

    (1) Spur certain white blood cells to eat foreign substances faster

    (2) Help stimulate production of antibodies by B cells

    (3) *Attack foreign cells, cells killed by viruses, and possibly cancer cells*

Natural Immunity

Natural immunity—Antigens lock on to sites on cell's membrane, producing antibodies, which work only on specific antigens that trigger them

    Ex— *Measles antibodies work only on measles virus*

Acquired Immunity

Acquired immunity—Immunity that is brought about artificially

    1. Vaccines— *killed or weakened viruses that make body produce specific antibodies to attack antigens*

    2. Passive immunity (versus active immunity, gained through illness or vaccine)—Gained from donor antibodies in gamma globulin

        Gamma globulin—a collection of certain proteins in donor blood

        —Lasts only a few weeks or months (versus active immunity, which is long-term or lifelong)

        Ex— *Babies must receive vaccinations after passive immunity starts to weaken*

Step 4. *Recite:* Review your notes by reciting to yourself. Use "recall words" to help you: Write words and phrases in the margins of your notes, and turn them into questions that will help you study your notes. Your instructor may wish to have pairs of students spend some time reciting to each other as well. He or she may also ask you to create and use flash cards to help you remember new terms in the reading.

Study Check: By the time you finish studying your notes, you should know the following:

- The meanings of and key information on all the boldfaced words.
- The two types of lymphocytes and their functions.
- What the process of natural immunity is.
- What the two types of acquired immunity are.
- The differences between active immunity and passive immunity.

■ Quiz on the Science Passage

Part A: Write each of the following terms in the blank by its definition.

antigens   gamma globulin   lymphocytes   vaccines

_____lymphocytes_____ 1. White blood cells that fight infections in various ways.

_____vaccines_____ 2. Substances made up of weakened or killed viruses used to stimulate immunity.

_____gamma globulin_____ 3. A collection of proteins in donor blood used to provide immunization against some diseases.

_____antigens_____ 4. Parts of pathogens that link up to human cells and cause damage.

Part B: Circle the letter of your answer choice for each of the following questions.

5. B cells are a type of
   a. antibody.
   b. antigen.
   c. lymphocyte.
6. __T__ *True or false?* Antibodies fight disease-causing agents that enter the body and link up to cells.
7. Natural immunity is provided by
   a. vaccines.
   b. antibodies.
   c. donor blood.

8. Acquired immunity is provided by
   a. vaccines.
   b. gamma globulin.
   (c) both of the above.

9. Active immunity comes from
   a. contracting a disease.
   b. receiving a vaccine.
   (c) both of the above.

10. A baby is born with
   a. active immunity.
   (b) passive immunity.
   c. both of the above.

Reading Literature and Making Inferences

The comprehension skills you've learned in this book apply to everything you read. But to get the most out of literature, you also need to be aware of several important elements that shape fiction. And you need to know how to make inferences. Following, then, are a few guidelines to help you understand fiction more fully.

Key Elements in Literature

Important elements in a work of literature are theme, plot, setting, characters, conflict, climax, narrator, and figures of speech:

- Look for the *theme,* or the overall idea, that the author is advancing. This is the very general idea that is behind the author's entire effort and unifies the work. For example, the theme in much of Katherine Anne Porter's writing is that separateness and misunderstanding are fundamental facts of the human condition.

- Make sure you understand the *plot*—the series of events that take place within the work. For instance, the plot of Philip Roth's short novel *Goodbye, Columbus* is that boy meets girl, they fall in love, and then—because of different values—they fall out of love.

- Observe the *setting,* that is, the time and place of the plot. The setting of *The Adventures of Huckleberry Finn,* by Mark Twain, for instance, is nineteenth-century America.

- Examine the *characters*—the people in the story. Each character will have his or her own unique qualities, behaviors, needs, and values.

611

- Be alert for the main *conflict* of a story. The conflict is the main struggle of the plot. It may be within a character, between two or more characters, or between one or more characters and some force in the environment. For example, the conflict in *Moby-Dick* is between the hunter Captain Ahab and the animal he hunts—a white whale (the Moby-Dick of the title).

- Watch for the *climax,* the final main turning point of a story. The main conflict of a story is usually solved or explained in a final way at this point in the plot. For example, the climax of Shirley Jackson's story "The Lottery" comes when a woman's neighbors surround her and stone her to death.

- Be aware of the *speaker,* or *narrator,* who tells the story and the *tone* of that speaker. Both strongly influence the character of a work. The speaker is not the author but the fictional voice the author uses to narrate the story. In Mark Twain's *Huckleberry Finn,* for instance, the speaker is the title character, not the author. The tone is the style or manner of a piece. It reflects the speaker's attitude and is strongly related to the author's attitude and purpose as well.

- Note *figures of speech,* expressions in which words are used to mean something other than they usually do. These expressions are often comparisons that make a special point. Examples of figures of speech are "I wandered lonely as a cloud" (William Wordsworth), "my love is like a red, red rose" (Robert Burns), and "the slings and arrows of outrageous fortune" (William Shakespeare).

Making Inferences in Literature

To get the most out of reading literature, it is very important to make *inferences.* In other words, you must "read between the lines" and come to conclusions on the basis of the given information. While writers of factual material often directly *state* what they mean, writers of fiction often *show* what they mean. It is then up to the reader to infer the point of what the writer has said. For instance, a nonfiction author might write, "Harriet was angry at George." But the novelist might write, "Harriet's eyes narrowed when George spoke to her. She cut him off in mid-sentence with the words, 'I don't have time to argue with you.'" The author has *shown* us the anger with specific details rather than simply stating its existence abstractly. The reader must observe the details about Harriet and George and infer that she is angry.

The following pages will give you practice in drawing inferences from three kinds of literary material: a poem, a biography, and a novel. In each case, read the literary piece presented and then answer the inference questions that follow.

A Poem

Nowhere is inference more important than in reading poetry. Poetry, by its nature, implies much of its meaning. Implications are often made through figures of speech. For practice, read the poem below. Note that definitions of the more difficult words are provided at the beginning.

When I Was One-and-Twenty
A. E. Housman (1859–1936)

■ Words to Watch

crowns, pounds, guineas: forms of English money

fancy: desire

in vain: with little consequence

rue: sorrow, or regret

> When I was one-and-twenty
> I heard a wise man say,
> "Give crowns and pounds and guineas
> But not your heart away;
> Give pearls away and rubies
> But keep your fancy free."
> But I was one-and-twenty,
> No use to talk to me.
>
> When I was one-and-twenty
> I heard him say again,
> "The heart out of the bosom
> Was never given in vain;
> 'Tis paid with sighs a-plenty
> And sold for endless rue."
> And I am two-and-twenty,
> And oh, 'tis true, 'tis true.

Activity

Answer each question by circling the inference most solidly based on "When I Was One-and-Twenty."

1. To "give . . . your heart away" is a figure of speech meaning
   - (a) to fall in love.
   - b. to be dishonest.
   - c. to become ill.
2. To "keep your fancy free" is a figure of speech meaning
   - a. don't charge others for your company.
   - b. don't be rich.
   - (c) don't desire only one person.
3. The wise man's advice was:
   - a. It's best to be poor.
   - (b) It's less costly to give riches away than to fall in love.
   - c. An expensive romance is never harmful.
4. When the speaker says, "But I was one-and-twenty,/No use to talk to me," the meaning is that he or she
   - a. welcomed the wise man's advice.
   - b. understood the wise man's advice.
   - (c) ignored the wise man's advice.
5. When he or she accepted the wise man's advice, the speaker
   - a. was twenty-one.
   - b. had just fallen in love for the first time.
   - (c) was twenty-two and had experienced a disappointing romance.

Following is an explanation of each item:

1. "To give . . . your heart away" is a fairly common figure of speech, and so you probably knew right away that it means to fall in love. The answer to this item is *a*.
2. Since *fancy* means "desire," "keep your fancy free" must mean to keep your desire free—of attachments. Thus the answer to this question is *c*—"don't desire only one person."
3. "Crowns and pounds and guineas," "pearls," and "rubies" all represent riches. Thus the wise man's advice was *b*—"It's less costly to give riches away than to fall in love."

4. Since it was "no use" for the wise man to talk to the speaker when he or she was twenty-one, we can infer that at that age, the speaker ignored the wise man's advice. Thus the answer to this question is *c*.

5. At first, the speaker didn't accept the wise man's advice, so we must infer that something happened between the ages of twenty-one and twenty-two to make him or her think differently. From the emotional end of the poem—"And oh, 'tis true, 'tis true"—we can infer that the speaker had an unhappy romance. The answer to this item is thus *c*.

An Excerpt from a Biography

Below is the passage that starts the literary autobiography *Growing Up* by the *New York Times's* columnist Russell Baker. Inference skills will be helpful in understanding the speaker, the characters, and the setting.

> At the age of eighty my mother had her last bad fall, and after that her mind wandered free through time. Some days she went to weddings and funerals that had taken place half a century earlier. On others she presided over family dinners cooked on Sunday afternoons for children who were now gray with age. Through all this she lay in bed but moved across time, traveling among the dead decades with a speed and ease beyond the gift of physical science.
>
> "Where's Russell?" she asked one day when I came to visit at the nursing home.
>
> "I'm Russell," I said.
>
> She gazed at this improbably overgrown figure out of an inconceivable future and promptly dismissed it.
>
> "Russell's only this big," she said, holding her hand, palm down, two feet from the floor. That day she was a young country wife with chickens in the backyard and a view of hazy blue Virginia mountains behind the apple orchard, and I was a stranger old enough to be her father.
>
> Early one morning she phoned me in New York. "Are you coming to my funeral today?" she asked.
>
> It was an awkward question with which to be awakened. "What are you talking about, for God's sake?" was the best reply I could manage.
>
> "I'm being buried today," she declared briskly, as though announcing an important social event.
>
> "I'll phone you back," I said and hung up, and when I did phone back she was all right, although she wasn't all right, of course, and we all knew she wasn't.
>
> She had always been a small woman—short, light-boned, delicately structured—but now, under the white hospital sheet, she was becoming tiny.

I thought of a doll with huge, fierce eyes. There had always been a fierceness in her. It showed in that angry, challenging thrust of the chin when she issued an opinion, and a great one she had always been for issuing opinions.

"I tell people exactly what's on my mind," she had been fond of boasting. "I tell them what I think, whether they like it or not." Often they had not liked it. She could be sarcastic to people in whom she detected evidence of the ignoramus or the fool.

"It's not always good policy to tell people exactly what's on your mind," I used to caution her.

"If they don't like it, that's too bad," was her customary reply, "because that's the way I am."

And so she was. A formidable woman. Determined to speak her mind, determined to have her way, determined to bend those who opposed her. In that time when I had known her best, my mother had hurled herself at life with chin thrust forward, eyes blazing, and an energy that made her seem always on the run.

She ran after squawking chickens, an ax in her hand, determined on a beheading that would put dinner in the pot. She ran when she made the beds, ran when she set the table. One Thanksgiving she burned herself badly when, running up from the cellar oven with the ceremonial turkey, she tripped on the stairs and tumbled back down, ending at the bottom in the debris of giblets, hot gravy, and battered turkey. Life was combat, and victory was not to the lazy, the timid, the slugabed, the drugstore cowboy, the libertine, the mushmouth afraid to tell people exactly what was on his mind whether people liked it or not. She ran.

Activity

Now put a check by the six inferences most solidly based on the words and images in the passage. Refer to the passage as needed when making your choices.

_____   1. Baker's mother knew she was remembering past events.

___✓___   2. Baker's mother thought she was actually living at the time of some memories.

___✓___   3. The author's mother's last bad fall must have affected her mind.

_____   4. Baker's mother predicted the day of her own funeral.

___✓___   5. Once she imagined that her funeral would take place that day.

___✓___   6. In describing the incident in which his mother said, "I'm being buried today," Baker uses the term "all right" with two different meanings.

_____   7. Baker's mother had been a calm woman with a patient, encouraging manner.

_____ ✓ _____   8. She was an energetic, blunt person.

_____   9. Baker chose to describe his mother more sentimentally than realistically.

_____ ✓ _____   10. His mother's travels "among the dead decades" caused Baker himself to remember earlier days.

Here are explanations for each of the ten inferences.

1 and 2. Because Baker's mother expected the real Russell to be only two feet high, we know that she was unaware of where she was and that she was mentally experiencing earlier times in her life. Thus, inference 1 is not well supported, but inference 2 is solidly based on the given details.

3. The first sentence of the passage connects Baker's mother's fall with her mind wandering "free through time." Therefore, the details of the passage also support inference 3.

4 and 5. Baker doesn't state that his mother's funeral took place on the day she said it would. This tells us that she did not predict the day of her funeral, but that she only imagined it was about to happen. You thus should have checked 5, but not 4.

6. Since the two uses of the term "all right" seem contradictory ("she was all right, although she wasn't all right"), we can assume that Baker intends them to have different meanings. Thus, the statement is a well-supported inference.

In writing "when I did phone back she was all right," Baker refers to his mother having overcome the false belief that she was being buried that day. But when he states "she wasn't all right, of course, and we all knew she wasn't," Baker refers to his mother's generally poor physical and mental condition, which she had not overcome.

7 and 8. The author's description of his mother as someone who had been "always on the run" tells us she was more energetic than calm. And because he describes her as someone with "fierceness in her" who "always told people exactly what was on her mind," sometimes sarcastically, we can conclude that she was more blunt than patient and encouraging. Thus, inference 7 is not well supported, but inference 8 is.

9. This inference is not supported by the passage. In discussing a senile parent, some writers might be tempted to dwell on their warmest, sweetest memories. Since Baker describes his mother as a blunt and impatient person who was often disliked, we can conclude that he has avoided sentimentality.

10. This inference is strongly based on the details of the passage. Baker remembers, for instance, how determined and energetic a person his mother was, running after chickens with an ax and once tumbling down the basement stairs after running up with the Thanksgiving turkey.

An Excerpt from a Novel

Now apply your inference skills to the beginning of Philip Roth's short novel *Goodbye, Columbus.*

From *Goodbye, Columbus*
Philip Roth

The first time I saw Brenda she asked me to hold her glasses. Then she stepped out to the edge of the diving board and looked foggily into the pool; it could have been drained, myopic Brenda would never have known it. She dove beautifully, and a moment later she was swimming back to the side of the pool, her head of short-clipped auburn hair held up, straight ahead of her, as though it were a rose on a long stem. She glided to the edge and then was beside me. "Thank you," she said, her eyes watery though not from the water. She extended a hand for her glasses but did not put them on until she turned and headed away. I watched her move off. Her hands suddenly appeared behind her. She caught the bottom of her suit between thumb and index finger and flicked what flesh had been showing back where it belonged. My blood jumped.

That night, before dinner, I called her.

"Who are you calling?" my Aunt Gladys asked.

"Some girl I met today."

"Doris introduced you?"

"Doris wouldn't introduce me to the guy who drains the pool, Aunt Gladys."

"Don't criticize all the time. A cousin's a cousin. How did you meet her?"

"I didn't really meet her. I saw her."

"Who is she?"

"Her last name is Patimkin."

"Patimkin I don't know," Aunt Gladys said, as if she knew anybody who belonged to the Green Lane Country Club. "You're going to call her you don't know her?"

"Yes," I explained. "I'll introduce myself."

"Casanova," she said, and went back to preparing my uncle's dinner. None of us ate together: My Aunt Gladys ate at five o'clock, my cousin Susan at five-thirty, me at six, and my uncle at six-thirty. There is nothing to explain this beyond the fact that my aunt is crazy.

"Where's the suburban phone book?" I asked after pulling out all the books tucked under the telephone table.

"What?"

"The suburban phone book. I want to call Short Hills."

"That skinny book? What, I gotta clutter my house with that, I never use it?"

"Where is it?"

"Under the dresser where the leg came off."

"For God's sake," I said.

"Call information better. You'll go yanking around there, you'll mess up my drawers. Don't bother me, you see your uncle'll be home soon. I haven't even fed *you* yet."

"Aunt Gladys, suppose tonight we all eat together. It's hot, it'll be easier for you."

"Sure, I should serve four different meals at once. You eat pot roast, Susan with the cottage cheese, Max has steak. Friday night is his steak night, I wouldn't deny him. And I'm having a little cold chicken. I should jump up and down twenty different times? What am I, a workhorse?"

"Why don't we all have steak, or cold chicken—"

"Twenty years I'm running a house. Go call your girlfriend."

Activity

Now answer each question by circling the inference most solidly based on the material in the excerpt.

1. The narrator of the story is
   a. Aunt Gladys.
   b. Aunt Gladys's nephew.
   c. Philip Roth.
2. The setting of the story is
   a. colonial America.
   b. nineteenth-century America.
   c. twentieth-century America.
3. The figure of speech comparing Brenda's hair to "a rose on a long stem" reflects
   a. the narrator's concern with flowers.
   b. the narrator's admiration of Brenda.
   c. Brenda's occupation.
4. We know that Brenda is
   a. a good swimmer.
   b. a lifeguard.
   c. both of the above.

5. *True or false?* __T__ Aunt Gladys's nephew probably wants to call Brenda to ask her out on a date.

6. Aunt Gladys's ideas

   (a)   about dating are old-fashioned.

   b.   make perfect sense to her nephew.

   c.   both of the above.

7. Brenda lives

   a.   in the city.

   (b)   in the suburbs.

   c.   at the country club.

8. We can assume that Doris

   a.   is related to the narrator.

   b.   is disliked by the narrator.

   (c)   both of the above.

9. We can assume that Aunt Gladys

   a.   belongs to the Green Lane Country Club.

   (b)   has never met Brenda Patimkin.

   c.   both of the above.

10. We can assume that the members of Aunt Gladys's family

   a.   dislike each other.

   (b)   have different tastes in foods.

   c.   have different working hours and so cannot eat together.

Reading for Pleasure:
A List of Interesting Books

On the following pages are short descriptions of some books that might interest you. Some are popular books of the last few years; some are among the most widely read "classics"—books that have survived for generations because they deal with basic human experiences that all people can understand and share.

Autobiographies and Other Nonfiction

I Know Why the Caged Bird Sings, Maya Angelou

> The author writes with love, humor, and honesty about her childhood and what it is like to grow up black and female.

Alicia: My Story, Alicia Appleman-Jurman

> Alicia was a Jewish girl living with her family in Poland when the Germans invaded in 1941. Her utterly compelling and heartbreaking story shows some of the best and worst of which human beings are capable.

Growing Up, Russell Baker

> A giant presence in his life, Russell Baker's mother also insisted that he make something of himself. In his autobiography, the prizewinning journalist shows that he did with an engrossing account of his own family and growing up.

In Cold Blood, Truman Capote

> A frightening true story about the murder of a family, the book is also an examination of what made their killers tick. Many books today tell gripping stories of real-life crimes. *In Cold Blood* was the first book of this type and may still be the best.

Sleepers, Lorenzo Carcaterra

> The author of this autobiography tells of the shocking abuse he suffered while in a detention home for boys and of the elaborate revenge that he and his friends later exacted against the guards. The book becomes impossible to put down, and anyone who reads it is unlikely to ever forget it.

Gifted Hands, Ben Carson, M.D.

> This is the inspiring story of an inner-city kid with poor grades and little motivation who turned his life around. Dr. Carson is now a world-famous neurosurgeon at one of the best hospitals in the world; his book tells how he got to where he is today. In *Think Big* and *The Big Picture,* two related books, Dr. Carson tells more of his story and presents the philosophy that helped him make the most of his life.

Move On, Linda Ellerbee

> A well-known television journalist writes about the ups and downs of her life, including her stay at the Betty Ford Center for treatment of her alcoholism.

The Diary of a Young Girl, Anne Frank

> To escape the Nazi death camps, Anne Frank and her family hid for years in an attic. Her journal tells a story of love, fear, and courage.

Man's Search for Meaning, Viktor Frankl

> How do people go on when they have been stripped of everything, including human dignity? In this short but moving book, the author describes his time in a concentration camp and what he learned there about survival.

The Story of My Life, Helen Keller

> How Miss Keller, a blind and deaf girl who lived in isolation and frustration, discovered a path to learning and knowledge.

Angela's Ashes, Frank McCourt

> The most popular nonfiction book published in recent years, this book tells the story of an Irish boy whose father was a drunkard and whose mother tried desperately to hold her family together. The poverty described is heartbreaking, and yet the book is wonderfully moving and often funny. You'll shake your head in disbelief at all the hardship, and at other times you'll laugh out loud at the comic touches.

The Autobiography of Malcolm X, Malcolm X and Alex Haley

> Malcolm X, the controversial black leader who was assassinated by one of his followers, writes about the experiences that drove him to a leadership role in the Black Muslims.

Makes Me Wanna Holler, Nathan McCall

A dramatic first-person account of how a bright young black man went terribly wrong—and was lured into a life of crime. McCall, now a reporter for the *Washington Post,* eventually found a basis for self-respect different from that of his peers, who are murdered, commit suicide, become drug zombies, or wind up in prison.

A Hole in the World, Richard Rhodes

Little more than a year old when his mother killed herself, Rhodes has ever since been conscious of "a hole in the world" where his mother's love should have been. In this true and terrifying account of his boyhood, he describes how he managed to survive.

Down These Mean Streets, Piri Thomas

Life in a Puerto Rican ghetto is shown vividly and with understanding by one who experienced it.

Fiction

Watership Down, Richard Adams

A wonderfully entertaining adventure story about rabbits who act a great deal like people. The plot may sound unlikely, but it will keep you on the edge of your seat.

Patriot Games, Tom Clancy

In a story of thrills and suspense, an agent for the United States government helps stop an act of terrorism. The terrorists then plot revenge on the agent and his family.

The Cradle Will Fall, Mary Higgins Clark

A country prosecutor uncovers evidence that a famous doctor is killing women, not realizing that she herself is becoming his next target. One typical comment by a reviewer about Clark's books is that they are "a ticket to ride the roller coaster. . . . Once on the track, we're there until the ride is over."

Note: If you like novels with terror and suspense, many of Mary Higgins Clark's books are good choices.

And Justice for One, John Clarkson

In this adventure-thriller, a former Secret Service agent seeks revenge after his brother is almost killed and a woman friend is kidnapped. Because of corruption in the police force, the agent must take the law into his own hands.

Deliverance, James Dickey

A group of men go rafting down a wild Georgia river and encounter beauty, violence, and self-knowledge.

Eye of the Needle, Ken Follett

A thriller about a Nazi spy—"The Needle"—and a woman who is the only person who can stop him.

Lord of the Flies, William Golding

Could a group of children, none older than twelve, survive by themselves on a tropical island in the midst of World War Three? In this modern classic, Golding shows us that the real danger is not the war outside but "the beast" within each of us.

Snow Falling on Cedars, David Guterson

This is a unique murder mystery. The story is set in the 1950s in an island community where a fisherman is found dead on his boat and another fisherman is quickly blamed for the death. The accused man is so proud that he refuses to defend himself for a crime he says he did not commit. Like all great stories, it is about more than itself. It becomes a celebration of the mystery of the human heart.

The Silence of the Lambs, Thomas Harris

A psychotic killer is on the loose. To find him, the FBI must rely on clues provided by an evil genius. Like some other books on this list, this was made into a movie that is not as good as the book.

Flowers for Algernon, Daniel Keyes

A scientific experiment turns a retarded man into a genius. But the results are a mixture of joy and heartbreak.

The Shining, Stephen King

A haunted hotel, a little boy with extrasensory perception, and an insane father—they're all together in a horror tale of isolation and insanity. One review says, "Be prepared to be scared out of your mind. . . . Don't read this book when you are home alone. If you dare—once you get past a certain point, there's no stopping."

Note: If you like novels of terror and suspense, many of Stephen King's books are good choices.

Watchers, Dean Koontz

An incredibly suspenseful story about two dogs that undergo lab experiments. One dog becomes a monster programmed to kill, and it seeks to track down a couple who know its secret.

Note: If you like novels with a great deal of action and suspense, many of Dean Koontz's books are good choices.

To Kill a Mockingbird, Harper Lee

A controversial trial, involving a black man accused of raping a white woman, is the centerpiece of this story about adolescence, bigotry, and justice. One review describes the book as "A novel of great sweetness, humor, compassion, and of mystery carefully sustained."

The Natural, Bernard Malamud

An aging player makes a comeback that stuns the baseball world.

Waiting to Exhale, Terry McMillan

Four thirty-something black women all hope that Mr. Right will appear, but this doesn't stop them from living their lives. One reviewer writes that McMillan "has such a wonderful ear for story and dialogue. She gives us four women with raw, honest emotions that breathe off the page."

Gone with the Wind, Margaret Mitchell

The characters and places in this book—Scarlett O'Hara, Rhett Butler, Tara—have become part of our culture because they are unforgettable.

A Day No Pigs Would Die, Robert Peck

A boy raises a pig that is intelligent and affectionate. Will the boy follow orders and send the animal off to be slaughtered? Read this short novel to find out.

Harry Potter and the Sorcerer's Stone, J. K. Rowling

The first in a series of award-winning stories that have captured the hearts of young and old alike, around the world. These funny, action-packed, touching books are about a likable boy who is mistreated by the relatives who take him in after his parents are killed. Then Harry discovers that he is a wizard, and his extraordinary adventures begin.

The Catcher in the Rye, J. D. Salinger

The frustrations and turmoil of being an adolescent have never been captured so well as in this book. The main character, Holden Caulfield, is honest, funny, affectionate, obnoxious, and tormented at the same time.

The Lord of the Rings, J. R. R. Tolkien

Enter an amazing world of little creatures known as Hobbits; you, like thousands of other readers, may never want to leave.

Charlotte's Web, E. B. White

This best-loved story, for children and adults, is about a little pig named Wilbur and his best friend, a spider named Charlotte. Wilbur is being fattened in order to be killed for a holiday meal; Charlotte must come up with a plan to save him.

Classics

Middlemarch, George Eliot

A long book that is likely to be one of the peak reading experiences of your life. Eliot writes with extraordinary insight and compassion about the problems that all human beings face in seeing themselves clearly and in coping with the difficulties of their lives.

The Scarlet Letter, Nathaniel Hawthorne

A compelling story, set in the days of the Puritans, about a young woman, her illegitimate baby, and the scarlet badge she wears as her punishment.

Moby-Dick, Herman Melville

Two of the most famous characters in fiction—mad Captain Ahab and Moby-Dick, the white whale—battle it out as hunter and hunted.

The Adventures of Huckleberry Finn, Mark Twain

A rich book filled with wit, understanding, moral insight, and very human characters—definitely *not* for children only. Many people argue that either this or *Moby-Dick* is the greatest American novel.

Writing
Effectively

This section of the book shows you how to write effective paragraphs and essays, describes the relationships between writing and reading, and provides some writing assignments.

What Is a Paragraph?

A *paragraph* is a series of sentences about one main idea, or *point*. A paragraph typically starts with a point, and the rest of the paragraph provides specific details to support and develop that point.

Consider the following paragraph, written by a student named Gary Callahan.

Returning to School

Starting college at the age of twenty-nine was not easy for me. For one thing, I did not have much support from my parents and friends. My father asked, "Didn't you get dumped on enough in high school? Why go back for more?" My mother worried, "Where's the money going to come from?" My friends seemed threatened. "Hey, there's the college man," they would say when I approached. Another reason that starting college was difficult was that I had bad memories of school. I had spent years of my life sitting in classrooms completely bored, watching clocks tick ever so slowly toward the final bell. When I was not bored, I was afraid of being embarrassed. Once a teacher called on me and then said, "Ah, forget it, Callahan," when he realized I did not know the answer. Finally, I soon learned that college would give me little time with my family. After work every day, I have just an hour and ten minutes to eat and spend time with my wife and daughter before going off to class. When I get back, my daughter is in bed, and my wife and I have only a little time together. Then the time on weekends goes by quickly, with all the homework I have to do. But I am going to persist because I believe a better life awaits me with a college degree.

The above paragraph, like many effective paragraphs, starts by stating a main idea, or point. In this case, the point is that starting college at age twenty-nine was not easy. A point is a general idea that contains an opinion.

In our everyday lives, we continually make points about all kinds of matters. We express such opinions as "That was a terrible movie" or "My psychology instructor is the best teacher I have ever had" or "My sister is a generous person" or "Eating at that restaurant was a mistake" or "That team should win the playoff game" or "Waitressing is the worst job I ever had" or "Our state should allow the death penalty" or "Cigarette smoking should be banned everywhere." In *talking* to people, we don't always give the reasons for our opinions. But in *writing,* we *must* provide reasons to support our ideas. Only by supplying solid evidence for any point that we make can we communicate effectively with readers.

An effective paragraph, then, not only must make a point but must support it with *specific evidence*—reasons, examples, and other details. Such specifics help prove to readers that the point is reasonable. Even if readers do not agree with the writer, at least they have in front of them the evidence on which the writer has based his or her opinion. Readers are like a jury: they want to see the evidence so that they can make their own judgments.

What Are the Goals of Effective Writing?

Now that you have considered an effective student paragraph, it is time to look at four goals of effective writing:

Goal 1: Make a Point.

It is often best to state your point in the first sentence of your paper, just as Gary did in his paragraph about returning to school. The sentence that expresses the main idea, or point, of a paragraph is called the *topic sentence.*

Goal 2: Support the Point.

To support your point, you need to provide specific reasons, examples, and other details that explain and develop it. The more precise and particular your supporting details are, the better your readers can "see," "hear," and "feel" them.

Goal 3: Organize the Support.

You will find it helpful to learn two common ways of organizing the support in a paragraph—listing order and time order. In "Recognizing Signal Words" on page 391, you learned about signal words, also known as *transitions,* that increase the effectiveness of each method.

Listing Order: The writer organizes the supporting evidence in a paper by providing a list of two or more reasons, examples, or details. Often the most important or interesting item is saved for last because the reader is most likely to remember the last thing read.

Transition words that show a listing order include the following:

one	second	also	next	last of all
for one thing	third	another	moreover	finally
first of all	next	in addition	furthermore	

The paragraph about starting college uses a listing order: It lists three reasons why starting college at twenty-nine is not easy, and each of those three reasons is introduced by one of the above transitions. In the spaces below, write in the three transitions:

_____   _____   _____

The first reason in the paragraph about starting college is introduced with *For one thing,* the second reason by *Another,* and the third reason by *Finally.*

Time Order: Supporting details are presented in the order in which they occurred. *First* this happened; *next* this; *after* that, this; and so on. Many paragraphs, especially ones that tell stories or give a series of directions, are organized in a time order.

Transition words that show time relationships include the following:

first	before	after	when	then
next	during	now	while	until
as	soon	later	often	finally

Read the paragraph below, which is organized in a time order. See if you can underline the six transition words that show the time relationships.

Della had a sad experience while driving home last night. She traveled along the dark, winding road that led toward her home. She was only two miles from her house when she noticed a glimmer of light in the road. The next thing she knew, she heard a sickening thud and realized she had struck an animal. The light, she realized, had been its eyes reflected in her car's headlights. Della stopped the car and ran back to see what she had hit. It was a handsome cocker spaniel, with blond fur and long ears. As she bent over the still form, she realized there was nothing to be done. The dog was dead. Della searched the dog for a collar and tags. There was nothing. Before leaving, she walked to several nearby houses, asking if anyone knew who owned the dog. No one did. Finally Della gave up and drove on. She was sad to leave someone's pet lying there alone.

The main point of the paragraph is stated in its first sentence: "Della had a sad experience while driving home last night." The support for this point is all the details of Della's experience. Those details are presented in the order in which they occurred. The time relationships are highlighted by these transitions: *while, when, next, as, before,* and *finally.*

Goal 4: Write Error-Free Sentences.

If you use correct spelling and follow the rules for grammar, punctuation, and usage, your sentences will be clear and well-written. But by no means must you have all that information in your head. Even the best writers need to use reference materials to be sure their writing is correct. So when you write your papers, keep a good dictionary and grammar handbook nearby.

In general, however, do not refer to them until you have placed your ideas firmly down in writing. As you will learn on the pages ahead, there will be time enough to make the needed corrections.

How Do You Reach the Goals of Effective Writing?

Even professional writers do not sit down and automatically, in one draft, write a paper. Instead, they have to work on it a step at a time. Writing a paper is a process that can be divided into the following steps:

Step 1: Getting Started through Prewriting

Step 2: Preparing a Scratch Outline

Step 3: Writing the First Draft

Step 4: Revising

Step 5: Proofreading

These steps are described on the following pages.

Step 1: Getting Started through Prewriting

What you need to learn first are strategies for working on a paper. These strategies will help you do the thinking needed to figure out both the point you want to make and the support you have for that point.

There are several *prewriting strategies*—ones that you use before writing the first draft of your paper.

- *Freewriting* is just sitting down and writing whatever comes into your mind about a topic. Do this for ten minutes or so. Write without stopping and without worrying in the slightest about spelling, grammar, or the like. Simply get down on paper all the information about the topic that occurs to you.

- *Questioning* means that you think about your topic by writing down a series of questions and answers about it. Your questions can start with words like *what, when, where, why,* and *how.*

- *Clustering* (also known as *diagramming* or *mapping;* see pages 412–413) is another strategy that can be used to generate material for a paper. It is helpful for people who like to do their thinking in a visual way. In clustering, you begin by stating your subject in a few words in the center of a blank sheet of paper. Then, as ideas come to you, put them in ovals, boxes, or circles around the subject, and draw lines to connect them to the subject. Put minor ideas or details in smaller boxes or circles, and use connecting lines to show how they relate as well. Keep in mind that there is no right or wrong way of clustering. It is a way to think on paper about how various ideas and details relate to one another.

- In *list making,* a strategy also known as *brainstorming,* you make a list of ideas and details that could go into your paper. Simply pile these items up, one after another, without worrying about putting them in any special order. Try to accumulate as many details as you can think of.

    It is natural for a number of such extra or unrelated details to appear as part of the prewriting process. The goal of prewriting is to get a lot of information down on paper. You can then add to, shape, and subtract from your raw material as you take your paper through the series of writing drafts.

Important Notes about Prewriting Strategies: Some writers may use only one of the prewriting strategies. Others may use bits and pieces of all four. Any one strategy can lead to another. Freewriting may lead to questioning or clustering, which may then lead to a list. Or a writer may start with a list and then use freewriting or questioning to develop items on the list. During this early stage of the writing process, as you do your thinking on paper, anything goes. You should not expect a straight-line progression from the beginning to the end of your paper. Instead, there probably will be a continual moving back and forth as you work to discover your point and just how you will develop it.

Finally, remember that you are not ready to begin writing a paper until you know your main point and many of the details that can be used to support it. Don't rush through prewriting. It's better to spend more time on this stage than to waste time writing a paragraph for which you have no solid point and too little interesting support.

Step 2: Preparing a Scratch Outline

A *scratch outline* is a brief plan for the paragraph. It shows at a glance the point of the paragraph and the main support for that point. It is the logical framework upon which the paper is built.

This rough outline often follows freewriting, questioning, clustering, or list making. Or it may gradually emerge in the midst of these strategies. In fact, trying to outline is a good way to see if you need to do more prewriting. If a solid outline does not emerge, then you know you need to do more prewriting to clarify your main point or its support. Once you have a workable outline, you may realize, for instance, that you want to do more list making to develop one of the supporting details in the outline.

Below is the scratch outline that Gary Callahan, after doing a good deal of preliminary writing, prepared for his paragraph on returning to school:

Example of a Scratch Outline

Starting college at age twenty-nine isn't easy.
1. Little support from parents and friends.
2. Bad memories of high school.
3. Not enough time to spend with family.

This helpful outline, with its clear point and solid support, became the foundation of Gary's paragraph.

Step 3: Writing the First Draft

When you do a first draft, be prepared to put in additional thoughts and details that didn't emerge in your prewriting activity. And don't worry if you hit a snag. Just leave a blank space or add a comment such as "Do later" and press on to finish the paper. Also, don't worry yet about grammar, punctuation, or spelling. You don't want to take time correcting words or sentences that you may decide to remove later. Instead, make it your goal to develop the content of your paper with plenty of specific details.

Step 4: Revising

Revising is as much a stage in the writing process as prewriting, outlining, and doing the first draft. *Revising* means that you rewrite a paper, building upon what has been done to make it stronger and better. One writer has said about revising, "It's like cleaning house—getting rid of all the junk and putting things in the right order." A typical revision means writing at least one or two more drafts.

Step 5: Proofreading

Proofreading, the final stage in the writing process, means checking a paper carefully for spelling, grammar, punctuation, and other errors. You are ready for this stage when you are satisfied with your choice of supporting details, the order in which they are presented, and the way they and your topic sentence are worded.

Use a grammar handbook to be sure about your grammar, punctuation, and usage. Also, read through the paper carefully, looking for typing errors, omitted words, and any other errors you may have missed before. Such proofreading is often hard to do—students have spent so much time with their work, or so little, that they want to avoid proofing. But done carefully, this important final step will ensure that your paper looks as good as possible.

Hints for Proofreading

1   One helpful trick at this stage is to read your paper out loud. You will probably hear awkward wordings and become aware of spots where the punctuation needs to be improved. Make the changes needed for your sentences to read smoothly and clearly.

2   Another helpful technique is to take a sheet of paper and cover your paragraph so that you can expose and check carefully just one line at a time.

3   A third strategy is to read your paper backward, from the last sentence to the first. Doing so helps keep you from getting caught up in the flow of the paper and missing small mistakes, which is easy to do, since you're so familiar with what you meant to say.

What Is an Essay?

An essay does the same thing a paragraph does: It starts with a point, and the rest of the essay provides specific details to support and develop that point. However, while a paragraph is a series of *sentences* about one main idea or point, an *essay* is a series of *paragraphs* about one main idea or point—called the *central idea* of the essay. Since an essay is much longer than one paragraph, it allows a writer to develop a topic in more detail. Despite the greater length of an essay, the process of writing it is the same as that for writing a paragraph: prewriting, preparing a scratch outline, writing and revising drafts, and proofreading.

Here are the major differences between a paragraph and an essay:

Paragraph	Essay
Made up of sentences.	Made up of paragraphs.
Starts with a sentence containing the main point of the paragraph (*topic sentence*).	Starts with an introductory paragraph containing the central idea of the essay, expressed in a sentence called the *thesis statement* (or *thesis sentence*).
Body of paragraph contains specific details that support and develop the topic sentence.	Body of essay contains paragraphs that support and develop the central idea. Each of these paragraphs has its own main supporting point, stated in a topic sentence.
Paragraph often ends with a closing sentence that rounds it off.	Essay ends with a concluding paragraph that rounds it off.

Later in his writing course, the student Gary Callahan was asked to expand his paragraph into an essay. Here is the essay that resulted:

For a typical college freshman, entering college is a fun and exciting time of life. It is a time not just to explore new ideas in classes but to lounge out on the grass chatting with new friends, to sit having soda and pizza in the cafeteria, or to listen to music and play cards in the student lounge. I see the crowds of eighteen-year-olds enjoying all that college has to offer, and I sometimes envy their freedom. Instead of being a typical freshman, I am twenty-nine years old, and beginning college has been a difficult experience for me. I have had to deal with a lack of support, bad memories of past school experiences, and too little time for my family.

Few people in my life are supportive of my decision to enter college. My father is especially bewildered by the choice I have made. He himself quit school after finishing eighth grade, and he assumes that I should hate school as much as he did. "Didn't you get dumped on enough in high school?" he asks me. "Why go back for more?" My mother is a little more understanding of my desire for an education, but the cost of college terrifies her. She has always believed that college was a privilege only the rich could afford. "Where in the world will all that money come from?" she says. And my friends seem threatened by my decision. They make fun of me, suggesting that I'm going to think I'm too good to hang around with the likes of them. "Ooooh, here comes the college man," they say when they see me approach. "We'd better watch our grammar."

I have had to deal not only with family and friends but also with unhappy memories of my earlier school career. I attended an enormous high school where I was just one more faceless kid in the crowd. My classes seemed meaningless to me. I can remember almost none of them in any detail. What I do remember about high school was just sitting, bored until I felt nearly brain-dead, watching the clock hands move ever so slowly toward dismissal time. Such periods of boredom were occasionally interrupted by moments of acute embarrassment. Once an algebra teacher called on me and then said, "Oh, forget it, Callahan," in a disgusted tone when he realized I didn't know the answer. My response, of course, was to shrink down in my chair and try to become invisible for the rest of the semester.

Furthermore, my decision to enter college has meant I have much less time to spend with my family. I work eight hours a day. Then I rush home and have all of an hour and ten minutes to eat dinner and spend time with my wife and daughter before I rush off again, this time to class. When I return from class, I am dead tired. My little girl is already asleep. My wife and I have only a little time to talk together before I collapse into bed. Weekends are a little better, but not much. That's when I try to get my papers written and catch up on a few chores around the house. My wife tries to be understanding, but it's hard on her to have so little support from me these days. And I'm missing out on a lot of special times in my daughter's life. For instance, I didn't realize she had begun to walk until three days after it happened.

So why do I put myself and my family through all these difficulties? Sometimes I'm not sure myself. But then I look at my little girl sleeping, and I think about the kind of life I am going to be able to give her. My college degree may make it possible for me to get a job that is more rewarding, both financially and emotionally. I believe I will be a better provider for my family, as well as a more well-rounded human being. I hope that the rewards of a college degree will eventually outweigh the problems I am experiencing now.

What Are the Parts of an Essay?

When Gary decided to expand his paragraph into an essay, he knew he would need to write an introductory paragraph, several supporting paragraphs, and a concluding paragraph.

Each of these parts of the essay is explained below.

Introductory Paragraph

A well-written introductory paragraph will often do the following.

1   *Gain the reader's interest.* On pages 637–638 are several time-tested methods used to draw the reader into an essay.

2   *Present the thesis statement.* The thesis statement expresses the central idea of an essay, just as a topic sentence states the main idea of a paragraph. Here's an example of a thesis statement.

> A vacation at home can be wonderful.

An essay with this thesis statement would go on to explain some positive things about vacationing at home.

- What is the thesis statement in Gary's essay? Find that statement on page 634 and write it here:

  _____

  _____

  You should have written down the next-to-last sentence in the introductory paragraph of Gary's essay.

3   *Lay out a plan of development.* The *plan of development* is a brief statement of the main supporting details for the central idea. These supporting details should be presented in the order in which they will be discussed in the essay. The plan of development can be blended into the thesis statement or presented separately.

Blended into a thesis statement: A vacation at home can be wonderful because you can avoid the hassles of travel, make use of your knowledge of the area, and indulge in special activities.

Presented separately: A vacation at home can be wonderful. At home you can avoid the hassles of travel, make use of your knowledge of the area, and indulge in special activities.

Note that some essays lend themselves better to a plan of development than others do. At the least, your introductory paragraph should gain the reader's interest and present the thesis statement.

- What is the plan of development in Gary's essay? Find the sentence on page 634 that states Gary's plan of development and write it here:

————————————————————————————————————

————————————————————————————————————

You should have written down the last sentence in the introductory paragraph of Gary's essay.

Four Common Methods of Introduction

1 *Begin with a broad statement and narrow it down to your thesis statement.* Broad statements can capture your reader's interest while introducing your general topic. They may provide useful background material as well. The writer of the introductory paragraph below begins with a broad statement about her possessions. She then narrows the focus down to the three possessions that are the specific topic of the paper.

> I have many possessions that I would be sad to lose. Because I love to cook, I would miss several kitchen appliances that provide me with so many happy cooking adventures. I would also miss the wonderful electronic equipment that entertains me every day, including my large-screen television set and my VCR. I would miss the two telephones on which I have spent many interesting hours chatting in every part of my apartment, including the bathtub. But if my apartment were burning down, I would most want to rescue three things that are irreplaceable and hold great meaning for me—the silverware set that belonged to my grandmother, my mother's wedding gown, and my giant photo album.

2 *Present an idea or situation that is the opposite of what will be written about.* One way to gain the reader's interest is to show the difference between your opening idea or situation and the one to be discussed in the essay.

> The role of computers in schools is constantly growing. Such growth is based on a widespread faith that computers can answer many of the learning needs of our students. Many people believe that it is just a matter of time before computers do all but take the place of human teachers. However, educators should be cautious about introducing computers into curriculums. Computers may interfere with the learning of critical language skills, they may move too fast for students to digest new concepts, and they are a poor substitute for certain real-world experiences.

3   *Tell a brief story.* An interesting incident or anecdote is hard for a reader to resist. In an introduction, a story should be no more than a few sentences, and it should relate meaningfully to—and so lead the reader toward—your central idea. The story you tell can be an experience of your own, of someone you know, or of someone you have read about. For instance, in the following introduction, the writer tells a simple personal story that serves as background for his central idea.

> I remember the September morning that I first laid eyes on Jill. I'd been calling clients at my desk at work when I heard a warm, musical laugh. There was something so attractive about the sound that I got up to get a cup of coffee and to find the source of that laugh. I discovered the voice to be that of a young, auburn-haired woman we had just hired from a temporary agency. Soon after, Jill and I began going out, and we spent the next two years together. Only recently have we decided to break up because of disagreements about finances, about children, and about our relationship with her family.

4   *Ask one or more questions.* The questions may be ones that you intend to answer in your essay, or they may show that your topic relates directly to readers. In the following example, the questions are designed to gain readers' interest and convince them that the essay applies to them.

> Does your will to study collapse when someone suggests getting a pizza? Does your social life compete with your class attendance? Is there a huge gap between your intentions and your actions? If the answers to these questions are *yes, yes,* and *yes,* read on. You can benefit from some powerful ways to motivate yourself: setting goals and consciously working to reach them, using rational thinking, and developing a positive personality.

- Which of the four methods of introduction described above does Gary use in his essay?

_____

_____

Gary begins with an idea that is the opposite of what he is writing about. His essay is about his difficulties with college life, but he begins with the idea that college "is a fun and exciting time" for some students.

Supporting Paragraphs

The traditional college essay has three supporting paragraphs. But some essays will have two supporting paragraphs, and others will have four or more. Each supporting paragraph should have its own topic sentence that states the point to be developed in that paragraph.

Notice that each of the supporting paragraphs in Gary's essay has its own topic sentence. For example, the topic sentence of his first supporting paragraph is "Few people in my life are supportive of my decision to enter college."

- What is the topic sentence for Gary's second supporting paragraph?

  _____

- What is the topic sentence for Gary's third supporting paragraph?

  _____

In each case, Gary's topic sentence is the first sentence of the paragraph.

Concluding Paragraph

An essay that ended with its final supporting paragraph would probably leave the reader wondering if the author is really done. A concluding paragraph is needed for a sense of completion. Here are two common methods of conclusion.

Two Common Methods of Conclusion

1 *Provide a summary and a final thought.* Using wording that is different from your introduction, restate your thesis and main supporting points. This review gives readers an overview of your essay and helps them remember what they've read. A final thought signals the end of the paper, as in the following concluding paragraph from the essay about personal possessions.

> If my home ever really did burn down, I would hope to be able to rescue some of the physical things that so meaningfully represent my past. My grandmother's silver set is a reminder of the grandparents who enriched my childhood, my mother's wedding gown is a glamorous souvenir of two important weddings, and my photo album is a rich storage bin of family and personal history. I would hate to lose them. However, if I did, I would take comfort in the fact that the most important storage place for family and personal memories is my own mind.

2 *Focus on the future.* A focus on the future often involves a prediction or a recommendation. This method of conclusion may refer in a general way to the central idea, or it may include a summary. The following conclusion from the essay about self-motivation combines a summary with a prediction. The prediction adds further support for the central idea.

> So get your willpower in gear, and use the three keys to self-motivation—set goals and work to reach them, think rationally, and develop a positive personality. You will find that a firm commitment to this approach becomes easier and easier. Progress will come more often and more readily, strengthening your resolve even further.

- Which kind of conclusion does Gary use to end his essay?

  _____

In his conclusion, Gary refers to his central idea in the context of the future. He makes hopeful points about what his and his family's life will be like after he gets a college degree.

Activity

Answer each of the following questions by filling in the blank or circling the answer you think is correct.

1. An effective paragraph or essay is one that
   a. makes a point.
   b. provides specific support.
   c. makes a point and provides specific support.
   d. does none of the above.

2. The sentence that states the main idea of a paragraph is known as the _____topic_____ sentence; the sentence that states the central idea of an essay is known as the _____thesis_____ statement.

3. Prewriting can help a writer find
   a. a good topic to write about.
   b. a good main point to make about the topic.
   c. enough details to support the main point.
   d. all of the above.

4. *True or false?* ___T___ During the freewriting process, you should not concern yourself with spelling, punctuation, or grammar.

5. One step that everyone should use at some stage of the writing process is to prepare a plan for the paragraph or essay. The plan is known as a(n) _scratch outline_.

6. When you start writing, your first concern should be
    a. spelling.
    b. content.
    c. grammar.
    d. punctuation.

7. Two common ways of organizing a paragraph are _listing_ order and _time_ order.

8. A thesis statement
    a. is generally part of an essay's introduction.
    b. states the central idea of the essay.
    c. can be followed by the essay's plan of development.
    d. all of the above.

Relationships between Reading and Writing

You may wonder why a section on writing is included in a book called *Reading and Study Skills*. Perhaps you felt that you were capable of becoming a good reader and skilled student without having the additional burden of producing written assignments placed on you. Reading and writing, however, are so closely interconnected that it is virtually impossible to be competent at one without being competent at the other. The two abilities work together in several ways:

- *Reading and writing are interrelated language skills.* Through reading, you learn, almost subconsciously, how good writers put sentences together and organize ideas. In addition, you acquire new vocabulary words. Through writing, you begin to use what you have learned by reading. You also gain intensive practice in being logical, a skill that is essential to understanding more difficult reading material.

- *Both reading and writing are processes.* You become a better reader, or a more skillful writer, by treating each task as a process. You preview, read, and reread. Or you prewrite, write, and rewrite. With each step, your skills become sharper and the end product—your understanding of what you have read or the paper you have written—becomes finer.

- *Both reading and writing are vital for communication.* Competence in reading and writing is an essential skill if you wish to make your voice heard and your ideas known. Shutting yourself off from either one can damage your life in two ways. First, your verbal abilities suffer because you have few language models and few chances to extend your word skills. Second, your message—whatever it may be, either in your personal life or on the job—is lost because you cannot get it across to other people.

Reading and writing, then, are so closely linked that practicing one helps the other—and neglecting one damages the other. This is why writing assignments have a role in this book, and why writing should be an important priority in your life as a student.

Writing Assignments

Following are a number of assignments based on chapters or reading selections in the book. Before attempting any of these assignments, reread the guide on pages 628–630.

1. Consider this study situation:

> Howard has trouble taking notes in all his classes. He is seldom sure about what is important enough to write down. Also, he has trouble organizing material when he does write it down. Often the only points he records are the ones the instructor puts on the board. The connections between these points are usually clear to him in class, for he spends most of his time listening carefully to the instructor rather than taking notes. However, several weeks later, when he is studying for a test, he has trouble remembering many of the relationships among points. His notes do not provide a complete, unified understanding of the subject but seem instead to consist of many isolated bits of information.
>
> One course that gives Howard special problems is sociology. In class the instructor asks students questions and uses their comments as takeoff points for discussing course ideas. Sometimes she is five minutes into an important idea before Howard realizes it is important—and he hasn't taken a single note on that point. He often winds up with such a frustrating shortage of notes that he decides not to go to class at all. In another course, biology, the instructor talks so fast that Howard cannot keep up. Also, Howard misspells so many words that it is often impossible for him to understand his notes when he tries to read them over weeks later, before an exam.

Write a paper in which you respond in detail to Howard's situation. Apply what you have learned in the chapter titled "Taking Classroom Notes" to explain at least three specific steps that Howard could follow to become an effective note-taker.

2. Consider this study situation:

> Cheryl has trouble managing her study time. She claims that the only time she can make herself study is right before a test. "If I'm not in a crisis situation with a test just around the corner," she says, "I usually won't study. When I'm in the right mood, I do try to study a bit to keep things from piling up. But most of the time I'm just not in the mood. Some mornings I get up and say to myself, 'Tonight you will do at least two hours of schoolwork.' Then, 95 percent of the time, I let something distract me." Cheryl recently had to face the shortcomings of her cramming method. She found herself with only one night to prepare for two exams and a report; the result was several disastrous grades.

Write a paper in which you respond in detail to Cheryl's situation. Apply what you have learned in the chapter titled "Time Control and Concentration" to explain at least three specific steps that Cheryl could take to control her time effectively.

3. Consider this study situation:

> For tomorrow's test in his Introduction to Business course, Gary has to know three chapters from the textbook. At 1:30 P.M. yesterday, he sat down with a yellow marking pen and started reading the first chapter. At 3 P.M. he wasn't even halfway through the first chapter, and he felt bored and worn out. The sentences were long and heavy and loaded with details. Gary's head became so packed with information that as soon as he read a new fact, it seemed to automatically push out the one before it. When he looked back at what he had covered, he realized he had set off most of the text in yellow. Gary decided then to stop marking and just read. But the more he read, the sleepier he got, and the more his mind kept wandering. He kept thinking about all the things he wanted to do once the test was over. At 5:15 P.M. he had just finished reading the first chapter, but he felt completely defeated. He still had to study the chapter, and he had no idea exactly what to study. On top of that, he had to plow through two more chapters and study them as well. He felt desperate and stupid—because he had waited so long to start with the text and because he was having such a hard time reading it.

Write a paper in which you respond in detail to Gary's situation. Apply what you have learned in the chapter titled "The PRWR Study Method" to explain at least three specific steps that Gary could take to study effectively through previewing, textbook marking, and note-taking.

4. Consider this study situation:

In two days, Steve will have a biology quiz in which he will have to write the definitions of ten terms that have been discussed in the course. As a study aid, the instructor has passed out a list of thirty terms that students should know thoroughly. Steve has gone through his class notes and textbook and copied down the definitions of the thirty terms. He tries to study the terms by reading them over and over, but he has trouble concentrating and merely keeps on "reading words." He decides to write out each definition until he knows it. Hours later, he has written out ten definitions a number of times and is still not sure he will remember them. He beings to panic because he is spending such an enormous amount of time for such meager results. He decides to play Russian roulette with the terms—to study just some of them and hope they are the ones that will be on the test.

Write a paper in which you respond in detail to Steven's situation. Apply what you have learned in the chapter titled "Building a Powerful Memory" to explain at least three specific steps that Steve could take to improve his memory.

5. Consider this study situation:

Most of the exams Rita takes include both multiple-choice and true-false questions as well as at least one essay question. She has several problems with such tests. She often goes into the test in a state of panic. "As soon as I see a question I can't answer," she says, "big chunks of what I do know just fly out the window. I go into an exam expecting to choke and forget." Another problem is her timing. "Sometimes I spend too much time trying to figure out the answer to tricky multiple-choice or true-false questions. Then I end up with only fifteen minutes to answer two essay questions." Rita's greatest difficulty is writing essay answers. "Essays are where I always lose a lot of points. Sometimes I don't read a question the right way, and I wind up giving the wrong answer to the question. When I do understand a question, I have trouble organizing my answer. I'll be halfway through an answer and then realize that I skipped some material I should have put at the start or that I already wrote down something I should have saved for the end. I have a friend who says that essays are easier to study for because she can usually guess what the questions will be. I don't see how this is possible. Essay tests really scare me, since I never know what questions are coming."

Write a paper in which you respond in detail to Rita's situation. Apply what you have learned in the chapters titled "Taking Objective Exams" and "Taking Essay Exams" to explain at least three specific steps that Rita could take to improve her performance on exams.

6. Consider this study situation:

> Pete had been out of school for ten years before he enrolled in college. During his first semester, his sociology instructor asked him to "compile a list of ten books and articles about single-parent families." In addition, Pete's business instructor asked him to do a research paper on "benefits of the Japanese quality circle in American companies." Pete dreaded these projects because he had no idea where or how to begin them. Before class one night, he walked into his college library and wandered around for a while, aimlessly and shyly. He felt especially intimidated by the people who sat typing in front of computer screens and seemed to know exactly what they were doing. Pete felt completely out of his element—like a visitor in a foreign land. He didn't even know what questions to ask about how to use the library.

Write a paper in which you respond in detail to Pete's situation. Apply what you have learned in the chapter titled "Using the Library and the Internet" to explain at least three specific steps that Pete could take to do a good job on his research assignments.

7. Read the selection about propaganda on pages 65–66. Then write a paper about an ad you have seen recently that uses several of the propaganda techniques discussed in the selection. Show specifically—by mentioning the name of the product and describing the language, slogans, characters, and settings in the ad—how the ad uses particular propaganda methods.

8. Review the section on effective writing on pages 67–68. An example given in the section to illustrate a "point" is "Proms should be banned." Write your own paper that presents a variation on this idea. Your point should be, "_____ should be banned for several reasons." The topic you choose could be one of the following or some other: smoking, grades, ads for alcoholic beverages on television, commercials aimed at children, hitchhiking, loud radios.

9. Read the section on concentration skills on pages 85–90. Then write a paper based on the idea that many students—from the youngest to the oldest—find it difficult to pay attention in school. Why might this be true? What aspects of school make it hard to pay attention? (Is it the setting? The teachers? The subject matter? The pressures? The boredom?) Write a paper on the steps a teacher could take to make it easier for students to pay attention. Make your steps practical ones that a concerned teacher at a specific level (primary school, high school, college) could take.

10. Read the selection about television on pages 498–500. Then write a paper about your own feelings toward television. Are you concerned about how much TV you and your family watch or about how TV is deadening communication within the family? Or do you have positive feelings about the role TV plays in your life? Write a paper explaining why you are *or are not* worried about the place of TV in your household. Back up your reasons with specific details about the hours spent watching TV, the kinds of shows on TV, or any other information that supports your reasons.

Acknowledgments

Reprinted by permission from *The American Heritage Dictionary, Third Paperback Edition.* Copyright © 1994 by Houghton Mifflin Company. Excerpts in Parts Three and Seven on pages 313, 315, 321, and 566.

From *The Autobiography of Malcolm X.* Copyright © 1964 by Alex Haley and Betty Shabazz. Reprinted by permission of Random House, Inc. Selection on page 485.

Stacy Kelly Abbott, "From Nonreading to Reading." Reprinted by permission. Selection on page 524.

Ronald B. Alder, "Visual Elements in Assertive Communication." Adapted from *Talking Straight.* Copyright © 1977 by Holt, Rinehart, and Winston. Reprinted by permission of Holt, Rinehart, and Winston, CBS College Publishing. Selection on page 457.

Lexine Alpert, "Flour Children." Originally appeared in the January 1990 issue of *In Health Magazine.* Reprinted by permission of the author. Selection on page 519.

Russell Baker, from *Growing Up.* Reprinted by permission of Don Congdon Associates, Inc. ©1982 by Russell Baker. Selection on page 615.

Jane Brody, "Fatigue." From Jane Brody's *The New York Times Guide to Personal Health.* Copyright © 1976, 1982 by The New York Times Company. Reprinted by permission. Selection on page 470.

Dr. Benjamin Carson and Gregg A. Lewis, "Dare to Think Big." Taken from *The Big Picture* by Dr. Benjamin Carson with Gregg A. Lewis. Copyright © 1999 by Benjamin Carson. Used by permission of Zondervan Publishing House. Selection on page 509.

Jean Coleman and John Langan, adapted from "Learning Survival Skills," in *Groundwork for College Reading,* 3rd ed. Copyright © 2000 by Townsend Press. Material in Part One on pages 28–35.

Rod Plotnik, from *Introduction to Psychology,* 2nd ed. Copyright McGraw-Hill, Inc. Reprinted by permission. Selection on page 126.

Marcia Prentergast, "Winning the Job Interview Game." Reprinted by permission of the author and Townsend Press. Selection on page 514.

Virginia Nichols Quinn, from *Applying Psychology,* 2nd ed. Copyright © 1984 by McGraw-Hill Book Company. Reprinted by permission. Selections on pages 118 and 466.

Scott Rego, "The Fine Art of Complaining." Reprinted by permission of the author and Townsend Press. Selection on page 489.

Philip Roth, from *Goodbye, Columbus.* Copyright © 1959 by Philip Roth. Reprinted by permission of Houghton Mifflin Company. Selection on page 618.

Marta Salinas, "The Scholarship Jacket," from *Nosotras: Latina Literature Today,* edited by María del Carmen Boza, Beverly Silva, and Carmen Valle. Copyright © 1986 by Bilingual Press/Editorial Bilingüe, Arizona State University, Tempe, AZ. Selection on page 503.

Richard T. Schaefer and Robert P. Lamm, from *Sociology,* 4th ed. Copyright © 1992 by McGraw-Hill, Inc. Selection on page 120.

Charles D. Schewe and Reuben M. Smith, from *Marketing.* Copyright © 1980 by McGraw-Hill, Inc. Reprinted by permission. Selection on page 137.

Rudolph E. Verderber, from *Communicate!* 9th ed. Copyright © 1999 by Wadsworth, Inc. Reprinted by permission of the publisher. Selection on page 133.

Drew H. Wolfe, from *Introduction to College Chemistry,* 2nd ed. Copyright © 1988 by McGraw-Hill. Reprinted by permission. Selection on page 139.

Photo Credits

Index

Instructor's
Guide

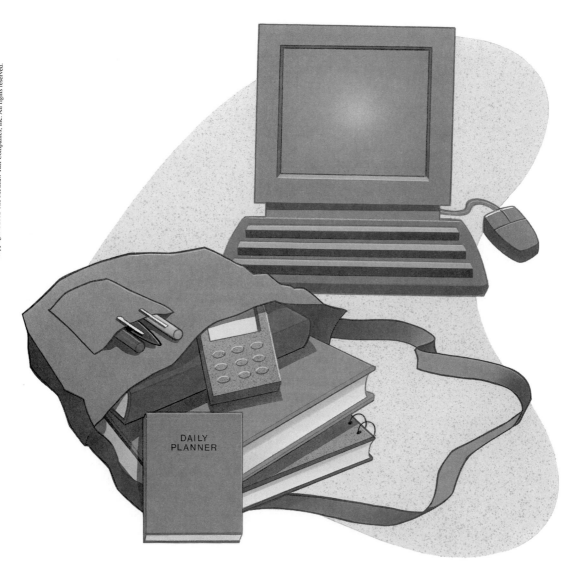

DAILY
PLANNER

Preview

This final section, the Instructor's Guide, provides a series of suggestions and strategies for instructors using the textbook. Included are specific ideas about starting and conducting the course, along with a model syllabus.

Note: An *Instructor's Manual and Test Bank,* providing thirty supplementary activities and tests along with the materials in this Instructor's Guide, is available separately for instructors who use *Reading and Study Skills* as a class text.

Suggested Approaches and Techniques

On the following pages, I describe briefly some approaches and techniques that have proved helpful while using the materials in the book.

1   I have found the following memory-building activity to be an invaluable one for the first class session: I ask the students to learn each other's first names. So that I do not get in the students' way while they are doing this, I leave the room for ten or fifteen minutes. When I return, I call for volunteers to introduce me, on a first-name basis, to all the people in the room.

Afterward, I ask students to describe *how* they went about mastering the first names of all the people in the class. They then have a chance to compare ideas with others on the memory processes that were used. They will probably discover that in most cases, the methods used to learn the names were similar. Additionally, they may realize for the first time that there *is* a definite process, or sequence of steps, involved in an act of memorization.

This activity has several benefits. Students learn each other's first names; they develop a sense of working together as a class; they surprise and please themselves with their success at the project; and they are prepared to learn the three basic steps in effective memorization described on pages 210–212.

2   I begin the semester with the chapter titled "Taking Classroom Notes" because students usually have one or more content courses along with their course or courses in developmental skills. They need to learn right away how to take effective notes in those courses.

One helpful device in teaching note-taking is to have instructors at your school videotape some "mini-lectures" in their disciplines, each lecture lasting about twenty minutes. The tapes can then be used for supervised practice in note-taking.

3   I do not proceed in an unvarying linear sequence. To combat lags in students' attention, I skip around freely and often provide practice in three or four skills within a three-hour class. The book's organization makes it easy to vary a class's activities.

4 I find that the chapter titled "Your Attitude: The Heart of the Matter" has more impact on students after the semester is about three weeks old. Students can look back to examine what they are or are not doing with their time in school.

I save the chapter on "Learning Survival Strategies" for several weeks later. This chapter also encourages students to evaluate themselves as students, and it provides a boost—moral support and positive thinking—at a time when it may be needed.

5 As the directions for some of the activities in the book will show, I believe that students can often learn effectively by working with each other. Just as attention will decline if one skill is worked on unremittingly, so it will drop if all activities are carried out in one way. For some activities, students should work silently at their seats while the instructor goes around, observes their work in progress, and offers comments. (This is the best time to provide feedback—at the moment a student is involved in a task.) For other activities, students can be asked to work in pairs; for yet other exercises, they can be divided into small groups of three or four. Such variety both sustains energy levels and enriches the learning process.

6 Skills work is hard work. It's not glamorous; trumpets don't sound, and the sky seldom turns technicolor. When students visibly flag, as they will if they are working hard, I sometimes announce a "milling-around break." Everyone stands up and mills around for a couple of minutes and gets the blood flowing again. Then we sit back down, noses to the grindstone again, a little fresher. I know an instructor who starts her classes with calisthenics; it may not be a bad idea.

7 I've found that grading students on most of their classroom and homework activities is an effective way of motivating them to put forth their best efforts. Accordingly, I may accumulate fifteen or more grades from a student in the course of a semester. When it is impractical both to grade many papers and to make individual comments on the papers, I note the most common areas of mistakes and discuss them in class rather than writing extensively on each paper.

In a typical class, where students with reasonable ability are making a reasonable effort, most of the grades should be good. The grades are invaluable because they show students that they are capable of success. Very often developmental students have received only negative feedback about their academic ability; positive reinforcement helps them blossom. The graded activities are also a constant check on whether a skill has been presented effectively in class. It is only natural at times that an instructor will miscalculate students' readiness to apply a particular skill. When this happens, a quiz can simply be marked with a check rather than with a number or letter grade.

8 Students' learning is often best measured by asking them to practice a skill, rather than by asking objective questions about the skill. In this regard, many of the activities in the book, particularly in the section on study skills, can be used as mastery tests. For example, Activities 4 to 6 on pages 63–69 can be used to measure students' skill at taking classroom notes.

At the same time, objective tests provide a traditional, detached way for both students and their instructor to evaluate progress. I have therefore devoted an entire part of the text (Part Seven) to a series of objective tests, and I have included a second series of these tests in the *Instructor's Manual*. These tests may be photocopied.

9 I think a strong attendance policy is vital for a developmental skills course. Following is part of an information sheet that I distribute to new classes:

> This is a skills course—not a lecture course where you can borrow a friend's notes afterward. Typically, one or more skills will be explained briefly in class, and you will then spend most of the class time practicing the skills, making them your own. You will be learning in the best possible way: through doing.
>
> Since much of the value and meaning of the course is the work done in class, you must be here on a steady basis. In a real sense, if you miss class, you are missing the course. Therefore, you should determine now to attend class faithfully; otherwise, you will be wasting your time and money.
>
> Grading will be tied in with attendance. Quizzes will be given at the start of, and during, many classes. If you are late or you miss class, you will receive a zero. Makeup tests will, as much as possible, be provided upon request. However, makeup grades will never count for as much as in-class grades.

When I started teaching this course a number of years ago, I made attendance a voluntary matter. Many of my students, not able to handle the winds of freedom, were blown away. I now believe that a firm attendance policy, tied in closely to grading, is in the best interest of most students.

A Model Syllabus

Following is a syllabus I have used as a general guide for the use of *Reading and Study Skills* with my reading students at Atlantic Cape Community College. The syllabus assumes a three-hour class meeting once a week for fifteen weeks. It also assumes time for review of homework activities or matters covered in previous classes. The first nine weeks of the course emphasize study skills, for these are skills that students need immediately for help with their other classes.

Very seldom are *all* the skills listed for a single class covered in that class. Instead, I focus on those skills most suited to the needs of the individual students involved. Instructors using the book will probably want to do likewise, emphasizing the skills most appropriate for their students.

Class 1

- Business matters. I hand out 4- by 6-inch slips of paper on which students write their names, addresses, and phone numbers; other courses they are taking; whether they are working full- or part-time; and their likely career goals.
- Introduction to the instructor and the course.
- Class exercise: The memory-building activity described on page IG-3 of this Instructor's Guide.
- Skill introduced: "Taking Classroom Notes." I advise students to take notes from the very start in their other classes. To underscore the importance of notetaking, I put the relentless facts about forgetting on the board (80 percent forgotten in two weeks; 95 percent in a month—see page 43). I suggest that students have a separate notebook (or section of a looseleaf book) for each course, and I cover briefly several other organizational hints (pages 43–45).
- Skill introduced: "Time Control and Concentration." I tell students to get a large monthly calendar, or make one. (I show them my own—a Sierra Club Wilderness Calendar with plenty of write-in space.) I also pass out more 4- by 6-inch slips and give students practice in preparing a "to do" list— a helpful skill, for they have a lot of items to remember at the very start of the semester.
- Assignment: To get *Reading and Study Skills* for the course and to fill in the "Guide to Courses" on the inside front cover of the book.

Class 2

- Skill covered: "Taking Classroom Notes." I put students into groups of fours, and they read the thirteen note-taking hints (as described on pages 43 ff). I put a grid on the board and ask someone from each group to write in the group's choices for the five most important note-taking hints. Here's the way the grid looks:

	Jack's Group	Betty's Group	Carol's Group	Maurice's Group
Most important				
Second most important				
Third most important				
Fourth most important				
Fifth most important				

The grid is then used as a basis for class discussion of the note-taking hints. There is no correct sequence, except that hint 1 should be in the first position. The sequence depends upon the needs and priorities of individual groups of students. The value of the grid is that it gets students to think actively about all the note-taking hints, and it's a good focal point for discussing the hints.

I also cover methods for studying class notes (pages 51–54 and Activity 2 on page 62) and handwriting efficiency (pages 52–57). Note that students are more interested in handwriting efficiency if it's presented with the sexier title *speed writing*.

- Skill covered: "Time Control and Concentration." I go through the activities on pages 75–78 and 83–84 (where I have students prioritize the items on Emily's "to do" list).

- Assignments:

  (1) Work through the "Introduction" on pages 1–8.

  (2) Complete "Time Control and Concentration" on pages 71–90, and do a weekly study schedule.

Class 3

- Test 1: I give students one of the classroom note-taking lectures on pages 63–69 *or* use a taped lecture prepared by a subject-area instructor on our faculty.
- Test 2: I give students ten to fifteen minutes to read and study pages 39–60 and prepare for a mastery test (pages 543–544) on taking class notes. It may be advisable to have students tear out the test (the test pages are perforated) and hand it in to you before they begin studying; you can then pass it back to them when they're ready to take the test.
- Skill covered: "Setting Goals for Yourself" (pages 20–27). I have students work in pairs or small groups and read through the entire chapter, answering the various questions as they proceed. Class discussion follows.
- Assignment: Read "Your Attitude: The Heart of the Matter" (pages 11–19) and write a paper responding in detail to one of the nine questions on page 19.

Note: In this class and following classes, I cover briefly in class or assign as homework (or both) the various word skills in Part Two, as needed by students. I also begin to introduce, as time permits, the various reading comprehension skills in Part Four (pages 361 ff). The main emphasis, however, remains on study skills.

Class 4

- Skill covered: "Textbook Study I: The PRWR Study Method." I present in turn the various points in the chapter (pages 93–106), and students work through the various activities that help them learn those points. We also do Activity 1 on pages 106–108.
- Skill covered: "Recognizing Definitions and Examples" on pages 361–367.
- Test: I give students ten to fifteen minutes to read and study pages 71–90 and prepare for a mastery test (pages 545–546) on time control and concentration.
- Assignments:
  (1) Complete the activities in "The PRWR Study Method" on pages 108–112.
  (2) Do the review test on definitions and examples on pages 366–367.

Class 5

- Skill covered: "Textbook Study II: Using PRWR." We do pages 113–121 in class.
- Skill covered: "Recognizing Enumerations" on pages 368–377.
- Test: The mastery test on definitions and examples on pages 573–574.
- Assignment: Do pages 122–128 and the review test on enumerations on pages 375–377.

Class 6

- Skill covered: "Building a Powerful Memory." I demonstrate the first memory step, organization, by having students group the nine shopping items on page 210. (I write the items on the board in random order before showing students the grouped items in the book.)
- We then read and work through the rest of the chapter and do several of the activities at the end.
- Test: I give students two mastery tests in PRWR: pages 547–549.
- Assignment: We begin "Applying PRWR to a Textbook Chapter," starting on page 150, in class, and students are then asked to work through Section Three (up to page 183) for homework.

Class 7

- Skill covered: We complete the textbook chapter in class (through page 204).
- Test: I allow students to use their notes to take the quiz on the textbook chapter on pages 205–206.
- Test: I give students ten to fifteen minutes to read and study pages 207–218 in preparation for a mastery test (pages 553–554) on memory-building.
- Skill covered: "Recognizing Headings and Subheadings" on pages 378–390.
- Assignment: Read "Learning Survival Strategies" on pages 28–35 and write a paper responding in detail to one of the last five questions on page 36.

Class 8

- Skill covered: "Taking Objective Exams." I always challenge students when they do Activity 1 on page 230. I explain that no student has ever gotten all ten of the "following directions" questions correct, but that if anyone does, I will on the spot give him or her an A for the course, and he or she may leave the classroom and not come back for the rest of the semester. So far, at least, no one has ever gotten all ten correct, but everyone has energetically tried.

- Test 1: I give students two tests on taking objective exams—the mastery tests on pages 555–556 and 559–560. I count only the grade of the one on pages 559–560.

- Test 2: I also test students on headings and subheadings, using the review test on pages 388–390 and the mastery test on pages 577–578. Again, I count only the second grade.

- Skill covered: "Recognizing Signal Words" (pages 391–400).

- Assignment: Do the review test on signal words on pages 399–400.

Class 9

- Skill covered: "Taking Essay Exams." I teach this unit by having students prepare their own outline of hints on taking classroom notes (taken from the thirteen hints on pages 43–51).

- Test: Students then study for and write an essay answer to the question, "Write an essay describing seven hints to remember when taking classroom notes." We then compare their answers with the answer on page 252.

- Assignments: Do Activity 4 on taking essay exams on page 254.

Class 10

- Skill covered: "Using the Library and the Internet." I lecture on the library and Internet for about half an hour, and we then descend *en masse* on the library and do most of the activities there. Students realize that they should ask questions about anything they don't understand, for they're preparing themselves to do the individualized (and graded) research activity that follows.

- Assignment: Each student chooses a different area to research from the activity on pages 274–276.

Class 11

- Test 1: Students have half an hour to prepare an outline answer for the question on page 557 and to study the outline. They then write an essay answer to the question.
- Test 2: Students are given ten to fifteen minutes to read and study pages 255–274 in preparation for a mastery test (pages 561–562) on the library and the Internet.
- Skill covered: "Recognizing Main Ideas" (pages 401–408).
- Assignment: Do the review test on main ideas on pages 407–408.

Class 12

- Test: Mastery test on main ideas on pages 581–582.
- Skill covered: "Knowing How to Outline." We go through pages 409–419.
- Skill covered: "Knowing How to Summarize." We go through pages 424–435.
- Assignments:
  (1) Do the review test on outlining on pages 420–423.
  (2) Do the review test on summarizing on pages 436–438.

Class 13

- Test 1: Mastery test on outlining on pages 583–584.
- Test 2: Mastery test on summarizing on pages 585–588.
- Skill covered: "Skim Reading." The five timed passages on pages 457–473 are extremely helpful in making students apply the comprehension skills learned in Part Four. If they do not take advantage of definitions, enumerations, and relationships between headings and subheadings, they will not take effective notes.
- Assignments:
  (1) Individualized work in the college reading lab. Any makeup work.
  (2) As needed, "Understanding Graphs and Tables" on pages 439–451 or any of the additional learning skills in Part Eight of the book.

Class 14

- Skill covered: "Rapid Reading." We do the first four selections on pages 485–502.
- Test: Skim-reading mastery test on pages 591–592.
- Assignments:
    (1) Individualized work in the college reading lab. Any makeup work.
    (2) As needed, any of the additional learning skills in Part Eight of the book.

Class 15

- Skill covered: "Rapid Reading." We do two additional selections chosen from those on pages 503–534.
- Test 1: Rapid-reading mastery test on pages 593–596.
- Test 2: Department-required final reading exam.